Karl Lamprecht
A German Academic Life (1856–1915)

STUDIES IN GERMAN HISTORIES
Series Editors: Roger Chickering and Thomas A. Brady, Jr.

PUBLISHED

Communal Reformation
Peter Blickle

Karl Lamprecht
A German Academic Life (1856–1915)
Roger Chickering

German Encounters with Modernity
Katherine Roper

Karl Lamprecht

A German Academic
Life (1856–1915)

Roger Chickering

Humanities Press
New Jersey

First published 1993 by Humanities Press International, Inc.,
Atlantic Highlands, New Jersey 07716

Library of Congress Cataloging-in-Publication Data
Chickering, Roger, 1942–
  Karl Lamprecht : a German academic life (1856–1915) / Roger
Chickering.
      p.   cm. — (Studies in German histories)
  Includes bibliographical references and index.
  ISBN 0–391–03766–8
  1. Lamprecht, Karl, 1856–1915. 2. Historians—Germany—Biography.
I. Title. II. Series.
D15.L3C45   1993
907'.202—dc20
  [B]   92–9140
                                          CIP

A catalog record for this book is available from the British Library.

Printed in the United States of America

D
15
L3
C45
1993

For Tom Brady

Contents

Preface   xi

List of Abbreviations   xvii

PART I. THE MAKING OF THE HISTORIAN
1. Jessen, Wittenberg, Naumburg   2
2. Göttingen, Leipzig, Munich   22
3. Cologne and Bonn   67

PART II. THE DESTRUCTION OF THE HISTORIAN
4. German History (Prise)   108
5. Nemesis   146
6. Ideology and Method   175
7. Axes and Knives   212
8. Banishment   254

PART III. THE HISTORIAN LIVES ON
9. German History (Reprise)   286
10. Universal History   334
11. Academic Reform   367
12. Culture and Policy   394
13. Interruptions   431

Bibliography   447

Index   480

Ich wurde in einer Gesellschaft gefragt, was wohl die
Haupteigenschaft eines Biographen sein müsse. Als ich
antwortete: "Die Liebe zum Helden," tritt jemand hierzu und
stellt die Frage: "Wie hat sich dann aber ein Selbstbiograph
zu verhalten?"

KARL LAMPRECHT, 1906

Preface

Und wenn ihr nach Biographien verlangt, dann nicht nach
jenen mit dem Refrain "Herr Soundso und seine Zeit,"
sondern nach solchen, auf deren Titelblatte es heissen
müsste, "ein Kämpfer gegen seine Zeit."

"The biographical form overcomes absolute interminability in the novel," writes
Georg Lukács. "The extent of the world is limited by the extent of the hero's
possible experiences, and the mass of these experiences is organized by the
direction that his development takes toward finding the meaning of life in
self-knowledge."[1] Lukács' observations speak as well to both the allurements
and the difficulties of biography as a form of historical writing. Biography
represents the most self-contained variety of history, for it organizes itself around
the life and career of a single subject. The challenge of biography is to plumb the
personal history of the subject to depths impossible or impractical in other
historical genres and, at the same time, to integrate personal and collective
history, to situate the subject in the cultural contexts that have—pace
Nietzsche—bound the rebel no less than Herr So-and-So.

I was originally drawn to biography by my frustrations over the inaccessibility
of the personal histories of some 8,000 persons who were the subjects of a
prosopographical study of patriotic societies in imperial Germany. The number
of people involved, as well as the paucity of surviving evidence, made it
impossible to test fully the hypothesis that personal experiences of early
socialization, professional training, and occupational strain contributed to the
proclivity of some people to become active in these nationalist organizations.
My fatigue with these organizations defeated the idea, which I had briefly
entertained, of doing a biographical case study of one of the nationalists. By
now, however, my curiosity about the intersection of personal and collective
history was awakened, and I decided to write a biography. To this degree, I was
what one student of the genre has called a "rare bird indeed," "the writer who
first decides to produce a biography and then begins to look for a suitable
subject."[2]

The selection of Karl Lamprecht as a "suitable subject" was nonetheless by no
means arbitrary. He was a member of several of the patriotic societies I had
studied. He was also active in the German peace movement, which I had
studied earlier. But the anomalies of his political behavior were less interesting
to me than was his spectacular role in the history of the profession to which he

and I both belong. I had reached a point in my own professional life at which I thought an intellectual stock-taking to be important, and a promising vehicle seemed to be the life of this historian, who compelled his own colleagues, most of them for the first time, to confront fundamental questions about the methodology and philosophy of their own professional practices. The fact that abundant documentary traces of the historian survived the upheavals that have beset his country since his death made the project seem practical as well.

I found Lamprecht an attractive subject above all, though, because he cut such a broad swath through the history of his own epoch. The "range of the hero's possible experiences" was extraordinary in his case. His life and career were set in many arenas, and his presence was everywhere unsettling. Personal history intersected not only with the history of the German historical profession, but with the history of the academic bourgeoisie, education, the politics of the German academy, numerous academic disciplines (or what the Germans call *Wissenschaftsgeschichte*), journalism, domestic politics, and even foreign policy. The historian's life thus touched repeatedly on the very issues of individuality and structure that he himself defined as the core of methodological controversy at the end of the last century.

Karl Lamprecht was the most famous and interesting historian in Wilhelmine Germany. His crusade on behalf of his grand theories of *Kulturgeschichte*, which purported to capture every facet of human history within a lawful regularity that he himself had defined, also made him the most controversial historian of his era. The controversy persists to this day. "To talk about Lamprecht," as one commentator wrote in 1979, "is to quarrel about him."[3] The persistence of controversy is a sign of how much the great *Methodenstreit*, which his theories provoked at the end of the last century, continues to color the study of history in Germany at the end of the present century. After decades of silence from German historians had ratified his defeat in the great methodological dispute, interest in Lamprecht revived in the 1960s, as the study of history broadened in the Federal Republic in the wake of the Fischer controversy. The revival of interest in social history drew attention to this would-be pioneer, whose downfall had evidently sealed the ascendancy of political history in Germany at the turn of the century. Sympathetic analyses of Lamprecht's work began to appear in West Germany, particularly from the seminars of Gerhard Oestreich and Karl-Georg Faber.[4] Here, in the words of Bernhard vom Brocke, the object was to make possible a "more unprejudiced appreciation" of the historian's "pathbreaking achievements," to "distinguish between the durable and the historically contingent [*Zeitbedingten*]" qualities of his work.[5] These analyses accordingly featured an effort to sort out those elements of Lamprecht's theories that anticipated a workable modern history of society and culture.

This renewed appreciation for Lamprecht had distinct limits, however. He enjoyed no sympathy among the young scholars who in the 1970s began to invoke the theories of Max Weber to promote the study of history as a "historical social science." Despite his own efforts to construct a rigorous science of history, Lamprecht was "in no sense a progressive force," argued Wolfgang Mommsen, one of the leaders of this effort. "No direct route," Mommsen added, led "from Lamprecht to a historiography which can be understood as a partner to a modern social history in the sense that Max Weber imagined."[6] The indictment from Bielefeld rehearsed the case that the great German sociologist himself had directed against his contemporary early in the century. Lamprecht was a charlatan, whose feckless campaign on behalf of his own confused theories wrecked the cause of social history in Germany for more than half a century.[7] The vehemence of the denunciations nourished the suspicion that these scholars were trying to underscore the distance of their own "historical social science" from the so-called *Strukturgeschichte*, which was associated with an earlier generation of west German historians, primarily Werner Conze and Otto Brunner, from whom direct ties could be traced back via the sociologist Hans Freyer to Lamprecht.[8]

Lamprecht long enjoyed a better reputation in the German Democratic Republic. Excepting only Jürgen Kuczynski, who, for reasons of his own, shared Max Weber's assessment, East German historians accepted the judgment originally formulated by Franz Mehring—that Lamprecht represented an "alternative to Ranke," a progressive among the bourgeois historians of imperial Germany, and that his early work, however confused, comported with the verities of historical materialism.[9] The collapse of the East German state has made this position difficult to defend any longer. Political circumstances and the dictates of academic survival in the "new *Bundesländer*" have accordingly bred new accents in the image of Lamprecht there. In some quarters at least, the historian is now being portrayed as an east German alternative to Weber, as the symbol of a broader, comparative methodology appropriate for the study of world history at the close of the twentieth century.[10]

The divergences in these judgments promise to keep the controversy over Lamprecht alive. The proposition that his theories offer a viable methodological alternative to Max Weber will be hard to sustain. But so will the argument that he has nothing to offer historians today, for it overlooks singular and durable achievements. Lamprecht's towering importance in the development of German regional history is evident to anyone who has labored in this field. Less appreciated today outside eastern Germany is the significance of his contribution to the study of world history: whatever his motives, he was practically alone among his contemporaries in awarding the dignity of a history to every people on earth. Finally, one has to marvel at the majestic panorama that he sought to capture of his own nation's history—his ingenious attempt to encompass every realm of the German past within the bounds of his analysis. He cheerfully underestimated the difficulties of writing a *histoire totale*; and little more than curiosity value attaches today to the elaborate analytical apparatus he constructed or to the eccentric answers it yielded. His great feat, nonetheless, was to pose the right questions.

The persistence of the controversy over Lamprecht makes the absence of a biography all the more remarkable. The theories that have made him so controversial simply cannot be divorced from his personal history; and it is difficult to foresee how a balanced judgment of his achievements and failures can be made until this vital connection is established. Because it attended uncritically to this connection, the only noteworthy attempt to produce a full Lamprecht biography to date also failed to yield a balanced judgment. Herbert Schönebaum was Lamprecht's last *famulus* in the Institute for Cultural and Universal History in Leipzig. After the historian's death in 1915, Schönebaum became the lonely custodian of the Lamprecht shrine; and the massive biographical manuscript that he completed in 1956 was a monument to his life's hero.[11] The manuscript was never published, in part because his hero was still under the profession's ban, in part because the author himself was politically compromised. The principal reason for its failure to appear, however, was that it was an exercise in hagiography. Although it brought together an enormous amount of material, its interpretive value was slight and its chief interest lay in its character as a memoir.

One ought not to underestimate the difficulties that Schönebaum faced. These were fundamental. They related to the structuring principle of a biography—to what Lukács has described, in another passage of his essay on the novel, as the "wandering of the problematic individual to himself."[12] Lamprecht is a difficult hero, a problematic individual by any standard. In the course of his "wanderings to himself," this extraordinary man, whose irrepressible energies intimidated his colleagues while he lived, also attempted to intimidate the biographer after his death. He insisted on setting the terms in which his own biography was to be read. His autobiographical understanding framed the experiences that are central to an account of his career; and, as Schönebaum's failure warns, the biographer who wishes to frame those experiences anew must not only accommodate but contest the hero's powerful claims.

I have been fortunate in having a broader methodological repertoire with which to approach this problematic hero. But some caveats are in order. I have employed methods and concepts from both psychology and what is known loosely nowadays as "discourse analysis." I have done so in both cases with misgivings, for I fear that I have been too cautious for the dedicated advocates of psychohistory or the "linguistic turn" and too incautious for their dedicated opponents. The use of tools from psychology impressed me as the only way to make sense of evidence that childhood experiences bore on the behavior of the adult historian. I have drawn from a variety known as the " psychology of the self," which addressed this evidence at a level of analysis I found persuasive and has proved of value to other historians whose work I respect.[13] This analysis is largely confined to the first chapter, where I have attempted to purge the text of all jargon and to confront questions of theory in the notes. Readers who are skeptical of the use of psychology in history are nonetheless forewarned. The analysis of narrative structures proved more difficult to confine, for it informs my reading not only of the *Methodenstreit* but of the historian's whole life. One final caveat: the second chapter contains an extended excursus into the intellectual and institutional development of the German historical profession in the nineteenth century. The survey is designed to set the background for Karl Lamprecht's dramatic entrance into the profession, but some readers may find that it rehearses a familiar story.

I have had an enormous amount of aid. I wish here to thank all those who read portions of the manuscript, offered advice, or supported my efforts in other ways. On the American side of the Atlantic they include Georg Iggers, Peter Loewenberg, Russell MacCormmach and the late Christa Jungnickel, Winston Maxwell, Susan Moseley, Isabel Paret, Peter Paret, Woodruff Smith, and my colleagues in Oregon, Howard Brick and Stanley Pierson. In Europe I profited from the assistance of Stig Foerster, Peter Griss, Wolfgang Hardtwig, Gangolf Hübinger, Thomas Nipperdey, Klaus Pabst, Hans Schleier, Manfred Schön, Luise Schorn-Schütte, Bernhard vom Brocke, Rüdiger vom Bruch, and Wolfgang Weber. To Amata Niedner I am grateful for the warmth with which she welcomed me into her family and gave me access to the private papers of her great-grandfather. I owe thanks to the staffs of all the many archives and libraries in which I worked on both sides of the Atlantic, particularly to the people who oversee the manuscript division of the university library in Bonn and the interlibrary loan office of the library of the University of Oregon. I could not have undertaken the project without the financial assistance of the Alexander von Humboldt Foundation, and the book would be appearing years hence but for the support of the Humanities Center of the University of Oregon and the Institute for Advanced Study in Princeton. To Alison Baker goes my loving gratitude for the forebearance with which she accepted the irrepressible intrusions of Karl Lamprecht into our life together.

Finally, to my dear friend and former colleague in Eugene, I owe a special debt. Our exchanges over the course of almost a quarter of a century have shaped my ideas about Lamprecht, German history, and myself as a scholar in more ways than I can articulate. This book is for him.

FREIBURG I. BR.

Notes

1. Georg Lukács, *Theorie des Romans* (Berlin, 1963), 70–71.
2. Samuel H. Baron, "Psychological Dimensions of the Biographical Process," in Samuel H. Baron and Carl Pletsch, eds., *Introspection in Biography: The Biographer's Quest for Self-Awareness* (Hillsdale, NJ, 1985), 2.
3. Karl-Heinz Metz, *Grundformen historiographischen Denkens: Wissenschaftsgeschichte als Methodologie. Dargestellt an Ranke, Treitschke und Lamprecht* (Munich, 1979), 484.
4. Karl-Georg Faber, "Ausprägungen des Historismus," *Historische Zeitschrift*, 228 (1979), 1–22; Gerhard Oestreich, "Die Fachhistorie und die Anfänge der sozialge-

schichtlichen Forschung in Deutschland," HZ, 208 (1969): 320–63; Bernhard vom
Brocke's entry in the NDB, 13: 467–72; and the most significant treatment of
Lamprecht to emerge from this milieu, Luise Schorn-Schütte, *Karl Lamprecht:
Kulturgeschichtsschreibung zwischen Wissenschaft und Politik* (Göttingen, 1984).

5. NDB, 13: 468.
6. HZ, 239 (1984), 621–22; Wolfgang J. Mommsen, "Max Weber und die historiographische Methode in seiner Zeit," StdSt, 3 (1983): 28–43.
7. The classic statement of the indictment is Hans-Josef Steinberg, "Karl Lamprecht,"
in Hans-Ulrich Wehler, ed., *Deutsche Historiker*, 9 vols. (Göttingen, 1972–1981), 1:
58–68.
8. See Winfried Schulze, *Deutsche Geschichtswissenschaft nach 1945* (Munich, 1989),
281–301; Jerry Z. Muller, *The Other God That Failed: Hans Freyer and the Deradicalization of German Conservatism* (Princeton, NJ, 1987); Georg G. Iggers, *The German
Conception of History: The National Tradition of Historical Thought from Herder to the
Present*, 2d ed. (Middletown, CT, 1983), 262; Roger Chickering, "An Uninvited
Guest," in James van Horne Melton and Hartmut Lehmann, eds., *Paths of Continuity: Central European Historiography from the 1930s through the 1950s* (Cambridge and
New York, 1993).
9. Hans Schleier, "Der Kulturhistoriker Karl Lamprecht, der 'Methodenstreit' und die
Folgen," in Schleier, ed., *Karl Lamprecht: Alternative zu Ranke. Schriften zur Geschichtstheorie* (Leipzig, 1988); cf. Jürgen Kuczynski, *Studien zu einer Geschichte der Gesellschaftswissenschaften*, 10 vols. (Berlin, 1975–1978), 5: 196. See also Matti Viikari,
*Die Krise der "historistischen" Geschichtsschreibung und die Geschichtsmethodologie Karl
Lamprechts* (Helsinki, 1977).
10. See the special issue on Lamprecht in *Comparativ: Leipziger Beiträge zur Universalgeschichte und vergleichende Gesellschaftsforschung*, Heft 4 (1992).
11. Herbert Schönebaum, "Karl Lamprecht: Leben und Werk eines Kämpfers um die
Geschichtswissenschaft 1856–1915," unpublished ms. (1956). Copies of the manuscript are in the university libraries in Bonn and Leipzig; cf. Muller, 286–87. In my
own view, however, as the footnotes in the present volume will attest, the manuscript has enormous value as the memoir of a man with unique access to Lamprecht
in his final years.
12. Lukács, 70.
13. See Thomas Kohut, *William II and the Germans: A Study in Leadership* (New York,
1991).

List of Abbreviations

AA	Auswärtiges Amt
ADB	*Allgemeine Deutsche Biographie*
AHR	*American Historical Review*
AKg	*Archiv für Kulturgeschichte*
ASg	*Archiv für Sozialgeschichte*
BA	Bundesarchiv, Koblenz
CEH	*Central European History*
DG	Karl Lamprecht, *Deutsche Geschichte*, 12 vols. (Berlin, 1891–1909). Subsequent editions indicated in parentheses.
DLZ	*Deutsche Literaturzeitung*
DS	Denkschrift
DWL	Karl Lamprecht, *Deutsches Wirtschaftsleben im Mittelalter*, 4 vols. (Leipzig, 1885–1886)
DZfG	*Deutsche Zeitschrift für Geschichtswissenschaft*
EB	*Ergänzungsband*
GfRGk	Gesellschaft für Rheinische Geschichtskunde
GG	*Geschichte und Gesellschaft*
GGA	*Göttingische Gelehrten-Anzeigen*
GLA	Generallandesarchiv, Karlsruhe
GStAD	Geheimes Staatsarchiv Preussischer Kulturbesitz, Berlin-Dahlem
GStAM	Geheimes Staatsarchiv Preussischer Kulturbesitz, Zweigstelle Merseburg
GWU	*Geschichte in Wissenschaft und Unterricht*
HJb	*Historisches Jahrbuch*
HT	*History and Theory*
HVjs	*Historische Vierteljahrschrift*
HZ	*Historische Zeitschrift*
IKUg	Institut für Kultur- und Universalgeschichte
IWWKT	*Internationale Wochenschrift für Wissenschaft, Kunst und Technik*
JbNöSt	*Jahrbücher für Nationalökonomie und Statistik*
JMH	*Journal of Modern History*
KE	Karl Lamprecht, *Kindheitserinnerungen* (Gotha, 1918)

KM	Kultusministerium
LW	Herbert Schönebaum, "Karl Lamprecht: Leben und Werk" (Unpublished manuscript, 1956), UB Bonn and UB Leipzig
LZbl	*Literarisches Zentralblatt*
MG	Karl Lamprecht, *Moderne Geschichtswissenschaft: Fünf Vorträge* (Freiburg im Breisgau, 1905)
MGM	*Militärgeschichtliche Mitteilungen*
MIöG	*Mitteilungen des Instituts für österreichische Geschichtsforschung*
NDB	*Neue Deutsche Biographie*
NL	Nachlass
PAAA	Politisches Archiv des Auswärtigen Amtes, Bonn
PF	Philosophische Fakultät
PJb	*Preussische Jahrbücher*
Rh	*Revue historique*
RK	Reichskanzlei
RS	Rundschreiben
RVjb	*Rheinische Vierteljahrsblätter*
StA	Staatsarchiv
StdSt	*Storia della Storiografia*
UA	Universitätsarchiv
UB	Universitätsbibliothek
VSWG	*Vierteljahrschrift für Sozial- und Wirtschaftsgeschichte*
VuG	*Vergangenheit und Gegenwart*
WaG	*Welt als Geschichte*
WL	Max Weber, *Gesammelte Aufsätze zur Wissenschaftslehre*. Ed. Johannes Winckelmann (Tübingen, 1982)
ZKg	*Zeitschrift für Kulturgeschichte*

Dates in the footnotes are listed according to the European format of day-month-year. Thus 10.5.15 is 10 May 1915.

Epigraphs at the heads of chapters are from Friedrich Nietzsche, "Vom Nutzen und Nachteil der Historie für das Leben," *Unzeitgemässe Betrachtungen* (*Werke*, 6 vols., ed. Karl Schlechta, Munich and Vienna, 1980), 1: 209–85.

Part I
The Making of
the Historian

1

Jessen, Wittenberg, Naumburg

"Erkenne dich selbst." Es ist ein schwerer Spruch.

Karl Georg Emil Lamprecht was born on 12 October 1849 in the Saxon village of Berg, near Eilenburg on the Mulda River, where his father was deacon in the local Protestant parish. With his blond hair and sturdy constitution, the child, whom his parents called Georg, could fairly be described as beautiful. He was also the object of his parents' deep affection. When he was three, the family moved from Berg to the town of Jessen, on the White Elster River in Prussian Saxony, where his father had received the pastorate. Here the child continued to thrive in an agricultural setting until early 1854, when diphtheria struck the town. On 1 March 1854, to the horror of his parents, the child died.

The dead child was one of four Karl Lamprechts to inhabit Jessen in the nineteenth century, and his death had a profound impact on both the first and fourth in the series. The first was the bereaved father, who, to judge by the surviving fragmentary evidence, commands no little interest in his own right, quite apart from his influence on the fourth Karl Lamprecht, the future historian.

Karl Nathaniel Lamprecht was born on 16 April 1804, into the family of one of the leading merchants in the small town of Ortrand in western Saxony.[1] Upon the death of his father in 1807, the boy began a lonely odyssey, which lasted more than three decades, through cities and towns in central Germany. He first moved with his mother to the Niederlausitz, to the town of Drebkau near Cottbus, where he began his schooling. Several years later he moved to a small village in the vicinity of Senftenberg, where he lived with his mother's brother, who was the local pastor, and intermittently attended the *Gymnasium* in Cottbus, some thirty kilometers away. In 1823 his education became more systematic. Despite the fact that he was, at nineteen, already old enough to have completed his *Abitur*, he was selected to fill the position reserved for boys from Ortrand at Schulpforta, the prestigious boarding school near the city of Naumburg. After he took his *Abitur* there in 1828, he acceded to the wishes of his mother and began to study law in Jena.

2

The circumstances of the next several years of his life remain obscure, but in all events they brought about his intellectual maturation.[2] Whether because of personal problems, political difficulties, or unencouraging professional prospects for jurists, he left Jena without completing his studies and enrolled in the theological faculty in Halle. When he arrived in Halle, the faculty was in the throes of a celebrated dispute between the neo-pietists and the rationalists. The dispute likely colored the young man's theological views, which emerged as something of a compromise between the two extremes locked in the controversy.[3] His beliefs matured in the tradition commonly known as *Vermitt-lungstheologie*, although they might also be characterized as liberal pietism. The influence of Friedrich Schleiermacher was central in his attempt to reconcile faith and reason, theology and philosophy.[4] From Schleiermacher he accepted the premise that reason was consistent with faith in a transcendent God who was both the source of religious feeling and the fundament of all human knowledge. With Schleiermacher he also believed that the capacity of human reason to comprehend the world was limited, for God remained ultimately hidden from knowledge. The highest object of human reason could accordingly be but to catch glimpses of God's hidden hand. If these beliefs emphasized humility in the exercise of reason, they were not altogether unsympathetic to philosophy. The elder Lamprecht later recalled that during his days as a student he had "dabbled in Hegel, Schelling, and Fichte," but that "Fichte, all in all, actually did a service for theology, in that he reduced all knowledge to imagination, opinion [*Dafürhalten*], to belief."[5]

In 1832, after he recovered from an attack of cholera, his odyssey continued. He first fell victim to the penury of the Prussian state and joined the ranks of unemployed aspirants for clerical positions. Like many others in his situation, he survived temporarily by teaching. During the next several years he served as tutor to the family of a Silesian nobleman, found employment as an instructor at a teachers' seminar in Altdöbern in the Niederlausitz, and taught Latin at a private school for the children of local notables in Calau. In Calau he also became engaged to Emilie Limburg, who was the daughter of the local postmaster and fifteen years his junior.[6] In 1844, after spending two years in Wittenberg at the Evangelical seminar, he finally, at the age of forty, received a clerical position in Berg. Shortly thereafter he married Emilie Limburg.

Karl Nathaniel Lamprecht had spent more than three decades without establishing roots or, evidently, any significant emotional ties. It is difficult to determine the emotional impact of these peregrinations, but he did not look back on them fondly, perhaps because his decision to abandon the law had frustrated his own aspirations and alienated him from his mother. The persistence with which he gave his children his own name might perhaps have symptomized personal disappointments and the hope of finding vicarious fulfillment. In any event, this period bred in him the emotional independence as well as the enormous energy, vivacity, and stormy temperament that were his chief character traits. In Berg he at last found a measure of stability and security, but he seems to have accepted it with more resignation than joy. His marriage, too, was marked less by passion than by comfortable companionship and a sense of obligation.

The first son was born in 1845, ten months after the marriage, and was christened Karl Hugo Lamprecht. Toward this son, who was called Hugo and who resembled Emilie in his mild and undemanding temperament, the father's relationship was governed by a love more proper than ardent. The underlying dynamic of the father's relationship to his second son, Georg, who was born four years later, cannot be fully reconstructed. However, it was extraordinarily powerful. The father idealized the child and saw in him, more than in any of his other children, the vicarious stilling of his own frustrations and the fulfillment of his own ambitions: this son was to become the jurist.

The emotional tie to his second son was the most intense the elder Lamprecht ever established with another human being. The death of the boy in 1854, two years after the family had moved to Jessen, inflicted an emotional blow from which the father never completely recovered; and it cast a shadow from which the next Karl Lamprecht, who was born two years thereafter, never escaped.

"His friendly little face is compensation for a lot that I have had to endure," wrote the father to a friend several weeks after the birth of another son on 25 February 1856.[7] It soon became clear, however, that the new child was not going to provide full compensation. While his wife expressed her gratitude that the Lamprecht family once again numbered two children, the father was now thinking in terms of three.[8] In his fantasy, Georg lived on, his growth and development now measured in relation to the third child.

The third son was christened Karl Gotthard Lamprecht. Unlike the two previous children, he was called by the same name as his father. In other respects, too, the situation of the new Karl Lamprecht was different, for the enduring trauma of the aggrieved father created an extraordinary situation, which was fraught with consequences for the child's development.

Outwardly this development conformed to the patterns and practices that have made the *Pfarrhaus* a legendary institution in German history.[9] The rectory in which the young Karl Lamprecht spent his early years was permeated with the spirit of Christian piety and paternal authority. His mother could almost stand as the prototypical *Pfarrfrau*. An unpretentious, pious, and occasionally melancholy woman, she was devoted to her husband and children, who returned her affections; but she placed no significant intellectual or emotional demands on any of them beyond her enforcement of the piety that pervaded the home.[10] She was, in her youngest son's words, "a woman who learned the cultivation of true modesty and humility, not the phantom of intellectual [*geistige*] superiority."[11]

The aura of superiority—intellectual and every other kind—attached instead to the father, who was the overwhelming figure in the boy's early life, the dominant influence in his emotional, ethical, and intellectual development. He was, in his son's own telling phrase, "a significant person [*ein bedeutender*

Mensch]."[12] Whatever the disappointments of his earlier life, the father remained a vivacious and impetuous man; his presence was comprehensive, and he exerted a captivating effect, like "an imposing officer in civilian clothing," on those who came in contact with him.[13]

The father dominated the emotional field in which the young Karl Lamprecht grew up. This field was replete with active paternal affection, but it was extraordinary in its composition. The boy's surviving brother Hugo was eleven years his senior, and soon after the birth of the last Karl Lamprecht, he left home for boarding school. Hugo's departure left the new child alone with his parents and emphasized the distance between this child and his father, who was fifty-two years his senior. But the problem of distance between father and son was significantly complicated by the continued presence, in the imagination of both, of the idealized Georg. "In my father's eyes," Lamprecht recalled, "the wonderfully beautiful, vigorous, blond Georg . . . was not dead; father always included him [*zählte ihn mit*]." The inclusion could only be invidious, for, as the historian continued, "in the mind of my father he [Georg] was every bit as important as I was [*galt im Grunde genau so viel als ich*]."[14]

The central fact of the boy's early development was thus that he found himself in constant competition for the attention, affection, and approval of his father, in circumstances all the more bewildering for the physical absence of his competitor. The dead child's presence as a standard of comparison was nonetheless real, and it persisted throughout Karl Lamprecht's youth. The historian later recounted the painful episode that occurred when he presented his father with the news that he had just negotiated one of the major passages in his own development by passing his *Abitur*. His father's immediate response was to muse that Georg would at that point just be undertaking his legal career.[15]

The impact of this situation on the boy's development can be reconstructed only in the most general terms and on the basis of fragmentary evidence, which comprises autobiographical recollections and the boy's correspondence with members of his family. The evidence nonetheless presents a consistent and compelling picture. That the situation inflicted significant injury upon him seems indisputable, although the stages through which the injury developed remain closed to anything but speculation. The critical challenge that the boy faced, like other children, was to construct an acceptable sense of his own autonomy, worth, and identity in an environment dominated by his parents.[16] The process has been variously described, in a modern idiom, as finding "narcissistic balance," achieving "the clear differentiation of oneself as a separate individual," or fulfilling the "primary need for respect, understanding, and being taken seriously."[17] The process began at the birth of the child and passed through numerous phases, each of which posed its own characteristic demands and problems, whose resolution left their imprint on the evolving structure of his character.

The circumstances in which the young Karl Lamprecht confronted this challenge can be apprehended only fleetingly, as the child himself became conscious of them and after the adult had distilled them in his reminiscences. They could scarcely have been better calculated, however, to nurture uncertainty about his own identity. The father's invocation of the dead child was a regular feature in the boy's early experience. Its first demonstrable effect was to spawn confusion in the boy's mind about the temporal and spatial limits of his own existence measured against that of his dead brother. One of the historian's earliest memories related to a small picture, entitled "Georg and the Chickens," which hung in the guest room of the rectory. Lamprecht confessed that as a young child he believed the picture to be his dead brother—not merely that it was a representation of the child, but, as he later explained, "that this very picture was itself my brother."[18] The young Lamprecht also spent hours alone in the local cemetery, which contained the grave of his brother. Here, he recalled, he watched the sun dance on the graves and thought of the souls of the dead, concluding that his own existence had no temporal bounds, "that I, unlike other people, was immortal."[19]

These recollections of the adult historian addressed a problem more fundamental than he himself could appreciate. It related to the limits of his self, to basic dimensions in the child's sense of identity. The evidence suggests that the phantom presence of his dead brother in his immediate environment confused fundamentally the young Karl Lamprecht's definition and understanding of himself as a discrete and autonomous human being, as someone important and worthy in his own right. The problem was that the principal arbiter of his worth and importance was a parent emotionally preoccupied with another child who was not physically there.

To cope with the problem, to provide both compensation and an early mode of self-healing for the injury that resulted, the child devised a number of strategies. These he acted out in play, in the realm that Erik Erikson has described as an "intermediate reality between phantasy and actuality."[20] Jessen was little more than a village surrounded by grain fields when Lamprecht was growing up in it. These fields bounded a social terrain within which he and his companions played together; the wider realm beyond the fields, however, exercised a special enticement on the boy, who appropriated it for his solitary exploration and enjoyment. "Even in my early years," he recalled, "I, unlike the others, felt the longing and drive to go further out and to become more familiar with the end of the fields and the solitude [Einsamkeiten] of uncultivated nature."[21] The lure of realms that lay beyond established limits became an essential theme in Lamprecht's life; its original power derived from the way this wider, unbounded space offered the boy what his home and the cemetery did not—a sense of freedom and autonomy that was uncomplicated in any manner by the presence of Georg.[22]

Long before it became a prominent feature of his career as historian, the motif of venturing out into realms beyond bounds acquired special significance in Lamprecht's relationship to his father. Although he was frequently exposed to the outbursts of his father's temper, the historian could recall his father's brandishing a cane only once, at the conclusion of what could well have been psychologically the most important venturing out of his life. Curious about what lay beyond the sandy plains that stretched out to the east of Jessen, the child one evening stole a ride on a wagon headed out of town in that direction. When he was eventually discovered and delivered home, it was well past midnight, and his father was, he remembered, "in a state of rage that he had never until then displayed toward me." The father also had the cane in his hand, but at this point in the drama the historian's memory lapsed, and he confessed to being unable to remember whether he actually received blows.[23] The lapse testified to the importance of an episode in which the child was at last the lone object of his father's emotional concern. In this fashion, the father's rage validated—so dramatically that it remained inscribed in the adult historian's conscious recollection—a behavioral motif that brought him exclusive recognition in the eyes of his father.

The boy was also an avid collector. Next to venturing out on solitary excursions, the act of collecting constituted the central motif of his play. His devotion to it was practically boundless. The objects of what he later called his "mania for collecting [*eifriger Sammelwut*]" included all the natural curiosities available to a boy growing up in an agricultural community—flowers and grasses, insects, and rocks, as well as shells, stamps, and seals acquired in trades with his companions.[24] Whatever this acquisitive obsession might suggest about the developing balance of drives in the boy's character structure, collecting was consistent with the other central motif of his playful behavior.[25] It, too, provided a means of self-affirmation or what Walter Benjamin has called "a process of renewal."[26] Objects from the fields—the realm beyond—could be brought back to what the historian described as an "especially valuable" storeroom next to the rectory, which he reserved for the cache.[27] Here, to use Benjamin's nice phrase, "the locking of individual items within a magic circle" symbolized the placing of new bounds around these objects, their ordered appropriation, arrayal, and redefinition in the service of the boy's emergent definition of himself.[28]

The twin motifs of collecting and venturing out beyond bounds were so central to the subsequent career of Karl Lamprecht that their prominence in his childhood play takes on special significance. Their emotional importance to the child appears to have been fundamental, insofar as they represented his principal means for constructing a sense of himself as a unique, autonomous, and worthy being. That this behavior provoked his father's wrath could only recommend it, for wrath represented recognition and validation—justification, in other words, in the eyes of the father.

The use of a religious term like "justification" to describe the young Lamprecht's quest for an acceptable sense of himself is hardly contrived. Religion was the primary idiom of his emotional and intellectual development, and it provided the terms in which his tensions with his father found expression.

Religion meant Lutheranism. The confession was endemic to the area in which the young Lamprecht grew up—so much so that this part of central Germany was known as the "Lutheran corner" (*der lutherische Winkel*), in which the figure of Luther still possessed, as the historian put it, the aura of a "modernized medieval saint."[29] For this child of the *Pfarrhaus*, the atmosphere of religion was pervasive, and its embodiment was his father.[30] In both his public and private roles, in the pulpit as well as in the rectory, the elder Lamprecht undertook the boy's instruction in the basic Biblical and Lutheran texts. In the course of this instruction, the father laid the foundations for the boy's world view, his ethical beliefs and the rough outlines of ideas that can be best described as metaphysical.

The elder Lamprecht's religious beliefs exemplified a tendency, common among liberal Lutheran theologians of the mid-nineteenth century, to embrace highly personal programs.[31] His antipathy to the bureaucracy and dogmatic orthodoxy of the high church went hand in hand with his tolerance and the residual pietism that colored his reception of Schleiermacher, who continued to be the most significant intellectual influence on him.[32] The basic tenet of the elder Lamprecht's views remained the belief in a transcendent, benevolent God whose works and will were revealed in the Scriptures but were also accessible, to a limited degree, to the God-given powers of the human intellect, once these powers were properly conditioned. Conditioning demanded—and here the influence of his pietism was most apparent—observance of a strict ethic of Christian piety, humility, and moderation. The ethic emphasized both the patient acceptance of human limitation and the disciplined effort needed to realize human potential.

The transmission of these views to the young Lamprecht took place in a loving yet monitory tone, which was echoed in the letters the father wrote once the boy left home for boarding school. "Only endure courageously, by straining all your powers," the father advised his son. "Let God's will be done, and in order that His good and merciful will be done, we too must do our part, and I am firmly convinced that you will neither forget nor hesitate to do yours."[33] The admonitions embraced a catalogue of habits of mind and character demanded of the pious Christian. "I hope to God," wrote the father to his fifteen-year-old son, that "you will be . . . attentive, steady [*ruhig*], obedient, calm, diligent, and distinguished [*erhaben*] in word and deed . . . with all due patience and quiet waiting for eventual recognition."[34] Christian piety, in the father's view, proscribed many temptations, the most reprehensible of which was intellectual arrogance, the presumption that human intelligence was somehow capable of grasping the totality of God's order. This temptation was the subject of another epistolary sermon to the fifteen-year-old boy. "May God admonish you to humility and to the insight that he who knows much still knows little in the total scheme of things. 'To the humble person God gives *mercy*.'"[35]

One feature of the young Lamprecht's moral education deserves special mention. In his homilies to his son, the elder Lamprecht portrayed the pursuit of

Christian virtue as a conflict between two tendencies that resided in the boy and not only contended for his soul but informed his very identity. "Your letter tells us that you have once again become our good Karl," wrote the father after his son, presumably in the form of the bad Karl, had been disciplined at school.[36] Reference to two conflicting sides of human nature was common in Lutheran moral teaching, but in the context of the father's habitual invocations of the idealized Georg as a role model, the repeated appeals to the son's "better, more noble self [*Ich*]" could do nothing to diminish confusion in the boy's mind over who the real Karl Lamprecht was.[37]

The young Lamprecht's assimilation of these admonishments informed his emerging consciousness of himself no less than it affected his relationship to his father. The assimilation took place within the psychological context of the child's search for an acceptable sense of himself; and if his modes of play represented one aspect of the search, the manner in which he accepted and rejected his father's teachings represented another.

By all outward indications, the boy's relationship to his father was one of devotion bordering on reverence. There is much to support the judgment of Karl-Heinz Metz that the father was the "great and admired reference-figure in the life of the boy."[38] The historian's conscious recollections of his father suggested a relationship of profound respect and affection; and the death of the old man in 1878 came as a severe blow to the twenty-two-year-old son.[39] Years after this event, the historian confessed to a colleague how much his father had provided him with abiding ideals. "A close tie to departed ones," he wrote in connection with his father, "always strengthens our ideals; the modern adult no longer enjoys a more profound education than through these [ideals]."[40]

During his father's lifetime, the boy's respect for his father seemed at times to reach the point of identification. The child's earliest surviving letters were directed to Hugo, who was then completing his theological studies. These letters are remarkable documents, for both their tone and their pretentious moralizing suggested the child's affectation of his father's persona. "I am very mad at you," carped the eleven-year-old boy at his twenty-two-year-old brother, who was evidently not a conscientious correspondent, "(but I don't mean it in a bad sense)."[41] "I am going to have the great goodness of heart," came another admonishment, "to forgive you your indolence and to write you."[42] Several years later, when his brother announced that he was going to ask a woman to marry him, the boy's ruminations on *les affaires de coeur* (in which he at the time had had no experience whatsoever) were difficult to distinguish in their tone from his father's sermons:

> Now, if it is the will of the good Lord, so let Him ordain it well and good in His wisdom [*Rathe*], and let everything turn out well. The saying has it that the heart's desire is the voice of fate, and certainly one can suppose that, if at all, this side of our sensuous feelings has a more elevated effect. Follow it yourself and believe that it is a reliable guide . . . . Not external things should be our guide, but rather that which is internal and eternal.[43]

The direct correspondence between the father and Hugo Lamprecht does not survive, but the wisdom offered by the young Karl Lamprecht upon his brother's passing his theological examinations in 1872 could, at least in its tenor, substitute for the paternal response. "You stand now at the end of your career," counseled the boy, "or at least at its goal, which will provide a secure basis and firm foundation for whatever changes the future may offer."[44]

Both the young Lamprecht's penchant for adapting his father's persona and the reverence he displayed to others for the man indicated an affection that was genuine but problematic. The boy's attitude suggested an ambivalence born of disappointment. His image of his father was idealized; it related to the father less as he was than as the boy wished him to be—a model of perfection and omnipotence.[45] But the boy's relationship to his father was ambivalent in another respect, for his sense of himself was linked to modes of behavior that challenged his father's authority.

Whatever the young Karl Lamprecht's paternalizing posture toward his brother might suggest about his identification with his father, the similarities in the tone of the letters corresponded to significant temperamental resemblances between the father and his younger son. These, too, created tensions in the relationship. The young Karl Lamprecht inherited his father's vivacious energy, impetuosity, and obstinacy, as well as the restlessness that had been such a feature of the father's early life. As the boy's devotion to his favorite pastimes bore witness, these character traits coalesced into a stubborn independence, which approached self-absorption, and an unquenchable, impatient curiosity. Like the modes of play to which they corresponded, the traits reflected as well the child's attempt to deal with the extraordinary demands placed upon his psychological development; and they symptomized an emerging sense of self which was not altogether secure or stable—a character structure which was, in the perceptive phrase of a scholar who knew him later, not "fully worked out [nicht vollkommen]."[46]

The father's sermonizing was one indication that the development of this sense of self had brought the boy into conflict with paternal authority. "My dear little Karl," read one letter to the schoolboy, "accustom yourself to being thorough [gewöhne Dich an Gründlichkeit]. Abandon no subject before it has become clear and lucid to you in all its aspects."[47] This injunction, like the father's repeated calls for patience, humility, and moderation, addressed the enduring absence of these traits in the boy. It was no coincidence, however, that the traits that were coming to define the boy's character were just those that made him the object of his father's concern and censure, for the child could doubtless intuit that resistance to his father's authority brought recognition.

Karl Lamprecht was plagued for the duration of his life by the problem of his own identity, but no evidence survives that he was conscious of the extent to which his self-definition emerged in conflict with his father's authority. Several pieces of evidence do suggest a subconscious awareness of the problem, however. The parts of the Bible that most intrigued the child during his religious instruction were books of the Old Testament that had resistance to authority as their theme.[48] One comprised the books of Chronicles, which can be read as a treatise on the consequences of obeying and defying divine authority. Suggestive, too, was the child's fascination with the apocryphal books of the Maccabees and the story, related in the book of Daniel, of the three young men in the oven, for in these cases the principal theme is the successful defiance of oppressive secular authority.

Several other episodes in the historian's later biography are relevant to the problem of his relationship to his father, for they suggest that the challenge to paternal authority might have been complicated not only by a sense of disappointment, but by feelings of rejection. In one of the volumes of his *magnum opus*, in the midst of a discussion of Luther, for whom he betrayed great sympathy, Lamprecht suddenly interjected a question about the reformer's relationship to his father. "Did the monastic order offer the young monk compensation for the lost love of his father?" And a little later in the same account, the historian drew attention to the young Luther's "horrible loneliness, his God-forsaken situation."[49] Feelings of rejection by his father would also make sense of Lamprecht's proclivity as a young adult to establish quasi-paternal relationships with significantly elder men.

Rejection worked both ways. An extended discussion of the historian's choice of a career and his abandonment of Christianity is out of place here. It suffices to note that in both contexts the son rejected positions identified with his father. Finally, if it did not symbolize an ultimate rejection of his father, the last act in the historian's life, his burial, was an unambiguous expression of his determination to maintain his distance. The cemetery in Jessen, where the historian spent many hours musing as a boy, does not contain his remains. There the father rests alone in the company of his favorite son.[50]

The young Karl Lamprecht spent a great deal of time alone. Collecting and wandering in the fields, the forms of play that nourished his sense of autonomy, were largely solitary pursuits. Nor did the independence, impetuosity, and restlessness that became increasingly pronounced in his character win him close friends. But other circumstances contributed to his isolation. These were social; and they, too, defined the boy's emergent awareness of himself.

Jessen numbered perhaps a thousand souls in the middle of the nineteenth century. Most of its inhabitants were occupied in farming grains or vegetables, making wine, and processing textiles. Industry, principally in textile processing, was small scale; the town was largely self-sufficient, and much of its internal commercial exchange was still based upon barter.[51] Not until the 1870s did a branch line connect the town by rail to the closest urban center in Wittenberg, which was five hours away by carriage.

The boy's social experience was conditioned by the place that his father occupied in the social structure of Jessen. The elder Lamprecht was the most prominent man in the town. His authority derived from his official position as *Oberpfarrer*, whch made him spiritual mentor to a Protestant community that comprised the great majority of the town's inhabitants. The position carried secular responsibilities as well. He was school inspector for the town and its environs. His position made him the town's chief statistician, record keeper, and the central figure in its charitable undertakings. He was also the highest-placed representative of the Prussian state in Jessen, and he cultivated close contacts with the artisans who dominated the town council.[52] His energy and vivacity emphasized his role as a prop of the community, for he was inclined to carry out his responsibilities conscientiously and to make his home a center of sociability. Like other pastors in these circumstances, however, he could not find full acceptance in his community, for his cultural background—the academic credentials his position required—made him practically unique in Jessen. It accentuated his status both as a notable and as an import from outside, a man whose children were not going to grow old in that town.[53]

The elder Lamprecht was conscious of the status he enjoyed and insisted on being paid the deference due him, but his position brought disadvantages as well as advantages to his youngest son.[54] The social distance which separated the young Lamprecht from the other children of the town nurtured his own temperamental proclivities toward solitude and independence. "Pastor's Karl," as he was commonly known, consequently found it difficult to relate to the children of artisanal and farming families who were growing up with him; and he had few friends.[55]

The social distance from his contemporaries spawned an aloofness in the boy, the consciousness that he was somehow different from the rest of his cohort and set apart from them by his endowments. His father did not entirely discourage this perception, and it only increased once the young Lamprecht began his formal schooling in the company of these other children.[56] Unlike them, he was growing up in a cultured home, in the expectation that he would pursue an academic career. Karl Lamprecht was being groomed, in other words, to join the country's cultured elite.

"There are few concepts," Rudolf Vierhaus has observed, "that have at the same time been used so often, with such different meanings, and whose accumulated connotations are so specifically German as 'Bildung.'"[57] Vierhaus' essay is a useful place to start in trying to understand the evolution of the idea of Bildung; but here it is germane only to emphasize several features of the concept's history that related directly to the experience of the young Karl Lamprecht.[58] "Education" is a less satisfactory translation of the word than "cultivation," for Bildung implied the shaping and development of the whole personality by means of exposure to the great achievements of human cultural endeavor. By the middle of the nineteenth century, the concept had undergone a certain reification, so that it also implied a body of knowledge and refined taste that one could acquire and display and that entitled one to reward. But the implications of the concept were so all-embracing that the word "religion" can with little exaggeration be used in connection with it, for as Thomas Nipperdey has written, it pertained to "'ultimate questions [*letzte Dinge*],' to ultimate human concerns."[59] The ethical moment in *Bildung* was thus of as much consequence as the ideological, aesthetic, and pedagogical dimensions of the concept. Self-cultivation, the achievement of culture, was a moral postulate that demanded the dedication of the whole person to the enduring wisdom and values that culture comprised.

The secularization of the concept of *Bildung*, the celebration of culture as a natural human achievement, took place in the course of the nineteenth century as the legacy of German neo-humanism of the *Goethezeit*. Nonetheless, the idea of *Bildung* had deep roots in the Lutheran tradition, particularly in Lutheran pietism; and these by no means disappeared in the nineteenth century.[60] They survived in the religious aura that continued to attach generally to the concept of *Bildung* and, more specifically, in the idea of a human vocation to engage in the obedient, disciplined cultivation of God-given abilities in order better to serve God. In the liberal Protestantism of the midcentury, the original ethic comported with the cultivation of the human intellectual potential; the purpose of this endeavor was now to descry the great general patterns of order and excellence in human existence—patterns that humans themselves understood to be culture but which ultimately reflected God's own higher design.

Like the sons of countless other German pastors, young Karl Lamprecht received, at the hands of his father, an education founded on this ethic. It was calculated to inspire attitudes appropriate to both Christian piety and the cultivation of the mind, or, more concretely, to academic success. The boy's education thus also addressed the practical, pedagogical aspects of *Bildung*. By the middle of the nineteenth century, *Bildung* practically demanded a pilgrimage through special institutions of learning, beginning with the *Gymnasium*, whose curriculum emphasized the disciplines thought to represent the basic vernacular of cultural achievement, the classical languages. From the perspective of both father and son, the problem was that the essential prerequisite for admission to the *Gymnasium* was a basic knowledge of these languages, especially of Latin.

Jessen was typical of small German towns, in that it supported only a communal *Volksschule*, whose curriculum did not extend beyond basic practical disciplines geared for children of rural folk who harbored no hope or ambition for post-elementary schooling of any kind. After being tutored for several years by his father, the young Lamprecht enrolled in this school at the age of nine, but he continued to receive essential parts of his education at home. The *Pfarrhaus* in Jessen was a center not only of sociability and power but of culture. Here the boy learned from his father the basics of Latin, as well as a little Greek; he participated in the small Latin reading circle which his father had organized among the handful of people in the area—the local physician and pastors from neighboring communities—who knew some Latin.[61] The boy was also encouraged to read widely and critically, and to sing and appreciate music. The elder Lamprecht himself exemplified the power of the German idea of *Bildung*; he was an intellectually alive and well-read man, and he directed his son's enormous curiosity and love of collecting into a passion for learning. It was doubtless greater testimony to the father's pedagogical labors than to those of the boy's schoolmaster that the young Lamprecht exhausted the offerings of the communal school two years later, in 1867, after he had distinguished himself, as his teacher reported, by his "unusual abilities in all subjects, as well as by his tireless diligence."[62]

In the spring of 1867, the eleven-year-old boy passed the required entrance examinations for the nearest Gymnasium, which was located in Wittenberg. He thereupon ventured out from Jessen for good, to return only during holidays. He later described the departure as the shattering of his dreams of a life of collecting in the freedom of nature, but he made the transition quickly enough to suggest that his idyllic recollections of life in Jessen were exaggerated. He boarded with the family of a bookseller, where, he reported, he had the good fortune "almost to rediscover his Vaterhaus."[63] If his rural background brought him any disadvantages, he soon overcame them. He performed well for his teachers, who praised him for his natural talents and diligence and scolded him only mildly for the restlessness which he continued to display in the new setting.[64] But from the outset, the Gymnasium in Wittenberg was merely a temporary station in his father's plans; and two years later the son enrolled in his father's alma mater.

The young Karl Lamprecht's departure from Jessen to Wittenberg in 1867 marked a rite of passage into the milieu that nurtured Germany's elite. The Gymnasium in which he enrolled was part of a network that had been built up in the kingdom of Prussia in the aftermath of the upheavals of the Napoleonic era. The purpose of these institutions was to prepare young men for the universities, where they would be trained to staff the upper echelons of the public bureaucracy. The Gymnasium was, in the words of Karl-Ernst Jeismann, a self-conscious, "well-organized educational institution, whose internal didactic and methodological conception was [now] better thought out than ever before."[65] Although the educational system that took shape early in the nineteenth century departed in significant respects from the lofty designs of the men who had inspired it during the era of reform, the Gymnasium was founded upon a classical, humanistic curriculum. The ultimate mission of the institution was preprofessional training of public elites, but in the ideology of the educators, this mission required the Bildung of the young men who attended these schools. This process in turn implied cultivating, principally by means of the study of classical languages, the fundamental habits of mind thought to be essential for political and cultural leadership.[66]

In 1867, there were just under 200 Gymnasien in Prussia, and Karl Lamprecht was one of about 55,000 boys undergoing the training they offered.[67] This privileged group, the bulk of whom were, like Lamprecht himself, non-noble sons of public officials and professionals, were placed in the charge of a distinguished corps of pedagogues. The men who taught in the Gymnasien were highly trained academics; many were active, publishing scholars, and, to judge by the frequency with which they populate academic memoirs, more than a few of them were fearsome pedants and disciplinarians.

The network of *Gymnasien* stood atop the hierarchy of the school system, but within this network itself there was an order that was less formally defined. Some of these institutions enjoyed better reputations than others by virtue of their traditions, endowments, faculties, and the kinds of students they attracted. The school to which Karl Lamprecht transferred in the spring of 1869 ranked, by any calculation, near the pinnacle.

Schulpforta was situated about four kilometers southwest of Naumburg, on the bank of the river Saale in the Prussian province of Saxony. It was founded as one of three so-called *Fürstenschulen* by Duke Moritz of Saxony in 1543 on the site of a secularized Cistercian monastery. Its reputation grew as a center of humanistic Protestant learning in the tradition of Melanchton, and its alumni included Klopstock, Fichte, Leopold Ranke, and Friedrich Nietzsche.[68] After the school came under Prussian jurisdiction in 1815, its reputation grew as a place for preparing boys of the Protestant-Evangelical confession for what its own staff described as a "more advanced academic [*wissenschaftliche*] life or a career in pure scholarship."[69] The Prussians incorporated it into the system of classical secondary schools they were then building. They also retained the practice of offering scholarships at the school to students from selected Saxon towns, and in 1869, after he had passed additional examinations, Karl Lamprecht was awarded the *Freistelle* reserved for Jessen.

Lamprecht was one of about 200 Protestant boys who were interned within the walls of the former monastery and given concentrated exposure to a rigid curriculum of Latin, Greek, German, French, history, geography, mathematics, natural science, Protestant religion, and gymnastics.[70] His aptitude proved greater for the languages and literatures and for history than for mathematics and the sciences, where his interest waned once instruction passed from taxonomy, which appealed to his collector's instincts, to experiment and exact analysis, which taxed his patience.[71]

On the whole, however, his performance in this regimen was outstanding, even among a group of boys whose academic preparation was often far stronger than his. His curiosity remained acute. He impressed his teachers with his energy and his powers of rapid comprehension. His voracious reading extended well beyond what his teachers assigned, and he committed vast quantities of information to memory. On his own time he studied Italian, Hebrew, art history, and piano. By his third year, he stood at the head of his class.

His academic performance was marred only by tensions with some of his teachers. These tensions reflected a significant problem. His restiveness at being an object of authority increased as the hold of his father was transformed in the distance between Jessen and Naumburg. Although the direct ties to home survived only in the form of holiday visits, the father remained a presence in the boy's life. The epistolary sermons that arrived regularly at the school, the inquiries into the boy's academic progress, the accountings that the penurious father demanded of his son's expenses, and the reports the rector periodically sent home to the father on the son's performance all served as reminders of the continuing dominion of paternal authority. Although he could not defy this authority directly, the boy did begin to resist the authority of others, be they older students who subjected him to ritual hazing, teachers whom he did not respect, or the father's surrogate at the school, the rector himself. On one occasion in his third year, the boy's insubordination took the form of circulating a clandestine newspaper that contained barbs at the faculty; when caught, he was disciplined and nearly expelled.[72]

During his years at Schulpforta, he found himself for the first time in close quarters among boys who were at least his social equals (one of them, let it be noted here, was Theobald von Bethmann Hollweg). Lamprecht had little difficulty winning acceptance among his peers in the course of their collective activities, particularly during the excursions which the students made during their free time into the surrounding countryside or to Naumburg and other places of interest and amusement.[73] He maintained few friendships, however; and these were with boys who both suffered and flattered the traits in his personality that had begun to develop in the child and were now, in the wake of academic success and in the absence of his father, becoming exaggerated in the adolescent. His aloofness developed toward arrogance, while his self-absorption and restiveness with authority fueled his ambition; these traits also underlay his penchant for asserting his own authority in intellectual self-display.[74] One of his friends recalled his "strong need to make known what was going on in his head [was in ihm lebte und nach Gestaltung rang]."[75] The pretentiousness of the letters he wrote to his brother at this time bore witness to the same proclivity, as did a fondness for using foreign words.

Around him formed a small clique (which did not include Bethmann Holl-weg). It comprised three or four boys who were captivated, if not intimidated by the intellectual energy and power he exuded. He called up vast amounts of information from memory, and he paraded it as his own erudition in front of his friends. If those in his orbit found his impatience, restlessness, and lack of tact occasionally disconcerting, they forgave him these traits, grateful to be in the presence of a boy whom they all acknowledged as their superior.[76] Whatever the company of these admirers did to satisfy Lamprecht's need to find acceptance, it did little to mute the emerging signs of grandiosity in his character or to restrain his growing ambition.

The years at Schulpforta not only witnessed the development of Lamprecht's ambition; they resolved the issue of where this ambition was to find an outlet. That he would enter an academic career was never in doubt. During his last years at Schulpforta, as the question of his future became more immediate, he weighed a number of obvious options for university study, including philology, theology, and the law.[77] The choice of theology was a common one for the son of a pastor, but in young Lamprecht's case, the ambivalence of his relationship with his father and the fact that his surviving brother had already chosen a career in this field presented insuperable barriers.[78] The choice of the law was even more burdened by association with Georg.

Lamprecht's decision to pursue studies in history was due largely to the influence of Friedrich Wilhelm Herbst, who succeeded to the rectorship of Schulpforta in 1873 and entered Lamprecht's life at a time when a decision was due. Herbst was a respected historian in his own right, a student of Ranke. In an epoch of growing teutophilia in the history curriculum in the secondary schools, Herbst was unusual in the breadth of his interests. He insisted that his students occupy themselves with the history of art, literature, and the economy, as well as with the history of peoples around the world.[79] Lamprecht, who was then in his last year at the school, found in Herbst a sympathetic and accessible man, who was willing to serve both as tutor and confidante—in fact, as something of a father figure.

The academic record had already suggested the student's aptitude for a career in scholarship, particularly in history—a discipline in which, it was reported, he possessed an unusual "range of knowledge" and capacity for "independent conceptualization of the material."[80] His academic virtues reflected the metamorphosis of the familiar motifs of collecting and venturing beyond established bonds. If the one now underlay his drive to assemble a broad body of knowledge, the other corresponded to his attraction to unconventional ways of interpreting this knowledge. He demonstrated the latter trait in his valedictory speech, in which he plotted Pericles' funeral oration as a curve.[81] Herbst's role was to encourage the boy's interest in history and to cultivate his interpretive skills, which struck the schoolmaster as refreshing and original. The success of Herbst's efforts was signaled early in 1874, when Lamprecht announced his decision to study history.[82]

Six months later, in September, after an intense summer of study at home, Karl Lamprecht passed the examinations for his *Abitur*. In passing him, the examining committee at Schulpforta expressed the hope that he would "someday with God's help succeed in achieving splendid goals in scholarship and life."[83] The eighteen-year-old graduate, whose short career as a scholar had already been crowned with success, harbored no doubt that he would fulfill this hope.

Notes

1. NL Lamprecht (Munich), Lamprecht-Stammbaum; UB Bonn, NL Lamprecht (L 2), Karl Nathaniel Lamprecht, Lebenslauf, 26.9.45. On the elder Lamprecht see KE, 28–31; LW, 3–6.
2. Lamprecht states flatly that his father enrolled first in Jena, but Schönebaum can find no evidence to support the assertion. I see no reason to doubt Lamprecht's version.
3. See Robert M. Bigler, *The Politics of German Protestantism: The Rise of the Protestant Church Elite in Prussia, 1815–1848* (Berkeley and Los Angeles, 1972), 99–104; Franz

Schnabel, *Deutsche Geschichte im Neunzehnten Jahrhundert: Die protestantischen Kirchen in Deutschland* (Freiburg i. Br., 1965), 265–74.
4. KE, 46. See Emanuel Hirsch, *Geschichte der neueren evangelischen Theologie in Zusammenhang mit den allgemeinen Bewegungen des europäischen Denkens*, 5 vols. (Gütersloh, 1964), 5: 281–91, 375–79.
5. NL Lamprecht (Korr. 66), Karl N. Lamprecht to Karl G. Lamprecht, Jessen, 1.3.75. The elder Lamprecht's expression was: "hegelten, schellingten und fichteten."
6. NL Lamprecht (L 1), Emilie Lamprecht, Für meine lieben Kinder (1882).
7. NL Lamprecht (L 1), Karl N. Lamprecht to Riecke, Jessen, 18.4.56.
8. NL Lamprecht (L 1), Emilie Lamprecht, Für meine lieben Kinder.
9. The literature on this subject is extensive. See Hartmut Lehmann, "'Das ewige Haus': Das lutherische Pfarrhaus im Wandel der Zeiten," in H. Look, ed., *"Gott kumm mir zu hilf": Martin Luther in der Zeitenwende* (Berlin, 1985), 177–200; Martin Greiffenhagen, ed., *Das evangelische Pfarrhaus: Eine Kultur- und Sozialgeschichte* (Stuttgart, 1984); *cf.* Wilhelm Baur, *Das deutsche evangelische Pfarrhaus: Seine Gründung und sein Bestand* (Bremen, 1878).
10. Historisches Archiv der Stadt Köln, NL Gustav von Mevissen, Lamprecht to Mevissen, Gross-Ballerstedt, 29.9.82; KE, 49–50; *cf.* Andreas Gestrich, "Erziehung im Pfarrhaus," in Greiffenhagen, 63–82; Barbara Beuys, "Die Pfarrfrau: Kopie oder Original?" in Greiffenhagen, 47–61; Hermann Werdermann, *Die deutsche evangelische Pfarrfrau: Ihre Geschichte in vier Jahrhunderten*, 3d ed. (Witten, 1935).
11. NL Lamprecht (Korr. 59), Lamprecht to Hugo Lamprecht, Pforte, 4.2.74. These traits suffuse the brief account of her life which she wrote for her children shortly before her death: NL Lamprecht (L 1), Für meine lieben Kinder (1882).
12. KE, 48.
13. Siegfried Hübschmann, "Karl Lamprecht," *Mitteldeutsche Lebensbilder* (Magdeburg, 1929), 4: 405.
14. Ibid., 11.
15. Ibid.
16. See Erik H. Erikson, *Identity: Youth and Crisis* (New York, 1968), 91–141; Erikson, *Childhood and Society*, 2d ed. (New York, 1963), 187–274.
17. Alice Miller, *Das Drama des begabten Kindes und die Suche nach dem wahren Selbst* (Frankfurt am Main, 1983), 70–71; Arnold M. Cooper, "Narcissism," in Silvano Arieti, ed., *American Handbook of Psychiatry*, 2d ed., 7 vols. (New York, 1981), 7: 309. See also Heinz Kohut, "Forms and Transformations of Narcissism," *Self Psychology and the Humanities: Reflections on a New Psychoanalytic Approach* (New York and London, 1985), 97–123; Kohut, *The Analysis of the Self: A Systematic Approach to the Psychoanalytic Treatment of Narcissistic Personality Disorders* (New York, 1971).
18. KE, 60.
19. Ibid., 11–12.
20. Erikson, *Childhood and Society*, 211–12, 222; *cf.* D. W. Winnicott, "Playing: Creative Activity and the Search for the Self," in Winnecott, *Playing and Reality* (London and New York, 1971), 53–64.
21. KE, 18–19; *cf.* Annie M. Popper, "Karl Gotthard Lamprecht (1856–1915)," in S. William Halperin, ed., *Essays in Modern European Historiography* (Chicago and London, 1970), 120. Lamprecht himself remarked on the parallels between this motif in his childhood play and his later scholarship. KE, 18–19. Popper alone of Lamprecht's subsequent commentators has appreciated the importance of this early fascination with the "realms beyond."
22. Georg's death represented the archetypical venturing out beyond bounds. It is tempting to speculate that the young Karl Lamprecht unconsciously identified with his deceased brother and sought to follow him in hopes of gaining the same kind of acceptance that his brother had in the eyes of their father. This interpretation

highlights the suicidal accents in the theme of venturing out. It sheds a suggestive light on the historian's behavior during the great crisis of his adult life, the *Methodenstreit*. It is difficult, however, given the paucity of evidence, to develop the analysis further at this level (*cf.* n. 45, below).

23. KE, 23–24, 65.
24. NL Lamprecht (L 6f), Lamprecht, Den Eltern (Lebenslauf); KE 34.
25. The evidence does not permit more than speculation on this problem, but see Sandor Rado, "Obsessive Behavior: So-Called Obsessive-Compulsive Neurosis," in Arieti, ed., *American Handbook of Psychiatry*, 3: 195–208; David Shapiro, *Neurotic Styles* (New York and London, 1965), 23–53.
26. Walter Benjamin, "Unpacking My Library: A Talk about Book Collecting," in Hannah Arendt, ed., *Illuminations* (New York, 1969), 61.
27. KE, 34.
28. Benjamin, 60.
29. KE, 47.
30. See Gestrich, 67, 71.
31. Schnabel, *Kirchen*, 271.
32. KE, 46, 51–53.
33. NL Lamprecht (Korr. 66), Karl N. Lamprecht to Lamprecht, Jessen, 13.5.74.
34. NL Lamprecht (Korr. 66), Karl N. Lamprecht to Lamprecht, Jessen, Erntefest 1871.
35. NL Lamprecht (Korr. 66), Karl N. Lamprecht to Lamprecht, Jessen, 1.11.71.
36. NL Lamprecht (Korr. 66), Karl N. Lamprecht to Lamprecht, Jessen, 25.4.74.
37. NL Lamprecht (Korr. 66), Karl N. Lamprecht to Lamprecht, Jessen, 23.10.74.
38. Metz, *Grundformen*, 462–63.
39. NL Lamprecht (Korr. 59), Lamprecht to Hugo Lamprecht, Jessen, 24.12.78; Lamprecht to Emilie and Hugo Lamprecht, Bonn, 22.7.82; Lamprecht to Hugo Lamprecht, Bonn, 9.10.86; Lamprecht to Hugo Lamprecht, Leipzig, 11.1.04.
40. Hessische Landesbibliothek, Wiesbaden, NL Erich Liesegang, Lamprecht to Liesegang, Strassburg, 29.12.89.
41. NL Lamprecht (Korr. 59), Lamprecht to Hugo Lamprecht, Jessen, 1.8.67.
42. NL Lamprecht (Korr. 59), Lamprecht to Hugo Lamprecht, Pforta, 7.12.72.
43. NL Lamprecht (Korr. 59), Lamprecht to Hugo Lamprecht, [Schulpforta] 3–4.2.74.
44. NL Lamprecht (Korr. 59), Lamprecht to Hugo Lamprecht, Pforta, 12.5.72.
45. Lamprecht reported a boyhood incident over which he long brooded, for it contradicted his "concept of the omnipotence of his parents." The incident involved his discovery that his mother could not read Latin (KE, 66). The historian failed, however, to mention any occasion on which he doubted his father's omnipotence. I am indebted to Kohut for this analysis, but I am not comfortable pursuing it further at this level, for I do not believe the historical evidence can sustain more detailed conclusions about the internal dynamics of Lamprecht's development. In Kohut's terms, however, the narcissistic trauma that the child suffered led to the repression of primitive grandiose fantasies, which under more normal circumstances would have been modified—in other words, limited. Consequently, a grandiose narcissistic self survived into adulthood to drive the historian's ambition to realize its archaic aims. Moreover, despite his tensions with his father, which remained largely subconscious, the child's traumatic disappointments with his father resulted in the creation of an "idealized parent imago," which lent ideational content to the historian's grandiose ambition and functioned as an ego-ideal of limitless perfection and omnipotence. See Kohut, "Forms and Transformations," passim; *Analysis of the Self*, esp. 25–28; Miller, 68–77; Otto Kernberg, "Pathological Narcissism in Middle Age," in *Internal World and External Reality: Object Relations Theory Applied* (New York and London, 1980), 135–54.
46. G. A. Rein, Politik und Universität, diktiert 1975–1976, 17. I am indebted to

Geoffrey Giles for making this manuscript available to me.

47. NL Lamprecht (Korr. 66), Karl N. Lamprecht to Lamprecht, Jessen, 9.8.71.
48. BA, NL Gottfried Traub (70), Lamprecht to Traub, Leipzig, 16.11.11; KE, 64–65.
49. DG, 5: 224–25; cf. LW, 295.
50. In his memoirs the historian told of a visit to the cemetery in 1913, when he was provoked to think of the "remarkable tie, which was now at least restored between the remains of my father and brother and which corresponded to the very remarkable behavior of my father while he was still living." KE, 10–11.
51. KE, 16, 35.
52. KE, 53–54; cf. Lehmann, "Das ewige Haus," 187–88.
53. See Wolfgang Marhold, "Die soziale Stellung des Pfarrers," in Greiffenhagen, esp. 185–186.
54. BA, NL Maximilian Harden, Lamprecht to Harden, Leipzig, 18.5.96; cf. KE, 55–56.
55. LW, 7.
56. NL Lamprecht (Korr. 66), Karl N. Lamprecht to Lamprecht, Jessen, 23.10.74.
57. Rudolf Vierhaus, "Bildung," in Otto Brunner et al., eds., Geschichtliche Grundbegriffe: Historisches Lexikon zur politisch-sozialen Sprache in Deutschland, 6 vols. (Stuttgart, 1972–1990), 1: 547.
58. See also Ralph Fiedler, Die klassische deutsche Bildungsidee: Ihre soziologischen Wurzeln und pädagogischen Folgen (Weinheim, 1972); Wilhelm Richter, Der Wandel des Bildungsgedankens: Die Brüder von Humboldt, das Zeitalter der Bildung und die Gegenwart (Berlin, 1971); Walter Horace Bruford, The German Tradition of Self-Cultivation: "Bildung" from Humboldt to Thomas Mann (Cambridge, 1975).
59. Thomas Nipperdey, Deutsche Geschichte 1800–1866: Bürgerwelt und starker Staat (Munich, 1984), 440.
60. See Anthony J. La Vopa, "Vocations, Careers, and Talent: Lutheran Pietism and Sponsored Mobility in Eighteenth-Century Germany," Comparative Studies in Society and History, 28 (1986): 255–86.
61. KE, 31, 38, 46, 65–66; cf. Gestrich, 78.
62. NL Lamprecht (L 1), Zeugnis, Carl Gotthard Lamprecht, 1865–1867; LW, 8.
63. NL Lamprecht (L 6f), Lamprecht, Den Eltern [Lebenslauf]; Georg Winter, "Karl Lamprecht," Die Gesellschaft, 17 (1898): 308.
64. NL Lamprecht (L 1), Censuren; LW, 8–9; Herbert Schönebaum, "Karl Lamprechts Verbundenheit mit seiner Heimat jenseits der 'Kindheitserinnerungen,'" Heimatkalender für den Kreis Jessen 1956 (Jessen, 1956).
65. Karl-Ernst Jeismann, Das preussische Gymnasium in Staat und Gesellschaft: Die Entstehung des Gymnasiums als Schule des Staates und der Gebildeten 1787–1817 (Stuttgart, 1974), 397. See Friedrich Paulsen, Geschichte des gelehrten Unterrichts auf den deutschen Schulen und Universitäten vom Ausgang des Mittelalters bis zur Gegenwart, 2d ed., 2 vols. (Berlin and Leipzig, 1896–1897), esp. 2: 313–58; Fritz Blättner, Das Gymnasium: Aufgaben der höheren Schule in Geschichte und Gegenwart (Heidelberg, 1960); Margret Kraul, Das deutsche Gymnasium 1780–1980 (Frankfurt am Main, 1974), esp. 47–90.
66. Leonore O'Boyle, "Klassische Bildung und soziale Struktur in Deutschland zwischen 1800 und 1848," HZ, 207 (1968): 584–608; Hajo Holborn, "Der deutsche Idealismus in sozialgeschichtlicher Beleuchtung," HZ, 174 (1952): 359–84.
67. Detlef K. Müller, Sozialstruktur und Schulsystem: Aspekte zum Strukturwandel des Schulwesens im 19. Jahrhundert (Göttingen, 1977), 48.
68. Paulsen, Unterricht, 2: 407–12.
69. NL Lamprecht (L 3b), Bekanntmachung für Eltern und Vormünder . . ., 10.2.64; cf. Friedrich Meinecke, Autobiographische Schriften, ed. Eberhard Kessel (Stuttgart, 1969), 29–30.

70. LW, 9–26; Schönebaum, "Lamprechts Verbundenheit," 35–37.

71. NL Lamprecht (59), Lamprecht to Hugo Lamprecht, Pforta, 23.10.70, 23.9.71.

72. NL Lamprecht (Korr. 66), Karl N. Lamprecht to Lamprecht, Jessen, 23.9.71; *cf.* Gestrich, 80–81.

73. E.g., NL Lamprecht (Korr. 59), Lamprecht to Hugo Lamprecht, Pforta, 25.1.73.

74. KE, 51.

75. NL Lamprecht (L 3a), Karl Gneisse, Erinnerungen eines Mitschülers aus Karl Lamprechts Pfortazeit, Colmar, 17.9.15.

76. Ibid. NL Lamprecht (L 3a), Friedrich Zimmer to Marianne Lamprecht, Zehlendorf, 6.8.15; Hans Laehr to Marianne Lamprecht, Schweizerhof zu Zehlendorf, 16.8.15. *Cf.* NL Lamprecht (Korr. 24), Gneisse to Lamprecht, Weissenburg, 9.6.85.

77. NL Lamprecht (Korr. 59), Lamprecht to Hugo Lamprecht, Pforta, 4.3.73; NL Lamprecht (L 3a), Zimmer to Marianne Lamprecht, Zehlendorf, 6.8.15; Schönebaum, "Verbundenheit," 36.

78. See Gestrich, 69; Sigrid Bormann-Heischkeil, "Die soziale Herkunft der Pfarrer und ihrer Ehefrauen," in Greiffenhagen, 160.

79. Ernst Weymar, *Das Selbstverständnis der Deutschen: Ein Bericht über den Geist des Geschichtsunterrichts der höheren Schulen im 19. Jahrhundert* (Stuttgart, 1961), 196–204.

80. NL Lamprecht (L 3a), Zeugniss der Reife für den Zögling der Königlichen Schule Pforta, 15.9.74; NL Lamprecht (Korr. 45), Lamprecht to Rodenberg, Leipzig, 3.3.02.

81. NL Lamprecht (L 3a), Zimmer to Marianne Lamprecht, Zehlendorf, 6.8.15.

82. NL Lamprecht (Korr. 59), Lamprecht to Hugo Lamprecht, Pforta, 11.3.74.

83. NL Lamprecht (L 3a), Zeugniss der Reife für den Zögling der Königlichen Schule Pforta, 15.9.74.

2

Göttingen, Leipzig, Munich

> Es ist ein Versuch, sich gleichsam *a posteriori* eine Vergangenheit zu geben, aus dem man stammen möchte, im Gegensatz zu der, aus der man stammt.

Karl Lamprecht was cut from the classic mold of German historians. In fact, his case conforms so faithfully to typical patterns of background and training among historians (and the German professoriate in general) that one might almost speak of him as a modal figure. Like countless other German intellectuals, he was the product of the *Pfarrhaus*, the son of a university-educated Lutheran pastor. He grew up in a part of central Germany that nurtured a disproportionate share of the country's historians, and he was educated in an elite school which, along with the famed Joachimsthal *Gymnasium* in Berlin, produced more of these scholars than any other secondary institution.[1]

Lamprecht's conformity did not end with his completion of the *Abitur* in 1874. In the formal pattern of his subsequent training in several of the country's foremost academic institutions, he was likewise indistinguishable from most of his professional peers. Yet the great problem of Karl Lamprecht's biography is his deviation from the intellectual orthodoxy that a great majority of his peers absorbed during the course of such training. Paradoxically, Lamprecht was also the classic renegade, the great marginal figure in the German historical profession.

Although the extent of his deviation became obvious only in the 1890s, indications of the direction it was going to take began to emerge during his university training. Salient character traits, whose roots lay in a problematic childhood, conditioned his response to the influences to which he was exposed in the German academy. These traits encouraged the development of intellectual preferences and work habits that later distinguished the historian from his peers, for better and worse.

The reasons for Lamprecht's decision to study in Göttingen are not entirely clear. During his last semester at Schulpforta he spoke of studying in Munich with W. H. Riehl, but his plans changed during the summer of 1874. An interest in medieval history figured in his decision, for Göttingen was strong in this field; but there were practical considerations as well.[2] One of these was the prospect of attending a university together with one of his close friends from Schulpforta. Another was financial. His feelings of dependence on his father became more burdensome as he grew older, not only because this bond served as a reminder of his father's authority. His father was seventy and in declining health when Lamprecht took his *Abitur*; and the old man's finances suffered in the 1870s as a consequence of the Prussian government's assault on the Catholic church, which resulted in the takeover by civil authorities of responsibilities hitherto overseen—for fees—by both the Protestant and Catholic clergy.[3] Lamprecht was in no position, however, to emancipate himself financially from his father, "to remove the burden," as he put it, "which [father] has been suffering partially on my account."[4] Academic training in mid-nineteenth century Germany was an extended process that demanded an ample income of those who hoped to complete it. He could thus hope at best to finish his training with as little complication and delay as possible.

His immediate concern was to arrange for a part of his training that was inconvenient but unavoidable for an eighteen-year-old male in the new German Empire. As a graduate of a *Gymnasium*, Lamprecht was entitled to another of the privileges and badges of the German educated elite—to fulfill his military obligation as a so-called one-year volunteer in the army.[5] Provided he could support and equip himself with a weapon and uniform, he was entitled to train with a regiment for a single year and then to qualify for a reserve commission.

The situation in Göttingen was well suited to his needs. The town garrisoned the Prussian army's 82nd infantry regiment, in which he could serve during his first two semesters while attending lectures in his free time. The university itself was one of the country's leading institutions of higher learning. Political turmoil had undermined the reputation its philosophical and legal faculties had built for it in the previous century, when it ranked as the foremost Protestant university in Germany; but its faculty nonetheless included some of the most accomplished scholars in the country, among them the jurist Rudolf von Ihering and the theologian Albrecht Ritschl.[6] The leading historians there were Ranke's student, the great medievalist Georg Waitz, and the ancient historian Curt Wachsmuth.

In October 1874 Karl Lamprecht arrived in Göttingen, rented a flat, reported to his regiment, and enrolled at the university. He soon discovered that the competing demands on his time made it difficult to strike roots in either the academic or military setting. During the first two semesters his primary commitment was of necessity to his regiment, with which he spent the better part of each day. He had little enthusiasm for military life, which he regarded as an imposition on his time. He was not physically agile, nor was he captive to the chauvinism that had already begun to breed among young men of his social class after the recent German military victory over France. The fact that he lived off-barracks prevented him from establishing personal ties within his unit. The regular officers, with whom he had the greatest social affinities, treated him with the mild contempt and resentment that they harbored for one-year volunteers as a species.[7] "My fondest wish," Lamprecht confessed after living almost a year in these circumstances, "is to get out of the military soon."[8]

He was also discovering the difficulty of breaking through the anonymity of student life at a German university, even though Göttingen's enrollment of just under 1,000 students makes the institution seem intimate by modern standards.[9] He could not expect to find in a student corporation the kind of admiration that he had enjoyed within his clique of friends at boarding school. He did hope to join a *Burschenschaft*, the Germania, but during his early contacts with the membership, he conveyed an air of arrogance that was not so much inappropriate in such an organization as it was precocious. He was rejected.[10] He later joined a choral society, but this organization did not figure significantly in his life. "I would hardly have believed that I would so quickly become accustomed to spending the greater part of my day alone: neither my nature nor my upbringing have fostered this feature in me, so I am all the more surprised to have learned it so soon."[11] This account of his circumstances was an early exercise in self-deception, for there was a great deal in both his nature and his upbringing to foster a preference for solitude, which his circumstances in Göttingen rewarded.

Lamprecht's academic work in his first year at the university was perforce independent and unsystematic, governed by the offerings available in the late afternoons and evenings, when he was free of his military obligations. This regimen came to an end in the fall of 1875. Late in the summer of that year, Lamprecht participated in regimental maneuvers, passed the required examinations, and was released from his unit with a precommissioned rank.[12] When he returned to Göttingen in the fall, he took up the study of history in earnest.

The development of history as an academic discipline at German universities in the nineteenth century has inspired an academic industry itself, and the literature on the subject is immense.[13] The volume of the literature testifies to the complexity of the story, to its many intellectual, political, social, and organizational dimensions. Much of the story is so well known that it requires little additional attention in the present context. However, several themes do recommend a brief, schematic excursus here, for they bear directly on the professional training of Karl Lamprecht.

The term "historicism" has appeared frequently in the literature to designate the tradition of historical thinking that took shape in Germany at the beginning of the nineteenth century. In the course of the subsequent evolution, fragmentation, and discrediting of this tradition, the term has taken on a life of its own; it has been used in so many different connections that its meaning has become problematic.[14] To argue here that the word and the tradition with which it is associated are best understood as an ideology risks compounding the problem with the introduction of another term that is no less problematic. The argument certainly calls for a straightforward and inoffensive definition of the second term. Terry Eagleton's is as useful as any. Ideology, he writes, comprises "the ideas, values and feelings by which men [and presumably women] experience their societies at various times."[15]

The virtue of this perspective on the development of the profession of history is the centrality it affords to the concept of experience. The view of history that became systematized and institutionalized in Germany in the late eighteenth and early nineteenth centuries—and subsequently became known as historicism—represented the attempt of a particular group of men (along with a few women) to interpret and make sense of their experience, to construct a vision of the past that would provide orientation for the present. Their problem was to forge, in the light of this experience, a speculative philosophy of history in the sense in which Professor Walsh has used this term, to demonstrate that human history proceeded in an intelligible pattern toward a goal acceptable to moral reason.[16] The enduring power of this way of viewing history was then due to its serviceability as an ideology amid rapidly changing historical circumstances.

The experience that first demanded interpretation was rooted in an era of cataclysmic change in Germany. The consolidation of monarchical absolutism in the late eighteenth century anticipated the more frontal and dramatic onslaught that the forces of republican and imperial France waged on hoary German institutions and conventions. Both the absolute monarchs and the French invaders justified their campaigns of eradication with appeals to doctrines drawn from what Ernst Troeltsch later defined as a naturalistic tradition—one whose governing concepts were uniformity, clarity, and the universal working of rational norms and principles, which were analogous, if not identical, to the laws of mathematics and natural science.[17] Implicit in this tradition was a view of history that deprecated its own subject matter. The past was to be judged in light of the universal, transhistorical, rational norms that alone imparted validity to institutions and customs; tradition and diversity were vestiges of unreason, obstacles to the rational reordering of human affairs. The study of history, as Troeltsch has written, was to consist in "the critical clearing away [*Wegräumung*] of the past."[18]

Reaction to the sweeping institutional transformations in Germany took many forms. The central intellectual feature of the reaction was an altered approach to history, an enhanced appreciation of the past as an object of study in its own right. This conception emerged unsystematically over the course of several decades; and it could build on antecedents established during the *Aufklärung*.[19] Its early proponents were a diverse group intellectually, but they numbered some of the greatest minds in the annals of German history. They included (and it is hardly necessary to add the names) historians in the local academies of the late eighteenth century (who sought to defend traditional institutions against centralization), philologists, the intellectual giants of the *Goethezeit*, romantic poets, philosophers, folklorists, jurists, geographers, theologians, and reform-minded statesmen.[20] All of them were highly educated; most of them were public officials of one category or another. Change impinged most directly on their experience in the form of violence against cultural traditions, political institutions, and norms of Gelehrsamkeit in which they had grown into intellectual awareness. The study of history thus offered them a bridge between present and past, a strategy for managing the experience of what Wolfgang Hardtwig has called "the collapse of institutional identity amidst social change that had become permanent."[21] History offered an ideological alternative to the invader's rationalism.

As these writers lent ideological support to the campaign against the French, they laid the foundations for the elevation of history to the status of an autonomous body of knowledge, which was to be understood in none but its own terms. Their rejection of the universalism of French imperial claims and their insistence on the unique validity of German institutions were anchored in a renunciation of all conceptual or normative systems as guides to the past. These systems, be they rooted in providence, revelation, nature, or reason, were repugnant for the violence they did to the diversity of the past; they imposed a sterile uniformity on human affairs and erased the singularity of every historical era and the unique historical development of every unit of human organization. Only in the light of its own development could the intricate diversity of human affairs be understood. "The world is no system; it is history," writes Professor Nipperdey of this emergent "method for intellectual discourse with the past."[22] The premise of the discourse was, to use Troeltsch's terms again, the "historicization of all our thinking about humanity, its culture, and its values"; and the controlling terms in the discourse were henceforth to be diversity, individuality, development, and the autonomy of the past.[23]

The new conception of history served at first to underpin a broad range of human sciences or Geisteswissenschaften; only gradually did it lead to the emancipation of history as an independent discipline at German universities.[24] The most prominent champions of the new orientation were not historians in the modern sense, and university professors of history played practically no role in its definition. In fact, there was no university chair devoted exclusively to history until 1804, and its occupant, Gabriel Gottfried Bredow in Helmstedt, did not stand out amid the likes of J. G. Fichte, Wilhelm von Humboldt, and Friedrich August Wolf. The establishment of history as a university discipline over the next three decades reflected the heightened prestige of historical studies, but it was more directly related to the reform of German higher education in the first decades of the nineteenth century.

This story, too, has been often told.[25] Its central feature was the heightened status and power afforded at German universities to the philosophical faculties, whose role had hitherto been to offer preparatory work for students enrolled in the other "higher" faculties, principally in law and theology. This change was the product of many considerations. The most lofty was the belief that the generation, dissemination, and acquisition of pure knowledge were virtuous pursuits in and of themselves and that cultivation of the personality required exposure to philosophy, literature, and the other humanistic disciplines represented in the philosophical faculties. Mundane considerations carried more weight, however. Study in subjects offered in the philosophical faculties became practical, for although many advocates of university reform were uncomfortable with the idea, cultivation was now serviceable as professional training. *Bildung* had become *Ausbildung*.

The reform of German universities was inseparable from the reform of secondary education. The propaedeutic functions previously reserved for the philosophical faculties at the universities devolved now to the *Gymnasien*, freeing university professors for more advanced research and instruction. More significantly, the expansion of the system of *Gymnasien* and other institutions of secondary education created a growing demand for teachers professionally trained in the humanistic disciplines at the universities. As a response to this pressure, the number of students who matriculated in philosophical faculties rose by more than 200 percent in the thirty years after the Peace of Vienna—in an era that had not yet seen the dramatic expansion of the natural sciences but did witness an increase of nearly 75 percent in the number of secondary school teachers trained.[26] In addition, the new prestige of the humanistic disciplines, as well as the conviction that these disciplines offered a valuable supplement to professional training, drew increasing numbers of students from the law and theological faculties—the future public officials and clerics—into the lectures and seminars of professors in the philosophical faculties.

Although these pressures worked to the benefit of philology and the other established disciplines in the philosophical faculties, they also led to the foundation of history as an autonomous discipline.[27] The same features in the new conception of historical study that had made it a potent ideological weapon against the French recommended its installation as a basic component of civic ideology in the postwar era, when the experience of state-building made insecure governments throughout Germany eager to invoke the sanction of tradition. The study of history accordingly became a staple in the education of teachers, clerics, and jurists alike. That history should be an independent discipline, as opposed to an adjunct to other disciplines like law, philosophy, or philology, was, however, by no means self-evident. The struggle for the emancipation of history was frequently bitter; it was played out in ministries of culture and at the level of institutional politics at universities everywhere in Germany. The historians' success was gradual but relentless. In 1810 there were four chairs of history at German universities; by 1830 there were fourteen, and in 1850 there were twenty-eight at nineteen German universities.[28]

These figures reflected the success of the historians in the enterprise of *Verwissenschaftlichung*—an untranslatable term that suggests the professionalization and institutionalization of the discipline.[29] The historians' challenge was to establish the integrity of their discipline by defining systematically its subject matter, methodologies, standards, goals, and modes of presentation in a manner that would distinguish it from competing disciplines.

Working out this definition was largely the achievement of Leopold Ranke. The great historian's reputation has suffered in the twentieth century, and the pillars on which it once rested, the originality of his views and the majestic objectivity of his scholarship, have not withstood the wear of critical scrutiny.[30] His contribution was nonetheless to construct, albeit unsystematically over the course of his long career, a compelling synthesis of ideas that others had worked out before him. Ranke's achievement was momentous enough to make understandable the almost divine aura that attached to him in the late nineteenth century, when he stood as the embodiment of the professional norms of German historical scholarship, the very symbol of its greatness.[31]

The point of immediate reference in Ranke's thinking about the nature and methodology of historical study was the intellectual edifice constructed by the greatest philosopher of the day, who was also his colleague in Berlin.[32] Hegel's speculative philosophy represented the most serious rival to the new conception of history; and philosophy's comprehensive claims were the greatest intellectual impediment to history's academic emancipation. The problem was that Ranke and Hegel professed the same subject—knowledge of history, of the coherent and intelligible patterns that the human past revealed. The immediate disagreement between the two scholars was over method. In Hegel's panorama, philosophical and historical truth, reason and history, were reconciled as the past played witness to the progressive unfolding and self-fulfillment of an absolute and immanent spirit of freedom. This panorama was a prodigious feat of deductive logic. Ranke objected to it for much the same reasons that the pioneers of the new conception of history had rejected French rationalism almost half a century earlier. Deductive reason could not, Ranke argued, provide knowledge of history. The observer of the human past who forced it into the conceptual constraints of any system, philosophical or dogmatic, could not know the truth revealed in the history of what he once called the "race of these creatures so many and varied [vielgestaltige], to which we ourselves belong."[33]

Ranke's premise was hence to insist on the diversity and absolute historicity of the past—the fact that every historical epoch, like each unit of human organization, was rooted in its own particular development and could be apprehended only in these terms. From this premise Ranke rejected not only Hegel's manner of access to the past through speculative reason, but also his dialectical vision of progress, which, no less than earlier linear visions of progress, entailed judging the past in light of transhistorical moral categories. "I would maintain that every epoch is immediate to God," as he put this proposition to the king of Bavaria, "and that its value consists not in what follows out of it, but in its very existence, its own proper self."[34]

Ranke's most famous formula, his determination to show "wie es eigentlich gewesen," was thus a great deal less simple than it sounded. Historical knowledge, understanding how things "really happened," required in the first place that the historian abandon all speculation, moral judgment, and every other sort of preconception; access to the past was to come instead in a manner that resembled induction, through immersion in the sources immediate to the epoch under scrutiny. The additional guidelines that Ranke prescribed for analyzing these sources reflected his intellectual debts to Barthold Georg Niehbuhr, Friedrich August Wolf, and August Böckh, the great philologists who, in the course of professionalizing their own discipline, had broadened it into ancient history.[35] Ranke appropriated the techniques of criticism that these men had developed for ancient texts. He adopted their basic insight into the historicity of the sources themselves, the fact that every document had a history of its own, that the sources were not only to be read critically for their authenticity and logical coherence, but analyzed within the historical context of their own origins.

Ranke's methodological injunctions raised their own problems, however. The first was the classic hermeneutical question of how the historian, the child of one unique and particular epoch, could relate to the events and characters of another. A second problem was related to the first. Ranke's paean to the variety and particularity of the past, his strictures against abstraction and prejudgment of any kind, and his insistence on the use of primary sources all dictated a strategy for the detailed analysis of particular historical events; but they seemed to offer no transition from a level of analysis where particularity was absolute to one where the historian could contend with the philosopher and offer statements about commonality, coherence, and patterns in historical development.

The relationship of the particular to the general occupied Ranke for the duration of his career, but his strategy for approaching the problem remained constant once he had resolved the hermeneutical issue. Once again, however, his ideas were unoriginal. Although Ranke counts as one of the principal exemplars of what Hans-Georg Gadamer has classified as the "romantic hermeneutics," the historian's ideas were fundamentally those of Schleiermacher and Wilhelm von Humboldt.[36] Ranke argued that interpreting historical sources, apprehending the truth contained in these documents, required the employment of a special critical faculty called *Verstehen* or *Einfühlung* in German. It was not to be confused with reason; it implied instead a more comprehensive, intuitive understanding of the past that almost corresponds to the word *divination*. Exercise of this faculty, he claimed, enabled historians to experience empathetically the mental world of the objects of their study. It also allowed them to transcend the limits of that world and to achieve an understanding of the great ideas that operated throughout history, linked the past to the present, and provided continuity, pattern, and meaning to history.[37]

The ontological postulate of Ranke's *Ideenlehre* was neo-Platonic. The ultimate reality of history was ideal. It comprised great transcendent ideas that spanned the epochs and informed the thoughts and behavior of historical actors and human communities. The epistemological implication of this position was that the quest for historical knowledge required special qualifications of those who undertook it. Professional training might hone but could not create the faculties essential to gaining objective knowledge of the past; intuitive understanding and the ability to strip oneself of the prejudice of one's own culture— the traits that underlay what Ranke called the "universality of sympathy"—were gifts analogous to artistic genius.[38] The study of history required talents that were more than intellectual, for it was an aesthetic endeavor.

Ultimately, though, it was a religious endeavor.[39] When Ranke's hermeneutic was keyed into a theological idiom (as it frequently was), it betrayed another profound debt to Schleiermacher, to whom he was personally close.[40] Ranke employed a colorful if not entirely consistent range of metaphors to emphasize the operation of divine purposes in human history. The most famous of these was his reference to the holy hieroglyph. "In all of history, God dwells, lives, is to be found," he wrote to his brother in 1820. "Every act testifies to Him; every instant preaches His name, but above all, I think, so does the coherence [Zusammenhang] of history. He stands there like a holy hieroglyph, perceived only in His external manifestations."[41] On other occasions Ranke spoke of the presence of the "thoughts of God" and the "breath [Anhauch] of God" in history. History reflected the operation of the hidden hand (or finger) of God, and the ultimate pattern and meaning of history was the "divine mystery." The study of history, Ranke once explained, was to penetrate "to the depths and most secret stirrings of life which guide humanity":

> . . . the directions in which humanity has exerted itself in every epoch, what it has strived after, what it has acquired and really attained. For one can conceive of this as a goal of divine knowledge. Precisely this we seek to penetrate with the aid of history.[42]

Historians thus occupied a "priestly office." Their charge was to decipher God's hieroglyphics in the unfolding of the past. The ethic of the office was ascetic. In the face of these divine mysteries, the historian's calling required self-renunciation, the "immersion" of the self in the object of study, the attainment of a state that Ranke once characterized in almost mystical terms as "the extinguishing of the self."[43]

Like no other German historian, Ranke sought to practice the "universality of sympathy" that his theory postulated. His corpus included studies in Italian, Spanish, Serbian, Ottoman, Venetian, French, and English, as well as German history. His Ideenlehre nonetheless harbored seeds of the profession's subsequent parochialism. Despite his suggestions that the historical study of the human experience ought to be as comprehensive as that experience itself, his own writings made it clear that one realm of this experience was privileged and that the others were not the proper concern of the professional historian. Ranke argued that the realm of politics and the state provided the essential transition from the particular to the general and represented the highest, most historically significant forms of human activity.[44] States were the "thoughts of God"; in Ranke's view, their interaction provided the most proximate indications of the designs of God in human history.

When Karl Lamprecht years later accused Ranke of smuggling metaphysics back into his vision of history, he was accused of blasphemy. But he was certainly correct. The reluctance of other historians to admit the truth of Lamprecht's charge reflected another of Ranke's achievements, which was to create a "theology of history" that fit so comfortably into the traditions of Lutheran Protestantism that its metaphysical assumptions invited no examination.[45] Above human history stood the divine order. This realization was the limit beyond which human knowledge of history could not extend into the nature of things. The highest to which the historian could aspire was the divination or intimation of the divine order—the kind of intellectual apprehension suggested by the German word *ahnen*. The highest object of historical knowledge was thus the great ideas that the past revealed and which hovered in their interplay at the convergence of the historical and the divine.

It was often quipped that Ranke was a better theoretician when he wrote history than when he wrote theory, but it is difficult to overrate the importance of the theoretical edifice he built for subsequent generations of historians. For all its ambiguities, it was a model of graceful balance and synthesis. It defined the methodological guidelines that insulated the study of history from speculative philosophy. In a way Hegel's system could not, it provided a philosophical foundation for historians to ground their research in the sources, to study, as the philosopher Eduard Spranger later put it, "the undiscoverable divine whole in the discoverable particulars."[46] Ranke's system admittedly obfuscated rather than resolved important issues of freedom and progress in history, but these issues were not as urgent to him as they were to his successors; and he could claim refuge in the incomprehensibility of the divine order. But Ranke harbored no doubt that this order was ultimately moral and benevolent, a "hidden harmony," and that its fulfillment would come in history. The most difficult problem was, as Georg Iggers has pointed out, that the sources of the optimism, credibility, and coherence in Ranke's system were also its points of vulnerability. Its integrity could not withstand the breakdown of the Protestant faith that provided its metaphysical guarantee.[47]

Karl Lamprecht put Ranke's theories, and the profession whose academic identity was founded upon them, to the sternest tests they faced in the nineteenth century. By the time Lamprecht first encountered them during his university training, though, the theories and the profession alike had adapted to new circumstances during the eventful decades of the midcentury. The name with which these adaptations were most directly associated was Johann Gustav Droysen, who joined Ranke in 1859 at the university of Berlin, where he reigned second only to his older colleague as the patriarch of the German historical profession.

The two scholars were not close temperamentally or politically. Ranke's magisterial vision of history was a product of the *Vormärz*, an era of comparative political tranquility, while Droysen's reflected the activism and aspirations of the educated middle class in the turbulent period that followed. The contrast between the two historians should not, however, be overstated. They were part of a common methodological and intellectual tradition; and in the end the beliefs they shared proved to be the more fundamental and enduring.

The two scholars agreed that history ultimately reflected the hidden hand of God. Droysen's dictum was that "From history, among other sources, we learn to understand God, and only in God can we understand history."[48] Droysen was trained as a philosopher, however, and his theory of history was more tightly reasoned and less immediately theological than Ranke's. The lectures he delivered regularly after 1858 on the principles of history constituted, along with his theoretical articles of the 1860s, what one philosopher has described as the "first comprehensive methodological canon of modern historiography."[49]

Droysen's theory was to serve several purposes. One represented a reprise of Ranke's effort to insulate the discipline of history from the challenge of speculative philosophy. Droysen, however, was responding to the challenge posed by a new and potentially more dangerous rival. Four years after the publication of *The Origin of Species*, he confronted the argument of the English historian T. H. Buckle that human history, no less than the natural world, was governed by immutable laws and that the study of history, if it hoped to claim the status of a science or *Wissenschaft*, would have to devote itself to the empirical discovery and verification of these laws. Droysen's reply to this claim was of enduring significance. It introduced the conceptual categories out of which champions of the German historical profession built lines of defense against what appeared, during the next several decades, to be unremitting assaults from the champions of science and positivism.

"If there is to be a '*Wissenschaft* of history,' and we too believe there is," Droysen argued,

> it means that there is a category of phenomena for which neither the theological nor the philosophical, neither the mathematical nor the physical mode of analysis [*Betrachtungsweise*] is suited, that there are questions for which answers are to be sought neither in speculation—be it theological (which has the absolute as its premise) or philosophical (which has the absolute as its goal)—nor in the kind of empiricism which conceives of the world of phenomena according to their quantifiable attributes, nor in any of the practical moral disciplines.[50]

Droysen thus defined history as the discipline that alone addressed a category of phenomena that were inaccessible to either speculative or empirical, inductive treatment. The object of this discipline, he observed, was a realm in which human behavior was unconstrained by natural forces or circumstances and hence was not subject to the kind of laws or regularities that determined the behavior of the phenomena that natural scientists studied. Droysen called the realm of history "the moral world," and he insisted that it was defined by the play of human choice, purpose, and free will. The constituents of this world he called "moral forces [*sittliche Mächte*]." He defined these in turn as "moral communities," freely formed to serve natural or ideal needs; and his enumeration of these communities included the family, nation, language and the arts, society, the economy, and the state.[51]

The tension between Droysen and Ranke lay not in the attempt to stake out a distinctive terrain for historical study, nor in the shape of that terrain, which both defined as the realm of free, moral action. Droysen believed no less than Ranke that the forces that operated in history were ideal and that the highest of these found expression in the state; and like Ranke, he emphasized that knowledge of these forces required the critical scrutiny of primary sources and an operation called *Verstehen*. The difficulties arose when Droysen enlarged his ideas about hermeneutics in a fashion that revealed how much he believed the study of history was the guide to political practice.[52]

Ranke viewed the great ideas of history as transcendent forces whose contemplation was the ultimate task (and reward) of the historian. Droysen disagreed. Ideas were the moral forces that unfolded progressively within history and linked every age in a great ethical continuum. "The ideas of the moral world are in and of themselves in the nature of the human being, but they unfold in the progressive movement of history; their unfolding is the content of history."[53] The act of historical understanding consisted in each age's moral appropriation of the past; this operation was possible because of the continuity of ethical forces at work in both present and past. "The ethical system of any epoch is only the speculative appropriation [*Fassung*] of what has hitherto unfolded."[54] The practical consequence of this proposition was that history posed the ethical (and political) imperatives that each era faced, so that the study of the past offered a diagnostic guide to the present.[55]

Droysen's emphasis on the progressive movement of moral forces in history betrayed his debt to Hegel, with whom he had trained; and it reintroduced teleological themes that Ranke had sought to purge in his own confrontation with the great philosopher's system.[56] At midcentury, however, Droysen's ideas provided a more compelling intellectual foundation for the activist generation of historians who succeeded Ranke and made up the so-called Prussian school.[57] The views of these scholar-politicians reflected the experience of the educated German middle class of the midcentury—the disillusionment born of the collapse of revolution in 1849, the subsequent struggle for constitutional reform and national unification, and the spectacular events of 1866 and 1870–1871. Droysen enjoyed the support of Heinrich von Treitschke, Heinrich von Sybel (Ranke's own student), and many less well-known historians when he insisted that the moral imperatives of history corresponded to the political program of the German liberals of a *kleindeutsch* persuasion and that historians were to guide the way toward this program's fulfillment. The course of history thus became, in the hands of these men, a secular teleology with a national-liberal coloration.[58]

The importance of the *Reichsgründung* in the history of the German historical profession is difficult to exaggerate. The meaning of the past and the fulfillment of history now stood revealed in a momentous political event. This conclusion began to obscure the philosophical tensions between Droysen and Ranke and to provide the common ground on which disciples of both men could affirm the singularity of their discipline and anchor it in politics. In the eyes of all, the achievement of national unity in 1871 represented a historical telos.[59] The assumptions on which this proposition rested were familiar. The distinctive object of historical study was the moral realm of ideas, free will, and purposeful human activity. The intellectual operation appropriate to the study of this realm was close attention to primary sources in combination with *Verstehen*, understood as a process of sympathetic intuition. The supreme institutional manifestation of this moral realm, and hence the proper focus of historical study, was the state, whose development alone provided meaning to the past.

Droysen's legacy was evident in the ease with which historians began to place the philosophy of history in the service of civic ideology in the new state, in whose cultured elite they themselves circulated. The primacy of the state in history corresponded, in their view, to the supremacy of the state over society, to the role of this institution as the guarantor of order against the social and religious forces that challenged the Bismarckian settlement. "The state is under all circumstances the most important product of human cultural endeavor," wrote one historian in 1878. The state, he continued in an allusion to anxieties that most of his colleagues shared, represented the great vessel of culture "which by protective enclosure or, if necessary, by compulsion preserves all the other fruits of civilization—by no means least the finest extracts [*Säfte*] of *Bildung*— from spoilation and destruction."[60]

The activism of the Prussian school waned after 1871, and the next generation of historians witnessed a "Ranke Renaissance," a reversion to the detachment, if not the tolerance, of the master. But this transition brought only a change in tenor; it did not impede the framing of a powerful orthodoxy that was devoted to political history and harbored an animus against Catholics, Jews, ethnic minorities, socialists, separatists, and other groups that seemed to challenge the integrity of the German state at home or the extension of its power abroad.[61] In this fashion, historians became perhaps the most ardent devotees of "statolatry" in imperial Germany, as they defended the state's authoritarian civic values and preached the morality of its power.[62]

In describing the period between 1850 and 1890, Josef Engel has written of the "golden age" of German historical studies. Historians, he writes, had elevated their profession to the status of an academic discipline (*Wissenschaft*), replete with "its own subject-matter, its own method, and its own center: the expanded concept of instruction and research appropriate to it."[63] Engel's characterization is only a little exaggerated. In the aftermath of the *Reichsgründung*, the buttressing of the intellectual foundations of a *Geschichtswissenschaft* and the alliance of its practitioners with the state accompanied the final stages in the consolidation of the discipline's institutional structure. A professional community of specialists emerged.

The pillars of this community were located in German universities.[64] At the time Lamprecht began his university studies, there were thirty-seven chairs of history at twenty universities within the frontiers of the new *Reich*. At many of these institutions the study of history had taken on the modern form of the seminar, in which professors provided advanced training in the criticism and interpretation of historical texts for students who were destined for the historical profession or secondary teaching.[65] The presence of these students, alongside those who already possessed advanced degrees and taught at the universities as unpaid instructors, guaranteed a dynamic atmosphere of scholarly exchange, which was further fostered by competition for students and faculty among these twenty academic "centers of *Bildung*."[66]

Students spread out from the historical seminars to the other centers of the profession. Local, regional, and state archives acquired an importance they had never before enjoyed. As doctoral students scoured the holdings of these repositories, the wisdom of organizing, managing, and publishing their documentary treasures became apparent. This pressure led in turn to the opening of additional career opportunities for historians, both in archival service and in editorial undertakings, of which the *Monumenta Historica Germaniae* was unique only in being the most ambitious.[67] The need to coordinate and promote the financing of these projects was a spur to the founding of local and state historical societies, whose model was the Historical Commission of the Bavarian Academy of Sciences.[68]

Over this entire structure loomed the university of Berlin.[69] Its five chairs of history were occupied in 1874 by Droysen, Treitschke (who succeeded to Ranke's chair in 1873), Theodor Mommsen (for ancient history), Karl Wilhelm Nitzsch, and Wilhelm Wattenbach, who was responsible for a range of subjects from paleography to sphragistics and numismatics, which were commonly taught in Berlin and elsewhere under the rubric of "auxiliary disciplines" (*Hilfswissenschaften*). The extent of Berlin's hegemony was documented in the fact that of the thirty-seven holders of chairs in history at German universities, thirty could trace their intellectual paternity in one way or another back to the capital. They had either studied with Ranke or Droysen personally or with one of their students, most frequently with Waitz or Sybel.[70]

Sybel's significance in the structure of the profession transcended his status as one of Ranke's first students.[71] He was the principal conduit between Berlin and the broader network of institutions of historical study. While he occupied a chair in Munich, he and Ranke founded the Historical Commission there and inaugurated its most extended project, the edition of the old imperial *Reichstagsakten*. In 1859 Sybel founded the *Historische Zeitschrift*, which quickly became under his editorial direction the leading journal in the profession.[72] In 1875 he moved to Berlin to become director of the Prussian archival system. Sybel was, in Friedrich Meinecke's phrase, an "academic grand seigneur."[73] Meinecke was in a good position to judge. His own early career in the Prussian *Geheimes Staatsarchiv* and the editorial offices of the *Historische Zeitschrift* was indebted to the power of this patron, who had contacts in the profession's every corner.

Sybel's power of patronage represented the single most tangible guarantee that the disciplinary norms that Ranke and Droysen had worked out would continue to govern the profession. It was hardly the only guarantee, for the barriers against deviancy were many. The homogeneity of background and cultural experience among aspirant historians was another. Still another was the elaborate set of procedures and standards that defined the stages through which every one of these students passed in the course of his professional socialization. The norms of the discipline informed the standards and guided the professors who oversaw the procedures. As a consequence it was unusual when a student who challenged these norms advanced even as far as the rite of initiation symbolized in the doctoral *Promotion*.[74]

The institutionalization of the profession's norms was possible only because this process enjoyed the support of the state, specifically of the bureaucrats who oversaw higher education in the Prussian ministry of culture and in equivalent offices in other German states. The ideal of *Wissenschaft* that guided the policies of these men was the legacy of the reform era, when the conviction reigned that the mission of universities was to pursue pure scholarship, the generation of knowledge for its own sake in original research. The disciplinary norms that defined *Geschichtswissenschaft* had roots in the same intellectual ground as this "research ethic" or *Wissenschaftsideologie*; and the prominence of primary research in the thinking of both Ranke and Droysen ensured that their conception of historical studies received official sanction. The practical consequence of this situation was that in history, as in other disciplines, the leaders of the profession served as advisers to officials, like Johannes Schulze in the Prussian ministry of culture, who made the critical appointments that determined the growth and direction of the discipline at German universities.[75]

The other consequence of this situation was to frustrate the hope, which had underlain university reform at the beginning of the century, that original research would ultimately lead to a grand interdisciplinary synthesis of knowledge. By midcentury it was clear that the research ethic was instead encouraging the fragmentation and specialization of the academy's disciplines. History again was no exception. Competition among young scholars for university positions was keen; and the standards of competition placed premiums on their staking out specialized fields for intensive research in constitutional, administrative, or diplomatic history.

In these circumstances German historical scholarship began, even during its "golden age," to display signs of sclerosis. Its pioneers had supplied a compelling defense of the discipline's identity, and its younger practitioners produced monographs and editions of breathtaking erudition. But this defense, which by its very nature had been a process of exclusion, had encouraged a narrow concentration on the history of affairs of the state, where the line between erudition and pedantry became difficult to distinguish. As the disciples of Ranke turned into *Fussnoten-Historiker*, technicians of detail and opaque prose, they promoted the fragmentation of their discipline to the neglect of the broader thinking about history that had always tempered Ranke's attention to the particular.[76]

Contemporaries recognized the problem. Theodor Lindner, one of Ranke's students, was not alone when, four years after the master's death, he delivered a general lament on the state of the historical profession. "Spirit and life have been banned," he wrote:

> [I]nstead of being directed over broad expanses, the gaze of students is being made myopic by the extreme concentration on detail [*Kleinigkeiten*]; judgment and perception of what is important and what is trivial [have] disappeared. It was forgotten that method is to be only the means to the end; the slow step became itself the goal, and instead of great leaders, only subalterns came forward.[77]

In view of the historiographical controversy that broke out soon after Lindner offered this commentary, there was no little irony in his analysis of the profession's narrowness and obsession with detail. The root of the problem, he argued, lay in the influence of Georg Waitz and his successor Julius Weiszäcker, the scholars with whom Karl Lamprecht had studied in Göttingen.

The institutional and methodological foundations of the discipline of history were already in place when Lamprecht entered the university of Göttingen in 1874. The significance of the profession's development transcended its practical impact on his professional training—the subjects he studied in lectures and seminars, the methods he learned, and the examinations he passed. It is not extending the metaphor too far to suggest that the real issue in the history of history in the early nineteenth century was where the methodological and conceptual bounds of the discipline were to be staked. Given the central importance that the motif of venturing out beyond established bounds had acquired in his personality, it was only consistent that Lamprecht soon became restive within the disciplinary confines he encountered.

His initial encounter with history in Göttingen brought him into contact with two of the most dedicated guardians of these bounds to be found anywhere in Germany. Georg Waitz was Ranke's first and favorite student.[78] Although in his political activism he stood closer to Droysen than to his teacher, he was the purest exponent of Ranke's doctrines of source criticism, which he practiced in his monumental eight-volume history of medieval German law. His reputation as the founder of the cult of detail was well deserved, and it spoke to a degree of thoroughness, conscientiousness, and caution that bordered on the obsessive and made him, as Sybel recalled, "distrustful of every attempt to summarize, to define, or to write a concluding word."[79] Waitz was more comfortable with documentary research and editorial scholarship than he was with exposition; and when, upon his retirement from Göttingen in 1876, he succeeded Georg Heinrich Pertz as director of the *Monumenta Historica Germaniae* in Berlin, it represented a fitting conclusion to his career.

Julius Weizsäcker was a fitting successor to Waitz in Göttingen.[80] Weizsäcker trained first in Protestant theology in Tübingen before he studied history with Ranke and Sybel (among others). He did his most notable work as the general editor of the *Reichstagsakten* for the period 1376–1431. Here he trained a generation of young scholars in editorial techniques and earned a reputation that rivaled Waitz's for caution and scrupulous attention to detail.

Waitz and Weizsäcker were unusual only in the extreme to which they pushed a methodological canon that even their critics like Theodor Lindner accepted. One of the strengths of the seminar in Göttingen was that it epitomized an ethic whose pietist roots survived in the legacy of Ranke. The strict techniques of documentary criticism and interpretation taught in Göttingen, and only a little less severely in other German historical seminars, were held to be the basic practical skills without which no serious historian could proceed. These techniques were no less fundamental to a professional ethos of *Gewissenhaftigkeit*—conscientiousness, scrupulousness, and patient inquiry. Meinecke's recollections of his seminar in Bonn emphasized just this aspect of the experience—that "there was something ethical involved." "The strict methodological rules that one learned in the seminars, the patient collection and testing of the sources, of their special characteristics and contexts—all that did not amount to professional pedantry [*Zunftpedantrie*]."[81] The ethic was in the end one of dedication and self-renunciation, reminiscent of Ranke's extinguishing of the soul. The pursuit of historical objectivity—the respect which bordered on reverence for the document as the repository of historical truth—seemed to demand the purging of the researcher's subjectivity and interpretive autonomy, or what one later critic of Waitz's school described as "the nearly total suppression of one's own person."[82]

It took a great deal of effort for a self-absorbed, impatient young man like Lamprecht to exist in an environment so pervaded by this ethic. When he first enrolled in Göttingen, Waitz was near retirement; and the contacts between the two were limited to Lamprecht's sitting in on the last tutorials that Waitz held in the seminar. The experience was sufficient, however, to stimulate the student's fascination for German medieval sources.[83] His interest in this subject was thus already well aroused when Weizsäcker arrived in Göttingen in April 1876 to offer a series of lectures and tutorials on the constitutional history of the Holy Roman Empire.[84]

Weizsäcker's influence on Lamprecht was short-lived but pivotal. During the two semesters in which the two worked together in 1876–1877, Weizsäcker provided direction to Lamprecht's work and entered into a personal relationship with him that was at times almost paternal. Despite his austere manner as a scholar and his reputation as a fierce critic of students, Weizsäcker was a sensitive and accommodating man who appreciated the almost obsessive energy with which his student approached his work; it also spoke for Weizsäcker's qualities that he encouraged a student whose breadth of interest so contrasted with his own intellectual caution.[85]

From the day he arrived, Lamprecht was determined to collect as broadly as he could from among the university's offerings. During his first year, however, military service restricted his studies. The list that Herbert Schönebaum has compiled of the lectures and exercises he might have attended at this time suggests that Lamprecht attempted to compensate in breadth for what his study had to sacrifice in coherence and direction.[86] In addition to Waitz's seminar, the list includes lectures in political economy with Georg Hanssen, the history of philosophy, the philosophy of religion, philology, art history, music history, and literary history. He also read voraciously on his own and immersed himself in the geography of central Europe.[87] After Weizsäcker's arrival, Lamprecht's pace accelerated as he began to concentrate on medieval history. He studied the history of the Germanic tribes of late antiquity with Wachsmuth, medieval legal history with the jurist Ferdinand Frensdorff (who had trained with Waitz), English constitutional development with Reinhold Pauli, and French constitutional and legal history with the jurist Theodor Warnkönig. His private readings now emphasized the medieval German epic.[88]

Although the frenetic pace of Lamprecht's study earned him the admiration of his professors, it was symptomatic of problems both temperamental and intellectual. In both his formal academic work and his private reading, his inclination was to roam broadly in order to gather an enormous store of historical information. Bringing all this information under analytical control was a more difficult challenge. Notebooks with elaborate but unpursued schemes for the periodization and topical organization of medieval history testified to the failure of the student's early efforts. Subjects such as local and urban French history, church-state relations, and medieval German history frustrated his patience and eluded his analytical grasp.[89]

The problem only intensified as he attempted to integrate subjects that lay beyond the purview of academic history. Studying the history of religion, art, literature, and philosophy drew his interest to cultural regions routinely ignored in conventional accounts of the development of political institutions. Ranke's works, which he read at this time with great admiration for their literary grace, could offer little help in these wider regions.[90] The fundamental difficulty was the analytical priority of the state; and it clashed with the position of a number of writers who were attracting his interest. One of these was the popular anthropologist in Munich, W. H. Riehl, with whom he had briefly considered studying. Riehl challenged the historians' priorities when he argued, as Lamprecht noted in an extended summary of this author's *Bürgerliche Gesellschaft*, that "society is inherently something natural, like the life of human beings in its various forms."[91] The state, by contrast, was a derivative phenomenon, an appurtenance grafted onto society in order to preserve the coexistence of the orders (*Stände*) that society naturally comprised.

Lamprecht also encountered the leading positivist thinkers of midcentury, whose challenge to state-oriented history was more systematic than Riehl's. Lamprecht's exposure to the classic texts of European positivism was due to the presence in Göttingen of Ernst Bernheim, then a private instructor, who became an advisor and friend to him during the semester when Waitz's chair was vacant.[92] Bernheim was beginning the methodological studies on which his reputation was subsequently to rest, and he found in Lamprecht an eager partner in discussion. Unlike the great majority of German historians, Bernheim believed that the reigning methodological canon had not sufficiently parried the challenge of natural science. He was convinced that historians had to confront more seriously the view, which was common to Buckle, Comte, Spencer, Du Bois-Reymond, Taine, and Marx, that the influence of a variety of natural, social, and cultural circumstances or structures conditioned human behavior and that the play of these circumstances could be analyzed in categories analogous to those of the natural sciences—in a way that admitted empirical testing and an element of predictability.[93] The uncomfortable implication of this view, which Droysen had rejected out of hand, was that human behavior was not free, either individually or in the collective context of the state. Bernheim himself could not abandon the idea of freedom in history, but he was prepared to admit that the play of prior circumstances did limit human freedom significantly and that historians accordingly had something to learn from the positivists.[94]

The extent to which Lamprecht sympathized with Bernheim's standpoint emerged in a critique he presented early in 1876 on Droysen's *Outline of the Principles of History*.[95] Much of this critique was a pretentious misrepresentation of Droysen's views, which the student dismissed as "poetry which flatters history"; but the presentation did suggest Lamprecht's discomfort with the proposition that history was the realm of free, moral action. "Nowhere," he remarked (wrongly), "does Droysen mention the influence of prior circumstances on historical development." Lamprecht's next description of Droysen's position was more accurate:

> . . . everything is a question of the volitional acts of human beings. He calls the historical world the moral cosmos only because the volitional acts of individuals are displayed in it, not because prior circumstances, which are created by the volitional acts of countless individuals, work in it.

When he turned a little later to his own ideas about the character of these *Zustände*, or prior circumstances, the critic betrayed some of the debts he had incurred in his reading. He also touched a nerve.

> The question arises here: do geographical conditions [*Beziehungen*] not play a role in history? Are coal and iron and steam entirely blameless for Bebel and Liebknecht? I do not believe it, even if I would prefer not, à la Buckle, to accord these factors the principal weight.

Lamprecht then suggested the possibility of a synthesis that would do justice to "this reciprocal action between nature and humanity, both of which act now in a giving, now in a receiving capacity; it is this reciprocity which lends such manifold variety to the course of history and makes the understanding of history so difficult."

Lamprecht also studied philosophy in Göttingen. He heard lectures on ethics and the history of philosophy with J. J. Baumann, but another of the university's philosophers had a more significant influence on him.[96] Rudolf Hermann Lotze remains one of the most fascinating, eccentric, and neglected figures in modern German intellectual history.[97] Trained as a physiologist and philosopher, at home equally in the natural sciences and the humanities, Lotze stood at the intersection of several disciplines; lines led to him from Spinoza, Leibniz, Herder, Kant, Hegel, Schelling, and Herbart, and from him to thinkers as diverse as Wundt, Windelband, and Husserl. He was a crucial figure in Lamprecht's intellectual development in two respects. In the first place, he was a pioneer in an area of philosophy that was, under the name of psychophysics or psychology, on the verge of becoming an autonomous discipline with ties to both the natural sciences and the humanities. Its object was the operation of the human mind, and its practitioners were building an impressive body of experimental evidence to suggest the regular patterns and physiological correlates of mental activity, from perception to emotion.[98] Lamprecht's introduction to this budding science of the mind further eroded his confidence in Droysen's claim that the distinct subject of history, the realm of ideas, was one of freedom and intentionality and hence was impenetrable to mechanical analysis.

Lotze was also arguably the greatest metaphysician since Hegel. His grand project was not unlike Bernheim's (in fact he exercised a significant influence on Bernheim). Lotze hoped to unify science and philosophy, mechanics and teleology, in a grand exercise in natural philosophy or what might be called inductive metaphysics. Above an indifferent, real world of phenomena which, he believed, had to be understood and explained mechanically, Lotze posited the essential, ideal unity of all existence, which lent purpose and value to the operation of mechanical laws. This unity, he reasoned, consisted in the great web of reciprocal relationships that encompassed all beings.[99]

Although Lamprecht could only with difficulty follow the complex reasoning of this "speculating Struwwelpeter" (as one of his many detractors called him), Lotze's philosophy brought intellectual excitement as well as a practical introduction to the great holistic systems of German idealistic philosophy. Lotze's great "*Kombinationsversuch,*" as Lamprecht later called it, the proposition that the unity of existence was constituted in relationships among all its components, stimulated the student's fertile imagination.[100] Lotze's thinking encouraged his own search for links among diverse realms of historical activity, even if it provided little guidance in the distinctions between analytical and analogical relationships. Lamprecht found this philosophy more attractive than Droysen's, for it could accommodate forces that were not ideal, political, or singular, although it resembled Droysen's in its goal and final design, in part because it had antecedents in the same philosophical tradition.[101] Discovering the laws of historical development and the mechanics of human behavior in the past could be the means of revealing unifying relationships, patterns, and moral purposes which Lotze, like Droysen, believed were ultimately ideal.

The two and a half years Lamprecht studied in Göttingen were crucial in his intellectual development. During this period the study of history took on direction and meaning for him, and the intellectual agenda that would occupy him for the rest of his life began to take shape.[102] His project became the construction of an analytical framework that did not suffer from the limitations of the reigning philosophy of history. He sought a framework broad enough to comprehend the conditions, structures, and reciprocal relationships of every phase of human activity in the past, as well as to descry the developmental patterns that gave meaning to human existence.

This project, which the word "bold" hardly begins to describe, subjected its author to every manner of difficulty during the course of his career. The difficulties began in Göttingen. They grew out of Lamprecht's straining at the bounds of academic history. While Droysen presented him with a convenient foil, Lamprecht experienced difficulties with his professors and fellow students. His reputation as the leading student of history in Göttingen rested on the phenomenal breadth of his learning, but breadth was not an unalloyed virtue, particularly when it extended into philosophy; and he was reputed to be a little eccentric. "Attending lectures in philosophy," he later told a colleague, "even in the history of philosophy, counted as a grave diversion [schlimme Entgleisung]."[103] Lamprecht could well have collided with Waitz but for the professor's early departure from Göttingen.[104] Professional friction was also an element in Lamprecht's relationship to Weizsäcker, who had little understanding or sympathy for his methodological ideas; but mutual admiration and personal affection tempered the tension between the two.[105]

Lamprecht's difficulties in Göttingen also had a more personal aspect, for the grand design taking shape in his mind required an assault on bounds that were disciplinary in more than one sense of the word. To speak of a religious crisis would be an exaggeration. In 1875–1876, though, the student underwent a period of religious doubt; and the beliefs that survived could be described only in the loosest sense as Christian. Lamprecht's doubts had probably been building for some time, but they crystallized when he began to study philosophy with Lotze and then, on his professor's recommendation, read Eduard von Hartmann's broadside, The Self-Disintegration of Christianity.[106] Lamprecht was struck by Hartmann's insistence on the unbridgeable contradiction between the modern spirit of scientific inquiry and criticism, whose object was the immanent regularities that governed the world, and a religion that was based on transcendental mysticism.[107] Hartmann's sharpest remarks were directed at the tradition in which Lamprecht himself had grown up—the liberal Protestantism of Schleiermacher, which Hartmann portrayed as "systematized muddleheadedness [Verschwommenheit]," the last pathetic attempt to marry Wissenschaft and Christian belief.[108] Hartmann's resolution of this contradiction lay in a "new world religion," a kind of universal pantheism; but Lamprecht was not yet prepared to follow him this far. Nonetheless, the philosopher's influence did encourage Lamprecht's abandonment of his own religious roots. For the duration of his life the historian remained religious, but his beliefs were henceforth empty of any specific Christian content. The best description of these beliefs was probably the one he himself offered shortly before his death, when he spoke of a "sincere and childishly simple religiosity, which is contained within the simple framework of a world-view and the genuine greatness of moral feeling."[109]

Lamprecht's religious experience was hardly unique. The embrace of a secular world view, the abandonment of all but the routine outward forms of Protestantism, was a common phenomenon within the German *Bildungsbürgertum* of the late nineteenth century (Lamprecht's experience was, for example, reminiscent of Jacob Burckhardt's).[110] But the long-term implications of Lamprecht's experience lent it special significance. His distancing himself from Christianity had both a metaphysical and an ethical dimension; and it was directed at two figures who remained associated in his eyes.[111]

The first was Ranke. Lamprecht signaled his rejection of a philosophy of history whose metaphysics imposed dogmatic limits on the pursuit of historical truth. Lamprecht's criticism of Ranke's *Ideenlehre* did not become systematic until his famous public attack twenty years later; but his opposition had long focused on the theology of Ranke's views, which, he insisted (correctly), derived directly from Luther. Lamprecht characterized as transcendental mysticism the doctrine that history was a reflection of God's hidden hand—that, as he charged, the "entire course of history constituted a divine secret."[112] The project emerging in Lamprecht's own mind was nothing less than to uncover the hidden hand, to "see God," as he later put it, "when we pluck the ripest fruits from the tree of knowledge."[113] That this Faustian undertaking was impious no longer concerned him.[114]

The second figure at whom the move away from Christianity was directed was his own father. The old man followed the development of his son's religious doubt with patience and understanding.[115] However, his own association with the beliefs that his son was now abandoning allowed no doubt that the younger Karl Lamprecht was engineering his full emancipation from his father's authority.

The implications of this step, its significance in the completion of the historian's self-image, emerged in a remarkable letter he wrote in June 1875, in the midst of his religious unrest.[116] The letter was to his brother, the pastor, in whom he had begun to find a regular and sympathetic audience for his concerns.[117] Hugo Lamprecht had been exiled to a small, indifferent rural parish in the Mark Brandenburg and was having his own doubts about theology as a profession. In this letter Karl Lamprecht posed the question of scholarship in a manner that would have bewildered both his father and Ranke. "Does one pursue academic studies primarily for the sake of other people?" He answered:

> My view is that if theology is a discipline, then one studies it above all for oneself. In order to satisfy *his own* urges, in order to clarify things for *oneself*: that is the reason above all why one studies, and egoism is not the least of the drives to scholarship.

Lamprecht was not meditating only on his brother's concerns. The ethic he invoked in this passage was his own reply to his father's pietism. He was embracing a new, autonomous ethic more appropriate to the great project that would earn the father's respect even as it vaulted the son beyond the bounds drawn by paternal admonitions to a life of Christian humility. When Lamprecht wrote to his brother of those "great spirits," who could dispense with the traditional forms of Christianity because they "have always placed themselves above dogma," he was referring to himself.

Even during his years in Göttingen, the study of history provided Lamprecht with an alternative to Christianity as the source of release, solace, and fulfillment in his life.[118] His emerging vision of history also furnished him with a compelling means of interpreting his own experience—as a member of the educated Protestant elite in Germany, but also as his father's son. All the elements that went into this vision were products of the tradition and milieu in which he matured and received his training. But the grandiosity of this vision and the enormity of its author's ambition suggested the deeper significance that the study of history had acquired for him. It was the source of self-esteem for a man whose youth had provided him with no others.[119]

On 25 February 1877, Karl Lamprecht celebrated his twenty-first birthday at a small party Weizsäcker and Bernheim had arranged for him at the professor's home. It was a gratifying show of support at a time when Lamprecht was beset with problems. He had arrived in Göttingen for the winter semester with the news that his father was terminally ill with diabetes.[120] His own health was a cause for concern, too. The pace and intensity of his work had aggravated a stomach disorder, possibly an ulcer.[121] In these circumstances his personal ties to Weizsäcker and Bernheim became closer, but they only eased a little the problem of his intellectual isolation in Göttingen. He had no real friends in a small provincial city that offered little diversion.[122] Beyond Bernheim, he could find little sympathy for the ideas about history that were exciting him the most.

The state of his father's health recommended both a hasty completion of his studies and a transfer to a university nearer home. Perhaps grateful to occupy his student with an orthodox topic, Weizsäcker proposed that a seminar paper that Lamprecht had written on the canon lawyer Ivo, Bishop of Chartres, serve as the basis of a dissertation that could be completed elsewhere. Armed with documents and notes for this project, Lamprecht left Göttingen in March 1877.

The universities closest to home were located in Halle and Leipzig. Of the two, Leipzig was the more attractive to a young man who had felt confined in a small university city. Although it had not yet entered the period of its most dramatic growth, the city of Leipzig had a population of more than 100,000 and was one of the country's leading commercial centers. The university, the only one in the kingdom of Saxony, was the largest in Germany with an enrollment of close to 3,000 students in 1877—almost three times that of the university Lamprecht had just left.[123] The university in Leipzig also enjoyed the generous support of the state's government, whose largesse reflected the enlightened policies of successive ministers of culture, who were determined to keep pace with the leading universities in Prussia.[124] The strength of the university lay in the philosophical faculty, particularly in the fields of economics, in which Wihelm Roscher held a chair, and experimental psychology, which had virtually been born in Leipzig. The pioneer of this discipline, Gustav Theodor Fechner (Lotze's mentor), lived on in Leipzig after his mantle had passed in 1875 to Wilhelm Wundt.

Lamprecht arrived in Leipzig in April 1877, took a small flat across the street from the Johannis cemetery, and enrolled in the university.[125] Among his fellow students, whom he pronounced to be more noisy and unruly than those in Göttingen, he flaunted the range of his knowledge and became known quickly, if not with much affection, as the "general historical oracle."[126] In these circles he established few personal ties, and he had no difficulty resuming a solitary existence in the larger city.

One aspect of his isolation was the unusual academic situation in which he found himself. He had completed a great deal of work in Göttingen, so his primary goal in Leipzig was to write a dissertation in but two semesters. The man in the most logical position to direct his work had himself just arrived in Leipzig. To judge from his career, Carl von Noorden was an extraordinarily restless man, whose association with the great names in the profession had failed to produce a comfortable sense of his own intellectual calling.[127] It was doubtless of some moment that his roots were Calvinist. As a young man he exhibited a passion for poetry and music, studied law and Sanskrit, and took a doctorate in philology. Then he turned to the study of medieval history, working with Ranke (with whom he was distantly related) and Sybel, who also took him on as an editor of the *Historische Zeitschrift*. Noorden demonstrated his loyalties to Sybel in a series of bitter scholarly and political polemics in the 1860s, before he abandoned activism in favor of a contemplative posture more similar to Ranke's. He also shifted his attention from medieval to modern history, where he wrote the volumes on which his reputation rested, on the history of Europe during the War of the Spanish Succession. With Ranke's aid he received a chair in Greifswald in 1868. Then, in rapid succession, he migrated to chairs in Marburg, Tübingen, Bonn, and finally in Leipzig, where he arrived in the spring of 1877 and remained until his death six years later. During his tenure in Leipzig he established the university's historical seminar.

Noorden's relationship to Lamprecht was curious, similar in some respects to Weizsäcker's. In addition to auditing Noorden's lectures on Europe in the seventeenth and eighteenth centuries, Lamprecht served as his *famulus* or student assistant. Although holding the position was an honor, Lamprecht resented the imposition on his time.[128] Noorden, who had been trained in the great traditions of German historical scholarship, was as skeptical as Weizsäcker had been about his student's interest in a comprehensive methodology; but like Weizsäcker, he was impressed almost to the point of intimidation by Lamprecht's "tumultuously wild presence [*tumultuanisch ungeberdiges Auftreten*]," by the range of Lamprecht's learning, and by the energy and independence with which he sought to integrate it.[129] Perhaps because their temperamental similarities created a bond, their personal relationship was warm, and Lamprecht was a frequent guest in Noorden's home.

The bond was not sufficiently strong, however, to make Noorden comfortable directing Lamprecht's dissertation. The problem was that the student no longer wished to write about Ivo of Chartres. In Leipzig he had strayed beyond the bounds of his discipline into another field, where the outlines of his vision of history took more specific shape under the tutelage of a figure who was more sympathetic to his intellectual designs.

The premise that Ernst Troeltsch described as "the historicization of all our existence," the idea that every aspect of human affairs could be properly understood only in the light of its own unique historical development, represented the basis of a general intellectual reorientation in Germany in the early nineteenth century. This premise was reflected not only in the foundation of history as an independent discipline, but in the terms in which the practitioners of a variety of other humanistic fields redefined their goals, subject matter, and methods. The names Savigny, Hegel, Grimm, and Schleiermacher attested to the significance which jurists, philosophers, philologists, and theologians alike attached to integrating the idea of historical development into their disciplines.

Perhaps with the exception of history itself, no discipline was more directly or durably affected by the new orientation toward history than economics. Although the professionalization of this discipline took place somewhat later, the establishment of the "historical school of national economy" resembled the emancipation of history, in that the discipline's pioneers sought to insulate it systematically from older traditions and the claims of rivals. In the case of economics, however, tradition and rival claims were more difficult to escape, and their imprint survived more prominently in the new discipline.[130]

The men whose names were associated with the so-called older historical school of national economy, Bruno Hildebrand, Carl Knies, and Wilhelm Roscher, had all trained as historians—Roscher with Ranke, Knies with Sybel. While their growing interest in the realm of economic activity represented a departure from the conventions of their historical training, the methods they adopted in the effort to redefine the study of economics lay well within these conventions. History offered the solvent to free the study of economics from the grip of the two traditions that had dominated the field. These were cameralism and classical economic theory—the one, in Roscher's words, "a kind of technology," the other "a kind of applied mathematics."[131] If cameralism reduced national economy to a field ancillary to the practical discipline of public administration, classical theory cast economic behavior in mathematical formulas and global abstractions.

The redefinition of the field thus took place on two fronts. Against the cameralists the historical economists argued, in the spirit of the humanistic academic reformers, that their field comprised a *Wissenschaft*, a systematic body of knowledge appropriate for study beyond any direct practical application it might yield. Against the classical theories of Adam Smith, David Ricardo, and their German disciples, the historical economists argued, as Ranke had argued against Hegel, that abstract theories, the effort to analyze the realm of economic activity in isolation, did violence to the historical diversity of economic behavior, as well as to the complex interaction between the economy and other realms of human activity. The historicity of economic behavior and its interdependence with politics and culture, they insisted, made careful source-based historical analysis of economic practices, institutions, and systems the only method appropriate to their discipline.

This argument entangled the economists, like the historians, in the problem of the universal and the particular—of relating the individual phenomena they studied to a realm in which they could draw conclusions about patterns and meaning in history. The logic of their argument implied the singularity of every economic system in every historical epoch and hence the impossibility of making comparisons among these systems or statements about critical questions like economic development. For a number of reasons, however, the economists shied away from these implications. In the first place, they had not shed all vestiges of the cameralist tradition, and their aspirations to offer policy recommendations required that their study of history suggest norms for guidance. In the second place, they soon faced an urgent new challenge in the form of historical materialism, a doctrine that fused classical theory with historical analysis and offered a historical panorama of economic development that was as imposing as it was unacceptable to a group of German university professors.

After Max Weber's devastating commentaries, there is little need to dwell on the inconsistencies and contradictions to which the early historical economists succumbed as they responded to these pressures.[132] It suffices to note that despite their rejection of the abstractions of classical theory, the founding fathers smuggled in general theories of historical development. These rested on the belief that economic behavior was governed by regular patterns or laws.[133] The historical economists believed that these patterns were empirically demonstrable and that they differed more in degree than in function from natural laws. The laws that governed human economic behavior, they argued, were specific to historical context and operated in a lesser order of certainty than natural laws, which addressed precise and universal relations of cause and effect and were couched in the idiom of mathematics and experimentation; the idiom of economic laws was instead analogy and the new language of statistics, which offered a quantifiable basis for measuring social phenomena and for reducing the problem of individual diversity to the observable regularities of a statistical series.[134]

The analogical tradition most cordial to these scholars was organic. Theories of economic development adapted effortlessly to metaphors of growth. In addition, organic analogies corresponded to what might be called a holistic or integrative mode of analysis, which addressed the interdependence and ultimate unity of all regions, material and ideal, in the life of a people (*Volk*) at any given moment of its history.[135] The economists thus found refuge against the charge that in privileging the economy in their analyses, they, no less than the classical theorists, had fallen prey to materialism. The economy did admittedly occupy a privileged position in their analyses, but organic analogies enabled them to emphasize the play of ideal forces in the motivation of economic behavior. In this fashion, the historical economists distinguished the emerging norms of their discipline from the traditions of mechanical analysis and analogy associated with the classical school. The centrality of these organic analogies also revealed the roots that their discipline had struck in an indigenous intellectual tradition that reached through Hegel and the romantics back to Herder.

The fact that academic history was a product of the same intellectual tradition underscored the affinities between the two new disciplines, particularly once the teleological admixtures associated with the Prussian school of historiography made the theme of moral and political progress as central to history as the theme of growth was to economics. Despite these affinities, the relationship between the two disciplines was not easy after the middle of the nineteenth century. The difficulties were due less to the theories of the economists, which admitted the constitutive role of the state in economic affairs, than to the growing parochialism of the historians—their preoccupation with the state as a free moral agent and their reluctance to make concessions to the constitutive role of economic forces in politics. The receptivity of the economists to theory, their penchant for speaking of regular patterns, if not laws of behavior and historical development, reinforced the historians' suspicions. And these lingered after the *Reichsgründung*, despite the succession of a younger generation of economists who emphasized historical research still further at the expense of theory.

The father of the German historical school of national economy, the most prominent and influential figure of its first generation, was Wilhelm Roscher.[136] He was also the school's most enthusiastic, ambitious, and naive theoretician. His confidence in the working of empirical laws in human behavior was not confined to the regularities of economic growth but extended to the interaction between economics and all other realms of human activity. Nor did the methodological difficulties of constructing an inductive metaphysics arouse in him the reservations that ultimately prevented Hildebrand and Knies from sharing his confidence. In the breadth of his aspirations he resembled Lotze, but his mind was not disciplined like Lotze's; and he failed to recognize the extent to which the laws he invoked were products of his own beliefs and fertile speculation. He was, however, for just this reason a great synthesizer and system builder. He was most responsible for pulling economics in the direction of those "irritatingly integrative sciences" (the expression comes from a modern philosopher) like psychology and sociology, whose practitioners stood closer intellectually to German economists in the late nineteenth century than they did to academic historians.[137]

Roscher was a child of the same Lutheran tradition as Ranke. Like his teacher, he made no claim to understand the ultimate essence of the cosmos, which remained the secret of God; like Ranke, he insisted that the scholar's greatest aspiration could be only to detect the workings of God's hidden hand. In Roscher's vision, however, this hand worked with greater regularity and left more intelligible traces. In an enormous corpus, which he produced over the course of more than half a century, Roscher worked out the contours of an all-embracing system of society and history. Its basic units were national groups (*Völker*)—organic entities whose morphologies displayed common developmental sequences that both testified to the operation of laws in history and made possible the drawing of analogies and analytical comparisons among different groups. Analyzing the causality of historical events meant, in his eyes, relating these events to the workings of historical laws. These laws governed not only the stages of historical development but the interaction among all the realms of activity—economic, political, and cultural—which the organic totality of the national group comprised.

Roscher argued that all economic systems underwent a developmental sequence that witnessed first the replacement of nature by labor and then the replacement of labor by capital as the dominant factor in production. The economic dimension of a nation's life was fundamental, but economic development proceeded in organic relationship to other phases of the *Volksleben*. Roscher claimed, for instance, that political and legal systems progressed in sequence from aristocratic to monarchical to democratic forms. Economic and political development was also intertwined in culture, the highest and purest expression of a nation's essential spirit or *Volksgeist*. But cultural endeavor, too, underwent a progressive movement through a series of *Kulturstufen*—epochs that Roscher identified, on the basis of his studies of literature, as the "typical" (in which the dominant literary form was the epic), the "conventional" (in which lyric poetry predominated), and the "individualistic" (which witnessed the appearance of memoirs, drama, and the writing of historical accounts). Roscher insisted finally that each nation's transit through all of these epochs constituted a common developmental cycle through phases of rise, maturation, and decline.

Roscher's wonderful mosaic was an inspiration to scholars who, in an era of growing fragmentation and specialization, had not abandoned hope in the unity of knowledge. Because it built so much on indigenous traditions, his vision was more attractive to German scholars than was Comtean positivism, a foreign doctrine (with which it had a lot in common). Roscher's system was also, as Weber later showed, a monument of methodological confusion. The critical problem was the ontological status of the bold generalizations that were the pillars of his system. Not only the stages through which human activity progressed in history, but the ideas of the *Volk*, the *Volksgeist*, natural laws, organic unity, the concept of development itself, and countless other ideas were not just heuristic categories in Roscher's eyes; they were the constituents of reality, and they were empirically validated by the actions of men and women throughout time. In the end, despite Roscher's homage to Ranke, the animating spirit in his system was Hegel's, except that Hegel was by far the more rigorous thinker.

"Roscher represents less a contrast to Hegel than a regression," Weber wrote. "Hegel's metaphysics and the rule of speculation over history have disappeared in Roscher; brilliant metaphysical constructions have been replaced with a rather primitive form of simple religious devoutness [Gläubigkeit]."[138]

Roscher had been teaching in Leipzig for almost thirty years when Karl Lamprecht first encountered him in 1877. Lamprecht's previous studies in the field of national economy had been limited to his work with Georg Hanssen in Göttingen. His interest in a broad analytical framework for the study of history had grown instead out of his frustrations with his own discipline and his work with Bernheim and Lotze. When Lamprecht arrived in Leipzig, Roscher was at the zenith of his fame, and he appealed powerfully to the interests and frustrations of a student whose restless imagination and search for a comprehensive theory of history resembled his own.

It took little time for Lamprecht to realize not only that Roscher's grand system comported with ideas he had encountered with Lotze and Bernheim, but that it provided intellectual slots for most of the historical information he himself had been collecting. He absorbed Roscher's teachings as rapidly as he could. He audited lectures on the basics of national economy, agricultural policy, public finance, and the history of social and political theory.[139] He also devoured Roscher's classic treatise, The System of National Economy, whose first volume had appeared in its thirteenth edition in 1875.[140]

"I am now auditing national economy with Roscher," Lamprecht wrote to his brother in July 1877, "and although it is theoretical, I have still been frequently provoked to inquire into various aspects of agriculture. It has to do with my work."[141] The work in question was his dissertation, which had changed significantly since he left Göttingen. The more he immersed himself in the study of economics, the more dreary became the prospect of a topic in constitutional history. He accordingly abandoned Ivo of Chartres in favor of a study in French economic history—a subject that had begun to interest him as a backdrop to Ivo's writings on the institution of the tithe.[142] The topic was more cordial to Roscher as well, who agreed to direct the work.

The dissertation Lamprecht completed at the end of 1877 showed the signs of Roscher's inspiration and direction.[143] It was an impressive work. On the basis of a close and imaginative reading of legal codes and monastic charters, it presented a profile of the agrarian economy of northeastern France in the eleventh century. The structure of the dissertation corresponded to Roscher's morphological categories. The first part treated the topography and resources— the forests, streams, meadowlands, and livestock—that constituted the natural bases of production. The second part analyzed the appropriation of these resources in settlements, field systems, and property relations. The third was devoted to the social organization of production, to agrarian estates, forms and degrees of servitude and obligation, and the role of law in solidifying relations of production and property. The final section of the dissertation examined the problem of mobilizing wealth in a natural economy and the nascent development of the handicrafts and commerce as harbingers of a monetized economy.

Lamprecht's analysis was careful and controlled. His generalizations rarely reached beyond the immediate confines of his topic. He mentioned the development of monarchical authority only in passing and dealt with the church only in its role in the system of production. His analysis of the sensitive problem of the tie between social relations and the legal system followed Roscher's circumspect lead in emphasizing the symbiotic nature of the relationship. On only a few occasions did the author provide hints of his broader analytical ambitions, but here, too, he did little more than paraphrase generalizations long associated with Roscher.

Roscher was pleased. The dissertation presented, he noted, "a rich picture of medieval economic and popular life." Roscher reported that the work was "conceived very much with a grand perspective [*sehr aus dem Vollen geschöpft*], carried out with great care in the particulars."[144] More interesting was the reaction of Noorden, the second reader, who had regarded a project in economic history with the skepticism common to his guild and perhaps with a little resentment over the desertion of his student. Noorden applied the historian's true test and checked the footnotes, which occupied close to two-thirds of the dissertation. At this stage in his career, Lamprecht's scholarship proved both exhaustive and accurate; and Noorden's doubts about the student's potential evaporated. "The author has worked with exemplary thoroughness and exactitude," he commented, and he added that the dissertation deserved "unconditional praise for its method and for the scholarly significance of its conclusions."[145] The readers' judgment was confirmed when Gustav Schmoller, who was then in Strassburg, accepted the dissertation for publication in the monograph series he was then inaugurating.

To complete his doctorate, Lamprecht needed only to pass examinations in three fields. That he would opt for history and national economy was clear; for the third he chose philosophy and read with Wilhelm Wundt, whose chair was officially in that field. Because his interest was already occupied with national economy, he was not tempted at this time to pursue psychology with Wundt; he concentrated instead on the history of philosophy, which he had studied in Göttingen. In February 1878 he passed his doctoral examinations with little difficulty. His examiners were all impressed by the wealth of his knowledge, and they noted only in passing that he displayed some unclarity of thought and that his knowledge was, as Roscher wrote, "clouded by a certain restlessness."[146]

This criticism touched problems whose significance was beginning to emerge. Lamprecht worked rapidly. His completion of a doctorate in only seven semesters was an achievement, particularly in view of his military service, which had consumed much of his time during two of them. The speed with which he worked attested to an astounding rapidity of comprehension, but it also betrayed the ever-impatient collector, whose attention was more easily occupied in gathering in broad fields than in assimilating what he had gathered. His appropriation of Roscher's system was hurried and uncritical; the fact that his training in philosophy was also shallow limited his appreciation for the system's methodological difficulties. But Roscher, too, was unaware of these difficulties, so his criticism of his student's restlessness was all the more telling. It came from a man whose own penchant for exuberant speculation was well known.

Roscher was a sympathetic critic. In the course of two semesters, he had become an admirer, a model, and another of Lamprecht's "fatherly friends."[147] Roscher had also become, for better or worse, the most important and enduring intellectual influence in Lamprecht's life.

Lamprecht's dissertation dealt with the realm that Roscher had designated "material culture"—the material bases of French society, the natural conditions and relations of production. The dissertation contained only a passing observation about cultural attitudes, popular morals, or what would today be called "mentalities."

> Everywhere the raw, untamed power of nature, everywhere the preponderance of sensuality over intellect, of passion over calculation. In this respect, the popular classes of that era, which were segregated legally and socially, resembled one another incomparably more with respect to their morals than [do] the social orders of our own day.[148]

This passage spoke to an interest that Lamprecht managed to suppress in his dissertation but had hardly abandoned. He hoped to find ways to relate the realms of "material culture" and "ideal culture" in a historical account. In this respect, too, Roscher's system seemed to offer a solution, insofar as it defined a series of integrated stages of cultural development in which literary genres served as indices. Lamprecht, however, hoped to broaden this strategy to encompass other art forms.

Lamprecht also read art history in Leipzig, although not formally or systematically. Through Noorden he met the resident art historian, Anton Springer. Springer was a Hegelian. Lamprecht found his thinking cordial, for Springer dismissed aesthetic judgment as analytically irrelevant and emphasized the commonalities that stretched across genres to link the works of art of a given historical epoch.[149] Lamprecht found another guide in the historian Georg Voigt, who had written an important book on the reception of classical art during the Italian Renaissance. On Voigt's advice, he first read Burckhardt.[150]

Lamprecht's interest in art history was sufficiently stimulated in Leipzig to figure in the decisions he now made. The state of his father's health and finances made some form of gainful employment essential, and the logical step was to take the state examinations to qualify for secondary teaching. When he returned home after his *Promotion* in February 1878, he agreed to this course but persuaded his father first to allow him an additional semester of study, so that he could, as he noted later, "fill a couple of special holes in my historical training."[151]

He chose to go to Munich. The main attraction was not the presence there of Riehl or two of Ranke's most distinguished students, Carl Adolf Cornelius and the historian of the medieval German monarchy, Wilhelm Giesebrecht; it was instead the artistic treasures housed in the city's museums. Lamprecht had little contact with the historians in Munich; most of his time at the university he spent auditing the lectures of J. A. Messmer in aesthetics and art history. But he spent the bulk of his time alone in Munich, reading art history, viewing the great collections in the Alte Pinakothek, and studying the development of medieval costumes.[152]

This last item was the clue to the figure who set Lamprecht's agenda in Munich. Jacob Burckhardt was, after Roscher, the most significant intellectual influence Lamprecht encountered in these years, even though he did not know the Swiss historian personally. Burckhardt's work not only confirmed ideas that Lamprecht had learned from Springer and Voigt about the historicity and broader cultural contexts of art. Lamprecht was fascinated as well by Burckhardt's portrayal of diverse aspects of culture—not only art and literature, but customs, costumes, folkways, beliefs, and morals—as components of a unified pattern defined by a common theme. "In reading the *Civilization of the Renaissance in Italy*," he later explained, "I was struck to see how every cultural epoch is delineated by a center of psychic life."[153] His reading of Burckhardt also convinced him that the art of a historical epoch represented a special kind of litmus for locating this center—that art represented a central expression of an era's cultural spirit or psychic ambience.

But the scope of Lamprecht's interest was broader than Burckhardt's, and his goals were more ambitious. Despite its majestic scope, Burckhardt's work was incomplete. To the extent that he emphasized politics as the soil out of which the culture of the Italian Renaissance grew, Burckhardt had, in Lamprecht's eyes, repeated the mistake of the German political historians and overlooked the material circumstances that shaped political history. "The most attractive task of historical research," he wrote in gentle criticism of Burckhardt, "consists in establishing the character of the psychic view which issues forth from a given combination of natural, economic, political, and social forces."[154] The student of Roscher envisaged, in other words, the writing of "total history." Burckhardt had shown how to locate the unified cultural patterns of a historical epoch; Lamprecht proposed to relate these patterns to the material bases of culture—to the relations of production, and to show how art, culture, politics, and material structures all evolved interdependently through progressive historical stages.

Finally, Burckhardt's work suggested to Lamprecht the pivotal analogy that tied this grand vision together.[155] The theme that lent cultural cohesion to Burckhardt's Renaissance was the development and expression of human individuality. The central theme in Lamprecht's dissertation was individual bondage (*individuelle Gebundenheit*) in a natural economy, the coercion and constraint of individual human beings in a network of obligation to family, community, and nature. Lamprecht reasoned that the phenomena that Burckhardt described in the realm of ideal culture corresponded to developments in the material realm, as the coming of a money economy undermined this network of constraint and cleared the way for a new system of productive relations based on competition and personal freedom. This insight was not original with Lamprecht; there were clear hints of it in Roscher (to say nothing of Marx).[156] But Lamprecht became its great exponent. He dedicated himself to working out its implications and trying to demonstrate its truth, for it became the cornerstone of his analysis of German history.

In the summer of 1878, during his last weeks in Munich, Lamprecht composed an essay that bore the title "On Individuality and the Understanding of It during the German Middle Ages."[157] It was a remarkable document. It marked the conclusion of his intellectual maturation, his first attempt to synthesize the various influences that he had encountered during his training and to formulate his own broad view of German history. The essay was also a programmatic statement, for it prefigured the major project of his life.

In its basic design, the essay was an attempt to fuse Roscher and Burckhardt. It purported to trace the evolution of the concept of individuality—of the individual human being as an autonomous entity—during the German Middle Ages, from the Carolingian era to the eve of the Reformation. Its argument, in brief, was that the concept of individuality emerged slowly and sporadically with the breaking down of the constraints exercised by tribe and family and with the rise of the idea of the German nation. The triumph of individuality came only with the transition from a natural to a money economy and the emergence of a genuine sense of national identity. The institutions that characterized a natural economy—compulsory participation in the three-field system and communal regulation of the harvest—represented a "complete regimentation [Bevormundung] of the individual by the village community."[158] This situation corresponded to a broad range of conventions and attitudes that likewise stifled the idea of individuality. The era's insecurity was not conducive to attitudes of foresight and calculation, in either economic or political affairs; nor did it encourage the development of a sense of individual possession (hence the forgeries of canonical documents). Laws of inheritance gave precedence to families at the expense of individuals; penal law did not recognize the importance of motive. Philosophy was the tool of the church, which played the role of collective conscience and interposed itself between the individual and God. In art and literature the dominant symbolic and epic modes allowed no room for individuality of style.

After a brief flowering in the late feudal knighthood, the culture of individuality came into its own with the growth of a money economy and the consequent development of the third estate, the Bürgerstand, which, unlike the knighthood, could claim to be a truly national class. The division of labor in the towns and cities bred the ideas of virtuosity and vocation. Cities became centers of political autonomy, cultivation, and patronage of the arts. The growing appreciation for the individual personality was mirrored in all phases of cultural life. Positive law emphasized the distinction between the private and public spheres, as private property became the norm. The popularity of nominalism and Aristotelian ethics testified to a new individualistic orientation in philosophy, while religious mysticism spoke to the direct tie between the individual and God. The emphasis on portraiture in art and literature corresponded to a new understanding of an individual's unique aptitude (*Beanlagung*). Finally, the money economy made for the flourishing of the middle-class family. "Loyalty and coarse respectability, competence and diligence in professional life are its pillars," Lamprecht observed. "With it the way was cleared for the education of children's character, and the development [*Durchbildung*] of the personality was made possible beginning in the first years."[159]

Lamprecht himself probably did not appreciate the irony of his undertaking. The essay attempted to demonstrate that individuality, the concept fundamental to the whole historicist tradition, had evolved historically in response to changes in relations of production. In fact, there was considerable confusion on this score, for Lamprecht appeared to argue as well that the idea of individuality developed according to its own logic; and his paean to the educated middle-class family left little doubt about the *telos*. This confusion was related to another problem. It was unclear in Lamprecht's account whether culture was to serve as an index of transformations in the material realm, for the two spheres tended to develop independently of one another—or rather, the ties between them were less analytical than analogical.

The essay nonetheless brought together an enormous range of material from the realms of the economy, law, politics, art, architecture, literature, philosophy, and popular morals. Although the analogies with which it attempted to integrate this material were often strained, they testified to the author's ingenuity. Lamprecht gave evidence in this early essay of the immense range of his learning and imagination, which had already led him to insights far beyond the vision of more conventional academic historians. The essay's conceptual problems, like the imprecision of language that frequently muddled it, could still perhaps be excused as signs of the author's youth, inexperience, and haste.

More than anything Lamprecht had yet produced, this essay was the product of his solitary meditations, and for this reason it was the most candid indication of the direction of his thinking and intentions. In Göttingen and Leipzig he had worked under the guidance of scholars who attempted to discipline his thinking and bridle his speculation. Even Roscher, who was the most willing to indulge the student's imagination, tried to encourage clarity. Lamprecht did not suffer their efforts gladly, but he did submit. His dissertation, while by no means a conventional piece of scholarship, was sound for just this reason. The essay he wrote in Munich was much bolder, and it raised more problems. It thus suggested both the advantages and the risks of Lamprecht's working without a restraining hand.

The essay that Lamprecht wrote on individuality marked the conclusion of another phase of his development as well. In this respect, the departure from Leipzig represented less of a break, for the terms in which he pondered the broader questions of his own growth and calling were the same as he had originally defined in Göttingen. In the midst of his religious doubts, and stimulated in all probability by his encounter with Hartmann, Lamprecht read Schopenhauer. To a young man who had just thrown off the constraints of his father's pietism and had fixed upon his own egoism as the driving force in his scholarship, an ethic of self-renunciation had little appeal; and Schopenhauer served as a foil rather than a source of inspiration. But abandoning Christianity in favor of an ethic of self-indulgence did not resolve his uncertainties either; and as he continued to grapple with the question of an acceptable ethic, the specter of Schopenhauer lingered.[160]

Lamprecht resolved these uncertainties in Leipzig, as he defined an ethic that guided him for the rest of his life. During his second semester there, as he completed his dissertation, he composed an ethical statement in the form of a sonnet, which he addressed to Schopenhauer with the title "To the Pessimists."[161] In it he rejected an ethic based either on self-renunciation or self-indulgence; he announced his commitment instead to an ethic of service. The critical strophe read:

> . . . nothing avails one's striving alone,
> Nothing is created by a person's spirit going off on its own:
> But he who has seen into the cosmos takes on the obligation
> To weave himself into the pattern of the omnipotent force.

The ethic was secular; it reflected, in addition to his reading of Schopenhauer, the influence of Kant, as well as, perhaps, *Faust II*. But it already had accents of sacrifice coupled with obligation that might be best characterized as Promethean.[162] The ethic represented, in all events, the adult's final adaptation of the motifs that had dominated his childhood.[163] The theme of sacrifice addressed his sense of being an outsider and failure to find acceptance; his sense of obligation pertained to a great scholarly achievement that would bring his ethical fulfillment, the vindication of his sacrifice, and the acceptance hitherto denied him.

Unless read in this context, the essay on individuality that Lamprecht wrote in Munich cannot be fully understood. It was an autobiographical document. Its most significant analogy linked the history of the German nation to the personal development and *Bildung* of Karl Lamprecht. The essay was about individual identity. It was set in the Middle Ages, an era which, he wrote, afforded "glimpses into the youthful life of a people."[164] The essay traced the historical maturation of a sense of personal identity through a series of phases analogous to those of human growth. Maturation meant liberation from stifling constraints, the achievement of a sense of personal autonomy and self-awareness. The developments that Lamprecht described reached a plateau of maturity on the eve of the Reformation. "Essential things had been accomplished in the development [*Ausbildung*] of free individuality"—most importantly, he explained, the escaping of the restrictive bounds imposed by tribe, family, and social exclusivity. He continued:

Legal chains which were too confining had, where necessary, become more flexible bounds of a moral or economic character, and at the same time morality was strengthened and grounded systematically; the economy was freed in its most salient points from the compulsion of antiquated legal constraints.[165]

Yet Lamprecht's story was not exclusively about liberation. In his account, German history revealed the perils of artificiality, premature development, and the disorientation of individuality.[166] Genuine maturation was simultaneously the story of transcending antiquated bounds and the grounding of individuality in new, more appropriate contexts. For this reason, Lamprecht insisted that national identity was an essential prerequisite for individual identity. For this reason, too, the climax of his account came with the appearance, in the late Middle Ages, of the urban corporations (*Genossenschaften*) and the educated middle-class family (which, but for the absence of Luther, could have been Lamprecht's own). These institutions provided not only the conditions for the fullest flowering of individuality, but the legitimate bounds to ensure that the individual would not become uprooted.[167]

This principal theme, the maturation of a sense of individual identity in a continuing process of transcending and redefining bounds, revealed the essay to be a veiled statement of the historian's understanding of his own growth—of his successful challenge to the constraints of paternal authority and disciplinary conventions, and his recognition of his own proper calling. The conclusion of the essay made the parallel inescapable. "One should not," he announced, "overlook what was still lacking."

> The individual still lacked a clear relationship to the transcendental [*übersinn-lich*] world—the drive to create such a world was disapproved of and suppressed by the church; there was no sense of history, no understanding of the circumstances and accomplishments of other eras; and more high-principled education in politics and more unprejudiced systematic knowledge [*Wissen-schaft*] were consequently lacking.[168]

The grandiosity of Karl Lamprecht's understanding of himself became evident in this passage. The culmination of the development of German individuality and of the German nation awaited the emergence of an overarching context, a definitive conceptual framework—in Walter Benjamin's phrase, an ultimate magic circle—in which to comprehend the significance of these developments and to provide the nation with a genuine sense of its own individuality and historical maturation. The history of the German nation's progressive self-fulfillment was at the same time the story of the man whose own self-fulfillment lay in the perfection of just this framework. Having ventured out as far as he could beyond the bounds that challenged his own maturation, Lamprecht proposed to construct an ultimate framework or conceptual boundary, in order to capture and bring order to the entirety of the German past. The result would not only be history, a framework for understanding the past; it would represent nothing less than a unified field of knowledge. And its discovery would establish Lamprecht as the German Empire's greatest historian, the true successor to Ranke.[169]

Notes

1. Wolfgang Weber, *Priester der Klio: Historisch-sozialwissenschaftliche Studien zur Herkunft und Karriere deutscher Historiker und zur Geschichte der Geschichtswissenschaft 1800–1970* (Frankfurt am Main, Bern, New York, 1984), esp. 59–101; Christian von Ferber, *Die Entwicklung des Lehrkörpers der deutschen Universitäten und Hochschulen 1864–1954* (Göttingen, 1956), 177–78.
2. NL Lamprecht (Korr. 59), Lamprecht to Hugo Lamprecht, Pforta, 11.3.74; LW, 27; Winter, "Lamprecht," 308.
3. GStAM, NL Friedrich Althoff (B Nr. 108/1), Lamprecht to Althoff, Bonn, 16.7.84; KE, 37.
4. NL Lamprecht (Korr. 59), Lamprecht to Hugo Lamprecht, Munich, 6.5.78.
5. See Lothar Mertens, "Das Privileg des Einjährig-Freiwilligen Militärdienstes," MGM, No. 1 (1986): 59–67.
6. Götz von Selle, *Die Georg-August-Universität zu Göttingen 1737–1937* (Göttingen, 1937), 291–323; Günther Meinhardt, *Die Universität Göttingen: Ihre Entwicklung und Geschichte von 1734–1974* (Göttingen, 1977), 70–86; Charles E. McClelland, *State, Society and University in Germany 1700–1914* (Cambridge, 1980), esp. 35–57.
7. Wilhelm Deist, ed., *Militär und Innenpolitik im Weltkrieg 1914–1918*, 2 vols. (Düsseldorf, 1970), 1: xx.
8. NL Lamprecht (Korr. 59), Lamprecht to Hugo Lamprecht, Göttingen, 18.9.75; LW, 27–28.
9. Franz Eulenburg, *Die Frequenz der deutschen Universitäten: Von ihrer Gründung bis zur Gegenwart* (Leipzig, 1904), 304.
10. NL Lamprecht (L 3a), Gneisse, Erinnerungen; LW, 31; Johannes Scholz, *Geschichte der Burschenschaft Germania in Göttingen während der Jahre 1871–1893* (Neustrelitz, 1931), 172–74.
11. NL Lamprecht (Korr. 59), Lamprecht to Hugo Lamprecht, Göttingen, 9.4.75.
12. He thereafter participated regularly in summer maneuvers. In the summer of 1880 he was promoted to lieutenant in a regiment of the *Landwehr* that was headquartered in Bonn. NL Lamprecht (Rh 1), Entwurf für das Gesuch an v. Arnim [1880].
13. For surveys see Heinrich Ritter von Srbik, *Geist und Geschichte vom deutschen Humanismus bis zur Gegenwart*, 2 vols. (Munich and Salzburg, 1951); Georg G. Iggers, *The German Conception of History: The National Tradition of Historical Thought from Herder to the Present*, 2d ed. (Middletown, CT, 1983); Georg von Below, *Die deutsche Geschichtsschreibung von den Befreiungskriegen bis zu unseren Tagen: Geschichtsschreibung und Geschichtsauffassung* (Munich and Berlin, 1924); Moriz Ritter, *Die Entwicklung der Geschichtswissenschaft an den führenden Werken betrachtet* (Berlin and Munich, 1919).
14. See Karl-Georg Faber, "Ausprägungen des Historismus," HZ, 228 (1979): 1–22; Heinrich Dilly, "Entstehung und Geschichte des Begriffs Historismus—Funktion und Struktur einer Begriffsgeschichte," *Geschichte allein ist zeitgemäss* (Giessen, 1978); Wolfgang Götz, "Historismus. Ein Versuch zur Definition des Begriffs," *Zeitschrift des Deutschen Vereins für Kunstwissenschaft*, 24 (1970): 196–212; Georg Iggers, "Historicism," *Dictionary of the History of Ideas*, 2 (1973): 456–64; Dwight E. Lee and Robert N. Beck, "The Meaning of Historicism," AHR, 59 (1954): 568–77;

cf. Thomas Nipperdey, "Historismus und Historismuskritik heute," in Eberhard Jäckel and Ernst Weymar, eds., *Die Funktion der Geschichte in unserer Zeit* (Stuttgart, 1975), 82–95.

15. Terry Eagleton, *Marxism and Literary Criticism* (Berkeley and Los Angeles, 1976), viii.

16. W. W. Walsh, *Philosophy of History: An Introduction* (New York, 1960), 121.

17. Ernst Troeltsch, *Der Historismus und seine Probleme: Das logische Problem der Geschichtsphilosophie* (Tübingen, 1922), 102–10.

18. Ibid., 103.

19. Horst Walter Blanke, "Die Wiederentdeckung der deutschen Aufklärungshistorie und die Begründung der Historischen Sozialwissenschaft," in Wolfgang Prinz and Peter Weingart, eds., *Die sog. Geisteswissenschaften: Innenansichten* (Frankfurt am Main, 1990), 109–12.

20. See Hans Peter Reill, *The German Enlightenment and the Rise of Historicism* (Berkeley and Los Angeles, 1975); Ernst Schulin, "Der Einfluss der Romantik auf die deutsche Geschichtsforschung," *Traditionskritik und Rekonstruktionsversuch* (Göttingen, 1979), 24–43. Although Blanke has recently drawn attention to their agendas, see also Below, *Geschichtsschreibung*, 4–17; Friedrich Meinecke, *Die Entstehung des Historismus* (Munich, 1959).

21. Wolfgang Hardtwig, "Von Preussens Aufgabe in Deutschland zu Deutschlands Aufgabe in der Welt: Liberalismus und borussianisches Geschichtsbild zwischen Revolution und Imperialismus," HZ, 231 (1980): 271.

22. Nipperdey, *Deutsche Geschichte 1800–1866*, 498.

23. Troeltsch, *Historismus*, 102.

24. Nipperdey, *Deutsche Geschichte 1800–1866*, 519; *cf.* Konrad H. Jarausch, "The Institutionalization of History in 18th-Century Germany," in Hans Erich Bödeker et al., eds., *Aufklärung und Geschichte: Studien zur deutschen Geschichtsschreibung im 18. Jahrhundert* (Göttingen, 1986), 25–48.

25. For a guide to the literature see Rüdiger vom Bruch, "Die deutsche Hochschule in der historischen Forschung," in Dietrich Goldschmidt et al., eds., *Forschungsgegenstand Hochschule: Überblick und Trendbericht* (Frankfurt and New York, 1984), 1–27; *cf.* Friedrich Paulsen, *Die deutschen Universitäten und das Universitätsstudium* (Berlin, 1902), esp. 60–82; McClelland, *State, Society and University*, 99–150.

26. Hans-Ulrich Wehler, *Deutsche Gesellschaftsgeschichte: Von der Reformära bis zur industriellen und politischen "Deutschen Doppelrevolution" 1815–1845/49* (Munich, 1987), 220; *cf.* Paulsen, *Universitäten*, 265–66.

27. Josef Engel, "Die deutschen Universitäten und die Geschichtswissenschaft," HZ, 189 (1959): 223–378.

28. Weber, *Priester*, 53. These figures do not include universities in Austria and Switzerland.

29. See Wolfgang Hardtwig, "Die Verwissenschaftlichung der Geschichtsschreibung und die Aesthetisierung der Darstellung," in Reinhart Koselleck et al., eds., *Formen der Geschichtsschreibung* (Munich, 1982), 147–91; Horst Walter Blanke, Dirk Fleischer, and Jörn Rüsen, "Theory of History in Historical Lectures: The German Tradition of *Historik*, 1750–1900," HT, 23 (1984): 351; *cf.* Charles E. McClelland, "Zur Professionalisierung der akademischen Berufe in Deutschland," in Werner Conze and Jürgen Kocka, eds., *Bildungsbürgertum im 19. Jahrhundert: Bildungssystem und Professionalisierung in internationalen Vergleichen* (Stuttgart, 1985), 233–47; Hans-Ulrich Wehler, "Professionalisierung in historischer Perspektive," GG, 6 (1980): 311–25; Peter Uwe Hohendahl, *Literarische Kultur im Zeitalter des Liberalismus 1830–1870* (Munich, 1985), 11–54.

30. *Rankeana* also comprises an enormous literature. For a guide see the masterful study by Leonard Krieger, *Ranke: The Meaning of History* (Chicago, 1977); *cf.* Rudolf

Vierhaus, "Ranke und die Anfänge der deutschen Geschichtswissenschaft," in Bernd Faulenbach, ed., Geschichtswissenschaft in Deutschland: Traditionelle Positionen und gegenwärtige Aufgaben (Munich, 1974), 17–34; Wolfgang Weber, Biographisches Lexikon zur Geschichtswissenschaft in Deutschland, Oesterreich und der Schweiz: Die Lehrstuhlinhaber für Geschichte von den Anfängen des Faches bis 1970 (Frankfurt am Main, 1984), 461; Srbik, 1: 239–92; Metz, Grundformen, 14–236.

31. Georg G. Iggers, "The Image of Ranke in American and German Historical Thought," HT, 2 (1962): 17–40.

32. Ernst Simon, Ranke und Hegel (Munich, 1926); cf. Herbert Schnädelbach, Geschichtsphilosophie nach Hegel: Die Probleme des Historismus (Munich, 1974).

33. Leopold von Ranke, Weltgeschichte, IX, 2, ed. Alfred Dove (1888), ix.

34. Ibid., 5.

35. R. Steven Turner, "Historicism, Kritik, and the Prussian Professoriate, 1790 to 1840," in Mayotte Bollack et al., eds., Philologie und Hermeneutik im 19. Jahrhundert (Göttingen, 1983), 2: 470–71.

36. See Hans-Georg Gadamer, Truth and Method (New York, 1975), 153–87.

37. See Manfred Riedel, Verstehen oder Erklären? Zur Theorie und Geschichte der hermeneutischen Wissenschaften (Stuttgart, 1978).

38. Ernst Cassirer, The Problem of Knowledge (New Haven, 1969), 237.

39. See Wolfgang Hardtwig, "Geschichtsreligion—Wissenschaft als Arbeit—Objektivität: Der Historismus in neuer Sicht," HZ, 252 (1991): esp. 2–8.

40. Simon, Ranke und Hegel, 36–45; cf. Carl Hinrichs, Ranke und die Geschichtstheologie der Goethezeit (Göttingen, 1954), esp. 99–160.

41. Quoted in Karl Kupisch, Die Hieroglyphe Gottes: Grosse Historiker der bürgerlichen Epoche von Ranke bis Meinecke (Munich, 1967), 10.

42. Ibid., 25–26.

43. Krieger, 5.

44. Iggers, Conception, 87; cf. Rudolf Vierhaus, Ranke und die soziale Welt (Münster, 1957).

45. Kupisch, 13–17; cf. Srbik, 1: 259.

46. Quoted in Fritz K. Ringer, The Decline of the German Mandarins: The German Academic Community, 1890–1933 (Cambridge, MA, 1969), 95.

47. Iggers, Conception, 69.

48. Johann Gustav Droysen, Historik: Rekonstruktion der ersten vollständigen Fassung der Vorlesungen (1857) Grundriss der Historik in der ersten handschriftlichen (1857/58) und in der letzten gedruckten Fassung (1882), ed. Peter Leyh (Stuttgart-Bad Cannstatt, 1977), 398.

49. Schnädelbach, Geschichtsphilosophie, 89; cf. Karl-Heinz Spieler, Untersuchungen zu Johann Gustav Droysens "Historik" (Berlin, 1970); Below, Geschichtsschreibung, 48; Cassirer, 257; Weber, Lexikon, 113–14.

50. J. G. Droysen, "Die Erhebung der Geschichte zum Rang einer Wissenschaft," HZ, 9 (1863): 1–22, reprinted in Historik, 456–57.

51. Ibid., 406–9.

52. Michael J. Maclean, "Johann Gustav Droysen and the Development of Historical Hermeneutics," HT, 21 (1982): 347–66.

53. Droysen, Historik, 404.

54. Ibid.

55. Jörn Rüsen, Begriffene Geschichte: Genesis und Begründung der Geschichtstheorie J. G. Droysens (Paderborn, 1969), 89–95; Hayden White, "Droysen's Historik: Historical Writing as a Bourgeois Science," The Content of the Form: Narrative Discourse and Historical Representation (Baltimore and London, 1987), 83–103.

56. Ibid., 102; Herbert Schnädelbach, Philosophy in Germany, 1831–1933 (Cambridge, 1984), 51.

57. See G. P. Gooch, *History and Historians in the Nineteenth Century* (Boston, 1959), 122–50; Günther List, "Historische Theorie und nationale Geschichte zwischen Frühliberalismus und Reichsgründung," in Faulenbach, *Geschichtswissenschaft*, 35–53; Volker Dotterweich, *Heinrich von Sybel: Geschichtswissenschaft in politischer Absicht (1817–1861)* (Göttingen, 1978), esp. 82–87; Metz, *Grundformen*, 237–423.

58. See Hardtwig, "Preussens Aufgabe," 265–324.

59. Ranke, Leondard Krieger has written, "tended to think of [German unification] not as the object of deliberate policy but as the product of a historical necessity about which there was little choice." Krieger, *Ranke*, 300.

60. Alfred Dove, on the occasion of Droysen's seventieth birthday, quoted in Below, *Geschichtsschreibung*, 78–79; *cf.* Wolfgang Hardtwig, "Geschichtsinteresse, Geschichtsbilder und politische Symbole in der Reichsgründungsära und im Kaiserreich," in Ekkehard Mai and Stephan Waetzoldt, eds., *Kunstverwaltung, Bau- und Denkmal-Politik im Kaiserreich* (Berlin, 1981), 47–74; Hans Schleier, *Sybel und Treitschke: Antidemokratismus und Militarismus im historisch-politischen Denken grossbourgeoiser Geschichtsideologen* (Berlin, 1965).

61. Hans-Heinz Krill, *Die Ranke Renaissance: Max Lenz und Erich Marcks* (Berlin, 1962); Hans Schleier, "Die Ranke-Renaissance," in Joachim Streisand, ed., *Studien über die deutsche Geschichtswissenschaft*, 2 vols. (Berlin, 1965), 2: 99–135.

62. The term "statolatry" is from Nicos Poulantzas, *Fascism and Dictatorship: The Third International and the Problem of Fascism* (London, 1974), 243.

63. Engel, "Universitäten," 347, 352.

64. On the organization of the profession see Hermann Heimpel, "Über Organisationsformen historischer Forschung in Deutschland," HZ, 189 (1959): 139–222.

65. See Wilhelm Erben, "Die Entstehung der Universitäts-Seminare," IWWKT, 7 (1913): 1344–45.

66. See Franz Schnabel, *Deutsche Geschichte im neuzehnten Jahrhundert: Die Erfahrungswissenschaften* (Freiburg, 1965), 158–77.

67. Gooch, 60–71; Srbik, 1: 233–36, 299–302.

68. See Theodor Schieder, "Organisation und Organisationen der Geschichtswissenschaft," HZ, 237 (1983): 265–87.

69. See Christian Simon, *Staat und Geschichtswissenschaft in Deutschland und Frankreich 1871–1914* (Bern, 1988), esp. 81–143; Max Lenz, *Geschichte der Königlichen Friedrich-Wilhelms-Universität zu Berlin*, 4 vols. (Halle, 1910–1918), 2: 356–57.

70. Weber, *Priester*, 210–22, 262–65.

71. On Sybel, see Dotterweich, *Heinrich von Sybel*; Walter Bussmann, "Heinrich von Sybel (1817–1895)," in *Bonner Gelehrte: Beiträge zur Geschichte der Wissenschaften in Bonn* (Bonn, 1968), 93–103; Weber, *Lexikon*, 595–96.

72. See Margaret F. Stieg, *The Origin and Development of Scholarly Historical Periodicals* (University, AL, 1986), 20–38.

73. Friedrich Meinecke, *Schriften*, 110.

74. See Robert Deutsch and Wolfgang Weber, "Marginalisierungsprozesse in der deutschen Geschichtswissenschaft im Zeitalter des Historismus," *Schweizerische Zeitschrift für Geschichte*, 35 (1985): 174–97.

75. The best guide to this problem is the work of R. Steven Turner: "The Growth of Professorial Research in Prussia, 1818 to 1848—Causes and Context," in Russell McCormmach, ed., *Historical Studies in the Physical Sciences* (Philadelphia, 1971), 3: 137–82; "The Prussian Universities and the Concept of Research," *Internationales Archiv für Sozialgeschichte der deutschen Literatur*, 5 (1980): 68–93.

76. See Ekart Kehr, "Moderne deutsche Geschichtsschreibung," in Hans-Ulrich Wehler, ed. *Der Primat der Innenpolitik: Gesammelte Aufsätze zur preussisch-deutschen Sozialgeschichte im 19. und 20. Jahrhundert* (Berlin, 1976), 256; Kupisch, 58.

77. NL Althoff (A I Nr. 73), Lindner to Althoff, Halle, 25.1.90.
78. Heinrich von Sybel, "Georg Waitz," *Vorträge und Abhandlungen*, ed. Konrad Varrentrapp (Munich and Leipzig, 1897), 309–13; Gooch, 110–14; Weber, *Lexikon*, 637.
79. Sybel, "Waitz," 311.
80. Sybel, "Worte der Erinnerung an Julius Weizsäcker," *Vorträge und Abhandlungen*, 315–20; Weber, *Lexikon*, 650.
81. Meinecke, *Schriften*, 59–60.
82. Srbik, 1: 299; *cf*. Hellmut Plessner, "Zur Soziologie der modernen Forschung und ihrer Organisation in der deutschen Universität," *Diesseits der Utopie* (Frankfurt, 1974), 132; Schnädelbach, *Philosophy*, 71.
83. LW, 34.
84. NL Lamprecht (L 5), Kolleghefte und Nachschriften, Göttingen.
85. NL Lamprecht (Korr. 53), Weiszäcker to Lamprecht, Berlin, 10.10.85; (Korr. 54), Franz Wolff to Lamprecht, Berlin, 29.7.82; NL Althoff (B Nr. 196/2), Weiszäcker to Althoff, Berlin, 10.4.84; *cf*. Meinecke, *Schriften*, 71, 73.
86. LW, 28–29.
87. NL Lamprecht (L 8), Geographische Arbeiten, Göttingen 1875. This file contains the many maps Lamprecht prepared of central European river systems, particularly of the Rhine. As if to document his priorities, he drew one on the back of an exercise he had written for his regiment on the development of firearms.
88. LW, 33–41.
89. NL Lamprecht (L 7), Auszüge, kurze Referate, Quellenstudien, Göttingen, 1874–1877.
90. NL Lamprecht (Korr. 59), Lamprecht to Hugo Lamprecht, Göttingen, 6.11.75; NL Liesegang, Lamprecht to Liesegang, Leipzig, 30.9.96.
91. NL Lamprecht (L 5), W. H. Riehl, "D. bürgerliche gesellschaft." On Riehl see Peter Steinbach's introduction to Wilhelm Heinrich Riehl, *Die bürgerliche Gesellschaft* (Frankfurt am Main, 1976), 7–44; Viktor von Geramb, *Wilhelm Heinrich Riehl: Leben und Wirken (1823–1897)* (Salzburg, 1954).
92. Herbert Schönebaum, "Karl Lamprecht und Ernst Bernheim," AKg, 43 (1963): 217–39; *cf*. Luise Schorn-Schütte, *Karl Lamprecht: Kulturgeschichtsschreibung zwischen Wissenschaft und Politik* (Göttingen, 1984), 31–33; Weber, *Lexikon*, 41.
93. See Cassirer, 243–55; *cf*. H. Stuart Hughes, *Consciousness and Society: The Reorientation of European Social Thought, 1890–1930* (New York, 1958), 36–37; W. M. Simon, *European Positivism in the Nineteenth Century: An Essay in Intellectual History* (Ithaca, NY, 1963).
94. Ernst Bernheim, *Geschichtsforschung und Geschichtsphilosophie* (Göttingen, 1880).
95. NL Lamprecht (L 7), Historik von Droysen.
96. Susan D. Schultz, "History as a Moral Force against Individualism: Karl Lamprecht and the Methodological Controversies in the German Human Sciences, 1880–1914," Ph.D. dissertation (University of Chicago, 1985), 68–69.
97. NL Lamprecht (Korr. 13), Lamprecht to Karl Brandi, Leipzig, 14.11.12. See Gerhard Lehmann, *Geschichte der Philosophie, VIII: Die Philosophie des neunzehnten Jahrhunderts*, 2 vols. (Berlin, 1953), 2: 20–29; ADB, 19: 288–91; Schnädelbach, *Philosophy*, 169–80; Thomas E. Willey, *Back to Kant: The Revival of Kantianism in German Social and Historical Thought, 1860–1914* (Detroit, 1978), 40–57.
98. Gardner Murphy and Joseph K. Kovach, *Historical Introduction to Modern Psychology* (New York, 1972), 114–17; Edwin G. Boring, *A History of Experimental Psychology* (New York, 1950), 261–70.
99. Hermann Lotze, *Mikrokosmus: Ideen zur Naturgeschichte und Geschichte der Menschheit*, 4th ed., 3 vols. (Leipzig 1884–1888); Gerhard Lehmann, "Kant im Spät-

idealismus und die Anfänge der neukantischen Bewegung," *Zeitschrift für philosophische Forschung*, 10 (1963): 449–51; Werner Sellnow, *Gesellschaft-Staat-Recht: Zur Kritik der bürgerlichen Ideologien über die Entstehung von Gesellschaft, Staat und Recht* (Berlin, 1963), 305–17.

100. DG, 11: 307; *cf.* DG, 8: 43; DG, 10: 296.
101. Ernst Bernheim, *Lehrbuch der historischen Methode und der Geschichtsphilosophie*, 3d ed., 2 vols. (Leipzig, 1908), 2: 732–34; *cf.* Bernheim, *Geschichtsforschung*, 83–88.
102. In 1894, in a letter to Friedrich Althoff, Lamprecht spoke of "an all-comprehensive account [*Gesamtdarstellung*] of German history," as "the dream of my life since my student days." NL Althoff (B Nr. 108/1), Lamprecht to Althoff, Leipzig, 28.6.94. He made the same point to Moriz Ritter. NL Lamprecht (Korr. 45), Lamprecht to Ritter, Leipzig, 29.9.93.
103. NL Lamprecht (Korr. 48), Lamprecht to Spranger, Leipzig, 22.1.12; (Korr. 13), Lamprecht to Brandi, Leipzig, 14.11.12; (Korr. 59), Lamprecht to Hugo Lamprecht, Leipzig, 5.7.77; LW, 100–101.
104. NL Lamprecht (Korr. 59), Lamprecht to Hugo Lamprecht, Göttingen, 6.11.75.
105. NL Lamprecht (Korr. 59), Lamprecht to Hugo Lamprecht, Göttingen, 26.11.76; UB Greifswald, NL Ernst Bernheim, Lamprecht to Bernheim, Leipzig, 27.10.96. The correspondence between Lamprecht and Bernheim will be published shortly in the *Archiv für Kulturgeschichte* by Luise Schorn-Schütte, whom I wish to thank for making available in manuscript the material from Greifswald. See also Antoine Guilland, "Karl Lamprecht," Rh, 121 (1916): 84.
106. Eduard von Hartmann, *Die Selbstzersetzung des Christentums und die Religion der Zukunft* (Berlin, 1874).
107. NL Lamprecht (L 5), v. Hartmann, "Selbstzersetzung des Christentums" (28.2.75); LW, 31.
108. Hartmann, 79.
109. NL Lamprecht (Korr. 24), Lamprecht to Giesing, Leipzig, 10.3.15; *cf.* NL Lamprecht (H 62a), W. Wundt, "Karl Lamprecht," 10–11; Peter Griss, *Das Gedankenbild Karl Lamprechts: Historisches Verhalten im Modernisierungsprozess der "Belle Epoque"* (Bern, 1987), 50.
110. On the problem of the secularization of German historical thinking in the nineteenth century see Wolfgang Hardtwig, *Geschichtsschreibung zwischen Alteuropa und moderner Welt: Jacob Burckhardt in seiner Zeit* (Göttingen, 1974), 96–119.
111. See Lamprecht, *Americana: Reiseeindrücke, Betrachtungen, Geschichtliche Gesamtansicht* (Freiburg, 1906), 72.
112. Lamprecht, "Rankes Ideenlehre und die Jungrankeaner," *Alte und neue Richtugen in der Geschichtswissenschaft* (Berlin, 1896), 33.
113. "Ueber geschichtliche Auffassung und geschichtliche Methode," ibid., 10–11.
114. See Theodor Kappstein, "Karl Lamprecht," *Reclams universum*, 33 (1915): 218.
115. NL Lamprecht (Korr. 66), Karl N. Lamprecht to Lamprecht, Jessen, 1.3.75, 7.4.75; KE, 52.
116. NL Lamprecht (Korr. 59), Lamprecht to Hugo Lamprecht, Göttingen, 27.6.75.
117. Hugo Lamprecht's letters to Karl Lamprecht have not survived, so it is difficult to reconstruct this relationship. The historian's letters to his brother furnished regular reports on his professional achievements.
118. NL Lamprecht (Korr. 59), Lamprecht to Hugo Lamprecht, Göttingen, 27.10.76.
119. Otto Kernberg has put this proposition in somewhat different terms. "A more severe type of narcissistic disturbance," he writes, "can be found in cases where the self has developed pathological identificatory processes to such an extent that it is modeled predominantly on a pathogenic internalized object, while important aspects of the self (as relating to such an object) have been projected onto object

representations and external objects. This severer type of narcissistic pathology refers to individuals who (in their intrapsychic life of object relations and in their external life) identify with an object and love an object standing for their (present or past) self." Kernberg, *Borderline Conditions and Pathological Narcissism* (New York, 1975), 323.

120. NL Lamprecht (Korr. 59), Lamprecht to Hugo Lamprecht, Göttingen, 21.10.76.
121. NL Lamprecht (Korr. 59), Lamprecht to Hugo Lamprecht, Göttingen, 21.1.77.
122. NL Lamprecht (Korr. 59), Lamprecht to Hugo Lamprecht, Göttingen, 14.3.77.
123. Eulenburg, *Frequenz*, 307.
124. Karl Czok, "Der Höhepunkt der bürgerlichen Wissenschaftsentwicklung 1871 bis 1917," in Lothar Rathmann ed., *Alma mater lipsiensis: Geschichte der Karl-Marx-Universität Leipzig* (Leipzig, 1984), 191–228; Herbert Helbig, *Universität Leipzig* (Frankfurt am Main, 1961), 64–94; Rudolf Kittel, *Die Universität Leipzig und ihre Stellung im Kulturleben* (Dresden, 1924), 25–37.
125. On Lamprecht in Leipzig, see LW, 42–58.
126. NL Lamprecht (Korr. 59), Lamprecht to Hugo Lamprecht, Leipzig, 18.5.77, 5.7.77.
127. Max Braubach, "Carl von Noorden 1833–1883," in *Bonner Gelehrte*, 162–69; Leo Philippsborn, "Carl von Noorden, ein deutscher Historiker des 19. Jahrhunderts," Ph.D. dissertation (Göttingen, 1963); Weber, *Lexikon*, 417. The papers of Herbert Schönebaum in the university library in Leipzig contain the manuscript of Werner von Noorden's biography of his father, "Carl von Noorden, ein akademisches Leben," 2d version (1944).
128. NL Lamprecht (Korr. 59), Lamprecht to Hugo Lamprecht, Leipzig, 5.7.77; LW, 56.
129. NL Lamprecht (Korr. 67a), Lamprecht to Leipziger Tageblatt, n.d. [May 1914], Konzept; Noorden to Maurenbrecher, Leipzig, 10.1.80, 25.1.80, cited in Noorden, 611–14.
130. Gottfried Eisermann, *Die Grundlagen des Historismus in der deutschen Nationalökonomie* (Stuttgart, 1956); Harald Winkel, *Die deutsche Nationalökonomie im 19. Jahrhundert* (Darmstadt, 1977), 82–101; Schnabel, *Deutsche Geschichte: Die Erfahrungswissenschaften*, 155–58; W. J. Fischel, "Der Historismus in der Wirtschaftswissenschaft dargestellt an der Entwicklung von Adam Müller bis Bruno Hildebrand," VSWG, 47 (1960): 1–31; Georg Jahn, "Die historische Schule der Nationalökonomie und ihr Ausklang—Von der Wirtschaftsgeschichte zur geschichtlichen Theorie," in Antonio Montaner, ed., *Geschichte der Volkswirtschaftslehre* (Cologne and Berlin, 1967), 41–50.
131. Eisermann, 130.
132. Max Weber, "Roscher und Knies und die logischen Probleme der historischen Nationalökonomie," WL, 1–145.
133. See Georg von Below, "Zur Würdigung der historischen Schule der Nationalökonomie," *Zeitschrift für Sozialwissenschaft*, 7 (1904): 367–91; Winkel, 175–80.
134. Theodore M. Porter, *The Rise of Statistical Thinking, 1820–1900* (Princeton, 1986), 149–92; Ulla G. Schäfer, *Historische Nationalökonomie und Sozialstatistik als Gesellschaftswissenschaften* (Cologne and Vienna, 1971), esp. 132–81.
135. See Hayden White, *Metahistory: The Historical Imagination in Nineteenth-Century Europe* (Baltimore and London, 1973), 15–16.
136. See Eisermann, 119–58.
137. Schnädelbach, *Philosophy*, 73; Schultz, "Moral Force," 29–38.
138. WL, 41.
139. NL Lamprecht (L 17), Kollegnachschriften Leipzig, 1877/78: Practische Nationalökonomik, Finanzwirtschaft, Geschichte der politischen und socialen Theorien als Vorschule jeder practischen Politik.

140. Roscher, *System der Volkswirtschaft: Die Grundlagen der Nationalökonomie*, 13th ed. (Stuttgart, 1875); LW, 52.
141. NL Lamprecht (Korr. 59), Lamprecht to Hugo Lamprecht, Leipzig, 5.7.77.
142. NL Bernheim, Lamprecht to Bernheim, Munich, 22.6.78; Schorn-Schütte, *Lamprecht*, 34; Guilland, 85; Griss, 38. Schönebaum claims that Lamprecht had already selected this topic with Weizsäcker's endorsement in Göttingen. LW, 41, but *cf.* 56. It is unlikely that Weizsäcker would find this theme cordial.
143. Karl Lamprecht, *Beiträge zur Geschichte des französischen Wirthschaftslebens im elften Jahrhundert* (Leipzig, 1878).
144. LW, 53.
145. Ibid., 53–54.
146. Ibid., 54.
147. Ibid., 257; NL Lamprecht (Korr. 45), Roscher to Lamprecht, Leipzig, 24.4.83.
148. Lamprecht, *Beiträge*, 95.
149. LW, 47–48; Guilland, 85; E. Mencke-Glückert, "Zur Vollendung von Karl Lamprechts deutscher Geschichte," *Das Deutschtum im Ausland* (March 1910): 125. On Springer see Udo Kultermann, *Geschichte der Kunstgeschichte: Der Weg einer Wissenschaft* (Frankfurt am Main, 1981), 213–21.
150. LW, 48–49.
151. NL Althoff (B Nr.108/1), Lamprecht to Althoff, Bonn, 16.7.84.
152. NL Lamprecht (L 15), Kollegnachschriften, Auszüge, München, 1878; LW, 60–63.
153. Guilland, 86. On Burckhardt see Hardtwig, *Burckhardt*, 148–87.
154. Guilland, 86.
155. Lamprecht, "Was ist Kulturgeschichte?" DZfG (N.F), 1 (1896–1897): 127–28.
156. NL Lamprecht (L 17), Kollegnachschiften, Leipzig, 1877/78, Roscher, Practische Nationalökonomik. Lamprecht's lecture notes include the proposition that "the economic restraint [*Bevormundung*] of the individual by his superiors gives way more and more, on higher levels of cultural development, to a system of commercial freedom."
157. NL Lamprecht (H 2), Über die Individualität und das Verständnis für dieselbe im deutschen Mittelalter (manuscript). Lamprecht published the manuscript for the first time with slight modifications in the concluding volume of his *Deutsche Geschichte*. DG, 12: 3–48.
158. NL Lamprecht (H2, 9); *cf.* DG, 12: 10.
159. NL Lamprecht (H2, 36–37); *cf.* DG, 12: 39–40.
160. NL Lamprecht (Korr. 59), Lamprecht to Hugo Lamprecht, Leipzig, 18.5.77.
161. NL Harden, Lamprecht to Harden, Leipzig, 30.7.07. The passage quoted read in German:

> . . . nichts frömmt das Einzelstreben,
> Nichts schafft des Menschengeistes Einzelrichtung;
> Doch wer das All erschaut, dem wird Verpflichtung,
> Sie einzuordnen in der Allmacht Weben.

162. See Hinrichs, 1–97.
163. In 1890 the historian wrote to Mathilde Mevissen that his education in his parents' home and his circumstances had accustomed him to regard "selfless creation [*selbstloses Schaffen*] as something taken for granted." NL Mevissen, Lamprecht to Mathilde Mevissen, Marburg, 20.10.90.
164. NL Lamprecht (H2, 2); *cf.* DG, 12: 4.
165. NL Lamprecht (H2, 43–44); *cf.* DG, 12: 47.
166. NL Lamprecht (H2, 15); *cf.* DG, 12: 26.
167. NL Lamprecht (H2, 33); *cf.* DG, 12: 35.

168. NL Lamprecht (H2, 44); *cf.* DG, 12: 47.
169. The parallels between his own career and Ranke's began to impress Lamprecht as early as his days in Schulpforta, their common alma mater. NL Lamprecht (L 3a), Friedrich Zimmer to Marianne Lamprecht, Zehlendorf, 6.8.15. Shortly after completing his doctorate, Lamprecht remarked on the storytelling talents of his niece: "[T]he historical proclivities of the Lamprechts have been decisive. I see her already shining as a second Ranke in the firmament of history." NL Lamprecht (Korr. 59), Lamprecht to Hugo Lamprecht, Leipzig, 23.2.78.

3

Cologne and Bonn

... das Vergangene und das Gegenwärtige ist eines und
dasselbe, nämlich in aller Mannigfältigkeit typisch gleich.

At the time he completed the essay on individuality, the prospects of Karl
Lamprecht's becoming an academic historian were not encouraging. The unconventionality of his interests had already contributed to his decision to leave
Göttingen and then to take his doctorate with an economist rather than a
historian. His work in Munich seemed to take him farther afield. The risks of
unconventionality became apparent when he sent a copy of the essay on
individuality to Noorden in Leipzig and inquired whether his professor would be
willing to supervise the further study necessary for a habilitation. Noorden was
bewildered by the essay and declined.[1] His reaction promised to be typical; and
for Lamprecht the experience could stand as an early lesson in the ways the
discipline of history defended its norms.

Even had Noorden been more accommodating to the student's inquiry,
Lamprecht faced practical obstacles that appeared to exclude the additional
period of study and long apprenticeship required of aspirants to university chairs.
He could no longer count on his father's support. So he began to ponder
alternative careers that the German historical profession offered to young men in
his circumstances. These careers were to be found in libraries, archives,
museums, and local historical societies, secondary teaching, and the more
uncertain occupation of journalism. Before he was compelled to commit himself, however, Lamprecht experienced a stroke of fortune. As a consequence,
not only did he continue his academic study, but in the next decade he
blossomed as a historian to the point where the parallels with Ranke were no
longer preposterous. He also found more personal fulfillment and happiness than
in any other period of his life.

Lamprecht weighed his options during the summer of 1878.[2] The most
promising was an offer that he owed to his place in the extended network that
linked the alumni of Schulpforta. The rector, Lamprecht's advisor Friedrich
Wilhelm Herbst, had once served as private tutor to the family of Wilhelm

Ludwig Deichmann, one of Cologne's leading bankers. After the death of the banker, Herbst had placed one of his students, Friedrich Zimmer, as tutor to the family of Deichmann's son, Theodor. Zimmer had been one of Lamprecht's close friends at boarding school; and when, in 1878, he prepared to resume his theological studies in Bonn, both he and Herbst suggested Lamprecht as a successor in Cologne.

As negotiations proceeded in Cologne, Lamprecht returned to Leipzig in the fall of 1878 to prepare for the state examinations that would qualify him to teach in secondary schools. In February 1879 he passed examinations in history, Latin, Greek, and geography. He was then offered the position of tutor in Cologne, as well as a teaching position in the Friedrich-Wilhelms *Gymnasium* in that city, where Herbst had also once been rector.[3]

"My future is assured," Lamprecht announced to his brother upon completing his examinations, "and thus a black spot disappears from our family's economic skies."[4] Economic independence represented the final stage in his emancipation from his father; but it came as an anticlimax. Shortly before Christmas in 1878, several months after his retirement, the old man died. Lamprecht's grief was genuine, and when he lamented the departure of this "often unappreciated soul," he was referring to his own failings.[5] But the blow was softened by the fact that he himself had already come to terms emotionally and intellectually with his father's failings. The inheritance was not large. The principal item was his father's desk, which became the locus of the historian's labors for the rest of his life—a reminder and fitting symbol of the presence that had inspired the intensity as well as the direction of those labors.[6]

In April 1879 Lamprecht took up residence in Cologne in the family of Theodor Deichmann. His responsibilities were divided between the *Gymnasium*, where he served as an apprentice teacher, and tutoring the banker's son, Carl Theodor, who was preparing to take entrance examinations for a *Gymnasium* in Dresden. "The position was splendid for me," Lamprecht recalled.[7] He was well paid. His rector was Oskar Jaeger, who was already emerging as a leading force in the country's pedagogical politics, a passionate defender of the classical curriculum as the corrective for the growing nationalistic parochialism of instruction in the schools.[8] Jäger was intellectually sympathetic to Lamprecht, an accomplished historian as well as a considerate supervisor. At home, the Deichmann family began to regard Lamprecht almost as one of their own. Deichmann soon offered him a position in the family's banking house. This offer Lamprecht refused; but he did accept Deichmann's commission to record the family's genealogy. The confidence he enjoyed in the eyes of the Deichmann family was not only flattering to the young man; it brought him the opportunity of a lifetime.

Gustav von Mevissen was the paragon of nineteenth century Germany's progressive entrepreneurial middle class, the embodiment of its energy, initiative, imagination, and its best intentions.[9] There was scarcely a major commercial or industrial undertaking in the Rhineland in which he was not involved.

As president of the Rhenish Railroad (*Rheinische Eisenbahn*) he oversaw the building of most of the railway network on the left bank. As director of the Schaafhausen Bank and then the Darmstädter Bank for Commerce and Industry, he not only promoted the area's industrialization but pioneered the organization of German industry into joint stock companies. He was also for decades the leading figure of Rhenish liberalism, serving as chairman of Cologne's chamber of commerce, deputy to the National Assembly in Frankfurt, and, after 1866 when he was ennobled, as a member of the Prussian House of Lords. If he was troubled after the foundation of the empire in 1871, the reasons lay not in frustration over the political settlement, for he was one of Bismarck's early supporters, but rather in his disappointment with his own class, whose growing devotion to its material fortunes was, he feared, clouding its social consciousness and blinding it to its civic obligations.

Mevissen, who was known with good reason as the "uncrowned king of the Rhineland," seemed almost larger than life. His disappointment with his own class reflected his most intriguing trait. Although he had no university training, he was a man of immense learning and vision, who was as comfortable among the country's academic elites as he was in the company of its leading businessmen. His own feelings of social and political obligation were rooted in a philosophy that bore the imprint of Hegel. His friendship with leading historians like Sybel, Treitschke, and Waitz grew out of common political experiences, but it reflected as well the deeper belief they all shared in the importance of culture and education for the nation's integrity and welfare.

In his later years, Mevissen's interests turned to philanthropy. Several of the projects that occupied him were devoted to the education of his own class in the higher values implied by the concept of *Bildung*. One project was the establishment of a business school (*Handelshochschule*) in Cologne in order, as he put it, "harmoniously to bind education and property" and "to enrich and embellish the life of the business elites [*Besitzenden*]" by providing the sons of these elites with exposure to humanistic learning as well as with practical training.[10] Another project grew out of his discussions with Sybel in the late 1860s, when the historian had held a chair in Bonn. The plan was to establish a society for the study of Rhenish and Westphalian history, in the hopes of promoting civic consciousness and pride among the region's business elites. At the time of Sybel's departure for Berlin in 1875, however, this project remained unrealized.

That Mevissen had ties to the Deichmann family was no coincidence given the extended marital network within the Rhineland's business elite. His wife's brother was married to Theodor Deichmann's sister.[11] Lamprecht's position with the Deichmann family thus brought him into Mevissen's orbit. Once Deichmann had satisfied himself about the competence and reliability of the family's tutor, he introduced Lamprecht to Mevissen in November 1879.[12] Mevissen, whose own career had owed much to his energy and imagination, was impressed by these traits in the young historian, as he was by Lamprecht's interest in the history of economic institutions. He immediately tendered an attractive offer.

Lamprecht was to serve as Mevissen's agent for Rhenish history. The immediate charge was to catalogue the 25,000 volumes in Mevissen's private library, but Mevissen had a broader agenda. He offered Lamprecht a generous stipend for a period of three years, as well as a free pass on his railways. With this support, Lamprecht was first to take his habilitation at the university in Bonn. He was then to promote the study of Rhenish history systematically, both by means of his own research into the history of the region's medieval economy and by reviving the plan for a Rhenish historical society, an organization that was to link the scholars at the university with those in archives and libraries throughout the region.[13]

"How can I thank you enough for all that you are and were to me?" Lamprecht wrote to his benefactor two decades later. "I bless the hour when you first talked to me after dinner at Deichmanns'; and I would not know what could compare with that hour in terms of internal benefits and rich consequences for future years."[14] Lamprecht had good reason to be grateful, for his relationship to Mevissen was the most significant emotional tie he established outside his immediate family. If it began as a contractual proposition, it soon developed into a close personal bond. Mevissen experienced no little vicarious fulfillment as his protégé pursued historical scholarship with the energy and imagination of an entrepreneur.[15] Lamprecht in turn learned to respect the business acumen, as well as the learning and vision of the man whom he called "the most significant mind [Kopf] I have met in the Rhineland."[16] But the emotional bond between the two ran deeper than mutual admiration. Mevissen came to regard Lamprecht almost like a son, and his feelings were reciprocated.[17] Lamprecht found in Mevissen the most significant of a series of father figures, a man who commanded authority and respect at the same time that he inspired trust and intimacy. "In innumerable questions, personal as well as scholarly," the historian confessed several years later, "you were my teacher and educator."[18] Mevissen was also the great patron whose power and influence helped ensure Lamprecht's professional career despite the unconventionality of the young man's interests.

The Friedrich-Wilhelm University in Bonn was founded in 1818 as a bastion of Protestant culture in the largely Catholic provinces that had fallen to Prussia in 1815.[19] The university was designed to be an instrument in the Prussianization of these provinces; and the history of the institution was plagued as a consequence by political and confessional tension. The centrality of the university's political mission also convinced the Prussian government to staff the institution with prominent scholars. Among the historians who taught there were Barthold Georg Niehbuhr, Friedrich Christoph Dahlmann, and Sybel, who founded the historical seminar upon his arrival in Bonn in 1861.[20]

Sybel left for Berlin in 1875, but his spirit of partisanship lingered. After Noorden briefly occupied it, Sybel's chair passed in 1877 to Wilhelm Maurenbrecher.[21] Maurenbrecher had begun as Sybel's protégé in Bonn. His research on Emperor Otto I and on the origins of the Counter-Reformation betrayed the conviction, which he shared with his teacher, that the political and confessional issues of his own day had deep roots in German history. Maurenbrecher also shared Sybel's passion for political engagement. When he moved to a chair in Dorpat, he distinguished himself in defending the cause of ethnic Germans in the Russian Baltic provinces; and after he returned to Germany, to a chair in Königsberg, he was a frequent speaker in public meetings and a contributor to political journals, notably to Gustav Freytag's *Grenzboten*. By the time he returned to Bonn, however, his most substantial scholarship was behind him, and his reputation rested primarily on his oratorical talents, which some compared to Treitschke's. His temperament and politics were also comparable to Treitschke's. He remained a passionate champion of the settlement of 1871 and the Protestant cause. Walter Goetz once described him as a "massive personality"; but the discrepancy between his forceful demeanor and his modest scholarly achievement lent him a certain pathos and made him appear, in Goetz's words, "larger than he really was."[22] Possibly for this reason, Prince William, the future Kaiser, found him captivating.[23] But perhaps because Maurenbrecher was more sensitive to his own failings, he was more comfortable in the company of students and younger colleagues than he was among his peers.

Moriz Ritter, the second member of the seminar, was in many respects the polar opposite of Maurenbrecher.[24] He was a Catholic. Like Maurenbrecher, he took his doctorate in Bonn, but not before he had he clashed with Sybel, who regarded him, as he regarded most Catholic scholars, as "tendentiously ultramontane." Ritter's education in history owed more to another of Ranke's students, Carl Adolf Cornelius in Munich, who served as protector to many young Catholic historians. Cornelius placed Ritter with the Bavarian Academy of Sciences and supervised his training in source criticism. While under Cornelius's tutelage, Ritter began the work for which he was best known, on the Counter-Reformation and the Thirty Years' War in Germany. While in Munich he, like many Catholic intellectuals, lived through the religious crisis provoked by the promulgation of the doctrine of Papal infallibility in 1870. He followed Ignaz Döllinger out of the Church and participated in the construction of a new church of "Old Catholics." It was a painful step, but Ritter's break with Rome suddenly made him an attractive candidate in Bonn when the chair in history that was reserved for Catholics fell vacant; and in 1873 he returned, with Sybel's blessing, to the Rhineland.

The two words most frequently used to describe Ritter were "conscientious" (*gewissenhaft*) and "uncompromising" (*unerbittlich*).[25] Both traits spoke to the critical introspection, as well as to the intellectual insecurities, that his status as an outsider had bred in him. If Maurenbrecher's past had encouraged a penchant for bluster and self-assertion, Ritter's early experiences in the profession fostered a sense of caution, a reluctance to take intellectual risks or to venture beyond the narrow area, which was bounded by the Religious Peace of Augsburg and the Peace of Westphalia, in which his scholarship was superb. He commanded more respect as a scholar than Maurenbrecher, but he was more distant and cool in his relations with his students, among whom he had a reputation as a relentless critic.

The other two historians in Bonn were scholars of less consequence. Arnold Schaefer, who occupied the chair in ancient history but taught modern history as well, was near the end of his career.[26] Karl Menzel, who was responsible for medieval history as well as the auxiliary sciences, was another of Sybel's protégés.[27] He had been an archivist in Weimar before Sybel brought him to Bonn in 1873; his best-known scholarship, on the history of Nassau and the Palatinate in the fifteenth century, was provincial in all senses of the word.

The group of historians in Bonn was larger than at most universities. However, the rivalries, temperamental friction, and resentments that operated there were like those in most faculties, except that they were played out in the shadow of Sybel, who, while he reigned in Bonn (and the expression is hardly exaggerated), had been the moving force in the hiring of Menzel, Ritter, and Maurenbrecher. If all three owed their positions to Sybel, only Ritter had unassailable scholarly credentials; Menzel's career was inconceivable but for his patron's favor. The situation was further clouded by the fact that Maurenbrecher had in the meantime broken with Sybel, while Ritter had no affection for his former colleague.

Into this family came Lamprecht. His arrangement with Mevissen called for his completing a habilitation in Bonn, so in January 1880 he traveled south to introduce himself to the faculty. Neither his plan for an economic history of the Rhineland nor the tone in which he spoke of a Rhenish historical society, a project once associated with Sybel, made a good impression. Maurenbrecher spoke of his "strange ideas [krumme Wege]," and Schaefer dismissed him as a "windbag."[28] But Lamprecht had powerful academic sponsors in addition to Mevissen. One was Sybel himself, who was Mevissen's friend and, at this point at least, favorably inclined to the young historian.[29] The other sponsor was Noorden, whose friendship with Maurenbrecher extended back to their days together as Sybel's students. Noorden had evidently suppressed his earlier reservations about his former student, for his advocacy of Lamprecht in Bonn was unqualified. To Maurenbrecher he wrote, "I regard his knowledge, the soundness of his will and understanding, his personality, and intellectual ability so high that I would without hesitation assign him to lead a section of the historical seminar."[30] Noorden described Lamprecht to Sybel as a "truly productive mind, the most competent [tüchtig] young historian whom I have yet had the privilege to teach."[31]

These endorsements eased a little the apprehension among the resident historians about the "gushing force" they were inviting into their midst.[32] Although resentments lingered over the pressure brought on them from outside, they consented to Lamprecht's habilitating in Bonn, to which he moved in April.[33] To support his habilitation, he wisely chose not to present the essay on individuality. Instead, he submitted a manuscript on the minor medieval chronicler Dietrich Engelhus, on whom he had been working sporadically for several months.[34] The manuscript was little more than a fragment of what was to have become a full and conventional edition. It failed to impress the historians in Bonn.[35] With Ritter's endorsement, Menzel wrote that the manuscript "gives the impression of great versatility and competent training, but reveals as well the author's pronounced proclivity for all too hasty and bold conclusions." Maurenbrecher chose to dwell instead on Lamprecht's doctoral dissertation, which he, like his friend Noorden, judged to be "undoubtedly" one of the "most competent historical dissertations of recent years . . . a brilliant piece of evidence for the range of reading and thoroughness, for the diligence and acuity of a young scholar."[36] The judgment of the historians was not unfair to either Lamprecht's potential or to the early signs of trouble in his work. The final verdict was charitable. The faculty accepted the manuscript on Engelhus and invited him to complete the final stages of the habilitation. Here he acquitted himself strongly in a colloquium on the election of Rudolf of Habsburg as emperor and in a public lecture on monastic reform in Lorraine in the tenth century.

In June 1880 Lamprecht received his habilitation and with it the *venia legendi*, the license to teach at the university. He now joined the ranks of the so-called private instructors, the *Privatdozenten* who made up the "unofficial university" throughout Germany.[37] It was a significant step in an academic career. The position of *Privatdozent* represented a holding stage in which aspirant scholars, most of whom were already in their late twenties or early thirties, waited for professorships to open. Depending on their fields, abilities, connections, and their luck, they could expect to wait from five to ten years for a call to a chair.[38] The difficulty was that the expansion of German higher education at the end of the century had already begun to work to their disadvantage. They provided cheap labor. They usually survived with difficulty on fees from their students and whatever outside income they could put together; aside from occasional stipends, the state provided them no support. Ministries of culture accordingly responded to the growth of university enrollments by entrusting an increasing share of the curriculum to them, particularly in introductory courses and in areas too specialized to justify establishing new chairs. As a result, the number of private instructors grew much more rapidly than the number of available chairs. Although the problem did not become acute until the turn of the century, chair holders were already almost a minority among those teaching at German universities in 1880.[39] Consequently, many if not most private instructors faced uncertain prospects of advancement to a chair, particularly if their credentials were in any way suspect—if, for instance, their scholarship or politics were heterodox, or if they were Jewish.[40] Even their relative flexibility and freedom to devote blocks of time to their research were not unmixed blessings, for their reputations as scholars depended on their productive use of this time; and the competition among them was fierce.

Lamprecht's experience was not altogether typical. He was younger, at twenty-four, than most of his fellow instructors and hence did not feel so immediately the pressure to find a stable career. He was also more fortunate in having a reliable source of income—first from Mevissen, then from a generous stipend from the university—to relieve him of the financial anxieties that plagued many of his peers.[41] "The life of the instructor," he could report to his brother, "is in many respects a quite extraordinarily pleasant one; one is master of one's time and energies."[42]

One of the reasons why he found this existence so pleasant was that he enjoyed teaching. His habilitation was in the history of the Rhineland in the Middle Ages. Over the next several years he offered lectures and tutorials on aspects of this subject, including—to Mevissen's satisfaction—a course on the history of Cologne, as well as courses on medieval economic history and the foundations of German history.[43] These courses were well attended, and he acquired a reputation as a "talented, enthusiastic, and exciting teacher."[44] Several of his students left testimonies to the power of his presence in the classroom. Some of these students later became his bitter enemies, so their testimony was hardly biased in his favor. Friedrich Meinecke recalled attending Lamprecht's lectures on economic history "with the greatest satisfaction" and that he was "gripped by Lamprecht's gushing and vivid lecture."[45] Georg von Below, who was then writing a dissertation with Ritter, also confessed his admiration for Lamprecht's enthusiasm, energy, and great range of knowledge.[46] These recollections spoke to characteristics that won Lamprecht a devoted following among his students, who regarded him, as one of them recalled, with a mixture of "total admiration and an almost childish trust." In this company, which recalled the clique that had formed around him at Schulpforta, he was "no longer the teacher, but rather the older friend."[47] He was also a benign and convivial mentor, who enjoyed the company of these admirers in his home, on excursions into the *Siebengebirge*, and in the town's taverns.[48] Something of his appeal to younger people is captured in the scene, described by Meinecke, of Lamprecht in a tavern together with Below, Meinecke, and Wilhelm Busch, who was writing a dissertation with Maurenbrecher. As Meinecke, the "youngster," looked on and Busch quipped about Below's obsession with his scholarship, Lamprecht quizzed Below about his dissertation "in a friendly and appreciative manner."[49]

Lamprecht also enjoyed more success in social relations with his peers than at any other time in his life. He took up residence in Bonn with his friend Friedrich Zimmer and Zimmer's brother, both of whom were studying theology. Through them he met a number of young theologians, philosophers, and natural scientists whom the pressures of an instructor's existence had thrown together in a small community. Their company brought him welcome relief from work, as well as most of the friendships he established with men of his own age.[50] His ties to Cologne enhanced his social standing in Bonn; and the support these ties provided was emotional as well as financial. The Deichmanns and Mevissens constituted practically a second family for him, particularly after the death of his mother in 1882.

Lamprecht's happiness in the Rhineland reflected an active social life and his success with his students. It was due primarily, however, to achievements of another kind.

The great upsurge of interest in history in the nineteenth century was a complex phenomenon. Its most prominent feature—the one associated with the names of Ranke, Droysen, Waitz, and Sybel—was the professionalization and establishment of the discipline at German universities. Below the academic heights of the profession, however, innumerable archives and historical societies fostered the study of state, regional, and local history.[51] Politics figured vitally in their history, too. The proliferation of these organizations in the aftermath of the Napoleonic Wars was the product of tensions that accompanied the redrawing of the map of Germany, the eradication of hundreds of territories that had been virtually sovereign for centuries, and the consolidation of lands with little common political tradition. In these circumstances, the study of history appealed both to those who sought to promote the settlement of 1815 by resurrecting common regional heritages and to those who resisted the same settlement in the name of traditional autonomies. In the event, cultivating local history might well have eased political tensions, for as Hermann Heimpel has observed in the case of the new Grand Duchy of Baden, deflecting local resentments into antiquarian pursuits tended to rob these feelings of their political force.[52]

The study of local and regional history took place largely outside the universities. The leading academic historians were disinterested in local history for the same reasons they idolized the nation-state. The anomaly that demonstrated the truth of this proposition was the prominence of academics from the university of Berlin in the Society for the History of the Mark Brandenburg. But no chair for regional history existed at a German university until after the turn of the century. The professionalization of the discipline meant that local historical societies (and their journals) were increasingly staffed by academically trained historians, but these organizations were populated in the main by educated laymen who were devoted to history as an avocation—by the "retired pastors and physicians" whom Theodore Mommsen and his colleagues at the universities ridiculed for their parochial interest in archaeological artefacts, genealogy, the restoration of monuments, and the history of local dynasties.[53]

Neither Mevissen nor Lamprecht could be accused of parochialism when they began to lay plans for promoting the study of Rhenish history. Resentments over the Rhineland's absorption into Prussia played no role whatsoever in Mevissen's thinking. He calculated instead that an awareness of Rhenish history would nurture civic pride among the region's inhabitants and a heightened sense of their responsibility to the nation as a whole. His project was to ally professional historians not only with archivists and amateurs, but with the Rhineland's mercantile elite.[54]

Lamprecht's interests were less political, more scholarly, but no less grand. He calculated that the Rhineland, a region whose political identity had never been unproblematic, represented an ideal case study for writing the kind of comprehensive history that his training and inclinations had led him to prefer.[55] At least in the Middle Ages, he reasoned, the foundation of the region's history resided not in its political institutions but in the development of its economy. "The details of political history can provide no sufficient basis for a general understanding of this era," he explained to Mevissen early in 1880. "The main emphasis [*Schwerpunkt*] of consistent historical development" lay instead "in the realm of real culture, in the history of the estates, of the law and the economy."[56] Lamprecht shared the prejudice against the provincialism of local history, and at one point he derided the "marasmus" (*Geschichtsmarasmus*) that Rhenish history was suffering at the hands of its practitioners.[57] Given the breadth of his own perspective, the primary appeal of regional history was practical. Writing the comprehensive history of an extended epoch required the restriction of its geographical scope. Lamprecht was convinced, however, that the history of the Rhineland exemplified tendencies that operated everywhere in Germany—that, as he put it in a letter to Schmoller, "here in the local is where the universal really appears clearly and immanently."[58]

Lamprecht initially interpreted his charge from Mevissen as a commission to write a comprehensive history of the Rhineland in the Middle Ages. Mevissen himself supported Lamprecht's idea, but he had higher priorities. He insisted that the historian's first obligation was to prepare the groundwork for a new regional historical society, whose immediate charge would be to inventory and publish documents of Rhenish history.[59] While Mevissen was recruiting donors in the business community, Lamprecht accordingly spent much of 1880 on Mevissen's railroad. He visited archives and libraries throughout the region, where he enlisted the participation of scholars and inspected manuscript holdings; before local antiquarian societies in Bonn and Cologne he held a series of lectures on aspects of Rhenish history. He also tried to keep interest alive at the university among the historians, who regarded the project with little enthusiasm, both because they, like most members of their guild, took a dim view of the way local history was practiced and because they resented the central role of their young colleague.[60]

Lamprecht's role was nonetheless critical to the success of the project, for he alone had ties to the scholars at the university, the librarians and archivists in the field, and the men with the money. The series of negotiations that led to the establishment of the Society for the Study of Rhenish History (*Gesellschaft für Rheinische Geschichtskunde*) gave ample evidence of the tensions that required resolution.[61] The patrons demanded a voice in determining the plan and contents of the society's editorial undertakings, while the historians insisted on autonomy in making decisions that pertained to scholarship.[62] That a formula was found for compromise owed largely to Lamprecht's mediation. The foundation of the society in Cologne on 1 June 1881 was thus a triumph for the young scholar who had brought in not only all four of the university's historians, but the legal historian Hugo Loersch from the law faculty, as well as the region's leading archivists, Konstantin Höhlbaum from Cologne, Woldemar Harless from Düsseldorf, and Wilhelm Becker from Coblence.[63] The lord mayor of Cologne became chairman of the board of directors, while the establishment of a separate committee of scholars, chaired by Arnold Schaefer and charged with planning the editions, seemed to guarantee the integrity of the scholarship. Lamprecht's mediating role was affirmed in his election, albeit in minor positions, to both the board of directors and the committee of scholars.

Lamprecht had good reason to be pleased with his accomplishments, but establishment of the society created difficulties he had not foreseen. His status changed. While he remained in the direct employ of Mevissen, he now became the agent of the new organization, or, more specifically, of the academic historians on the scholars' committee, who were his colleagues in Bonn. Tensions in Bonn were thus transferred to Cologne during the first years of the new society's existence. The historians approached the editorial projects in what one might call a Waitzian spirit of source criticism; the editions were to be exhaustively prepared and to feature documents that related to political and constitutional development. Lamprecht, who was less enthusiastic about editing documents in this fashion than about writing the economic history of the Rhineland, proposed instead a series of editorial projects that addressed the history of prices, interest rates, and tariffs. Most of these proposals the scholars' committee rejected, citing the carelessness of Lamprecht's planning.[64] As a consequence, the output of the new organization was meager in its first years.[65]

Lamprecht's response to the frustration of his plans was characteristic. He sought a broader forum. He first appealed directly to Mevissen. He then tried to disarm criticism of his projects by enlisting the support of Schmoller, Roscher, and other leading economists.[66] When all these efforts failed, he began to lose interest in the Society for the Study of Rhenish History. He also signaled his defiance by joining the board of directors of another, more traditional local history organization, the Historical Society for the Lower Rhine (*Historischer Verein für den Niederrhein*), which also operated out of Cologne.[67]

Lamprecht's frustrations with his colleagues in the Society for the Study of Rheinish History also cast into a new light another project in which he had become involved. The new historical society was but one of the avenues Mevissen envisaged for promoting interest in the history of the Rhineland. Another was to provide a focal point for regional scholarship in a new journal. The opportunity arose fortuitously in 1880, when the publishers of one of the existing local journals offered its editorship to Felix Hettner, the director of the provincial historical museum in Trier, who agreed on the condition that Lamprecht join him.[68] The original plan was to publish the journal as the organ of the Society for the Study of Rhenish History. However, Lamprecht's conflicts with his colleagues from Bonn persuaded him to keep the journal beyond their reach and to broaden its regional basis beyond the Rhineland; and these ideas met with the approval of both Hettner and Mevissen, who helped underwrite the project.

In the *Westdeutsche Zeitschrift für Geschichte und Kunst* Karl Lamprecht acquired what amounted to a personal organ, in which he could promote regional history according to his own conceptions without the restraining hand of the academic historians in Bonn. Hettner was responsible for the Roman era, while the medieval and modern periods fell to him. His intention was, as he wrote to one potential contributor, to edit a journal "in the grander style," in which he could "bring general and provincial research into contact and reconcile them."[69] The thematic emphasis was to reflect his interests. "My efforts," he explained, "will be devoted to giving as much place as possible to economic history."[70]

In the event, the journal, which began to appear early in 1882, was distinguished less by its innovative scholarship than by several other features, which addressed the need to bring together a diverse readership throughout western Germany, from Switzerland to the Low Countries. Each quarterly number comprised three sections.[71] The first section corresponded to a suggestion from Mevissen; it contained essays of broad general interest for lay readers as well as professional historians.[72] The second section brought more specialized articles and book reviews. A majority of the essays in both these sections were on topics in political or constitutional history. Lamprecht's efforts to recruit contributions in economic history were not as successful as he had hoped, but he did introduce his readers to the scholarship of economists, anthropologists, and art historians—among them Wilhelm Arnold, Eberhard Gothein, and Anton Springer—as well as to the work of foreign scholars such as Henri Pirenne and P. J. Blok. The most impressive feature of the journal, however, was the third section, which contained systematic bibliographies, guides to manuscript collections in local and regional archives, and surveys of museum holdings. Supplements to the journal carried additional guides to archival holdings and reports from local historical societies throughout the region.

The journal bore Lamprecht's imprint in its format and exhaustive bibliographies, many of which he prepared himself on the basis of his journeys.[73] He had established himself at the center of an extended network, which comprised local historians, archivists, and librarians and made up the core of the journal's contributors, as well as its readership. The blossoming of the journal was measured not only in the growth of this readership to nearly 400, but also in the lavish praise showered on the editors, one of whom was becoming a major force in the Rhenish historical community.[74]

Lamprecht's achievement as editor of the *Westdeutsche Zeitschrift* was impressive by any accounting, but it represented only one aspect of his emergence as a leading scholar of the Rhineland. His role as editor must have required considerable self-restraint, for he could have filled several volumes of the journal with the results of his own scholarship. The journal's success was due in large part to him, but he regarded his editorial work, like his activity in the Society for the Study of Rhenish History, as a necessary diversion; and his enthusiasm for it soon diminished, too. "The past year has cost me a lot of work, which was embodied not in scholarly articles, but in mountains of letters," he complained to Mevissen in 1882. "Now, however, this stage of organizing is over, and I can turn with all the more heart and soul to scholarly work."[75] The energy and determination with which he did so impressed even those who knew him well. He spent his free time in sorties into the Rhineland from his base in Bonn, storming archives and libraries, visiting museums, churches, and ruins. The inveterate collector was in his element. "Everywhere it was a question of raising new treasures, getting acquainted with old ones—all in the loveliest part of Germany."[76] "I almost might envy you," Ernst Bernheim commented in 1883, "the freedom with which you are able to pursue your own innermost inclinations."[77] The freedom of movement that made this idyll possible was the product of modern technologies; it was threatened when the Prussian state took over Mevissen's railroad in 1881, but petitions to the ministry and the university preserved Lamprecht's free pass.[78]

Lamprecht's collecting campaign in the Rhineland seemed at times to be less the result of a coherent research design than an attempt to satisfy an insatiable drive. Some archivists came to dread his visits, which were normally unannounced. One of his friends recalled that the historian often boarded trains in the morning out of Bonn with no idea where he was going.[79] But these impressions were erroneous. Few historians have conducted their research more in accordance with a plan than did Lamprecht.

Mevissen set Lamprecht's specific agenda, but the patron only provided a geographical focus for an enterprise whose intellectual inspiration had come from Roscher and Burckhardt and whose contours were already apparent in the essay on individuality. Lamprecht proposed to write the comprehensive history of the medieval Rhineland. Because he insisted that the foundations of this history lay in the realm of "real" or material culture, his goal was, in the first place, to reconstruct the material bases or structures of life—the natural preconditions, the organization of production, and the legal buttressing of social structure. He planned to undertake this reconstruction in much the same way as he had approached the history of northern France in his dissertation. Now, however, he wished to explore in greater detail the relation of other spheres of activity to these foundations. The history of art was to provide both access and an index to developments at the level of ideal culture, where attitudes, tastes, and moral sensitivities took form. His other major goal was to situate politics in this edifice, to address the question, as he put it to Bernheim, of "where in truth does the central point of [political history] lie, where [lies] its more general significance?"[80] Lamprecht had little enthusiasm for the history of political events and institutions, however; he regarded it as superficial and ephemeral in the full scheme of things. Nonetheless, his ambitions promised to make his treatment of politics pivotal to his argument, as well as controversial. He hoped to challenge a dominant tradition in German historiography by demonstrating that the realm of politics was not situated at the foundation of Rhenish history during the Middle Ages—that this realm was instead conditioned by more profound material and cultural structures.

Lamprecht published close to two dozen studies in national and regional journals during his first five years in the Rhineland.[81] Most of these articles were based on archival materials that he gathered during his frequent excursions, and they addressed critical points in his research design. He studied the migration, settlement, and early economic organization of Germanic tribes in the Rhineland during the Roman era.[82] These studies were remarkable for their use of the novel theory, which had been developed systematically by the legal historian Wilhelm Arnold, that the distribution of localities' names (Ortsnamen)—particularly of the suffixes in these names—could be used to trace early patterns of migration and settlement.[83]

Lamprecht's work in art history demonstrated the same preference for the novel approach. He published several studies on the illumination of medieval manuscripts.[84] His most ambitious project was to compare the illumination of the initial letter in manuscripts of the Carolingian era with those of the Kaiserzeit, as well as with ornamentation found on archaeological relics of earlier epochs.[85] He argued that the increasing symmetry, complexity, and accuracy of design, and the growing prominence first of animal and then plant forms in ornamentation all testified to stages in the development of collective aesthetic sensitivities, or, to use his own expression, "the nation's power of perception in ornamentation [ornamentale Anschauungskraft der Nation]."

Lamprecht's most conventional studies were in political history, but they, too, betrayed hints of their author's unorthodox inclinations. He built on the theme of his habilitation lecture and examined the significance of the so-called letters of consent (Willebriefe), which regulated the reclamation of crown lands at the time of the elevation of Rudolf of Habsburg to the imperial throne in 1273.[86] The historian went beyond analyzing these documents in the conventional context of the growth of the constitutional powers of the electors. Instead, he attempted to relate the history of these letters to the evolving financial foundations of royal and princely power in Germany.

All of these essays represented preliminary studies, or, as he explained to one local historian, a part of his training—his "Vorbildung"—for the main project, the history of the medieval Rhineland, which he had begun to plan soon after sealing his agreement with Mevissen.[87] The contours of what he hoped would be his "masterpiece" emerged quickly. By 1883 the first part of the study was complete, and he had found a publisher who was willing to take on a project that had grown, as he himself admitted, to "almost pompous" proportions.[88] The first volume to appear, in May 1885, was a documentary supplement.[89] If its editorial format was conventional, its contents were not; the volume presented an assortment of more than 300 charters, registers, deeds, inventories, leases, administrative decrees, and other documents that pertained to the history of landholding and agrarian production in the Hunsrück and Eifel regions of western Germany. A second volume, which appeared later the same year, was more unusual.[90] It presented statistical analyses of close to 30,000 documents drawn from dozens of monastic and other ecclesiastical holdings in the same region, in the first instance from the large abbeys of Prüm, Mettlach, and St. Maximin. The most valuable of these documents were the so-called

Weistümer and *Urbare*, which fixed, inventoried, and registered manorial assets, rights, and obligations. Lamprecht used them to analyze not only the economic organization of the estates, but problems of transportation, tariffs, the circulation and value of coinage, and the fluctuation of prices.

Two additional volumes of narrative and description followed in 1886 to bring to completion a monumental undertaking.[91] The last two volumes alone comprised more than 1,600 pages. Paradoxically, the subject of the work was far more narrow than its title, *German Economic Life in the Middle Ages*, suggested. The analysis was confined to central-western Germany, principally to the valley of the Mosel River. But Lamprecht detailed the economic history of this region from the third to the fifteenth centuries, from the era of its settlement by Germanic tribes until the eve of the Protestant Reformation. The work represented less a coherent narrative than a series of long analytical essays. An introductory chapter extended his earlier research into a survey of Germanic settlement, patterns of landholding, social organization, and legal institutions. The historian then turned to the topography, demography, and natural resources of the Moselland; to population growth; to the progress of settlement; and to the clearing of forests in the early Middle Ages. The third part of the study was a tour de force that examined the symbiosis of economic and legal structures and the devolution of juridical powers onto the autonomous local Germanic economic communities (*Markgenossenschaften*). The fourth and fifth parts were devoted to the technologies and organization of agrarian production and the emergence of a manorial economy.

Until this point, the structure of Lamprecht's study resembled that of his dissertation, except that he was covering a far broader chronological sweep in far greater detail. Lamprecht now proceeded to analyze the dynamic connection between economic forces and political development, as he examined the emergence of the territorial state out of the manorial economy in the later Middle Ages. He turned first to the growing concentration of manorial landholdings (*Grossgrundbesitz*)—the economies and political calculations that fostered it, the patterns of servitude and administrative networks that grew up to support it, and its subsequent evolution, under the impact of rising land values, into a system based on various forms of leaseholding. The historian then followed the development of the largest of these landholding systems into quasi-political units, which built systems of taxation, arrogated juridical powers, and established networks of military strongholds to suppress civil disorder. A long excursus then analyzed the impact of economic and political transformations on the social structure and conditions of the agrarian population. Here Lamprecht argued that demographic pressure, inflation, and the rising burden of rents produced a general crisis in the countryside by the fifteenth century. The final part of the study traced the further development of consolidated political units into virtually sovereign territorial states, in which the growing impact of a money economy made possible the employment of regular armed services and civil bureaucracies.

A schematic survey can do scant justice to Lamprecht's achievement.

Although he was compelled to postpone a systematic consideration of ideal culture for a future study, the scope of his effort was breathtaking nonetheless.[92] The emphasis fell on the interaction between economic organization and the development of legal and political institutions, but the historian also presented a comprehensive account of the reciprocal relationships among demographic trends, technology, the organization of production, social structure, the law, and politics. His analysis did not grant systematic priority to any of these spheres. He argued, for instance, that the development of the manorial system was due to the interplay of economic imperatives, changes in legal jurisdictions, and political calculation. Still, the burden of his argument clearly challenged the analytical primacy of political categories. "The manorial system," he concluded, "not the old Empire, is the cradle of the modern state."[93] The state, in other words, was a derivative phenomenon; it emerged out of a complex of economic and legal institutions. The crucial steps along the way of German political development were the symbiosis of legal and economic institutions after the collapse of Carolingian power, the erasure of the distinction between public and private law in manorialism, and the reestablishment of a public realm of law and politics with the emergence of semisovereign territories out of the manorial system.

These assertions fueled an already intense historiographical debate. Lamprecht's argument was not original, but his study added force to a position staked out by Karl Wilhelm Nitzsch, Gustav Schmoller, and the Austrian historian, Karl Theodor Inama-Sternegg. A detailed examination of the debate, which soon focused on Lamprecht himself, is premature here; but it is germane to emphasize how central the medieval origins of the modern state were to Lamprecht's conception of history. This theme provided the historical juncture at which the particular realms of history—society, law, and politics—came together into a comprehensive whole. The theme also ratified Lamprecht's broad vision of local history, for it provided the point at which the particularities of locality and region coalesced into national history. These junctures were analytical rather than analogical; they enabled the historian to address issues of cause and effect across disparate realms of history. The exiguousness and ambiguity of the surviving sources made many of his conclusions seem dubious, but he and his critics could at least address a common fund of evidence with a common set of questions.

The manorial roots of the state represented but one of the many controversial issues Lamprecht raised. In fact, the range of his study was so broad and its detail so rich that nearly everyone who read it found some provocation.[94] On the whole, however, the initial reaction from the great names in the field gratified the historian's feelings that he had produced a masterpiece. "My first impression is understandably one of great astonishment," wrote Inama-Sternegg, the leading historian of the German medieval economy.[95] Waitz greeted the work with "true astonishment at your energy, the amount and significance of your activity."[96] "New testimony to your enormous energy," was the verdict of

Weizsäcker, who was now teaching in Berlin.[97] Weizsäcker's colleague Schmoller offered congratulations to a scholar who, though "so young, completed so great a work so quickly."[98] Nor was the praise confined to letters of congratulation. Schmoller's review called Lamprecht's study "a very great, epoch-making, scholarly step forward."[99] Otto von Gierke, the historian of medieval corporations, expressed amazement at an "achievement which, one could think, contained the results of a life's work."[100] August Meitzen, the Berlin economist who was the leading authority on the history of Prussian agriculture, called Lamprecht's volumes "an essential reference," "indispensable for every study in this field."[101]

German Economic Life in the Middle Ages was, as even his enemies conceded, Karl Lamprecht's greatest piece of scholarship, the work in which his accomplishment most matched his ambition.[102] His borrowing of methodologies from economists, philologists, geographers, archaeologists, and ethnologists to bring massive materials under control was unprecedented. In the historiography of the medieval German economy and law, his study stood out in the distinguished company of studies by Inama-Sternegg, Hanssen, Meitzen, Arnold, Georg von Maurer, Eberhard Gothein, and Nitzsch. The work's reputation suffered from the subsequent discrediting of its author, but its grand scope, provocative conclusions, and innovative exploitation of statistics and tools from other disciplines have ensured its place as a monument of German historiography.[103] Many of its conclusions have withstood the test of subsequent scholarship, and as recently as 1955, one authority called it an "indispensable handbook" for scholars of Rhenish history.[104]

At the time of their publication, these volumes established their author's reputation as possibly the most promising young force in the profession. "People began to talk about him," one of his students in Bonn remembered.[105] Indeed, nowhere did they talk more about him than in Bonn, where his success made his professional future an acute political question.

Lamprecht's relations with the historians in Bonn remained uneasy. Most of the older scholars had little understanding or sympathy for the direction of his research, and bad feelings lingered on both sides over the confrontations within the Society for the Study of Rhenish History, which had resulted in the rejection of his editorial projects.

Lamprecht was closest to Arnold Schaefer, who had attempted to soothe his feelings in Cologne. Schaefer was the eldest of Lamprecht's colleagues, and his interests were the broadest. His death in November 1883 robbed Lamprecht of a potential ally on the faculty, as well as a man for whom he had begun to develop a genuine affection.[106]

Lamprecht's relationship with Maurenbrecher warmed gradually. As Noorden's close friend, Maurenbrecher felt a special obligation to the young historian whose potential he, like his friend, rated high despite the unorthodoxy of Lamprecht's work and the carelessness that marred much of it.[107] Menzel, the provincial historian, probably felt the most threatened by Lamprecht; and the relationship between the two men remained bad. Menzel complained in 1885 of Lamprecht's "pushy [*streberisch*], hasty, ever-bustling personality [*vielgeschäftiges Wesen*], to which is added a good measure of unreliability and dishonesty."[108] The charge of dishonesty was unfair, but Menzel's close ties to Sybel, to whom he aired this opinion, made his enmity a significant liability.

Lamprecht's most intriguing relationship was with Ritter. By temperament and intellectual inclination the two scholars had nothing in common. Ritter's stern reserve and distrust of abstraction clashed with Lamprecht's volubility and penchant for the unorthodox. The clash surfaced not only in the Society for the Study of Rhenish History, but in Ritter's uncomprehending reaction to Lamprecht's excursions into art history—a field which, Ritter insisted (as he pronounced Lamprecht lost to the profession), bore no relationship to "real" history.[109] Yet Lamprecht respected Ritter more than he did his other colleagues in Bonn, and he accepted Ritter's advice and direction, albeit grudgingly at the time.[110] "You know how much stock I place in your judgment," he confessed later, "perhaps because I know that we are separated temperamentally by a deep chasm, which will perhaps never allow us to come to a complete understanding, and because I know, on the other hand, that you are an entirely honest and incorruptible judge."[111] Despite all the circumstances that weighed against it, a life-long affection did develop between these two historians, as their contrasts formed a complementary bond that was nurtured by the complete absence of malice in either man.

Even had Lamprecht enjoyed the unqualified confidence of all the historians in Bonn, the chances of his finding a more secure position there were not auspicious. There were four chair holders in history in Bonn, but the historical seminar enrolled but twelve students in the summer semester of 1883.[112] Like others in his position, Lamprecht thus prepared to enter the conventional career track to a chair, which led to vacancies created by retirements or resignations at universities elsewhere. His problem was that he lacked a powerful academic patron in his field. No one in Bonn could be expected to push his candidacy with much enthusiasm. Roscher, his *Doktorvater*, was not a historian. Weizsäcker, with whom he remained close, had supervised neither his dissertation nor his habilitation; Noorden, whose support had been erratic in any event, died late in 1883. The uncertainty of Lamprecht's finances added urgency to his situation. His stipend from the university was due to expire in the fall of 1884, and he was reluctant to renew his dependence on Mevissen.[113]

Lamprecht used all the means at his disposal. He began early to cultivate relations to leading figures elsewhere in the field. He was in touch with his former professors, as well as with Schmoller, Sybel, and Treitschke.[114] His tie to the economist Meitzen was particularly close after the two toured the Eifel and the Ardennes together in the summer of 1883, in order to inspect traces of Germanic settlements in the layout of modern field systems.[115] The fact that most of these scholars resided in Berlin was one of the reasons they were important to an aspiring young scholar, for they were well situated to bring him to the attention of the most powerful academic patron in Germany.

It is an exaggeration to credit Friedrich Althoff alone with building the finest university system in the world at the end of the nineteenth century. But his was surely the leading role.[116] As head of the department for higher education under a succession of Prussian ministers of culture from 1882 to 1907, he oversaw the expansion of that state's universities and their adaptation to an era of dynamic industrial growth. The fact that the state's expenditures on higher education doubled during his tenure was at least in part due to his vision, resourcefulness, and receptivity to innovation. Much of the additional money he channeled into the natural sciences, medicine, and the technical disciplines. The price of this largesse, from which the humanities and the new social sciences also benefited, was the growth of the bureaucratic power of his so-called ministry of the mind in Berlin, the erosion of the universities' financial autonomy, and their control over academic appointments. In the *"Wissenschaftsstaat"* over which he presided, Althoff wielded immense power over appointments. Beyond the lines of responsibility that linked him to administrators and faculty leaders at each Prussian university, he constructed an informal network of confidants throughout the country, on whom he relied for information and advice (and gossip).[117] Because his influence and powers of persuasion were so pervasive, and because he shared most of the values of the German academy, he overturned formal faculty votes less frequently than did his predecessors.[118] He nonetheless acted ruthlessly when the occasion demanded, and academics feared him for his "benign brutality" as much as they respected him.[119] "If you reject my good will," he once told a young scholar, "you are a child."[120] The advice was only realistic, for no one had more power than Althoff to make or break an academic career. "Whoever did not oblige him stood mercilessly in dread of his might," noted one commentator. "In this way, many a scholarly star has risen like a comet in the radiance of the imperial sun, only to disappear when Althoff desired it."[121] His intrusions into faculty affairs and the sovereign contempt with which he treated academics provoked widespread resentment in the community of scholars; but these men were primary beneficiaries of his policies, and the enormous prestige they themselves enjoyed in imperial Germany testified to the success of his rule.

Lamprecht first came to Althoff's attention early in 1884. The historian owed his introduction to the mediation of Meitzen and two of Althoff's closest confidants, the legal historian Ludwig von Cuny, who had endowed the stipend that supported Lamprecht in Bonn, and Schmoller.[122] Meitzen supported Lamprecht's cause by submitting to Althoff the proofs of the documentary volume for the *Economic Life*. Weizsäcker joined the chorus of those urging Althoff to help the young historian.[123] So did Roscher's most famous student. Treitschke's sympathy for Lamprecht, once awakened in the 1880s, persisted until the older scholar's death in 1895; and it reflected the broad range of Treitschke's historical interests, which animated his later work and belied his reputation as the country's fiercest political historian.[124]

In April 1884 Althoff conveyed his "warmest sympathies" to Lamprecht and offered him an additional stipend. He also agreed to support Lamprecht's candidacy for a chair in Bonn, although not in history but in economics.[125] Neither the resident economist in Bonn, Erwin Nasse, nor the resident historians were prepared to install Lamprecht in a chair, but the sudden intervention of Althoff forced their hand. They proposed that Lamprecht apply instead for an extraordinary professorship in economic history. In May, Lamprecht accordingly submitted a petition to the faculty, which he supported with a package of his publications and the proofs of his documentary volume.[126] His case thus rested primarily on an edition of documents, many of which were drawn from a project that the Society for the Study of Rhenish History had earlier rejected. With Menzel in the lead, the historians had little difficulty demonstrating Lamprecht's shortcomings as an editor. The new volume represented "a step forward" in comparison to the earlier project, Menzel announced after a detailed reading, but Lamprecht was still no accomplished editor: "[H]is documentary collection is full of careless and hurried mistakes, both major and minor." The final report from the historians acknowledged Lamprecht's unusual energy and provocative scholarship, but emphasized his failings, chief among them an absence of self-criticism and "a frequent lack of caution, thoroughness, and maturity of judgment." This report, which the full faculty endorsed, recommended an instructor's stipend for Lamprecht and reconsideration for promotion when his major study was complete.[127]

The historians could cite a long list of errors, omissions, inconsistencies, and contradictions in Lamprecht's work, so their judgment was not unfounded. Lamprecht was bitter nonetheless. "The hitch in the whole affair," he wrote to his brother as the deliberations dragged on, "is that I am much too independent for the gentlemen here, that they have not been able to tie me down."[128] This judgment was not unfounded either, insofar as Lamprecht had resisted his colleagues' attempts both to restrain his unconventionality and to encourage care in his scholarship. But if the historians in Bonn had little success in these efforts, they failed altogether to restrain his quest for promotion in another forum and according to another set of rules.

Whether or not Althoff construed the faculty's action in Bonn as an act of defiance is not clear. In August 1884 he again assured Lamprecht, who had kept him well informed about events in Bonn, of his "fullest sympathies."[129] The next month Lamprecht went to the capital to meet with his many patrons, including for the first time with Althoff himself. In Berlin, the historian reported (in familiar terms), "I collected many nice faces—I hope enough [of them] to exchange next semester for the sour-pusses in Bonn [sauerköpfigen Bonner]."[130] The presence of Prince Leopold of Prussia in his classroom in the fall suggested that this hope was not idle, as did his nomination to a chair at the Academy of Art in Düsseldorf and to an editorial position at the Academy of Sciences in Munich.

Lamprecht's prospects brightened, too, when Maurenbrecher left Bonn in the fall of 1884 to fill Noorden's chair in Leipzig. Maurenbrecher was not an enemy, but his reservations about Lamprecht's judgment and carelessness limited his enthusiasm about promotion. Maurenbrecher's replacement was Alfred Dove.[131] This remarkable, troubled man paused several years in Bonn in the course of a long search for professional and personal bearings. Dove was an accomplished historian—a student of Ranke, Droysen, and Philip Jaffé—but he was also a brilliant stylist and journalist, whose talents had been honed at the side of Gustav Freytag. Commitment to a career in either field seemed like a betrayal of the other, so he vacillated, both professionally and emotionally. He was not a malicious man, although he could give that impression, for by the time he arrived in Bonn from a chair in Breslau, the burden of uncertainty had brought his sardonic sense of irony to the point of cynicism. It was unlikely that Lamprecht would find a reliable friend in him, but upon his arrival Dove did take Lamprecht's side; and his ties to Althoff, with whom he himself had just negotiated the move from Breslau, made him an important ally.[132]

The story now ended quickly. Early in 1885, Althoff made his intentions dramatically clear in a visit to Bonn. In February Lamprecht petitioned again for promotion and supported it with the proofs of the second, statistical volume of his huge study.[133] The historians needed no more persuasion. Neither Ritter nor Menzel could overlook additional evidence of carelessness, but they concluded that the new volume justified the promotion. Dove was more enthusiastic. Lamprecht's problems, he argued, were due to his taking an "untrodden path in a new direction" and would disappear once the pace of his work became more moderate.[134] The philosophical faculty endorsed the historians' vote, and Lamprecht was formally named extraordinary professor of history in June 1885.

The immediate significance of Lamprecht's promotion was only symbolic, for it brought no remuneration, and he continued to live on stipends that the university and Althoff had provided. But the circumstances of the promotion were of the utmost importance. Althoff's patronage ensured Lamprecht's professional future; there could henceforth be little doubt that he would receive a chair. Moreover, the events of 1884–1885 retraced a familiar pattern in Lamprecht's life. Repudiated initially by his colleagues in Bonn, he ventured outside the institution to plead his case in a higher forum. In doing so, he learned an important lesson in German academic politics, that the people who mattered most in the academy were not necessarily its members. During the next several years, the network that he cultivated included—in addition to his established patrons in Berlin—the empress, the crown prince, Prince William, the Prussian minister of culture, and Ranke, whom he visited shortly before the old man's death in May 1886.[135] There was more than a little symbolism in this visit, for Lamprecht's promotion also had far-reaching implications for the future of the historical profession in Germany.

The term *Kulturgeschichte* is as difficult to translate into English as it is to specify in German. As it was commonly understood at midcentury, the term applied to a broad genre of historical writing that was defined primarily by the fact that its emphasis lay outside politics and the state. It represented, as Ernst Cassirer has written, a "many-colored picture," an "odd assortment"; and to call the genre "cultural history" requires an understanding of the word "culture" comprehensive enough to include virtually every dimension of the human experience—society, economy, law, education, ideas, art, literature, folkways, and morals, as well as politics.[136]

Cultural history was the obverse side of the discipline that took hold at the universities. If academic history was defined by its exclusive concentration on politics, cultural history tended to be panoramic. Its inspiration and scope were Herderian, although many of the early products of the genre were modeled on Voltaire's famous historical studies. Cultural histories were written largely for a popular audience by men who were not professional historians. The most widely read histories in nineteenth century Germany were of this sort. They included the vast catalogues of institutions, manners, and morals that authors such as Wilhelm Wachsmuth, Wilhelm Drumann, Georg Friedrich Kolb, Johannes Scherr, and Henne am Rhyn compiled.[137] The most accomplished products of the genre were Riehl's paean to the German peasantry and Gustav Freytag's to the German middle class, his *Bilder aus der deutschen Vergangenheit*.[138]

The terms on which the discipline of history consolidated at the universities encouraged the exclusion of *Kulturgeschichte* from the historical seminars. To this extent it is accurate to call cultural history an *Oppositionswissenschaft*, or, as one contemporary described it, "the cinderella among the historical disciplines."[139] Lectures on cultural history or on the historical development of realms outside the state fell for the most part to scholars in other disciplines. Aside from the ancient historians, whose interest in nonpolitical themes was dictated by a paucity of political sources, few academic historians chose to write or lecture in this genre. The small group of historians at the universities who were associated with *Kulturgeschichte* labored in protest against the prevailing trends in their own profession, as they undertook to repair the fragmentation of the discipline. They emphasized the economic, social, cultural, and moral circumstances or structures which, they argued, provided the essential context for political history. The most famous early exponent of cultural history in the academy was Ranke's critic, Heinrich Leo, who taught in Halle and produced large-scale surveys of Italian, Dutch, and European history.[140] Another leading representative of this tradition was Karl Wilhelm Nitzsch in Berlin—a man who, as one of his students recalled, "had his own ideas."[141] To the vexation of many of his colleagues, Nitzsch argued that the failure of the medieval German monarchy was due to geographical circumstances and economic backwardness. His controversial studies of the economic foundations of Roman and German history gave rise to the quip that he viewed hog food as the foundation of history.[142] The quip was misleading, for Nitzsch's surveys were sensitive as well to the history of ideas, art, and literature. His treatment of these subjects was admittedly by no means as rich as the work of a third major figure, Jacob

Burckhardt, at whose hands *Kulturgeschichte* was practically defined by an emphasis on art and literature. However, Burckhardt's refusal to treat political history
in isolation, his insistence on anchoring political institutions and practices
within their cultural context, situated him within a broader historiographical
tradition.[143]

Burckhardt was a representative figure in another regard. Like most of the
scholars who were attracted to cultural history, he occupied a marginal position
in German historiography. Marginality could be geographical, as it was in his
case or in that of some Austrians, such as Adam Wolf, for whom the events of
1866 made political history problematic.[144] Cultural history tended to appeal for
similar reasons to local historians in the many regions of Germany that had been
rendered politically marginal during the nineteenth century. The model to
which these historians could look was Justus Möser's seminal history of the city
of Osnabrück. Finally, marginality was also confessional in the new Germany.
Unification and the *Kulturkampf* brought great professional disadvantages to
Catholic scholars and emphasized the Protestant accents that political historiography had carried since its inception. In these circumstances, cultural
history became an appealing alternative, not to say a weapon, in Catholic
historiography. One of the grandest pieces of German cultural history ever
written was Johannes Janssen's *Geschichte des deutschen Volkes*, which scandalized the Protestant establishment in assaulting one of the central propositions in
the dominant historiography, the lionization of Luther as a national hero.[145]

Cultural history thus became institutionalized on the periphery of the German
historical profession, where it languished in an air of dilettantism, if not political
suspicion. Its devotees were less likely to be found in the academy than in the
local historical *Vereine*.[146] A handful of journals, such as the *Vierteljahrschrift
für Volkswirtschaft und Kulturgeschichte* and the *Zeitschrift für deutsche Kulturgeschichte*, served their interests.[147] But these journals were more popular than
scholarly; and in part because academic historians avoided them, they tended to
be short-lived.

"As long as the area that cultural history is to encompass has not been
distinctly delimited," wrote Ottokar Lorenz in 1886, "research done in this area
will always have something dilettantish about it."[148] This view was widely held.
In an era of specialized scholarship, the critical failing of *Kulturgeschichte* was its
lack of definition. Its subject matter was amorphous and all-encompassing.
While its concern for areas other than politics implied a practical boundary with
academic history, it did not resolve the question of disciplinary frontiers
elsewhere—for example, with economics, church history, or art history. Nor
could cultural historians lay claim to a distinctive methodology. Most of them
were rooted in the same intellectual soil as the political historians and worked
with similar assumptions. Like the political historians, they sought to portray
each historical epoch in its own unique terms, through a process of sympathetic
intuition. Their perspective was merely more inclusive, and their efforts were
oriented toward the broader cultural unities of the past. Because they wrote

more in the spirit of Herder than of Ranke, their surveys were in practice, as one detractor noted, like rococo picture galleries—exercises in compilation and description, in which diverse cultural realms stood together not in any analytical relationship, but instead as expressions of a *Volksgeist* or some other higher organic unity.[149]

The writing of cultural history was thus accompanied by little theoretical or methodological reflection. Nor was cultural history associated in any special or unique way with the doctrines of Comte, Darwin, Taine, or Buckle. The leading spokesman of a positivist theory of history in Germany was Emil Du Bois-Reymond, a physiologist, who found little resonance among practicing historians of any sort.[150] The closest German counterpart to Thomas Henry Buckle was admittedly a cultural historian, Friedrich Heller von Hellwald, whose *Die Culturgeschichte in ihrer natürlichen Entwickelung* appeared in 1875. But the search for the laws thought to govern history was a more legitimate undertaking among historians at midcentury than it was later; and among those who joined it in their youth were eminent scholars such as Sybel and Bernhard Erdmannsdörffer.[151]

In the 1880s, however, developments in a neighboring discipline made *Kulturgeschichte* the object of more serious academic concern; they also clouded the definition and popular understanding of this genre still further. At the universities, cultural history had become the province of scholars outside the historical seminars—particularly of economists. The premise that had informed the professionalization of economics at the hands of Roscher, Knies, and Hildebrand was the historicity of all economic activity. Insofar as it treated the political and cultural factors that historically shaped economic institutions and behavior, the scholarship of German economists fell under the expansive purview of *Kulturgeschichte*. In the thinking of the "older school" of historical economists, however, history remained in the end an ancillary discipline. While these men used history to establish their methodological distance from the classical economists, they also emphasized their distance from the historians, for they insisted that the goal of their discipline was to construct general theories of economic behavior. The role of historical scholarship was accordingly to provide the material with which to illustrate, modify, and refine these theories by grounding them in historical context. As one later critic put it, the economists proposed to pour "historical sauce over a classical entrée."[152]

The generation of scholars who followed these patriarchs proposed to deemphasize the theoretical component, or perhaps more accurately, to postpone it. The leading figure of the new generation was Knies' student, Gustav Schmoller, who during his early career at the universities of Halle and Strassburg established impressive credentials as a historian with a series of monographs on the history of administrative institutions and economic policy in Prussia in the age of absolutism and on the history of guilds in Strassburg.[153] By the time he moved to Berlin in 1882, he was one of the country's most prominent scholar-activists, a leader in the *Verein für Sozialpolitik*, an advisor to ministers and politicians, and the editor of one of the most respected academic journals, which was known popularly as *Schmollers Jahrbuch*. Schmoller was also the leading spokesman for a group of scholars who were known as the "younger school" of historical economics. To him fell the role of defending the methodological agenda that distinguished this school not only from the historical economists of Roscher's generation, but from the advocates of a revitalized neo-classical economics who congregated in Vienna around Karl Menger.[154]

"The object that I have always had in mind," Schmoller told the Prussian Academy of Sciences on the occasion of his election in 1887,

> has been really to achieve and complete what Hildebrand, Knies, and Roscher tried to do for German economics: to liberate the discipline entirely from the dogmatism of Anglo-French utilitarianism, to place it on a foundation that is psychologically and historically deeper and more secure.[155]

"Dogmatism" was a charge that Schmoller directed against the "older school" and the neo-classical economists alike. By this term he meant their proclivity to abstraction, their construction of theories of economic behavior that took insufficient account of the particularities of historical context. However, his position exposed him to attack from two sides, for his views on methodology were not entirely consistent with his own practice. Economists, particularly those in Vienna, accused him of narrow empiricism, a devotion to "historical micrographics," while academic historians in Germany attacked him for violating his own precepts, particularly in embracing a value-laden theory of economic growth and *Kulturstufen*.[156] Schmoller's views are perhaps best characterized as an analytical posture, or a preference for the particular, rather than as a systematic statement of method. The study of economic behavior made him sensitive to the structures and regularities of human action, which he sought to analyze with the aid of statistics. But he never embraced the more extravagant claims made on behalf of statistical analysis as a key to unlocking predictable laws of behavior.[157] Nor was he comfortable with economic theory. Theory, he insisted, could only be constructed after a basis of historical facts had been scrupulously assembled. He argued, in other words, that the historical sauce had to constitute the stock for the entrée. "I am always so conscious of the endless complexity of all social and historical phenomena," he once pleaded, that "I cannot ever see over the multiplicity of causes to the point where I might divorce my own theories from their groundwork [*Untergrund*] and portray them as abstract and absolute truths."[158]

Schmoller's forceful advocacy of history over theory was as significant for the writing of history in imperial Germany as it was for his own discipline. Around him gathered a talented group of economic historians, many of whom were his own students or disciples. The group included Karl Bücher, Wilhelm Stieda, Ignaz Jastrow, August von Miaskowski, Ludwig Elster, Gustav Schönberg, Richard Kaufmann, and Eberhard Gothein, as well as Meitzen and Inama-Sternegg. Their vehicles included the *Jahrbücher für Nationalökonomie und*

Statistik and Schmoller's own journal, as well as a series of historical monographs in which they conceded nothing to the political historians in the rigor of their scholarship. In its breadth, however, their scholarship far exceeded that of the political historians. The economists emphasized the historical impact of political forces and cultural norms on economic behavior. They could look for models to Schmoller's own studies on the intersection of politics, public administration, and economic development in Prussia; but the range of their interest was extraordinary. It encompassed political, constitutional, and legal history, demography, geography, agriculture, financial policy, colonial policy, navigation, and the position of women. To the extent that their research had a theoretical scaffolding, Schmoller and Bücher supplied it (albeit with different nuances) in the form of a theory of coordinated political and economic growth through progressive phases, which corresponded to the geographical units of village, city, territory, and state.

The scope of this scholarship suggested that the historical economists were the heirs to the broad legacy of cultural history. As industrial growth and social dislocation increasingly set the political agenda in the new German empire, these economists added a new dimension and power to the concept of *Kulturgeschichte*. They seemed to mark out a subgenre in which the accents were fastened onto the history of the economy and society. They introduced social and economic history into the curricula at German universities.[159] Because their historical scholarship was free of the taint of dilettantism, it suggested a compelling alternative not only to the more popular variety of cultural history, but to the political history practiced in the academy.

Although the scholarship of the economic historians implied a challenge to the historical primacy of the state, the political historians were slow to take alarm; and not until the late 1880s did they begin to rally behind the slogan "political history versus cultural history." In the first place, the methodological tensions between economic and political historians remained ill defined. Schmoller's strictures against premature abstraction were reminiscent of Ranke's charges against Hegel; and they spoke to assumptions that the economists and political historians continued to share, despite the historians' intransigent suspicion of theory, statistics, and analysis of material structures. The differences between the two disciplines seemed to reside principally in the definition of subject matter; but these differences did not appear insuperable either. The state and politics were central elements in the scholarship of the economists; so political historians could speak of a welcome division of labor, in which economic history served as an auxiliary discipline to their own. Finally, it reassured the political historians to see this division of labor preserved in university faculties. The economists had their own seminars; and after the deaths of Leo in 1878 and Nitzsch in 1880, no holder of a chair in history could be characterized as an advocate of cultural history, however defined.

In these circumstances Lamprecht's promotion in 1885 was a significant event. His interests, his achievements as a scholar, and his success as an editor had earned him a place in the front ranks of the country's economic historians. His exhaustive bibliographical reviews were valued contributions to the *Jahr-bücher für Nationalökonomie und Statistik*.[160] He was well known to the established scholars in the field like Schmoller, Bücher, and Inama-Sternegg.[161] He was also an acknowledged leader among a group of younger historical economists who were waiting, in insecure circumstances similar to those he himself had known, on the periphery of their profession. These scholars included Gothein, Jastrow, Robert Hoeniger, Paul Hinneberg, and his own former student, Erich Liesegang.[162]

Lamprecht's many ties and affinities with the economists had already recommended the possibility of a chair in economics. But he always regarded himself as a historian, and his ambition was to receive a chair in history. His interest in *Kulturgeschichte* guided him throughout his training; it extended back to his school days, when he contemplated studying with Riehl in Munich.[163] Lamprecht's understanding of this term was broad even by the standards of the economists, and it recalled the panoramic aspirations of the cultural historians of the early nineteenth century. Cultural history, he believed, required a perspective more comprehensive than an economist's, for its object was to encompass a field far broader than the development of material culture. However essential, Schmoller's impulse was insufficient without Burckhardt's.

Lamprecht made no secret of his preferences for history, least of all to his patrons. In a memorandum he prepared for Althoff, he described his goals in unambiguous terms. "In my view," he wrote, "it is the office of the historian to comprehend the era to which he has devoted himself—in my case, it is for the time being the German Middle Ages—in all of its facets, in its spiritual as well as its material culture."[164] Althoff was receptive to this argument, despite the clash it portended with reigning views in the historical profession. He decided to promote the career of Karl Lamprecht after extensive consultation with his advisors and in full awareness of its implications. The man whose advice weighed most heavily in Althoff's decision was surely Schmoller, who not only was Althoff's closest confidant in matters that involved this field, but who had a direct interest in the outcome.[165] Althoff's decision was a signal that *Kulturge-schichte*, the historical profession's stepchild, which had hitherto invited historical economists into the company of amateur historians and dilettantes, would be offered a new bridgehead within the historians' guild.

In May 1886 Ranke and Waitz died within twenty-four hours of one another. The symbolism of the events impressed the young historian in Bonn, who wrote that "the entire generation of historians is passing on—think of how old Giesebrecht and Sybel, [Karl] Hegel and Wattenbach are!—and we younger ones are presenting no suitable successors."[166] Lamprecht was not being candid, for by the middle of 1886 he had begun to think of himself as a "suitable successor." Two volumes of his vast study had appeared amid great acclaim; he now enjoyed the support of powerful patrons, and his future seemed assured. Proofs of the last two volumes of the magnum opus, which he hoped would clinch the matter, arrived in the summer of 1886, just as events of great personal moment intruded.

It was not unusual for a male child of the *Bildungsbürgertum* to grow up with little contact with members of the opposite sex. Lamprecht had no female siblings. Apart from a friendship which he formed in Jessen with the daughter of a mason, his only contacts with females as a boy were with adult women—his mother, his aunts, and a succession of maids.[167] The environment at boarding school was exclusively male; the only liaisons with women it offered were with prostitutes in town, but there is no evidence that Lamprecht participated in any of these adventures.[168] University life, too, was more conducive to male than to female company, but Lamprecht tended to avoid both in his devotion to study.

His circumstances changed upon his arrival in the Rhineland. Employment in the Deichmann household and his ties to Mevissen's family brought about his introduction into Cologne's high society. In Bonn, where the academic elite set the tone, the social atmosphere was more modest, but his position at the university gave him access to the company of men and women his own age. After an awkward initial period in which he, like any eligible newcomer, endured the rites of being "sniffed out," social diversion in these circles became a regular part of his life.[169]

In these circumstances and in this phase of his life, the prospect of marriage ceased to be remote. His own inchoate ideas on the subject had grown out of observing his parents' relationship and his brother's experiences with marriage and family. His occasional remarks left little doubt, however, that his feminine ideal resembled his own mother. That a suitable wife was to be Protestant and of at least modest means needed no emphasis. Her beauty, he explained, was to consist less in physical attractiveness than in her inner virtues, among which he stressed humility, modesty, and the absence of intellectual pretensions.[170]

Zitta von Stintzing, the daughter of a law professor in Bonn, evidently embodied this ideal. In July 1882 Lamprecht suddenly announced that he could "never lose his love and respect" for the woman and that he intended to ask for her hand.[171] It was an impulsive decision for a young man of no secure means or station; and it came to nothing. Lamprecht found a sympathetic but sensible confidant in Moriz Ritter, who pointed out the practical consequences of the step and advised postponement.[172] When the young woman left Bonn shortly later, the relationship ended.

The episode was too brief to leave emotional scars deeper than a general sense of disappointment. Lamprecht was attracted to the idea of quiet, stable companionship. His social involvements had been a welcome source of release, but frivolity did not come naturally to him; nor was he entirely comfortable in the company of large numbers of his peers. As his friends began to leave Bonn, he found party life less attractive, but he had few alternatives.

His principal source of release remained, as always, his scholarship, but completion of his *Economic Life* brought a pause in the furious pace at which he had worked. It also represented an emotional climax that left him bored, lonely, and vulnerable. "I suddenly no longer have any idea what I ought to do, and I notice to my astonishment that there are twenty-four hours in a day," he remarked to his brother early in August 1886.[173] To make matters worse, he was physically uncomfortable again with the stomach disorder, which the intensity of his work had aggravated. In the hopes of treating this ailment, if not his malaise, he departed late in August for the Black Forest, where his physician had prescribed a cure.

Mathilde Mühl was from Strassburg. Her father, Gustav Mühl, had been director of the municipal library as well as a poet of some local renown before his death in 1880.[174] In August 1886 she arrived in the company of her mother and sister at the same resort where the historian was taking the cure. On 27 August Lamprecht joined them for lunch. Six days later he asked Mathilde Mühl to marry him; the next day, 3 September, she accepted. If Lamprecht had had any doubts, they were overwhelmed in his euphoria. "'My little bird' is not what one would call pretty," he told his brother the next day. "On the whole what predominates is her charm: I have never seen such an engaging spectacle."[175] Several days later he reported, "What the days since the 3rd have revealed, how endlessly much I have experienced, how different I have become. This transformation, the firm confidence in the eternal duration of our union—that makes me calmer than I often used to be, and constantly cheerful."[176] The rapture dimmed a little, when, a week later, his fiancee took to bed, her nerves exhausted. A physician arrived from Strassburg to explain to the anxious historian that she had experienced similar problems before, but that the difficulty was intestinal and merely required rest. A tentative wedding date was set for the next spring.

Ernst Kraepelin first used the term dementia praecox in 1896 to describe a group of degenerative psychiatric disorders. Fifteen years later Eugen Bleuler redefined Kraepelin's categories as varieties of a single disorder, which he thought to be characterized by the splitting of personality functions.[177] He named the disorder schizophrenia; one of its varieties he called paranoid schizophrenia. Disagreements persist to this day over the diagnosis and etiology of this frightful illness, but in order to appreciate the achievement of these psychiatrists at the turn of the century, one need only consider the bewilderment, arrogant incomprehension, and finally the deceit of the physicians who presided over the deterioration of the woman whom Karl Lamprecht had chosen to marry.

Early in October the historian returned to Bonn, where his emotions vacillated through a series of reports from Strassburg, which told of repeated nervous attacks, confinements, periods of recuperation, and renewed assurances from the doctors.[178] That Mathilde Mühl had long been a very sick woman was known at least to her mother, for whom the historian's impulsive decision presented an unexpected opportunity to secure an unfortunate daughter's future. A man less optimistic, guileless, or less prone to self-deception than Lamprecht might have grown suspicious once the reports from the doctors counseled marriage as the best cure for her problem—"the sooner the better."[179] After relapses occasioned several postponements, the historian followed their advice, and the couple wed in May 1887 in Strassburg.

In the summer of 1887 they moved into a small house near Bonn in Poppels-dorf, where they were able, thanks to an increase in Lamprecht's stipend and a generous gift from Mevissen, to live modestly but in circumstances appropriate for an ambitious young professor. An active social life to support these ambitions was out of the question, however, so the couple's contacts were limited to quiet visits with a few close friends and colleagues, including the Ritters and the Doves.[180] Delusional episodes of jealous rage, followed by periods of langor and confinement, became regular features of the Lamprechts' life together. The doctors whom they consulted offered contradictory prognoses. The birth of a daughter in the spring of 1888, which some of the physicians had recommended as a cure, brought only temporary respite.[181]

Lamprecht's affection for the woman, although strained during these episodes, was genuine; and his commitment to her was lifelong. But the fluctuations in her condition shook him profoundly. Only during the intervals of her lucidity could he indulge the optimism that was natural to him and which his professional prospects alone would have justified. Anxieties at home and the planning of his next project confined his scholarship to a few editorial projects and the publica-tion of essays, most of which were derivative.[182] Still, the publication in 1886 of the final volumes of his *Professorenbuch*, as he referred to it (with good reason), ensured that his name would begin to appear on lists of nominees for vacant chairs.[183]

Althoff's influence, if not his authority, extended well beyond the frontiers of the state of Prussia. Even before Lamprecht married, the historian's name had been on lists in Basel and for the polytechnical university in Zurich, where the death of the cultural historian Johannes Scherr created a vacancy at the end of 1886. Lamprecht probably would have received the second position but for his reluctance to accept exile in Switzerland.[184] Nominations for positions in Tübingen, Halle, Breslau, and Münster came to nothing but were reminders that Althoff had not lost track of him.[185]

Althoff still hoped to place Lamprecht in Bonn, despite the continuing problem of too few students and too many historians at that institution. Creat-ing a chair for Rhenish history in Bonn would delight Mevissen but would establish an expensive precedent at other universities.[186] Althoff's solution was instead to tailor another position to fit Lamprecht's unusual talents. Early in 1889 the historian received a new extraordinary professorship in Bonn, this time with a regular salary and assurances of an eventual chair.[187] Lamprecht's com-mission was to teach cultural history as he himself understood the subject; several months later his commission was broadened to include lectures in economics.[188]

This could be only a temporary solution, however, for it pleased neither the historians nor the economists in Bonn. Althoff accordingly resolved the problem of Lamprecht's future himself, in a demonstration of the power that made him such a formidable force in German higher education. Early in 1890, the departure of Conrad Varrentrapp for Strassburg opened a chair in history in Marburg. The faculty nominated two political historians and included Lamprecht's name, albeit with little enthusiasm, as a third choice. Althoff thus defied only the spirit, not the letter of the faculty's wishes, when on 22 January 1890 he named Karl Lamprecht to the chair.[189]

Notes

1. LW, 67; Winter, "Lamprecht," 309.
2. Noorden to Sybel, 7.6.78, in Noorden, 608; NL Bernheim, Lamprecht to Bernheim, Munich, 22.6. 1878.
3. LW, 72–74.
4. NL Lamprecht (Korr. 59), Lamprecht to Hugo Lamprecht, Leipzig, 19.2.79.
5. NL Lamprecht (Korr. 59), Lamprecht to Hugo Lamprecht, Jessen, 24.12.78.
6. In 1882 Lamprecht told his mother of "the thought of our good father, which rises up out of the couch across from me when I sit at the desk in the quiet of the night." NL Lamprecht (Korr. 59), Lamprecht to Emilie and Hugo Lamprecht, Bonn, 22.7.82.
7. NL Althoff (B Nr. 108/1), Lamprecht to Althoff, Bonn, 16.7.84; cf. LW, 74–77.
8. Weymar, 205–26; EB, 2,2: 424; cf. Friedrich Marcks, *Oskar Jäger* (Leipzig and Berlin, 1930); James C. Albisetti, *Secondary School Reform in Imperial Germany* (Princeton, 1983), 143.
9. Joseph Hansen, *Gustav von Mevissen*, 2 vols. (Berlin, 1906); Justus Hashagen, "Gustav von Mevissen," ADB, 53, 772–88; Konstantin Höhlbaum, "Gustav von Mevissen," HZ, 94 (1899): 72–79; Karl Lamprecht, "Gustav von Mevissen als Förderer der Geschichtswissenschaft," *Nationalzeitung*, no. 551 (1899).
10. Hansen, 2: 627–36; cf. Fritz Redlich, "Academic Education for Business: Its Development and the Contribution of Ignaz Jastrow," in *Steeped in Two Cultures: A Selection of Essays* (New York and Evanston, 1971), 213–16.
11. Hans Carl Scheibler and Karl Wülfrath, eds., *Westdeutsche Ahnentafeln* (Weimar, 1939), 1: 109–70.
12. Herbert Schönebaum, "Gustav Mevissen und Karl Lamprecht: Zur rheinischen Kulturpolitik von 1880–1890," RVjb, 17 (1952): 180–96.
13. NL Althoff (B Nr. 108/1), Lamprecht to Althoff, Bonn, 16.7.84; NL Lamprecht (Korr. 59), Lamprecht to Hugo Lamprecht, Cologne, 23.1.80.
14. NL Mevissen, Lamprecht to Mevissen, Leipzig, 31.12.98.
15. NL Lamprecht (Korr. 37), Mevissen to Lamprecht, Godesberg, 23.5.90.
16. NL Lamprecht (Korr. 59), Lamprecht to Hugo Lamprecht, Bonn, 14.6.82, 25.11.82.
17. NL Lamprecht (Korr. 59), Lamprecht to Hugo Lamprecht, Bonn, 22.9.81, 23.11.86; NL Mevissen, Lamprecht to Mevissen, Herrenalb, 28.3.86.
18. NL Mevissen, Lamprecht to Mevissen, Prague, 26.9.90; Leipzig, 27.12.96; NL Traub (70), Lamprecht to Traub, Leipzig, 16.11.11.
19. See Friedrich von Bezold, *Geschichte der Rheinischen Friedrich-Wilhelms-Universität von der Gründung bis zum Jahre 1870* (Bonn, 1920); Max Braubach, *Kleine Geschich-*

te der Universität Bonn 1818–1968 (Bonn, 1968); McClelland, State, Society, and University, 146.

20. Paul Egon Hübinger, Das Historische Seminar der Rheinischen Friedrich-Wilhelms-Universität zu Bonn: Vorläufer, Gründung, Entwicklung. Ein Wegstück deutscher Universitätsgeschichte (Bonn, 1963).

21. Walther Hubatsch, "Wilhelm Maurenbrecher 1838–1893," in Bonner Gelehrte, 155–61; P. Hübinger, 173–77; Weber, Lexikon, 369.

22. Walter Goetz, "Walter Goetz," in Sigfrid Steinberg, ed., Die Geschichtswissenschaft der Gegenwart in Selbstdarstellungen, 2 vols. (Leipzig, 1925), 1: 136–37; cf. Goetz, Historiker in meiner Zeit: Gesammelte Aufsätze (Graz, 1957), 1–87; Georg von Below, "Georg von Below," in S. Steinberg, 1: 7; cf. Meinecke, Schriften, 57.

23. Wilhelm II, Aus meinem Leben (Berlin and Leipzig, 1927), 160.

24. Stephan Skalweit, "Moriz Ritter 1840–1923," in Bonner Gelehrte, 209–24; Walter Goetz, "Moriz Ritter (1940–1923)," HZ, 131 (1925): 472–95; cf. Goetz, Historiker, 198–223; P. Hübinger, 13–18; Weber, Lexikon, 479.

25. Meinecke, Schriften, 63–65; Below, "Below," 10.

26. Roderich Schmidt, "Arnold Schaefer 1819–1883," in Bonner Gelehrten, 170–89; P. Hübinger, 114–16; Weber, Lexikon, 497–498.

27. M. Ditsche, "Karl Menzel 1835–1897," in Bonner Gelehrte, 225–30; P. Hübinger, 98–103; Weber, Lexikon, 379.

28. Noorden to Maurenbrecher, 13.1.80, in Noorden, 613.

29. The precise nature of Sybel's involvement at this stage in the negotiations is difficult to determine. He certainly knew about Mevissen's plans and did nothing to block them. NL Lamprecht (Korr. 59), Lamprecht to Hugo Lamprecht, Cologne, 23.1.80; Noorden to Sybel, 9.3.79, 5.1.80, in Noorden, 609–11.

30. Noorden to Maurenbrecher, 10.1.80, in Noorden, 611–12. Noorden's correspondence with Maurenbrecher has been published by Herbert Schönebaum, "Carl von Noorden und Wilhelm Maurenbrecher im Austausch über die geistige Entwicklung des jungen Karl Lamprecht," AKg, 44 (1962): 379–87. Noorden's role in this whole affair is problematic. He himself had refused to supervise Lamprecht's habilitation, either in the fall of 1878, as Schönebaum claims, or in the summer of 1879. See Schönebaum, "Noorden und Maurenbrecher," 381; cf. Ursula Lewald, "Karl Lamprecht 1856–1915," in Bonner Gelehrte, 232–34. It is difficult to believe that Noorden wished to deceive Maurenbrecher; perhaps the explanation for his ambivalent behavior is that he did not trust himself to discipline Lamprecht's talents.

31. Noorden to Sybel, 5.1.80, in Noorden, 610–11.

32. Ibid. The expression was Noorden's.

33. UA Bonn, Phil. Fak., Lamprecht to PF, Bonn, 19.4.80.

34. LW, 86–89.

35. Nor did it impress Hermann Heimpel, who edited Engelhus' chronicle for the Monumenta many years later: NL Lamprecht (Munich), Heimpel to Else Rose-Schütz, Göttingen, 15.8.57. Lamprecht's manuscript was never published: NL Lamprecht (Rh 1).

36. UA Bonn, Phil. Fak., G. vom Rath RS, Bonn, 21.4.80.

37. See Alexander Busch, Die Geschichte des Privatdozenten: Eine soziologische Studie zur grossbetrieblichen Entwicklung der deutschen Universitäten (Stuttgart, 1959); Franz Eulenburg, Der "akademische Nachwuchs": Eine Untersuchung über die Lage und die Aufgaben der Extraordinarien und Privatdozenten (Leipzig and Berlin, 1908); Klaus Dieter Bock, Strukturgeschichte der Assistentur: Personalgefüge, Wert- und Zielvorstellungen in der deutschen Universität des 19. und 20. Jahrhunderts (Düsseldorf, 1972), 31–68; Paulsen, Universitäten, 222–30; McClelland, State, Society, and University, 259–61.

38. Weber, *Priester*, 145–56.
39. Eulenburg, *Nachwuchs*, 11.
40. Lamprecht's friend Ernst Bernheim was more fortunate than most Jews in this respect, for he did finally receive a chair in Greifswald, but only after waiting there a quarter of a century as extraordinary professor and having been passed over for chairs elsewhere. "That he is a Jew you undoubtedly know," wrote Sybel to Althoff as an addendum to an otherwise favorable letter about an open chair in Königsberg in 1891. NL Althoff (Nr. 184/1), Sybel to Althoff, Tutzing, 7.7.91. Max Lehmann was less charitable. A Jew, he explained, could not be an unprejudiced judge of the Middle Ages, an epoch in which the Christian church was so central. NL Althoff (B Nr. 110/2), Lehmann to Althoff, Marburg, 4.7.91. On another occasion Lehmann advised against naming a Jew to a chair in Marburg, because "it seems to me to lie as much in the interest of the university as of the state not to give further nourishment to the anti-Semitism that exists here." GStAM, Rep. 76-Va, Sekt 12, Tit. VII, Lehmann to Althoff, Marburg, 18.1.91.
41. NL Althoff (B Nr. 108/1), Lamprecht to Althoff, Bonn, 16.7.84.
42. NL Lamprecht (Korr. 59), Lamprecht to Hugo Lamprecht, Bonn, 23.4.83.
43. Schönebaum, "Mevissen und Lamprecht," 183.
44. UA Bonn, Phil. Fak., Dove Aufzeichnung, Bonn, 11.8.85.
45. Meinecke, *Schriften*, 63.
46. Below, "Below," 13–14.
47. NL Lamprecht (M 6), speech by Karl Doren in "Karl Lamprecht zum Gedächtnis. Gedenkfeier im Institut für Kultur- und Universalgeschichte (16.5.15)," 24. Alfred Dove, who was his colleague for several years in Bonn, complained that Lamprecht's directives to his students "were more conducive to docility [*Folgsamkeit*] than to independence." Dove to Otto Ribbeck, Bonn, 19.11.90, in Friedrich Meinecke, ed., *Ausgewählte Aufsätze und Briefe*, 2 vols. (Munich, 1925), 2: 142–144.
48. NL Lamprecht (Korr. 17), Paul Clemens to Lamprecht, n.p., 23.2.05.
49. Meinecke, *Schriften*, 63–64.
50. NL Lamprecht (Munich), Otto Wallach, Lebenserinnerungen, ms.; NL Lamprecht (Korr. 59), Lamprecht to Hugo Lamprecht, Bonn, 14.11.80, 14.5.83.
51. There is an extended literature on this subject. For good introductions see Klaus Pabst, "Historische Vereine und Kommissionen in Deutschland bis 1914," in *Vereinswesen und Geschichtspflege in den böhmischen Ländern* (Munich, 1986), 13–38; Alois Gerlich, *Geschichtliche Landeskunde: Genese und Probleme* (Darmstadt, 1986), esp. 42–76; Luise Schorn-Schütte, "Territorialgeschichte—Provinzial-geschichte—Landesgeschichte: Ein Beitrag zur Wissenschaftsgeschichte der Landes-geschichtsschreibung," in Helmut Jäger et al., eds., *Civitatum communitas: Studien zum europäischen Städtewesen* (Cologne and Vienna, 1984), 390–416; Hartmut Boockmann et al., *Geschichtswissenschaft und Vereinswesen im 19. Jahrhundert: Beiträge zur Geschichte historischer Forschung in Deutschland* (Göttingen, 1972); Rudolf Kötzschke, "Nationalgeschichte und Landesgeschichte," in Pankraz Fried, ed., *Probleme und Methoden der Landesgeschichte* (Darmstadt, 1978), 13–37; Heimpel, "Organisationsformen," 189–220.
52. Heimpel, "Organisationsformen," 197.
53. Ibid., 212.
54. Hansen, 1: 836–40.
55. See Ursula Lewald, "Karl Lamprecht und die Rheinische Geschichtsforschung," RVjb, 21 (1956): 279–304; Max Braubach, *Landesgeschichtliche Bestrebungen und historische Vereine im Rheinland* (Cologne and Opladen, 1955), esp. 16–18; Hermann Aubin, "Aufgaben und Wege der geschichtlichen Landeskunde," in Fried, *Probleme und Methoden*, 39–40.

56. NL Mevissen (GfRGk, Handakt Lamprecht), Lamprecht, Über eine Rheinische Geschichte im Mittelalter, Cologne, 2.1.80.
57. Lewald, "Geschichtsforschung," 283.
58. GStAM, NL Gustav Schmoller, Lamprecht to Schmoller, Bonn, n.d. [1881]; see Griss, 88–103.
59. Lamprecht later claimed that the idea of a historical society to publish documents was his: NL Liesegang, Lamprecht to Liesegang, Leipzig, 17.7.95; cf. NL Lamprecht (Korr. 27), Hansen to Lamprecht, Cologne, 15.12.02. The original idea for the society, however, dated back to 1868. Lamprecht's correspondence with Mevissen suggests that he had little enthusiasm for editing and publishing documents and that he regarded his history of the Rhineland as his Hauptaufgabe. NL Mevissen (GfRGk, Handakt Lamprecht), Lamprecht, Übersicht über das Jahr Juni 1880–1881, Bonn 20.5.81; cf. Lewald "Geschichtsforschung," 285.
60. Noorden to Maurenbrecher, 5.12.80, in Noorden, 613; LW, 155–56.
61. LW, 107–10; Braubach, 16–18; Lewald, "Geschichtsforschung," 284–85.
62. NL Mevissen (GfRGk, Handakt Lamprecht), Protokoll über die Beratung des Statutenentwurfs, Cologne, 5.12.80.
63. Everhard Kleinertz, "Joseph Hansen (1862–1943)," in Joseph Hansen, ed., Preussen und Rheinland von 1815 bis 1915: Hundert Jahre politischen Lebens am Rhein (Cologne, 1990), 284.
64. NL Schmoller, Lamprecht to Schmoller, Bonn, n.d. [1881]; NL Bernheim, Lamprecht to Bernheim, Bonn, 10.7.80, 29.11.81; LW, 114–16, 126–27; Schönebaum, "Lamprecht und Mevissen," 186.
65. Johannes Müller, Die wissenschaftlichen Vereine und Gesellschaften Deutschlands im neuzehnten Jahrhundert: Bibliographie ihrer Veröffentlichungen, 2 vols. (Berlin, 1883–1917), 1: 123, 665–66.
66. NL Schmoller, Lamprecht to Schmoller, Bonn, 7.6.81.
67. Braubach, 12–13; LW, 121.
68. NL Mevissen (GfRGk, Handakt Lamprecht), Lamprecht, Übersicht über das Jahr Juni 1880–1881; Lewald, "Geschichtsforschung," 285–86.
69. UB Leipzig, NL Eduard Zarncke, Lamprecht to Zarncke, Bonn, 11.3.83.
70. UB Leipzig, NL Karl Bücher, Lamprecht to Bücher, Bonn, 6.6.83.
71. NL Lamprecht (Kr. 2), Westdeutsche Zeitschrift für Geschichte und Kunst, Prospect.
72. GStAM, NL Heinrich von Sybel (B1 Nr. 25), Lamprecht to Sybel, n.p., n.d. [1882].
73. LW, 129–31.
74. NL Lamprecht (Korr. 29), Hettner to Lamprecht, 1.1.83; (Kr. 2), Bisher vorliegende Urteile über die Westdeutsche Zeitschrift.
75. NL Mevissen, Lamprecht to Mevissen, Bonn, 19.5.82.
76. NL Lamprecht (Korr. 59), Lamprecht to Hugo Lamprecht, Bonn, 3.10.80.
77. NL Lamprecht (Korr. 9), Bernheim to Lamprecht, Göttingen, 9.2.83.
78. NL Mevissen, Lamprecht to Eisenbahnminister, n.d. [1880]; UA Bonn, Phil. Fak., PF to Kuratorium, Bonn, 28.1.82.
79. NL Lamprecht (L 3a), Zimmer to Marianne Lamprecht, Zehlendorf, 6.8.15; (Korr. 24), Gneisse to Lamprecht, Weissenburg, 9.6.85.
80. NL Bernheim, Lamprecht to Bernheim, Gross Ballerstedt, 30.12.80.
81. LW, 90–111, 125–27. Herbert Schönebaum has compiled Lamprecht's bibliography. "Lamprechtiana: Verzeichnis der Schriften Karl Lamprechts und der von ihm in Referat und Korreferat betreuten Dissertationen," Wissenschaftliche Zeitschrift der Karl-Marx-Universität Leipzig, 5 (1955–1956): 7–21. Although it is itself not free of omissions, Schönebaum's supersedes the older compilation of Rudolf Kötzschke, "Verzeichnis der Schriften Karl Lamprechts," in Karl Bücher, ed., Worte zum Gedächtnis an Karl Lamprecht (Leipzig, 1916), 13–27.

82. "Zwei Notizen zur ältesten deutschen Geschichte," *Zeitschrift des Bergischen Geschichtsvereins*, 16 (1880): 173–90; "Die ältesten Nachrichten über das Hof- und Dorfsystem, speziell am Niederrhein," *Zeitschrift des Bergischen Geschichtsvereins*, 16 (1880): 191–99; "Fränkische Ansiedelungen und Wanderungen im Rheinland," *Westdeutsche Zeitschrift für Geschichte und Kunst*, 1 (1882): 123ff; "Fränkische Wanderungen und Ansiedlungen im Rheinland," *Zeitschrift des Aachener Geschichtsvereins*, 4 (1882): 189–250; "Recht und Wirtschaft zur Frankenzeit," *Historisches Taschenbuch*, 2 (1882): 43–67, 76–89.

83. Gerlich, 140–67.

84. "Der Bilderschmuck des Codex Egberti zur Trier und des Codex Epternacensis in Gotha," *Jahrbücher des Vereins von Alterthumsfreunden im Rheinland*, 70 (1881): 56–112; "Bilderzyklen und Illustrationstechnik im späteren Mittelalter," *Repertorium für Kunstwissenschaft*, 7 (1883): 405–15; "Verse und Miniaturen aus einer Evangelienhandschrift der Kölner Dombibliothek," *Neues Archiv der Gesellschaft für ältere deutsche Geschichtskunde*, 9 (1883): 620–23.

85. Karl Lamprecht, *Initial-Ornamentik des VIII. bis XIII. Jahrhunderts* (Leipzig, 1882).

86. "Die Entstehung der Willebriefe und die Revindication des Reichsgutes unter Rudolf von Habsburg," *Forschungen zur deutschen Geschichte*, 21 (1881): 1–19; "Zur Vorgeschichte des Consensrechtes der Kurfürsten," *Forschungen zur deutschen Geschichte*, 23 (1883): 63–116.

87. UB Bonn, Autografen-Sammlung, Lamprecht-Richard Pick, Lamprecht to Pick, Bonn, 24.7.82.

88. NL Lamprecht (Korr. 59), Lamprecht to Hugo Lamprecht, Bonn, 14.6.82, 25.11.82, 106.83; LW, 127–28.

89. *Deutsches Wirtschaftsleben im Mittelalter: Untersuchungen über die Entwicklung der materiellen Kultur des platten Landes auf Grund der Quellen. Zunächst des Mosellandes. III: Quellensammlung* (Leipzig, 1885).

90. *Deutsches Wirtschaftsleben im Mittelalter . . . II: Statistisches Material, Quellenkunde* (Leipzig, 1885).

91. *Deutsches Wirschaftsleben im Mittelalter . . . I: Darstellung*, 2 vols. (Leipzig, 1886).

92. NL Schmoller (133), Lamprecht to Schmoller, Bonn, 17.2.88, 12.2.88. See Matti Viikari, *Die Krise der "historistischen" Geschichtsschreibung und die Geschichtsmethodologie Karl Lamprechts* (Helsinki, 1977), 165–207.

93. DWL, 1,2: 1506.

94. NL Lamprecht (Korr. 12), G. Blondel to Lamprecht, Lyon, 19.11.86; (Korr. 24), Gierke to Lamprecht, Heidelberg, 21.11.86; (Korr. 48), H. Soltbeer to Lamprecht, Göttingen, 14.7.88.

95. NL Lamprecht (Korr. 32), Inama-Sternegg to Lamprecht, Vienna, 22.4.86.

96. NL Lamprecht (Korr. 52,1), Waitz to Lamprecht, Berlin, 26.9.85.

97. NL Lamprecht (Korr. 53), Weizsäcker to Lamprecht, Berlin, 16.11.86.

98. NL Lamprecht (Korr. 46), Schmoller to Lamprecht, Berlin, 5.12.86.

99. "Die soziale Entwickelung Deutschlands und Englands hauptsächlich auf dem platten Lande des Mittelalters," *Schmollers Jahrbuch*, 12 (1888): 203–18.

100. JbNöSt, 48 (1887), 526–34; cf. LW, 159–62.

101. DLZ, Nr. 51 (18.12.86): 1833–37; HJb, 8 (1887): 502–19.

102. Georg von Below judged it to be Lamprecht's "most valuable, his really valuable book." *Geschichtsschreibung*, 97.

103. Hermann Aubin, "Aufgaben und Wege der geschichtlichen Landeskunde," in Fried, *Probleme und Methode*, 39; Gerlich, 71–73; Kay Hoffmeister, "Karl Lamprecht: Seine Geschichtstheorie als Ideologie und seine Stellung zum Imperialismus" (Ph.D. Dissertation, Göttingen, 1956), 19–20; cf. Thomas F. X. Noble, *The Republic of St. Peter: The Birth of the Papal State, 680–825* (Philadelphia, 1984), 149.

104. NL Lamprecht (Munich), Ursula Lewald to Rose-Schütz, Bonn, 4.8.1955.

105. NL Lamprecht (M 6), Karl Lamprecht zum Gedächtnis, 23.
106. NL Lamprecht (Korr. 46), Schaefer to Lamprecht, Bonn, 21.6.83; (Korr. 59), Lamprecht to Hugo Lamprecht, Bonn, 10.12.83.
107. Noorden to Maurenbrecher, 17.10.82, 21.3.83, in Noorden, 614–15.
108. Menzel to Sybel, 17.2.85, quoted in P. Hübinger, 133, n. 148.
109. NL Bernheim, Lamprecht to Bernheim, Bonn, 22.6.83; LW, 100–101; NL Lamprecht (Korr. 45), Lamprecht to Ritter, Leipzig, 20.6.92.
110. NL Schmoller, Lamprecht to Schmoller, Bonn, 12.2.88.
111. NL Lamprecht (Korr. 45), Lamprecht to Ritter, 11.10.94.
112. NL Lamprecht (Korr. 59), Lamprecht to Hugo Lamprecht, 22.7.83.
113. NL Althoff (B Nr. 108/1), Lamprecht to Althoff, Bonn, 16.7.84.
114. NL Lamprecht (Korr. 59), Lamprecht to Hugo Lamprecht, 14.10.83.
115. NL Bernheim, Lamprecht to Bernheim, Bonn, 2.8.83; Lewald, "Geschichtsforschung," 290.
116. On Althoff see especially Bernhard vom Brocke, "Hochschul- und Wissenschaftspolitik in Preussen und im Deutschen Kaiserreich 1882–1907: Das 'System Althoff,'" in Peter Baumgart, ed., Bildungspolitik in Preussen zur Zeit des Kaiserreichs (Stuttgart, 1980), 9–118; cf. Arnold Sachse, Friedrich Althoff und sein Werk (Berlin, 1928); K.-H. Manegold, "Das 'Ministerium des Geistes': Zur Organisation des ehemaligen preussischen Kultusministeriums," Die deutsche Berufs- und Fachschule, 63 (1967): 512–24.
117. NL Althoff (A I Nr. 73). The letters in this file contain evaluations of historians that Althoff solicited from other historians.
118. Because they realized that Althoff could install a professor over their objections, faculties took care to discourage his inclination to do so. In 1891 the faculty in Marburg demonstrated one technique. "On the subject of Professor Pflugk-Harttung," Max Lehmann wrote to Althoff, "there reigns an unusual harmony of views, not only among the faculty members here, but . . . also among all my acquaintances: he is a combination of careerist and Yankee, by turns pushy and presumptuous, and despite the endless number of his 'works' he is so uncultivated that he commits, for example, errors in Latin so glaring that they would shame a young schoolboy." GStAM, Rep. 76-VA, Sekt 12, Tit. VII, Lehmann to Althoff, Marburg, 18.1.91. Abschrift. The curator of the university then pleaded in Berlin against the appointment, which, he predicted, would "result in an unholy uproar in academic circles here" and undermine his own effectiveness. Steinmetz to Gossler, Marburg, 7.2.91. Pflugk-Harttung was not appointed.
119. vom Brocke, "System Althoff," 109.
120. Ibid., 104.
121. Ibid., 37.
122. NL Althoff (B Nr. 108/1), Lamprecht to Cuny, Bonn, 13.3.84; Cuny to Althoff, Berlin, 14.4.84; NL Lamprecht (Korr. 36), Meitzen to Lamprecht, Berlin, 13.3.84; NL Schmoller, Lamprecht to Schmoller, Bonn, 27.3.84. It is tempting to think that Mevissen, who knew Althoff, was also involved, but there is no conclusive evidence. Cf. Lewald, "Geschichtsforschung," 292–96; Lewald, "Karl Lamprecht," 236–39; LW, 143–46; Schorn-Schütte, Lamprecht, 52–54.
123. NL Lamprecht (Korr. 17), Cuny to Lamprecht, Berlin, 25.5.84.
124. NL Althoff (B Nr. 196/2), Weizsäcker to Althoff, Berlin, 10.4.84; NL Lamprecht (Munich), Herbert Schönebaum, "Henrich von Treitschke und Karl Lamprecht: Dr. Erich Madsack gewidmet zu seinem 70. Geburtstag am 25. September 1959" (Privatdruck). On Treitschke see also Srbik, 1: 396; Bernhard vom Brocke, Kurt Breysig: Geschichtswissenschaft zwischen Historismus und Soziologie (Lübeck and Hamburg, 1971), 133–41; Georg Iggers, "Heinrich von Treitschke," in Hans-Ulrich

Wehler, ed., *Deutsche Historiker*, 9 vols. (Göttingen, 1972–1981), 2: 76.

125. NL Lamprecht (Korr. 59), Althoff to Lamprecht, Berlin, 10.4.84. Abschrift.
126. UA Bonn, Phil. Fak., Lamprecht to Ritter, Bonn, 10.5.84.
127. UA Bonn, Phil. Fak., Historisches Sektion to PF, Bonn, 25.6.84.
128. NL Lamprecht (Korr. 59), Lamprecht to Hugo Lamprecht, Bonn, 29.6.84; cf. Below, "Below," 14–15. Lamprecht's bitterness was directed primarily at Ritter, whom he called his "fanatical opponent." This charge was unfair. Ritter, who was dean of the faculty at the time, played little role in the deliberations. (Korr. 59), Lamprecht to Hugo Lamprecht, Bonn, 20.7.84.
129. NL Lamprecht (Korr. 3), Althoff to Lamprecht, Berlin, 14.8.84; LW, 146–47.
130. NL Lamprecht (Korr. 59), Lamprecht to Hugo Lamprecht, Bonn, 19.9.84.
131. Carl Arnold Willemsen, "Alfred Dove 1844–1916," in *Bonner Gelehrte*, 254–59; Weber, *Lexikon*, 110–11.
132. NL Lamprecht (Korr. 59), Lamprecht to Hugo Lamprecht, Bonn, 21.12.84; (Korr. 19), Dove to Lamprecht, 22.1.85; NL Althoff (Nr. 30/2), Dove to Althoff, Bonn, 27.1.87; UB Freiburg, NL Alfred Dove, Lamprecht to Dove, Leipzig, 6.6.12.
133. UA Bonn, Phil. Fak., Lamprecht to Schönfeld, Bonn, 3.2.85.
134. Ibid., Schönfeld to Philosophische Fakultät, Bonn, 3.2.85.
135. NL Mevissen, Lamprecht to Mevissen, Bonn, 6.11.86; NL Lamprecht (Korr. 59), Lamprecht to Hugo Lamprecht, Bonn, 10.11.86; LW, 171–72.
136. Cassirer, 267; Below, *Geschichtsschreibung*, 63–84; Gooch, 523–42; Ernst Schaumkell, *Geschichte der deutschen Kulturgeschichtsschreibung* (Leipzig, 1905). See also Rudolf Vierhaus, "Kulturgeschichte," in Klaus Bergmann et al., eds., *Handbuch der Geschichtsdidaktik*, 3d ed. (Düsseldorf, 1985), 187–90; Volker Hartmann, *Die deutsche Kulturgeschichtsschreibung von ihren Anfängen bis W.H. Riehl* (Marburg, 1971); Winfried Schulze, *Soziologie und Geschichtswissenschaft: Einführung in die Probleme der Kooperation beider Wissenschaften* (Munich, 1974), 22–23; Gerhard Ritter, "Zum Begriff der 'Kulturgeschichte,'" HZ, 171 (1951): 293–302.
137. Friedrich Jodl, *Die Culturgeschichtsschreibung: Ihre Entwickelung und ihr Problem* (Halle, 1878).
138. See Srbik, 2: 139–45.
139. NL Lamprecht (M 6), Doren in "Karl Lamprecht zum Gedächtnis," 26; Thomas Nipperdey, "Die anthropologische Dimension der Geschichtswissenschaft," in *Gesellschaft, Kultur, Theorie: Gesammelte Aufsätze zur neueren Geschichte* (Göttingen, 1976), 41.
140. See Srbik, 1: 315–18; Iggers, *German Conception*, 67–69; Weber, *Lexikon*, 345–46.
141. Max Lehmann, "Max Lehmann," in S. Steinberg, 1: 212.
142. Srbik, 1: 318–19; I. Jastrow, "Karl Wilhelm Nitzsch und die deutsche Wirtschaftsgeschichte," *Schmollers Jahrbuch*, 8 (1884): 148–71; Georg Winter, "Die Begründung einer sozialstatistischen Methode in der deutschen Geschichtsschreibung durch Karl Lamprecht," ZKg, 1 (1893–1894), 196–219; Simon, *Staat und Geschichtswissenschaft*, 61–62. See also Bruno Opalka's introduction to Karl Wilhelm Nitzsch, *Geschichte des deutschen Volkes bis zum Augsburger Religionsfrieden* (Stuttgart, 1959), 1: 7–64; Weber, *Lexikon*, 414–15.
143. See Hardtwig, *Burckhardt*; Felix Gilbert, *History: Politics or Culture? Reflections on Ranke and Burckhardt* (Princeton, 1990), 81–92; Srbik, 2: 145–70; Weber, *Lexikon*, 77–79.
144. Srbik, 2: 84–122; cf. Günter Fellner, *Ludo Moritz Hartmann und die österreichische Geschichtswissenschaft: Grundzüge eines paradigmatischen Konfliktes* (Vienna and Salzburg, 1984), esp. 80–99.
145. Srbik, 2: 33–74.
146. Hartmann, *Kulturgeschichtsschreibung*, 87–95.

147. Wolfgang Zorn, "'Volkswirtschaft und Kulturgeschichte' und 'Sozial- und Wirt-schaftsgeschichte': Zwei Zeitschriften in der Vorgeschichte der VSWG 1863–1900," VSWG, 72 (1985): 458–67.
148. Ottokar Lorenz, Die Geschichtswissenschaft in Hauptrichtungen und Aufgaben kritisch erörtert (Berlin, 1886), 178.
149. Jodl, 23; cf. Nipperdey, "Anthropologische Dimension," 41–42.
150. Günter Mann, "Geschichte als Wissenschaft und Wissenschaftsgeschichte bei Du Bois-Reymond," HZ, 213 (1980): 75–100; cf. Lorenz's review of Du Bois-Reymond's article "Kulturgeschichte und Naturwissenschaft": "Die 'bürgerliche' und die naturwissenschaftliche Geschichte," HZ, 39 (1878): 458–85.
151. Jodl, 63–81; Below, Geschichtsschreibung, 82.
152. Quoted in Rüdiger vom Bruch, "Gustav Schmoller," in Notker Hammerstein, ed., Geschichtswissenschaft um 1990 (Stuttgart, 1988), 220.
153. See, in addition to the article of Rüdiger vom Bruch cited above, the same author's "Gustav Schmoller," in Wolfgang Treue and Karlfried Gründer, eds., Berlinische Lebensbilder: Wissenschaftspolitik in Berlin. Minister, Beamte, Ratgeber (Berlin, 1987), 175–93; Karl Heinrich Kaufhold, "Gustav von Schmoller (1838–1917) als Histo-riker, Wirtschafts- und Sozialpolitiker und Nationalökonom," VSWG, 75 (1988): 217–52; Carl Brinckmann, Gustav Schmoller und die Volkswirtschaftslehre (Stuttgart, 1937); Otto Hintze, "Gustav von Schmoller," Deutsches Biographisches Jahrbuch (1917–1920), 124–34; Fritz Hartung, "Gustav von Schmoller und die preussische Geschichtsschreibung," Schmollers Jahrbuch (1938): 277–302.
154. Dieter Lindenlaub, Richtungskämpfe im Verein für Sozialpolitik: Wissenschaft und Sozialpolitik im Kaiserreich vornehmlich vom Beginn des "neuen Kurses" bis zum Aus-bruch des ersten Weltkrieges (1890–1914) (Wiesbaden, 1967), 96–106; Gerhard Ritzel, "Schmoller versus Menger: Eine Analyse des Methodenstreits im Hinblick auf den Historismus in der Nationalökonomie," Ph.D. dissertation (Basel, 1950).
155. Quoted in Bruch, "Schmoller" (in Treue), 187.
156. Ibid., 183; Below, "Zur Würdigung," 221–37; Winkel, 177–78.
157. See Theodore M. Porter, "Lawless Society: Social Science and the Reinterpreta-tion of Statistics in Germany, 1850–1880," in Lorenz Krüger et al., eds., The Probabilistic Revolution, 2 vols. (Cambridge, MA, 1987), 1: 351–76.
158. Quoted in Kaufhold, 225.
159. Gerhard Oestreich, "Die Fachhistorie und die Anfänge der sozialgeschichtlichen Forschung in Deutschland," HZ, 208 (1969): 320–63.
160. "Die wirtschaftsgeschichtlichen Studien in Deutschland im Jahre 1883," JbNöSt, 43 (1884): 113–77; "Die wirtschaftsgeschichtlichen Studien in Deutschland im Jahre 1884," ibid., 45 (1885): 313–88.
161. NL Lamprecht (Korr. 14), Bücher to Lamprecht, Basel, 10.1.89; (Korr. 13), Lujo Brentano to Lamprecht, Strassburg, 27.6.86.
162. NL Lamprecht (Korr. 31), Hoeniger to Lamprecht, Berlin, 8.3.85; (Korr. 32), Jastrow to Lamprecht, Berlin, 22.2.90; (Korr. 35), Liesegang to Lamprecht, Berlin, 6.1.90; cf. Lindenlaub, 132–34.
163. NL Lamprecht (Korr. 59), Lamprecht to Hugo Lamprecht, Pforta, 11.3.74; NL Bernheim, Lamprecht to Bernheim, Munich, 22.6.78; UA Bonn, Phil. Fak., Lamprecht to PF, Bonn, 19.4.80.
164. NL Althoff (B Nr. 108/1), Lamprecht to Cuny, Bonn, 13.3.84. "I am convinced that he is very qualified to do Kulturgeschichte," Meitzen wrote to Althoff at the end of 1884, "and that he is broadly [mehrseitig] qualified by virtue of the serious studies he has undertaken." NL Althoff (B Nr. 129/2), Meitzen to Althoff, Berlin, 1911.
165. vom Brocke, "System Althoff," 82–83; Brinckmann, 115.
166. NL Lamprecht (Korr. 59), Lamprecht to Hugo Lamprecht, Bonn, 30.5.86.
167. KE, 38, 61–62.

168. NL Lamprecht (L 3a), Gneisse, Erinnerungen eines Mitschülers aus Karl Lamprechts Pfortazeit, Colmar, 17.9.15; *cf.* Albisetti, 54–55.

169. NL Lamprecht (Korr. 59), Lamprecht to Hugo Lamprecht, Bonn, 14.11.80. "[M]an wird, nun den Berliner Ausdruck anzuwenden, angeschnuppert."

170. NL Lamprecht (Korr. 59), Lamprecht to Hugo Lamprecht, Pforta, 3–4.2.74; Göttingen, 3.1.75.

171. NL Lamprecht (Korr. 59), Lamprecht to Emilie and Hugo Lamprecht, Bonn, 22.7.82.

172. NL Lamprecht (Korr. 59), Lamprecht to Emilie Lamprecht, Bonn, 26.7.82; NL Lamprecht (Munich), Ursula Lewald to Rose-Schütz, Bonn, 14.4.57.

173. NL Lamprecht (Korr. 59), Karl Lamprecht to Hugo Lamprecht, Bonn, 8.8.86.

174. DG, 11: 582.

175. NL Lamprecht (Korr. 59), Lamprecht to Hugo Lamprecht, Herrenalb, 4.9.86.

176. NL Lamprecht (Korr. 59), Lamprecht to Hugo Lamprecht, Herrenalb, 7.9.86.

177. Josef Bleuler, *Dementia Praecox oder die Gruppe der Schizophrenien* (Leipzig, 1911). See Jules R. Bemporad and Henry Pinsker, "Schizophrenia: The Manifest Symptomology," in Arieti, *Handbook of Psychiatry*, 3: 524–39.

178. NL Lamprecht (Korr. 59), Lamprecht to Hugo Lamprecht, Bonn, 9.10.86–9.4.87.

179. NL Lamprecht (Korr. 59), Lamprecht to Hugo Lamprecht, Bonn, 4.12.86, 13.12.86, 5.4.87. It is tempting to speculate that the historian must have been aware at some preconscious level of a grave problem in the woman he was courting. I shall not indulge this temptation beyond noting Otto Kernberg's conclusion that adults with narcissistic disorders frequently seek out relationships with persons who have strong dependencies. Kernberg, "Pathological Narcissism in Middle Age," 135–54.

180. BA, NL Walter Goetz (36), Lamprecht to Ritter, Leipzig, 5.1.13; NL Lamprecht (Korr. 19), Dove to Lamprecht, Bonn, 14.5.90.

181. NL Lamprecht (Korr. 59), Lamprecht to Hugo Lamprecht, Bonn, 13.5.88.

182. *Skizzen zur rheinischen Geschichte* (Leipzig, 1887); Karl Menzel et al., eds., *Die Trierer Adahandschrift* (Leipzig, 1889).

183. NL Lamprecht (Korr. 59), Lamprecht to Hugo Lamprecht, Bonn, 10.6.83.

184. NL Lamprecht (Korr. 59), Lamprecht to Hugo Lamprecht, Bonn, 6.3.87; LW, 181–82.

185. NL Mevissen, Lamprecht to Mevissen, Bonn, 15.5.88; NL Althoff (Nr. 30/2), Dove to Althoff, Bonn, 27.1.87; NL Lamprecht (Korr. 59), Lamprecht to Hugo Lamprecht, Bonn, 18.7.88; LW, 187.

186. NL Althoff (Nr. 30/2), Dove to Althoff, Bonn, 27.1.87.

187. NL Lamprecht (Korr. 3), Althoff to Lamprecht, Berlin, 31.12.88; (Korr. 59), Lamprecht to Hugo Lamprecht, Bonn, 17.2.89; UA Bonn, Kuratorium (IV E IIc80, 1 I), Gossler to Gandtner, Berlin, 15.1.89.

188. UA Bonn, Kuratorium (IV E IIc80, 1 I), Gossler to Gandtner, Berlin, 26.9.89.

189. GStAM, Rep. 76–VA, Sekt. 12 Tit. VII, Niese to Steinmetz, Marburg, 18.1.90; Althoff to Lamprecht, Berlin, 21.1.90; LW, 204.

Part II
The Destruction of
the Historian

4

German History (Prise)

Dies ist ein Gleichnis für jeden einzelnen von uns: er muss
das Chaos in sich organisieren, dadurch, dass er sich auf
seine echten Bedürfnisse zurückbesinnt.

It is tempting to portray Karl Lamprecht as a tragic hero. The elements of his
early biography fit easily into the schema: a difficult childhood surmounted in
dedication to learning; a challenge to the reigning norms of the discipline; drive
and ambition rewarded in achievement, acclaim, and recognition as a leading
force in the profession. The next phase of the story can with little difficulty be
presented as the vengeful destruction of the hero at the hands of those whose
conceptions he had challenged. Compelling as the theme of tragic heroism
seems, the verdict on its suitability is best withheld, for there are aspects of the
story that do not fit well. Here, though, it is useful to hold onto the theme at
least long enough to confront a problem which so far has received only passing
attention. Moriz Ritter once referred to it as the "dark sides [*Schattenseiten*] of
Lamprecht's scholarship [*Arbeitsweise*]."[1] One might as well call it the hero's
tragic flaw.

Karl Lamprecht's impulsive energies were not disciplined by patience, caution, or a disposition to self-criticism. The capaciousness of his intellectual grasp
was extraordinary, as was the speed at which he assimilated enormous amounts
of material. But the signs of carelessness and haste that marred his early
scholarship betrayed the price he paid. The problems surfaced persistently at
several levels in his work. A few examples can suffice. The short book he
published in 1882, on the ornamentation of initial letters in medieval manuscripts, revealed several kinds of flaws. The book comprised a short essay,
followed by a collection of drawings to illustrate the essay and a register of the
manuscripts from which the illustrations were drawn. In a number of instances,
the dates the historian assigned to the drawings simply did not correspond to the
dates he assigned to the manuscripts in the register. These discrepancies were
annoying symptoms of the author's haste; more serious were the analytical
problems in the text itself. Here Lamprecht provided an imaginative commentary on the ornamentation of artefacts and manuscripts from three different

epochs. On the basis of this commentary, he ventured conclusions about the evolution of collective aesthetic tastes over the course of a millennium. The leap from the particular to the general was breathtaking, but, as one critic pointed out, it was baseless. It breezed over every intermediate level of analysis—even the effort to establish the representativeness or commensurability of the objects being compared; the historian's selection of artefacts and manuscripts was arbitrary and took no notice of paleographic particulars that might have associated the manuscripts with a specific illuminator, school, or scribal tradition at a specific time.[2]

This criticism spoke to a grave failing, which one might characterize as chronic analytical impatience. Its roots were temperamental. The historian's instinctual preferences were to collect masses of material and to surround them hastily by means of broad generalizations, as if the very mass of the material justified a high level of abstraction. For errant details that evaded his theories he had no patience, nor was he sympathetic to the need to reconcile inconsistency, assimilate nuance, and integrate material on intermediate levels of generalization. Georg von Below had these preferences in mind when he once quipped about Lamprecht's ability "immediately to support an error with a theory."[3]

Even Lamprecht's best work suffered from the hurried pace of its preparation. The fact that *Economic Life in the Middle Ages* was a huge, unwieldy study was due only in part to the immensity of the topic; it was due as well to the author's failure to digest and consolidate the masses of material he had brought together. But the fundamental flaw in this work reflected the historian's understanding of regional history. His insistence that regional history be oriented toward larger issues was supposed to overcome the parochialism of the genre; in fact, to Lamprecht the appeal of this orientation was the analytical shortcut it seemed to offer to a high level of abstraction. In a remarkable passage in the *Economic Life*, he explained that the object of his study was to study "specific developments" in the history of material culture "in a specific area." The specificity of context would not, however, limit the general validity of the study's conclusions because, he continued, "the design of the study" was to be arranged so that "in the sequence of the specific accounts, at least those main developmental stages are highlighted whose existence a subsequent, pure, historical account would have to [!] posit."[4] Here the historian simply eliminated the transition from the particular to the general by positing the identity of the two; he assumed that the general was present in the particular and that the particular served not as the basis for the inductive approach to the general, but rather merely as illustration for general propositions whose validity was (somehow) already established. Regional diversity was irrelevant or incidental, primarily a question of asynchronism (or what would today be called uneven development).[5]

Lamprecht's careless use of the language abetted his hurried excursions to high levels of abstraction. His language, too, was capacious, in the sense that he employed words less to designate or specify things than to surround or contain them; modifiers brought substantives into their thrall simply by being close to them. The essay on individuality spoke of "most individually developed [durchgebildeten] contemporaries" and "physiological tribal feelings."[6] Lamprecht's language was inventive but sloppy; and he often took refuge in neologisms or foreign words to relieve himself of the demands of precision. The resulting ambiguities then masked the porosity, if not the untenability, of his generalizations.

Lamprecht's early prose also abounded in words whose function was to negate, reverse, or qualify a train of thought. The category included not only conjunctions like "but" (in German: aber, allein, doch), which signaled a direct assault on the sense of a foregoing clause, but words that implied more subtle reservations, like "nevertheless," "still," "though," and "admittedly" (his favorites: freilich, zwar, indes). Their profusion testified to the historian's determination to retain generalizations in the face of details that threatened to invalidate them. In the essay on individuality he cited the phenomenon of popular mysticism in the late Middle Ages as an aspect of that era's heightened individuality. The proposition raised an obvious problem. "It is clear," he conceded, mysticism "wants in the last analysis the extinction [Ertödtung] of individuality for the purpose of a complete rapturous merging with God." "But," he continued in a labored attempt to salvage his general proposition, what mysticism "certainly achieved was the strongest conceivable orientation to the uniqueness, the subjective moral as well as intellectual capacities of every human being."[7]

As this example suggested, Lamprecht's careless use of language created special problems in his construction of analogies. This student of Roscher inherited his mentor's confidence that analogies documented essential similarities and that they could be used to trace patterns of historical development. Like Roscher, he believed that analogies represented building blocks of inductive logic, but he failed to subject them to critical examination, to test whether their elements bore any analytical relationship to one another beyond some intuited resemblance.[8] He was blind to the danger that they could be merely the capricious products of his own linguistic inventiveness. And since he contrived analogies hastily as well, they frequently served only to sow confusion. The essay on individuality, of which even the historian's most loyal admirer has noted that "boldness surpassed conclusiveness," again provides a case in point.[9] The nature of this essay's subject, individuality, was never clear. The analogies with which Lamprecht traced the manifestations of individuality in distinct cultural spheres rested on a singular imprecision of language, as he referred interchangeably and with no evident regard for context to "individuality" (Individualität), "individual" (Individuum), "individualization" (Individualisierung), "individual life" (Einzelleben), "self-consciousness" (Selbstbewusstsein), "personality," "character," and "subjectivity." His penchant for reifying all these concepts in contorted metaphors only made matters worse. One passage illustrates the difficulty. Its subject is fifteenth century works of art:

. . . their content points to an epoch of uncommonly strengthened personality. . . . The right of individuality is won and it [individuality] moves freely still in self-imposed bounds; personality has not yet absolutely arrived; it does not yet intrude into the open, it still wants only to count as such [as personality].[10]

These problems all grew out of the same temperamental proclivity. Lamprecht's restless energies were directed outward, beyond the bounds of the orthodox, toward appropriating the new or unknown, and experimenting with the untried. Whatever he had intellectually appropriated soon exhausted his interest. Repetition, correction, consolidation, and refinement taxed his patience. Convention and routine bored him. His enthusiasm for both the Society for the Study of Rhenish History and the *Westdeutsche Zeitschrift* waned rapidly once the novelty of the undertaking gave way to routine.[11] He tired of even his own thoughts once he had committed them to paper. He complained of having to deliver the same lecture more than once; and his lectures frequently underwent substantial changes even as he delivered them.[12] When he wrote for publication, on the other hand, he rarely made more than superficial revisions in his initial drafts before he rushed them to the publisher.[13]

The historian's impulsiveness first led to tragic consequences in the summer of 1886. The private tragedy of his marriage was not an irrelevant factor in the public tragedy that he experienced several years later. Whether or not he anticipated or desired much intellectual dialogue in his marriage, the emotional collapse of his wife deprived him of the intimate company of another adult and encouraged his self-absorption.[14] His reaction to his wife's ordeal was to seek refuge in work, at his father's desk, where his temperamental inclinations were amplified. His energies became increasingly furious and resistant to discipline, as the need to cope helped turn what he described as the "loyal enthusiasm of the author for his material" into an obsession.[15]

Lamprecht's difficulties remained under control when he was in Bonn. For one thing, uncertainty over the nature and seriousness of his wife's disorder did not yet preclude optimism. For another, he remained in the proximity of two elder colleagues, Ritter and Dove, who urged patience, restraint, clarity, and concentration on him.[16] He did not accept their criticism graciously, but it was no coincidence that he produced his best scholarship at a time when he felt pressure to abide by their counsel. His departure removed all the constraints. "So all the knots are untied," was Dove's reaction when he learned of Lamprecht's appointment in Marburg, "and from now on you are your own man in every respect."[17] There was more than a hint of irony in Dove's remark, for he knew Lamprecht well enough to foresee what might happen; but for better or worse, Karl Lamprecht was now free to follow his own inclinations.

Mevissen was sad to see Lamprecht leave the Rhineland for Marburg, but his congratulations emphasized the obvious significance of the move. "With this appointment you have reached the next goal in your well-founded aspirations, and you have won a life in a secure position from which you can with peace of mind wait to see where the paths of life and your own achievements will carry you."[18] Lamprecht appeared to have reached a plateau in a remarkable career. At thirty-three he was the youngest *Ordinarius* for history in Germany, and there was much to suggest that he would become a major force in the profession.

Marburg fell into the notorious category of the small provincial university when Lamprecht received his call. Its enrollment was only about 700 students.[19] Apart from the tranquil charm of the area and a reasonable cost of living, Marburg's principal advantage, from Lamprecht's perspective, was its proximity to the Rhineland, where he had sunk emotional and professional roots.[20] He resigned from the board of directors of the Society for the Study of Rhenish History; but he remained involved in the affairs of that organization, including several of its editorial projects. He also retained his position with the *Westdeutsche Zeitschrift*.[21]

The historical seminar in Marburg, where Lamprecht's appointment was to a chair in medieval history, was smaller than in Bonn.[22] Benedictus Niese was the ancient historian. The chair for modern history was occupied by one of the profession's more interesting figures. Max Lehmann had trained with Ranke, Droysen, and Jaffé in Berlin.[23] In 1875 Sybel installed him in the Prussian state archive, as well as in the editorial offices of the *Historische Zeitschrift*, where he served until his call to Marburg in 1888, when he was forty-three. In the meantime he published a biography of Gerhard Scharnhorst that is to this day unsurpassed. Meinecke, whose early career was a replica of Lehmann's, once described him as a "bundle of nerves in a slender, snake-like figure."[24] Meinecke also used the word "leonine" (*löwenhaft*) to describe Lehmann's moralism, which was rigid, easily irritated to passion, and involved him in several public disputes with his colleagues. Lamprecht had good reason to be anxious about his relations with him, for the two scholars had already quarreled over Lamprecht's demand to respond to articles critical of him in the *Historische Zeitschrift*.[25] In the event, Lehmann was an accommodating colleague, and if he harbored resentments over the way Althoff's protégé stormed the seminar and attracted students, he hid them well.[26] As a gesture of conciliation, Lehmann opened the *Historische Zeitschrift* to Lamprecht, who in 1891 published an essay in social history, on the origins of the German urban middle class in the fourteenth and fifteenth centuries.[27]

Lamprecht's wife did not accompany him to Marburg. Within days of his receiving the call, the birth of a second daughter brought on a breakdown that resulted in the woman's institutionalization.[28] The two children arrived in Marburg later in the spring, along with a governess. The absence of their mother cast a shadow over a situation that seemed otherwise, as Lamprecht described it to his brother, "as good for a young *Ordinarius* as could possibly be imagined." His colleagues' solicitude over his personal difficulties was touching, but more gratifying was the realization that elevation to a chair had brought more authority, respect, and independence than he had ever known and that his status entitled him to acceptance as an equal among his colleagues. "I can say that I feel more at ease than in Bonn," he continued. "A lot of it admittedly has to do with the independence I have achieved, which has to boot brought me straight away onto a fairly high level in the historical profession." And he added, with a sense of surprised relief, that he relished his independence all the more because Lehmann was "obliging enough to let me enjoy it entirely."[29] Lamprecht had little time to enjoy his situation in Marburg, however, for his sojourn there was little more than an interlude. Within months of his arrival, he arrived on yet a higher level in the profession.

Lamprecht's appointment in Marburg was part of one of the periodic reshufflings among holders of university chairs occasioned by retirements, deaths, or other circumstances. Lamprecht's entry into this circle of *Ordinarien* was made possible when Hermann Baumgarten in Strassburg left it, to be replaced by Varrentrapp from Marburg. From the perspective of young instructors on the perimeter of the circle, these sometimes convulsive realignments were welcome spectacles, and in 1890–1891 there was much to watch. Dove decided to leave Bonn and return to journalism as an editor of the *Münchner Allgemeine Zeitung*; two additional vacancies appeared in Berlin with the death of Weizsäcker and the creation of a new chair, while in Leipzig the declining health of Georg Voigt opened still another. The situation in Bonn was quickly resolved when Reinhold Koser, who had been an extraordinary professor in Berlin, accepted the chair, as Lamprecht's former colleagues signaled that they did not want him back.

Lamprecht was soon caught up, however, in the flux created by two of the other vacancies. The new chair in Berlin went to Max Lenz, who had taught in Breslau; Lenz's successor in Breslau was Goswin Freiherr von der Ropp, who had taught in Giessen. With the chair in Giessen now open, Ropp and his colleague in Giessen, Wilhelm Oncken, approached Lamprecht, who refused the overture in the calculation that the position did not represent a significant enough step forward to justify another move so soon.[30]

The offer that arrived in December 1890 was too tempting to refuse. The moving force behind the call to succeed Voigt in Leipzig was Lamprecht's former colleague in Bonn, Wilhelm Maurenbrecher, who had been at the Saxon university since 1884. Whatever doubts Maurenbrecher might once have had about Lamprecht's work had by now disappeared. In his report to the search committee in Leipzig in November 1890, Maurenbrecher dismissed the "isolated mistakes and precipitous conclusions" in Lamprecht's early work and stressed instead his "extraordinary energy and his acuity of vision, which always penetrates to the heart of problems," as well as his demonstrated success in the classroom.[31] Other members of the committee, including Lamprecht's *Doktorvater* Roscher, leaned toward Eberhard Gothein, despite the argument that Gothein was really an economist and that Lamprecht was the broader scholar.[32] Maurenbrecher, the faculty member with the most immediate interest in the appointment, overpowered the opposition; the faculty placed Lamprecht, whom

it characterized as a "unique scholarly personality," at the top of the list.[33] On
the day before Christmas the offer went to Marburg. Althoff, although disappointed to see the historian leave Prussian service, put up no resistance; and
Lamprecht, who hardly exaggerated when he spoke of a "colossal career move,"
accepted immediately.[34]

The city to which Lamprecht returned in April 1891 had, like its university,
changed dramatically since he left it thirteen years earlier.[35] Leipzig's population
had almost trebled, although its growth was abetted by the incorporation of
surrounding communities; in the remaining ten years of the century the number
of inhabitants nearly doubled again. The city remained the commercial hub of
central Germany, as well as the center of German printing and publishing; but it
had grown into an industrial metropolis around a core of metal processing,
engineering, and electro-technical firms. The city center, including much of the
university, had been rebuilt in the 1880s and early 1890s.

The university's enrollment had grown, too, to over 3,000 students, although
there were now fewer students in Leipzig than in Berlin or Munich.[36] Nonetheless, the university in Leipzig was then basking in "its greatest splendor," as
the economist Lujo Brentano recalled; and its reputation as a center of
learning was second only to Berlin's.[37] One of the faculty's great strengths lay in
medicine. Another was in the natural and social sciences, where the university's
reputation rested not only on the work of individual scholars, like the chemist
Wilhelm Ostwald and the geographer Friedrich Ratzel, but on an uncommon
spirit of intellectual exchange, which marked the efforts of a number of these
scholars to link the natural and social sciences in a common methodology.
Roscher, whose chair Brentano briefly occupied, had been one of the leaders in
these efforts before his retirement in 1889; but by the time of Lamprecht's arrival
in Leipzig, the most renowned figure was Wilhelm Wundt, whose laboratory
had established Leipzig as the leading center of experimental psychology in
the world.

"I have taken care of my 238 visits, presented my card in my inaugural
lecture, and have thus been received," the historian reported to Mevissen
shortly after settling in Leipzig. "These formalities have fortunately given me the
impression, though, that I am gladly accepted here and that I fit in."[38] It helped
that Lamprecht knew many of his new colleagues from his student days. Apart
from his old ties to the historians and to Roscher (who, despite his role on the
search committee, was not sorry to see his student return), close relationships
developed immediately with Wundt and the geographer Ratzel, two scholars of
broad intellectual range who were intrigued by the project taking shape in
Lamprecht's mind.[39] Other colleagues found him in their audiences as an
auditor when they lectured.[40] His visibility in the faculty thus rose rapidly during his first years in Leipzig. He served on search committees for a Germanist,
an art historian to succeed Springer, and two economists, one of whom was
Karl Bücher.[41]

Lamprecht's stature grew as well on the peripheries of university life in Leipzig. From Mevissen he had learned the academic advantages of cultivating contacts outside the academy, and the traditions of the university in Leipzig encouraged interaction with the civic and business elites in that city and in Dresden, the capital of the kingdom. The historian became a frequent speaker before businessmen's organizations. He also ingratiated himself with the king, who was an amateur historian—"half-*historicus*," Lamprecht called him—of some accomplishment.[42] And in 1892 the historian was named a member of both the Saxon Academy of Sciences and the Royal Jablonowski Society of Sciences, an organization that attempted to promote German-Polish understanding by sponsoring an annual essay competition.[43]

In the historical seminar Lamprecht quickly became a dominant force. He was appointed to be codirector of the seminar along with Maurenbrecher, in the understanding that his primary teaching responsibilities would lie in the Middle Ages. The other members of the seminar were the ancient historian Curt Wachsmuth, with whom Lamprecht had studied in Göttingen, and another of Lamprecht's acquaintances from his student days, Wilhelm Arndt, a sorry but not atypical figure who, now at the age of fifty-two, had been waiting for a chair for fifteen years while teaching the *Hilfswissenschaften* in Leipzig as extraordinary professor.[44] Maurenbrecher was accustomed to ruling with a heavy hand, and for the sake of domestic peace it was probably fortunate that his health began to fail soon after Lamprecht's arrival. Lamprecht had strong ideas about the organization of a seminar, and if his short stay in Marburg had prevented his instituting changes at that university, he was determined to put his ideas into practice in Leipzig.

The historical seminar in Leipzig, which Noorden had founded in 1877, was, like historical seminars at other German universities, the narrow and exclusive preserve of the chair holders. Its function was to train a select group of doctoral students in the methodologies of source criticism. Instructors and extraordinary professors who were habilitated at the university were normally required to offer their lectures and exercises outside the seminar. Lamprecht, who had endured the slights and constraints of this system in Bonn, proposed to broaden the seminar by incorporating all the instructors and turning it into a center for all those who wished to study history at the university. The first phase of these reforms was complete within a year, and its beneficiaries were the corps of *ausserordentliche* professors, which included (in addition to Arndt), Wilhelm Busch, Georg Erler, and Felician Gess. Henceforth they were allowed not only to hold their own classes within the framework of the seminar, but to participate in the planning of each year's offerings. Lamprecht also moved to coordinate these offerings in response to students' needs, to increase the weight of cultural history in the curriculum as well as in the seminar's library, to make study space available in the seminar for all students of history, and to provide them with advice and supervision.[45] The significance of these reforms can be judged from the testimony of Walter Goetz, who had completed his doctorate in Leipzig in

1890 but returned to habilitate several years later, after Lamprecht's arrival. "Never before at any German university," he recalled of the reformed seminar he found, "was the student of history offered, so rich and systematically organized, so exhaustive a selection of lectures and tutorials."[46] The growing enrollments in the seminar suggested that students appreciated what they were offered.

The reform of the seminar required a good deal of perseverance. The historian soon learned, as he noted to Mevissen, that "the path does not lead over roses."[47] Maurenbrecher's opposition to the dilution of his domain with junior faculty was foreseeable; more surprising was the restiveness of the younger instructors themselves, who were less impressed with the benefits than the burdens of Lamprecht's reforms, particularly once he began to advocate opening history courses to students from all faculties.

One obstacle to reform disappeared late in November 1892, when Maurenbrecher died. Lamprecht was now undisputed leader in the seminar, and he first exercised his power by persuading the faculty to bring Lehmann to Leipzig from Marburg to succeed Maurenbrecher; Lamprecht also persuaded Althoff to let Lehmann leave Prussia and Lehmann himself to accept the call.[48] It is not certain whether Lamprecht acted out of affection for his former colleague or in an attempt to be open-minded with those who differed with him. In all events, bringing Lehmann to Leipzig created a stir in the profession. For all his eccentricities, Lehmann was one of the leading representatives of the dominant school of political history; and at the time of his departure for Leipzig, the political historians were preparing to do battle with the aggressive variety of cultural history that had become associated with Lamprecht.

Lamprecht's private ordeal continued, meanwhile, toward a resolution of sorts. As he exchanged residence in Marburg for quarters in the Thomasstrasse in the center of Leipzig, his wife wandered through a series of institutions, where she underwent a series of conflicting diagnoses, until she arrived in the fall of 1891 in an asylum near Leipzig, at the resort of Kösen. Here the doctors assured the historian that his wife's condition was far from hopeless, that she was suffering from nervous *désequilibrium* (a condition, they noted, more frequently encountered in France), that her episodes of paranoia had resulted from taking the wrong medication (sulfanol), and that with the aid of their own continuing supervision and a strong diet of fats, she might well recover.[49] At first, developments seemed to justify Lamprecht's relief and renewed optimism. By the fall of 1892 his wife had recovered sufficiently to rejoin her family in Leipzig. But the joy was short-lived. Within days the delusionary episodes returned; and early in 1893 Mathilde Lamprecht returned to the asylum. "I don't need to tell you what I have suffered," the historian wrote to his brother in the aftermath. "It is frightful, and I am no longer able to deal with new blows the way I could with the earlier ones."[50] In the event, he now became more skeptical of the doctors' cheerful prognoses and settled into a routine of visiting his wife on weekends, as he suffered through "the eternal ups and downs" with which the psychosis took its course.[51]

Karl Lamprecht lived the rest of his life, for all intents and purposes, as a bachelor father. His daughters were the focus of his private emotions, while the prospect of adding to his wife's misfortune precluded any thought of terminating the marriage.[52] Instead, he found another woman to anchor a reconstituted family. Emma Bruch, a thirty-eight-year-old friend of his wife from Strassburg, entered Lamprecht's employ in 1892 as another in a series of housekeepers and governesses. She remained for the rest of the historian's life, the surrogate mother to his children, a capable head of the household, and eventually a trusted friend. If her relationship with him ever exceeded these bounds, the two hid the fact with masterful discretion.[53] There is every reason to believe, however, that once he left the Rhineland in 1890, the historian was wedded exclusively to the great project that he had begun there.

"Some six years of the most strenuous work now lie behind me," read the message with which Lamprecht presented the final volumes of his *Economic Life* to Deichmann in 1886. This work would, he hoped, represent "a sufficient technical foundation for my life's project [*Lebensaufgabe*], a history of German culture."[54] The historian's plans to write a comprehensive cultural history originally took shape during his days as a student in Munich; and the regional studies he undertook in the Rhineland were as much a diversion as they were preparation. In 1882 he received a tempting offer to write a cultural history of the German Middle Ages, in which the emphasis was to fall on the interaction of real and ideal culture. The publisher, who well recognized the popular appeal of this genre and feared being preempted in the market, pushed Lamprecht to write it immediately, however, and the historian, who was busy on other projects, eventually backed out.[55] In fact, Lamprecht hoped initially that the *Economic Life* would itself present just such a cultural history, but the enormity of the material that he had gathered forced him to forego systematic treatment of the ideal realm in the study he completed in 1886.

This failing he began to repair as quickly as the emotional turmoil of his engagement and marriage would allow (or require). By the fall of 1887 he had begun the preliminary planning for a cultural history of Germany, and the project became his principal professional occupation during his last years in the Rhineland.[56]

The challenge he faced was to expand the already broad concept of the *Economic Life* in three directions.[57] The scope of historical study was to be enlarged geographically, topically, and chronologically. Lamprecht was least troubled by the first of these dimensions, by the problem of encompassing all of Germany in his account. Because he assumed that regional history represented national history in microcosm and that his extensive encounter with local particulars had already oriented him sufficiently to general themes, the historian of the Rhineland could confidently aspire to be the historian of all Germany.

On the strength of his earlier work, Lamprecht was also comfortable in treating the history of material culture—the realm that he understood to comprise the circumstances imposed by nature, demography, economics, social structure, and law—as well as the tie between material culture and political development. His attention now focused on what he called the "parallel development of mental [geistige] circumstances" or the realm of ideal culture.[58] This realm he understood to comprise an intellectual, ethical, and aesthetic dimension. His object was to define links among these dimensions, as well as between them and the various dimensions of material culture.

Enlarging the geographical and topical scope of historical study in this way increased the burdens of synchronous analysis. Enlarging the chronological scope to include the entire span of German history, from the tribal era to his own day, raised problems of diachronous analysis that the historian had not systematically confronted before. He had these problems in mind when he wrote early in 1888 to Schmoller of the "great virtues of cultural history" and specified, in a telling expression, the insight it offered into "chronological bounding [zeitliche Abgrenzung]."[59] The question of periodization had been peripheral in his large study of the Middle Ages; he had been content to employ a standard schema of the German historical economists, which stressed the transition from a natural to a money economy in the late Middle Ages. In the new project, however, the great chronological expanses seemed to require a more comprehensive framework for defining the essential stages through which historical development passed.

Periodization emerged in fact as the crux of the whole undertaking once the historian concluded that the definition of historical periods held the key to both synchronous and diachronous analysis. These periods, he concluded, not only bounded the essential chronological units that gave pattern and meaning to development; they also defined essential commonalities that stretched across and unified all dimensions of human existence at any given moment of historical development. Periodization thus offered the cultural historian the tools to integrate vast amounts of material and to overcome the analytical incoherence that had earned cultural history the label "archaeology of bric-a-brac."[60] Periodization would provide, as Lamprecht put it in a criticism of one product of this genre, "an organic way to conceptualize German historical development," and to solve "the problem of the reciprocal impact of ideal and material culture."[61]

Paradoxically, in view of the great controversy his work soon provoked, the methodology that Lamprecht adopted in planning this immense undertaking was entirely unsystematic. Its assumptions were unexamined, and the possibility of its broader applicability did not at the time occur to him. The methodology took shape electically, as the historian confronted the specific problems he had set himself. He began only with two working premises, one of which he regarded as the methodological legacy of Ranke, the other of Roscher. The first was a hostility to theory. He insisted that speculation, deduction, and all metaphysics be banished from the study of history, that induction from the particulars, as these were preserved in original sources, was the only valid procedure for framing conclusions about the meaning of history.[62] Nor did Lamprecht believe that his second premise violated the first. Like Roscher, he held that analogy was the historian's principal tool for relating the particulars of the past to one another and for building general conclusions. Analogies enabled the historian to reach across the diverse realms of human behavior in history, to construct parallels, similarities, and contrasts among different cultures and epochs, and hence to descry intrinsic patterns of historical development.[63]

The deficiency of Lamprecht's capacity for self-criticism was nowhere more evident than in the regularity with which he violated his own premises. This violation was perhaps the most systematic feature of his methodology. His abuse of analogy and his impatience with induction have already been cited. However unsystematic or unspoken his methodological assumptions, they were based on audacious speculation and a variety of theoretical propositions that reflected the influences that the historian had assimilated since his student days.

The specific imprint of these influences in his work is difficult to reconstruct. Part of the difficulty lies in the extraordinary range of his reading; little scholarship of consequence in history, art history, social theory, or economics escaped his attention. But another part of the difficulty was temperamental. He read voraciously but unsystematically. He appropriated ideas and theories rapidly and aggressively, whenever and wherever he found them useful, without much respect for the identity or integrity of his sources. Whatever interested him, one of his friends observed, he "assimilated in a flash [*blitzschnell*]" and "submerged [it] in the never completely calm waves of his principles [*wissenschaftliche Ueberzeugungen*]."[64] In his haste, he took little notice of the intellectual contexts in which ideas were set, nor, for that matter, was he interested or well trained in analyzing systematically the ideas of other people. As a consequence, he was able to gather up an extraordinary mélange of ideas that coexisted unstably in his capacious grasp. Traces of them are easily identified, for they surfaced throughout his magnum opus amid the waves of his principles, in various mutations and orders of priority, often as truncated fragments of theories or intellectual systems whose postulates clashed.

Pursuing these traces in Lamprecht's work would be an exhausting and probably futile undertaking; it would result in a long list.[65] It suffices to emphasize that his methodology was anchored in theories associated with two different philosophical traditions. The impulse in his quest for historical unities came from the synthetic, organic strain of German historicism, which had descended from Spinoza, Leibniz, Herder, Hegel, and the German romantics to the writings of the early cultural historians, where it resisted the specialization that the academics were imposing on the discipline of history. Lamprecht's exposure to this tradition came principally through the mediation of Lotze in Göttingen and Roscher in Leipzig. Roscher's influence was more immediate and practical, for he introduced Lamprecht to the study of political economy and drew his attention to the centrality of the material realm in a unifying schema of developmental epochs. This indigenous tradition was basic to Lamprecht's theory of history, but onto it the historian grafted elements of another philosophical tradition whose roots ran deeper outside Germany. Its central proposition was that both the interdependence among the realms of human activity and the successive epochs of historical development were governed by a dynamic that operated regularly, in patterns analogous to scientific laws. The sources of this theory were the writings of Comte and the other leading representatives of the positivist tradition, including Marx, whom Lamprecht had encountered in his work with Bernheim in Göttingen.

A series of sketches that Lamprecht prepared between 1887 and 1889 documented the evolution of his thinking about the periodization of German history.[66] Each period, or Zeitalter, was to mark off a distinct developmental stage and to delimit an essential unity among all aspects of life—economy, society, politics, moral awareness, aesthetic perception, and intellectual activity. From his reading of Burckhardt, Lamprecht had earlier concluded that aesthetic perceptions represented the most direct expression of the unity of a given era. The periods that he listed in his first schematic draft were accordingly defined by their dominant artistic styles. Lamprecht borrowed liberally from Roscher's nomenclature and designated his periods the "Symbolic" (to 350 A.D.), the "Typical" (350–1050), the "Conventional" (1050–1450), the "Subjectivistic" (1450–1850), and the "Impressionistic" (1850 to his own day).[67] In subsequent drafts, these periods underwent modification. The historian eliminated "Impressionism" and added (again with one of Roscher's labels) a new, "Individualistic" period, which separated the Conventional from the Subjectivistic period, which he in turn redefined to span the late eighteenth century to his own day.

Lamprecht next satisfied himself that essential parallels linked all the dimensions of mental activity or ideal culture in any period, that analogies could be drawn among prevailing aesthetic, moral, and intellectual concepts. Thus in the Symbolic era, for instance, he concluded that symbolic representation in art corresponded to the dominance of mythology and to ethical concepts that could, he reasoned, have only symbolic, not substantive, meaning because they were tied exclusively to the satisfaction of bodily needs and desires.[68] The analytical unity among the elements of material culture occupied the historian less in his planning, for he was confident that his work on the medieval economy had established causal links that led from economic organization to social structure and political development.

Lamprecht's periodization was an exercise in what would today, in the language of a quite different tradition, be called mediation.[69] The object was to modulate among levels within a unified whole, in this case the totality of life in a given historical period. Lamprecht's principal means in this exercise was analogy. He employed it not only to correlate the different dimensions of ideal culture, but to establish the pivotal link between this realm and the realm of material culture. The transition emerged not, as might have been expected, out of the aesthetic dimension of ideal culture, but instead from the moral. In Lamprecht's reasoning, moral awareness corresponded to experience (*Erfahrung*). Experience in turn not only had material circumstances as its referent, but, as he noted in one of his drafts, "experience must in essence be thought of as adequate to circumstances [*adäquat der Zustände*]."[70] It was significant that the historian chose a foreign word, whose meaning in the context was anything but clear, to formulate so crucial a postulate in his schema; the "adequacy" of experience was henceforth to guarantee the correlation between material and ideal culture. Lamprecht argued that moral awareness—and (by analogical extension) aesthetic perception and intellectual activity—related to the experience of human existence in a collective context (*menschliches Beisammensein*), which he understood to mean both society and politics.[71] For the prototypical instance, the historian returned to his essay on individuality to retrieve its central analogy of constraint (*Gebundenheit*): he reasoned that the evolution of forms of bondage and dependence in society and politics corresponded to prevailing ideas of collective identity and obligation, until the loosening of the bonds of feudalism led to a more profound kind of moral awareness, which was based on the psychological experience of the individual.[72]

Both the early drafts and the logic of the historian's thinking implied the temporal and analytical priority of the material realm over the ideal.[73] The foundation of mental activity was experience of the material realm of work, society, and politics. The motor of historical development lay accordingly in the material realm, from which impulses later produced corresponding mental changes. "Developments in material culture," he wrote in one draft, "reveal [*äussern*] their social, and even more their ideal effect naturally only after a certain time, after the course of several generations."[74] The drafts did not directly address the problem of analytical priorities within the material realm itself. The historian's earlier studies of economic life had implied, however, that the organization of work was the foundation on which both social relations and the structure of politics took shape. The same conclusion was implicit in Lamprecht's brief notes on the subject of historical dynamics, in which he simply took over from Roscher and Hildebrand the idea of a fundamental progression from a natural to a money economy.

Lamprecht was soon accused of being a historical materialist. He had admittedly read Marx, and many features of the historian's early drafts invited the comparison; but the charge was unfair, to Marx no less than to Lamprecht.[75] The consistency, coherence, and discipline in Marx's thought were utterly foreign to Lamprecht's thinking, which was becoming so restless that it defied every label. The planning drafts were supposed to clarify his thoughts and set systematic foundations for the volumes he was about to publish. In the event, the drafts laid bare a number of fundamental ambiguities and inconsistencies that cried out for clarification. To cite but one more, the time lag that separated economic development from its social and cultural effects (sometimes,

Lamprecht noted, by centuries) drew into question the very integrity of historical periods as organic units. "Related and mutually dependent periods of material, social, and mental development never fall chronologically together," he asserted, without pondering the implications of what he had written.[76] Bernheim, to whom he sent copies of the drafts for comment, was sympathetic to the undertaking but raised penetrating questions about the limits of analogy and the permissibility of employing categories drawn from art history to characterize entire historical epochs. In his haste and absorption in his own ideas—and in the expectation that the act of writing would clarify his thoughts further—Lamprecht disregarded the criticism and overlooked the ambiguities.[77] As a result, problems already evident in the drafts soon surfaced again in the published volumes, where they were intensified, compounded, or superseded, as the historian compulsively altered his views and confounded the resemblances to historical materialism or any other coherent body of thought.

Lamprecht was oblivious of many of the failings of his work, but not of the professional risks inherent in any such bold and unconventional undertaking.[78] He could expect no support from his colleagues in Bonn, so he worked alone and shared his plans with no professional historians save Bernheim, who was then teaching in Greifswald. By the spring of 1889 he had proceeded from his preliminary sketches to an outline for a first volume, which he wrote in less than a year and dispatched to the publisher at virtually the same moment as he received the call to Marburg.[79] The coincidence was calculated, for the security of his new position reduced significantly the risks of publication.[80] The first of a projected four volumes appeared with a dedication "to the memory of my dear father" in the fall of 1890, during Lamprecht's brief sojourn in Marburg. The project, which he had already begun to call his *Lebenswerk*, thereupon grew at a furious pace amid the turmoil in his home and the dislocation of the move to Leipzig.[81] A second volume appeared in the middle of 1892, a third several months later. A fourth and fifth followed shortly thereafter, before the storm of controversy over his work finally compelled the historian to pause in 1895.

Karl Lamprecht's *German History* proved to be his *Lebenswerk*, but hardly in the sense he had hoped. The volumes he published between 1890 and 1895 destroyed his reputation in the German historical profession. The bitter debate they provoked was a complex spectacle, which had as much to do with the German historical profession as it did with the flaws in Lamprecht's work. Still, these volumes let loose the storm, and the effort to analyze the broader implications of the controversy best begins with them.

They present enormous problems. The first five volumes of the *German History* reached from the earliest recorded phases of the tribal era to the Peace of Westphalia in 1648. The chronological span alone makes it difficult in a schematic survey to do justice to the vast riches these volumes contained, to say nothing of the questions they raised.

The first volume, which Lamprecht wrote entirely in Bonn, covered more than a millennium. An introductory chapter, a sketch of the history of German national consciousness, introduced the five *Zeitalter* with which he proposed to structure the course of German history. The account proper began with the prehistoric Germanic tribes, whose early migrations, tribal organization, political, military, and economic institutions, and culture it described. It then traced the encounter of the Germanic peoples with Rome, the development of confederations among the tribes as they became sedentary, the emergence of the Frankish kingdom, its political, social, and economic institutions, and finally Germanic culture of the so-called *Stammeszeit* down to the eighth century A.D. The range of the material the historian presented was extraordinary. The most striking and controversial sections of the volume were those in which he drew on archaeological and ethnological findings to analyze the earliest institutions and culture of the Germanic peoples. His discussion of the "natural" forms of family, clan (*Geschlecht*), and tribal (*Stamm*) organization included the remarkable proposition that these institutions were originally built on primitive communism and matrilineal kinship systems (or what in German is called *Mutterrecht*), before they gave way in the first centuries A.D. to private property and the monogamous, patrilineal family.[82] The provenance of this idea was transparent, for Friedrich Engels was not the only German scholar to be fascinated in the 1880s by Lewis Henry Morgan's thesis that institutions based on matrilineality were common to "ancient societies."[83] Lamprecht's appropriation of the ethnologist's ideas was remarkable only because, as Bernheim attempted to warn him, there was not a shred of historical evidence to suggest that early Germanic institutions conformed to the pattern—a fact that Lamprecht's tortured appeals to Tacitus could not conceal.[84]

In his analysis of Germanic culture, Lamprecht applied his scheme for historical periodization. He began with a discussion of the early material foundations of this culture—the organization of society for military purposes and the social stratification that accompanied the development of pastoral agriculture. From there he turned to the "content of mental life that derived [*abgeleitet*] from these social and material preconditions."[85] His examination of the character of "every operation of internal life which had aesthetic valence and found external expression" persuaded him that mental life was symbolic; and he labeled the first period, which extended several centuries into the Christian era, accordingly.[86] Aesthetic attention, he claimed, was riveted in the Symbolic era to the striking deed, the powerful emotion, or, in ornamentation, to the simple motif that served as the image of more abstract but imperfectly understood action. The ethical analogue of this aesthetic principle consisted of symbolic legal rituals and a set of simple moral precepts, which reflected the absence of any sense of individual personality in the face of the massive constraints exercised by family, clan, and tribe. Finally, he argued, the intellectual world of the Germanic peoples was populated in this period by a plethora of deities, which were symbolically represented in human form but bore no ethical relevance to human behavior.

Lamprecht's definition of Symbolism was not equal to the analytical burdens he placed on it as the essential, unifying feature of a specific period. The historian admitted that "significant remnants" of Symbolism "blossomed" throughout the Middle Ages until they enjoyed a renewed "resurrection" in Dürer, "the most German of all painters."[87] The distinction between Symbolism and "Typism," the artistic style that followed and lent its dominant imprint to the next period (which began in the fourth century A.D.), was also porous (not to say obscure). The Typical era was marked by the establishment of the tribal states, which, Lamprecht argued, mediated "progress towards a more autonomous conception of the individual personality."[88] The principal aesthetic genres of Typism were the poetry of the epic saga, in which the fate of the nation was typified in the form of heroes, and new, more lively forms of ornamentation ("epic, as it were"), in which objects, particularly animals, were portrayed "only as types, only in their most external contours."[89] Early Christianity, which "intruded most decidedly onto the individual [drängte sich aufs bestimmteste dem Einzelnen auf]," evidently represented the moral and intellectual analogue, although the historian did not press the argument; nor did he clarify the distinction between a "type" and a "symbol."[90]

The discussions in Lamprecht's first volume that were devoted to the Germanic migrations of the early Christian era and to the aesthetics of ornamentation drew from his earlier work. The second and third volumes of the German History derived even more extensively from the Economic Life in the Middle Ages, and this fact helps explain the speed with which the historian wrote them during his year in Marburg and his first eighteen months in Leipzig. The second volume began with the establishment of the Carolingian monarchy and concluded on the eve of the election of Frederick Barbarossa as emperor in 1152. Political events marked this volume's chronological boundaries, and much of it consisted of a conventional narrative of the bewildering politics of the early Middle Ages—the attempts by Carolingian, Ottonian, and Salian rulers to establish stable bases of imperial rule, the resistance of the Saxons and other groups to these attempts, the alliance between the church and the emperors, Italian politics, the growing conflict between the empire and the Papacy, and the culmination of this conflict in the investiture struggle. Lamprecht's analysis of the social foundations of politics rehearsed the conclusions he had reached in his earlier work about the spread of manorialism, bonded service, and the usurpation by the large landowners of juridical, military, and political power.

Lamprecht's discussion of the cultural ramifications of social and political change was more systematic and persuasive in the second volume than in the preceding one. Manorialism, he argued, loosened the bonds of family, clan, and Markgenossenschaft and produced a "unique, typical constraint [Gebundenheit] of the personality" during the Ottonian era.[91] The era had not yet discovered the subjective dimension of personality, so moral precepts in the Typical period were still anchored externally and formally in law. Thinking, too, remained oriented to the particular and concrete; language reflected an inability to generalize or deal in abstract terms. The polemics and satires of the eleventh century, for example, displayed Typical characteristics in repeating the same formulaic expressions, thoughts, and images.[92] The heroes of sagas were typical figures who lacked internal dimensions; their moral world was governed by the simple dichotomy of good and evil. Aesthetic perceptions responded only to the depiction of contours and external features in ornamentation. Finally, the reception of Christianity reflected the sensitivities of the Typical period. Early German Christianity featured a "tangible, direct supernaturalism," asceticism, and a naive belief in miracles; it showed neither an inclination toward contemplation nor an attempt to reconcile faith and reason. "The era of the Ottonians did not yet philosophize," the historian concluded, "least of all religiously."[93]

The third volume of the *German History* began with a surprise. Here Lamprecht introduced a "rule," according to which the "course of development of natural [*urwüchsige*] nations" could be distinguished not by five, but by "three periods of growing culture." These he designated "in the traditional terminology" as "antiquity [*Vorzeit*], Middle Ages [*Mittelalter*], and the modern age [*Neuzeit*]."[94] His reasons for introducing a new schema were a mystery until he explained that antiquity corresponded to Symbolism, the Middle Ages to Typism and Conventionalism, and modern times to Individualism and Subjectivism. That the breaks between some of his five periods were more significant than others had remained merely an implication until this stage of the account.

Despite this volume's initial diversion and despite its "rather confused and diffuse subject-matter" (as even the author admitted), it was the most coherent and successful volume of the entire series.[95] It dealt with the final phase of the Middle Ages (in Lamprecht's new scheme)—the period of Conventionalism (in the old)—which fell together with the age of the Hohenstaufens. Lamprecht went over a lot of ground that was familiar from his earlier work, as he addressed social and political developments stimulated by the coming of a monetary economy: he examined the early growth of towns, the loosening of manorialism in favor of freer forms of leaseholding in the countryside, the evolution of the largest estates into quasi-sovereign institutions at the expense of the monarchy, and the appearance of occupational groups (*Berufsstände*), knights and burghers, in the countryside and towns, respectively.

The central section of the third volume treated the society and culture of the knighthood, which the historian analyzed under the rubric of the Conventional. As he employed it, the term described a set of precepts, tastes, and beliefs geared to social constraint. "Virtue now means social propriety [*Anstand*], morality its rules [*Lehre*]."[96] The term applied to the veneration of women and devotion to modish styles. In ornamentation and the lyric, the Conventional meant that the depiction of people and action was confined to surface features: "the sense for the outline of things is developed, but the power is lacking to appropriate the reality of these things according to their true essence."[97] Lamprecht's discussion of Conventionalism did nothing to quiet the growing suspicion that his historical periods, at least in the scheme of five, were built on his own aesthetic sensitivities, for he made clear his distaste for the artificiality and superficiality of this era's culture. The problem, he explained, was that the culture of Conventionalism was to a large extent a foreign import from the west.

The concluding section of this volume was an impressive survey of the periphery of the empire in the thirteenth and fourteenth centuries, when imperial power was collapsing in Germany. In his analysis of developments in Flanders and Holland and in the parts of eastern Europe that Germans colonized, Lamprecht demonstrated how geographical and demographic circumstances encouraged colonialization and conditioned social, legal, and political institutions, as well as aspects of ideal culture in the colonized areas.[98]

In May 1892, as he was completing the third volume, Lamprecht wrote to Bernheim that he was "completely exhausted and will need several years before I can go on."[99] His exhaustion did not last long. Within weeks he reported to another friend that he was mobilizing to "push into another land" and already "sitting half in the era of the Reformation."[100] The obsessive momentum of his work in the next months bespoke the traumatic impact of his wife's temporary return and reinstitutionalization. "In the bad stages I plunged into work," he told Bernheim in February 1893.[101] To Mevissen he wrote several months later, "this German History is like a vampire."[102] Despite the fact that he was now treating an era in which he had not read systematically since his student days, Lamprecht poured out three additional installments in the next two years. He completed the volume on the Reformation first, early in 1894. A volume on the fourteenth and fifteenth centuries followed several months later, and in July 1895, after a furious period of writing which he undertook, as he confessed, "in extremis," he extended the account to the conclusion of religious warfare in the middle of the seventeenth century.[103]

The fourth volume of the series set the stage for the Reformation with a survey of the period that extended from the election of Rudolf of Habsburg as emperor in 1273 to the end of the fifteenth century. The volume suffered noticeably from the haste with which the historian wrote it. Long segments were devoted to narrating struggles among emperors, foreign powers, popes, lesser prelates, church councils, princes, lesser nobles, estates, and cities. Lamprecht's disheveled account reduced these developments, whose complexity was formidable enough to tax the skills of the most patient narrator, to complete disarray. Much more successful was his analysis of social developments, particularly the rise of the cities and the burgher class of merchants and craftsmen. This development he cast in the context of a growing rift between the cities and the countryside, which was caused by the uneven growth of the money economy and exacerbated by the lack of central political authority. In these circumstances, the burghers replaced the knights at the forefront of the nation's development. The vivid chapters that Lamprecht wrote on the rise of the guilds and on everyday life inside city walls were among the best of the entire oeuvre.[104]

Lamprecht argued that the principal features of the burghers' social experience were the constraints imposed by family and urban corporations (Genossen-

schaften). These constraints were looser than the "narrow bounds of medieval thought and perception," and they corresponded to Conventionalism, which informed the ideal culture of burgher society in much the same way as it had the culture of the knighthood.[105] The portraiture, historical accounts, and even the autobiographies of this period failed to penetrate beneath the external features of their subjects, to depict more than "strong conventional types" associated with specific families or social groups.[106] Caricature and satire were hence popular genres. The spread of Christian mysticism was an analogous development: "it was still a movement of constrained spirit, but it pushed powerfully against the ultimate bounds of the old church and the medieval character [*Wesen*]."[107] Gothic architecture pushed literally against the bounds of the old church, but like chivalry, it was a French import and had unfortunate consequences. Its "all-dominating influence" stifled the development of free national traditions in ornamentation and sculpture.[108] Conventional constraints were likewise at work in painting. "Color was still a conventional extra feature [*Beigabe*]," the historian noted, "it did not yet have a life of its own, much less any connections to related colors or to light."[109] Finally, poetry, drama, and the songs performed in tournaments all reflected, in analogous fashion, a greater sense of freedom and individuality without escaping the conventional bonds of family, social group, and religion.

In the first part of the fifth volume of Lamprecht's *German History*, these bonds were sprung. This volume was the most remarkable yet, for it read like a collaborative effort in which Ranke and Burckhardt had joined forces with Engels. After another hurried narrative excursion into the politics of the reign of the emperor Maximilian I, Lamprecht turned to economic and social conditions. Here he took up a theme from the fourth volume, the widening rift between town and countryside occasioned by the uneven spread of a monetized economy. Now, however, the historian painted a picture of growing revolutionary tension in both arenas. In the cities the "hypertrophy of the money economy," the increasing concentration of wealth and power of capital, undermined the spirit and solidarity of the urban corporations and spawned a restive proletarian class.[110] In the countryside, on the other hand—and here Lamprecht rehearsed the findings of his *Economic Life*—social crisis was the product of overpopulation, underdevelopment, the decline of manorialism, and the attempt of landholders to extort ever higher fees and services from the impoverished peasantry.

Lamprecht's vision of social conflict was probably less indebted to Engels than to Engels' source, Wilhelm Zimmermann, but it was provocative nonetheless. In his survey of the polarization of class relations in the cities, the historian at one point spoke of the "foundation of a great, powerless [*unmündig*] community" and posed the question: "And what would happen if this community became conscious of its legitimate social and political demands *vis-à-vis* the ruling classes and sought to realize these demands in an uprising [*im Kampf*] against the existing constitution?"[111] In the next chapter, however, on "the development of individualistic society" in the towns, Lamprecht's perspective changed abruptly, as he turned to another social repercussion of the monetized economy. Now he spoke of the triumph of individualism and the final undermining, in the upper middle class, of the medieval bonds of corporation and family. "Intelligence and a spirit of adventure ruled; one transcended oneself [*man trat aus sich heraus*]; personality counted for something [*galt*], and its development was consequently subjected to vigorous education."[112] This development then reached its pinnacle in an "advance of limitless significance [*ein unendlicher Fortschritt*]," in the formation of what Lamprecht called "the classes of immaterial production, the teachers and physicians, the academics, and artists, and by no means least, the fully professional public officials."[113]

On this social foundation, Lamprecht played Burckhardt to Germany's history and documented the cultural postulates that marked the dawn of the modern age and the onset of the period of Individualism. The basic feature of the period was the new power of individuals to comprehend themselves as discrete beings, separate from their surroundings; the result was "the individuality of observation and hence the naturalism [*Naturwahrhaftigkeit*] of representation."[114] Individualism was reflected in the greater realism of graphic art, the new sensitivity in portraiture and literature to the inner life of the subject, in the rise of neo-Platonic realism, as well as in individual piety and the cultivation of higher learning. "The cultivation, even the cult of the personality was the order of the day," Lamprecht wrote in introducing his discussion of humanism.[115] The historian's views on the subject of humanism were ambivalent, however: the revival of classical learning was critical to the new era, but it threatened, in the wrong hands, to degenerate into sterile intellectualism and abstraction, "boundless vanity," and isolation from the pulse of the nation. The problem, which Erasmus exemplified, was familiar. Humanism, like chivalry and Gothic architecture, was a foreign import. In his survey of the German humanists, the historian thus labored to minimize the Italian influence (and to maximize the Flemish). Dürer, who in an earlier volume had embodied the vitality of Symbolism, now stood as the great representative of the Individualist era, "the greatest and most German of our painters."[116]

Having set the stage with social conflict, vibrant individualism, and foreign intrusions (a category that included the machinations of the Papacy), the historian introduced the Great Man. "It was Luther," he announced, "who cleared the way for Individualism in the most profound regions of spiritual life, in the religious and philosophical, in that he placed the individual person before the divine principle directly, without the intrusion [*Dazwischenkunft*] of any sacral institution."[117] Luther's achievement was the creative renewal of Christianity in a purer, German form, as he extended the principles of the new era into the most profound dimension of human existence and reduced all the constraints on individuality to a personal faith in God. Lamprecht's Luther was cut from a Rankean mold, a man who waged a "heroic personal struggle, within himself as well as within the abandoned ranks of Christianity, for the truth and validity of his teachings."[118] And, the historian concluded, the broad popular resonance of these teachings was due above all to "the person of the Reformer."[119]

It remained for Lamprecht to show how a Rankean Luther could fit into a decidedly un-Rankean interpretation of the revolutionary upheavals of the 1520s. Lamprecht treated the Peasants' War at great length and with no little sympathy. His sudden endorsement of Luther's own position on the uprising was thus unexpected; and it resulted in a conundrum. In a hurried conclusion to the narrative, the historian explained that the peasants' movement was out of step—"in a certain sense reactionary"—despite the inspiration it took from those monuments of Individualism, Luther's teachings. The communalism that this movement advocated was a throwback to the constraints of a natural economy.[120] Out of step, too, were the religious radicals, like Münzer, whose individualism repudiated all constraint. "Lutheranism was necessary for the time," Lamprecht concluded. Luther was the great representative of Individualism, but of an "individualism bridled [*gegängelt*] by authority."[121]

The second half of the fifth volume, which appeared separately and brought the account to 1648, not only failed to resolve this riddle; it added innumerable others. It was devoted almost entirely to political narrative, which Lamprecht composed in great haste, without much enthusiasm or reflection. The only notable sections of the book were those that returned to the developmental divergence between the town and countryside. Lamprecht argued now that the rift widened in the second half of the sixteenth century as a consequence of commercial decline in central Europe; rural Germany, particularly that part of it that remained Catholic, retreated into the backwardness of a natural economy, while the Protestant towns became the loci of the more advanced culture of Individualism. But even this argument faded into the general confusion of Lamprecht's attempt to recount the politics of religious conflict, international rivalry, and territorial consolidation.

"So, in an unmistakable disruption of all the unifying elements in its political life, the nation faced a dubious future, in which salvation could only come from the vigorous development of the individual states."[122] By the time he closed the second half of the fifth volume with this observation, Lamprecht really was exhausted. He had lived with the project without interruption for more than five years, in what he described to Mevissen as "a permanent state of intellectual pregnancy."[123] Now, in the summer of 1895, the historian looked forward to a long pause in order to collect material for the subsequent volumes, which were to bring the account to his own day. In the event, the pause lasted far longer than he had anticipated, and before he could again take up the *German History*, all his considerable energies were absorbed in the defense of the first volumes.

Lamprecht's *German History* has been described in many ways. Sam Whimster captured a consensus of the judgments when, in a recent essay, he called it "a strange work by any standard."[124] It is difficult, even today, not to marvel at the grand vision, ingenuity, scope, and ambition of this project, whose goal was to capture the entirety of the German past. Lamprecht's account touched on the history of life-styles, diet, manners, tastes in clothing, sexuality, the role of women, the family, child rearing, education, popular religion, and a host of other topics that have since attracted the interest of social historians. In the perspective of another century, Lamprecht seems to have asked all the right questions of German history. Yet any attempt to understand the historian's work must also concede that practically everything that his critics said about it was true. Lamprecht set out to demonstrate the coherence of all aspects of German history, but the results of his labors—the answers he found to his questions—were so marred by error and inconsistency that they appeared to leave German history in chaos. Lamprecht's critics will soon have their turn. But because none of them sought to understand the historian's work in the light of his biography, a number of observations are first in order.

Lamprecht has not lacked defenders. A sympathetic tradition of exegesis has grown out of the effort to reconcile the inconsistencies in the historian's work and to build his system more coherently and persuasively than he himself was able to do.[125] It is tempting to borrow from a modern idiom and say that the interpretive challenge has been to impose structure upon a text that the author himself inadvertently deconstructed. The difficulty is that posing the challenge in these terms slights the vital connection between the text and the author's personal history. It does so in two ways. In the first place, it minimizes the extent to which the errors, inconsistencies, and confusion—the features that lent the text its chaotic or "deconstructed" character—were essential aspects of the historian's work, the products of deeply ingrained habits of his mind. Interpreting them away in the search for a historiographical system produces an unhistorical picture of the text. This interpretive strategy also obscures the fact that the "self-deconstruction" of the German History was only superficial. A close reading of the text reveals a narrative structure that endowed both national and personal history with meaning.

The German History was an immense exercise in collection and classification. Every detail of the past was to be fitted into a hierarchy of categories, at the top of which stood Lamprecht's five historical periods. His strategy at every level was to build generalizations like containers, into which he could deposit the facts that he had collected from the fields of the past. The whole enterprise extended a familiar motif in the historian's life; and it foundered on temperamental unsuitabilities that were also familiar. Lamprecht gathered details furiously, but he abstracted carelessly and in great haste. The results were evident on virtually every page of the work, primarily in the form of facts that did not belong in the containers into which the collector had hurriedly thrown them.

In those countless instances where he was too rushed even to notice the problem, the result was a simple contradiction. The following paragraph, quoted in its entirety, is a classic instance. Its subject is the survival of the corporative (genossenschaftliche) institutions of the Germanic tribes in the Roman provinces:

> And beyond the tribes [Sippenverbände], even the corporate idea of the
> Germanics increased in significance in the provinces. Organized in hundreds

[*Hundertschaften*], the east Germanics move into their empires; they come as warring conquerers. In keeping with the sense of this organization, it would have been fitting that they adopted corporate economic practices when they settled on the new land [*dass sie sich markgenossenschaftlich im neuen Lande niedergelassen*]. In view of the dense population of the Imperium, that was not possible; nowhere were free spaces available for large-scale corporative appropriation, and from another direction the political character of the conquest led to long-term quartering in the manner of Roman warriors. Thus the organization of the fields could hardly be founded on the Germanic pattern; [this] system of farms [*Hufensystem*] stretches even today from the north only to the middle of what is today France.[126]

All the material in the paragraph contradicted the proposition announced in the topic sentence. Into a container marked "survival of Germanic corporate institutions" the historian placed an impressive series of facts that demonstrated the failure of these institutions to take root.

A variation of this difficulty was the quick improvisation of a new generalization to accommodate the facts that did not fit the old. "In all events, the crusades gradually lost their religious impact." With this proposition the historian began a discussion of developments in the twelfth and thirteenth centuries. The next paragraph dealt with the same era and began: "Above all, these new experiences of the crusades worked in the area of religion."[127] Lamprecht's analysis of territorial consolidation in the fourteenth century included the observation: "Thus the upper as well as the lower classes were obligated to the princes; and only the highest state power was lacking to subordinate both [groups] to the prince as subjects." The next sentence introduced a new paragraph and a new proposition: "This [state] power, too, had long been developed."[128]

Often a sequence of contradictions extended over long passages. In speaking of resistance to Papal policies in the fourteenth century, the historian concluded that the German people (*Volk*) "had begun to become a political whole, a nation tending toward its own immanent unitary development." Six years and seven pages later, the cities foresook the emperor for the Pope; a little later the nation "began to awake and to side solidly against the Pope and for the emperor." Then "national consciousness, which had long been excited, bestirred itself." Several pages after that, however, "the moral power of the Papacy in Germany, over the princes and the people, was still unbroken and insurmountable—but only until the next page, where "the national emerged," and the Papacy "encountered the nation" when it "acted against the imperial throne."[129]

Even in the cases where the historian appeared to recognize the contradictions, he could not bring himself to rethink his generalizations or reorder his facts. Instead, as if removing the facts from the container and leaving it empty, he introduced a series of qualifications that all but negated his original generalization. In a discussion of a meeting of the German princes in Aschaffenburg in July 1447, Lamprecht observed that "increasing moral pressure" from King Frederick III "very soon" led to "concessions by a majority of the princes."

"*Freilich*," the historian conceded, "to be sure, several important princes were not quickly to be won." The several recalcitrants included the duke of Austria, the electors of Brandenburg, Cologne, Trier, Saxony, and the elector Palatine. In fact, Lamprecht noted in concluding this paragraph on Frederick's success, the last four of these princes thereupon turned against the German king and struck a deal with the king of France.[130] The proliferation of negating or qualifying words like *freilich* was the signal that Lamprecht was in trouble with the facts and was reshaping the container. In one passage, seven such words marked the contorted effort of four successive sentences to produce a consistent argument. In the fourteenth century, he wrote, "a single great opponent, France," loomed at the western borderlands of the *Reich*:

> It was not [*nicht*] as if there already reigned an active national antagonism between French people and Germans. To be sure [*gewiss*], this opposition was intuitively felt, but [*aber*] its development into an intellectual tenet was still prevented by the survival of the universal imperial idea. Nonetheless [*indes*], its absence was, for all that [*doch*], also no [*kein*] obstacle to prevent the French from acting against the empire ever more powerfully with hundreds of small annexations. But [*aber*] this policy had over and over again to place limits on the empire as a whole.[131]

The catalogue of the historian's difficulties included all the familiar infelicities of style and the gratuitous use of neologisms, foreign words, and incongruous metaphors; but these difficulties only compounded the confusion sown by what one friendly critic called Lamprecht's "urge to classify [*Klassifikationsbedürfnis*]" and by the attendant strategies for building generalizations.[132] Extending the list of examples would produce a volume of commentary as long as the *German History* itself. Most of the problems resulted from the collision of the historian's penchant for grand abstraction with an impatience so restless that he found almost unbearable the thought of reworking words that he had once committed to paper.

The most successful parts of the *German History* were those in which the generalizations addressed social and economic trends. At times—when, for example, he discussed the development of guilds—Lamprecht's strategy anticipated the construction of what would later be called ideal types. He was most interested and comfortable in working in these areas, where the data addressed long-term patterns of behavior and accommodated the kind of abstract analysis he preferred.

The sections devoted to political narrative unfortunately made up the better part of the first five volumes. These sections had nothing to recommend them. They were conventional and ill integrated with the other sections, and they suffered the most from the historian's haste. Lamprecht was not well suited to writing political history. He found it boring.[133] He had no patience for the singularity of events, nor, as he himself recognized, did he have much aptitude for depicting historical figures.[134] His self-absorption was a profound liability in this connection, for it drained him of any real interest in the motivations of

other human beings. His portrayals of historical figures were often flat, formulaic, irrelevant to the account, and based on dubious anecdotes. They were also
demanding on participles. The emperor Conrad II he described as "Sharp and
strict, frugal and self-contained [*zusammenhaltend*], filled with irreconcilable
hate for his enemies, frightfully passionate with respect to everyone, ruthlessly
striving for his goals, now and then beyond the bounds of law."[135] About Rudolf
of Habsburg the historian wrote: "He was thin and oversized, with a small head,
from whose face, furrowed with anxious wrinkles, two intelligent eyes looked
forward expectantly, beardless, with straight, long-waved hair which only
loosened at the end; he displayed his fingers and narrow feet: he was the
half-merchant knight."[136] Ulrich von Hutten was

> a man in the best years of maturing manly strength, with the incredible energy
> of a lust for life despite an incurable illness, thirsting for freedom, driven by
> the most powerful fantasies as far as the greatness and fortune of his estate
> [*Stand*] were concerned, endowed as well with all the means of democratic
> eloquence, though not without an aristocratic gift for form, no great scholar,
> no distinguished poet, but an agitator by God's grace, open and wonderfully
> committed finally to everything that was spiritually great.[137]

Lamprecht's political narrative was a chaos of undigested detail. Events simply
occurred, without cause, as if political actions required no motivation. His
inconsistencies ensured that the account lacked coherence, too. Even the more
lucid passages exuded the historian's boredom. On events in the north at the
end of the tenth century, he wrote:

> At the same time, a period of internal unrest began in Denmark, to which
> German rule fell victim. The Christian, German-minded king Harald Blåtand
> was murdered, the bishoprics fell apart, archbishop Adaldag of Hamburg-
> Bremen died with a broken heart on 28 April 988. In the dissolution of all
> existing conditions, the heathens of the north invaded; king Erich of Sweden
> conquered Denmark and expelled the new king Sven, as he had conquered
> Norway and driven away king Olaf.[138]

Despite the prominence of politics in the *German History*, Lamprecht's disin-
terest in the subject was the most systematic indicator of his methodological
views. The first five volumes retained the analytical priorities of the preliminary
drafts and appeared to argue that political developments and ideal culture were
epiphenomena of more basic changes in material culture. But the only direct
discussion of methodology came in perfunctory pronouncements that the historian distributed as asides throughout the volumes. The most remarkable and
extended of these dicta was a single paragraph that appeared without warning in
the fourth volume, as an addendum to a discussion of the Swiss saga. Here
Lamprecht charged that the writing of political history resembled the composition of the saga: both lacked a scientific foundation and relied on the imagination of a storyteller. By contrast, he announced, cultural history offered the prospect
of "a new era of historical scholarship," the means of achieving "complete scientific
truth" with a new method based on inductive psychology.[139]

He did not pursue this provocation. Nor did he extend his discussion of the laws of historical dynamics beyond a series of apodictic observations dispersed incidentally throughout the text. One, for instance, contained another provocation.

"The fates of those nations to which the privilege of self-development is granted proceed their own way, according to their own laws, and even the most distinguished sons of these nations have no more freedom in the face of these laws than the freedom of will that the average person has in the small world of his circumstances."[140] This proposition remained as little developed as a law he subsequently announced about cultural transfer:

> The essence of historical development rests for the most part on the fact that typical aspects of the culture of more highly developed nations are transferred onto youthful nations, that these aspects live on in the youthful nation and are unified with the new achievements of the receiving nation into more beautiful blossoms, which promise better fruit.[141]

Although these brief statements on methodology seemed designed to offend his colleagues in the profession, the historian failed to elaborate. Nor did he consistently observe his own pronouncements. It was difficult to reconcile his law, which shackled the distinguished sons of nations, with his remarks about "the dominating [beherrschenden] antagonism of great personalities in German history."[142] This remark was also an early indication of the limits of Lamprecht's materialism. There were others. "Ideas are mightier than deeds," he observed later, "they overcome the world of historical material."[143] "Here too," he remarked in connection with social unrest early in the sixteenth century, "the strength of thought overcomes every other force of historical development."[144] These statements suggested how extensively the historian's inconsistency affected his methodology, but they also reflected a deeper contradiction that ran throughout the initial volumes of the German History and provided the most compelling evidence that even at this stage in his career, Lamprecht was no materialist.

The German History recounted the history of German national consciousness. In a preface to the first volume, which was designed to introduce both the subject matter and the conceptual framework of his whole work, Lamprecht sketched the development of national consciousness through the five historical periods. He defined his subject as the "historically developed agreement of all members of the nation [Volksgenossen] in the most essential questions of individual as well as collective existence."[145] He portrayed German history as the story of the nation's halting progress toward full self-consciousness, the development of a "feeling of nationality" that originally rested on the "homogeneity [Gleichartigkeit] of the national individuals."[146]

This proposition raised a number of problems. In the first place, it implied the existence of a sense of national unity, albeit in a primitive form, from the dawn of recorded history in the Symbolic period. The attempt to document the presence of national consciousness among the Germanic tribes, even as they slaughtered one another, drew the historian into some of his most awkward contradictions.[147] At the root of this problem lay another, which also occasioned no little confusion.[148] The historian never defined the nation, that historical subject whose destiny consisted in achieving full consciousness of itself. But the omission was not inadvertent. In Lamprecht's account the nation had no historical definition, for it was not a historical category. The *Volk* was eternal. It was an ideal, metahistorical unity—a moral force uniting all *Volksgenossen* from the beginning of history. The nation's progressive self-realization in history was ultimately an epistemological process; it related to the apperception of a transcendent idea, of a reality whose ontological status was exempt from history. The historical priority of material conditions in Lamprecht's account hence stood curiously juxtaposed to the philosophical priority of ideal culture, where national consciousness resided. The provenance of Lamprecht's ideas was well disguised in an ingenious mixture of sources, but his philosophical debt in these volumes was in all events less to Marx than to Hegel and Ranke.

Postulating national unity in these terms fulfilled an important practical function in the *German History*, and it offered the key to some of the problems in Lamprecht's earlier work. It enabled him to speak of a *"Volksindividualität"* and to draw evidence virtually at random in order to document the unity of the nation's cultural development in a given period.[149] Frankish institutions in the Rhineland, the ornamentation of manuscripts in abbeys in the Mosel valley, the chivalric poetry of a thin social stratum, or the religious ideas of a single Saxon monk all acquired representative significance as expressions of an organic whole, which Lamprecht variously called a "German personality," the *"Volksseele,"* or (when a foreign word seemed in order) a "temperamental complex [*Gemütskomplexion*]" in which all Germans shared.[150] In this fashion the historian postulated the very historical unity he claimed to be demonstrating.

Lamprecht failed to recognize the methodological difficulties in the *German History*, in part because of the haste with which he wrote, in part because these difficulties had become integral features of his style and approach to historical scholarship. But his failure was also due to the intensity and immediacy of his own involvement in his subject. The structure of these volumes betrayed their autobiographical meaning; German history served as a metaphor for social and personal experience.

"All literature must be read as a symbolic meditation on the destiny of community."[151] Whether or not one accepts Frederic Jameson's judgment as a general proposition (or is willing to accord Lamprecht's work the status of literature), the *German History* was preeminently a meditation on *Gemeinschaft*; and it reflected the anxieties of a social group whose cultural authority in that community was being challenged. An extended discussion of Lamprecht's political views must await a subsequent chapter. Here it is sufficient to emphasize the influence of Gustav von Mevissen, who awakened and nurtured the historian's concerns about the fragmentation of German society in an industrial age and about the mission of the country's educated elite to repair the situation. Lamprecht was like Treitschke in this respect, and his great admiration for the older historian reflected a shared sense of civic obligation and a common belief that the object of historical scholarship was ultimately to serve the community's abiding collective values.[152]

Lamprecht's German History, like Treitschke's German History in the Nineteenth Century, was accordingly a paean to the moral power residing in a national community that had endured centuries of fragmentation—in political disunity, foreign despoilation, religious cleavage, economic dislocation, and social antagonism. Lamprecht's history was incomplete when he broke it off at the Peace of Westphalia, but its dénouement was not difficult to anticipate. The plot of his narrative, to borrow via Hayden White from Northrop Frye, was comic.[153] German history was moving toward fulfillment, which would come with the transcendence of fragmentation and with the community's internal reconciliation. A dramatic high point of the account was to come in 1871 with the achievement of political unity and a centralized state, the mediating agency that the community had historically lacked.

In identifying the year 1871 as a telos of German history, Lamprecht's plot was conventional. It resembled in this regard the accounts with which Treitschke and the other protagonists of the Borussian school were constructing an orthodoxy in imperial Germany. However, the fulfillment of community was only one of the plots in Lamprecht's German History. It was entwined in several parallel subplots, and not all of these were conventional.

The first was about culture, in the sense implied by the German word Kultur. Lamprecht did not define this concept in the German History either, but his account made it clear that culture was foremost an ethical matter. It related to the regulation of behavior. Cultural progress meant the transition from collective to individual constraint, from external compulsion to internal discipline and freedom. Primitive civilizations were "ruled by dark drives," which were bridled by the collective compulsion exerted by family, clan, and tribe.[154] The development of culture then passed, in Lamprecht's analysis, through stages characterized successively by the appearance of legal order, the discipline of social convention, and the emergence of a sense of individual moral duty. It was no coincidence that culture developed through the same stages, marked out by the same historical periods, as did national consciousness, for the two were ultimately the same. Culture was originally but the collective component of national consciousness.

In the period of Individualism, in the first stage in the modern era, however, cultural progress modulated into psychological development. The idea of individual personality appeared, and with it the internalization of constraint, the conscious and willing embrace of the nation, and the substitution of internal authority—conceived initially in Protestant terms as personal faith in God—as the final sanction for behavior. Lamprecht stopped before he could extend this theme, but its implications were already clear. Culture had become in the modern age a question of cultivating personality; *Kultur* could now be recognized as *Bildung*. And the historian's incidental remarks suggested that cultural development would soon culminate in the full emancipation of personality and that this achievement would be marked by Kant's founding a secular ethic based entirely on the authority of human understanding.[155]

The social correlate of cultural development was the subject of a second subplot in the *German History*. Lamprecht recounted the emergence of the urban *Bürgerstand* as the leader of the German nation, the group that "set the national tone," generated the nation's wealth, and represented the most reliable prop for a strong German monarchy.[156] The greatest achievement of this class, however, was to provide an elite group of intellectuals, professionals, and public officials, who were, as the historian rhapsodized, "ennobled" by their *Bildung*.[157] In the era of Individualism these men assumed cultural leadership of the nation and became the arbiters of taste, the vanguard of the Protestant Reformation, the indispensable prop of modern administration, and the embodiment of the modern symbiosis of culture and personal development.

The centrality of this theme represented but one of the ways in which Lamprecht's work was permeated with the values and anxieties of the nineteenth century heirs of this early Protestant *Bildungsbürgertum*. To cite but a few additional instances in which the *German History* read like a contemporary commentary, the historian emphasized Charlemagne's views about monogamy and the nuclear family. He lamented the backwardness of the peasantry, the insularity of the aristocracy, and the evils of big cities and unrestrained capitalism. He dilated on the virtues of university education, on the stifling force of Catholicism, and the perils of ethnic conflict in central and eastern Europe. The *German History* was about Lamprecht's own class. It was an essay on the meaning of a social experience he shared, an attempt to ground the cultural authority of the imperial German *Bildungsbürgertum* in the context of the nation's full historical experience.

The *German History* was finally an essay on personal experience. The subject of its third major subplot was Karl Lamprecht. Many of the historian's digressions made sense only in the light of his own autobiography. His account of Frankish institutions offered repeated observations on the protective obligations of monogamous marriage, in which the wife "looked up to her husband, not as his property but as his charge [*Schützling*]."[158] These passages reflected not only the views of his class on this institution, but his anxieties about his own marriage, which at the time was undergoing its initial blows in Bonn. Other indices of the personal relevance of German history abounded. They included the allusion to Luther's abandonment by his father, the repeated references to the national significance of solitude, the paean to the *Pfarrhaus* and "its best sons," and the pronouncement that the writing of history was "the most telling indication of the intellectual attainment" of an era.[159]

But the *German History* was an autobiographical document in a more profound sense. It was an extended restatement of the essay on individuality. It was about national growth, defined in an analogy to human maturation—a process that featured increasing control of primal, arbitrary urges, first by the "external forces of existence," later by means of legal and then moral discipline.[160] Growth had both a social and a psychological dimension. The loosening of outer, institutional constraints corresponded to the increasing subjection of the individual will to the intellect. "The practical freedom of the will," wrote the historian in an allusion to Goethe, "is in fact identical for the most part with the determination of our will by our powers of understanding [Verstand]."[161] In Lamprecht's schema, the onset of the modern era directed moral development into Bildung, the cultivation of the intellect, which he understood as transcendence to progressive levels of understanding. The first stage was the self-transcendence required to comprehend the individual as a discrete and autonomous being. The next was the intellectual comprehension of collective bonds, the transformation of national feelings into the "clearly understood, outwardly manifested consciousness" of nationality.[162] Luther's achievement in the period of Individualism was to broaden intellectual autonomy to the bounds of personal faith, and Kant was soon to eliminate even this constraint by bringing ethics within the domain of understanding. Personal growth thereafter meant the unfettered pursuit of Wissenschaft, broadening the range of human understanding and the systematization of knowledge.

Lamprecht paused before he could bring this theme to its conclusion. Nonetheless, occasional remarks in his text, as well as the logic of his own argument, pointed toward the conception of a vast intellectual panorama, a Weltbild analogous to the perfected landscape whose artistic reproduction, he observed, required the transcendence of nature, a condition in which "one [der Mensch] is able to remove oneself entirely from nature, when one frees oneself to a high degree from a naive relationship to nature, when one is alienated from it."[163] The fulfillment of personal growth, the ultimate feat of Bildung, was to come in transcending the final constraints to understanding the entire panorama of existence, which meant historical understanding or, more accurately, the understanding uniquely afforded by Kulturgeschichte.

The issue of whether Karl Lamprecht ever in fact achieved any kind of self-transcendence is not pertinent here. The German History, however, was his account of his own personal growth. The progress of Germany through the successive periods of its history was a metaphor for his own emancipation by stages from the constraints on his intellectual development. These constraints, too, were symbolized by his father and Ranke. The first were the external constraints laid down by his family (in an environment dominated, as he emphasized repeatedly, by a natural economy).[164] The next were the conventional views of the profession that he intended to join. The last were the moral and intellectual constraints of Protestant Christianity. The goal of the historian's growth thereupon became to transcend all bounds, to understand the entire past, and frame the ultimate intellectual landscape. The success of the project would bring the fulfillment of both German history and its historian.

Lamprecht's first volumes concluded with Luther's achievement and in anticipation of Kant's. After Kant's there was only Lamprecht's.

Lamprecht was drawn to the theme of personal fulfillment and transcendence in German history. He saw it epitomized in the Parzifal and Faust motifs, both of which represented, in his view, "the longing of an honest heart to escape the narrow conventions [*Schlackenformen*] of their era and to find higher fulfillment."[165] He was particularly fascinated by the case of Luther, where the same theme had strong connotations of "heroic personal struggle" and vindication in the face of adversity.[166] Well might the historian have been sensitive to the parallels between the Reformer's experience and his own, for by the time he wrote the volume on the Reformation, he had challenged his own share of narrow conventions and was beginning to pay the price in adversity.

Notes

1. UA Bonn, Phil. Fak., Schönfeld to PF, Bonn, 3.2.85.
2. MIÖG, 4 (1883): 630–33.
3. Below, "Below," 13–14.
4. DWL, 1: 1485–86. I have tried to make syntactical sense of this dreadful sentence, but fairness demands that Lamprecht be allowed to speak in his own language: "So war es unsere Aufgabe, in der Geschichte der materiellen Kultur auf bestimmtem Boden bestimmte Entwicklungsreihen untersuchend zu verfolgen und dabei die Anordnung der Untersuchung so zu treffen, dass in der Reihenfolge der einzelnen Darstellungen immerhin schon jene hauptsächlichsten Stufen ihrer Entwicklung zur Geltung gelangen, welche eine spätere reine Geschichtsdarstellung aufzustellen haben würde." *Cf.* ibid. 1: vi.
5. This view admittedly reflected prejudices common to Rhenish regional patriotism, one of whose postulates was that this part of Germany was the early focus of advanced culture, the "Pflanzstätte unserer nationalen Bildung." See Wilhelm Arnold, "Zur Geschichte des Rheinlands," *Westdeutsche Zeitschrift für Geschichte und Kunst*, 1 (1882): 1–35.
6. NL Lamprecht (H2, 11, 31); *cf.* DG, 12: 12, 32.
7. NL Lamprecht (H2, 38); *cf.* DG, 12: 41.
8. Several years later Lamprecht wrote that "inductive reasoning [*Induktionsschluss*] is nothing other than analogical reasoning [*Analogieschluss*] improved after long effort." EB, 2, 1: 70.
9. Herbert Schönebaum, "Vom Werden der Deutschen Geschichte Karl Lamprechts," *Deutsche Vierteljahrsschrift für Literaturwissenschaft und Geistesgeschichte*, 25 (1951): 100.
10. NL Lamprecht (H2, Heft 2, 41). Lest clarity is thought to be lost in translation, the passage reads: "ihr Inhalt weist hin auf eine Epoche ungemein erstarkter Persönlichkeit. . . . Das Recht der Individualität ist errungen und bewegt sich frei noch in selbsterzogener Schranke; die Persönlichkeit steht noch nicht absolut da, sie drängt sich noch nicht hervor, sie will noch Nichts als solche gelten." *Cf.* DG, 12: 44.
11. LW, 271.
12. Below, "Below," 13–14; Peter Schumann, *Die deutschen Historikertage von 1893 bis 1937: Die Geschichte einer fachhistorischen Institution im Spiegel der Presse* (Göttingen, 1975), 112, n. 1.

13. NL Lamprecht (DG 4). The manuscripts for the volumes of the *Deutsche Geschichte* in this file reveal nothing more than minor corrections once Lamprecht had written the text in longhand.

14. NL Lamprecht (Korr. 58). The correspondence between the historian and his bride suggests little intellectual depth in the relationship even before her condition deteriorated.

15. NL Sybel, Lamprecht to Sybel, Marburg, 12.7.90; LW, 208.

16. Dove to Otto Ribbeck, Bonn, 19.11.90, in Dove, *Aufsätze und Briefe*, 2: 142–44; Dove, "Karl Lamprecht," ibid., 1: 315; NL Schmoller, Lamprecht to Schmoller, Bonn, 12.2.88; NL Lamprecht (Korr. 45), Lamprecht to Ritter, Leipzig, 29.12.93.

17. NL Lamprecht (Korr. 19), Dove to Lamprecht, Bonn, n.d. [February 1890].

18. NL Lamprecht (Korr. 37), Mevissen to Lamprecht, Cologne, 3.3.90.

19. Eulenburg, *Frequenz*, 307.

20. NL Althoff (B Nr. 108/1), Lamprecht to Althoff, Bonn, 24.1.90.

21. NL Mevissen, Lamprecht to Mevissen, Bonn, 1.3.90; Marburg, 22.11.90.

22. A. von Premerstein et al., "Zur Geschichte des Historischen Seminars," in H. Hermelink and S. A. Kaehler, *Die Philipps-Universität zu Marburg 1527–1927: Fünf Kapitel aus ihrer Geschichte. Die Universität Marburg seit 1866 in Einzeldarstellungen* (Marburg, 1927), 735–41.

23. Lehmann, "Lehmann," in S. Steinberg, 1: 207–32; Waltraut Reichel, *Studien zum Wandel von Max Lehmanns preussisch-deutschen Geschichtsbild* (Göttingen, 1963); Günter Vogler, "Max Lehmann," in Streisand, 2: 57–95; NDB, 14: 88–90; Weber, *Lexikon*, 340–41.

24. Meinecke, *Schriften*, 88.

25. NL Lamprecht (Korr. 35), Lehmann to Lamprecht, Berlin, 3.4.88; Lamprecht to Lehmann, n.d. [January 1890].

26. NL Lamprecht (Korr. 35), Lehmann to Lamprecht, Marburg, 24.2.90, 27.2.90; NL Liesegang, Lamprecht to Liesegang, Marburg, 18.7.90; cf. LW, 210, 221.

27. Lamprecht, "Der Ursprung des Bürgertums und des städtischen Lebens in Deutschland," HZ, 67 (1891): 385–424; cf. Theodor Schieder, "Die deutsche Geschichtswissenschaft im Spiegel der Historischen Zeitschrift," HZ, 189 (1959): 47.

28. NL Mevissen, Lamprecht to Mevissen, Baden-Baden, 5.4.90; NL Lamprecht (Korr. 59), Lamprecht to Hugo Lamprecht, Marburg, 4.8.90; Eger, 29.9.90.

29. NL Lamprecht (Korr. 59), Lamprecht to Hugo Lamprecht, Marburg, 3.6.90.

30. NL Lamprecht (Korr. 45), Ropp to Lamprecht, Giessen, 2.6.90; GStAM, Rep. 76–Va, Sekt. 12, Tit. VII, Ropp to Lamprecht, Giessen, 18.6.90; LW, 210. The beneficiary of the shuffle was ultimately Konstantin Höhlbaum, the archivist from Cologne, who succeeded Ropp in Giessen.

31. UA Leipzig, Phil. Fak., PA 675, Maurenbrecher et al., Erster Kommissionsbericht, 10.11.90.

32. UA Leipzig, Phil. Fak, PA 675, Protokoll der 2. Sitzung der Kommission, 16.11.90. In their preference for Gothein these men had the support of Dove: Dove to Ribbeck, Bonn, 19.11.90, Dove, *Aufsätze und Briefe*, 2: 142–44. Roscher was probably not opposed to Lamprecht personally but hoped, like Lujo Brentano, to use the occasion to hire another economist. Cf. Marie Luise Gothein, *Eberhard Gothein: Ein Lebensbild* (Stuttgart, 1931), 80; LW, 215.

33. UA Leipzig, Phil. Fak., PA 675, Maurenbrecher to Dekan, Leipzig, 20.12.90; StA Dresden, 10281/203, Ratzel to KM, 22.12.90.

34. GStAM, Rep. 76–Va, Sekt. 12, Tit. VII, Lamprecht to Althoff, Werneck, 26.12.90; NL Lamprecht (Korr. 59), Lamprecht to Hugo Lamprecht, Marburg, 29.12.90. The playing out of the musical chairs had its irony. Lamprecht's depar-

ture brought Ropp to Marburg from Breslau. Georg Kaufmann left the academy in Münster to fill the vacancy in Breslau, while Kaufmann's chair in Münster went to a young extraordinary professor from Königsberg, Georg von Below.

35. See Czok, "Höhepunkt," 191–97; *cf.* Karl Czok, *Karl Lamprechts Wirken an der Universität Leipzig* (Berlin, 1984), 7–8.
36. Eulenburg, *Frequenz*, 306–7.
37. Lujo Brentano, *Mein Leben im Kampf um die soziale Entwicklung Deutschlands* (Jena, 1931), 147.
38. NL Mevissen, Lamprecht to Mevissen, Leipzig, 29.5.91.
39. NL Mevissen, Lamprecht to Mevissen, Leipzig, 23.12.91; NL Lamprecht (Korr. 44), Ratzel to Lamprecht, Leipzig, 10.7.93; NL Liesegang, Lamprecht to Liesegang, Leipzig, 30.5.94.
40. NL Mevissen, Lamprecht to Mevissen, Leipzig, 24.5.93.
41. LW, 222–23.
42. NL Bernheim, Lamprecht to Bernheim, 23.6.92.
43. UB Leipzig, Jablonowski Gesellschaft (2.3), Roscher RS, Leipzig, 14.11.92; NL Lamprecht (Korr. 59), Lamprecht to Hugo Lamprecht, Leipzig, 6.1.92; LW, 226.
44. NL Lamprecht (Korr. 4), Arndt to Lamprecht, Leipzig, 28.11.85; Weber, *Lexikon*, 16, 631.
45. NL Mevissen, Lamprecht to Mevissen, Leipzig, 10.10.91; StA Dresden, VB 10228/1, Lamprecht to Seydewitz, Leipzig, 29.4.93; LW, 227–28; Karl Czok, "Karl Lamprecht (1856–1915)," in Max Steinmetz, ed., *Bedeutende Gelehrte in Leipzig*, 2 vols. (Leipzig, 1965), 1: 96–97.
46. Goetz, "Goetz," 154–55.
47. NL Mevissen, Lamprecht to Mevissen, Leipzig, 22.7.91.
48. NL Althoff (A I Nr. 73), Lamprecht to Althoff, Leipzig, 15.12.92; (B Nr. 110/2), Lehmann to Althoff, 14.12.92.
49. NL Lamprecht (Korr. 59), Lamprecht to Hugo Lamprecht, 26.9.91; NL Liesegang, Lamprecht to Liesegang, Leipzig, 10.10.91; NL Mevissen, Lamprecht to Mevissen, Leipzig, 10.11.91.
50. NL Lamprecht (Korr. 59), Lamprecht to Hugo Lamprecht, Leipzig, 4.11.92, 11.2.93.
51. NL Mevissen, Lamprecht to Mevissen, Leipzig, 24.5.94.
52. LW, 578.
53. In an agitated letter to his brother in September 1894, the historian indicated that he had in the past had to deal with advances from some of his housekeepers, who hoped to take the place of the absent wife. "I do not want to claim of Frau Bruch that she, too, does not harbor the seed of such a thought in the depths of her soul. But this much is clear: if [this thought] is there, it is stored very deep." NL Lamprecht (Korr. 59), Lamprecht to Hugo Lamprecht, Vienna, 10.9.94.
54. NL Lamprecht (Korr. 38), Lamprecht to Deichmann, n.d. [1886]. Entwurf.
55. NL Lamprecht (Korr. 25). G. Grote'sche Verlagsbuchhandlung to Lamprecht, Berlin, 15.7.82; 20.7.82; 5.2.86; UB Bonn, Autografen-Sammlung, Lamprecht to Richard Pick, Bonn, 24.7.82; *cf.* Herbert Schönebaum, "Unausgeführte Vorhaben wissenschaftlicher und kulturpolitischer Art und die Forschungsinstitute Karl Lamprechts," *Forschungen und Fortschritte*, 33 (1959): 118.
56. NL Lamprecht (Korr. 59), Lamprecht to Hugo Lamprecht, Bonn, 24.10.87; 18.7.88; 21.10.88.
57. See Herbert Schönebaum, "Vom Werden der Deutschen Geschichte Karl Lamprechts," *Deutsche Vierteljahrsschrift für Literaturwissenschaft und Geistesgeschichte*, 25 (1951): 94–111.

58. UA Bonn, Phil. Fak., Lamprecht to Ritter, 10.5.84.
59. NL Schmoller, Lamprecht to Schmoller, Bonn, 17.2.88.
60. Schumann, *Historikertage*, 110.
61. Quoted in Schönebaum, "Unausgeführte Vorhaben," 118.
62. Alfred Dove, "Karl Lamprecht," in *Aufsätze und Briefe*, 1: 315–16; Metz, *Grundformen*, 509, 538; Karl Czok, "Der Methodenstreit und die Gründung des Seminars für Landesgeschichte und Siedlungskunde 1906 an der Universität Leipzig," *Jahrbuch für Regionalgeschichte*, 2 (1967): 17.
63. NL Lamprecht (H 62a), Wilhelm Wundt, Karl Lamprecht, 17–18.
64. Alfred Doren, "Karl Lamprechts Geschichtstheorie und die Kunstgeschichte," *Zeitschrift für Aesthetik und allgemeine Kunstwissenschaft*, 11 (1916): 387.
65. See, for example, Franz Arens, "Karl Lamprecht," PJb, 203 (1926): 194–203.
66. NL Lamprecht (WW 55a), Periodiserung in der Geschichte, 1888–1889. Entwürfe. Schönebaum has reproduced these drafts with minor errors in LW, 188–94. *Cf.* Schorn-Schütte, *Lamprecht*, 55–59.
67. NL Lamprecht (WW 55a), Disposition der geistigen Kultur, 20.2.88; LW, 188–89.
68. NL Lamprecht (WW 55a), Wie hängt d. Entwicklung der aesthet. Kultur mit d. Entwicklung der Moral zsmm?; LW, 192–93.
69. See Frederic Jameson, *The Political Unconscious: Narrative as a Socially Symbolic Act* (Ithaca, 1981), 27–28.
70. NL Lamprecht (WW 55a), Entwicklung der sprachlichen Ausdrucksmittel für die Erfahrung; LW, 189–90.
71. Ibid.
72. Ibid.; Periodisierung; LW, 193–94.
73. NL Lamprecht (W 55a), Geschichtliche Grundlagen für die Entwicklung von Erfahrungsbegriffen; LW, 191–92.
74. NL Lamprecht (W 55a), Formen der Entwicklung sprachlichen Ausdrucks für die Erfahrung (Anmerkung: Zur chronologischen Abgrenzung der Perioden); LW, 190.
75. Karl H. Metz, "Der 'Methodenstreit in der deutschen Geschichtswissenschaft (1891–1899)': Bemerkungen zum sozialen Kontext wissenschaftlicher Auseinandersetzungen," StdSt, 6 (1984): 5; Metz, *Grundformen*, 466.
76. LW, 191.
77. Schönebaum, "Vom Werden," 111.
78. NL Sybel (B1 Nr. 25), Lamprecht to Sybel, Marburg, 9.1.91; NL Althoff (B Nr. 108/1), Lamprecht to Althoff, Leipzig, 28.6.92; NL Lamprecht (Korr. 3), Lamprecht to Althoff, Leipzig, 30.11.93, Konzept.
79. NL Lamprecht (Korr. 59), Lamprecht to Hugo Lamprecht, Bonn, 22.11.89, 16.2.90; (Korr. 31), Hoeniger to Lamprecht, Berlin, 5.1.90.
80. NL Harden, Lamprecht to Harden, Leipzig, 27.6.96.
81. NL Lamprecht (Korr. 59), Lamprecht to Hugo Lamprecht, Bonn, 16.2.90; LW, 278.
82. DG, 1: 79–95.
83. The provenance can be traced through Schmoller, whose review of *Deutsches Wirtschaftsleben* included the gentle criticism that Lamprecht's account would have profited from a reading of Morgan: "Die soziale Entwickelung Deutschlands und Englands hauptsächlich auf dem platten Lande des Mittelalters," *Schmollers Jahrbuch*, 12 (1888): 208. Lamprecht's exposure to Morgan came through the work of Ralph Dargun: see HZ, 71 (1893): 489; Schmoller, "Zur Würdigung," 29; Below, "Zur Würdigung," 7: 160–70; Spiess, 21, 43.
84. NL Lamprecht (Korr. 9), Bernheim to Lamprecht, Greifswald, 21.4.90; DG 1: 104–105.
85. DG, 1: 170.

86. Ibid., 172.
87. Ibid., 179.
88. Ibid., 332.
89. Ibid., 334.
90. Ibid., 359.
91. DG, 2: 179.
92. Ibid., 184.
93. Ibid., 198.
94. DG, 3: 3.
95. NL Lamprecht (Korr. 59), Lamprecht to Hugo Lamprecht, Leipzig, 15.3.92.
96. DG, 3: 195.
97. Ibid., 231.
98. Ibid., 297.
99. NL Bernheim, Lamprecht to Bernheim, Leipzig, 20.5.92.
100. NL Liesegang, Lamprecht to Liesegang, Leipzig, 23.7.92.
101. NL Bernheim, Lamprecht to Bernheim, Leipzig, 27.2.96.
102. NL Mevissen, Lamprecht to Mevissen, Leipzig, 6.7.93.
103. NL Liesegang, Lamprecht to Liesegang, Leipzig, 2.12.95.
104. DG, 4: 211–52.
105. Ibid., 252.
106. Ibid., 260.
107. Ibid., 271.
108. Ibid., 288.
109. Ibid., 291.
110. DG, 5: 75.
111. Ibid., 70.
112. Ibid., 119.
113. Ibid., 125.
114. Ibid., 164.
115. Ibid., 136.
116. Ibid., 217.
117. Ibid., 7.
118. Ibid., 150.
119. Ibid., 272.
120. Ibid., 347.
121. Ibid., 358.
122. Ibid., 767.
123. NL Mevissen, Lamprecht to Mevissen, Leipzig, 24.7.95.
124. Sam Whimster, "Karl Lamprecht and Max Weber: Historical Sociology within the Confines of a Historians' Controversy," in Wolfgang J. Mommsen and Jürgen Osterhammel, eds., *Max Weber and His Contemporaries* (London, 1987), 270.
125. In addition to the modern commentaries by Luise Schorn-Schütte, Karl-Heinz Metz, and Matti Vikaari, see the older studies by Erich Gabert, "Karl Lamprechts Theorie der Geschichtswissenschaft: Darstellung und Versuch einer psychologischen Analyse," Ph.D. dissertation (Leipzig, n.d.); Adolf Kuhnert, *Der Streit um die geschichtswissenschaftlichen Theorien Karl Lamprechts* (Gütersloh, 1906); Emil Jakob Spiess, *Die Geschichtsphilosophie von Karl Lamprecht* (Erlangen, 1912); Erich Rothacker, *Ueber die Möglichkeit und den Ertrag einer genetischen Geschichtsschreibung im Sinne Karl Lamprechts* (Leipzig, 1912); Friedrich Seifert, *Der Streit um Karl Lamprechts Geschichtsphilosophie: Eine historisch-kritische Studie* (Augsburg, 1925).
126. DG, 1: 248–49.
127. DG, 3: 167–68.

128. DG, 4: 308.
129. Ibid., 90–116.
130. Ibid., 431.
131. Ibid., 125.
132. NL Lamprecht (Korr. 8), Arnold Berger to Lamprecht, Bonn, 22.11.96; *cf.* Cassirer, 292. Eduard Engel, one of the most formidable guardians of linguistic purity, was scandalized by the historian's use of the language. Lamprecht, he wrote, was a "Meister des nebelspaltenden Ueberganges," the holder of the prize for "unerträgliche Wortmacherei." Eduard Engel, *Deutsche Stilkunst* (Vienna and Leipzig, 1922), 371, 395; *cf.* Metz, *Grundformen*, 582–90.
133. NL Mevissen, Lamprecht to Mevissen, Leipzig, 31.12.94; NL Bernheim, Lamprecht to Bernheim, Leipzig, 13.3.95.
134. NL Liesegang, Lamprecht to Liesegang, Leipzig, 4.5.94.
135. DG, 2: 248.
136. DG, 4: 48.
137. DG, 5: 330. The passage was worse than it appears here, for the entire description was in the form of a long appositive phrase; the predicate, "seemed," followed only at the end.
138. DG, 2: 165.
139. DG, 4: 133–34.
140. DG, 2: 51.
141. DG, 4: 3.
142. DG, 1: 216.
143. DG, 4: 43.
144. DG, 5: 115.
145. DG, 1: 3.
146. DG, 5: 134.
147. For example, DG, 1: 210–16.
148. For example, DG, 1: 234. "Gingen auch Goten und Wandalen, Rugen, Turklingen und andere Stämme des Ostens der unmittelbar deutschen Entwicklung verloren, ja erzeugte ihr Ausscheiden eine schmerzliche Lücke im Zusammenhang des nationalen Gebietes, so überbrückten sie andrerseits in mutiger Selbstaufopferung den Abgrund, der zwischen der romanischen und germanischen Gruppe der europäischen Völkerfamilie nur zu leicht hätte entstehen können." I have no idea what this passage means.
149. Rudolf Kötzschke, "Karl Lamprecht," in Rudolf Kötzschke and Armin Tille, *Karl Lamprecht: Eine Erinnerungsschrift der deutschen Geschichtsblätter* (Gotha, n.d.), 9.
150. DG, 3: 208–209; *cf.* DWL, 1: 119.
151. Jameson, *Political Unconscious*, 70.
152. Deutsche Staatsbibliothek, Berlin, NL Heinrich von Treitschke (7), Lamprecht to Treitschke, Leipzig, 20.6.92; 9.12.94; Hessisches Staatsarchiv Marburg, NL Hermann Grimm, Lamprecht to Grimm, Leipzig, 2.5.96. The dissertation of Susan Schultz presents a convincing analysis of this theme in Lamprecht's work: see Schultz, "Moral Force," esp. 127–89.
153. White, *Metahistory*, 163–91; Northrop Frye, "Historical Criticism: Theory of Modes," *Anatomy of Criticism: Four Essays* (Princeton, 1971), 43–52.
154. DG, 1: 297.
155. DG, 5: 12.
156. DG, 2: 343; DG, 4: 197.
157. DG, 5: 126–27.
158. DG, 1: 107, 110–11.
159. DG, 3: 52; DG, 4: 256; DG, 5: 288, 364–65.

160. DG, 1: 318.
161. DG, 2: 183.
162. DG, 5: 134.
163. Ibid., 133.
164. KE, 16, 35, 39.
165. DG, 3: 140.
166. NL Mevissen, Lamprecht to Mevissen, Leipzig, 2.12.95; NL Lamprecht (Korr. 59), Lamprecht to Hugo Lamprecht, Leipzig, 1.4.93; LW, 295.

5

Nemesis

Nun ist sogar noch eine fürchterliche Spezies von Histo-
rikern übrig, tüchtige, strenge und ehrliche Charaktere—
aber enge Köpfe.

It began early in 1887 as another of the pedantic quarrels that were regularly fought out in the pages of German academic journals. Lamprecht's review of the book in question was not unappreciative; but it emphasized the author's obses-
sion with detail and the book's lack of overall coherence and design. The review also chided the author for his failure to cite the appearance of a unit of currency, the Rhenish *gulden*, in dating a central fourteenth century document. The reply from the aggrieved author disregarded Lamprecht's broader criticism and pointed out, on the basis of Lamprecht's *Economic Life in the Middle Ages*, that the Rhenish *gulden* had appeared earlier than Lamprecht had claimed in the review. Lamprecht retorted that the author had misinterpreted the passage in question in the *Economic Life* and had overlooked others. The author's next rejoinder not only quoted chapter and verse from Lamprecht's own work, but revealed that in several passages of his magnum opus, Lamprecht had written of "Rhenish *gulden*" but had cited documents that referred instead to "Bohemian *gulden*." Although Lamprecht protested that the misreading resided in the edition of the documents he had used, he had suffered a minor but unambiguous public humiliation. He thereupon announced that in view of his antagonist's "most inappropriate [*befremdlichen*] means of scholarly debate," he was cutting off all further dialogue with him.[1] In the event, the exchange between the two scholars continued in one forum or another for more than a decade, and it had fateful consequences.

Georg von Below, the author of the book under review, was a far less typical figure in the profession than was Karl Lamprecht.[2] He was born in 1858, two years after Lamprecht, into one of East Prussia's great noble families, which for centuries had provided the Prussian state with distinguished soldiers and statesmen.[3] Like Lamprecht, though, he bore the weight of painful childhood experiences. When he was three, he contracted polio and emerged from the ordeal with his left arm badly underdeveloped. Several years later a fall from a horse crippled his right arm. These misfortunes ruled out a military career and left the child bitter and frustrated, particularly after a painful series of operations failed to restore the use of his right hand. The constant presence of officers at the family estate near Gumbinnen doubtless served to increase his frustrations, as did the departure of his younger brother for a career in the army. His success at the *Gymnasium* in Gumbinnen first suggested that he might find in scholarship an alternative outlet for his great energies, his urge to prove himself in spite of his handicaps, and the resentments he was never entirely able to allay.[4]

In 1878 he entered the university in Königsberg, where he studied agriculture and law. He then transferred to Bonn to study history with Ritter and Maurenbrecher. He brought to his studies the deep Lutheran piety common to most young German historians, as well as "tenacious, genuinely Prussian energy" (the words are Ritter's) and a devotion to conservative political ideals, which was not so common among a group of young academics whose inclinations were usually national liberal.[5] His most striking traits, however, were the extraordinary intensity and critical acuity of his mind; and he asserted these traits with a ferocity that might almost be described as military (or perhaps Clausewitzian), as if the ethos of his profession demanded that divergent positions be sought out, their weak points exposed, and their foundations attacked until destroyed.[6]

Below and Lamprecht first met in Bonn, after Below had returned from a semester in Berlin. A more complete temperamental and intellectual dissimilarity is difficult to imagine. Lamprecht was then beginning to blossom as a scholar; he exuded an intimidating self-confidence that bordered on arrogance and contrasted with Below's self-conscious reserve. Lamprecht's intellectual energies were directed toward synthesis and the grand, comprehensive vision whose medium was the extended historical survey. Below's energies were no less intense, but they were analytical, attuned to fine distinction, uncomfortable with abstraction; and they tended to find expression in the short monograph and review.[7] The contrast between the two young historians was rendered explosive by traits they shared. The mixture of ambition and insecurity was volatile in both; and although Lamprecht was not as combative by temperament, both men were easily provoked.

The relationship between the two was nonetheless cordial at first. Lamprecht introduced Below to economic history, and if the student's enthusiasm for the subject was more reserved than the instructor's, Below nevertheless described himself as one who had followed Lamprecht's words in the classroom "most attentively."[8] Lamprecht was more accessible than the dour Ritter, with whom Below's relationship was as difficult as Lamprecht's.[9] Lamprecht provided welcome assistance with Below's dissertation, on the election of German cathedral chapters in the Middle Ages.[10] The two remained in contact after Below left Bonn for Marburg, where he habilitated with Varrentrapp and Max Lenz on the strength of a critical edition of the documents of the territorial diets in Jülich and Berg—a project commissioned by the Society for the Study of Rhenish

History. The first public sign of tension between the two young scholars appeared late in 1886, when Below commented critically on a lecture that Lamprecht delivered to the Society for the Study of Rhenish History.[11] Lamprecht's response came early the next year in his review of Below's *Habilitationsschrift*, which occasioned the polemical exchange and sealed the antagonism.

The intellectual grounds of the antagonism emerged shortly thereafter, when Below created a sensation in the profession with two ferocious articles in the *Historische Zeitschrift* on the origins of the medieval towns.[12] In these articles he lashed out at what he called the "currently reigning view" that the towns emerged out of the patrimonial system, that their inhabitants were originally enserfed, and that the judicial powers that the towns exercised originated as extensions of patrimonial law. Instead, he argued, the towns were entities entirely separate from manorialism. Both in their functions as markets and in their ability to defend themselves behind walls, the towns owed their existence to concessions (*Regale*) that rested upon public authority, derived ultimately from royal power, and had nothing to do with patrimonialism. The jurisdictions of patrimonial and municipal courts—the one private, the other public—were accordingly, Below insisted, at no time and in no way conflated.

Below's efforts to draw the bounds between the towns and the patrimonial system presented an early illustration of his methodological preference for separation and distinction over inclusion and synthesis. The articles also had broader implications. They intensified a historiographical dispute over patrimonialism that had been building for decades.[13] The debate was extraordinarily complicated and arcane, but it had important ramifications. In part these were political, for the controversy touched on the origins not only of the towns, but of guilds and capitalism; and it was conducted in an era of partisan debate in Germany over the deficiencies and excesses of capitalism, the fate of the guilds, and the broadening of municipal autonomy.[14]

Of more immediate relevance to the historical profession, however, was the fact that the debate provided the terrain on which the proponents of two conflicting visions of history clashed. The underlying methodological and philosophical issue was the origin of the modern state. In his articles in the *Historische Zeitschrift*, Below provided an uncompromising statement of one of the conflicting positions. He characterized the towns as repositories of public law, which were exempted from the jurisdiction of manorial law. Towns thus represented vehicles of continuity in public law and state sovereignty throughout the Middle Ages; and they documented the fundamental distinction between public and private law—in other words, between politics and society. The other position held that public law disappeared in the German Middle Ages in the wake of the collapse of Carolingian power, only to reemerge later out of the womb of patrimonialism. The corollary of this so-called *Hofrechtstheorie* was that the state and public authority emerged only as derivatives of anterior developments in the private realm of *Grundherrschaft*. If the one position implied the priority of political history—the proposition that the state was the principal agent of historical development—the other implied the historical primacy of society over politics.

The *Hofrechtstheorie* could trace its lineage back to the work of Karl Friedrich Eichhorn and Georg von Maurer, but by the time Below took the field against it, it had become a cardinal tenet in the historiographical trend now known variously as economic history or *Kulturgeschichte*, which was emerging as an alternative to the political history favored by the German academy.[15] The principal representatives of this genre were featured in Below's articles, but not in a flattering light. Among the "so-called economic historians" whose work fell under the young historian's critical knife were Nitzsch, Inama-Sternegg, Gierke, Arnold, and Schmoller, as well as Lamprecht. Below laid down the gauntlet to all the adherents of what he later labeled the "Nitzsch cult," those scholars who, whether they called themselves cultural or economic historians, had challenged the primacy of the state and politics.[16]

In his crusade Below could be confident of a lot of sympathy, not only from Heinrich Brunner and Rudolf Sohm, the legal scholars on whose theories he relied for his case on the continuity of public law, but from most of the leading figures in the historical profession, including Sybel and Lehmann, the men who controlled the *Historische Zeitschrift*.[17] Below brought to a head concerns that had been building among political historians for some years, and he addressed the kinds of frustrations that moved Ludwig Weiland to write from Göttingen: "Thank God that someone has finally torn these things away from the economic historians who have reduced everything to a hopeless snarl."[18] The only reservations these men had were about the "unmannerly tone" of Below's polemic, but the political historians were clearly happy to have him represent their case.[19] The role was satisfying as well to Below, for it meant that this scion of the great family could, in his own fashion, serve the state after all.

"Below seems to be making himself into your intimate enemy," Dove wrote to Lamprecht after the appearance of the first of Below's articles in the *Historische Zeitschrift*.[20] Lamprecht had good reason to be alarmed over the articles, for he himself had recently emerged as the principal younger proponent of the kind of history that Below attacked. Although Lamprecht's scholarship had only peripheral relevance to Below's immediate topic, Below subjected it to extended criticism that verged on ridicule. He not only accused Lamprecht of misunderstanding the "basic character [*Wesen*] of medieval administration" but devoted long footnotes to tearing apart, document by document, conclusions Lamprecht had reached in his *Economic Life in the Middle Ages*.[21]

Lamprecht was furious. He immediately demanded that the *Historische Zeitschrift* permit him a rebuttal.[22] Lehmann's refusal served early notice that this journal was not going to be a neutral forum in the exchange. It suggested as well that Below enjoyed an advantage in a contest in which the stakes were higher than injured pride. Below's attack came at an inopportune time for Lamprecht, who was still in Bonn awaiting a call to a chair. He thus had to be concerned about the delicate state of his professional reputation, particularly because his opponent was now an immediate rival, whose attack seemed part of a transparent strategy to win a professorial appointment.[23]

Below's next assault in the *Historische Zeitschrift* caused additional alarm. His long review of Lamprecht's *Economic Life in the Middle Ages* appeared in the fall of 1889, after much anticipation and a delay that invited questions about the motives of reviewer and editor alike.[24] The verdict on Lamprecht's scholarship was severe. "There is hardly a sentence," Below announced, "which one can accept without criticism." The work's principal weakness (and Below insisted that it was common to the whole genre of economic history), was the author's failure to work inductively. Lamprecht's massive citations were "for the most part simply pearls arrayed on the string of aprioristic constructions." The constructions to which Below most objected were those with which Lamprecht attempted to couple the emergence of the state to economic development. The bulk of the review comprised an impassioned attempt to defend the thesis that territorial sovereignty (*Landeshoheit*) did not grow out of *Grundherrschaft*. It emerged instead, Below contended, out of public authority that had originally been vested in the imperial office before it devolved onto the so-called *Grafschaften*; accordingly, all officials who exercised public judicial powers did so on the residual basis of this authority. The review bore all the hallmarks of the savage scholarship for which Below was becoming notorious, but the caustic charges of error, contradiction, and confusion were more insulting this time than convincing. On one of the few occasions in his career, the reviewer was on the defensive, and he conveyed the impression of a man struggling to rescue his own views from Lamprecht's massive evidence.

The clearest sign that Below's assault had failed came within a matter of weeks, when Lamprecht received the call to the chair in Marburg. Althoff, at least, had evidently not been impressed by the attack. Lamprecht would have been even more gratified had he known that Below's name had appeared alongside his own in third place on the list submitted by the faculty in Marburg and that Althoff had chosen him over his younger rival.[25] Appointment to the chair also afforded Lamprecht a measure of revenge. As he left for Leipzig a year later, he discovered that Below was Lehmann's favorite candidate for the now vacant chair in Marburg. Lamprecht's parting gesture was to sabotage Below's candidacy—a step that led to the young historian's exile to a professorship at the academy in Münster until 1897.[26]

In the meantime, Lamprecht had begun to focus his energies on writing the *German History*, and his role became more peripheral as Below's battles moved to another theater. Below turned his fire on Berlin, in the direction of Schmoller.[27] His immediate targets were two young historical economists at the university, Ignaz Jastrow and Robert Hoeniger, with whom Lamprecht had close ties. With Lamprecht's support and encouragement, they engaged Below in a polemical exchange that reverberated throughout the academic press and was as vicious as it was pedantic.[28] The point of the debate was hidden amid recriminations over the appropriateness and accuracy of footnotes.[29] To the initiated observer, though, the issue was the validity of the kind of economic history that both Schmoller and Lamprecht represented. While its vehemence could perhaps be attributed to the temperament of the contestants, the exchange was another symptom of the deeper tensions that were gathering in the German historical profession, eroding the consensus within it, and subverting the bounds of civility that had once governed academic discourse. The dispute was conducted in a tone well described by the German word *Gehässigkeit*; and before it was over, it had prompted charges of anti-Semitism (Hoeniger and Jastrow were both Jews), provoked Hoeniger to challenge Below to a duel (which because of his disability Below could not accept), and damaged the careers of both the young scholars who had taken Below on.[30]

As Lamprecht watched the spectacle from Marburg and then from Leipzig, the intensification of his feelings about Below ensured that the antagonism between these two scholars would become difficult to contain. He began to view Below's behavior as an ethical rather than an academic problem. He convinced himself that Below was dishonest. As early as 1888, terms like "lies and deceit [*Lug und Betrug*]" and "falsification [*Fälschung*]" began to surface in Lamprecht's correspondence as characterizations of his antagonist's scholarship.[31] In 1890, he referred in print to Below's "immaturity and untruthfulness [*Unreife und Unwahrhaftigkeit*]."[32] As Below's polemic with Hoeniger and Jastrow reached its final stages in 1892, Lamprecht was speaking of Below as "morally dead," an "intriguer," and a "pathological character."[33] Lamprecht seemed to be arming himself for the renewal of his own direct confrontation with his antagonist. A confrontation was imminent in all events, for rumors had begun to circulate that Below was preparing a review of the first volumes of Lamprecht's *German History*.

Friedrich Meinecke tells in his memoirs of spending several weeks in 1891 with Otto Hintze in Switzerland hiking around Lake Lucerne. Their conversations were animated, Meinecke reports, for they had to do with pressing historiographical questions—whether the proper subject of history was the collectivity or the individual and whether historical development operated according to laws.[34] The immersion of the two young historians in these questions suggested the broader context of Below's early polemics against the economic historians over patrimonialism. One observer of the profession in this epoch has spoken of a search for "a new Archimedean point," around which the Rankean legacy of political history might be broadened or perhaps replaced.[35] A sense of flux pervaded the German historical profession in 1890, as did anticipation that major issues were about to be engaged.

Many of these issues emerged in a celebrated exchange over the theme of *Kulturgeschichte*, which began shortly after Below launched his attacks. It was probably more than a coincidence that the next historian to come to the public defense of the profession's reigning values was by social background also an outsider—more so, in fact, than Below himself. Dietrich Schäfer was a child of the working class; his roots were in the shipyards of Bremen.[36] In the course of his wanderings among university chairs, which brought him eventually (in 1903) to Berlin, this student of Treitschke and Waitz paused for several years in Tübingen, where in 1888 he presented his inaugural lecture on "The Proper Domain [Arbeitsgebiet] of History."[37]

Schäfer's object was to refute the idea that a "new era of historical writing" had arrived with Kulturgeschichte, that the several varieties of scholarship that emphasized mass phenomena and popular life offered a valid alternative to the history of the state and politics. Schäfer offered two lines of defense of political history, both of them more practical than philosophical. The first was to point out the historical connection between state-building and the writing of history, the fact that the great monuments of historiography were inconceivable without the state as both their object and context. As he himself put this proposition, "A healthy and powerful state [Staatswesen] is the indispensable precondition for the vital and powerful writing of history."[38] Schäfer's other argument was to emphasize methodological weaknesses in cultural history to which even the genre's proponents were sensitive. The subject matter proper to cultural history, he noted, was amorphous and ill defined beyond the vague sense that it had to do with all matters other than politics and the state. More seriously, the genre could offer no distinctive methodology either to synthesize this vast subject matter or to support judgments about its historical significance.

As Schäfer portrayed it, political history alone offered the practical tools to achieve the comprehensive vision of the past that the cultural historians claimed to pursue. The development of the state, he insisted, represented the dominant theme in human history, the only index with which to gauge the significance of every other facet of human behavior; the state accordingly provided the essential focus for integrating the history of all realms of human activity. To the extent that his argument had a philosophical foundation, it drew directly from Droysen. "Moral forces," Schäfer explained, "are the ones that govern history."[39] The repository of the highest order of moral force was the state, the institution whose claims on its members were the most compelling and comprehensive. Accordingly, both practical and moral imperatives defined "the relationship of people to the state" as the proper focus of the historian's activity—as "the proper domain of historical writing." The history of the state furnished the only viable context for the study of those subjects that so fascinated the cultural historians. "Obligations to the state and to one's people [Volkstum]," Schäfer concluded, provided the framework "within which alone family and society, as well as religious and legal order, achieve secure shape."[40] Schäfer's argument was thus that cultural history could, if practiced properly with an eye to political context, serve as a welcome auxiliary to political history, but that any sharp distinction between the two genres was illusory.

This claim quickly drew a rejoinder from the young historical economist Eberhard Gothein, who was then teaching at the technical university in Karlsruhe.[41] Gothein's career was already displaying significant similarities to Lamprecht's.[42] He was a student of the historian Erdmannsdörffer and the economist Knies, as well as a disciple of Burckhardt. Like Lamprecht, Gothein regarded himself as a cultural historian. He, too, wrestled with the challenges of synthesizing the material and ideal realms of history; and his scholarly career testified to the same difficulties of staking out an intellectual terrain for *Kulturgeschichte* along the academic boundaries that divided economics and history. He was, however, a more cautious scholar than Lamprecht, with whom he was briefly a rival for professorial chairs; his ambitions were lower, he took fewer risks, and he made fewer enemies. In fact, his brief polemical defense of cultural history was something of an aberration in his career.

"Political history remains a necessary and valuable undertaking, but general, cultural history demands the integration and subordination [of political history]."[43] Gothein's defense of this proposition read like a paean to Herder. Cultural history, he argued, addressed the higher unity of all facets of human spiritual development; politics was but one of these facets. Gothein conceded to Schäfer, however, that politics occupied a privileged position in some historical epochs. Other concessions soon followed, as Gothein revealed the extent to which he and Schäfer were working from common philosophical assumptions. Because history was properly concerned with the development of the human spirit, Gothein insisted that "cultural history in its purest form is the history of ideas." In this sense, he noted, the genre's early pioneers included a great historian, recently deceased, for whom the actions of the state were but expressions of higher ideas (in this case God's).[44] With a bow to two of Ranke's colleagues in Berlin, Droysen and Wilhelm Dilthey, Gothein also acknowledged the primacy of free will and moral ideas in history. The only consideration that Gothein could now invoke against Schäfer's claims for political history was itself political. Gothein denied that the state represented the highest moral force in history. "Humanity's greatest moral progress has not come through the state," he observed, "but in resistance to it; progress can always be traced back to the opposition of the individual's moral consciousness to a political order that had become immoral."[45]

The rejoinder Schäfer issued two years later was anticlimactic.[46] There was no need for him to offer new arguments beyond emphasizing the similarities between Gothein's position and his own. But Schäfer did dwell briefly on the political implications of Gothein's historiographical preferences. He suggested that the new interest in cultural history reflected the subjection of scholarship to the "entrepreneurial spirit of book publishers" and the "playground of popularity."[47] The impression was difficult to resist, he warned, that behind the calls for cultural history lurked a political agenda animated by "the slogans of human rights, liberty, equality, fraternity."[48]

Although it was conducted in a tone much more civil, this curious exchange between Schäfer and Gothein raised the same issue as Below's polemic against the economic historians.[49] In both cases, the debate was over the primacy of the state as the object of historical study. But although Schäfer and Gothein addressed the issue more directly, they broke off their debate before they engaged underlying methodological problems. The fact that the two contestants shared so many assumptions resulted in a more tepid dialogue than many observers wished, Lamprecht among them; and it blocked more than a cursory discussion of fundamental questions.[50] But neither Gothein nor Schäfer was prepared temperamentally or intellectually to explore these questions further.

In fact, despite the interest it provoked in the historical profession, their polemic served less to bring clarity to the discussion of cultural history than to suggest the extent to which *Kulturgeschichte* had become a *Reizwort*, the symbol around which fronts were solidifying in a dispute over issues whose full dimensions were still undefined.[51] The alarm sounded by Schäfer and Below reflected not only the visceral apprehension that this term was beginning to arouse among academic historians, but also a growing sense of confidence among those who thought of themselves as cultural historians.

Georg Steinhausen was giving voice to this confidence when, in 1893, he wrote that "Cultural history may in fact [still] be the discipline of the future, but one can already see the dawn of this future."[52] Steinhausen, who was then the university librarian in Jena, had just taken over the *Zeitschrift für deutsche Kulturgeschichte*. This "Journal for Remarkable Things," as Below once called it, had languished under the editorship of a retired archivist who catered to the antiquarian interests of a circle of librarians, archivists, *Gymnasiallehrer*, and other amateur historians.[53] Steinhausen, who was also the author of a two-volume history of letter writing in late medieval Germany, brought a new sense of purpose to the journal. He was determined to add rigor to its scholarship, to enlist the cooperation of academics, and to purge cultural history of its reputation for dilettantism.[54] The presence of academic historians and economists in the ranks of his early contributors, among them Lamprecht, Gothein, and Friedrich von Bezold, lent a measure of credibility to his efforts.

Steinhausen began then to call for the establishment of independent university chairs of cultural history.[55] In support of his demands he could point to the growing frequency with which courses in this subject were being offered at German universities—an observation that the research of Gerhard Oestreich has more recently confirmed.[56] At the universities, however, *Kulturgeschichte* implied the somewhat more rigorously defined field of social and economic history; and its professors were economists rather than historians.[57].

The near-absence of academic historians in the ranks of those who were promoting the several varieties of cultural history suggested the deeper tensions that the growing prominence of this genre was provoking in the German historical profession. The interest in *Kulturgeschichte* was due to a convergence among several groups on the profession's periphery, where sensitivity to contemporary social problems was evidently greater than in the profession's academic core. The most prominent of these groups comprised the historical economists, many of whom hoped to enlist scholarship in the cause of social reform. Many of these men were active in the *Verein für Sozialpolitik* and soon became leading figures in the emergence of sociology as an academic discipline.

The economists were joined by a more diverse group, drawn from what one might characterize as the historical profession's second tier, chiefly the academically educated historians whose careers had stopped short of university chairs. The *Zeitschrift für Kulturgeschichte* was their forum; Steinhausen was their spokesman, and if his own career was at all representative, professional resentment against the academic historians was an element in their enthusiasm for cultural history.[58] The most significant component of this group included the men who taught history in the classical secondary schools and whose interest in cultural history was in part a product of concerns similar to the economists'. They proposed to reform the curricula of the *Gymnasien* in order to address contemporary social problems more effectively. Pedagogical reforms in Prussia and other states in the early 1890s addressed this concern and gratified the advocates of cultural history generally. Directives from ministries of culture mandated more attention to social and economic developments in the curricula of the secondary schools, in order to promote an awareness of the "perniciousness of all attempts to alter the social order by force."[59]

These strides did not, however, resolve the problems that had long plagued *Kulturgeschichte*. Those who promoted it seemed to make up such a diverse coalition that it remained difficult to identify even the common areas of their interest. The greatest common bond among those who described themselves as cultural historians remained the conviction that they represented a viable complement or alternative to the political history practiced in the universities. However, a great deal of what passed as cultural history was still bereft of theoretical reflection; and it addressed the minutiae of manners and morals, of *Lebkuchen* and *Totenbretter*, with little sense for historical context. The only consensus on method among the cultural historians appeared to be that all phases of human activity belonged in the historian's purview and that the writing of history ought not to be confined to matters of the state. This proposition not only offered little guidance to a subject matter specific to cultural history; it was unobjectionable as well to most political historians, who could argue along with Schäfer that politics provided the only possible focus for an analytical synthesis of the many realms of human activity. In this light Gothein's defense of cultural history was an effort in bridge-building. In appealing to Droysen, Dilthey, and Burckhardt, it emphasized methodologies and interpretive categories common to political and cultural history—that both were concerned with the play of ideas and moral forces, that both properly emphasized the singular and individual in history, and that both accordingly demanded a hermeneutic of *Verstehen*, or interpretive understanding.

Gothein's concept of cultural history represented but a mild challenge to reigning views within the historical profession, for it proposed only a broadening of subject matter without any modification of method. The challenge to political history on another front—the one manned by Below—was more serious, for it involved a more coherent definition of subject matter; it also had more troubling methodological implications, which the polemics of the late 1880s had begun to draw out.[60] Although Schmoller's disciples worked with many of the same assumptions as the political historians, their scholarship emphasized a specific realm of human activity that could contest the supremacy of the political and that invited the use of interpretive categories that seemed to threaten the historians. The study of material *Zustände*, the economic and social structures of human behavior, appeared to privilege the collectivity over the individual as the object of analysis; it also emphasized the regularity over the singularity of behavior and accorded preference to causal analysis—at least in the sense of statistical correlation—over the play of intentionality and free will. Although he did less to define cultural history than to catalogue it as a realm distinct from politics, Steinhausen seemed to support this view to the extent that he, too, spoke of the importance of *Zustände* as the defining mark of cultural history and suggested that the proper object of the genre was "the mass, the type."[61]

Steinhausen and most economists nonetheless defended the validity of political history as it was traditionally practiced. Even if they challenged the primacy of politics in history, they conceded that singularity, ideal forces, and moral freedom were the proper concepts for analyzing the history of the state. Their position was rather that the effort to comprehend the entirety of the past, to understand the workings of all the conditions that operated on human behavior, required a plurality of methods. A similar outlook informed the sympathetic treatment of cultural history in Ernst Bernheim's influential treatise on the philosophy and methodology of history, the first edition of which appeared in 1889. Here Bernheim advocated a cooperative division of labor among historians, philologists, economists, sociologists, and others whose work drew them to study the past.[62]

Few cultural historians were prepared to move beyond this position and to argue that the analytical strategies appropriate to the material realm of *Zustände* were applicable to all phases of history and offered the only legitimate basis for historical scholarship. The most radical and ambitious variety of cultural history was distinguished by the belief in just such a uniform methodology, which would synthesize the study of all facets of history into a single comprehensive *Wissenschaft* that emphasized regular patterns of behavior. The vision was basically that of the positivists, who had not enjoyed much support in Germany. By the late 1880s, however, their cause had been encouraged by strides made in statistics and psychology, which suggested the possibility of subjecting all facets of human behavior, including the political and mental, to common categories of causal analysis. Those who advocated this vision were still not numerous in Germany, but in 1889 one of them obtained a hearing in—of all places—the *Historische Zeitschrift*. Here the young historical economist, Paul Hinneberg, attacked the distinction between the human and natural sciences and argued that the study of the regularities (*Gesetzmässigkeiten*) that operated in all areas of history was the only defensible basis of a historical *Wissenschaft*.[63]

Hinneberg's provocation drew no immediate response. The many issues of subject matter and method that the discussion of cultural history had raised remained unfocused. They came to a head several years later, when the only academic historian prominently associated with *Kulturgeschichte* embraced the most extreme and uncompromising position yet defined.

A spirit of rancor was abroad in the German historical profession in the early 1890s, and it unsettled the camp of the political historians as well. Here Max Lehmann unleashed a bitter dispute when he challenged the Borussian symbology at one of its foundations and argued that Frederick the Great had started the Seven Years' War in an act of aggression.[64] Defense of the orthodox view—that Frederick had responded to an Austrian attack in 1756—fell to Albert Naudé, a young student of Reinhold Koser in Berlin.[65] Lehmann's campaign on behalf of his views provided additional evidence of his tenacious moralism, and it cost him a lot of good will in the profession. It also led to his break with Sybel. In December 1892, Lehmann decided to leave Marburg for Leipzig, only to learn that the ministry proposed to appoint Naudé as his successor. In his effort to block his rival's candidacy, Lehmann circulated a series of letters with scurrilous charges, which prompted Sybel—who with Treitschke was the leading representative of the symbology that Lehmann had assaulted—to demand a formal recantation. Lehmann predictably refused, so Sybel removed him from the editorial staff of the *Historische Zeitschrift* in March 1893.[66]

When Lehmann moved to Leipzig to join Lamprecht in the spring of 1893, he was an unhappy man. His decision to leave Marburg had not been enthusiastic, and he was apprehensive about working with Lamprecht, for despite his clash with Sybel and his other colleagues, Lehmann remained loyal to the historiographical fundaments of political history.[67] The vigor of his apprehensions became clear soon after his arrival when, in his inaugural lecture to the Leipzig faculty, he addressed some of the issues raised in the recent controversies over *Kulturgeschichte*. The lecture was entitled "History and Natural Science."[68] In it he rejected every attempt to work out a unified methodology and to frame laws of historical development. The realm of history did not admit of the regularity and predictability of nature. History, he insisted, was instead the realm of the free personality: "the social and political structures of the past are themselves all creations of personalities and receive their individual character by this means." Lehmann pleaded his case with appeals to Droysen and Ranke, as well as to Luther, Stein, Bismarck, and the other heroes in the pantheon of German historicism. More offensive was his gratuitous attack on the work of several of the scholars in his audience. His remarks on the impropriety of statistics, theories of economic development, and geographical explanation in historical analysis fell at the feet of Bücher, Roscher, and Ratzel. His rejection of analogy was likewise directed at the faculty's historical economists. "Analogies are permitted for the natural scientist; to the historian they are forbidden, for they violate the sources [*Überlieferung*]." Lehmann garnished this pronouncement with a swipe at Schmoller, as he charged that "the situation of the guilds in Strassburg allows no reliable [sicheren] conclusions about the situation of the guilds in Basel."

The principal target of Lehmann's remarks, however, was his colleague in the historical seminar. Lamprecht had been the driving force behind Lehmann's appointment in Leipzig, and he had insisted on hiring a political historian in the interests of balance in the seminar. He accepted Lehmann's lecture, as he wrote to Mevissen, as an "invitation to dance," a challenge to constructive dialogue.[69] Lamprecht's response to his colleague came in a lecture to his own introductory course. Here he suggested that circumstances imposed limits on human freedom in history in the same manner as an individual's freedom of movement was limited by the deck of a moving ship.[70] Lamprecht appeared to offer a compromise when he insisted that "the principal task of the historian, but also the greatest thrill [Reiz] of historical research, consists in balancing the force of freedom off against the force of necessity, the personal against the structural, in every epoch and in every sequence of events." But he immediately undercut the offer with the assertion, which he was shortly later to repeat in the fourth volume of the German History, that the historical study of personality, freedom, and genius was not in the final analysis a scientific undertaking; it demanded instead the gifts of an artist. "When the historian devotes himself to the sympathetic understanding [of genius], he becomes completely an artist; now the flight of historical imagination rules uncontrolled and uncontrollable."

If Lamprecht hoped that these remarks would lead to a constructive exchange with his colleague, he miscalculated. Arguably, no member of the German historical profession was less suited by temperament to compromise than Lehmann—a man who, Schmoller once complained, looked upon those who disagreed with him "as intellectually or morally defective."[71] Lehmann's inaugural lecture compounded the strains he had brought with him from Marburg, and he became agitated. He and Lamprecht clashed over the dissertation of one of Lamprecht's students.[72] The other students in the seminar, most of whom sided with Lamprecht in the exchange over method, deserted his lectures.[73] Soon Lehmann broke off contacts with all his colleagues. The opening of a chair in Göttingen provided him a way out, and in July 1893, after only three months, he fled from Leipzig, complaining of the quality of life in the big city and the "tyrannical inclinations" of his colleague there.[74]

The bizarre circumstances of Lehmann's departure from Leipzig were the talk of the profession. They also raised a number of questions. Lehmann's attack on Lamprecht was greeted, as one of Lamprecht's friends reported, with "jubilations of applause [Begeisterungsjubel]" in Berlin, and Lehmann might well have hoped to build bridges back to these circles, as well as to escape association with a colleague whose scholarship he had concluded was unsound.[75] It is also possible that Althoff encouraged his move back to Prussian territory in order to save Lehmann and Lamprecht from one another.[76] In all events, this episode represented a last preliminary salvo in the greatest methodological controversy the profession had ever seen; and it prefigured the mutual incomprehension as well as the personal enmities between the opposing sides. It was also the direct prelude to an episode well described as grotesque.[77]

Success in the German historical profession demanded close attention to what might be called the politics of the academic review. Who reviewed a book and in which journal were decisions of vital significance; no aspiring historian could afford to be indifferent to them or to the power they placed in the hands of journal editors and scholars with connections to these men. Lamprecht's experience as editor of the *Westdeutsche Zeitschrift* had afforded him early insight into the strategies of reviewing; and he applied the lessons to his own work. Sending complimentary copies of the four volumes of his *Economic Life* to Meitzen, Gierke, and Schmoller represented a large investment for author and publisher alike; the dividends came, as Lamprecht had hoped, in the form of laudatory reviews from these scholars in important journals. The historian planned to promote the *German History* in a similar fashion and planted a number of favorable early reviews.[78] This practice had its risks, though. In one early review, Lamprecht's close friend, the archivist Georg Winter in Marburg, was so extravagant in his praise of the work—he claimed to detect "the spark of Ranke's spirit" in it—that he embarrassed even the author.[79]

Lamprecht's opponents were themselves adepts of the same politics, and they had the advantage of access to the profession's leading journal. It is unclear whether Lehmann or Sybel commissioned the review of the *German History* in the *Historische Zeitschrift* late in 1892, but the decision was an unambiguous sign of the antagonism toward Lamprecht in the editorial offices of this journal.[80] The commission went to Below. Before the review could appear, however, Lehmann's move to Leipzig forced him to reconsider the decision, in the calculation that another malevolent review from Below in his journal would destroy his relationship with his new colleague in Leipzig. Threatening his resignation from the editorial board, Lehmann persuaded Sybel that "anyone other than Below" should review Lamprecht's volumes.[81] Below then withdrew the review and placed it in the *Deutsche Zeitschrift für Geschichtswissenschaft*, which Ludwig Quidde edited in Munich.

Lehmann's subsequent removal from the editorial board of the *Historische Zeitschrift* and then his falling out with Lamprecht altered the situation radically in the spring of 1893 and cleared the way for the appearance of Below's review in Sybel's journal. Sybel's hostility to Lamprecht appears to have been long-building but muted by his friendship with Mevissen.[82] Sybel now emerged, in all events, as a driving force in the campaign against cultural history's leading protagonist. He had no difficulty in persuading Below to retrieve the review from Quidde in May and to send it back to Berlin, where he himself then "sharpened it in fundamental respects" and published it in November.[83]

Below's long review of the first three volumes of Lamprecht's *German History* established both the tone and the parameters for much of the debate that followed.[84] Given Below's fastidious sense of scholarship (to say nothing of his repugnance for Lamprecht), the failure of the review to engage the larger historiographical issues raised in these volumes was perhaps to be expected. The explosion of errant detail transfixed the reviewer. The bulk of the review—some twenty pages—comprised a list, drawn from selected passages, of specific factual errors, contradictions, and instances of confusion, ambiguity, and misinterpretation of sources. Below's only excursions into substantive criticism were his incidental strictures against the *Hofrechtstheorie*, Lamprecht's use of the theory of matrilinearity, and the slighting of political history. Yet the massive litany of Lamprecht's failings constituted the most profound indictment Below knew how to frame: Lamprecht could not get his facts straight. The inaccuracies, the unreliability of the conclusions, the imprecisions and tastelessness of style, and the want of empathy for historical figures were more than symptoms of the author's haste; they were, Below charged, evidence of his unprofessionalism and his transgressions against the most fundamental axioms of historical scholarship.

Below's attack came as no surprise to Lamprecht, who had heard of the review's peregrinations as early as May 1893. His anger was thus already building when he learned that Lehmann had abetted Below with a formal statement that he regarded his former colleague as an "arrant swindler" and "at best a feuilltonist."[85] Lamprecht's impulsive response bespoke his frustration and rage, as well as his hope of undercutting the impact of Below's review.[86] A few days before the appearance of the review, he accused Below in print of "moral delinquency [*sittliche Verwahrlosung*]" and of having lied publicly—an allusion to the exchange in 1887, forgotten by all but Lamprecht himself, over the Rhenish *gulden*.[87]

Lamprecht's spectacular charges threw the profession into consternation, for they threatened to take the dispute well beyond the bounds of academic discourse. Lamprecht's remarks were libelous (as were Lehmann's); they raised the specter of legal action or even a duel, either of which promised a scandal. Below's physical handicap once again precluded a duel, so the profession's leaders struggled to keep the affair in their own hands, out of the courts and the newspapers. The course of events now demonstrated the futility, not to say the frivolity, of Lamprecht's action. As even his friends recognized, he stood little chance of vindication in the courts given the weakness of his legal case; on the other hand, the unorthodoxy of his scholarship was certain to undermine his position in any forum of his professional peers.[88]

The resolution of the affair presented an extraordinary spectacle, which helped fortify the battle lines in the *Methodenstreit*. The proposal to set up a board of arbitration in Berlin came from Moriz Ritter, one of the few men who enjoyed the confidence of both Lamprecht and Below.[89] The difficulty was that neither party to the dispute was in Berlin, so the tortuous negotiations over the composition of the board fell to their surrogates. Below insisted that the board be composed exclusively of historians, among whom he enjoyed overwhelming support, while Lamprecht's only friends in Berlin were young economists like

Hoeniger and Liesegang.[90] It was already impossible to find anyone who was neutral. Lamprecht was evidently under enormous stress. With the advice of Arndt and Bücher (but no lawyer), he complicated the negotiations with erratic interventions from Leipzig, which only antagonized the potential arbitrators— both those who initially sympathized with him, like Schmoller, and those, like Max Lenz and Hans Delbrück, who did not.[91] The affair ended in Lamprecht's humiliation. In March 1894, before a board could be assembled, he abruptly agreed to issue a public retraction of his charges against Below, as well as a promise, in which Below joined, to cease the polemic.[92]

The vindication of Below mystified Lamprecht, whose understanding of the implications and likely consequences of the dispute remained clouded by his moralism and loathing for his antagonist. He was little aware of the embarrassment and resentment that his own behavior created as the affair resonated throughout the profession. Lamprecht was oblivious, too, of the damage the episode had inflicted on him. "In the meantime things have begun to turn a little," he wrote to Mevissen in May 1894, "and there are many even within the honorable profession who—at least when they are alone—no longer hold me to be a complete fool [*einen dummen Fasler*]."[93] The historian was deceiving himself. In the aftermath of the affair he stood completely isolated. Not a single *Ordinarius* in history had sided with him, and the personal sympathy that Below enjoyed among the academic historians was difficult in most cases to distinguish from an endorsement of Below's judgment on Lamprecht's scholarship. The dispute earned Lamprecht new enemies; and it discomfited important friends, among them Schmoller and Treitschke, who had reason to question the wisdom of their previous support.[94]

The repercussions of the controversy with Below soon began to affect every phase of Karl Lamprecht's professional life. They immediately cast a shadow over some of his accomplishments.

Lamprecht was, as one of his students recalled, a "master of the dangerous gift of forgetting things too quickly."[95] He dismissed the whole affair as a minor incident and returned to work. The lingering ordeal at home likewise retreated before a frenetic expenditure of energy on the fourth and fifth volumes of the *German History*. To those in his proximity he conveyed the impression of an indomitable drive, or as one of his colleagues described it, of the "onrushing, momentous, conquering power [*Wirksamkeit*] of his scholarship."[96] A series of successes at his university and in the wider profession helped sustain his optimism and made it easier to disregard the signs that more adversity was on the way.

The departure of Max Lehmann at the end of the summer semester in 1893 left the chair for modern history open once again. Despite the recent unhappy experiences, Lamprecht remained determined to recruit a political historian with a Prussian emphasis to Leipzig. His disputes with Below and Lehmann, however, dimmed his prospects for success and cast a Byzantine air over the politics of the appointment.

Lamprecht's initial preference for the Frederician scholar Reinhold Koser suggested that revenge played a role in his calculations. The gesture of appointing Naudé's *Doktorvater* to succeed Lehmann was attractive, as was the thought of a raid on Bonn, where Koser now occupied a position that Lamprecht had once coveted. Late in November 1893 Lamprecht persuaded the search committee, the philosophical faculty, and the ministry in Dresden of the virtues of this choice, and the call went to Bonn.[97] Koser quickly turned it down, possibly with the coaxing of Lehmann and others "in Berlin."[98] The call from Leipzig next went to Berlin itself, to the Leipzig faculty's second choice, the military historian Hans Delbrück, who in January 1894 likewise declined the offer.[99] These refusals and Delbrück's subsequent involvement in Lamprecht's arbitration proceedings with Below were clear signs of the difficulty of insulating affairs in Leipzig from the enmities being fueled in the capital. So was the involvement in these proceedings of Max Lenz, who made no secret of his resentment that his own candidacy for the chair in Leipzig had failed—a casualty, he claimed, of his association with Sybel.[100]

In these circumstances, the appointment of Erich Marcks to the chair in Leipzig early in 1894 was a stroke of fortune for Lamprecht. Marcks was a student of Treitschke and Hermann Baumgarten.[101] His *Habilitationsschrift* on the sixteenth century French Protestant leader Coligny reflected his own Huguenot roots; it also established his reputation as one of the rising stars in the profession and won him a call to a chair in Freiburg in 1892, when he was only thirty. He accepted the call to Leipzig two years later at the urging of Treitschke but with anxieties about his new colleague there.[102] In the event, he and Lamprecht quickly established a comfortable relationship, which was based on intellectual and temperamental contrasts that made Marcks an unusual complement to Lamprecht. The medium of Marcks' scholarship was biography. Here he practiced the art of sympathetic understanding with the sensitivity of an aesthete and a spirit of impartiality that invited comparisons to Ranke's. Marcks' most enduring scholarship comprised a series of highly crafted essays—on Philip II of Spain, Elizabeth I of England, and Louis XIV of France, as well as on leading personalities of his own nation's past, among them Goethe, Bismarck, and the emperor William I.[103] His belief in the importance of the great historical actor and in the other canons of the discipline was balanced by traits that allowed him to work in the vicinity of Lamprecht, whose vitality he at first found both exciting and intimidating.[104] Marcks' preference for historical portraiture corresponded to an intellectual reserve, and he was little interested in generalizations about method or theory. His reserve was temperamental as well, and he was reluctant to take sides in the *Methodenstreit* or to criticize his new colleague.[105]

The addition of Marcks to the historical seminar in Leipzig accompanied the establishment of a chair in the auxiliary disciplines. Lamprecht had long pressed for this change, citing the university of Berlin as a model.[106] His success allowed him to relieve Wilhelm Arndt's long frustration as an extraordinary professor, as well as to reward a colleague who had provided loyal if intemperate counsel during the arbitration negotiations with Below. Arndt's sudden death soon thereafter, at the beginning of 1895, was thus not only a blow to Lamprecht personally, but a challenge to his vision of the seminar.[107] His hope of filling the position with his friend Ernst Bernheim foundered on the ministry's determination to hire only an extraordinary professor.[108] Another project, briefly vetted, suggested the limits of Lamprecht's respect for academic convention. With Marcks' support, he entered negotiations with Bismarck in the hope of using the vacant position to lure the former chancellor's papers to Leipzig. This unusual plan then collapsed on the faculty's reluctance to pay the price, which was to appoint Bismarck's candidate, Horst Kohl, who had not habilitated, had taught only in a *Gymnasium*, and whose principal qualification was that he edited the *Bismarck-Jahrbuch*.[109] In the end, Lamprecht at least had the satisfaction of seeing an additional *Ordinarius* in the seminar, as the candidate who was the ministry's choice for the position used a counter-offer from Marburg to negotiate a full professorship in Leipzig.[110]

Gerhard Seeliger, the new professor of *Hilfswissenschaften* in Leipzig, is remembered primarily for his role in Lamprecht's ordeals. In many accounts the role has not flattered him. He has played the Beckmesser figure, the *Nörgler* whose petty criticism, limited horizons, and obstinate commitment to convention blocked the imaginative efforts of his colleague to reform instruction in Leipzig. There is much to support this view of Seeliger, but it does little justice to his accomplishments as a scholar, which Lamprecht himself admired, or to the difficulty of the situation he entered in 1895.[111]

Seeliger was an Austrian.[112] He was born in Galicia in 1860. He studied in Vienna, in the *Institut für österreichische Geschichte* with Theodor Sickel, and in Berlin with Weizsäcker, Wilhelm Wattenbach, and Harry Bresslau. In 1887 he completed his habilitation in Munich with Hermann Grauert and remained there as a *Privatdozent* until his call to Leipzig. His interests lay primarily in legal and constitutional history. A series of publications on the institutions of the *Hofmeister*, the imperial archchancelleries, and the so-called Carolingian capitulations (*Kapitularien*) established his reputation as the profession's leading authority in the science known as diplomatics, or the interpretation of old documents.[113] By virtue of his inclinations and his training at the hands of some of the profession's most fastidious scholars, he was at home in the close scrutiny of primary sources, but he had little understanding or sympathy for historical scholarship severed from its documentary moorings.[114] A lack of imagination was not in itself a problem, but Seeliger, who had something of the air of a military officer, was not a deferential man like Marcks.[115]

The diversity of interest and style among the three young chairholders in Leipzig seemed at first nonetheless to make a wholesome combination. Lamprecht's energy, versatility, and his "gushing facility of give-and-take" initially captivated Seeliger no less than Marcks.[116] In the fall of 1895 the three professors recast the curriculum in the seminar in a manner that clearly reflected

Lamprecht's experience and vision. "Without exact knowledge of economic, social, legal, and constitutional history," read the new guidelines, "one cannot attain a deeper understanding of political history, nor [can one attain] an understanding of intellectual history without at least a knowledge of art history."[117] Students in Leipzig were henceforth counseled to study all facets of medieval and modern history, as well as to take a broad range of supporting work in philology, philosophy, law, economics, and geography. The seminar's growing enrollments attested to the appeal of this comprehensive curriculum. Once he opened them to students from all faculties, Lamprecht's introductory lectures on cultural history attracted hundreds of students into the largest auditorium in the university.[118] The ranks of the instructional faculty expanded with the arrival of several *Privatdozenten*, including Erich Brandenburg and Felix Solomon from Berlin, Gustav Buchholz from Bonn, and Walter Goetz. To encourage contact among them, as well as among students, the regular faculty, and teachers and other interested people from the city, Lamprecht established a regular series of lectures and colloquia known as the *Historische Abende*.[119] "It was a happy moment," one of Marcks' students recalled of the Leipzig seminar in 1896: "a mutual give-and-take among eminent professors and students full of idealistic ambitions."[120]

In his efforts to reform the seminar, Lamprecht had ample opportunity to hone his political skills in negotiations with several different constituencies and agencies. He soon became a familiar figure in Dresden, where he won the confidence and friendship of the minister of culture, Paul von Seydewitz. The seminar was but one topic of their consultations. Another was the establishment of an organization for Saxon history. Lamprecht began to plan this project shortly after his arrival in Leipzig, but the initial reorganization of the seminar preoccupied his energies. Only in the spring of 1893 did he convene a group of historians, economists, philologists, and jurists from the faculty to plan an organization to link the university's scholars with archivists, librarians, and interested laypeople throughout Saxony and to oversee the publication of the kingdom's most important archival collections.[121] The model for the project was the Society for the Study of Rhenish History, but the absence of a patron like Mevissen complicated Lamprecht's efforts, for he had to deal not only with academics, archivists, librarians, and museum directors, but with the politicians who controlled access to the public purse.[122] Although the king, the amateur historian, gave his approval to the project in 1893, negotiations dragged on for three years before the state diet in 1896 officially established the Royal Saxon Commission for History and provided it with an annual subsidy of 10,000 marks. Most of the commission's members were scholars at the university, but Lamprecht also involved businessmen and civic leaders, whom he persuaded to provide subscriptions to augment the organization's budget.[123] The historian's principal difficulties were not with the politicians, who were willing to concede autonomy to the scholars, but instead with the director of the state archives in Dresden, Paul Hassel, a student of Sybel. The difficulties were reminiscent of problems Lamprecht had experienced in Cologne. Once again, he proposed to emphasize the publication of documents on Saxon cultural history—on topics such as the history of settlement, agriculture, manufacture, and the Peasants' War in central Germany. The plan that the commission adopted at the end of 1896 was thus a compromise that demonstrated Hassel's inclinations, as well as his power, for it emphasized the publication of administrative documents and the correspondence of the state's political and military leaders.[124] Establishment of the commission was nonetheless another significant achievement for Lamprecht. It provided another forum for the promotion of cultural history, albeit not to the extent he himself had wished, and its editorial projects offered employment opportunities for his students. The commission also represented a tribute to Mevissen, who had taught its principal founder the civic importance of local history and the virtues of allying academic scholars with the community's elite.

There was much to justify Lamprecht's hope that Leipzig would soon rival Berlin for primacy in historical scholarship and become renowned as the center for the study of cultural history. His ambitions to promote his vision as an alternative to political history extended well beyond his home territory, however; they were directed at reform in the profession at large. His broader projects developed in response to a series of transitions and institutional innovations in the profession, which produced several significant opportunities.

One opportunity arose on the heels of another historian's misfortune. The political views of Ludwig Quidde were already known to be eccentric when, early in 1894, he published a pamphlet that purported to be a study of the Roman emperor Caligula but was in reality a thinly disguised parody of the reigning German emperor.[125] The act resulted in Quidde's professional ostracism, and it made his position as editor of the *Deutsche Zeitschrift für Geschichtswissenschaft* untenable.[126] By the end of the year the publisher, Paul Siebeck in Tübingen, had found in Leipzig a team of historians who were willing to take over the journal.[127] Arndt's death and replacement by Seeliger stalled the preparations, but by the end of 1895 the Leipzig historians publicly announced the takeover. Although Seeliger was to be nominally the managing editor, Lamprecht was the moving force in the enterprise. From Mevissen he raised the capital to initiate publication; he alone among the new editors had significant editorial experience, and he hoped to model the journal after the format of the *Westdeutsche Zeitschrift* with a balance of general and specialized articles, bibliographies, and news of the profession.[128] The editorial program was a compromise, which accorded a prominent place to political history; but Lamprecht assumed that the new journal would challenge the *Historische Zeitschrift* for leadership in the field and become a forum for the work of cultural historians. The editors would, their prospectus announced, "encourage in equal degrees traditional historical research and the kind that has recently begun to develop, by accepting articles on the history of structures [*des zuständlichen Lebens*] as well as political history." "Book reviews," the prospectus continued in a passage that Lamprecht wrote as a slap at Below, "should avoid nonessential petty criticism [Einzelkritik] as much as possible and seek to evaluate the scholarly quality of new books from broader perspectives."[129] The initial issues of the journal appeared in 1896 with articles by a number of scholars close to Lamprecht, among them Bernheim, Schmoller, Kurt Breysig, and Carl Köhne.[130]

As negotiations over the new journal proceeded, Lamprecht received another attractive offer. The volumes collectively known as The History of the European States (Europäische Staatengeschichte) were one of the monuments of nineteenth century German historiography.[131] The founder of the series was the publisher Friedrich Perthes, whose unsuccessful attempt in the early 1830s to turn Ranke into a journal editor was but one facet of a campaign to popularize the study of history as the foundation of enlightened patriotism. In 1829, as part of the same campaign, he persuaded Arnold Ludwig Heeren and Friedrich August Ukert to edit a collection of studies for a popular audience on the histories of the European states. Heinrich Leo's vast survey of the Italian states made up the inaugural entry. By the time Wilhelm Giesebrecht assumed the editorship in 1874, the series comprised six dozen volumes, many of which were grand treatises by the profession's luminaries, including Droysen, F. C. Dahlmann, Johann Karl Pfister, and Gustav Stenzel. The volumes produced under Giesebrecht's direction became narrower in scope, however, as the profession's growing specialization eroded the original conception of the series.

Giesebrecht died in 1889. Five years later Perthes' grandson, the heir to the publishing house, approached Lamprecht with a proposal to oversee the resumption of the series. Lamprecht agreed once he received assurances of a free hand.[132] As he explained in the foreword to the first volume he commissioned, his intentions were to rejuvenate the series in the spirit of its original editors and to emphasize cultural history.[133] The prominence of economic and ethnological themes in the volumes by Henri Pirenne on medieval Belgium, M. G. Schybergson on Finland, and by Ludo Moritz Hartmann on medieval Italy served early notice that the series would henceforth be another forum for what Lamprecht was already calling the "triumphant new standpoint."[134]

Lamprecht's determination to promote this "new standpoint" likewise guided his participation in the early attempts to bring a measure of organizational unity to the diverse sectors of the German historical profession.[135] The idea of holding regular meetings among academic and nonacademic historians from Germany, Austria, and Switzerland originated in Munich; and the principal concern was the still lively topic of secondary-school reform, the place of history in the curriculum as it evolved to address contemporary social and political issues. In the first of these meetings, in Munich in the spring of 1893, Lamprecht played only a peripheral role.[136] But what he saw there convinced him of the advantages of the undertaking. Archivists, librarians, and Gymnasiallehrer not only constituted the vast majority of the profession, but they also made up the constituency that was most receptive to the kind of history he himself championed. That these congresses might become an instrument of this history was evident in the enthusiasm with which the delegates in Munich discussed the role of *Kulturgeschichte* in the reformed secondary curriculum. As the director of one *Gymnasium* pointed out, instruction in cultural history represented "the ways and means to fight social democracy."[137]

The second congress, in April 1894, was a much larger and more elaborate affair. It met in Leipzig.[138] With the aid of subsidies from the state government and Mevissen, Lamprecht orchestrated it to great effect.[139] His fear that his dispute with Below would mar the occasion proved unfounded, and close to 400 delegates appeared. For the keynote address he recruited Schmoller to "open the eyes" of the delegates about social and economic history.[140] His primary accomplishment at the congress was to set up a conference group among representatives of state and regional historical societies, who agreed to meet regularly in order to coordinate the publication of historical documents.

A third congress of historians met a year later in Frankfurt, where a principal item of business was the history curriculum in the universities. The basis of the deliberations was a memorandum prepared in Leipzig, which reflected curricular changes there and called for more comprehensive instruction in history at the university level.[141] Lamprecht had by now emerged as the leading figure in these congresses. There was thus reason to believe that he would also become a dominant force in the organization, the Association of German Historians (*Verband deutscher Historiker*), which the historians in Frankfurt established to coordinate the regular holding of subsequent congresses.

Lamprecht's success in this venture was impressive, but it was not unalloyed. The absence of leading academic scholars from the historians' congresses was as conspicuous as Lamprecht's prominence; it was also largely due to Lamprecht's prominence.[142] But Lamprecht's inability to interest the country's foremost historians in the congresses, or to persuade other German universities to host these gatherings, was just one sign of difficulties that were beginning to plague him.[143] His trouble with the state archivist in the Saxon historical commission was another. So was the sparse representation of prominent historians on the list of contributors to his new journal. So was the refusal of other historians, such as Naudé, Koser, Dove, and Otto Hintze, to write for the Perthes series once he took it over.[144] All of these difficulties were related. They symptomized the general mobilization taking place in Berlin and other academic centers in Germany. Lamprecht's enemies were preparing for war.

Notes

1. The exchange took place in the columns of the *Deutsche Literaturzeitung* over the course of several months: DLZ, 8 (26.2.87): 9308–10; (19.3.87): 347–48; (14.5.87): 741–42; (16.7.87): 1070. NL Lamprecht (Korr. 7), August Fresenius to Lamprecht, Berlin, 26.6.87.

2. See Below, "Below"; Minnie von Below, *Georg von Below: Ein Lebensbild für seine Freunde* (Stuttgart, 1930); Ludwig Klaiber, "Verzeichnis der Schriften Georg von Belows," *Aus Sozial- und Wirtschaftsgeschichte: Gedächtnisschrift für Georg von Below* (Stuttgart, 1928), 343–55; Otto Gerhard Oexle, "Ein politischer Historiker: Georg von Below," in Hammerstein, 283–312; Metz, *Grundformen*, 493–97; Jürgen Kuczynski, *Studien*, 5: 192–99; NDB, 2: 32–33; Weber, *Lexikon*, 36–37.

3. Oskar Pusch, *Von Below: Ein deutsches Geschlecht aus dem Ostseeraum* (Dortmund, 1974), 498–500.

4. M. von Below, 21–26, 36. Below's wife insisted, in the face of charges to the contrary, that her husband was never in the least affected by his handicap. Her assertions are difficult to believe.

5. NL Althoff (Nr. 153/2), Ritter to Althoff, Bonn, 2.2.86.

6. See Oexle, 289.

7. Hermann Aubin, "Georg von Below als Sozial- und Wirtschaftshistoriker, VSWG, 21 (1928): 1–31; Srbik, 1: 11; 2: 208.

8. NL Lamprecht (Korr. 7), Below to Lamprecht, Düsseldorf, 10.6.85; cf. Below, "Below," 13–14.

9. NL Goetz (NL Ritter, 174), Below to Ritter, Marburg, 26.5.87; Below, "Below," 10; M. von Below, 44–46.

10. NL Bernheim, Lamprecht to Bernheim, Bonn, 27.7.81.

11. LW, 180; NL Lamprecht (Korr. 7), Below to Lamprecht, Marburg, 25.11.86, 20.1.87.

12. "Zur Entstehung der deutschen Stadtverfassung," HZ, 58 (1887): 193–244; HZ, 59 (1888): 193–247.

13. It raged on for decades afterwards, until the 1930s when Otto Brunner resolved it, in a fashion, by demonstrating the anachronism of the very terms in which it was defined—the purported dichotomy between public and private law in the German Middle Ages. See E. W. Böckenförde, *Die deutsche verfassungsgeschichtliche Forschung im 19. Jahrhundert: Zeitgebundene Fragestellungen und Leitbilder* (Berlin, 1961), esp. 197–209; cf. T. Knapp, "Zur Geschichte der Landeshoheit," *Württembergische Vierteljahrshefte für Landesgeschichte*, 38 (1932): 9–112; Alfons Dopsch, "Stand der Forschung auf dem Gebiete der älteren deutschen Verfassungs- und Sozialgeschichte," *Die Geisteswissenschaften*, 12 (1913–14): 323–27; Otto Brunner, *Land und Herrschaft: Grundfragen der territorialen Verfassungsgeschichte Oesterreichs im Mittelalter* (Darmstadt, 1970), esp. 146–64; cf. Jürgen Habermas, *Strukturwandel der Oeffentlichkeit: Untersuchungen zu einer Kategorie der bürgerlichen Gesellschaft* (Neuwied and Berlin, 1962), 17–25.

14. Luise Schorn-Schütte, "Stadt und Staat. Zum Zusammenhang von Gegenwartsverständnis und historischer Erkenntnis in der Stadtgeschichtsschreibung der Jahrhundertwende," *Die alte Stadt*, 10 (1983): 228–66; cf. Jürgen Fröhling, "Georg von Below—Stadtgeschichte zwischen Wissenschaft und Ideologie," ibid., 6 (1979): 54–85; Simon, *Staat und Geschichtswissenschaft*, 19–22.

15. Alfons Dopsch, "Zur Methodologie der Wirtschaftsgeschichte," in *Kultur- und Universalgeschichte: Walter Goetz zu seinem 60. Geburtstag* (Leipzig and Berlin, 1927), 522. Not all economic historians subscribed to the *Hofrechtstheorie*, however. Cf. Eberhard Gothein, *Wirtschaftsgeschichte des Schwarzwaldes und der angrenzenden Landschaften* (Strassburg, 1892), 309–21.

16. Below, "Zur Würdigung," 305.

17. NL Althoff (B Nr. 9/2), Below to Althoff, Marburg, 5.12.87; Below, "Below," 23. Just how broad Below's support extended was evident in the remarks of the young Catholic historian Aloys Schulte, who wrote to Lamprecht in 1890 that "the polemics into which Below plunges with such pleasure are really repugnant to me, but one cannot overlook the fact that he has rendered a service. Specifically, he has

done away with Nitzsch." NL Lamprecht (Korr. 47), Schulte to Lamprecht, Karlsruhe, 27.4.90.

18. NL Althoff (B Nr. 9/2), Below to Althoff, Marburg, 5.12.87.
19. NL Althoff (Nr. 30/2), Dove to Althoff, Bonn, 18.6.89; (Nr. 186/3), Treitschke to Althoff, Berlin, 20.6.89; (Nr. 73), Weiland to Althoff, Göttingen, 21.1.91; (Nr. 73), Ritter to Althoff, Bonn, 21.1.91.
20. NL Lamprecht (Korr. 19), Dove to Lamprecht, Bonn, 12.7.87.
21. HZ, 58: 196, 201–2; HZ, 59: 197, 214–15.
22. NL Lamprecht (Korr. 35), Lamprecht to Lehmann, Bonn, 1.9.87; Lehmann to Lamprecht, Berlin, 22.8.87.
23. NL Liesegang, Lamprecht to Liesegang, Strassburg, 29.12.89.
24. HZ, 63 (1890): 294–309; *cf.* HZ, 59: 235; NL Lamprecht (Korr. 7), Below to Lamprecht, Marburg, 3.12.86; Lamprecht to Harry Bresslau, Bonn, 19.11.89, in Paul Hirsch, ed., "Briefe namhafter Historiker an Harry Bresslau," WaG, 14 (1954): 225–26; LW, 205.
25. GStAM, Rep. 76–VA, Sekt 12 Tit. VII, Niese to Steinmetz, Marburg, 18.1.90.
26. NL Althoff (A I Nr. 73), Lehmann to Althoff, Marburg, 18.1.91; (B Nr. 108/1), Lamprecht to Althoff, Marburg, 20.1.91; Lamprecht to Bresslau, Marburg, 22.2.91 in Hirsch, 226–27.
27. GGA, Nr. 23 (1888): 883–94.
28. NL Lamprecht (Korr. 31), Hoeniger to Lamprecht, Berlin, 7.1.90, 2.2.90, 2.5.90; (Korr. 35), Liesegang to Lamprecht, Berlin, 22.5.90; NL Liesegang, Lamprecht to Liesegang, Friedrichsroda, 8.9.92.
29. Jastrow, "Erwiderung betreffend die 'Jahresberichte der Geschichtswissenschaft,'" *Mitteilungen aus der historischen Litteratur*, 17 (1889): 92–116; Carl Koehne, *Der Ursprung der Stadtverfassung in Worms, Speier und Mainz* (Breslau, 1890), esp. 360–88; Robert Hoeniger, *Professor Georg von Belows "Detailpolemik": Ein Nachwort zu dessen Arbeiten über städtische Verfassungsgeschichte* (Berlin, 1892); Below, *Der Höniger-Jastrow'sche Freundeskreis* (Düsseldorf, 1892).
30. NL Lamprecht (Korr. 10), Below Notiz (Abschrift), Münster, 13.12.92; NL Mevissen, Lamprecht to Mevissen, Marburg, 24.7.90; Leipzig, 7.6.98; NL Althoff (A I Nr. 73), Lenz to Althoff, Berlin, 5.7.91; *cf.* M. von Below, 60; Ute Frevert, *Ehrenmänner: Das Duell in der bürgerlichen Gesellschaft* (Munich, 1991), 9–10. On Jastrow, see Redlich, "Academic Education for Business," 199–201, 222–32.
31. NL Mevissen, Lamprecht to Mevissen, Bonn, 15.5.88; Lamprecht to Bresslau, Bonn, 14.12.88, in Hirsch, 225.
32. DLZ, (1890): 1462–64.
33. NL Bernheim, Lamprecht to Bernheim, Leipzig, 20.5.92, 23.6.92, 26.7.92; NL Liesegang, Lamprecht to Liesegang, Leipzig, 24.5.92. NL Lamprecht (Kr. 10) contains a pile of notes on which Lamprecht tried out aphorisms for possible use against Below. One read: "bei irgendeiner Entstellung: Das ist nicht Caricatur oder die von Hrn v. B. zärtlich geliebte freie Phantasie über ein gegebenes Thema—das ist hallucinatorischer Blödsinn."
34. Meinecke, *Schriften*, 95.
35. J. Engel, 355.
36. See Hans-Thomas Krause, "Dietrich Schäfer: Vom Schüler Treitschkes zum ideologischen Wegbereiter des ersten Weltkrieges," Ph.D. dissertation (Halle/Wittenberg, 1968); Krause, "Die alldeutsche Geschichtsschreibung vor dem ersten Weltkrieg," in Streisand, 2: 207–19; Kurt Jagow, ed., *Dietrich Schäfer und sein Werk* (Berlin, 1925); Roger Chickering, "Max Weber und Dietrich Schäfer," in Wolfgang J. Mommsen and Wolgang Schwentker, eds., *Max Weber und seine Zeitgenossen* (Göttingen, 1988), 462–75.
37. Dietrich Schäfer, *Das eigentliche Arbeitsgebiet der Geschichte* (Jena, 1888); reprinted

in Schäfer, *Aufsätze, Vorträge und Reden*, 2 vols. (Jena, 1913), 1: 264–90. References here are to the reprinted text.

38. Schäfer, *Arbeitsgebiet*, 277.
39. Ibid., 281.
40. Ibid.
41. Eberhard Gothein, *Die Aufgaben der Kulturgeschichte* (Leipzig, 1889).
42. NL Lamprecht (Korr. 25), Gothein to Lamprecht, Karlsruhe, 8.7.85. See Wolfgang Zorn, "Eberhard Gothein 1853–1923," in *Bonner Gelehrte*, 260–71; Marie Luise Gothein, *Eberhard Gothein: Ein Lebensbild* (Stuttgart, 1931), esp. 74–78; HZ, 129 (1924): 476–90; Peter Alter, "Eberhard Gothein," in Wehler, ed., *Deutsche Historiker*, 8: 40–55; NDB, 6: 654–56.
43. Gothein, *Aufgaben*, 3.
44. Ibid., 49.
45. Ibid., 54.
46. Dietrich Schäfer, *Geschichte und Kulturgeschichte: Eine Erwiderung* (Jena, 1891). The tract also appears in *Aufsätze, Vorträge, Reden*, 1: 292–351, from which the following citations are drawn.
47. Ibid., 337.
48. Ibid., 335.
49. See Seifert, 9–15; Oestreich, "Fachhistorie," 326–31.
50. NL Althoff (B Nr. 108/1), Lamprecht to Althoff, Bonn, 21.2.90; GStAD, NL Friedrich Meinecke (Nachtrag 1), Meinecke to Below, Berlin, 1.12.97.
51. Gangolf Hübinger, "Kapitalismus und Kulturgeschichte," in Rüdiger vom Bruch, et al., eds. *Kultur und Kulturwissenschaften um 1900* (Stuttgart, 1989), 28.
52. Steinhausen, "Zur Einführung," ZKg, 1 (1893–1894): 2.
53. GGA, Nr. 7 (1892): 293. On Steinhausen see Georg Steinhausen, "Georg Steinhausen," in S. Steinberg, 1: 233–74; Goetz, "Georg Steinhausen," in *Historiker*, 391–92. On the journal see Wolfgang Zorn, "Zwei Zeitschriften," 462.
54. NL Lamprecht (Korr. 49), Steinhausen to Lamprecht, Jena, 29.5.93; *cf.* Georg Steinhausen, *Geschichte des deutschen Briefes: Zur Kulturgeschichte des deutschen Volkes*, 2 vols. (Berlin, 1889–1891).
55. Steinhausen, "Professoren der Kulturgeschichte?" ZKg, 2 (1894–1895): 192–98.
56. Oestreich, "Fachhistorie," 333–36.
57. Excepting only Lamprecht, Oestreich's survey of these offerings lists no chair holders in medieval or modern history. Adalbert Wahl, Kurt Breysig, and Otto Hintze were all *Privatdozenten* or extraordinary professors at the time they read cultural history.
58. See Steinhausen, "Steinhausen," esp. 5–6, 24–26.
59. Quoted in Albisetti, 237; *cf.* ibid., 146–47; EB, 2, 2: 423–30; Bernheim, "Geschichtsunterricht und Geschichtswissenschaft," esp. 29–34; Bernheim, *Lehrbuch der historischen Methoden und der Geschichtsphilosophie*, 716–17; Klaus Goebel, "Des Kaisers neuer Geschichtsunterricht: Aenderungen des preussischen Lehrplans 1915 und ihre Vorgeschichte," GWU, 25 (1974): esp. 709–10.
60. GGA, Nr. 7 (1892): 280–96.
61. ZKg, 1 (1893–1894): 3.
62. Ernst Bernheim, *Lehrbuch der historischen Methode* (Leipzig, 1889).
63. Paul Hinneberg, "Die philosophischen Grundlagen der Geschichtswissenschaft," HZ, 60 (1889): 18–55.
64. HZ, 141 (1930): 449–50.
65. Weber, *Lexikon*, 405–6.
66. Vogler, 73–74; Reithel, 76–84; Schieder, "Historische Zeitschrift," HZ, 189 (1959): 39–40.

67. NL Althoff (B Nr. 110/2), Lehmann to Althoff, Marburg, 14.12.92 (Abschrift); (A I Nr. 73), Lehmann to Althoff, Leipzig, 25.5.93.
68. ZKg, 1 (1893–94): 245–48; cf. *Zukunft*, 17 (1896): 252–55.
69. UA Leipzig, PA 679, Commission für Wiederbesetzung der durch den Tod von Prof. Maurenbrecher erledigten Professur für Geschichte, 12, 21, 24, 30.11.92; NL Mevissen, Lamprecht to Mevissen, Leipzig, 24.5.93; NL Lamprecht (Korr. 59), Lamprecht to Hugo Lamprecht, Leipzig, 19.5.93.
70. ZKg, 1 (1893–4): 248–50.
71. Reithel, 74.
72. Schönebaum, "Treitschke und Lamprecht," n. 9.
73. NL Althoff (A I Nr. 73), Heinrici to Althoff, Leipzig, 8.7.93; NL Bernheim, Lamprecht to Bernheim, Leipzig, 24.7.93; NL Lamprecht (Korr. 15), Buchholz to Lamprecht, Bonn, 18.7.93.
74. Lehmann, "Lehmann," 222.
75. NL Lamprecht (Korr. 31), Hinneberg to Lamprecht, Berlin, 25.7.93; (Korr. 9), Bernheim to Lamprecht, Greifswald, 16.7.93; Lehmann, "Lehmann," 222; LW, 243.
76. NL Althoff (A I Nr. 73), Meier to Althoff, Göttingen, 14.6.93; 9.7.93.
77. LW, 282.
78. NL Liesegang, Lamprecht to Liesegang, Leipzig, 23.7.92; NL Lamprecht (Korr. 31), Hinneberg to Lamprecht, Berlin, 25.7.93.
79. *Nationalzeitung*, 8.2.93, cited in HZ, 71 (1893): 465; NL Lamprecht (Korr. 54), Winter to Lamprecht, Magdeburg, 15.3.93.
80. Sybel asserted that Lehmann commissioned the review: Deutsche Staatsbibliothek, NL Delbrück, Sybel to Delbrück, Berlin, 10.1.93. Below later wrote that he had prepared the review "*auf Sybels Veranlassung.*" Below, "Below," 24; cf. Schieder, "Historische Zeitschrift," 47–51.
81. NL Meinecke (21), Lehmann to Meinecke, Marburg, 6.1.93, 18.1.93.
82. NL Lamprecht (Korr. 10), Lamprecht to Sybel, n.p. 4.9.93. The historiographical conflict was probably sufficient to explain Sybel's hostility, but there are hints that he also resented Lamprecht's success in the Rhineland, as well as the young historian's ties to Sybel's enemies there. Deutsche Staatsbibliothek, Berlin, NL Heinrich von Treitschke, Lamprecht to Treitschke, Leipzig, 16.10.93; LW, 310; cf. Lewald, "Lamprecht und die Rheinische Geschichtsforschung," 284, n. 24.
83. NL Sybel (B1 Nr. 3), Below to Sybel, Münster, 4.5.93; NL Meinecke (2), Below to Meinecke, Münster, 25.7.93; Meinecke, *Schriften*, 117.
84. HZ, 71 (1893): 465–98.
85. NL Bernheim, Lamprecht to Bernheim, Leipzig, 24.5.96; NL Lamprecht (Kr. 10), Below to Hinneberg, Laschnehlen, 29.8.93; Lamprecht to Lehmann, Leipzig, 21.9.93 (Abschrift). Lehmann then wrote to Meinecke in the editorial office of the *Historische Zeitschrift* that he was ready to declare publicly "that the evaluation of Lamprecht's book was never an object of disagreement between Sybel and me and that I thoroughly subscribe to Below's unfavorable verdict" on the book. NL Meinecke (21), Lehmann to Meinecke, Göttingen, 7.11.93.
86. NL Meinecke (2), Below to Meinecke, Gumbinnen, 29.8.93.
87. DLZ (11.11.93): 1434. Lamprecht was certain that Below knew, but concealed the fact that the original misreading of "Rhenish *gulden*" for "Bohemian *gulden*" was in the edition from which Lamprecht had cited the document in question. The original misreading was established in the exchange, however; and even if one is prepared to suspect the worst of Below, it is difficult to see how the incident supported the charge that he lied.
88. NL Lamprecht (Kr. 10), Liesegang to Lamprecht, 8.12.93; Hinneberg to Lamprecht, Berlin, 12.12.93.

89. NL Lamprecht (Kr. 10), Ritter to Lamprecht, Bonn, 3.1.94.
90. NL Lamprecht (Kr. 10), Jastrow to Lamprecht, Berlin, 27.11.93; Below to Hinneberg, Münster, 23.12.93; NL Meinecke (2), Below to Meinecke, Münster, 2.12.93. Lamprecht's principal advisors were Hoeniger, Liesegang, and Hinneberg. Hinneberg, however, was involved in the legal difficulties, for he was the responsible editor of the *Deutsche Literaturzeitung*, the journal in which Lamprecht had published his charges against Below.
91. NL Lamprecht (Kr. 10), Liesegang to Lamprecht, n.d. [January 1894]; Lamprecht to Lenz, Leipzig, 18.1.94; Liesegang to Lamprecht, Berlin, 19.1.94; Hinneberg to Lamprecht, Berlin, 21.1.94; NL Delbrück, Lamprecht to Delbrück, Leipzig, 19.3.94.
92. DLZ (24.3.94): 375–76; LW, 282–83.
93. NL Mevissen, Lamprecht to Mevissen, Leipzig, 25.5.94.
94. NL Lamprecht (Korr. 45), Lamprecht to Ritter, Leipzig, 6.1.94. Paul Scheffer-Boichorst, the medievalist at the university of Berlin and no friend of Lamprecht, was Althoff's informant on the progress of the affair. NL Althoff (A I Nr. 73), Scheffer-Boichorst to Althoff, Berlin, 15.1.94; NL Lamprecht (Kr. 10), Scheffer-Boichorst to Lamprecht, Berlin, 27.1.94.
95. Doren, "Geschichtslehre," 388.
96. NL Meinecke (25), Erich Marcks to Meinecke, Leipzig, 17.6.94.
97. UA Leipzig, PA 716, Lamprecht to KM, Leipzig, 27.11.93; NL Liesegang, Lamprecht to Liesegang, Leipzig, 29.11.93; 30.11.93.
98. NL Bernheim, Lamprecht to Bernheim, Leipzig, 24.12.93; NL Lamprecht (Korr. 53), Wenck to Lamprecht, Marburg, 14.7.93. Below pushed for the expeditious publication of his review in the *Historische Zeitschrift* in the hope of influencing the search in Leipzig. To Sybel he noted that "my criticism could, if it appears in time, have the effect (naturally to a *very* modest degree) of preventing people from listening to him so positively [*unbedingt*]." NL Sybel (B1 Nr. 3), Below to Sybel, Münster, 15.10.93.
99. NL Althoff (A II Nr. 117), Sydewitz to Delbrück, Dresden, 30.12.93 (Abschrift); Delbrück to Sydewitz, Berlin, 4.1.94 (Abschrift).
100. NL Lamprecht (Korr. 3), Lamprecht to Althoff, Leipzig, 30.11.93 (Konzept); (Kr. 10), Liesegang to Lamprecht, Berlin, 19.1.94.
101. On Marcks see Pierre Wenger, *Grundzüge der Geschichtsschreibung von Erich Marcks* (Zürich, 1950); Krill, *Rankerenaisance*; Karl Stählin, "Erich Marcks zum Gedächtnis," HZ, 160 (1930): 496–533; Weber, *Lexikon*, 363–64.
102. NL Treitschke (6), Treitschke to Marcks, Berlin, 22.12.93 (Abschrift); NL Treitschke (17), Marcks to Treitschke, Freiburg, 24.12.93, 10.2.94.
103. Erich Marcks, *Männer und Zeiten: Aufsätze und Reden zur neueren Geschichte*, 2 vols. (Leipzig, 1911); cf. Krill, 124, 139.
104. NL Treitschke (7), Marcks to Treitschke, Leipzig, 8.4.94.
105. NL Meinecke (25), Marcks to Meinecke, Freiburg, 20.12.93; NL Lamprecht (Kr. 10), Marcks to Lamprecht, Freiburg, 30.11.93.
106. NL Liesegang, Lamprecht to Liesegang, Leipzig, 11.6.94.
107. Lamprecht to Bresslau, Leipzig, 14.1.95, in Hirsch, 227; NL Lamprecht (Korr. 59), Lamprecht to Hugo Lamprecht, Leipzig, 15.1.95.
108. UA Leipzig, PA 885, Lamprecht to KM, Leipzig, 11.3.95; NL Bernheim, Lamprecht to Bernheim, Leipzig, 13.3.95, 23.3.95.
109. NL Lamprecht (Korr. 33), Lamprecht to Frau von Arnim, Leipzig, 13.1.95; Chrysander to Lamprecht, Friedrichsruh, 30.1.95; Lamprecht to KM, Leipzig, 21.3.95; Walter Goetz to Marianne Lamprecht, Tübingen, 20.4.18.
110. NL Bernheim, Lamprecht to Bernheim, Leipzig, 25.5.95.

111. NL Lamprecht (Korr. 47), Seeliger to Lamprecht, Munich, 20.5.86.
112. Rudolf Kötzschke, "Gerhard Seeliger," HVjs, 20 (1922): 482–96; HZ, 125 (1922): 552–55; Weber, *Lexikon*, 545. See also Seeliger, "Karl Lamprecht," HVjs, 19 (1919–1920): 133–44. Despite suspicions raised by his name, Seeliger was not a Jew. He was, as Sybel assured Althoff, "ein reiner und evangelischer Germane." NL Althoff (B Nr. 184/3), Sybel to Althoff, 1.4.95.
113. NL Althoff (B Nr. 184/3), Sybel to Leonhard, Berlin, 21.3.95.
114. Goetz, "Goetz," 154–55.
115. Halvdan Koht, "Aus den Lehrjahren eines Historikers," WaG, 13 (1953): 153.
116. Seeliger, "Lamprecht," 134.
117. NL Liesegang, Lamprecht to Liesegang, Leipzig, 17.10.95: Ratschläge für das Studium der mittleren und neueren Geschichte.
118. StA Dresden, VB 10228/1, Lamprecht to Seydewtz, Leipzig, 21.3.96; NL Mevissen, Lamprecht to Mevissen, Leipzig, 27.12.96; NL Lamprecht (Korr. 59), Lamprecht to Hugo Lamprecht, Leipzig, 1.5.96.
119. LW, 260–62.
120. Stählin, 497.
121. Herbert Schönebaum, "Karl Lamprechts wissenschaftlicher Anruf an Rheinland und Sachsen und an die gesamte deutsche Nation," *Hamburger Mittel- und Ostdeutsche Forschungen* (Hamburg, 1957), 153–57; Czok, "Lamprecht," 95; LW, 245–48.
122. NL Mevissen, Lamprecht to Mevissen, Leipzig, Ende Oktober 1895.
123. NL Bernheim, Lamprecht to Bernheim, Leipzig, 23.1.96; NL Liesegang, Lamprecht to Liesegang, Leipzig, 12.9.96; NL Mevissen, Lamprecht to Mevissen, Leipzig, 1.4.97; LW, 298–99; Kötzschke, "Lamprecht," 12.
124. LW, 337–39.
125. NL Lamprecht (Korr. 43), Quidde to Lamprecht, Munich, 16.7.93; Hans-Ulrich Wehler, ed., *Ludwig Quidde, Caligula: Schriften über Militarismus und Pazifismus* (Frankfurt M., 1977); Reinhard Rürup, "Ludwig Quidde," in Wehler, *Deutsche Historiker*, 3: 124–47; Roger Chickering, *Imperial Germany and a World Without War: The Peace Movement and German Society, 1892–1914* (Princeton, 1975), 85–88.
126. See Stieg, 85–101.
127. NL Mevissen, Lamprecht to Mevissen, Leipzig, 31.12.94.
128. NL Mevissen, Lamprecht to Mevissen, Leipzig, 24.7.95, Ende October 1895; NL Bernheim, Lamprecht to Bernheim, Leipzig, 5.4.95.
129. NL Meinecke (25), Marcks to Meinecke, Leipzig, December 1895, Anlage: Buchholz et al., RS, Freiburg and Leipzig, December 1895.
130. DZfG, N. F., 1 (1896–1897), *Jahrbücher* and *Monatsblätter*.
131. J. Caro, "Die europäische Staatengeschichte von Heeren, Ukert und Giesebrecht," in K. Lamprecht, ed., *Allgemeine Staatengeschichte* (Gotha, 1907), 3–12.
132. UB Leipzig, NL Wilhelm Stieda, Lamprecht to Stieda, Leipzig, 20.7.94.
133. LW, 264.
134. NL Schmoller, Lamprecht to Schmoller, Leipzig, 11.2.94.
135. On these congresses see Schumann, *Historikertage*; Gerhard Ritter, "Die deutschen Historikertage," GWU, 4 (1953): 513–21; Karl-Dietrich Erdmann, "Geschichte, Politik und Pädagogik—aus den Akten des deutschen Historikerverbandes," GWU, 19 (1968): 2–21; also in Erdmann, *Geschichte, Politik und Pädagogik: Aufsätze und Reden* (Stuttgart, 1970), 384–407.
136. NL Liesegang, Lamprecht to Liesegang, Leipzig, 10.5.93; cf. *Bericht über die 1. Versammlung deutscher Historiker in München* (Stuttgart, 1893).
137. ZKg 1 (1893): 139; Schumann, 25.
138. *Bericht über die 2. Versammlung deutscher Historiker in Leipzig* (Stuttgart, 1894).

139. NL Mevissen, Lamprecht to Mevissen, Leipzig, 4.4.94.
140. NL Schmoller, Lamprecht to Schmoller, Leipzig, 5.4.93.
141. *Bericht über die 3. Versammlung deutscher Historiker in Frankfurt am Main* (Stuttgart, 1895).
142. Dove to Ritter, Munich, 4.3.94, in Dove, *Aufsätze und Briefe*, 2: 169; Bücher to Schulte, 3.6.95, in Braubach, "Briefe," 378, n. 4.
143. NL Treitschke (7), Lenz to Treitschke, Berlin, 29.3.95; Lamprecht to Treitschke, Leipzig, 17.10.93; NL Lamprecht (Korr. 45), Lamprecht to Ritter, Leipzig, 6.1.94.
144. UB Freiburg, NL Alfred Dove, Lamprecht to Dove, Leipzig, 3.3.96; NL Lamprecht (Korr. 67), Hintze to Lamprecht, Berlin, 1.2.96; LW, 264.

6

Ideology and Method

Nun, wir wollen es zugeben, aber damit steht dann auch
der Satz fest: soweit es Gesetze in der Geschichte gibt, sind
die Gesetze nichts wert und ist die Geschichte nichts wert.

Late in 1893, within weeks of the publication of Below's assault on the *German History*, Lamprecht's work suffered a more damaging review. Paradoxically, this one was positive. "Despite all its weaknesses," the reviewer noted, "Lamprecht's *German History* remains a work of great merit." "No one will put these . . . volumes down," he wrote, "without receiving the most diverse stimulation and instruction."[1] The problem was that among the readers to whom the reviewer recommended Lamprecht's work, there was not a single academic historian. The review appeared in *Die Neue Zeit*, the foremost cultural journal of German social democracy; and the reviewer was Franz Mehring, the country's leading Marxist historian and literary critic. Mehring's judgment of Lamprecht's volumes was thus geared to an explicit ideological commitment. When he described them as a "major and significant step forward in bourgeois historiography," he was praising their proximity to a genre of historical writing in which Marx, Engels, Karl Kautsky, and he himself set the standard. Mehring noted the passages in Lamprecht's work that seemed to betray a lingering commitment to idealism, but he chose to dwell on the parts that emphasized "that in every historical epoch the content of spiritual life must be derived, to a greater or lesser degree, from material and social preconditions." On balance, Mehring concluded, Lamprecht stood "practically on the ground of historical materialism."

If Lamprecht were troubled by what one of his friends called this "social democratic glorification" of his work, he gave no evidence of it in his writings.[2] The fourth and fifth volumes of the *German History*, which he was then writing, maintained the approach that had earned him Mehring's accolade. Elsewhere in the profession, however, Mehring's review of Lamprecht's work caused a sensation, for it confirmed the worst suspicions about the ideological consequences of the kind of history Lamprecht advocated.[3] Mehring was not the first to invite the association of Lamprecht's name with Marx's.[4] Below's fear that the socialists could "easily make capital" out of cultural history was widely shared among a group of scholars who tended, as Ekart Kehr later wrote, to "identify social history with socialist history."[5]

The near-simultaneous publication of the reviews of early volumes of the German History by Mehring and Below announced the real beginning of the Methodenstreit. The two reviews also marked out the poles around which the elements in the case against Lamprecht tended to gravitate. Below's emphasized a failure of professional technique—Lamprecht's penchant for carelessness and committing errors of fact and detail. Mehring's review spoke to the broad conceptual ramifications of this failure, as it laid bare the ideological perils that awaited the historian who ventured beyond bounds prescribed by the profession's codes. Lamprecht's challenge was to remove the debate from these poles and to set it on terms that addressed the methodological issues that he himself regarded as pivotal. The historian only gradually became aware of how formidable this challenge was and how it threatened his professional survival.

In a burst of activity, Lamprecht finished writing the second part of the fifth volume of his German History early in the summer of 1895. His elation at the conclusion of this effort reflected his relief at bringing to an end a narrative account of politics and religious warfare that had never much engaged his interest. The elation reflected as well a belief that he had passed a major hurdle in the completion of his life's work and that he could look forward to an extended period of study and reflection as he prepared the next volumes, which were to treat the seventeenth and eighteenth centuries. "Sunny land now lies before me," he wrote to Liesegang, "and I am proceeding at a hearty pace."[6]

His plans did not include mounting a defense of his first volumes. The renewal of the attack on these volumes later in the same year took the historian by surprise. Although signs of trouble were accumulating everywhere, even amid his triumphs in the profession, he had persuaded himself that his difficulties were little more than the doings of Below and others who feared and envied him. The charges that were now directed at his methodology were more difficult to ignore, however, for they were more systematic and penetrating than Below's had been.

Lamprecht was ill prepared to parry them. His principal difficulty was that despite his ambition to revolutionize the study of history, he had never reflected systematically on questions of historical methodology, nor had he intended to. His observations on this subject had comprised little more than a series of incidental statements, which he posed as apodictic pronouncements in the volumes of his German History or in book reviews and other occasional pieces.[7] Here they served principally to bewilder and provoke those who had read the German History with skepticism.[8]

Lamprecht's pronouncements suggested a dichotomy between two distinct historical methodologies. The one, he argued, was devoted to the description of the unique and singular in the past, principally the acts of states and great persons. Its goal was the account of wie es eigentlich gewesen, and its most accomplished exponent was Ranke. By contrast, Lamprecht explained, the object of the other, or "new" historical method was an account of *wie es eigentlich geworden*. The significance of this distinction was not entirely clear, for it was absurd to claim that Ranke was uninterested in development; but here Lamprecht alluded to a deeper realm of historical analysis, the substratum of economy and society, which conditioned the development of political institutions and provided structural restraints on human behavior.

These assertions seemed to confirm Mehring's judgment that the historian was flirting with historical materialism. Lamprecht appeared to argue that politics and the free moral action of individuals were epiphenomenal or peripheral to a deeper realm of circumstance and collective action, or to what he called in one essay the "permanent flux of economic, social and legal transformations whose configuration conditions [*ausmacht*] constitutional structures at any given time."[9] The provocation extended further, however. Not only was the realm of economy and society analytically prior to the political; it was, Lamprecht insisted, uniquely accessible to tools of analysis that distinguished the new historical method and imparted to the results of this method a higher degree of objective validity than could be claimed by a method which, like the old one, so rested on the unrestrained imagination of the historian. Lamprecht variously called the new method "evolutionary," "morphological," or "genetic"; and he emphasized its affinities to the methods of the natural sciences. He claimed that it addressed the great underlying tendencies in history, whose development proceeded according to patterned if not lawful regularity. Only the historian equipped with the new method could, he concluded, pull together the "masses of material [*Stoffmassen*]" and discover the essential unity among the realms of human action in any historical epoch.[10]

These pronouncements were not themselves free of contradiction or ambiguity, but they staked out the basic oppositions according to which Lamprecht appeared to define the issue of methodology. The terms *gewesen* and *geworden* signaled a conceptual divide, which corresponded to two series of opposing terms—static description versus dynamic analysis, *Verstehen* versus *Erklären*, singular versus collective, freedom versus structures, individual versus collective action, transcendent versus immanent forces, and political history versus *Kulturgeschichte*. The final and most provocative opposition was only implied; but it was lost on none of Lamprecht's friends or enemies. It pitted the symbol of the old method, Ranke, against the most prominent and ambitious champion of the new.

By the time Lamprecht concluded the fifth volume of the *German History*, both his ambitions and the tendency of his thinking on method were well known. He had thrown down the gauntlet to his academic colleagues. The terms in which he presented the challenge could not have been better calculated to offend and alarm those who defended the profession's traditions. Nor could it have come as a surprise when these scholars responded by closing ranks.

The momentum of the *Methodenstreit* built slowly, and despite provocations at the outset from both sides, the issues were only gradually defined. The initial encounters pertained to what one might call the professional geography of the controversy. They served primarily to mark off the forum within which the contest was to be decided.

One of the remarkable features of Lamprecht's *German History* was its broad appeal outside the academy. Two thousand copies of the first volume sold within three years of its publication—an extraordinary feat for a title by a professional historian.[11] In 1894 a second edition of this volume appeared. Two years later all five volumes were in their second edition. Most of the favorable notices that greeted them were written by historians who had not habilitated, and many of these reviews appeared in the popular press.[12] Lamprecht's success at the congresses that preceded the founding of the Association of German Historians could be interpreted as additional evidence of his wide appeal; and it confirmed the impression that much of his audience was to be found in the profession's second tier, particularly among the secondary-school teachers.[13]

Apprehension over Lamprecht's popularity pervaded the early reviews of his work by academic historians. Below set the tone. In his analysis of the "chorus" of "rapturous praise" for Lamprecht's volumes in the "popular and semi-popular" press, he stressed the paucity of qualified reviewers. In these circumstances, Below explained, admiration for Lamprecht's work grew in direct proportion to the reviewer's ignorance.[14] The references in other academic reviews to the opinions of "naive [*urteilslose*] but influential *literati* in the entertainment papers or even the devotional press" spoke to the same point, as did remarks from the academic reviewers about the "undertones of modern journalistic style" in Lamprecht's volumes.[15]

These comments might well have betrayed resentments over a colleague's commercial success, but they also represented an act of corporate self-assertion. The verdict on Lamprecht's achievement was not to be left in the hands of amateurs. The historians' success in laying this claim remanded the *Methodenstreit* into the institutional strongholds from which an exclusive circle of professionals governed the discipline. By the mid-1890s this circle comprised about a hundred scholars—the chair-holders in history at imperial Germany's twenty-one academic centers, along with their apprentices, most of whom taught at the universities as *Privatdozenten*. Nothing in the history of the profession, however, suggested that all these academic centers would exert equal weight in the controversy; and several incidents in the early phase of the *Methodenstreit* confirmed the lesson of the arbitration proceedings between Lamprecht and Below. One of these centers preponderated.

Heinrich von Sybel's sudden death on 1 August 1895, brought on a crisis in the office of the *Historische Zeitschrift* in Berlin. Sybel had been the virtual embodiment of the journal, particularly after the stormy departure of Lehmann two years earlier. Lehmann's successor was one of Sybel's students, Friedrich Meinecke, who was also an archivist in the Prussian state archive in Berlin. Meinecke oversaw most of the editorial work of the journal with cautious competence; but he was young, inexperienced outside the archives, and wielded little power on his own. The question of the journal's future was thus clouded; and it was complicated further by the impending takeover of the profession's other major journal, the *Deutsche Zeitschrift für Geschichtswissenschaft*, and the removal of this rival to Leipzig.

Lamprecht did not mourn Sybel's passing, and he moved quickly to exploit the uncertainty in Berlin in the hope of engineering another, more spectacular takeover. To Rudolf Oldenbourg, the publisher of the *Historische Zeitschrift*, he laid out the prospect of a "single really great journal," which would issue from the merger of Oldenbourg's journal with the one that Lamprecht and his colleagues were preparing to publish in Leipzig.[16] Oldenbourg's receptivity to the plan was due in part to enthusiastic intervention on Lamprecht's behalf by the geographer Friedrich Ratzel, who was the publisher's close friend; it was due as well to Oldenbourg's anxiety over the "powerful competition" that was now threatening in Leipzig.[17]

Although he was not yet a commanding figure in the profession, Meinecke was well connected to the men who were; and he shared all their apprehensions about Lamprecht.[18] Consequently, when Oldenbourg asked for his "unadorned and detailed" opinion of a merger that might well cost him his job, Meinecke could scarcely contain himself.[19] "In blunt terms," he replied, "what Lamprecht proposes would be a great act of impiety against Sybel and against the direction in which the H. Z. has steered."[20] Under Sybel's guidance, Meinecke noted, the journal's policy had been "decisively to hold the front" against "the inedible mush that Lamprecht has been cooking up in materialism [*den materialistisch durchsäuerten Urbrei Lamprechts*]." The consequence of Lamprecht's becoming editor—or, as Meinecke characterized it, Lamprecht's "rape of the H. Z."— would be to drive off the bulk of the contributors and readers, certainly the "most able and loyal" of them, and to provoke the establishment of a rival journal to serve their needs.

Oldenbourg's enthusiasm for the merger now evaporated in the face of a campaign that Meinecke mobilized in late August to keep the journal in Berlin, or at least in the hands of historians of orthodox views.[21] Meinecke sealed his success early in September, when he persuaded Treitschke, the most famous historian in Berlin and the only scholar whose stature in the profession had rivaled Sybel's, to become editor-in-chief. Treitschke's challenge, as Meinecke described it in an unmistakable allusion to the danger just averted, was to nurture the "younger generation" and to "ward off harmful tendencies."[22]

The new arrangement provided that Meinecke remain as assistant editor. In this capacity he prepared the obituary for Sybel, which appeared in October 1895 in the *Historische Zeitschrift* and read like a public commentary on recent events.[23] As much as the glorious developments of midcentury had vindicated Sybel's vision of history, he wrote, the historian had died in apprehension for the future, as he sadly watched the growing intrusion of "materialistic thinking into our discipline"—the suggestive word that Meinecke used to describe this phenomenon was "invasion" (*Einbruch*).[24] The malady reflected the "loosening of the tie between politics and history," which, Meinecke conceded, might well have been a product of broader trends since 1871; but he also spoke of the disappearance of the "direct political impulse" that had animated the historians of Sybel's generation. The challenge of materialism and positivism was thus only part of the problem as Meinecke saw it. Ranke's heirs were unable to meet the challenge, for they had lost their instinct for politics and were falling prey to aestheticism and the "danger of internal enervation [*Erschlaffung*]." Meinecke's essay left little doubt, however, that the impulse for the profession's regeneration was to come from Berlin rather than Leipzig.

When he first addressed the profession in his new role as editor of the journal, Treitschke also alluded to the challenge from Leipzig. The *Historische Zeitschrift* would not, he announced, change course under his direction; it would remain devoted simply to history, whose stuff, he insisted, was the "world of moral freedom," "the world of will and action," and whose proper objects of study were the "*res gestae* of peoples, the actions of states and their leading men." Treitschke's remarks on *Kulturgeschichte* contained only the mild concessions that Schäfer had made several years earlier. Research in the history of literature, art, and the economy could be a supplement, valuable to the degree that it bore on politics. However, the historian's "proper realm, where he is master," Treitschke observed, "is the world of political acts and the moral laws that govern this world." The farther removed an area of human activity was from the state, "the less does it belong to history." Treitschke's controlling analogy was the history of chemistry, in which "the accent [*Ton*] falls undoubtedly in chemistry." "The same is true of all works of cultural history," he concluded: "the deeper they delve into technology or into a consideration of literary or antiquarian issues, the more they distance themselves from history."

It is difficult to understand the words of thanks that Lamprecht sent to Treitschke after reading this piece, unless a hasty reading or Lamprecht's long devotion to his older colleague led him to mistake the context of an appreciative but incidental reference to Freytag.[25] Treitschke's argument contained much more to cheer Meinecke than Lamprecht. Treitschke in fact had made it clear that he, at least, did not lack the "direct political impulse" that Meinecke had recently invoked. The editor reminded his readers that the *Einbruch* of which Meinecke had warned was objectionable for additional reasons. The historian who was interested in cultural history ought under no circumstances, Treitschke warned, to "sink to the level of subservient recorder of foreign intellectual endeavors and, misunderstanding human nature, to value intelligence and 'improvement' [Treitschke here used the English word] higher than moral will." Treitschke's installation as editor of the *Historische Zeitschrift* was thus an unmistakable sign that those who sought to challenge the profession's traditions and reigning methods would find no succor in Berlin.

Then Treitschke died. The crisis that broke in Berlin in April 1896 had less immediate impact on the journal, where the mantle passed smoothly to Meinecke, than on the university, where the question of Treitschke's successor arose. Lamprecht had long coveted a position at the nation's leading university.[26] He regarded himself, as he confessed to a colleague, as the man "born to be Treitschke's successor," the one who best combined Treitschke's passion for scholarship in the service of the nation with his success in the classroom.[27] At first glance, however, Lamprecht's designs on the now vacant chair were fatuous. His scholarship was anathema to the Berlin historians, and his erratic behavior during the arbitration with Below had left behind animosities in the capital that bordered on hatred. But the decision about Treitschke's successor was not the historians' alone to make; and Lamprecht had important friends elsewhere in the philosophical faculty in Berlin. Among the scholars thought to be favorable to his candidacy were the economists Adolf Wagner, Meitzen, and Schmoller, as well as the philosopher Friedrich Paulsen, the classicist Ernst Curtius, and the art historian Hermann Grimm, whom Lamprecht knew personally.[28] Lamprecht's most formidable ally, though, was Althoff, whose plans were in fact eventually to bring the historian to Berlin; these plans remained intact amid the early turmoil of the *Methodenstreit*, which Althoff had followed with the detached skepticism of a man who frequently watched academics quarrel.

Althoff was the pivotal figure in the political intrigue that ensued, but the outcome demonstrated the limits of even his power. Hoeniger and Liesegang once again served as intermediaries for Lamprecht, while the historian showered potential supporters with offprints.[29] The coalition against him worked with a determination that befitted their dread of having Lamprecht in their midst. Its core comprised the historians, particularly Lenz, Delbrück, and Paul Scheffer-Boichorst, as well as Theodor Mommsen, whose retirement more than a decade earlier had not shorn him of his influence.[30] Their entreaties persuaded Althoff that a badly riven faculty was too great a price to pay for a scholar of Lamprecht's energy and breadth of interest.[31] In June he succumbed to the pressure.

Althoff's decision had the virtue of economy, for the man who moved into Treitschke's chair in 1896 had already been made *Ordinarius* at the university the year before. The appointment of Hans Delbrück was in some respects an act of impiety to Treitschke, for the two scholars had broken over questions of social policy in 1889, when Treitschke resigned in anger from the board of the *Preussische Jahrbücher*, which they had edited together since 1883.[32] Although Delbrück had trained with Sybel and Treitschke, his career, like Lamprecht's, illustrated the risks of unorthodox historical scholarship. Delbrück's expertise was in military history, a field commonly taught not at the universities but at the military academies. However, his views on the subject brought him the enduring hostility of the soldiers; these views also earned him, like Lamprecht, the praise of Franz Mehring.[33] In truth, there was something almost Lamprechtian about Delbrück's approach to the history of warfare, his broad emphasis on the social, political, and technological forces that underlay the organization of armies and the operations of these bodies in combat.[34]

Delbrück never deprecated political history the way Lamprecht did, for he was too much the student of Clausewitz not to regard warfare primarily as an act of state. The similarity of their interests nonetheless kept relations between the two scholars initially cordial enough that Lamprecht tried to lure him to Leipzig in the aftermath of Lehmann's departure in 1893.[35] Their enmity developed shortly thereafter during the negotiations surrounding the arbitration between Lamprecht and Below. Lamprecht's charges that Delbrück had acted dishonestly in these negotiations were groundless, but the affront bought Lamprecht an enemy he could ill afford.[36]

Delbrück's accession to Treitschke's chair sealed the consolidation of forces against Lamprecht in Berlin. Repulsing the threat of Lamprecht's incursion made the historians at the university, like the editor of the *Historische Zeitschrift*, more determined in the defense of the profession's values and methods. Through Delbrück, the Berlin historians also controlled access to the influential *Preussische Jahrbücher*, a journal which, at least with respect to Lamprecht, was already looking like the "twin sister" of the *Historische Zeitschrift*.[37] While there was much in this constellation to justify the impression of a "kind of rivalry between Leipzig and Berlin," it was an unequal rivalry.[38] Berlin remained the center of the historical profession in Germany, the hub in an academic network of power and influence that was mobilizing against its errant member, who remained isolated in Leipzig.

The renewal of the attack on Lamprecht's scholarship in the summer of 1895 indicated the scope and strength of this network. The first to come to the defense of the discipline's orthodoxy was a young scholar in a tenuous position in the profession. That Felix Rachfahl should be, as one of his professors put it, "one of the first to bell the cat" was a comment on the effectiveness of the profession's rituals of socialization.[39] Rachfahl was a Silesian Catholic, the son of a schoolteacher. Despite—or perhaps more accurately, because of—these disadvantages of confession and social origin, he felt driven to succeed in a profession that had little ideological or political tolerance for Catholics, most of whom, should they complete the rigors of academic training, were banned to the recesses of the profession or to the small preserves that were marked off for Catholics by statute in confessional chairs. Rachfahl's approach to this challenge was to embrace the profession's dominant values. Conspicuous features of his training were Protestant. He avoided Catholic professors. Between his promotion in Breslau and his habilitation in Kiel, he studied in Berlin with Max Lenz, a scholar who, on the strength of his biography of Luther and his fierce attacks on the Catholic cultural historian Johannes Janssen, was known as possibly the most Protestant historian in Germany. During the course of his training, in which he specialized in the history of Pomerania in the late Middle Ages, Rachfahl also became, like Lenz, a disciple of Ranke, the figure who symbolized like no other the comfortable symbiosis of German historical scholarship and Lutheran theology. Rachfahl had no interest in a confessional chair, but his credentials retained a blemish that none of his efforts could entirely remove, so he waited thirteen years as extraordinary professor, first in Kiel and then, appropriately, in Halle/Wittenberg, before he received an *Ordinariat* in Königsberg in 1903.

Rachfahl's polemic against Lamprecht in the mid-1890s thus represented an episode in the young scholar's long struggle to demonstrate the orthodoxy of his own views. Years later, he described his feelings of alarm over the "jubilant applause" and the "enthusiastic and aggressive disciples" Lamprecht had attracted, and how he himself felt it necessary to "strip him of his nimbus."[40] It is more likely that Rachfahl responded to an invitation from Lenz to examine the fourth volume of Lamprecht's *German History*, which dealt with the period that most of Rachfahl's own research covered.[41] In all events, Rachfahl's review of this volume, which appeared in July 1895 in the *Deutsche Literaturzeitung*, was more balanced and temperate in tone than Below's, although its thrust was similar.[42] Rachfahl praised the conception of Lamprecht's volume, the effort to present a "comprehensive treatment of German history with a thorough consideration of internal, specifically economic conditions." The difficulties had to do with execution; and in Rachfahl's eyes, they were numerous. Chief among them were an exaggeration of the importance of economic factors and a treatment of political history that lacked "the care one would have desired." The bulk of the review, which addressed the second category of difficulties, was an essay in a genre already becoming known in the controversy as *Detailkritik*. Rachfahl rehearsed at length the same kinds of omissions, inaccuracies, artless characterizations, and errors of fact and interpretation that Below had already identified as the salient features of Lamprecht's scholarship in the first three volumes. Rachfahl's conclusion was also similar to Below's. Despite the riches it contained, Lamprecht's volume was not only a seductive menace for the naive lay reader but an offense to the profession's standards—to what Rachfahl himself called its "most noble postulate," that historical scholarship be distinguished by its "dedication to its material" and the "exactitude of its craftsmanship [*Sorgfalt der Arbeit*]."

Rachfahl's review contained only brief references to issues of methodology and philosophy of history. When Lamprecht himself drew attention to this failing in a rejoinder, Rachfahl felt obligated, as he wrote to Delbrück in September 1895, to take up Lamprecht's "basic conception of history" in a longer essay, which he published in Delbrück's journal early the next year.[43] The character of this essay, which rambled through several different issues, suggested that Rachfahl was collecting his thoughts on methodology for the first time. Most of his criticism was directed at Lamprecht's attempt to trace political development to economic factors, specifically his effort to link the dissolution of the medieval monarchy to the emergence of manorialism in a natural economy and to tie the subsequent centralization of power in the territories to the expansion of a money economy. Rachfahl objected to this schema on several grounds, including the violence it did to the vast complexity of German political development in the Middle Ages. But his greatest objection was that Lamprecht had perverted the foundations of German history.

In the most revealing section of his essay, Rachfahl examined the disintegration of the medieval monarchy. He rejected outright the proposition that conditions in the economic sphere could have caused developments in the political. The explanation for the disintegration of the state, he insisted, lay in another realm. And he invoked a venerable authority. The decline of the patrimonial state of the Carolingian and Ottonian epochs was due in his view to the "linking of the effects of the undeveloped idea of the state [Staatsidee] with the effects of the principles [Prinzipien] of theocracy and feudalism." He continued:

> The idea of the state's cohesion retreated into the background relative to the ecclesiastical-religious idea and the social idea, which rests upon the diversity of occupations and property-holding; the forces that were carried by these ideas burst the unity of the body politic, intent on arrogating its functions.[44]

One could ransack the writings of Ranke without finding a more blunt appeal to the Ideenlehre or to the powers of agency that enabled ideas to retreat, rest, carry, destroy, construct, and avail themselves. Rachfahl's position was that ideas were the motive forces in history, that they were eternal, and that social forces and structures acquired significance only as they were placed in the service of these ideas. Social and economic structures were important in the decline of the monarchy, Rachfahl conceded; they were, "so to speak, the most important instrument of which [the ecclesiastical-theological and the social ideas] availed themselves [sich bedienten] in destroying the old unity of the state and constructing new constitutional forms."[45]

Rachfahl wrote as if the train of his logic were self-evident, as it probably was to most of his readers. So was the indignation with which he proceeded to the political consequences of Lamprecht's attempt to "dissolve the development of the state into an economic process." This perspective held no explanatory value for the great events of the past, at least those that Rachfahl chose to parade. "Was it the effects of a money economy," he asked,

> that called the Prussian Volk to the colors in 1813, that in our own century inspired the hearts of countless Germans for the great ideas of national unity and freedom, that won the battles of the last great wars, that are to be thanked for the proclamation of the empire in the hall at Versailles, the rebirth of the German Reich in new splendor?[46]

Lamprecht's "one-sided view of history, which was so bereft of all ideal elements," could only lead to "a historical materialism," Rachfahl warned. He did not have to specify which one.

Rachfahl turned then to the provocations contained in the passage in Lamprecht's fourth volume, which addressed the question of historical knowledge. Here Lamprecht had announced that political history could lay no claim to the status of Wissenschaft, for it could offer no guarantee of its own objectivity. It imposed no control on the imagination of the historian who described the singular event and unique historical personality. Because it could never divest itself entirely of its fictional character, political history was a "distant descendent of the saga."[47] By contrast, Lamprecht had argued, the true science of history (and he clearly meant cultural history) had as its object the regular patterns of human behavior, which the historian was to analyze inductively, on the basis of masses of instances and by means of a "refined psychology," which Lamprecht characterized as a kind of "mechanics of the human sciences."

Rachfahl dismissed Lamprecht's vision of a scientific history with the remark that it was an "extension [*Fortbildung*] of the old, well-known contention of positivism."[48] Lamprecht's charges about the failings of political history occupied him at greater length, however, for the parallel with the saga was an affront. Rachfahl gestured once again to Ranke in his defense of the profession's hermeneutic tradition. He conceded that imagination played a vital role in the study of history; but the historical *Wissenschaft*, like every other discipline, was governed by "a system of rules and principles" that "bound and limited" the imagination. In history, he noted caustically, the system was called "the historical method." Of the historian it demanded "the disciplining of the free play of imagination through the hard work of [sympathetic] understanding," respect for the evidence, and the use of those operations of criticism and control "which alone assure reliable knowledge of the objective facts and the coherence of events." The guarantee of historical truth, of the objectivity of the facts and the validity of general propositions, was hence the honesty and conscientiousness of the historian. "If not absolute objectivity, then at least the highest possible degree of objectivity is to be attained where truthfulness [*Wahrhaftigkeit*] is the foundation and truth the goal of serious and methodical research."[49]

The historical method of which he spoke was finally, Rachfahl insisted, the only valid system of rules and principles for the analysis of the past. Here he rejected Lamprecht's claim that the distinction between political and cultural history was in the last analysis one of method—that attention to the structures and regularities of the past required an altogether different system of rules and principles than did historical description of the singular and unique. Rachfahl's retort was familiar to those who had followed the exchange between Schäfer and Gothein. He argued that the past presented a uniform object of knowledge that was accessible alone to what he had just defined as the historical method. All cultural institutions were built of the "perceptions, feelings, and strivings of historical personalities"; the state was the highest, most inclusive of these institutions and hence the most worthy of study.[50] The difference between political history and cultural history properly conceived was thus merely one of subject matter or, more accurately (and here he echoed Treitschke), one of differing degrees of immediacy to politics.

This essay was a valuable exercise, as even Lamprecht conceded.[51] Some of Rachfahl's arguments were ingenuous, heavy-handed, and inconsistent, but they provided a straightforward statement of the profession's governing beliefs. His essay laid out the points of disagreement in a way that seemed to invite dialogue on issues of the methodology and philosophy of history. The essay also inadvertently drew attention to the problems that were going to make dialogue impossible. The central problem was the charged implications of the word "method"; and the problem was more than semantic. Rachfahl denied that the distinction between political history and cultural history, at least as Lamprecht understood the terms, was a question of method. He insisted that Lamprecht's approach to the past was instead a facet of a world view, which Rachfahl, like Meinecke, was quick to label materialism or positivism. The charge was invidious not only because of the political connotations of these labels; the term "world view" itself connoted an order of intellectual commitment that the axioms of "the historical method"—the one and only—proscribed as philosophical or ideological, but in all events as prejudicial to an objective analysis of the past.

Rachfahl was right. Lamprecht's ideas about methodology were rooted in a comprehensive vision of the past, which the term "world view," even as Rachfahl used it, accurately described. The problem was that Rachfahl was more sensitive to the nature of his opponent's philosophical commitments than he was to his own. This problem was not his alone, however. Much of the frustration of the *Methodenstreit* was due to a general absence of critical introspection, the refusal of most of the participants to examine the foundations of their own methodological ideas with the critical energy they expended on the positions they opposed. Lamprecht was no exception to this pattern, as he demonstrated when his turn came to examine the views of his opponents.

In a letter he wrote to Hermann Grimm on the day Treitschke died in April 1896, Lamprecht reported that he was "living entirely in these matters" of methodology. Finally, the old school had, "at least in the person of one of its younger, less well known representatives," he noted in an allusion to Rachfahl, "condescended to take up the methodological questions that now have burning importance."[52] Although he was surprised by the challenge that both Rachfahl and Meinecke had laid down, he welcomed it as an opportunity to set out his position more forcefully and to emphasize the gulf that separated him from his antagonists. That this confrontation would be resolved in his favor he never doubted. If the controversy began on a negative note, he continued in the letter to Grimm, "the gentlemen are going to have to condescend to come out with a positive system—and then it will become clear that they have none. I am afraid that the historians in the Berlin guild are going to win no laurels in this business."

Lamprecht's remarks to Grimm betrayed the limitations of his understanding of the dispute that was beginning to engulf him. He approached the controversy with optimism and self-confidence, in the conviction that his own ideas merely required elaboration to be self-evident to anyone who examined them in a spirit of intellectual honesty and good faith. "My position seems unassailable to me," he wrote early in the polemic; and he never wavered in this belief.[53] He was blind to his own failings. Hostility to his ideas he found difficult to comprehend; he tended to regard it less as an intellectual than a moral problem, whose root lay in the envy and malice of Below and his circle of friends in Berlin. When he learned of Mommsen's opposition to his succeeding Treitschke, Lamprecht was baffled. "I don't understand his judgment at all," he wrote to Liesegang, "I can understand his position only on the assumption that he has never read anything I have written."[54] Incomprehension and naiveté characterized Lamprecht's defense of his cause throughout the *Methodenstreit*; and they lent an aura of pathos to the outcome.

There was also an element of pathos in Lamprecht's inability to present a consistent and systematic statement of his views on methodology. Once his attention was engaged in the polemic, he became obsessed with it. But he approached it with the same impulsiveness and furious energy that had disfigured the first volumes of his *German History* with heedless errors and contradictions. The fact that the early phases of the controversy coincided with uncertainty and emotional stress over the situation in Berlin did nothing to calm the historian's disposition, nor did lingering anxieties over his wife's condition and the fact that he himself was suffering at the same time with chronic bronchitis.[55] Consistency had never been his strength, but the replies to his critics that he now dashed off often failed to reflect his evolving views by the time they appeared in print.[56] Yet in these circumstances Lamprecht had not only to defend his ideas about historical method but to formulate them from the ground up. Below was correct when he later remarked that Lamprecht "built up his system" for the purpose of disarming criticism of his *German History*.[57] Soon, in fact, the polemic acquired a momentum of its own, which drove the historian, who found it difficult to discipline his imagination under any circumstances, into ever more extreme positions.

Lamprecht's first major statement on methodology, which appeared in pamphlet form early in 1896, was his reply both to Rachfahl's articles and to Meinecke's obituary for Sybel.[58] Both critics had emphasized the same conclusion that Mehring's review had invited, that the real issue was not method but ideology—the extent to which Lamprecht's views about German history were implicated in materialism or positivism. Lamprecht himself had clearly grown uneasy over this charge by now, and his reply addressed it as a central theme. His argument was that the distinction between political and cultural history, or, as he now referred to them, between the old and new directions of historical research, had nothing to do with *Weltanschauung*; it was entirely a question of method. The difference between the two directions, Lamprecht argued, lay in the categories of explanation that each employed. One used the principle of intentionality or teleology to represent historical acts as singular events, understandable as goals or outcomes of the purposive behavior of individual human beings. This was the explanatory strategy of the old, descriptive, political history; the strategy was attractive, he noted, because it was concrete, easy to understand, and comported with what he described as the "unrefined [*un-*

geläuteren], original, empirical human consciousness."[59] Whatever he meant by this phrase, it was not complimentary, for in his view the principle of intentionality survived as an obstacle to scientific historical analysis.

Lamprecht's description of the new direction, whose destiny was to overcome this obstacle, was not a model of lucidity, either. He introduced the concept of "generic behavior." "Is there not an endlessly extended realm of routine and generic behavior," he asked,

> in which—because all those who stand in the same historical life-situation [*Lebenshaltung*] also behave in essentially the same way—the individual moment of behavior retreats completely in the face of the generic uniformity [*Gleichmässigkeit*] of all actions?[60]

Intentionality was not appropriate to explain behavior in this "endlessly extended realm." Here human beings behaved not as free individuals who consciously willed the outcomes of their acts, but instead as members of collectivities, who responded typically, and often unconsciously, to motive forces that resided in the structures of collective "life situations." The object of the new direction of historical research, Lamprecht announced, was to explain the workings of collective forces in history. But because their operation was regular, these forces were accessible to methods of empirical study, statistical analysis, and explanation based on the principle of causality. These methods made the new "structural" history fully *wissenschaftlich*. They provided the means for verifying the conclusions and guaranteeing the objectivity of historical research. The old "personal" history could never, by contrast, aspire to the full status of science; its characteristic features—its devotion to the singular and its reliance on the historian's intuitive reconstruction of the past—were in this respect its defects; and they rendered the genre captive of its "novellistic bent [*romanhafter Zug*]."[61]

Lamprecht's assurance that the teleological and causal methods of historical analysis were nonetheless complementary, that the two were only "quantitatively distinguished," seemed difficult to reconcile with some of his earlier pronouncements; nor did it quiet suspicions that he had become a thorough-going positivist, whose project was to study human history with the intellectual tools of the natural scientist.[62] The most novel feature of Lamprecht's argument was his resolute denial that the "causal method" of the new history entailed any philosophical or ideological implications that might justify calling it the outgrowth of a world view. He insisted that there was nothing metaphysical about the principle of causality. In a passage that raised questions not only about his concessions to the teleological method, Lamprecht explained that

> once human events have become completely transparent [*bei voller Durchsichtigkeit des menschlichen Geschehens*], all acts, even those of eminent individuals, will in the final analysis have to be explained in terms of the causal nexus; the causal principle is to this extent [*insofern*] an absolute postulate of our thought, independent of any metaphysical system.[63]

It is necessary to pause briefly at this remarkable passage, for it laid bare the philosophical root of Lamprecht's problem. The premise of his position throughout the controversy was the validity of the "causal nexus" as a principle of historical explanation. In this passage he appealed to the *Critique of Pure Reason* in order to show that this premise rested upon no prior assumption about the roots of human behavior, that it was instead an epistemological category or, in Kantian terms, an "absolute postulate of our thought." Lamprecht neglected, however, to mention that causality was but one "postulate of our thought" and that Kant's functions of judgment also included singularity and particularity, the foundations of his opponents' method. Another offense lurked in the bewildering exercise that followed. The historian argued that the validity of the "causal principle" as an "absolute postulate" rested on an explanatory obligation to employ the "causal nexus"; this explanatory obligation rested itself, however, on the validity of the selfsame causal principle.[64] The proposition was at once a tautology and a symptom of the dreaded "ontological fallacy," which Lamprecht himself later deprecated as the "conflation of thinking and reality."[65] Here he committed it. His characterization of historical reality—and with it his whole methodology—rested henceforth on the ontological validity of epistemological categories.

With the fallacy disguised in the opacity of his prose, Lamprecht turned with much more critical insight to the metaphysics of his opponents. His essay on "Ranke's Doctrine of Ideas and the Neo-Rankeans" was the most effective polemic he ever wrote.[66] His survey of Ranke's own pronouncements made it difficult to deny that the great historian had himself embraced a comprehensive world view. Lamprecht laid bare the mysticism in Ranke's thinking and his profound debt to Lutheran theology and idealistic philosophy, particularly to Fichte. The great ideas, which provided both the motive forces and the categories of understanding in Ranke's view of history, were in the last analysis, Lamprecht argued, documents of the historian's personal faith, mystical entities that he believed to be manifestations of God. They were not, however, valid categories of historical explanation, for they were ultimately geared to a transcendent realm beyond both history and human understanding. The consequences of this *Weltanschauung* for Ranke as historian were, Lamprecht pointed out, that he "had to regard the great contexts of history as manifestations of the divine, revelations of a God who stands above the world that is accessible to our reason."[67]

This assault on the profession's most hallowed symbol earned Lamprecht no friends in the academy, but it provided him a powerful tool to attack what he now labeled the ideology of the neo-Rankeans, for whom his opponent Rachfahl stood as a vulnerable representative.[68] Rachfahl's characterization of German political development Lamprecht found, with good reason, to be "completely Rankean," "thoroughly governed by ideas."[69] For Rachfahl no less than Ranke, Lamprecht noted, ideas were transcendent categories, which provided the teleology of historical action "from above and from without"; but Rachfahl, like

Ranke, persistently broke off or obfuscated the analysis just as it reached the point of linking ideas to their historical determinants, which Lamprecht insisted were immanent and structural.[70]

Lamprecht's attack on the *Ideenlehre* was effective for being uncompromising and unusually consistent. The historian followed it, however, with a qualification that not only seemed to signal a change in his own thinking but undermined much of his case against the neo-Rankeans. He had opened himself to the accusation of materialism when he argued that the structures that most fundamentally conditioned behavior were social and economic. When he returned from Ranke to Rachfahl, his discomfort with the accusation was apparent. He began to waver. In speaking of the ideas that informed German constitutional history in the early Middle Ages, he observed that behind these ideas "stand very simple developmental facts [*Entwicklungsvorgänge*], which in their deepest foundations lead to roots that are chiefly economic [*vornehmlich wirtschaftliche Wurzeln*]." But he added: "This is admittedly not always the case."[71] "I am by no means saying anything I haven't before," began the labored attempt to elucidate. "In every epoch of our political life there are, in addition to the operation [*Wirksamkeit*] of social and economic factors, operations that come from other sides," by which he meant the spiritual. His objections, he explained, pertained only to the "hyperidealistic view that spiritual forces alone were the constitutive forces, alongside which economic (and social) factors functioned [*Momente liefen*] only as unessential 'conditions' [*Bedingungen*]." Lamprecht's conclusion to this passage then removed all certainty about where he stood:

> Spiritual and "material" factors [*Wirkungen*] are of the same rank and can therefore at the moment of their influence come into effect [*zur Wirkung gelangen*] in fundamental independence of one another; they are coordinate [*koordiniert*], and without doubt in the area of constitutional history, social and economic factors [*Momente*] are indeed at most times easier to recognize and also the more powerful.[72]

Lamprecht's position now seemed so eclectic as to defy categorization. He appeared to argue that material and spiritual factors represented two altogether autonomous categories of causation, that material factors "essentially constituted" collective behavior in some epochs and in some areas, while spiritual factors predominated in others. The only thing that was clear from this muddy passage was that Lamprecht was on the defensive, for he ended with a plea for the "equal entitlement" of economic factors in historical analysis.[73]

"So many sentences, so many absurd assertions," came the retort from Rachfahl, who was losing his patience.[74] He was not impressed by Lamprecht's apparent retreat from materialism, but he did insist that the operation of ideas in history was no mystical process; it could be demonstrated empirically. Ideas, he explained, were "purposive contexts [*Zweckzusammenhänge*]," the "general views of entire social groups, entire peoples, and entire generations."[75] But he remained a vulnerable target, for he left open the question of where these views came from, and he continued to convey the impression that ideas intervened as active agents. Some of his remarks on this subject rivaled Lamprecht's own in their obscurity. Of the "social idea" he wrote that it was "dependent in its origin, to a certain degree," on relations of property and profession, but that this idea was capable of "simultaneously developing to independent efficacy" and of "availing itself of economic relations."[76]

Although Meinecke, too, was becoming impatient with what he called the "evolutions" of Lamprecht, his response in the *Historische Zeitschrift* to Lamprecht's charges shortly later had the virtue of brevity, clarity, and candor.[77] Meinecke's devotion to Ranke was less uncritical than Rachfahl's, for like Lamprecht, he was uncomfortable with the view that impersonal ideas intervened as motive forces in history.[78] But he also recognized the futility of isolating historical method from metaphysical context, so he quickly cut through much of the confusion that Lamprecht and Rachfahl had together generated. "It will now be clear," he wrote of himself and Lamprecht, "that in fact we are separated by world view." Lamprecht was a positivist. And Meinecke admitted that he himself was an idealist, in the sense that he believed a priori in a "minimal spark" of freedom in every individual human being, a "free x," which contributed to the make-up of every historical structure and resisted causal analysis under the rubric of "generic behavior."

Meinecke's observations were refreshing, but they provided no basis for resolving the controversy. Admitting that historical method required metaphysical premises was no more a solution for Lamprecht, who aspired to make history into a discipline as inductive as natural science, than it was for Rachfahl and Lamprecht's other opponents, for whom Ranke symbolized the liberation of history from the thrall of both philosophy and natural science. Indeed, given the agendas of the participants, it is difficult to see how the controversy could have produced a consensus on questions of method or theory. Lamprecht's antagonists were already beginning to regard the exchange with him as futile. Rachfahl's public reference to Lamprecht's "garb of wordy, hard-to-unsnarl, sophistical, pseudo-philosophical dialectics" typified the ill will and bemusement Lamprecht was calling forth.[79] In all events, the dialogue on substantive issues was already drawing to a close. While Lamprecht developed his views on method in ever more extravagant fashion, his opponents were becoming reluctant to engage him any longer at this level of abstraction. Instead, they prepared to remove the focus of the controversy to more accessible flaws in his scholarship.

"I admittedly challenged you," Lamprecht wrote in May 1896 to Meinecke, who had complained about the tone of Lamprecht's attack on him, "just as I would challenge any statement by an author of the old direction from whom I had reason to expect constructive statements which would clarify the existing conflicts."[80] Lamprecht's remarks suggested that he was still confident that constructive dialogue would produce a consensus between him and the more open-minded of his academic colleagues. On this score, too, he was deluding himself. Signs of his isolation in the profession were everywhere; and decisions he himself now made only compounded the problem.

Lamprecht's growing isolation had immediate practical consequences. The initial exchanges in the polemic confirmed the hostility of the *Historische Zeitschrift* and *Preussische Jahrbücher* and ensured that the pages of these two journals would be closed to him.[81] His search for an alternative outlet disclosed other sensitive problems. His prospects for exploiting the *Deutsche Zeitschrift für Geschichtswissenschaft*, the journal that he had recently brought to Leipzig, were limited by the apprehensions of his colleagues on the editorial board. As the polemic continued, both Seeliger and Marcks became increasingly reluctant to see the new journal committed to a position that so clashed with the traditions in which they had themselves been trained.[82] Nor did Lamprecht find much support among his nominal allies in the editorial office of the *Zeitschrift für Kulturgeschichte*, where Steinhausen, who was trying to cultivate a broader constituency of scholars, was not prepared to allow Lamprecht to speak in their name.[83] In these circumstances, as he watched the doors close on him, Lamprecht again ventured out.

Maximilian Harden was arguably the most significant journalist in German history.[84] His was certainly a remarkable career, which began with a break with his psychotic father and progressed through episodes of acting, translating, writing literary criticism, and collaborating with Max Reinhardt in the *Deutsches Theater*, before it peaked in 1892 when he founded *Die Zukunft*, the journal through which his name became respected, feared, and villified over the next thirty years. That this moody, insecure Jew, whose formal education did not extend beyond the age of thirteen, should be drawn to Karl Lamprecht bespoke affinities stronger than the contrasts in their backgrounds. Both were driven by intense but restless energy, which they expended on an immense range of intellectual interests; both were crusaders, who were fearless in challenging those in power and paid for their efforts in contempt and ostracism. To speak of either Harden or Lamprecht as an outsider would be overstating the case, for both men circulated easily among sectors of imperial Germany's elites; but both occupied difficult positions within their professions, and this fact vitally affected their conceptions of themselves, just as it drew them together.

The overture came early in 1894 from Harden, who had learned of the scandal that Lamprecht's dispute with Below was threatening to visit on the historical profession.[85] The resolution of the dispute kept it out of the press, but Harden persuaded Lamprecht to publish occasional pieces—one an excerpt from the fifth volume of the *German History*—in *Die Zukunft*.[86] Lamprecht's growing problems within the profession cast his association with the journalist in a new light. Harden had a seamy reputation among the academic historians, who dismissed him, as Marcks wrote to Treitschke, as "merely a sensationalist."[87] But Harden, whose journal enjoyed a readership of close to 10,000, offered access to a forum within Germany's educated classes that stretched far beyond the academy. The journal could be, in Lamprecht's suggestive term, a "pulpit" from which to "speak to a broad audience [*weithin*]."[88] To his brother, the historian described Harden as "a very ephemeral spirit"—as a distasteful, but valuable ally; but "anyone who wishes to preach to the multitudes [*Tausende*]," he continued, "has to disregard the fact or accept the risk that the pulpit on which he stands perhaps has a rotten step."[89]

Lamprecht stood there a long time—so long that he could later describe Harden's journal in a different metaphor, as the "archive of the historiographical dispute."[90] The first half of his reply to Rachfahl and Meinecke originally appeared early in 1896 in *Die Zukunft*. Thereafter, Harden not only opened its pages to the polemical essays that Lamprecht supplied with increasing frequency, but he became one of the historian's principal advisors.[91] The advice was limited to questions of tactics, though, and Harden offered little to discourage Lamprecht's impulses to fight.[92] Harden's motives in the affair were, as usual, complex. To the extent that he understood the historiographical issues, his sympathy for Lamprecht's position was genuine. But other calculations were at work. His association with an eminent academic flattered his self-esteem, while he was shrewd enough to recognize the opportunity that this academic's professional difficulties presented for the fortunes of his journal.[93]

Lamprecht's association with Harden signaled the formal breakdown in communication between the historian and his opponents. The tie to the journalist implied Lamprecht's acceptance of his own professional isolation. It also marked the beginning of his attempt to retaliate by demonstrating the broader isolation of the German historical profession. The *Methodenstreit*, Lamprecht was beginning to believe, was to be resolved in a wider public forum, in which the central issue would be the competence of his enemies to pass judgment on his scholarship. Harden's journal was thus to be a vehicle to remove the debate beyond the confines of the profession, into a forum where another arbiter presided— where the historian himself was alone qualified to judge his own work.

The expansion of the public audience whom Lamprecht proposed to address contrasted with the shrinking circle of historians with whom he carried on any meaningful exchange about the issues that dominated the controversy. His preference for independence was long documented, but as the crisis intensified, the number of people on whom he relied for advice dwindled still further, as did the range of questions on which he was prepared to accept their counsel.[94]

Lamprecht showered the profession with copies of his methodological essays and polemical tracts.[95] Some of his colleagues responded at length with gentle and benevolent criticism, which offered constructive suggestions about many of the stylistic and conceptual difficulties that his opponents were to emphasize shortly in a much different spirit.[96] Lamprecht either ignored these suggestions or committed them to a pile of notes for revisions, never undertaken, in subsequent editions of his *German History*.[97] The only professional historian in whom he confided was Bernheim, who remained in Greifswald—too far away to have much immediate influence on the evolution of his views. Liesegang, who was still *Privatdozent* in economics in Berlin, was Lamprecht's man in the enemy's camp and his most trusted advisor throughout the dispute, but Liese-gang's advice, like Harden's, addressed questions of tactics more than substance.

Circumstances, as well as the historian's temperamental preferences, pre-cluded his seeking help among his colleagues in the historical seminar in Leipzig. The death of Arndt had deprived him of the only man in the seminar with whom he was personally close. He well recognized that neither Seeliger nor Marcks sympathized with his views on methodology. Domestic harmony thus recommended that the seminar remain insulated as far as possible (or as long as possible) from the professional controversy. With the exception of Buchholz, who inclined toward Lamprecht's side, the *Privatdozenten* in the seminar likewise kept their distance.[98]

Lamprecht had already begun to seek a different order of counsel elsewhere in the philosophical faculty in Leipzig. The extent of Karl Bücher's influence on him is difficult to reconstruct because of the paucity of written correspondence betweeen the two men, who saw each other almost every day.[99] Lamprecht, who had early been impressed with Bücher's work on the population and guilds of Frankfurt in the late medieval era, was a driving force behind the economist's call to Leipzig from Karlsruhe in 1892.[100] The historian's expectation that he and his new colleague would, as he wrote to Karlsruhe, enter into "wide-ranging cooperation" was quickly rewarded.[101] Bücher arrived in Leipzig with most of his archival work behind him, and he was at a point in his career when his interest turned to what he called the "general questions of national economy," to the broader theoretical implications of his empirical research.[102] The volume that he published shortly thereafter, in 1893, presented the fruits of his reflection in the form of a theory of economic growth.[103] In it he argued that economic systems evolved historically through broadening realms of exchange among producers and consumers; the essential stages of this growth he characterized as "domestic economy [*Hauswirtschaft*]," "municipal economy [*Stadtwirtschaft*]," and "national economy [*Volkswirtschaft*]."[104]

The attempt to impose this bold scheme on the past was much more to Lamprecht's taste than it was to the political historians', who, with Below in the lead, drew attention to a wealth of historical particulars that Bücher's stages failed to comprehend.[105] Lamprecht himself was more drawn to Bücher's intent than he was to the specifics of the theory. His own work rested on a theory of economic growth associated with Roscher and Bruno Hildebrand, which defined the stages of development in terms of the modes rather than the realms of exchange. The volumes of the *German History* that Lamprecht prepared after Bücher's arrival in Leipzig nonetheless revealed an attempt to amalgamate the two theories and to argue that the growth of a money economy after the millennium corresponded to the transition from a domestic, manorial economy to one increasingly dominated by the towns.[106]

The bond between the two men grew close. They were drawn together by similarities of background and temperament, as well as by their common intellectual interests.[107] Both had grown up in rural settings. Bücher was the son of a peasant; like Lamprecht, he looked upon his first-hand encounter with a rural economy as an essential feature of his professional development.[108] Like Lamprecht, he had studied medieval history in Göttingen (with Waitz), before he took a doctorate in ancient history with Arnold Schäfer in Bonn. Bücher shared as well Lamprecht's penchant for the grand historical vision. He was perhaps at the core a philosopher of history, for his great ambition was, as Goetz later remarked, "to penetrate into the final secrets of economic development."[109] In this ambition he was drawn to the vitality, imagination, and enthusiasm of his colleague, whom he found to be "a great energizer [*ein grosser Anreger*]." "In the endless joy with which he worked," Bücher recalled of Lamprecht, "he revealed a sense of power that practically knew no ends."[110]

The relationship was not untroubled. Like many others, Bücher was discomfited by the "erratic, unsettled, and unpredictable" elements in the historian's nature.[111] Bücher himself had an erratic side; he was quarrelsome and found it difficult to retain friends.[112] The two clashed over whether to call Lehmann and then Marcks to Leipzig, for Bücher had little understanding for Lamprecht's desire to bring intellectual balance to the historical seminar. Bücher, too, had fought with members of the Prussian historical school; and his verdict on their views—he spoke of "journalism applied to the past"—had at least the virtue of consistency.[113] The friendship between historian and economist nevertheless endured these encounters in search committees. Bücher provided loyal counsel to Lamprecht during the preliminary skirmishes in the methodological controversy, particularly during the arbitration negotiations, when his caution served as a brake. As the dispute intensified, however, Bücher's doubts began to grow about the wisdom of Lamprecht's tactics and the defensibility of methodological views that he believed the historian had not adequately thought through. "He is too erratic [*fahrig*]," Bücher wrote to his friend Aloys Schulte in June 1895, "he is always jumping from one ambitious project to another."[114] Lamprecht's reluctance to accept Bücher's advice thus registered a certain cooling in their relationship, as the beleaguered historian turned late in 1895 in a new direction for help and found it in the institute of another of his Leipzig colleagues.

Lamprecht first met Wilhelm Wundt as a student in Leipzig, but Wundt played no significant role in his life at this time, beyond serving as his examiner in philosophy. In 1879, a year after Lamprecht's departure from Leipzig, Wundt laid the basis for his reputation as the "founder of modern psychology," when he established the world's first institute for experimental psychology at the university in Leipzig.[115] At the heart of the institute's agenda were the reaction-time studies, which measured intervals between the administration of stimuli to subjects and the carrying out of prescribed responses. In format and technique these studies resembled the so-called psycho-physical experiments, which

Fechner and the physiologist Ernst Heinrich Weber had developed earlier in the century in order to explore the relationship between sensation and perception, between the physical world and the operations of the mind. Although Wundt had himself trained as a physiologist (in the laboratory of Heinrich von Helmholtz, among other places), he rejected the proposition that mental phenomena could be reduced to processes in the brain or neurological system. Instead, his reaction-time experiments rested on the premise of "psycho-physical parallelism," the theory, originally developed by Fechner, that operations of the mind worked in parallel with physiological processes, but that mental operations were autonomous, purely psychological in character. Furthermore, Wundt was convinced that these mental operations could be analyzed experimentally, their workings glimpsed during the milliseconds that separated stimulation from response in his subjects.[116]

Although the disciplinary roots of psychology lay principally in physiology, Wundt, like most other pioneers in the field, occupied a chair in philosophy. Unlike these other scholars, however, Wundt was guided by a vision that was philosophical in the broadest sense. A determination to establish psychology as a discipline independent of physiology played a part in his insistence that the study of the mind be divorced from the study of the body; but in his broader view, psychology offered a scientifically valid theory of knowledge, the epistemological foundation not only for a system of philosophy, but for every Geisteswissenschaft.

The central tenet in Wundt's system was the principle of psychic causality. He insisted that the operations of the mind, no less than the processes that governed the physical world, were lawful. These mental operations, which he described generally as perception, apperception, volition, and emotion, were of a distinct order and independent of physical processes; but categories of cause and effect were appropriate to an analysis of every mental act, even though the dynamic complexity of mental processes made them impossible to predict. Perhaps the most remarkable feature of Wundt's epistemological doctrines was his assertion that the central mental process was volition, that every thought was an act of will, that it involved conscious choice and purpose. Causality embraced teleology.

The work performed in the Leipzig institute was designed in the first instance to provide empirical support for Wundt's theories.[117] But this scholar's fertile mind far outpaced the capacity of his laboratory—or anyone else's—to supply him with experimental proof. To explain the workings of the human mind, he worked out an elaborate set of laws and principles, which included a "law of psychic resultants," a "law of psychic relations," and a "law of psychic contrasts." The most fundamental was the "principle of creative synthesis," which postulated that any fusion of mental elements produces a psychic complex greater than the sum of its parts, in the manner that the combination of musical notes produces a chord. Wundt invoked this principle to demonstrate the distinction between the physical realm, in which the law of the conservation of energy applied, and the realm of the mind, in which the generation of new psychic energy by creative synthesis provided the dynamic of the mind's development. And in order to analyze this process, too, Wundt devised a set of developmental laws, which comprised a "law of mental growth," a "law of the heterogeneity of purposes," and a "law of dialectical development."

The Hegelian ring to this last law suggested but one of the many sources that fed into the elaborate philosophical system that Wundt constructed on the basis of his psychological principles. In a prodigious outburst of scholarship in the 1880s, he laid out this system in a series of encyclopedic treatises on method, the psychology of ethical norms, and metaphysics.[118] Insofar as he emphasized the action of autonomous mental processes in the structuring of experience, he stood in the line of Kant and his disciples of the early nineteenth century, such as Johann Friedrich Herbart.[119] However, Wundt's philosophical vision was too all-encompassing and his intellectual preferences were too holistic to rest content with a set of theories that implied the dualism—or ultimately even the parallelism—of spirit and matter, the mind and the physical world.[120] To bridge this gulf, to demonstrate the fundamental unity of all existence, Wundt reached further back into the traditions of German idealism, to Spinoza and especially to Leibniz. The dualism of mind and matter he now dissolved into a question of perspective. He explained that the physical sciences and psychology, the sciences of matter and the mind, referred alike to experience, the one to experience mediated by mental constructs called natural laws, the other to the actual, immediate experience of the experiencing subject.

Wundt's insistence that the mind structured reality invited the conclusion that reality was itself ideal. The psychologist embraced this conclusion in a manner that revealed the extent of his debt to Leibniz. All dimensions of existence were united, he believed, under the reign of an immanent causality that was ultimately teleological or entelechial. Everywhere in existence he described the operation of will and purpose; the constituents of nature, from the lowest organisms to humanity, he regarded as "voluntary units [*Willenseinheiten*]." The hierarchy of these units—he might as well have called them "monads"—corresponded to ascending degrees of spiritual autonomy and consciousness; and this hierarchy represented the ordering principle, the lawful harmony of all existence. "Nature," as he put it, "is the prelude [*Vorstufe*] to spirit."

As this proposition made clear, Wundt's vision was finally historical: its salient feature was psychogenesis—the immanent, lawful development of spirit, not only of the individual mind, but of all consciousness.[121] The principle of creative synthesis underlay the development of ever higher, more advanced forms of thought, collective consciousness, and collective will, which found expression in language, religion, and ethical systems. Wundt was convinced, however, that analyzing the development of these higher forms of mental life exceeded the capacities of laboratory experiment, and he called instead for a social psychology of the human race, whose foundation was to be ethnological and historical. So, upon the completion of his treatise on metaphysics in 1889, Wundt himself prepared to undertake this vast project, his *Völkerpsychologie*, to which he then devoted the last decades of his long life.[122]

Wundt's many sobriquets attested to an extraordinary career. He has been variously called "an epigone of classical German idealism," "the German Spencer," and of course "the Leibniz of the nineteenth century."[123] William James once described him as "a sort of Napoleon of the intellectual world"; and while this remark was not kindly intended, it was apt.[124] There was indeed something almost imperial about the grand system that Wundt constructed eclectically, on the basis of his own wide reading, and then employed to impose a tenuous harmony among a multitude of theories not easily reconciled. In Wundt's writings one finds traces, some more substantial than others, not only of Kant, Spinoza, and Leibniz, but of Aristotle, Heraclitus, Herbart, Fechner, Lotze, Herder, Fichte, Schopenhauer, Comte, Feuerbach, F. A. Lange, Helmholtz, Du Bois-Reymond, Buckle, and Hegel.[125] Hegel's influence was minor; the dialectic was based too much on contradiction for the taste of Wundt, whose ideas about developmental laws came instead primarily via Haeckel from Darwin and Spencer.

Wundt regarded his own achievement as the grand synthesis of philosophy, the *Geisteswissenschaften*, and the natural sciences into a unified theory of knowledge. He insisted that his conclusions were consistent with the experimental findings of his laboratory. Few of his peers were convinced, however, for it was not difficult to see the extent to which his system grew out of his restless ingenuity and imaginative use of analogies, like the linking of physical and psychic causality. The pillars of his thought were the universal operation of causality and the unified character of existence; both, he thought, were empirically valid as "postulates of our thought"—propositions that he held to be psychological, but which contemporary thinkers more rigorous than he, such as Friedrich Avenarius and Ernst Mach, were already showing to be empirically unsupportable.[126] In the end, Wundt's inductive metaphysics might be better described as a kind of godless pantheism, a psychogenetic spiritualism that verged, despite its author's protestations to the contrary, on mysticism.[127]

Nevertheless, on the strength of his experimental work, Wundt was the most famous psychologist in the world when, in 1891, Karl Lamprecht returned to Leipzig to join him on the faculty. Although Lamprecht was Wundt's junior by almost a quarter-century, similarities of background, temperament, interests, and intellectual ambition quickly drew these two system-builders together.[128] Wundt enjoyed great respect in the Leipzig faculty, and late in 1893 Lamprecht confessed he, like many of his colleagues, had come under Wundt's "philosophical aegis."[129] The tie between the two scholars soon grew stronger, as both became involved in bitter debates that portended their professional isolation.

Although Wundt's difficulties were less acute than Lamprecht's, they were painful. A series of attacks on the theory of psychophysical parallelism in the early 1890s accompanied the defection of two of his ablest students, Oswald

Külpe and Hugo Münsterberg, who converted to the view that mental phenomena were rooted in physiological processes.[130] The attack on Wundt's theories then broadened in a celebrated exchange which began in 1894, as Wilhelm Dilthey and Hermann Ebbinghaus clashed over the scope and character of the discipline of psychology, specifically over whether its methodological affinities lay closer to the natural sciences or the *Geisteswissenschaften*.[131] Wundt was not a direct party to the exchange, but he was caught in the cross fire. At first glance, Dilthey's position was the more cordial to his views. In pleading for a "descriptive psychology," Dilthey argued that spiritual phenomena were autonomous of physical processes and hence inaccessible to the explanatory (*erklärende*) strategies of the natural sciences, like physiology. The difficulty for Wundt was that Dilthey proceeded to reject causal explanations of any kind in the study of the mind. Ebbinghaus' acerbic reply in defense of causality brought no comfort to Wundt either, for Ebbinghaus joined Külpe and Münsterberg in insisting that the causes of all psychic phenomena were physiological.

The attacks on Wundt and Lamprecht thus intensified at roughly the same time, and it was not difficult to see methodological and ideological parallels in the issues confronting the two scholars. The specter of materialism loomed large in both cases. Wundt accused those who supported Ebbinghaus of falling prey to a "peculiar variety [*Spielart*] of materialism" when they reduced psychology to the study of processes in the brain.[132] Wundt's polemic against the practitioners of "psycho-physical materialism" continued for the next several years. Revisions of his texts registered an attempt to portray psychology as an "idealistic" discipline, to remove it from all association with physiology, and to emphasize its cultural dimension and its affinities with humanistic disciplines such as ethnology and history.[133]

The intellectual collaboration between Wundt and Lamprecht now solidified in a community of beleaguerment.[134] The psychologist and the cultural historian both found themselves defending the scientific credentials of the disciplines they practiced. Both understood this challenge to hinge on the principle of causality, which they struggled to rid of the taint of materialism. In Lamprecht Wundt found a valuable ally. The historian's comprehensive perspective on the past and his views on immanent laws of development accorded well with the psychologist's plans to use cultural history to buttress his theories of mental development.[135] For Lamprecht the appeal of collaboration was even greater, for his situation was more perilous. His authority was less secure than Wundt's and his reputation more vulnerable. Wundt's theory of psychogenesis appeared to resolve many of the historian's difficulties. It offered a new metaphor in which to address the problem of historical development, particularly to deal with the relationship between material and ideal culture, to bring ideal culture under the sway of causal analysis, and to relocate the dynamic of historical development in a way that would make it hard to portray him any longer as a materialist.

Evidence of Wundt's influence first surfaced in Lamprecht's work in 1894. The passage on the saga in the fourth volume of his *German History* contained no footnote, but the source of its inspiration was transparent. Lamprecht wrote of the need for a "refined psychology" to serve the Geisteswissenschaften in the way that mechanics served the natural sciences. Subjecting historical data to "analysis by inductive psychology," he noted, promised to lead to "more reliable (vollkommeneren) scientific truths" and a "new epoch of historiography."[136] Lamprecht began to explore the implications of this proposition for his own work only after the completion of the fifth volume and the onset of the polemic on method. In the fall of 1895, during his initial preparations for the next volumes of his German History, he began to read in the philosophy of the seventeenth and eighteenth centuries, where he encountered Spinoza and Leibniz, who drew him directly to Wundt.[137] The discussions between Lamprecht and Wundt evidently became intense at the end of the year, for the psychologist's imprint became increasingly salient in the methodological essays that Lamprecht published in the next months. The historian's defense of causality in his initial response to Rachfahl and Meinecke, which he wrote in January 1896, was, as a footnote confirmed, a labored rendition of some of Wundt's theories.[138] And when Lamprecht sought in the same essay to characterize causality as an "absolute postulate of our thought," he enclosed his system in the same fallacy as Wundt's, in a metaphysical principle disguised as a psychological truth.

Lamprecht's next essay consummated his embrace of Wundt's system. He dashed it out in March 1896 "with my heart's blood," as he wrote to Liesegang.[139] He overrode the apprehensions of his editorial colleagues in Leipzig and placed it in the second number of their new journal, where it appeared in June. Its publication came too late to affect decisions in the capital about Treitschke's successor, but Lamprecht could be confident that the piece would provoke his opponents.[140]

The article was perhaps the most remarkable document of the entire Methodenstreit.[141] It was Lamprecht's personal manifesto. Its title, "What Is Cultural History?" signaled an attempt to provide Kulturgeschichte with a definition free of all ambiguity; it also announced his arrogation of the field, his claim to prescribe the scope, method, and ultimately the results of historical research. It demonstrated how far afield the historian had ventured in order to retrieve the elements of a grand synthesis, whose comprehensiveness was to be both its great attraction and the mark of its validity. The facility with which he incorporated the work of economists, philosophers, sociologists, geographers, ethnologists, and physiologists revealed a design to reconcile history with every other field of knowledge. For all its virtuosity, though, Lamprecht's synthesis was not original: it was suffused with the thinking of his colleague.

This point was immediately clear. "Everyone agrees," Lamprecht proclaimed at the start, "that psychology must be the basis of the study of history."[142] As the "uncontested foundation" of Geschichtswissenschaft, he then described a purely Wundtian psychology, which took psychic causality as its premise and studied the laws of mental processes, using experiment to analyze simpler phenomena and social psychology for the more complex. In this manner, the historian pointed out, the discipline had discovered the fundamental law of mass psychic phenomena:

> Whenever a majority of people feels, has an idea [*sich vorstellt*], or wills something in common, the collective feeling, the collective conception, or the collective will is not identical with the sum of the individual factors, but instead harbors in addition a psychic moment of a qualitatively different character, which manifests itself as reputation [*Beleumdung*] and slander, as public opinion, patriotism—in sum, as the social sentiment [*Stimmung*] of those circles that make up the majority of these people. [143]

This passage presented the new fulcrum on which Lamprecht's system was henceforth to rest. In translating Wundt's principle of creative synthesis into a collective historical context as the "law of historical resultants," the historian was following the psychologist's own lead. [144] Lamprecht now invoked the principle to identify the underlying forces in history. And on this subject, at least, he removed all ambiguity. These forces were not material. Once collective will or collective consciousness emerged as an "excess [*Überschuss*]" beyond the "individual factors" in any "social formation"—from the smallest voluntary groups to the nation—it became, by the laws of psychic mechanics, a "psychic force [*psychische Macht*]," which acted as a motivating (in other words as a causal) factor on the members of the collectivity whom it imbued. [145]

Isolating psychic forces as the motor of historical development seemed to bring Lamprecht remarkably close to Ranke's position. In order to discourage this conclusion, he attempted to emphasize the distinction between his theories and the *Ideenlehre*. He explained that what he now called "collective psychic forces" were not transcendent ideas, like Ranke's; they were instead "fully immanent" forces, for they derived from the psychic constitution of individual human beings and were the causes, not merely the conditions, of human behavior.

These distinctions could not fully allay the suspicion that the historian had rejected one kind of *Ideenlehre* in favor of another, but they did prepare the ground for the reappearance, albeit in a slightly different guise, of the concept of generic behavior. [146] To the extent that they lived within the thrall of these immanent collective forces, individual human beings could be regarded as typical, as *Gattungexemplare*—identical group members, whose personal idiosyncrasies need not detain the historian who employed what Lamprecht now characterized as the generic, collectivistic method in order to analyze their behavior scientifically, in the light of causality. [147]

Lamprecht argued that these collective ideas were immanent in nations of the world, which he now portrayed as the "most natural" units of historical development. [148] The evolution of these ideas lent pattern to history, and comparing the process across national frontiers was the great interpretive challenge facing the historical profession. Lamprecht also claimed to have discovered the laws that governed the process everywhere. In order to explain the play of immanent causality in the morphology of history's underlying spiritual forces, he introduced an array of categories, factors, rules, and principles that bore a close resemblance to Wundt's.

Several features of this new system were of particular significance, for they highlighted the way the historian's views were evolving in response to the trying circumstances he faced. The first feature was the new status he accorded to economic structures and systems of exchange, whose development through stages had seemed in his earlier writings to provide the motor of historical change. He now used the unwieldy term "socio-psychic" to describe the under-lying "factors" of history. The only thing "social" about them, however, was the context of their operation; in essence they were spiritual, for they derived ultimately from basic psychic processes in the individual mind, which Lamprecht identified as imagination, emotion, and volition. In its "most primitive" collective operation, he explained, imagination became the socio-psychic "factor" of language, emotion became the "simplest expressions of heightened emotional life," and volition became the "factor" of economic activity, which in turn evolved through progressive stages, from a natural to a money economy.[149] In this fashion, the historian psychologized modes of production and exchange and reduced them to evolving modes of psychic expression. The theory of economic stages thus survived in his new system only as a form of spiritual development.

The laws that governed this development operated generally, Lamprecht continued, to produce ever higher levels of collective spiritual expression out of all the basic mental processes. This expression took the form of custom, myth, art, religion, ethics, law, and science. In all cases, he explained, the causal mechanism was the same. It lay in the accumulation or intensification of psychic force. Again, the key was the principle of creative synthesis, for it dictated that the building of psychic force result everywhere in "qualitatively new" forms of expression.[150]

The initial part of Lamprecht's article seemed designed to bewilder his friends as well as his enemies. It addressed questions of interest to ethnologists, psychologists, and physiologists, but its relevance to the concerns of historians was often obscure. In the rest of the article, Lamprecht resurrected some more familiar themes, as he returned to the subject of history, which he now defined as "chronologically gradated [abgestufte] experience."[151] The discussion brought a degree of relief to his friends, but it only offered further offense to his enemies.

Lamprecht first invoked the law of historical relations. This was another of Wundt's contrivances, but one which suggested that Wundth had been listening to Lamprecht, for it postulated the holistic conclusions that the historian had long been claiming to prove.[152] "The sum of all socio-psychic factors at any given time constitutes a unity," Lamprecht explained. This unity "must itself therefore be subject to a continuous morphological process [Abwandlung] that can be divided up into periods."[153] "The great question" had to do with the character of these periods; and Lamprecht was ready with a familiar answer. His five epochs, which had marked the procession of German history from Symbolism to Subjectivism, returned to center-stage. Each of these *Kulturzeitalter* was now defined by what he called an "overarching psychic organism [*psychischer Gesamtorganismus*]" or, in a musical analogy (borrowed from Roscher), a "spiritual diapason"; these terms were meant to suggest a "general psychic disposition" that suffused and unified every facet of material and ideal culture in a given epoch.[154]

To explain the historical succession of these epochs, the historian had only to employ once again the principle of creative synthesis. Now he argued that the mechanism of historical change was the intensification of *Geistesleben*. The growth in intensity of the "socio-psychic life" of one epoch eventually produced a qualitative transition to the next. As indices of this process he noted, on the strength of his own work, that over time "nuances became finer, affects more balanced, the energy for understanding and perceiving things more penetrating."[155] A money economy he characterized as "a more intensive form of economic activity" than a natural economy. Dürer, a representative of the Individualist epoch, the historian found to be more intensive than the artists of the Conventional era, while Adolf Menzel, who lived in the Subjective epoch of the nineteenth century, had a "more intensive concept" of art than Dürer.[156]

Lamprecht could not see the trap into which his devotion to analogy had drawn him. He believed that levels of psychic activity could be calibrated empirically, like hydraulic pressure. In his view, the measurability of "psychic intensity" was the guarantee that history could be a wholly inductive, scientific field of scholarship whose results could be replicated. "The definition of typical socio-psychic stages of development has the character of statistical induction," he wrote in a passage that suggested a lot about the limits of his understanding of statistics as well.[157] "Only the numbers are missing," he continued, but he insisted that evidence provided by other sources, like art, was no less reliable. Accordingly, his historical epochs were "statistical quantities [*Grösse*]," which located "conclusively available [*bündig vorhandene*] correlations" and hence, he thought, causal relationships among patterns of collective behavior empirically observed.[158] One could, for example, speak of an "almost historically lawful structure of natural economy," for he was confident that statistics could demonstrate "that in times when a natural economy was in full bloom, practically no one who lived in the realm of the natural economy lived otherwise than by a natural economy [*naturwirtschaftlich*]."[159] The traps were many and deep.

The reign of causality, statistical regularity, and historical laws in Lamprecht's system left little room for spontaneity, idiosyncrasy, arbitrariness, imagination, or free will—on the part of either the individual subjects of history or the historian who studied them.[160] The function of historians in Lamprecht's vision was to collect historical data, to analyze these data statistically, and to demonstrate how they illustrated the laws of historical causality. Historians were, as he put it, to "exhibit the most ardent endeavors to subject historical phenomena to causal inferences [*Schlüsse*]."[161] Behavior that eluded this kind of analysis he regarded as a blemish, a symptom of the lingering imperfections of statistical techniques. Like Wundt, he believed that no facet of human behavior escaped psychic causality or the constraints of culture. Teleology and causality merged in the play of what he called "inner determinism." The idea of freedom, he noted in a defiant gesture to his opponents, could be sustained only on ignorance. Freedom was a "mode of behavior in which the causal stimuli are not completely evident [eine Weise des Handelns unter nicht völlig ins Evidente zu setzenden kausalen Anstössen]."[162]

Lamprecht's analytical assault on freedom and individuality stood in curious tension with one other central feature of his system. The central theme in history remained, in his view, the progressive emergence of individuality out of collective constraints. In the vernacular of his new system, the historian spoke of higher cultural epochs in which the "diapason of socio-psychic factors" was characterized by "special intensity and differentiation of individual psychic phenomena [Lebenserscheinungen]." In these circumstances, he went on, individual personalities were distinguished by the "highest differentiation and intensity" of their "psychic achievements."[163] Lamprecht was thus left with a paradox. To study a historical process whose telos was heightened individuality, he had worked out an analytical framework that accorded individual freedom no role. In this fashion his analytical categories seemed to preclude the very process they were constructed to comprehend.

Lamprecht did not see the paradox. It was but one of the many inconsistencies and ambiguities that he left behind in his haste to complete this article. But this paradox would probably have survived more careful review of the manuscript, for in the last analysis it was no paradox. It allowed for one great exception. This conclusion emerged near the end of the article, when the historian suggested that the "intensification of individuality" applied in unique ways to himself. He returned to the question, "What is Kulturgeschichte?" and he replied, "I think the problem is quite simple to solve." The great task now confronting the profession, he proclaimed, was simply to demonstrate the validity of Karl Lamprecht's system.[164] He consigned every one of his colleagues to the role of epigones. Their charge was to hone the edges of a system whose "core is indestructable"—to bring together evidence of the immanent rule of causality in history, to compare manifestations of each era's diapason, and to verify Lamprecht's ideas about the succession of cultural epochs.[165] Historians were henceforth to collect material to put into Lamprecht's boxes. Their work was also to celebrate a great creative feat, which made Lamprecht's own status unique in history. When he wrote of individuality's "psychic achievement," Lamprecht was referring in the first instance to his own, which was to transcend history in order to subject it definitively to human understanding. Another philosopher of immanent development had once described the process as the self-realization of spirit; Lamprecht preferred to call it individual personality's highest intensification.[166] It was, in all events, no generic achievement.

Late in June 1896 Lamprecht wrote to Harden with some thoughts on the article that he had just published. He closed the letter with the remark that *"Perrumpendum est."*[167] The "breakthrough" to which he alluded was to be the clarification of positions in the *Methodenstreit*. Once again, however, his hopes were frustrated, for his article only muddled the issues further. "What Is Cultural History?" was by any account a bewildering essay, an extraordinary brew in which most of the intellectual sources that flowed into Wundt's work surfaced anew in Lamprecht's language. The article registered the conclusion of the historian's retreat from all appearances of materialism and his open commitment to intellectual traditions that his opponents shared. But he undertook this commitment on his own extravagant terms. His vision of psychogenesis rested on an eccentric reading of Kant, which enabled him to bring the ideas of Leibniz, Herder, and Hegel into uneasy combination with those of Darwin and Comte. The mixture was so laced with grandiose claims and metaphors of natural science that his opponents found his new offering scarcely less distasteful than the old ones.

Publication of this essay did mark a turning point of sorts in the *Methodenstreit*. Lamprecht had managed at least to defuse the issue of ideology. In doing so he climbed to a high level of theoretical abstraction, where he believed he would enjoy an advantage over his opponents as the debate about method continued. However, he was almost immediately forced back down, as the terms of the debate changed, and its focus shifted to his enormous disadvantage.

Notes

1. Franz Mehring, "Deutsche Geschichte," *Die Neue Zeit*, 12 (1893–94): 443–48, 475–80, reprinted in *Gesammelte Schriften*, 15 vols. (Berlin, 1980), 7: 496–510; *cf.* Metz, *Grundformen*, 497–99.
2. NL Lamprecht (Kr. 10), Hoeniger to Lamprecht, Berlin, 13.1.94.
3. See Friedrich Aly, "Der Einbruch des Materialismus in die historischen Wissenschaften," PJb, 81 (1895): 199–214.
4. Lehmann, for one, did so in his inaugural lecture in Leipzig: ZKg, 1 (1893–1894): 246.
5. NL Sybel (Bl Nr. 3), Münster, 4.5.93; Kehr, "Neuere deutsche Geschichtsschreibung," 257; *cf.* Seeliger, "Lamprecht," 136; Seifert, 20.
6. NL Liesegang, Lamprecht to Liesegang, Leipzig, 2.12.95.
7. DG 4: 133–34; "Vorwort," DG 1 (2): v–xi; "Die Herrlichkeit Erpel: Ein wirtschafts-, sozial- und verfassungsgeschichtliches Paradigma," *Beiträge zur Geschichte vornehmlich Kölns und der Rheinlande. Zum 80. Geburtstage Gustav v. Mevissens* (Cologne, 1895), 1–26; *cf.* his review of Inama-Sternegg's *Deutsche Wirtschaftsgeschichte des 10. bis 12. Jahrhunderts*, in JbNöSt, 64 (1895), 294–98. These three essays are reprinted in Hans Schleier, ed., *Karl Lamprecht: Alternative zu Ranke. Schriften zur Geschichtstheorie* (Leipzig, 1988), 125–42. Schleier's anthology also includes Lamprecht's response to Max Lehmann in ZKg, 1 (1894), 248–50, which belongs to the same genre. See also Schleier's introductory essay in the

anthology, "Der Kulturhistoriker Karl Lamprecht, der 'Methodenstreit' und die Folgen," esp. 19; cf. Seifert, 15–22; LW, 285.

8. See Dove to Ritter, Munich, 19.3.95, in Dove, *Aufsätze und Briefe*, 2: 177–78; HZ, 76 (1896): 478–79.
9. JbNöSt, 64 (1895): 294; Schleier, *Alternative*, 138.
10. DG, 1 (2): ix–x.
11. NL Althoff (B Nr. 108/1), Lamprecht to Althoff, Leipzig, 20.9.94.
12. See, for example, the notices in the *Jahresberichte für Geschichtswissenschaft*, 14 (1891): II, 6, 379; 15 (1892): II, 36, 48–50; 16 (1893): II, 68.
13. NL Mevissen, Lamprecht to Mevissen, Leipzig, 27.12.92.
14. HZ, 71 (1893): 465–66.
15. DLZ, (6.7.95): 842; HZ, 77 (1896): 385.
16. Lamprecht to Friedrich Ratzel, Rathen a/Elbe, 9.8.95, in Schieder, "Historische Zeitschrift," 82. Schieder has published the pertinent correspondence from the Oldenbourg Archive in ibid., 79–101; cf. Schönebaum, "Treitschke and Lamprecht," 5.
17. Schieder, "Historische Zeitschrift," 82–86.
18. Several months before Sybel's death, Meinecke wrote to Below that his own "judgment of Lamprecht was already more or less the same as yours [*der Richtung der Ihrigen*], and I would never trust him [Lamprecht] in matters that demanded responsible action:" NL Meinecke (Nachtrag 1), Meinecke to Below, 7.3.95.
19. Schieder, "Historische Zeitschrift," 85.
20. Ibid., 88–90.
21. Ibid., 90–92.
22. NL Treitschke (7), Meinecke to Treitschke, Berlin, 10.9.95; Schieder, "Historische Zeitschrift," 95–96, 99. Lamprecht's ambitions to take over the *Historische Zeitschrift* foundered as well on the reluctance of Erich Marcks (whom Lamprecht had not originally consulted) to offend Meinecke, his *Duzfreund*. Ibid., 94; NL Meinecke (25), Marcks to Meinecke, Leipzig, 12.95.
23. HZ, 75 (1895): 390–95.
24. He was not the only observer to use this word. Cf. Aly, "Einbruch."
25. NL Treitschke (7), Lamprecht to Treitschke, Leipzig, 22.12.95.
26. "Only Berlin remains for me," wrote Lamprecht upon receiving the call to Leipzig in 1890: NL Lamprecht (Korr. 59), Lamprecht to Hugo Lamprecht, Marburg, 29.12.90; cf. LW, 316; Schönebaum, "Treitschke and Lamprecht," 5–6.
27. NL Grimm, Lamprecht to Grimm, Leipzig, 6.5.96; cf. Lamprecht, "Zum Gedächtnis Heinrichs von Treitschke," *Zukunft*, 16 (1896): 108–12.
28. NL Lamprecht (Korr. 31), Hoeniger to Lamprecht, Pontresina, 22.8.96; NL Liesegang, Lamprecht to Liesegang, Leipzig, 8.7.96; NL Grimm, Lamprecht to Grimm, Leipzig, 2.5.96; LW, 316.
29. Treitschke bequeathed a paradox. Liesegang, a devoted student of both Treitschke and Lamprecht, was named executor of Treitschke's literary estate. NL Liesegang, Lamprecht to Liesegang, Leipzig, 20.5.96.
30. NL Lamprecht (Korr. 31), Hoeniger to Lamprecht, Pontresina, 22.8.96; (Korr. 17), Cuny to Lamprecht, Berlin, 4.8.96; NL Liesegang, Lamprecht to Liesegang, 25.7.96.
31. NL Althoff (A II Nr. 117), Althoff to Bosse [?], n.d., Konzept; vom Brocke, "System Althoff," 83–84.
32. See Annelise Thimme, *Hans Delbrück als Kritiker der Wilhelminischen Epoche* (Düsseldorf, 1955); Arden Bucholz, *Hans Delbrück and the German Military Establishment: War Images in Conflict* (Iowa City, 1985); Gordon A. Craig, "Delbrück: The Military Historian," in Peter Paret, ed., *Makers of Modern Strategy: From Machiavelli*

to the Nuclear Age (Princeton, 1986), 326–53; Simon, *Staat und Geschichtswissenschaft*, 113–15; NDB, 3: 577–78; Weber, *Lexikon*, 103–4.
33. Mehring, "Eine Geschichte der Kriegskunst," *Gesammelte Schriften*, 8: 134–200.
34. Bucholz, 41–42.
35. NL Lamprecht (Korr. 18), Delbrück to Lamprecht, Berlin, 29.7.93.
36. NL Delbrück, Lamprecht to Delbrück, Leipzig, 19.3.94; UB Bonn, NL Aloys Schulte, Lamprecht to Schulte, Frankfurt, 17.10.95.
37. Schieder, "Historische Zeitschrift," 20.
38. NL Bernheim, Lamprecht to Bernheim, Leipzig, 24.11.97.
39. NL Althoff (B Nr. 112/2), Lenz to Althoff, Berlin, 4.1.97. On Rachfahl see Rachfahl, "Felix Rachfahl," in S. Steinberg, 2: 199–222; Weber, *Lexikon*, 459.
40. Rachfahl, "Rachfahl," 210–11.
41. LW, 312.
42. DLZ, (6.7.95): 840–51.
43. NL Delbrück, Rachfahl to Delbrück, Kappitz, 26.9.95; Kiel, 11.11.95; "Deutsche Geschichte vom wirthschaftlichen Standpunkt," PJb, 83 (1896): 48–96.
44. Ibid., 75.
45. Ibid., 77–78.
46. Ibid., 83.
47. DG, 4: 133–34.
48. Rachfahl, "Wirtschaftlichen Standpunkt," 89.
49. Ibid., 90.
50. Ibid., 92.
51. NL Bernheim, Lamprecht to Bernheim, Leipzig, 23.1.96.
52. NL Grimm, Lamprecht to Grimm, Leipzig, 28.4.96.
53. NL Liesegang, Lamprecht to Liesegang, Leipzig, 17.7.95.
54. NL Liesegang, Lamprecht to Liesegang, Leipzig, 25.7.96
55. NL Lamprecht (Korr. 59), Lamprecht to Hugo Lamprecht, Leipzig, 26.6.96.
56. NL Liesegang, Lamprecht to Liesegang, Leipzig. 17.7.96. Here the historian remarked about a reply he had just written to Rachfahl: "Auf die zuerst versuchte Weise ging es nicht, das war mir nach Absenden des Ms klar."
57. Below, *Geschichtsschreibung*, 96.
58. *Alte und Neue Richtungen in der Geschichtswissenschaft* (Berlin, 1896). The first section of this pamphlet (pp. 1–13) appeared simultaneously as "Die gegenwärtige Lage der Geschichtswissenschaft," *Zukunft*, 14 (1896): 247–55.
59. *Richtungen*, 5.
60. Ibid., 6. It is possible that Lamprecht drew here from the work of the Belgian statistician Quetelet, who had introduced the idea of the "average person."
61. Ibid., 18.
62. Ibid., 7.
63. Ibid., 8.
64. Cf. Viikari, *Krise*, 223; Schultz, "Moral Force," 150.
65. DG, 10: 255; cf. DG, 6: 133; DG, 10: 241–42.
66. *Richtungen*, 26–79; cf. Viikari, *Krise*, 230.
67. *Richtungen*, 35–36.
68. Ibid., 71.
69. Ibid., 52.
70. Ibid., 64–66.
71. Ibid., 69; cf. Lamprecht, "Das Arbeitgebiet [sic] geschichtlicher Forschung," *Zukunft*, 15 (1896): 25–28.
72. Ibid., 69–70.
73. Ibid., 70.

74. PJb, 84 (1896): 542–55.
75. Ibid., 549.
76. Ibid., 552.
77. NL Meinecke (Nachtrag 1), Meinecke to Below, Berlin, 18.11.95; HZ, 77 (1896): 262–66.
78. See Ernst Schulin, "Meineckes Leben und Werk: Versuch einer Gesamtcharakteristik," in *Traditionskritik*, 119; cf. Metz, *Grundformen*, 487.
79. PJb, 84: 553.
80. NL Meinecke (21), Lamprecht to Meinecke, Leipzig, 11.5.96.
81. NL Althoff (B Nr. 108/1), Lamprecht to Althoff, Leipzig, 15.11.96; NL Liesegang, Lamprecht to Liesegang, Leipzig, 28.1.96; LW, 269.
82. NL Liesegang, Lamprecht to Liesegang, Leipzig, 24.10.95; NL Meinecke (25), Marcks to Meinecke, Leipzig, n.d. [early 1896].
83. Schönebaum, "Unausgeführte Vorhaben," 119.
84. B. Uwe Weller, *Maximilian Harden und die "Zukunft"* (Bremen, 1970); Harry F. Young, *Maximilian Harden, Censor Germaniae: The Critic in Opposition from Bismarck to the Rise of Nazism* (The Hague, 1959); Peter Berglar, "Harden und Rathenau: Zur Problematik ihrer Freundschaft," HZ, 210 (1969): 75–94; Walter Frank, "Apostata: Maximilian Harden und das wilhelminische Deutschland," in *"Höre Israel!": Studien zur modernen Judenfrage* (Hamburg, 1941), 15–108.
85. NL Harden, Lamprecht to Harden, Leipzig, 24.3.94.
86. "Die Gesellschaft Jesu," *Zukunft*, 10 (1895): 449–55; "Historikertag und Umsturzvorlage," *Zukunft*, 11 (1895): 203–5.
87. NL Treitschke, Marcks to Treitschke, 4.4.95. This judgment did not prevent Marcks from publishing in Harden's journal himself.
88. NL Liesegang, Lamprecht to Liesegang, Leipzig, 1.5.95.
89. NL Lamprecht (Korr. 59), Lamprecht to Hugo Lamprecht, 24.7.95.
90. NL Harden, Lamprecht to Harden, Boppard, 17.4.10.
91. NL Harden, Lamprecht to Harden, Leipzig, 9.8.97; NL Lamprecht (Korr. 27), Harden to Lamprecht, Berlin, 31.7.97.
92. NL Lamprecht (Korr. 27), Harden to Lamprecht, Berlin, 31.12.96. "Es würde mich ungemein freuen, wenn Sie auch die weiteren Phasen des Kampfes in der Zukunft behandeln würden, wie mich jeder Beitrag von Ihnen hoch erfreut. Ich glaube auch, dass nichts die Tanten mehr ärgert, als die Tatsache, dass Sie vor einem grösseren Publikum zeigen, wie einseitig die Einwände Ihrer Feinde (nicht: Gegner) sind." Harden also agreed to plant a favorable review of Lamprecht's fifth volume in *Zukunft*. NL Harden, Lamprecht to Harden, Leipzig, 23.1.96.
93. In these circumstances, Harden's overtures to Erich Marcks during the *Methodenstreit* were suspicious: "Hoffentlich senden Sie bald wieder etwas für die 'Zukunft.' Wollten Sie nicht Lamprecht als Gegenstück zu Sybel behandeln." GLA, NL Erich Marcks (72), Harden to Marcks, Berlin, 24.11.95.
94. Schönebaum is wrong when he argues that Lamprecht "thankfully accepted suggestions from his opponents." LW, 420.
95. NL Lamprecht (Korr. 57), Verzeichnis für litterar. Austausch, ausgelegt 15 Nov 93 [April 1896 Versendungsliste DG Anhänger].
96. NL Lamprecht (Korr. 8), Berger to Lamprecht, Bonn, 22.11.96; (Korr. 49), Stieda to Lamprecht, Schliersee, 8.9.95, 13.9.95.
97. NL Liesegang, Lamprecht to Liesegang, Leipzig, 14.1.95; LW, 300–301.
98. NL Lamprecht (Korr. 15), Buchholz to Lamprecht, Leipzig, 19.9.96.
99. On Bücher see Bertram Schefold, "Karl Bücher und der Historismus in der deutschen Nationalökonomie," in Hammerstein, *Geschichtswissenschaft*, 239–67; Goetz, "Karl Bücher," *Historiker*, 277–85; Heinz Barthel et al., "Karl Bücher: Seine

politische und wissenschaftliche Stellung," in Ernst Engelberg et al., eds., *Karl-Marx-Universität Leipzig 1409–1959: Beiträge zur Universitätsgeschichte*, 2 vols. (Leipzig, 1959), 2: 78–91; NDB, 2: 718–19; Schorn-Schütte, *Lamprecht*, 88–89; Lindenlaub, 129–32. Bücher's memoirs were published only in a first volume, which broke off before his call to Leipzig: Bücher, *Lebenserinnerungen: 1847–1890* (Tübingen, 1919).

100. UB KMU Leipzig, NL Karl Bücher, Lamprecht to Bücher, Bonn, 6.6.83; NL Lamprecht (Korr. 14), Bücher to Lamprecht, Basel, 10.1.89.

101. NL Bücher, Lamprecht to Bücher, Leipzig, 20.5.92.

102. Max Braubach, "Aus Briefen Karl Büchers an Aloys Schulte: Ein Beitrag zur deutschen Wissenschaftsgeschichte zwischen 1890 und 1925," in Otto Brunner et al., eds., *Festschrift Hermann Aubin zum 80. Geburtstag*, 2 vols. (Wiesbaden, 1965), 1: 384.

103. Karl Bücher, *Die Entstehung der Volkswirtschaft: Vorträge und Versuche* (Tübingen, 1893).

104. See Winkel, 109–10, 177–78.

105. See Below, "Ueber Theorien der wirtschaftlichen Entwicklung der Völker, mit besonderer Rücksicht auf die Stadtwirtschaft des deutschen Mittelalters," HZ, 86 (1901): 1–77; *cf.* Below, "Zur Würdigung," 367–91.

106. DG 4: 185, 190, 206; DG 5: 4.

107. The families were close as well. NL Schulte, Lamprecht to Schulte, Leipzig, 24.1.95; NL Lamprecht (Munich), Bücher to Else Lamprecht, Leipzig, 19.6.19.

108. Schefold, 242.

109. Goetz, "Bücher," 281.

110. Karl Bücher, *Worte zum Gedächtnis an Karl Lamprecht* (Leipzig, 1916), 10–11.

111. Ibid., 2.

112. Goetz, "Bücher," 280.

113. Braubach, "Aus Briefen Büchers," 394.

114. Ibid., 399.

115. The classic account is Boring, A *History of Experimental Psychology*, 316–45. See also D. B. Klein, A *History of Scientific Psychology: Its Origins and Philosophical Backgrounds* (New York and London, 1970), 816–82; Murphy and Kovach, *Historical Introduction to Modern Psychology*, 159–80. On the risks of relying on the accounts of the American functionalist psychologists, who had little sympathy or understanding for the philosophical roots of Wundt's entire enterprise, see Kurt Danziger, "Wundt and the Two Traditions in Psychology," in R. W. Rieber et al., eds., *Wilhelm Wundt and the Making of a Scientific Psychology* (New York and London, 1980), 73–87. For introductions see Peter Petersen, *Wilhelm Wundt und seine Zeit* (Stuttgart, 1925); Wolfram Meischner and Erhard Eschler, *Wilhelm Wundt* (Cologne, 1979); Erhard Eschler, "Wilhelm Wundt (1832–1920)," in Max Steinmetz, ed., *Bedeutende Gelehrte in Leipzig*, 2 vols. (Leipzig, 1965), 1: 79–84; Ludwig J. Pongratz, *Problemgeschichte der Psychologie* (Munich, 1984), esp. 99–106; Wilhelm Wundt, *Erlebtes und Erkanntes*, 2d ed. (Stuttgart, 1921).

116. David Robinson, "Wilhelm Wundt and the Establishment of Experimental Psychology, 1875–1914: The Context of a New Field of Scientific Research," Ph.D. dissertation (University of California, Berkeley, 1987), esp. 64–112.

117. Kurt Danziger, "Wundt's Psychological Experiment in the Light of His Philosophy of Science," *Psychological Research*, 42 (1980): 109–22.

118. *Logik: Eine Untersuchung der Prinzipien der Erkenntnis und der Methoden wissenschaftlicher Forschung*, 2 vols. (Stuttgart, 1880–1883); *Ethik: Eine Untersuchung der Tatsachen und Gesetze des sittlichen Lebens* (Stuttgart, 1886); *System der Philosophie* (Leipzig, 1889).

119. For analyses of Wundt's philosophy see Edmund König, W. *Wundt als Psycholog und als Philosoph* (Stuttgart, 1902); Alfred Arnold, *Wilhelm Wundt: Sein philosophisches System* (Berlin, 1980); Meischner and Eschler, 69–92; Lehmann, *Geschichte der Philosophie*, 144–56.

120. Theodore Mischel, "Wundt and the Conceptual Foundations of Psychology," *Philosophy and Phenomenological Research*, 31 (1970–1971): 1–26; cf. H. V. Rappard, "A Monistic Interpretation of Wundt's Psychology," *Psychological Research*, 42 (1980): 123–34; Klein, 836.

121. See Peter Petersen, *Der Entwicklungsgedanke in der Philosophie Wundts* (Leipzig, 1908), esp. 89–108.

122. *Völkerpsychologie: Eine Untersuchung der Entwicklungsgesetze von Sprache, Mythus und Sitte*, 10 vols. (Leipzig, 1900–1920). See Eno Beuchelt, *Ideengeschichte der Völkerpsychologie* (Meisenheim am Glan, 1974), 23–29.

123. Meischner and Eschler, 81; Arnold, 50; Paula Relyea Anderson, "Gustav von Schmoller (1838–1917)," in Halperin, *Historiography*, 295.

124. Willem van Hoorn and Thom Verhave, "Wundt's Changing Conceptions of a General and Theoretical Psychology," in Wolfgang G. Bringmann et al., eds., *Wundt Studies: A Centennial Collection* (Toronto: 1980), 72.

125. Arnold, 41–56; Van Hoorn and Verhave, 106–7; Eschler, "Wundt," 80, 82; Solomon Diamond, "Buckle, Wundt, and Psychology's Use of History," *Isis*, 75 (1984): 143–52; David E. Leary, "German Idealism and the Development of Psychology in the Nineteenth Century," *Journal of the History of Philosophy*, 18 (1980): 309–10.

126. See David F. Lindenfeld, *The Transformation of Positivism: Alexius Meinong and European Thought, 1880–1920* (Berkeley and Los Angeles, 1980), esp. 1–57.

127. See Arnold, 107–8, 127–30.

128. NL Mevissen, Lamprecht to Mevissen, Leipzig, 29.5.91; NL Bernheim, Lamprecht to Bernheim, Leipzig, 24.12.93; NL Lamprecht (Korr. 45), Lamprecht to Ritter, Leipzig, 29.12.93; cf. Schorn-Schütte, *Lamprecht*, 83–86; Boring, 327–28; Schultz, "Moral Force," 169. That both were sons of pastors was hardly unusual in this milieu; more remarkable was the fact that both were given the names of elder siblings who had died in infancy. Wolfgang G. Bringmann et al., "Wilhelm Wundt 1832–1920: A Brief Biographical Sketch," *Journal of the History of the Behavioral Sciences*, 11 (1975): 287–97.

129. NL Mevissen, Lamprecht to Mevissen, Leipzig, 10.10.93.

130. Kurt Danziger, "The Positivist Repudiation of Wundt," *Journal of the History of the Behavioral Sciences*, 15 (1979): 205–30; Robinson, 192–98, 205–16. For the institutional context of Wundt's difficulties see Mitchell G. Ash, "Academic Politics in the History of Science: Experimental Psychology in Germany, 1879–1914," CEH, 13 (1980): 255–86.

131. Wilhelm Dilthey, "Ideen über eine beschreibende und zergliedernde Psychologie," *Sitzungsberichte der Akademie der Wissenschaften zu Berlin 1894* (Berlin, 1894), 1309–1407, reprinted in his *Gesammelte Schriften*, 14 vols. (Berlin and Stuttgart, 1921–1966), 5: 139–240; Hermann Ebbinghaus, "Über erklärende und beschreibende Psychologie," *Zeitschrift für Psychologie*, 6 (1896): 161–205. See Robinson, 202–4; Michael Earmarth, *Wilhelm Dilthey: The Critique of Historical Reason* (Chicago, 1978), 169–78, 184–86.

132. Wilhelm Wundt, "Über die Definition der Psychologie," *Philosophische Studien*, 12 (1896): 13.

133. Wundt, *Grundriss der Psychologie* (Leipzig, 1896); Robinson, 197–98, 212; cf. Solomon Diamond, "Selected Texts from Writings of Wilhelm Wundt," in Rieber, 155–77.

134. See Spiess, 45–61; Viikari, *Krise*, 238; Cassirer, 284–85; M. Norton Wise, "How Do Sums Count? On the Cultural Origins of Statistical Causality," in Krüger, *Probabilistic Revolution*, 1: 399–406.
135. Wilhelm Wundt and Max Klinger, *Karl Lamprecht: Ein Gedenkblatt* (Leipzig, 1915), 9, 13; Wundt, *Logik*, 2d ed., 2: 321–28; *cf.* ZKg, 3 (1895): 329.
136. DG 4: 133–34.
137. NL Lamprecht (Korr. 59), Lamprecht to Hugo Lamprecht, Leipzig, 15.10.95; LW, 299.
138. *Richtungen*, 5–8, *cf.* DG, 7: 100.
139. NL Liesegang, Lamprecht to Liesegang, Leipzig, 26.3.96.
140. NL Harden, Lamprecht to Harden, Leipzig, 26.6.96.
141. "Was ist Kulturgeschichte? Beitrag zu einer empirischen Historik," DZfG, N.F. 1 (1896–1897): 75–150.
142. Ibid., 77.
143. Ibid., 81.
144. Wundt, *Logik*, 2d ed., 2: 408–10.
145. "Was ist Kulturgeschichte?" 81–82.
146. See Seeliger, "Lamprecht," 142; Engelberg, "Methodenstreit," 143–44.
147. "Was ist Kulturgeschichte?" 82, 86.
148. Ibid., 98.
149. Ibid., 123–25.
150. Ibid., 124–25.
151. Ibid., 124.
152. Wundt, *Logik*, 2d ed., 2: 410–13.
153. "Was ist Kulturgeschichte?" 126.
154. Ibid., 109, 127.
155. Ibid., 128.
156. Ibid., 132.
157. Ibid., 133; *cf.* Wise, 405.
158. "Was ist Kulturgeschichte?" 135.
159. Ibid., 134.
160. See Wolf Lepenies, *Die Drei Kulturen: Soziologie zwischen Literatur und Wissenschaft* (Munich and Vienna, 1985), 305–6.
161. "Was ist Kulturgeschichte?" 89.
162. Ibid.
163. Ibid., 143.
164. Ibid., 144–45.
165. Ibid., 130.
166. See Cassirer, 281–82.
167. NL Harden, Lamprecht to Harden, Leipzig, 26.6.96.

7

Axes and Knives

*Denn sie wollen nicht, dass das Grosse entstehe: ihr Mittel
ist, zu sagen, "seht, das Grosse ist schon da!"*

The great debate that raged in the German historical profession during the 1890s was a bitter, exciting spectacle. It dominated the pages of academic journals. It was the topic of debate at scholarly conferences, the subject of seminars and lectures at the universities, and a factor in the politics of faculty appointments.[1] The dispute was, in addition, too intense to contain within the profession; and it spilled out, via the connections of its principal participants to popular journals, to engage the interest of the broader educated public in Germany.

The *Methodenstreit* bewildered contemporary observers, and questions about its significance linger still. In the last analysis, however, the dispute represented perhaps as clear an instance of a "paradigm conflict" as a humanistic discipline can offer.[2] At issue was the validity of what one might well call a "disciplinary matrix," a governing set of assumptions about the study of the past that the community of academic historians in Germany had shared, from midcentury until the late 1880s, with near-unanimity and a conviction that was as unreflecting as it was unchallenged. Common embrace of these assumptions was the foundation of *Geschichtswissenschaft*; it defined the discipline of history as it was institutionalized and practiced as a "normal science" in the German academy.

These assumptions had long structured what might be called, in another idiom, the professional discourse with the past.[3] They isolated the facets of the past that were appropriate for inclusion. They regulated the grammar of the discourse—the methodological parameters, the analytical questions and categories, and the explanatory strategies with which the past was to be investigated and understood. Finally, these assumptions extended to the standards of significance and value with which the past was to be ordered, so that they also to a large extent determined the outcome of the discourse.

To call these assumptions ideological is neither to discredit them nor to impugn the imposing body of scholarship produced by historians who were dedicated to them. It is rather to emphasize the extent to which these assump-

212

tions were oriented to the social, political, and professional experience of the men who constructed and protected the academic discipline of history in Germany in the nineteenth century. The paradigm organized that experience in a powerful vision of the past. It offered compelling assurances for a group of scholars who were anxious to legitimize the constitutional settlement of 1871 and to defend a social and confessional order beset by a variety of challenges. The paradigm enabled them as well to justify the leading role that members of the academy played in this order and to define the distinctiveness of the academic discipline that they themselves practiced.

By 1890, the symbol supreme of this paradigm, the embodiment and exemplar of its practices, ideals, and achievement, was the figure of Leopold von Ranke.[4] The issue is not pertinent whether the historian's epigones, who were proud to call themselves neo-Rankeans, were guilty of misinterpretation as they mined what Leondard Krieger has called the "open quarry" of his legacy and as they fashioned what they retrieved to fit their own experience and needs; it suffices to note that their views on the fundamental tenets of Ranke's legacy marked out a consensus within the German academic community.[5]

The most fundamental of these tenets was an emphasis on singularity, diversity, and individuality in history, a rejection of all abstract systems of laws, norms, or other concepts that implied the limitation of the freedom of historical actors to make moral choices. Only by approaching the past in this fashion, unencumbered by all prior judgments and speculative assumptions, could the historian grasp the objective truths that history revealed. The strategy appropriate to perceiving historical truth was immersion in the primary sources and interpretation of these documents by means of sympathetic intuition or *Verstehen*, an operation that stood in contrast to the categories of causal explanation implied by the word *Erklären*.

Although they claimed that the hallmark of their approach to history was its *Voraussetzungslosigkeit*, its objectivity and freedom from every prejudice or a priori belief, the historians who followed Ranke embraced (no less than had Ranke himself) a series of postulates that subverted these claims. The motive forces in history, they insisted, were the ideas that informed the purposive behavior of all historical actors, be they individual human beings or human communities. The highest of these communities was the state, whose development accordingly constituted both the essential theme of history and the proper focus of historical study.

This last postulate was the most neuralgic point. The historical primacy of the state implied both a political agenda and an exclusionary definition of the discipline. Both had come under duress by the 1880s. The doctrine of the state's primacy served as an ideological buttress against democratic reform of an authoritarian constitution; and embrace of this doctrine discouraged a sympathetic understanding of either the forces building for political reform or the broader social transformations that nurtured them.

The want of sympathy for these forces was not only political. Academic historians regarded the state as the distinctive subject matter of their discipline. The protection of professional identity and integrity was thus a central motive in their resistance to the growing popularity of new academic disciplines—economics in the first instance, but also sociology, geography, and ethnology—which took these broader forces as their principal objects of study and sought to comprehend realms of social experience not directly tied to the state or political development.

The immediate challenge to the historical profession's reigning paradigm came in the form of *Kulturgeschichte*. The growing currency of this genre was the product of the same broader developments that bred interest in the social science disciplines. To many academic historians, in fact, cultural history looked like the Trojan horse of these disciplines in the fortress of the profession. It was initially by no means clear, however, that the new genre threatened the reigning paradigm. Many of its practitioners subscribed to the same methodological postulates as the political historians. The issues around which much of the *Methodenstreit* revolved thus had to do with the level at which cultural history could be engaged, the extent to which the new genre could be accommodated within the reigning paradigm. The preliminary skirmishes between Schäfer and Gothein had suggested the terms of an accommodation at the level of subject matter. The two scholars appeared to agree that political history required only a greater sensitivity to the wide range of historical forces that bore on political development, that it was both possible and desirable to bring broader realms of human activity within the topical as well as the methodological purview of political history. Not all observers saw the problem in these terms, however. Some of the leading practitioners of cultural history called instead for an accommodation at the level of methodology. The methods of the political historians were not, they argued, appropriate for studying the history of all realms of human action, so the paradigm required broadening to admit a plurality of methods. The problem was whether concessions on this level could be contained. As at least some political historians suspected, questioning the unique validity of the paradigm's methods struck at its foundations.

These issues weighed too heavily on the German historical profession to be ignored. Had it come in different circumstances, the confrontation might well have left the profession more receptive to accommodation at some level with the concerns of those who practiced *Kulturgeschichte*. In the event, the confrontation came in the most uncompromising manner imaginable, and the main reason was the scholar who insisted on forcing the *Methodenstreit* into a paradigm conflict. Karl Lamprecht was not interested in compromise or accommodation, for he believed from the start that the controversy was about the most fundamental issues. His essay on Ranke was an onslaught on his opponents' sacred symbol, and it signaled his intention to challenge the paradigm that Ranke represented. So did Lamprecht's attempts in his early essays to deflect the controversy from issues of detail and ideology, which he regarded as irrelevant, onto questions of method.

If many in the profession found Lamprecht's challenge bewildering, the reasons lay only partly in the novelty of an attack on the established paradigm. The nature of Lamprecht's rival paradigm was anything but clear; the ambiguities and inconsistencies that riddled his polemical essays reflected not only his inveterate carelessness, but the volatility of his position. His initial emphasis on the socioeconomic foundations of politics, and on their accessibility to statistical and causal analysis, drew the charge that he was a materialist and a positivist. He quickly retreated, but his abrupt embrace of idealism in a Wundtian guise did not signal his acceptance of the profession's dominant beliefs; it brought instead a more radical challenge. He now appeared to argue that the operation of laws regulated all facets of history—the realm of ideas and moral behavior as well as material *Zustände*—and that only a methodology based on causal analysis could comprehend the patterns of historical development.

Lamprecht's challenge led to the profession's consolidation. If the dispute provoked German historians into a more self-conscious examination of methods and theories they had long employed, their counterattack on Lamprecht also betrayed the ideological commitments that underlay their own practices. Stigmatizing Lamprecht as a materialist was more than a professional reproach; it was calculated to insinuate foreign influence, subversion, and association with a doctrine that one high official described in 1895 as "the demonic power that undermines religious life and poisons the nation's soul."[6]

The counterattack was calculated in addition to insulate the profession from foreign influences of another sort. Lamprecht's opponents were determined to rededicate the discipline of history to the precepts that had guided it during its professionalization, a process that one scholar characterized in 1893 as "emancipation" from its "earlier bondage [*Dienstbarkeiten*] to theology, philosophy, and law."[7] Lamprecht embodied the threat of new bondage to social and natural science; resistance to this threat demanded the uncompromising defense of the discipline's bounds, its traditional canon, distinctive subject matter, and methodology.

Thus the *Methodenstreit* escalated. As one observer has put it well, the one side demanded "more than could be granted," while the other "defended more than could be preserved."[8] The ensuing breakdown of communication was probably unavoidable. Most of the participants in the dispute were young scholars, who were neither well trained in philosophy nor otherwise prepared to debate theoretical issues.[9] As posturing, deliberate obfuscation, and personal enmities compounded the rhetorical confusion, the two sides began to address their arguments to different constituencies. All these features emphasized the paradigmatic dimensions of the conflict, which would have frustrated communication in any circumstances. Dialogue broke down for want of a common language. Publication of Lamprecht's manifesto in the summer of 1896 made this problem acute. Ostensibly an outline of the (new) principles of the new paradigm, it presented, as one of the historian's perceptive colleagues noted, a grammar of a new language for historical discourse.[10]

Lamprecht's opponents were neither willing nor able to use his language. Their triumph came when they compelled him to use theirs.

The Association of German Historians met for its fourth congress in Innsbruck in September 1896. Austrians preponderated among the participants, but the presence of Below and Meinecke, Felix Stieve, and Karl Theodor von Heigel from Munich, and Heinrich Ullmann from Greifswald was a hopeful sign that this organization was beginning to expand into the leading ranks of the German historical profession. Lamprecht chose not to attend, citing the state of his health.[11] His polemic against the political historians was nevertheless the subject of a spirited exchange, which followed a lecture by the Austrian historian, Rudolf von Scala, on "Individualism and Socialism in the Writing of History."[12] The protocol did not reveal what was said in the corridors, but Meinecke returned to Berlin convinced that three-quarters of those at the conference sympathized with him.[13] Lamprecht, who was kept informed by friends who had been there, concluded that he could be "*very* pleased with the proceedings" and that most of the participants, particularly the Austrians, were on his side.[14] The impressions of the two historians were not as contradictory as they seemed. They tended to confirm the principle that support for Lamprecht's views was greatest among the German profession's marginal groups, for Austrian scholars fell prominently into this category. His next polemical exchange was thus especially disheartening, for it reflected the erosion of sympathy for him within another of these marginal groups.

Heinrich Finke was much more Catholic than Felix Rachfahl.[15] He was the son of a Westphalian peasant. That a child of these circumstances should pursue an academic career in imperial Germany was itself remarkable—the more so because Finke was unwilling to follow Rachfahl's route and to earn academic advancement by concealing his Catholicism. Finke studied Catholic theology and philosophy in Münster. After a short residence as a tutor in Frankfurt, where he met Johannes Janssen, he took up history in Tübingen and received his doctorate in 1880 with Bernhard Kugler. He then moved to Göttingen to study with Weizsäcker. After working for several years in Berlin as a stenographer in the Reichstag and a correspondent for a number of Catholic newspapers, he returned to scholarship, first as an archivist in Schleswig and then as a research fellow in the Vatican archives. One of the products of his research in Rome, an edition of the documents relating to the Council of Constance, enabled him to habilitate in Münster, where he was also named extraordinary professor in 1891.

Finke's academic career began in the lingering shadow of the *Kulturkampf*, and his scholarship was shaped by the pressure that this experience imposed on every Catholic intellectual who endured it. His response to this pressure brought him into the company of the young Catholic scholars who, primarily under the aegis of the *Görres-Gesellschaft*, attempted to reconcile Catholicism with the demands of modern scholarship, the fundaments of which had been laid by Protestants.[16] Finke's efforts were testimony to the influence of Weizsäcker, who suggested a level of basic research, putatively free from the demands of evalua-tive judgment, at which this reconciliation could best be achieved. Finke thus devoted his immense energies to editing the documents of pre-Reformation Europe, particularly those that pertained to the church councils; and the editorial achievements of this "ox of the archives," as he became known, were the principal basis of his reputation.

There is little reason to doubt Finke's own account of the origins of his dispute with Lamprecht, except to add that he and Below both taught in Münster at the time and were close friends.[17] Lamprecht's fourth volume covered the era that Finke knew best; several passages, he recalled, were so offensive to his sensitivi-ties that he resolved to look more closely into Lamprecht's scholarship. Finke, who was quarrelsome by temperament, probably needed little encouragement from Below to launch an attack that promised to enhance his visibility within the community of German Catholic scholars.[18]

Lamprecht was a vulnerable target. Although his ties to organized Christian-ity had long lapsed, he had by no means freed himself of the confessional prejudices that permeated the Protestant academic bourgeoisie in Germany. These prejudices, and the ignorance on which they rested, were the principal items in a long critique that Finke published early in 1896 on Lamprecht's treatment of the church in both the fourth and fifth volumes of his *German History*.[19] "Without any knowledge of medieval Catholic life, without any knowledge of Catholic rites [*Kultus*], and above all, without any understanding of [the church's] depth and beauty, Lamprecht has attempted to prove his case by the tinkling of banal phrases [*mit seichtem Phrasengeklingel*]."[20] To demonstrate this point, Finke compiled a long list of factual errors, distortions, dubious anecdotes, and tasteless characterizations "inappropriate in a dignified work of history."[21] These defects so marred Lamprecht's account that Finke judged it a "step backwards"; it did not deserve the label of serious scholarship.[22] He ascribed much of the difficulty to Lamprecht's haste, his failure to let the work mature; but there was a deeper problem that related to the integrity of Lam-precht's research. The historian embraced views, Finke argued, that had long been repudiated in a large body of Catholic historical scholarship about which Lamprecht knew nothing. From this observation followed Finke's most serious charge. He demonstrated the extent to which Lamprecht's treatment of theo-logical issues in the late Middle Ages rested on unattributed borrowings from the third volume of Adolf Harnack's *History of Dogma*; Lamprecht's originality, Finke remarked, consisted only in compounding, by his hasty misreadings, the errors and misconceptions contained in his source.[23] Finke also touched on the ideological issues at stake when he noted that Lamprecht's "socio-statistical" method was sensitive only to the financial bases of the church's decline and ignored the "thinking, perceptions, weaknesses, and virtues" of the masses.[24]

Lamprecht was shaken by this attack, but he was too preoccupied with his other opponents to respond immediately.[25] His reply several months later, in the fall of 1896, was itself an index of his lingering preoccupations; but it did him little credit.[26] Most of the issues he either ignored or obfuscated in an ill-tempered and patronizing attack on Finke's Catholicism. Finke's charges were "frivolities," the products of "religious fanaticism."[27] Finke's heart, Lamprecht charged, "had roots in two soils, one German and one Roman." The implication was familiar: German Catholic historians were not qualified to write German history. Finke's attack demonstrated only that he had "confused our national affairs," Lamprecht continued, "by introducing the circumstances, interests, and ideals of his universal church."[28] He pronounced Finke's historiography a relic of medieval thought; "the higher realm of an unprejudiced genetic perspective"— by which he meant his own—was "naturally" closed to Finke, "like every truly clerical historian."[29] Amid these charges, Lamprecht dismissed—in a footnote and without further comment—Finke's "repeated, completely unmotivated, though admittedly concealed reproach" that he had used Harnack's work without attribution.[30]

Although it limped on for several months, the exchange could hardly be productive given these terms of address.[31] Lamprecht's remarks hit Finke with particular force, but they were calculated to offend every Catholic historian in the country, in the same measure as they played to the confessional sympathies of most of Lamprecht's colleagues.[32] Lamprecht had no grounds for surprise when the journal of the *Görres-Gesellschaft* joined the chorus of his critics with a review of the polemic by the Swiss Catholic, Gustav Schnürer.[33] Despite its criticism of Lamprecht's "characteristic vacillations" and the "pathetic and murky evolutionist dreams" that underlay the historian's writing style, Schnürer's essay was a model of balance and detachment, for he sympathized with Lamprecht's intent and well recognized that his own attack was putting him in the company of Protestant historians whose confessional bias was more ferocious than Lamprecht's.

The polemic thus created strange alliances, and it cost Lamprecht the good will of a camp that was otherwise receptive to cultural history. The universalism of Lamprecht's vision, his deprecation of the history of the state, his sensitivity to popular culture, and his positive reception of Janssen's work found more resonance in German Catholic scholarship than among those who occupied the chairs of history in imperial Germany.[34] However, the methodological dispute highlighted elements in Lamprecht's vision that were anathema to Catholic historians, particularly the questions of materialism and free will, while the historian's own response to criticism from this quarter brought confessional antagonisms into play. As a consequence, it became difficult for Catholic scholars, who might in other circumstances have harbored some sympathy for Lamprecht, to come to his support as the attack on him intensified.

Max Lenz harbored no sympathy for Lamprecht whatsoever. Lenz was the son of a lawyer in Greifswald; and like Lamprecht, he grew up in a pious and cultured Lutheran milieu.[35] He was only six years older than Lamprecht, but he belonged to a different cohort, whose seminal experience was the war that interrupted his studies in Bonn in the summer of 1870. The nation-state that emerged from this war became the focal point of Lenz's work for the rest of his life. After recovering from wounds he suffered at Campigny, he resumed his studies in Greifswald, where, after spending a semester in Berlin, he completed his doctorate in 1875. The two most important intellectual influences on the student were Sybel, whom he encountered in Bonn, and Bernhard Erdmanns-dörffer, one of his professors in Greifswald as well as his sister's husband. While Sybel's partisanship helped rivet Lenz's interests on the history of the Prusso-German state, Erdmannsdörffer suggested a different mode of intellectual engagement as he turned the student's attention to Ranke.

Lenz then advanced rapidly to a position of prominence in the new state's academic network. Sybel's patronage brought him an archival position in Marburg, where he also habilitated with Conrad Varrentrapp in 1876. He remained in Marburg until 1888, first as extraordinary professor and then, in 1885, as *Ordinarius*. In 1888 he moved to Breslau, to the chair earlier occupied by his brother-in-law; and two years later he became the first occupant of a new chair in the capital.

By the time he arrived in Berlin, Lenz was known as Luther's biographer, Janssen's antagonist, and the leading exponent of a Rankean approach to history. His intellectual position lay along the axis that ran, as he often described it, "from Luther to Bismarck," and linked the two poles of modern German history, the liberation of the German spirit from the shackles of Rome and the great political events he had himself witnessed in 1870–1871.[36] To this extent, his views diverged little from the gospel of the Borussians; but his position was complicated by tensions generated along another axis, which ran from Sybel to Ranke. Lenz's insistence on the virtues of detachment and contemplative analysis of the objective forces of history was doubtless sincere; but it did not square well with his own passionate sense of commitment, which had nearly cost him his life on the battlefield in France before it drove him into the public in the 1880s as one of the fiercest champions of *Kulturprotestantismus*, the belief that Protestant Christianity imparted both meaning to German history and a sanction to the new state's civic culture. Lenz was, as one of his student's put it, a Rankean "without the proper dowry of a Rankean temperament."[37]

The Rankean legacy weighed uneasily on him in another respect. Like Erich Marcks, the other scholar most associated with the "Ranke Renaissance," Lenz worked comfortably with well-delineated topics, particularly in the medium of biography, where his subjects included Gustav Adolf, Napoleon, and Bismarck, in addition to Luther. His most enduring scholarship was a monumental history of the university of Berlin. But when he labored on higher plains of abstraction and synthesis in search of Ranke's grand perspective, his political commitments collided with his pretensions; his celebrated attempt in 1900 to extend the theme of Ranke's essay on "The Great Powers" was music to the ears of Admiral Tirpitz.[38]

Lenz thus contended with the burdens as well as the distinctions that attached to his role as epigone and custodian of Ranke's legacy. His insecurities found vent in personal traits that were foreign to his hero—in his querulousness, which often showed signs of malice, and in his boundless vanity. One of his friends recalled that Lenz was a *Mann der Selbstbehauptung*, a man who encountered opposing views more in a spirit of domination and self-assertion than intellectual exchange.[39] A less sympathetic observer, Lamprecht's friend Paul Hinneberg, once remarked that Max Lenz worshipped but two gods, one of them Ranke, the other Max Lenz.[40]

There was nothing Rankean about the vendetta that Lenz waged against Lamprecht. His views about the genre of cultural history hardened only after his move to Berlin, for while in Breslau he had announced plans for a comprehensive *Kulturgeschichte* of the Reformation, a work analogous to Burckhardt's and conceived as the definitive Protestant reply to Janssen.[41] Lenz was never able to bring the project to fruition, but whether his frustrations affected his attitude toward Lamprecht is a matter of speculation.[42] His response late in 1890 to the first volume of Lamprecht's *German History* was, in all events, not positive. He found the book "so unbelievably confused, trivial, and in parts arrogant," as he wrote from Berlin to Erdmannsdörfer, "that I was dumbfounded."[43]

Given the nature of the intellectual issues at stake in the *Methodenstreit*, and given the symbolic centrality of Ranke, it was natural that Lenz ranked high among Lamprecht's enemies. The personal animosity that exacerbated this antagonism grew out of a rumor that Lamprecht had blocked Lenz's call to Leipzig in 1893; the animosity was then sealed early the next year during the negotiations over the arbitration between Lamprecht and Below.[44] The doubts that Lamprecht expressed during these negotiations about Lenz's impartiality as an arbitrator were not without foundation; but they were tactless and left Lenz, the neo-Rankean who put great stock in his ability to be impartial, "literally trembling with rage."[45]

Within three months of this episode, Lenz had a copy of the first part of Lamprecht's fifth volume, which covered the era of the Reformation. He also had an invitation from Meinecke to review the book in the *Historische Zeitschrift*.[46] Lenz waited two years. By his own testimony, he agreed to publish the review only reluctantly, after Meinecke's repeated encouragement, although perhaps also with an eye to Lamprecht's candidacy for Treitschke's chair; in the meantime, though, he had encouraged his student Rachfahl to enter the fray against Lamprecht.[47]

Lenz's long-awaited "bomb" finally appeared in September 1896.[48] His approach tended more toward Below's than Rachfahl's, for although he opened his essay with an impassioned defense of Ranke, he chose to ignore questions of theory. Lenz's review was, like Below's, an extended critique of the facts, except that Lenz's discussion was geared more to deficiencies in Lamprecht's interpretive schema. This schema must have struck Lenz as curious, for in significant respects, particularly in its glorification of Luther, it resembled his own (and Ranke's); and Lenz's own biography of the Reformer was one of the few sources that Lamprecht acknowledged using. On the other hand, the broader context into which Lamprecht had placed the Reformation was repellent. Lamprecht's picture of "proletarian" and "socialistic" revolutionary ferment in urban and rural society was offensive enough; worse was his emphasis on the transition from a natural to a money economy and the basic divide which, he claimed, this process tore open between town and countryside. Apart from its materialistic premise, Lamprecht's view clashed with an axiom of Lenz's thinking: it challenged the proposition that the reception of Luther's teachings bound Germans of all stations together in a great common national experience—that, as Lenz explained it, "the new teachings were popular everywhere from the beginning and remained so in spite of the social catastrophes and religious crises that they had to overcome."[49] The bulk of Lenz's review comprised an assault on Lamprecht's idea of a dualism between town and countryside. The reviewer's arsenal contained a long string of facts, which, he argued, Lamprecht had ignored or misinterpreted because they undermined his analytical framework and established the commonalities of urban and rural experience. Lenz dilated on the alliance of peasants and urban handicraftsmen during the uprisings of the early 1520s. He argued that geographical and social mobility blurred distinctions between city and countryside in the early sixteenth century. He noted the cooperation between the cities and the rural nobility in the construction of territorial states. He insisted that rural backwardness and peasant poverty were not as great as Lamprecht's "deductions" had led him to believe. Lamprecht's vision of this era was, in sum, worse than inadequate. His theory of a dualism between a monetary economy in the towns and a natural economy on the land had obscured "as if in the fog," Lenz charged, "the clearest, definitively proven historical conditions."[50]

Lenz's review was shrewd. Unlike the attacks by Below and Rachfahl, it focused not on the sections of Lamprecht's volume that dealt with political history, but on those that treated social and cultural developments. A detailed critique of the inconsistencies in Lamprecht's analysis of German humanism was part of the same strategy. So, too, was a brief and unlikely passage on religious affairs, in which Lenz came to the defense of the "ultramontane" criticism to which Finke had just subjected Lamprecht's views.[51]

Lenz's was the most serious attack Lamprecht had yet faced. Lenz was more established, and he exercised more influence in the profession than the other scholars who had criticized Lamprecht in print. His strictures demanded a response, for they could not be dismissed as the product of confessional fanaticism or differences of philosophy and methodology. Nor could Lamprecht take refuge in the claim that he had frequently employed to parry the *Detailkritik* of his other opponents, whom he accused of operating "as if the decision about the great questions at issue were to be decided by reference to a minor lapse committed here or there."[52] The plea began to ring hollow that the factual errors in Lamprecht's scholarship were irrelevant—trivial flaws that were inevitable in a work of such grand scope—and that to dwell on them merely obfuscated the larger methodological issues.[53] Lenz's point was that the countless errors of fact and interpretation were intimately related to the larger methodological issues, for they symptomized the untenability of Lamprecht's vision of German history. Lenz's essay contained its own share of untenable claims about the Reformation, but it did suggest a level on which the various strains of the methodological controversy could be drawn together and resolved. For despite his carelessness, Lamprecht was no less committed than his opponents to an ideal of historical accuracy; his claim in the end was that his "collectivistic" methodology provided a fuller and more accurate vision of the past.

Yet Lamprecht remained reluctant to pitch the exchange in these terms. To do so would require a retreat from the high level of abstraction to which he had advanced with Wundt's help and where he believed he had scored a major victory over his opponents; worse, it would require a retreat of another kind, into a reexamination of specific historical problems that he had long resolved to his own satisfaction and hence no longer found interesting. "I naturally will not answer," he wrote to Bernheim. The attack had, he confessed, initially occasioned "a few hours of consternation," but his tranquillity had returned once his sympathizers had assured him that Lenz's tone, his obsession with "animosities and trivialities," had been self-defeating.[54]

Lamprecht changed his mind and decided to reply, in part at least because of reports from Berlin, where the enthusiastic reception of Lenz's essay gave cause for concern.[55] Lamprecht's response was grudging, however, and it represented little more than an incidental part of an agitated essay that he published in November 1896 on questions of method and theory.[56] He used this rambling reformulation of his most recent position to take shots not only at Lenz, but also at Rachfahl, Delbrück, and even Lehmann, who had removed himself from the controversy after his departure to Göttingen. The fault line in the historical profession, Lamprecht now explained, ran between the exponents of "collectivistic cultural history" and the "individualistic history of persons." The one was interested in how historical structures served as immanent causes of typical patterns of behavior; the other was devoted to singularity, individual free will, and the motive force of transcendent ideas. Among the failings of the "individualists'" perspective, the historian continued, was their inability to see the forest for the trees, their preference for the part over the whole, the individual over the group, and the exception over the rule. Because their perspective "basically admits neither historical types nor historical mass movements," these historians were "not able to understand these phenomena, either critically or constructively."[57]

The controlling word in this context was "critically," as Lamprecht turned briefly to Lenz, whose criticism he characterized as a classic illustration of the problem. The critic's arsenal of facts—all of them, Lamprecht conceded, indisputably true—demonstrated only an obsession with isolated details; these details represented but incidental exceptions to the "typical development"—to the historical regularities that Lamprecht had identified. Lenz was blind to the overarching "pattern" [Zusammenhang] of the mass movement," Lamprecht complained, and when the critic occasionally addressed the larger question, he betrayed his "elementary misconceptions."[58] Lamprecht's contention was not altogether unfounded; and the bearing of Lenz's facts on Lamprecht's generalizations would have rewarded much more discussion. Lamprecht, though, was not interested in further discussion. Instead, he concluded that the content and vehemence of the review from Lenz, a leading figure in the "individualists'" camp, were indications that "certain circles of this group are beginning to despair of a general defense of their position."[59]

Even for a man as given to self-deception as Lamprecht, this pronouncement was bizarre. As he himself seemed to recognize elsewhere in the same essay, the grounds for mounting concern, if not yet desperation, were in his own camp. The dispute had become bitter, he noted, and at stake was "nothing less than the intellectual existence of one of the scholars."[60] The agitation that marked this essay was evident as well in the tone of his rejoinder to Finke, which he framed at the same time. Both documents suggested the toll that the controversy was taking on its central figure.

Lamprecht turned forty in February 1896. The dispute over method was in its early phases, and the occasion offered the historian a serene moment in which to ponder both his accomplishments, which for a man his age were considerable, and his ambitions, which still seemed attainable. "Contemplating what I have sought and achieved—even more, contemplating things personal and general— all is coming together in these days," he wrote to his brother shortly thereafter.[61] The developments of the following months put an end to the serenity and made it difficult to believe that "all is coming together." Lamprecht was entering the most trying period of his life.

As the polemic consumed ever more of his time and professional energies, the historian had to cope with enduring difficulties at home. His wife now resided in an institution not far from the university, in the suburb of Thonberg; although the arrangement made frequent contact possible, her periodic visits at home brought as much frustration as joy, for "incessant difficult episodes" punctuated her moments of lucidity.[62] "It is frightful," Lamprecht confessed to his brother in November 1896, "and sometimes I do not think I can hold out."[63] His wife's shadow was long. The institutionalization of her sister late in 1896 indicated that the illness might be hereditary, and the historian's mood turned from despair to alarm and anxiety over the fate of his two daughters.[64] He had in addition to contend with the frequent intrusions of his mother-in-law. This difficult and unhappy woman was jealous of the affection her granddaughters had developed for their governess; her resentments were ill disguised and exacerbated the dislike and distrust the historian had developed for her.[65]

Lamprecht himself had little but gratitude for the governess, Emma Bruch. She held the household together in every practical sense and enabled him to enjoy his daughters, who were the principal objects of his affection and the source of whatever domestic relief his life still offered. The children were also his companions on extended summer excursions, which, as his professional difficulties increased, grew in importance as a means of escape.

In the fall of 1896, in order to escape the pollution of the central city, the historian moved the family into new quarters in the northern suburb of Gohlis, from which he could commute by tram to the university.[66] The move was inconvenient and traumatic, for it removed him further from his wife; but he undertook it on the urging of his doctors, whom he was consulting about still another affliction.[67] For a period of almost two years, from early 1895 to the end of 1896, he suffered from a stubborn bronchial infection, which discomforted and worried him—about the state of his finances as well as his health—and interfered with his teaching. After it yielded to lung surgery in the fall of 1896, a gastrointestinal disorder set in again and vexed him for another two years.[68]

The growing strains of the controversy might well have contributed to his physical ailments; but these strains posed a more direct threat to his psychological well-being. The Methodenstreit was one of those "moments of sharp attack" that required, as he later observed to Ritter, a "heightening of self-consciousness."[69] The personal stakes in the controversy were higher for him than for any of the other participants, for his emotional investment in it was of a distinct order. The body of scholarship that was the object of controversy was more than a survey of German history; it was at the same time an intimate personal statement and a grandiose exercise in self-display. Remarks charged with autobiographical significance documented Lamprecht's heightening of self-consciousness during the polemic, and they confirmed that the real issue was the historian's own history. In the preface to the second edition of the first volume of his German History, he confessed that he had begun the project with no distinct readership in mind, but instead "above all for myself." His purpose, he continued, was to "clarify my views about our people's past."[70] He meant his own past as well, for his great project was to comprehend a collective process of maturation that he had experienced personally. In a remarkable passage in his reply to Lenz, he characterized the terminus a quo in his process as a stage in which "personality was still bounded" and systematic knowledge (Wissenschaft) could only exist "in the sense of a childishly directed mania for collecting [eines kindlich gerichteten Sammeleifers] from one's own very limited experience."[71] In both its collective and personal contexts, maturation meant intellectual growth, the "unbinding of higher intellectual life," the incorporation of ever broader ranges of human experience into the realm of understanding. As he explained in "What Is Cultural History?," the essay that announced the terms of his own fulfillment, the nation's fulfillment lay in framing a view of the past that would make possible the "advance from the wealth of concrete particulars to knowledge of that which is at once universal and most profound."[72]

The historian emphasized in the same essay that he held "the core of my system [Auffassung] to be indestructable."[73] Despite the ordeals he endured in its defense, he did cling for the rest of his life to the intellectual edifice that he had constructed with Wundt's aid in 1896. Subsequent modifications were minor, for this system represented the completion of the agenda that had guided his labors since his days as a student, and in a sense since his childhood. It structured the nation's history as it structured his own. It framed a sense of himself within an extraordinary accomplishment, which signified the transcendence of history itself—the ultimate venturing out to enclose the past entirely within the bounds of causality.

Lamprecht's intellectual position was fraught with difficulties. His pretensions drove him far beyond the accepted bounds of historical method, to advocate views that his opponents were quick to condemn as ideological or metaphysical. The historian's inability to recognize the truth in their charges was due only in part to the deficiencies in his philosophical training; it reflected a deeper problem that inhered in his intellectual posture, as well as in what might be called—generously—his theory of knowledge.[74]

Like most of his opponents, Lamprecht believed in the accessibility of objective historical knowledge.[75] Like them, he also believed that apprehending the patterned structures of history demanded only that the scholar contemplate the particulars of the past with the proper technical skills, methodological training, and scrupulous impartiality. In Lamprecht's eyes, however, it violated none of these precepts to insist at the same time that his own achievement rested on a privileged epistemology. The guarantee of his system's validity, of its claim to the status of historical truth, resided, he believed, in its provenance. The historian's faith in the reliability and power of his own imagination was as boundless as it was naive and resistant to challenge. "Nothing in history is clear to me," he confessed to Grimm early in 1897, "which I have not brought completely under the control of my imagination."[76] His belief that he had arrived at his theories "by a purely empirical route," that every historian who followed this route "would have discovered the same results," was doubtless genuine; but it, too, was based ultimately upon a faith in his unique power to decipher the past.[77]

Lamprecht's confidence in the ordering powers of his own mind was the basis of his philosophy of history. It gestated within the holistic intellectual traditions of German idealism, which in his experience converged in the figures of Lotze, Roscher, and Wundt. This confidence was not foreign to the rest of his profession, but most historians were compelled to temper it, both in theory and practice, in their reverence for the documents. Lamprecht's faith in the powers of his mind was in no way tempered; it was suborned instead by proclivities that had deep roots in his past—his self-absorption, impulsiveness, restlessness, and his preference for solitude. During the polemic these traits encouraged his retreat into a characteristic posture that might well be described as solipsistic. Gerhard Seeliger used the term "auto-suggestion" to describe the problem.[78] Lamprecht's system was enclosed within high and rigid conceptual barriers. These not only sealed it against criticism from without but admitted considerable flexibility within, which surfaced externally as the historian's inconsistency. The psychiatrist Willy Hellpach, who studied history in Leipzig in the late

1890s, had occasion to watch this mechanism in operation. He recalled that Lamprecht "gushed over with insights and impressions; he seized in a flash what was consistent in them and ignored what did not seem to mesh." "Whatever would not submit to his own ideas," Hellpach continued, the historian "instinctively turned it away."[79]

When Hellpach described this behavior as part of the "romantic's drive for self-preservation," he touched upon one of the most intriguing and poignant features of the Methodenstreit. The controversy threatened Lamprecht's integrity in the most basic sense. That he survived the ordeal emotionally at all, particularly in view of the other strains in his personal life, was testimony to his vitality, his boundless belief in himself, and his instincts for self-preservation, all of which were heavily taxed.[80] His naiveté and capacity for self-deception had contributed to the breakdown in communication with his colleagues; these traits now disguised the desperation of his situation and nurtured illusions that were probably essential to his psychological survival.

Lamprecht was comfortable with solitude, and he persuaded himself that isolation, together with the incomprehension and hostility of others, were the prophet's burden. Since his student days he had regarded himself as a Promethean figure (albeit in anticipation of a happier fate), and in the pressure of battle this ethos took on moralistic and messianic accents. He could explain the resistance to his ideas only in terms of ignorance, dishonesty, and malice; and as his efforts to relieve his opponents' ignorance went unrewarded, he inclined to view their opposition in terms of moral failings.

The growing arrogance of his commentary owed much to this outlook. But the arrogance also reflected his penchant for trivializing the opposition, for casting it, as he explained to Harden, in an "amusing" light.[81] He found comfort, he wrote to Liesegang, in representing the whole conflict "from a distance," so that "all these things seem almost comical."[82] These remarks sounded forced, but Lamprecht did portray the Methodenstreit, as he portrayed all of German history, in a way that corresponds to the conception of comedy as a narrative mode.[83] Both his private and public commentaries on the dispute were emplotted in the necessities of his own grand system. The plot featured the hero's struggle against ignorance and envy; its dénouement lay in the final acceptance, amid general acclaim, of his views. "I am simply marching in step with the development of modern ideas," he wrote in 1897 to Althoff with a plot summary, adding that this development could not "be held up by any foolish [unverständig] obstruction."[84]

Yet as Hellpach's allusions to literary genre suggested, elements in Lamprecht's behavior during the crisis are perhaps better analyzed under the rubric of romance.[85] Lamprecht's dramatic rendition of the Methodenstreit featured the confrontation of momentous forces, a struggle between the "old" and the "new"; and it yielded in the end to a great personality with a mission.[86] The proportions of the heroism were romantic in White's sense, as was the lonely hero's ultimate vindication. The plot was to culminate not merely in the hero's public acceptance, but in his transcendence of the dramatic conflict.

Viewing the dispute in these terms was a way of coping. These strategies assumed greater importance as the historian's ordeal continued and his optimism became increasingly difficult to sustain, at least in the eyes of those close to him. That the controversy was taking a great toll on him was clear to those who had to endure first-hand his emotional agitation, which made it physically difficult for him to sit for long periods of time and gave rise to extreme fluctuations of mood.[87] Lethargy was nowhere in his character; so his agitation found vent in irritability, suspicion, and arrogance, as well as in moments of euphoria that accompanied the occasional encouraging development.

"He still has his 'admirers,'" wrote Bücher to Aloys Schulte at the height of the controversy, "but he cannot see that they mean nothing to him as long as none of them takes a public stand on his behalf."[88] Bücher's lament betrayed his own frustrations with his colleague, but it was not entirely accurate. Some of Lamprecht's admirers, such as Wundt, Liesegang, and Bücher himself, were not historians, so their public intervention would have brought him little if any benefit. Others among his admirers did come to his public defense; but few of them counted for much in the German historical profession. The encouraging commentaries on his work and the praise for his performance in the methodological dispute came as a rule either from German scholars buried deep in the recesses of the profession or from Austrians and other foreigners with whom he was in contact, such as the Belgian scholar Pirenne.[89]

Lamprecht did not lack sympathizers closer to the centers of academic power in Germany, but these men were in a dilemma. They recognized the eccentricities in his scholarship, but they regarded the *Methodenstreit* as a deplorable spectacle, which jeopardized a legitimate attempt to make German historiography more sensitive to the influence of social and cultural structures and to the operation of collective forces. The polarization of views threatened these scholars, too, as it made efforts at compromise and mediation difficult. Although he lacked the power in the profession that he coveted, Georg Steinhausen represented the views of a number of important scholars, who adopted a strategy of defending Lamprecht against the more extreme claims of his opponents while defending *Kulturgeschichte* against the more extreme claims of Lamprecht. The curious commentary on the dispute that Steinhausen published in September 1896 reflected the dilemma. He rejected the charge that Lamprecht was a materialist, but he otherwise found that the best defense of the historian's methodology was to emphasize its similarities to Freytag's.[90]

Gustav Schmoller faced similar difficulties. He was not technically a historian, but he was closer than perhaps any other economist to the historical profession; and his ties extended to both camps, so he found the dispute painful.[91] His basic sympathies lay with Lamprecht; in fact, he admired the very aspects of Lamprecht's work that had originally drawn fire from the historical seminar at his own university in Berlin. Schmoller was himself well acquainted with the charge that economic history was implicated in materialism, but he was too seasoned a scholar to be bothered much by it. As a neo-Kantian, he was likewise comfortable with the proposition that no scholar wrote history without prior heuristic commitments. Schmoller was consequently bemused by Lamprecht's contorted attempts to parry the charge of materialism and to disavow every trace of a *Weltanschauung* in his work.

Schmoller kept a low profile during most of the *Methodenstreit*. He spoke out only on two occasions in 1896, when he delivered gentle criticism that could be construed as an attempt to save Lamprecht from his own confusion.[92] In a lecture before the Berlin Historical Society and then in a contribution to the discussion that followed Scala's talk at the *Historikertag* in Innsbruck, Schmoller argued that Lamprecht's attack on Ranke was unfair, that his professions of pure empiricism and objectivity were idle, and that he would do well to recognize the extent of his own theoretical commitments.[93] But Schmoller was a cautious man. The mounting allegations of contradictions and flaws in Lamprecht's scholarship weighed on him, for they confirmed apprehensions that had originated several years earlier, when he found long passages from his own work paraphrased without attribution in Lamprecht's volumes.[94] Although Schmoller preferred to view this problem in the light of his colleague's haste, he began to back away, as he later confessed, "rather too much under the impression of the attacks."[95]

Schmoller was not the only scholar to back away. No one was more pained by the intensification of the controversy over Lamprecht's work than Ernst Bernheim.[96] Not only had he been Lamprecht's friend and loyal advisor for twenty years; he had devoted his career to working out a methodological compromise between the positions opposed in the controversy. "In my view," he wrote to Lamprecht in 1893, in the wake of Lehmann's departure from Leipzig, "the great conflict [*Gegensatz*] between individualism and socialism (or better: the operation of the masses) . . . cannot be resolved by the one-sided domination of one of the two positions, but only by their thorough-going [*durchgreifende*] reconciliation."[97] As sensitive as he was to the influence of social and cultural structures on individual behavior, Bernheim rejected every attempt to eliminate moral freedom from historical analysis and to reduce human action to the play of law and necessity.

Bernheim's notes on the manuscripts that Lamprecht sent him registered his reservations about the direction of his friend's work, but they produced little impact. The second edition of Bernheim's manual on historical method, which appeared in 1894, addressed the growing dispute in the profession with only a brief remark, but its tone might have given Lamprecht pause. Those who studied the past, Bernheim wrote, should concern themselves "as seriously as possible" with the new currents of materialism. "One must view them as a hostile power, whose weaknesses one must learn to recognize precisely, whose advantages one must appropriate fully in order to check and triumph over them."[98] Lamprecht's subsequent preoccupation with questions of method and theory damaged their relationship (as did misunderstandings about the failure of Bernheim's candidacy for a position in Leipzig in 1895).[99] Bernheim recognized that the author of the *German History* was no materialist in any conventional sense; but in Lamprecht's theoretical writings he found symptoms of the real object of his concern, the attempt to deploy the assumptions and methods of the natural sciences in the study of history. Bernheim found his friend's posture in the *Methodenstreit* troubling in another respect. Lamprecht's insistence on the originality of his methodological insights—his disavowal of all philosophical antecedents—struck Bernheim as an exercise in dissimulation and possibly a personal slight, for the friendship between the two men had developed in Göttingen during intense discussions of Comte, Buckle, Marx, and other positivists, to whom Bernheim was convinced Lamprecht was indebted.[100]

The growing controversy thus strained Lamprecht's relationship with one of his few close friends in the profession. He was fortunate that his actions did not sever another tie that he valued. Moriz Ritter's involvement in the dispute was inadvertent. He sympathized more with Lamprecht personally than with his view of history, but in 1893 he published an essay that could be read as a cautious attempt to strike a compromise position in the dispute then building between his former students, Lamprecht and Below.[101] Here Ritter suggested that the central theme of historical development lay in the interaction between society and state, between groups organized for the pursuit of sectorial ambitions and the power that was embodied in the community. Ritter's observations seemed to emphasize the importance of the social context of politics and human behavior, but insofar as he insisted on the centrality of politics in historical development, his position comported with the views defended by Schäfer in his exchange with Gothein.

Three years later, in his reply to Lenz, Lamprecht unearthed Ritter's essay in support of his own position.[102] As Ritter had characterized it, the state's role could be understood, Lamprecht claimed, as the imposition of harmony though justice and law—in other words, as an "act of immanent morality." In fact, Lamprecht continued, the whole confrontation between state and society could, in Ritter's description, be seen as a process of "increasingly intense domination." Therefore, he announced, Ritter stood "on the side of collectivism in the sense that he accepts the immanent development of historical necessities."

Ritter was embarassed. From Lamprecht's pen, the words "immanence" and "collectivism" carried connotations that he could not accept in his own work. In a private letter, he wrote that he had "several reservations" about Lamprecht's remarks.[103] He was prepared, like Lamprecht, to speak about an "immanent" law of historical development, but only in the sense that this law described the "direction presented to us for orienting our powers and capacities toward the realization of specific purposes." In no sense, however, did historical development exclude human freedom or the "incalculable diversity" of individual behavior. History, Ritter admitted, was about the interaction between individuals and larger collectivities (*Gesamtheiten*), but to posit the existence of "a collective will, a collective mind and a collective perception" he dismissed as a sign of "Wundtian obscurity." With these reservations Ritter cut the ground out from under Lamprecht's position, but this letter to Lamprecht was conspicuous among the documents of the Methodenstreit for its grace and good will, and the personal bond between the two men survived.

Both Bernheim and Ritter attempted to steer Lamprecht toward a more moderate formulation of his position. When he wrote of the reciprocal interaction of individual freedom and structural constraint, Ritter suggested possible terms for the "reconciliation" that Bernheim hoped to see. When a similar suggestion was proffered late in 1896 from the enemy's camp, it provided the most hopeful sign that the dispute might find a constructive resolution.

Otto Hintze's interest in methodological questions reflected the unusual breadth of his training and the practical problems he encountered in his early scholarship.[104] As a student at the university of Berlin he imbibed the methodological traditions of the German historical profession at the feet of its foremost representatives, Droysen, Treitschke, and Waitz, as well as Weizsäcker, under whose direction he produced a conventional dissertation on William of Orange in 1885. That Hintze's subsequent career as a historian would not be conventional was assured two years later, when he moved into the orbit of Schmoller and became a collaborator in the Acta Borussica, the great edition of sources on the domestic development of Brandenburg-Prussia. Hintze's contributions to the series in the early 1890s included a monumental history of the Prussian silk industry and a profile of the state's bureaucracy at the accession of Frederick the Great to power in 1740. The central theme of both projects was the interaction of state and society in an age of mercantilism, the impact of political decisions on the evolution of economic structures, as well as the limits imposed by institutions, such as the bureaucracy, on the freedom of individual leaders to make political decisions.

Hintze's research compelled him to confront in practice the central issues in the Methodenstreit. His penetrating analysis of structural constraints and collective forces distinguished his scholarship from the work of the other young scholars who led the attack on Lamprecht in the name of individual freedom.[105] Below's judgment, that Hintze's eccentricity was due to "the same ingenium as Schmoller's," was no compliment.[106] Meinecke, who shared some of Below's reservations, was nonetheless one of Hintze's closest friends and invited him in the summer of 1896 to respond to Lamprecht's manifesto, "What Is Cultural History?"[107] Meinecke also later judged Hintze's short essay, which appeared in the Historische Zeitschrift at the end of the year, to be the best commentary on Lamprecht's work to emerge during the controversy; and subsequent commentators have tended to agree.[108]

Hintze's evaluation of Lamprecht's achievement seemed anomalous in the pages of this journal. The charge that Lamprecht was a materialist he rejected out of hand. Hintze described the German History as a "remarkable step forward" toward a "social-psychological perspective" in history; this perspective he called "perhaps the most significant historiographical achievement since the end of the last century." Its hallmark, Hintze remarked, was its focus on the collective context of human action, the recognition that the principal "driving forces of history" were human beings in "social formations [*gesellschaftliche Verbindungen*], in which the collective spiritual forces are created that constitute the living core of all institutions."

At this point in the essay, Lamprecht's delight must have matched Meinecke's doubts about the wisdom of asking Hintze to write it. The rest of the article brought more to comfort Meinecke than Lamprecht. Hintze turned to the contrasts that Lamprecht had drawn between the individual and collective contexts of behavior and between the methods appropriate for the historical analysis of each. The problem, Hintze argued, was Lamprecht's tendency to construct absolute dichotomies, to "eliminate completely the individual moment" from social history and treat the members of social groups "simply as examples of generic types [*Gattungsexemplare*]." This distinction Hintze rejected. Groups were made up of individuals. Collective purposes emerged out of "individual psychic acts," and they constantly changed in response to changes in the "individual impulses on which they rest." With a bow to Meinecke, he observed: "The individual moment thus may not be neglected as an element in collective phenomena; in this moment lies the source of the specific individuality of the group, as well as the most important motor for its on-going development." But, with a bow to Lamprecht, he also stressed that "the life of the individual appears everywhere embedded in the life of communities." In place of Lamprecht's dichotomies, though, Hintze invoked a continuum, along which every historical act was situated between the poles of freedom and necessity. "Between what one might call the organic development or growth of historical formations and the apparently completely free act of a public leader's will, there is thus no distinction in principle, but rather only a difference of degree." The interplay, in other words, between individual freedom and collective restraint, the singular and the typical, was at every moment dynamic and reciprocal.

There is much to support Winfried Schulze's conclusion that in this essay Hintze trod "the narrow middle path" between the constructions of Lamprecht and the dominant views of the academic historians.[109] The essay was a model of generosity and conciliation. It made significant concessions to both sides while drawing elements from each into a possible synthesis. By molding the principal issues into metaphors of continuity rather than dichotomy, the essay appeared to offer the terms on which the methodological conflict might be resolved and the differences between the two sides composed into questions of emphasis or preference within a broader consensus, or in Hintze's own terms, along a common axis of historical inquiry.

The appearances were deceptive. On the deeper question of method Hintze offered no compromise, for here his claims were as preemptive as Lamprecht's. Lamprecht's speculations about the origins of the more highly developed mental processes he dismissed as "rather irrelevant"; the subjects of history were human beings at "the stage of fully developed consciousness." Hintze added: "We arrive at an understanding of them in no other way than by an act of artistic apperception based on research." Hintze's allegiance was to the hermeneutical tradition that Lamprecht was proposing to eliminate in the name of empiricism and causal analysis. The reciprocal interaction of groups and individuals was an "enormously complicated phenomenon," Hintze continued in an allusion to Dilthey, "which one can describe and sort into its components [zergliedern] but which one cannot rationally explain [erklären] in its totality on the basis of its simple elements." In the end Hintze, too, returned to the position that Schäfer had staked out in his debate with Gothein: the accommodation with cultural history was to occur at the level of subject matter, not method. The continuum Hintze envisaged was to make possible an expansion of historical research into broader realms, into the study of "not only the great chains and peaks, but the base of the mountains"; all along this continuum, however, a familiar hermeneutic, based on sympathetic intuition and focused on the individual moment in the past, was to rule.

Lamprecht interpreted Hintze's position nevertheless as a capitulation in Berlin. "At least three-quarters of my views now seem to me in the clear [im Trocknen]," he wrote to Harden late in November 1896.[110] The next day he announced to Grimm that Hintze's article revealed that "victory is already four-fifths mine."[111] A response, which the historian immediately published in Die Zukunft, bore the title "A Turning Point in the Historiographical Dispute."[112] Here Lamprecht took the pose of historian to the dispute as well as participant. He claimed that the methodological controversy was coming to a conclusion, that his opponents had now reached the position from which he had started two decades earlier. Hintze's image of a continuum he read as a formula for the "equable [gleichmässige] impact of individual and collective forces" and as an admission that structures were immanent causal factors in history. On these terms he accepted Hintze's position as a consensus gentium. "However," he continued, there were still "several not insignificant differences." These had to do with method. The methods appropriate for dealing with individual and collective forces were not, Lamprecht insisted, the same. The one tied a series of individual phenomena into a coherent narrative (Erzählung); the other used statistical data and other "mass observations" to isolate similarities, typical features, and "essential" patterns of collective behavior.

But Lamprecht was himself in a mood to compromise. He drew another dichotomy, this time between theory and practice. The methods of individualistic and collective history were logically different, he explained, but in the practice of research and writing, they were "mutually complementary" and were to be "treated as equals." Hintze's continuum now posed the block to compromise, insofar as he used it to "dissolve" social history back into individual history, "to salvage a little of the arbitrary freedom of the individual." Lamprecht was right about Hintze's intentions, but he undercut the credibility of his own gesture of conciliation when he insisted that "in the final analysis the great social-psychological forces rule over [*beherrschen*] the individual forces." And it was difficult to see in the end how Lamprecht expected this truth to provide room for compromise in either theory or practice. "How can anyone want to place historical significance [*Werth*] on the specific personal components of individual motivations?" "To do so," and here he pointed at both Hintze and Meinecke, "would be to misunderstand in the worst way the principle that what is historical can only be the most essential features of the past." That the essential features of the past were collective needed no emphasis.

The letter that Liesegang wrote in January 1897 was an indication of the kind of advice Lamprecht was now receiving. Liesegang assured the historian that he was emerging as the victor in the debate and that the difference between him and Hintze was not great.[113] Liesegang was twice wrong. Lamprecht's response had changed no minds in Berlin, and disagreements continued over fundamental questions of method. In the end, the exchange between Lamprecht and Hintze had done little more than add some clarity to the issues.[114] Still, at no time did the prospects seem better than in early 1897 for a resolution or workable compromise in the *Methodenstreit*. The resumption of the polemic between Lamprecht and another antagonist in the spring of the same year indicated the areas of intellectual agreement between the two sides. However, it also suggested that personal animosities had made compromise impossible.

Lamprecht's "What Is Cultural History?" had included an arrogant postscript addressed to Felix Rachfahl. In it Lamprecht announced that Rachfahl had "fundamentally completely" "adopted my views"—an indication, he concluded, of "general conceptual confusion" on his opponent's part.[115] Rachfahl accepted the provocation, for he was convinced that the confusion was Lamprecht's and that many of the methodological and philosophical distinctions between the "old" and "new" directions had dissolved in Lamprecht's embrace of a Wundtian *Ideenlehre*. His response to Lamprecht's manifesto appeared shortly after Hintze's essay.[116] It ranged over a number of issues, dealing with some more harshly than others, but it was more penetrating and philosophically informed than his earlier contributions to the debate; and it raised questions of a different order than Hintze's about the nature and extent of the disagreement between the two camps.

Like Hintze, Rachfahl rejected the dichotomy between individual and collective or generic behavior, but his resolution of the dichotomy appeared to offer a major concession to Lamprecht. Rachfahl agreed that all behavior was subject to causality. But he added a reservation. In human behavior causality was teleological. "The causal nexus [*Kausalzusammenhang*] is always a purposive context [*Zweckzusammenhang*]." The human experience of causality, he insisted, took the form of a connection between motive and action, and the principal task of the historian was to recreate this nexus to the extent permitted by the sources.

From this proposition, which both Lamprecht and Wundt could endorse (so could Max Weber), Rachfahl made two telling points. The first concerned the question of whether the sway of causality was necessary and absolute—whether the connection between cause and effect (or, in human behavior, between motive and action) was governed by necessity or admitted freedom of choice. With Hume as his authority, Rachfahl dismissed this whole question as a matter of speculation, appropriate for philosophers or perhaps natural scientists, but not for historians, whose sources allowed only provisional conclusions on the basis of actual cases. Any historical method that featured causal necessity as a universal principle rested on a metaphysical premise. "Whoever proposes a theory like this," Rachfahl declared, "should not try to parade it in front of us as the documented [gesichertes] result of scholarly study; he is erasing the line between belief and knowledge."

Rachfahl's second point pertained to the ontology of collective ideas or what he called, in Lamprechtian terms, "socio-psychic contexts." These, he conceded, represented the collective purposes that individuals "took up" as motives. However, to define these collective contexts as necessary causes of individual behavior was to cloud the problem of historical causation in the operation of transcendent forces, whose efficacy, he claimed, rested on nothing but the metaphysical belief of the historian. Another concession to Lamprecht then sealed the case. Ranke, too, Rachfahl admitted, had lapsed on occasion into metaphysical speculation; he had written as if the great ideas in history were transcendent forces. Rachfahl's conclusion was then ineluctable: Lamprecht's theory of immanent social-psychic forces tended in the last analysis toward a "refurbished and adulterated [erneute und verfälschte] edition of Ranke's theory of ideas."

Rachfahl's argument was effective as well as perverse. He drew out the assumptions that Lamprecht shared with his opponents, but he couched them in terms that he knew Lamprecht could not accept. The affinities that he cited between Lamprecht and Ranke were invidious, for they challenged the symbolic core of Lamprecht's understanding of the methodological dispute. But Rachfahl's intent was not to forge a compromise; it was to destroy Lamprecht's credibility and his claim to originality.

Lamprecht's harried reply betrayed how much Rachfahl had hurt him.[117] Personal enmities were also at work, for Lamprecht calculated—not without reason—that Rachfahl was working in the service of Lenz. Lamprecht's response comprised a disjointed series of apodictic pronouncements, which were self-evident to him alone and suggested that he had not taken his opponent's argument seriously. They also confounded the issues that Hintze and Rachfahl had begun to clarify. Rachfahl had, he announced, "completely misunderstood" his position in "a frequently comic fashion." The problem of causal necessity Lamprecht dismissed with the remark that his own theory embraced only "statistical causality," which, he explained, operated with "necessary regularity but not with absolute consistency." Individual freedom was a metaphysical concept; causality was not. To construe historical phenomena as "causally necessary, that is, as regular," had nothing to do with "metaphysical necessity"; it was instead, Lamprecht declared, a "formal postulate," a "characteristic and indispensable requirement of all scholarly [*wissenschaftlichen*] thought." The historian then closed with an extended discussion of Wilhelm von Humboldt's theory of ideas—evidently in the hope that the excursus would demonstrate the distance between his own theories and the tradition in which Ranke stood.

The renewed polemic between Lamprecht and Rachfahl had a bizarre sequel.[118] In his discussion of the transcendent character of Ranke's ideas, Lamprecht had quoted a passage from Rachfahl's essay that seemed to emphasize just this point, and he had exclaimed, "Exactly my opinion." "He scarcely suspected how right he was," came the rejoinder from Rachfahl, who pointed out that Lamprecht had quoted a paraphrase of his own language. The episode represented another minor humiliation for Lamprecht, but the hasty misreading of his opponent's essay suggested that the issue of his carelessness was more than incidental to the controversy. In fact, this issue now became mortal.

"He is probably a student of Delbrück or Lenz?" Hermann Oncken, who was the object of Lamprecht's inquiry to Liesegang, was indeed a student of Max Lenz.[119] He took his doctorate with Lenz in Berlin in 1891. After serving for three years as an archivist in the ducal archives in his native Oldenburg, he returned to Berlin to habilitate with the same scholar on the strength of a biography of the sixteenth century count Christoph of Oldenburg. The extent of Lenz's influence was evident in Oncken's subsequent work—in his veneration of Ranke, his devotion to the history of the state, his preference for biography, and the fluid line between his scholarship and his politics.[120] Oncken, however, was also at home in the archives, and his skills in criticism later made him one of the country's most distinguished editors of source collections. Shortly before completing his habilitation, he practiced these skills on Lamprecht.

He did so with the encouragement of his mentor. Lenz's review of the fifth volume of the *German History* had noted incidentally that much of Lamprecht's text appeared to comprise long, unattributed, and frequently inaccurate excerpts from standard secondary accounts, such as Friedrich von Bezold's book on the Reformation, Hermann Baumgarten's biography of Charles V, and Ritter's work on the Counter-Reformation. "It would be dreary but easy work," Lenz suggested, to examine the rest of Lamprecht's volume; and he predicted that "every page, in fact practically every line, would give offense."[121] To his student Lenz then recommended some dreary but easy work. After months of this labor, Oncken submitted the results, again on Lenz's recommendation, to Hans Delbrück.[122]

The essay that Hermann Oncken published in the *Preussische Jahrbücher* in July 1897 was one of the most lethal book reviews ever written.[123] It brought virtuosity to the art of *Detailkritik* in a line-by-line examination of sections of Lamprecht's fifth volume, principally its second half, which dealt with political developments in the late sixteenth and early seventeenth centuries. Oncken began with the mistakes—the dates that were wrong (sixteen in a space of one hundred pages), the garbled sequences of events, the misidentified characters, and the manifold inconsistencies or contradictions of fact. There was nothing novel in this kind of exercise, except that Oncken's catalogue delved further into the origins of Lamprecht's errors. In the process it also revealed how the historian had managed to write the volume so rapidly. By means of parallel texts, Oncken demonstrated that Lamprecht had, without even a gesture toward his sources, lifted most of the account from standard surveys by four other scholars—Bezold's, Ritter's, K. Theodor Wenzelburger's on the Netherlands, and Georg Winter's on the Thirty Years' War.[124] Lamprecht had attempted to disguise his sources and, as the reviewer put it, to "appropriate facts" by means of mannered stylistic alterations and ornaments, which Oncken characterized as *Effekthascherei*. But Oncken also proved that the historian could not even plagiarize well, for in his haste Lamprecht had misread the sources, overlooked their nuances and qualifications, and if they were themselves in error, repeated or compounded the mistakes.

As the mass of the revelations built up, Oncken's assault gathered momentum. The grim culmination came when he uncovered additional similarities between Lamprecht's work and Ranke's. In one passage, Lamprecht's source was the popular survey of the Thirty Years' War written by his close friend Winter, the archivist who had announced in 1893 that one could not overlook "the spark of Ranke's spirit" in Lamprecht's work. Oncken showed, again by parallel texts, not only that Lamprecht had drawn his account from Winter's book, but that Winter had in turn lifted much of his text from the third volume of Ranke's *German History in the Era of the Reformation*. "I think," Oncken remarked, "that we have seen in this case the muddy drains [*trübe Kanäle*] through which Ranke's spirit is occasionally absorbed by his worthy epigones."[125] Oncken's judgment was harsh, but on the strength of his evidence he could hardly be accused of exaggerating. Lamprecht's work, he found, was "sloppy in content, sloppy in form":

> . . . an example will not soon be found of an author who copies and plagiarizes his sources in such a fashion, who in like manner lines them up superficially and shuffles them into confusion, who misunderstands and flattens everything that comes into his hands so that he might dress it up in the baubles of his pompous turns-of-phrase and then send it out into the world as his original wisdom.[126]

Oncken later confessed that he looked back on this review with second thoughts, but at the time he wrote it he was fervent.[127] As his recitation of Lamprecht's errors lengthened, his indignation grew. He was convinced that the central issue was moral. Lamprecht had violated the "historian's first and self-evident obligation" to conduct research "conscientiously and thoroughly." Lamprecht's "honesty and self-integrity [*Wahrhaftigkeit gegen sich selber*]" thus stood under indictment. "We are not talking here about ideology," Oncken wrote, "nor about basic views on historical philosophy or writing, nor about the method by which one attains results; we are talking only about the modest virtues of elementary loyalty to one's scholarly obligation."[128]

It would be an exaggeration to say that Oncken's review changed the direction of the *Methodenstreit*. Below and others had already drawn attention to Lamprecht's careless errors; Rachfahl had in fact subjected the same volume to a critique that anticipated Oncken's.[129] But Oncken's review, whose prodigious attention to detail might in other circumstances have made it a wonder of German pedantry, delivered such a massive and thorough indictment of Lamprecht's scholarship that it established the framework within which the historian's whole enterprise was finally judged. Oncken charged that Lamprecht's errors were neither occasional nor inadvertent; nor were they, as Lamprecht was wont to claim, irrelevant to his broader vision of German history. "What are we to make of the grand design [*grossen Zusammenhängen*]," Oncken asked, which is constructed "on the rotten foundation of his research?"[130] Oncken's accusations provided the *Methodenstreit* at last with a common language of discourse, which was geared to the ethic of scholarship; and Lamprecht was compelled to respond in this language, for the central issue was now his own moral failure.

Even as he succumbed to this compulsion, Lamprecht enclosed himself within his illusions. He assured his brother that he had only to deal with the "small aftermath" of a struggle in which he had already triumphed.[131] He informed Harden that he had begun to look more closely at his "detail-opponents" and had found "unbelievable things."[132] Several weeks later Harden learned that "Oncken can be very nicely and calmly pinned to the wall."[133] The historian persuaded himself that Oncken was but the creature of Lenz and Delbrück, who envied Lamprecht's success.[134] "The fight must be concentrated against D. and L.," he told Harden. "O. belongs under the table."[135] In the event, the historian launched a counterattack in the summer and fall of 1897 against all three of his opponents. The polemic now descended into its penultimate phase, in which it resembled low comedy but for the desperation of the man in the role of the clown.[136]

Lamprecht first replied to Oncken in *Die Zukunft*. Here he resorted to equivocation, prevarication, and wild claims. He noted in his own defense that experts in the field had read the proofs of the volume under fire. To the charge that he had made unattributed use of his sources, he pointed to a brief postscript to his fifth volume, in which he had expressed a debt to several scholars, including Bezold, Wenzelburger, Ritter, and Winter, for "large parts of this volume." Besides, he explained, there was no room in his book for footnotes. Some of the factual errors he acknowledged, but he pleaded in extenuation that he had been fatigued when he wrote the book. Then he announced that most of the errors were *Druckfehler*, printers' errors, and that Oncken, who should have recognized them as such, could select a representative to look at the relevant passages of the manuscript. Then Lamprecht declared that the errors were trivial and irrelevant to his argument anyway: they pertained to political history in a period (1550–1650) of "relatively little general significance." To this tired and improbable defense he added a novel theory of historical compilation, according to which "absolutely true" excerpts were impossible to gather. Excerpting from the sources, he explained, inevitably did violence to them, particularly in an enterprise like his own, which required the historian to mold the singularity of political events into the continuities of cultural history. This proposition led to his final defense, which was to impugn his critic. "Who after all is Herr Oncken?" In Lamprecht's judgment, Herr Oncken was a docile tool of Max Lenz and a scholar of little consequence or experience, who was not qualified to "talk about questions of historical composition."[137]

When the historian turned to Delbrück and Lenz, he revealed another device in the repertory of his defenses. He called it employing "the framework of their own charges"; in another idiom it might be called projection.[138] He accused Delbrück of taking over without attribution a number of theories about the early Germanic *Hundertschaften*, which Lamprecht himself had established in the first volume of his *German History*. To document this charge, Lamprecht tried to emulate Oncken and reproduced lengthy excerpts from Delbrück's work and his own; but these demonstrated only the frivolity of Lamprecht's claims, for they revealed that Delbrück had cited his scholarship generously.[139]

Lamprecht dealt at more length with Lenz, but most of his response comprised a feckless attempt to apply *Detailkritik* to Lenz's scholarship. He examined three pages of Lenz's Luther biography; then, on the basis of several superficial similarities, he claimed that Lenz had plagiarized in clumsy fashion from an earlier biography of Luther by Julius Köstlin. Lenz, he announced, had "stumbled even in the simplest cases in making excerpts and compiling."[140] These claims were groundless, too. But they were more convincing than his strictures against Lenz's style (which he called "familiar in the bad sense and sloppy") and against Lenz's use of foreign words, which Lamprecht, whom no one could accuse of a sense of irony, scored as "*moderne Gallizismen und antike Latinismen*."[141]

Lamprecht lacked the patience, as well as the grounds, to subject his opponents' scholarship to the kind of scrutiny that they had given his. The most effective part of his counteroffensive against Lenz came when at long last he defended his interpretation of the Reformation against the substantive objections that Lenz had raised to his central argument—that the dualism of natural and monetary economy caused a widening gulf between town and countryside. In the end, though, Lamprecht confounded his own case. He concluded his defense with a long excursus, which purported to demonstrate, also against Lenz's objections, that popular unrest in both rural and urban areas had a "proletarian" and "socialistic" character in the early sixteenth century. This proposition required the unsuspecting historian to emphasize the close "interconnection [*Zusammenhang*] between town and countryside," which was exactly the argument with which Lenz had attacked his interpretive schema in the first place.[142]

Lenz saw no need to respond.[143] Delbrück did, for he had been challenged in his capacity as editor as well as scholar. He loathed Harden, with whom he was already involved in a nasty dispute over other matters. When Lamprecht criticized his decision to publish Oncken's review, Delbrück lashed back at both the historian and the journalist.[144] After dismissing Lamprecht's charges of unattributed use of material from the *German History*, he not only accepted editorial responsibility for Oncken's review but endorsed Oncken's findings. He could no longer, he declared, ascribe to Lamprecht's *German History*, "any scholarly value at all." Then he threw acid:

> It seems to me that the relationship between Herr Harden and Herr Lamprecht offers the possibility for resolving the dispute to the satisfaction of all parties. Let Lamprecht abandon his claim to be a scholar, let him give up his chair in Leipzig and join the editorial board of *Die Zukunft*. He will then be in the appropriate place for a man of his character and approach to scholarship, and he will never lack the recognition he deserves.

"As far as I am concerned, this dirt does not touch me," came Lamprecht's reply.[145] But Harden now intervened to settle some scores of his own. He reminded Delbrück of the painful dispute with Treitschke in the editorial offices of the *Preussische Jahrbücher*. Harden called his rival a "lamentable, comic figure" in politics, the editor of a "monthly journal that is wasting away," and a historian who had succeeded only in producing "some charming [*hübsche*] things" in his accounts of ancient battles.[146] The two publicists thereupon sued one another for libel. The fact that Delbrück's suit extended to Lamprecht's charge of unattributed borrowing then raised the intriguing prospect that the *Methodenstreit* might be resolved by judicial action.[147]

By the time the court threw out both suits early in 1899, the *Methodenstreit* had been resolved in another forum. Oncken's charges were much more damaging than Delbrück's; and they withstood all Lamprecht's attempts to discredit them. Early in 1898 Oncken counterattacked.[148] He revealed that Lamprecht had refused to grant access to the manuscript as a check for the *Druckfehler*.[149] To Lamprecht's claims that only a handful of errors were genuine and that he had relied on a plethora of sources for his account, Oncken produced another catalogue of mistaken dates and plagiarized passages; this one culminated in a page-by-page demonstration of how Lamprecht had, without a single footnote, based virtually all of a fifty-page passage on Winter's survey. Now Oncken's verdict was savage. He observed that Lamprecht could not have discredited his own theories and methodology more hopelessly than by "trying himself to put them into practice."

Delbrück was not expressing a neutral opinion when he wrote that Oncken's attack had delivered the "death blow" to Lamprecht's vision of history.[150] But Delbrück did speak for the great majority of Germany's academic historians. So did Lenz, who described Lamprecht in November 1897 as "a drowning man who is grasping for planks."[151] The *Historische Zeitschrift* condemned Lamprecht's defense for its "unbelievably weak arguments."[152] Similar sentiments were rife outside the academy as well, even among Lamprecht's erstwhile supporters.[153]

"Worse than weak" was the judgment of Franz Mehring, who was admittedly disappointed over Lamprecht's disavowal of materialism.[154] Perhaps the most telling testimony to the lethal impact of Oncken's revelations came years later, from Lamprecht's student and chronicler Herbert Schönebaum, who was also the most devoted admirer the historian ever had. In his account of the *Methodenstreit*, Schönebaum conceded that Oncken's attack had succeeded; the mass of errors uncovered in his hero's work, he confessed, was "terrifying [*erschreckend*]."[155]

In April 1898 the Association of German Historians congregated in Nuremberg. As in the past, the organization provided a sympathetic forum for Lamprecht. Those in attendance were predominantly archivists, librarians, and secondary teachers; and they included a number of Lamprecht's own students and friends from Leipzig.[156] In this forum the historian was a celebrity, the subject of a long and appreciative article in the local press.[157] The highlight of the congress was a lecture that he delivered to a large and enthusiastic public audience in the city hall. Here he explained how his own theories represented the culmination and synthesis of German historiography since Herder.[158] It was a moment of personal triumph, and it confirmed the historian's own conviction that he had been the victor in the methodological dispute.[159]

The next day, however, a heated debate took place over the origins of feudalism in Germany.[160] At issue was a new hypothesis that feudalism accompanied the Germanic settlement and that bondage did not, as had been commonly thought, emerge only later, after the decline of communal forms of economy that the Germanic tribes had brought with them. The specific issues were less significant than the fact that German academic historians dominated the debate and that, with the exception of Lamprecht, they formed a phalanx in rejecting the new theory as the work of economists, who were unschooled in traditional methods of historical research.

The events in Nuremberg were an apt indication of the situation in the German historical profession as the *Methodenstreit* drew to a close. Lamprecht was the most famous and interesting historian in Germany, and he continued to enjoy sympathy both within segments of the profession and in the broader public. He was utterly isolated, however, in the commanding heights of the profession, where the retreat into traditional concepts and methods was in full order.

In the fall of 1897 Lamprecht wrote Harden that his "absolutely devastating [*schlagende*] arguments" had "checkmated Delbrück as much as it is possible to be checkmated." This conclusion, he confided, was based on the "unambiguous judgment of the people" who had read his attack on the Berlin scholar.[161] Lamprecht's claim did not exaggerate the views of those people who were communicating with him. During the most intense stage of the dispute, the historian received encouragement from a large and devoted group of followers, who included current and former students in Germany and abroad, colleagues in

Leipzig from outside the seminar, and a network of acquaintances in the lower tiers of the historical profession. These people tended to be as extravagant in their praise as the historian's enemies were in their criticism; and the adulation nurtured the same illusions in the historian as did the criticism. "As I have often emphasized to my professional colleagues as well as to laypeople," came one of the more sober messages from a *Gymnasialdirektor* in Nuremberg, "I continually regret that they make much less effort to understand you than to get the better of you."[162] "Your criticism is frequently devastating and delightful," came another.[163] "With what poise and good humor you manage to hit the weaknesses in those insufficiently thought-out arguments," read still another comment on one of Lamprecht's polemical outbursts.[164] Georg Winter, who had himself not fared well in the controversy, suggested the tone of the support for Lamprecht within this circle of admirers when, in 1898, he described his friend as "a young, thoroughly original, brilliant, as well as an incomparably fruitful and creative scholar."[165] Lamprecht's complaint in 1898, that "I am learning nothing" from the dispute, was directed toward his enemies; but it applied with equal force to his friends.[166]

In the places that counted, Lamprecht no longer had any friends. As Hans Schleier has recently pointed out, Lamprecht's performance forged a broad academic alliance, which included the heirs of the Borussian political historians (such as Meinecke), neo-Rankeans, Catholics, and even economic historians like Schmoller.[167] In the face of this front, Althoff, the great patron to them all, could hardly take seriously the assurances from Leipzig that Lamprecht's desperate opponents were fleeing the field.[168] When in April 1898 the historian experienced one of Althoff's notorious snubs, it was a signal that Althoff had abandoned his former protegé.[169]

Others now left him, too. In Bonn Ritter was conspicuously silent.[170] Lamprecht's relations with his old friend Alfred Dove, who in 1897 had returned to scholarship in Freiburg, broke off in a frosty scene in Leipzig after an exchange in print, in which Lamprecht called Dove's view of Ranke naive and Dove chided him in return for misquoting Ranke.[171] The collapse of another friendship was more painful. In 1899 Bernheim commented publicly for the first time on the methodological dispute.[172] His remarks were hard, for they implied that Oncken's criticism was valid on a higher plane as well and that Lamprecht had unwittingly committed a kind of philosophical plagiarism. Although Bernheim exaggerated the case, there was some validity to his argument that Lamprecht had taken basic ideas without acknowledgement from Comte. Bernheim characterized Lamprecht's *German History* as "a concrete application of positivistic principles in the grand style," and he scored his friend's "complete ignorance of the literary context and character of his own work." In the final analysis, he argued, Lamprecht's central idea of cultural epochs, defined now as stages in the nation's psychic development, was "Comte's great principle, which Lamprecht has here unknowingly taken over and applied with a few modifications to our nation's history." Someone less self-absorbed might have anticipated the growing strains on Bernheim's patience, but Lamprecht regarded publication of this commentary as an act of treachery. He broke off all contact in 1899.[173]

Bernheim's charges were particularly painful because they echoed accusations that were hurled with much less hesitancy during the final assault on Lamprecht from the enemy's camp. Meinecke planned to follow up Oncken's attack with a last reckoning over questions of method and theory. His attempt to recruit Dilthey for the effort failed, and he was reluctant himself to contend with what he regarded as Lamprecht's "confused mixture of half-truths and contradictions."[174] In December 1897 he received an offer that he quickly accepted, although he later had reason to regret the decision.

Georg von Below had remained quiet during most of the Methodenstreit, in keeping with the terms of his settlement with Lamprecht in 1894 and because the controversy was pitched at a level of theoretical abstraction at which he was not yet practiced or comfortable.[175] But as the debate intensified, he found silence more difficult; and he began to study the methodological literature in anticipation of entering the fray once more. Meinecke's acceptance of his offer to examine Lamprecht's theories provided both the occasion and some guidelines for his reentry. Below should, Meinecke counseled, present a "short and concise" summary of the dispute; he should emphasize Lamprecht's "horrible confusion" and point out, for the sake of "foreigners" who had the wrong impression, that the reaction in Germany to Lamprecht was due not to hostility to positivism, but to the "dishevelment [Unsauberkeit] of his thought, paired [as it is] with tasteless vanity."[176]

The essay that Below published in the Historische Zeitschrift in July 1898 did not entirely accord with Meinecke's counsel.[177] It was not short and concise. Below gave instead the impression of a man whose long-building frustrations had found release in a torrent. "Even when it is rotten, the tree does not ordinarily fall by itself." Therefore, he announced, "One must use the axe." The axe in this case was to be his own critical commentary on Lamprecht's theories. In the course of it, Below marched through all the issues already raised in the debate—materialism, freedom and necessity, historical laws, individual and collective action, Ranke's theory of ideas, and Lamprecht's carelessness; to no one's surprise, in every instance Below set his flag on the side of Lamprecht's opponents. The thrust of his attack was twofold. In the first place (and here he anticipated Bernheim), he argued that Lamprecht's claim to being the great innovator, the theoretician who had introduced the concept of "genetic" history, rested on his ignorance of his own antecedents. But while Bernheim underscored Lamprecht's debt to Comte, Below introduced the theme that subsequently informed his own writings in historiography; he insisted that credit for introducing a theory of history that featured the collective development of national groups belonged to Herder and the German romantics.

Below's second charge was broader. Lamprecht's theories of development, he argued, had distorted this historiographical tradition beyond recognition and violated the bounds of the historical discipline. Despite Meinecke's suggestion,

Below made no concessions to positivism. He noted that an intellectual system built on the primacy of structures, collective action, historical necessity, causality, laws, and stages of development might well appeal to philosophers, economists, and sociologists in Germany (and, he added with a gesture to Meinecke, to historians abroad); but these postulates were all incompatible with the foundations of German historiography, which in Below's view lay in the primacy of the singular, individual, and contingent in history—in the study of those aspects of the past that resisted schematization in the name of any principle whatsoever.

Below's essay was a tour de force through the now mountainous literature of the *Methodenstreit*. It revealed the extent of his reading in the theoretical literature, in sociology, economics, and in philosophy, where his debt was clear to Dilthey, Wilhelm Windelband, and particularly to Heinrich Rickert.[178] Below also displayed once again the rhetorical skills that made him a fearsome polemicist. But Lamprecht was by now an easy target, and it served only rhetorical purposes to describe him as one of "those courageous men who, in wild and triumphant jubilation, run through open doors."[179] Whether because of the author's difficulty in restraining his enmity or his inexperience in dealing with issues of theory, Below's essay represented a clear retreat from the level to which Hintze and Rachfahl had brought the exchange on theory and method.

Below's axe was dull. His picture of German romanticism was itself romanticized; and Lamprecht had already published a much more discriminating analysis of Herder's place in the development of German historiography.[180] Below's principal difficulty, however, was one he shared with most of the other scholars who participated in the dispute. He subjected his opponent's beliefs to closer examination than he did his own; and he failed to appreciate that the criteria used in his criticism could be turned against his own position. Like Rachfahl, he dismissed causality and historical laws as metaphysical propositions, which Lamprecht had smuggled into his theories in the garb of empirical truths. Below's own position amounted to a paean to individuality, freedom, and variety as the subjects distinctive to the study of history. "Life's highest value for man," he wrote, "lies in the fact that he can develop independently, that he can achieve something, that he is an individuality."[181] Below did not address the epistemological foundation of this proposition, and his occasional remarks suggested his confusion. In the end, though, it was clear that he arrogated for his own premise the status that he denied to Lamprecht's. "The formation of the concept of personality" Below called "a product of properly understood empiricism."[182] The historian, he explained in another passage, "sees himself everywhere compelled [*genöthigt*] to confirm empirically the individualism of human actions."[183]

The truth of the principle of individuality—its power to prescribe the historian's agenda and his perspective on the past—was self-evident to Below. That he felt compelled to justify it at all was a sign of his apprehensions. In his eyes, Lamprecht's theories threatened the autonomy of the German historical profession, whose corporate identity rested alone on a common commitment to individuality in the study of the past. Below observed that Ranke and "every normal German historian" emphasized the "moment of freedom" in history.[184] For a historian to embrace causal explanation would be to "renounce the autonomy of his discipline."[185] But Below also inadvertently conceded that the relationship between paradigm and corporate solidarity was reciprocal. In a passage that revealed that Lamprecht had no monopoly on naiveté, Below wrote that "unprejudiced historical observation of the particularities of the course of history" was the most powerful antidote against a "materialistic view of history." "Why after all," he continued, "are there, for all intents and purposes, no adherents of materialism among academic historians?"[186]

Below's impassioned essay did not bring the execution of Lamprecht (that distinction belonged elsewhere); but it did help explain why there were no materialists among the academic historians in Germany. The essay provided the most ingenuous statement of the corporate anxieties that had fueled opposition to Lamprecht during the dispute.[187] Below's position was that Lamprecht represented the importation of the tools of the natural sciences into history. Lamprecht's triumph would signal the abandonment of the distinctive methods and research agenda that had defined the historical discipline's autonomy. In Below's commentary the political motif was never far from the surface, so that Lamprecht's enterprise took on the connotations of treachery to the profession; Lamprecht's success would mean history's capitulation to forces with which it stood in "irreconcilable, hostile opposition."[188] That Below used *feindlich* to describe history's relationship to the natural sciences suggested the power of professional resistance to innovation of any kind.

"A bunch of nonsense," was Lamprecht's instinctive reaction. "Let them cook in their own fat; I have more positive things to do."[189] He quickly changed his mind and drew up a long response to Below, which Meinecke agreed to distribute as a supplement to the *Historische Zeitschrift* in January 1899.[190] This essay was more coherent than many of his others, but it did nothing to still the professional anxieties that Below had addressed. With an appeal to Kant, Lamprecht tore down the disciplinary walls that Below had sought to construct around history. Lamprecht's argument suggested that he, too, had read Rickert, but his premise was that individuality and singularity were simply not categories of systematic thought (*Wissenschaft*). Systematic thought, he insisted, was based on judgment (*Urteil*), which entailed comparison (*Vergleich*), which in turn entailed subsuming the individual within the typical, general, and regular. But these principles, drawn from what he called "today's epistemological theory," had far-reaching ontological consequences.[191] "The individual is, from the standpoint of our view today—and probably forever—irrational and therefore an object not of scholarship but of art. This principle applies to the individual equally as a physical and a psychic entity."[192] In order to survive as a scholarly discipline, Lamprecht wrote, history had to stand on the "firm ground" of the "recognized principles of the epistemological theory of its day."[193] This epistemological imperative dictated a single methodology for understanding all realms of existence. And the practical consequence was that historians had to accept cultural history "as the *historische Grundwissenschaft*," the basis of the discipline of history.[194]

Lamprecht devoted the bulk of this essay to describing the basis of the discipline in terms that were familiar to anyone who had even casually followed the dispute in the profession. In one passage, though, the historian briefly laid open the most troubling but least-mentioned issue in the dispute. Below's repudiation of all historical schematization in the name of historical contingency implied a consequential relativism. On this ground, Below had dismissed Lamprecht's theories, but not his own. Well might Lamprecht condemn Below's "profoundly dogmatic position," his penchant for "discovering the relative" in history while exempting his own methodological principles, and his "latent conviction that he need only assert while others try modestly to provide evidence."[195] The great problem was of course that Below could, with equal justification, make the same claims of Lamprecht, whose methodological views rested no less insecurely on an idiosyncratic reading of Kant.

Lamprecht's reply was haughty in the extreme, in part because he hoped to provoke his opponent into prolonging the polemic. Below reacted as anticipated and demanded that Meinecke permit him a full rebuttal in the *Historische Zeitschrift*. Meinecke, however, had had enough. "For God's sake no more," he pleaded with Below, who, he now realized, was not the one to drive Lamprecht from the field.[196] "The man is not yet to be silenced," he wrote. "He is a hydra." In these circumstances Meinecke concluded, as he instructed Below, that the way to deal with Lamprecht, at least for the time being, was "to let him scrawl away."[197]

Meinecke's thinking prevailed. Below contented himself with a brief reply to Lamprecht early in 1899, after which the academic historians fell silent.[198] For all practical purposes, the *Methodenstreit* was over. It ended in an unambiguous verdict on Lamprecht. It also brought the German historical discipline's rededication to practices that both Georg von Below and Thomas Kuhn could characterize as normal.

Notes

1. Czok, *Lamprechts Wirken*, 13; Schleier, "Der Kulturhistoriker," 25.
2. See Kurt Bayertz, *Wissenschaftstheorie und Paradigmabegriff* (Stuttgart, 1981); *cf.* David A. Hollinger, "T. S. Kuhn's Theory of Science and Its Implications for History," AHR, 78 (1973): esp. 378–89; Thomas S. Kuhn, "Second Thoughts on Paradigms," *The Essential Tension: Selected Studies in Scientific Tradition and Change* (Chicago and London, 1977), 293–319; Jörn Rüsen, *Historische Vernunft: Grundzüge einer Historik I. Die Grundlagen der Geschichtswissenschaft* (Göttingen, 1983), 24–29; Horst Walter Blanke, *Historiographiegeschichte als Historik* (Stuttgart-Bad Cannstatt, 1991), 393–439; Richard Rorty, *Philosophy and the Mirror of Nature* (Princeton, 1979), 322–33.

3. See Richard Terdiman, *Discourse/Counter-Discourse: The Theory and Practice of Symbolic Resistance in Nineteenth-Century France* (Ithaca, 1985), esp. 54–59; *cf.* Walsh, 95.
4. Engelberg, "Methodenstreit," 147–48; *cf.* Hans Schleier, "Die Auseinandersetzung mit der Rankeschen Tradition Ende des 19. Jh. in Deutschland: Die deutschen Historiker und die Herausforderungen an die Geschichtswissenschaft," *Jahrbuch für Geschichte*, 32 (1985): 271–87; Iggers, "Image of Ranke," 18.
5. Krieger, 9; *cf.* Krill, esp. 80–81, 105, 256–57; Schleier, "Ranke-Renaissance," 111.
6. Quoted in Lamprecht, "Was ist Kulturgeschichte?" 147–48, n. 2.
7. Erdmann, "Geschichte, Politik und Pedagogik," 394. The words are Alfred Dove's.
8. Alexander Demandt, "Natur- und Geschichtswissenschaft im 19. Jahrhundert," *HZ*, 237 (1983): 58.
9. See Blanke, "*Historik*," 341, 350; Dietrich Fischer, "Die deutsche Geschichtswissenschaft von Droysen bis Hintze in ihrem Verhältnis zu Soziologie," Ph.D. dissertation (Cologne, 1966), 11.
10. NL Lamprecht (Korr. 8), Arnold Berger to Lamprecht, Bonn, 22.11.96. "Sie haben sich bei der Neuheit des Versuchs gewissermassen eine neue Sprache schaffen müssen."
11. LW, 330.
12. *Bericht über die vierte Versammlung deutscher Historiker zu Innsbruck 11. bis 14. September 1896* (Leipzig, 1897), 38–46; Schumann, *Historikertage*, 79–82.
13. NL Lamprecht (Korr. 35), Liesegang to Lamprecht, Berlin, 29.9.96.
14. NL Liesegang, Lamprecht to Liesegang, Leipzig, 30.9.96; NL Harden, Lamprecht to Harden, Leipzig, 18.9.96.
15. Bernd Mütter, *Die Geschichtswissenschaft in Münster zwischen Aufklärung und Historismus* (Münster, 1980), 251–83; Mütter, "Die Geschichtswissenschaft in der alten Universität und Akademie Münster von der Aufklärung bis zum Historismus (1773 bis 1902)," *Westfälische Zeitschrift*, 126/27 (1978): 158–61; Goetz, *Historiker*, 246–55; *HZ*, 160 (1939): 534–45; *NDB*, 5: 162; Weber, *Lexikon*, 147.
16. Mütter, 261–71; Christof Weber, "Heinrich Finke zwischen akademischer Imparität und kirchlichem Antiliberalismus," *Annalen des Historischen Vereins für den Niederrhein*, 186 (1983): 139–65.
17. Finke, "Finke," in S. Steinberg, 1: 106–8; *cf.* Helga Oesterreich, "Die Geschichtswissenschaft an der Universität Münster," in Heinz Dollinger, ed., *Die Universität Münster 1789–1980* (Münster, 1980), 352. In 1890 Lamprecht used his influence with Mevissen to block Finke's appointment to an archival position in Cologne, for which he favored his friend Joseph Hansen; but there is no evidence that Finke knew of Lamprecht's role. NL Mevissen, Lamprecht to Mevissen, Marburg, 28.10.90, *cf.* Kleinertz, 276–77.
18. Max Braubach, "Zwei deutsche Historiker aus Westfalen: Briefe Heinrich Finkes an Aloys Schulte," *Westfälische Zeitschrift*, 118 (1968): 10, 26.
19. *Die kirchenpolitischen und kirchlichen Verhältnisse zu Ende des Mittelalters nach der Darstellung K. Lamprechts: Eine Kritik seiner "Deutschen Geschichte"* (Rome, 1896).
20. Ibid., 96.
21. Ibid., 19.
22. Ibid., vi, 18.
23. Ibid., 20, 28–29, 36–38, 42, 119.
24. Ibid., 104.
25. LW, 313–14.
26. DZfG (Monatsblätter), N. F. 1 (1896–97): 267–75.
27. Ibid., 273.
28. Ibid., 269.
29. Ibid., 274–75.

30. Ibid., 270, n. 1. Finke's reproach was admittedly repeated, but it was neither unmotivated nor concealed.
31. Finke, *Genetische und klerikale Geschichtsauffassung: Eine Antwort an Professor Dr. Karl Lamprecht* (Münster, 1897); Finke, "Erklärung," DZfG (Monatsblätter), N. F. 2 (1897–98): 46; Lamprecht, "Gegenerklärung," ibid, 46–55.
32. "Finke haben Sie wunderhübsch heimgeleuchtet. Diese Ultramontanen behandelt man gewiss am besten mit leise-überlegenem Spott." NL Lamprecht (Korr. 23), Geffken to Lamprecht, Leipzig, 5.1.97; (Korr. 29), Helmolt to Lamprecht, Leipzig, 5.1.97.
33. Gustav Schnürer, "Lamprechts Deutsche Geschichte," HJb, 18 (1897): 88–116; *cf.* Schnürer, "Zum Streite über Lamprechts deutsche Geschichte," ibid., 21 (1900): 776–85.
34. Finke, "Finke," 106–8; DG 1 (2): ix; *cf.* Schleier, "Der Kulturhistoriker," 21.
35. Friedrich Graefe, ed., *Max Lenz zum Gedächtnis: Lebenslauf und Gedenkaufsätze* (Berlin, 1935); Otto Westphal, "Max Lenz (1850–1932)," *Hansische Geschichtsblätter*, 57 (1932): 29–37; Felix Rachfahl, "Max Lenz und die deutsche Geschichtswissenschaft," HZ, 123 (1921): 189–220; HZ, 147 (1932–1933): 265–68; Srbik, 2: 6–9; NDB, 14: 231–33; Weber, *Lexikon*, 343–44.
36. On Lenz's historiography, the literature on the "Ranke-Renaissance" is instructive. Krill, *Ranke-Renaissance*; Schleier, "Ranke-Renaissance"; Wolfgang J. Mommsen, "Ranke and the Neo-Rankean School in Imperial Germany: State-Oriented Historiography as a Stabilizing Force," in Georg G. Iggers and James M. Powell, eds., *Leopold von Ranke and the Shaping of the Historical Discipline* (Syracuse, NY, 1990), 124–40. See also John L. Herkless, "Ein unerklärtes Element in der Historiographie von Max Lenz," HZ, 222 (1976): 81–104.
37. HZ, 267 (1932–1933): 267; *cf.* Krill, 13, 256–57.
38. See Ludwig Dehio, "Ranke and German Imperialism" in *Germany and World Politics in the Twentieth Century* (London, 1965), 38–71; *cf.* Charles E. McClelland, *The German Historians and England: A Study in Nineteenth-Century Views* (Cambridge, 1971), 210–11.
39. HZ, 222 (1932–1933): 267.
40. NL Lamprecht (Kr. 10), Hinneberg to Lamprecht, Berlin, 19.9.93.
41. NL Sybel (B1 Nr. 26), Lenz to Sybel, Breslau, 15.11.89. Lenz also had positive things to say in 1891 about Bernheim, Hoeniger, and Jastrow. NL Althoff (A I Nr. 73), Lenz to Althoff, 5.7.91, 4.11.91.
42. Lamprecht himself was convinced that they did. DZfG (Monatsblätter), N. F., 2 (1897–1898): 50.
43. Lenz to Erdmannsdörffer, Berlin, 20.10.90, 23.12.90, quoted in Oestreich, "Fachhistorie," 331–32, n. 44. In the earlier letter Lenz announced that he disapproved of Lamprecht's *Economic Life in the Middle Ages* as well: "ich kannte sie nicht, missbilligte sie aber."
44. NL Liesegang, Lamprecht to Liesegang, Leipzig, 3.2.94.
45. NL Lamprecht (Kr. 10), Liesegang and Hoeniger to Lamprecht, Berlin [January 1894]; Lamprecht to Lenz, Leipzig, 22.1.94.
46. NL Meinecke (Nachtrag 1), Meinecke to Below, Berlin, 24.4.94.
47. NL Althoff (B Nr. 112/2), Lenz to Althoff, Berlin, 12.10.96; NL Delbrück, Rachfahl to Delbrück, Breslau, 9.4.96; NL Harden, Lamprecht to Harden, Leipzig, 18.9.96; Schultz, "Moral Force," 206.
48. Max Lenz, "Lamprecht's Deutsche Geschichte, 5. Band," HZ, 77 (1896): 385–447; NL Harden, Lamprecht to Harden, Leipzig, 18.9.96. Meinecke wrote to Below that the review "pleased him very well." NL Meinecke (Nachtrag 1), Meinecke to Below, Berlin, 9.8.96.
49. HZ, 77: 442.

50. Ibid., 410.
51. Ibid., 445–46.
52. Lamprecht, "Zum Unterschiede der älteren und jüngeren Richtungen der Geschichtswissenschaft," HZ, 77 (1896): 259, n. 1.
53. See "Alte und neue Richtungen," iii; "Was ist Kulturgeschichte?" 76; DZfG, N. F. 2 (1897–1898): 50.
54. NL Bernheim, Lamprecht to Bernheim, Leipzig, 27.10.96; NL Harden, Lamprecht to Harden, Leipzig, 18.9.96.
55. NL Liesegang, Lamprecht to Liesegang, Leipzig, 30.9.96.
56. "Die geschichtswissenschaftlichen Probleme der Gegenwart," Zukunft, 17 (1896): 247–55, 300–311.
57. Ibid., 306.
58. Ibid., 305.
59. Ibid., 251.
60. Ibid., 248.
61. NL Lamprecht (Korr. 59), Lamprecht to Hugo Lamprecht, Leipzig, 3.3.96.
62. NL Lamprecht (Korr. 59), Lamprecht to Hugo Lamprecht, Leipzig, 1.5.96.
63. NL Lamprecht (Korr. 59), Lamprecht to Hugo Lamprecht, Leipzig, 14.11.96.
64. NL Lamprecht (Korr. 59), Lamprecht to Hugo Lamprecht, Leipzig, 12.10.96; (Korr. 31), Hoeniger to Lamprecht, Berlin, 21.1.98.
65. NL Lamprecht (Korr. 59), Lamprecht to Hugo Lamprecht, Leipzig, 25.9.97.
66. NL Mevissen, Lamprecht to Mevissen, Leipzig, 2.5.97; LW, 328, 336–37.
67. NL Mevissen, Lamprecht to Mevissen, Leipzig, 27.12.96; LW, 337.
68. NL Lamprecht (Korr. 59), Lamprecht to Hugo Lamprecht, Leipzig, 26.6.96; NL Mevissen, Lamprecht to Mevissen, Leipzig, 26.10.97; NL Liesegang, Lamprecht to Liesegang, Leipzig, 31.7.98.
69. NL Goetz (36), Lamprecht to Ritter, Leipzig, 5.1.13.
70. DG 1 (2): vi.
71. "Die geschichtswissenschaftlichen Probleme der Gegenwart," 247.
72. "Was ist Kulturgeschichte?" 145.
73. Ibid., 130.
74. See Metz, Grundformen, 537.
75. To this extent, all the participants in the Methodenstreit were noble dreamers. See Peter Novick, That Noble Dream: The Objectivity Question in the American Historical Profession (Cambridge and New York, 1988).
76. NL Grimm, Lamprecht to Grimm, Leipzig, 4.1.97.
77. "Was ist Kulturgeschichte?" 127.
78. Seeliger, "Lamprecht," 134.
79. Willy Hellpach, "Geschichte als Sozialpsychologie, zugleich eine Epikrise über Karl Lamprecht," Kultur- und Universalgeschichte: Walter Goetz zu seinem 60. Geburtstage (Leipzig and Berlin, 1927), 511. There is a sensitive discussion of this problem in Metz, Grundformen, 471.
80. See Koht, "Lehrjahren," 156; Metz, Grundformen, 472.
81. NL Harden, Lamprecht to Harden, Leipzig, 10.8.96.
82. NL Liesegang, Lamprecht to Liesegang, Leipzig, 7.7.95.
83. Frye, 43–48.
84. NL Althoff (B Nr. 108/1), Lamprecht to Althoff, Leipzig, 15.9.97.
85. Hellpach, "Geschichte als Sozialpsychologie," 511; see White, Metahistory, 8–9.
86. See Schmoller, "Würdigung," 38–39; Kötzschke, "Lamprecht," 27; Viikari, Krise, 260; Spiess, 23; Sirbik, 2: 234.
87. NL Lamprecht (Korr. 59), Lamprecht to Hugo Lamprecht, Leipzig. 10.10.98; Goetz, "Goetz," 155.

88. Braubach, "Briefe Büchers," 399.
89. NL Lamprecht (Korr. 39), Neuwirth to Lamprecht, Prague, 8.1.97; (Korr. 2), Sigmund Adler to Lamprecht, Vienna, 10.1.97; (Korr. 27), Lamprecht to Hannak, Leipzig, 22.6.99; (Korr. 56), Zwiedinek to Lamprecht, Graz, 15.1.97; E. Hannak, "Lamprechts Deutsche Geschichte und die neue Richtung in der Geschichtswissenschaft," *Zeitschrift für das österreichische Gymnasium* (1897), 293–308; Henri Pirenne, "Une polémique historique en Allemagne," Rh, 62 (1897): 50–57; F. Neubauer, "Die Kulturgeschichte auf den höheren Lehranstalten," *Zeitschrift für das Gymnasialwesen*, 41 ((1897): 257–66; Mathieu Schwann, "Lamprechts Deutsche Geschichte," *Zukunft*, 15 (1896): 120–25. Lamprecht himself suggested Schwann to Harden as a reviewer. See also Lamprecht, "Neuere Litteratur zu den historisch-methodologischen Erörterungen," DZfG, N. F. 2 (1897–1898): 121–23.
90. Steinhausen, "Der Streit um die Kulturgeschichte," *Die Nation*, Nr. 51 (19.9.96): 763–66; *cf.* LW, 330–31.
91. NL Marcks (74), Schmoller to Marcks, 28.6.98; Viikari, *Krise*, 115.
92. Lamprecht himself, in all events, believed that Schmoller had taken his side. NL Harden, Lamprecht to Harden, Leipzig, 18.9.96.
93. "Die Beurteilung Rankes durch K. Lamprecht," *Sitzungsberichte der Historischen Gesellschaft zu Berlin*, 258. Sitzung (8.6.96); *Bericht über die vierte Versammlung deutscher Historiker*, 42–45; Schultz, "Moral Force," 125; LW, 317–18, 329–30.
94. Schmoller, "Zur Würdigung," 29.
95. NL Liesegang, Lamprecht to Liesegang, Leipzig, 12.9.96; Schmoller, "Zur Würdigung," 28, 51; Popper, 140; *cf.* Schmoller, *Grundriss der allgemeinen Volkswirtschaftslehre*, 2 vols. (Leipzig, 1904–1908), 2: 663–64.
96. Schönebaum, "Lamprecht und Bernheim," 231–36, is not reliable.
97. NL Lamprecht (Korr. 9), Bernheim to Lamprecht, Greifswald, 16.7.93. Schönebaum, "Lamprecht und Bernheim," 232, has misread the word "Versöhnung" in this letter as "Erörterung."
98. Bernheim, *Lehrbuch der Historischen Methode*, 2d ed. (Leipzig, 1894), vi.
99. StA Dresden, VB 10281/203, Helmolt to Waentig, Dresden, 18.12.09. Schönebaum has blown the issue of Bernheim's failed candidacy into the cause of the breach between the two men. "Lamprecht und Bernheim," 233; LW, 267. The episode caused disappointment on both sides, and perhaps some ill will on Bernheim's, but the breach occurred four years later over another issue.
100. See Bernheim, *Lehrbuch der Historischen Methode und der Geschichtsphilosophie*, 3d ed., 2 vols. (Leipzig, 1908), 2: 715–17. Here Bernheim noted that he had emphasized the importance of Comte in his primer, *Geschichtsforschung und Geschichtsphilosophie*, which he published in 1880 ("long before there was any talk of Lamprecht") and which Lamprecht had himself repeatedly cited. Bernheim's primer grew out of discussions that he had conducted with his students in Göttingen. Bernheim had on another occasion drawn Lamprecht's attention to the similarities in his work to the ideas of Comte. NL Lamprecht (Korr. 9), Bernheim to Lamprecht, Greifswald, 24.4.89. At the end of 1897, Lamprecht confessed to his friend that as a student he "had been the most excited by you and learned the most from you about things that really have to do with history." NL Bernheim, Lamprecht to Bernheim, Leipzig, 31.12.97. See also Simon, *European Positivism*, 243–4.
101. "Der Streit zwischen politischer und Kulturgeschichte," *Beilage zur Münchner Allgemeinen Zeitung*, Nr. 262 (1893); *cf.* Ritter, *Die Entwicklung der Geschichtswissenschaft an den führenden Werken betrachtet* (Munich and Berlin, 1919), 421–61.
102. "Die geschichtswissenschaftliche Probleme der Gegenwart," 304, 306–7.
103. NL Lamprecht (Korr. 45), Ritter to Lamprecht, Bonn, 30.11.96.
104. See Felix Gilbert, "Otto Hintze 1861–1940," in Gilbert, ed., *The Historical Essays*

of Otto Hintze (New York, 1975), 3–30; Jürgen Kocka, "Otto Hintze," in Wehler, *Historiker*, 3: 41–64; Otto Büsch and Michael Erbe, eds., *Otto Hintze und die moderne Geschichtswissenschaft* (Berlin, 1983); Heinrich Otto Meisner, "Otto Hintzes Lebenswerk," HZ, 164 (1941): 66–90; NDB, 9: 194–96; Weber, *Lexikon*, 241–42.

105. Lamprecht was so impressed that he attempted to recruit Hintze to write the volume on Prussia in the Perthes series. Although Hintze eventually declined, citing his work on the *Acta Borussica*, the correspondence between the two remained cordial throughout: NL Lamprecht (Korr. 67b), Hintze to Lamprecht, Berlin, 1.2.96.

106. NL Meinecke (Nachtrag 1), Meinecke to Below, Berlin, 16.10.99; *cf.* Friedrich Meinecke, *Ausgewählter Briefwechsel*, ed. Ludwig Dehio and Peter Classen (Stuttgart, 1962), 19.

107. Meinecke, *Schriften*, 123. See Winfried Schulze, "Friedrich Meinecke und Otto Hintze," in Michael Erbe, ed., *Friedrich Meinecke Heute* (Berlin, 1981), 122–36.

108. "Ueber individualistische und kollektivistische Geschichtsauffassung," HZ, 78 (1897): 60–67. The essay appears in English translation as "The Individualist and the Collective Approach to History," in Gilbert, *Historical Essays*, 357–67. See Schleier, "Ranke-Renaissance," 117; Metz, *Grundformen*, 504.

109. Schulze, "Otto Hintze und die deutsche Geschichtswissenschaft um 1900," in Hammerstein, *Geschichtswissenschaft um 1900*, 327.

110. NL Harden, Lamprecht to Harden, Leipzig, 29.11.96.

111. NL Grimm, Lamprecht to Grimm, Leipzig, 30.11.96.

112. "Eine Wendung im geschichtswissenschaftlichen Streit," *Zukunft*, 18 (1897): 23–33.

113. NL Lamprecht (Korr. 35), Liesegang to Lamprecht, Berlin, 5.5.97.

114. The exchange continued indirectly without resolution for the next several years. NL Lamprecht (Korr. 31), Hintze to Lamprecht, Berlin, 24.4.98; HVjs, 3 (1900): 448–49.

115. "Was ist Kulturgeschichte?" 147.

116. "Ueber die Theorie einer 'kollektivistischen' Geschichtswissenschaft," JbNöSt, 68 (1897): 659–89. The article appeared here after Rachfahl had been turned away by Schmoller, who was unsympathetic; by Meinecke, who was trying to convince Dilthey to write about methodological questions; and by Delbrück, who was planning something else to present to Lamprecht. NL Delbrück, Rachfahl to Delbrück, Kiel, 15.1.97.

117. "Individualität, Idee und sozialpsychische Kraft in der Geschichte," JBNöSt, 68 (1897): 880–900; *cf.* Schultz, "Moral Force," 258–59.

118. JbNöSt, 68 (1897): 901–2.

119. NL Liesegang, Lamprecht to Liesegang, Leipzig, 7.7.97. On Oncken see Klaus Schwabe, "Hermann Oncken," in Wehler, *Historiker*, 2: 81–97; Felix Hirsch, "Hermann Oncken and the End of an Era," JMH, 18 (1946): 148–58; Goetz, *Historiker*, 377–79; Weber, *Lexikon*, 424–25.

120. Rüdiger vom Bruch, *Wissenschaft, Politik und öffentliche Meinung: Gelehrtenpolitik im Wilhelminischen Deutschland (1890–1914)* (Husum, 1980), 215–26.

121. HZ, 77 (1896): 443.

122. Oncken himself insisted that Lenz did not inspire the attack on Lamprecht—that he himself decided to write it on the basis of his "private studies," that he wrote it "from start to finish without any influence from elsewhere," and that he decided independently to send it to Delbrück, whom he did not know at the time. *Lamprechts Verteidigung* (Berlin, 1898), 13; LW, 363–64. Despite both Oncken's testimony and his own, it is difficult to believe that Lenz was not involved. In February 1897 Oncken sent Delbrück the manuscript with the remark: "Falls Sie

den Aufsatz Herrn Prof. Lenz, der s. Z. die Güte hatte, zuerst mit Ihnen darüber zu sprechen, mitzuteilen für gut halten sollen, so würde ich nichts dagegen einzuwenden haben." NL Delbrück, Oncken to Delbrück, Berlin, 16.2.97.

123. "Zur Quellenanalyse modernster deutscher Geschichtsschreibung," PJb, 89 (1897): 83–125.

124. Friedrich von Bezold, *Geschichte der deutschen Reformation* (Berlin, 1890); Moriz Ritter, *Deutsche Geschichte im Zeitalter der Gegenreformation und des Dreissigjährigen Krieges (1555–1648)* (Stuttgart, 1889); K. Theodor Wenzelburger, *Geschichte der Niederlande*, 2 vols. (Gotha, 1879–1886); Georg Winter, *Geschichte des dreissigjährigen Krieges* (Berlin, 1893).

125. Ibid., 117.

126. Ibid., 119.

127. StA Oldenburg (271–314), NL Hermann Oncken, Johannes Haller to Oncken, Tübingen, 18.3.17. From Berlin, Robert Hoeniger reported that Oncken was "no malicious character. He has merely become honestly indignant, in his rather narrow-minded way, over the small errors that he was able to uncover in your *German History.*"

128. "Quellenanalyse," 122.

129. MIöG, 17 (1896): 468–78.

130. Oncken, "Quellenanalyse," 121.

131. NL Lamprecht (Korr. 59), Lamprecht to Hugo Lamprecht, Leipzig, 27.7.97.

132. NL Harden, Lamprecht to Harden, Leipzig, 11.7.97.

133. NL Harden, Lamprecht to Harden, Leipzig, 6.9.97.

134. NL Liesegang, Lamprecht to Liesegang, Leipzig, 7.7.97.

135. NL Harden, Lamprecht to Harden, Leipzig, 15.11.97.

136. "Der Ausgang des geschichtswissenschaftlichen Kampfes," *Zukunft*, 20 (1897): 195–208; "Meine Gegner," ibid., 21 (1897): 109–21, 199–208, 240–252; *Zwei Streitschriften, den Herren H. Oncken, H. Delbrück, M. Lenz zugeeignet* (Berlin, 1897); PJb, 89 (1897): 348–52.

137. "Meine Gegner," 202–3.

138. NL Harden, Lamprecht to Harden, Leipzig, 7.9.97.

139. "Meine Gegner," 203–8.

140. Ibid., 240–46.

141. *Streitschriften*, 49.

142. Ibid., 72–73.

143. HZ, 80 (1898): 342–43.

144. "Lamprechts Deutsche Geschichte," PJb, 90 (1897): 521–24.

145. "Epilog," *Zukunft*, 22 (1898): 448–50.

146. Ibid., 450–53.

147. NL Harden, Lamprecht to Harden, Leipzig, 3.6.98; NL Delbrück, Below to Delbrück, Marburg, 14.12.98; Delbrück, "Herr Lamprecht und Herr Harden," PJb, 92 (1898): 175; ibid., 95 (1899): 391–92, 552–55. Delbrück was prepared to produce Otto von Gierke, who had once thought highly of Lamprecht's work, to testify as an expert witness against Lamprecht's charge of unattributed borrowing. See also Weller, 357; Young, 75.

148. *Lamprechts Verteidigung: Eine Antwort auf Zwei Streitschriften* (Berlin, 1898).

149. Ibid., 15. NL Delbrück, Oncken to Delbrück, Berlin, 6.11.97. For Lamprecht's second thoughts about letting Oncken see the manuscript: NL Harden, Lamprecht to Harden, Leipzig, 15.11.97.

150. PJb, 90 (1897): 521.

151. NL Marcks (72), Lenz to Marcks, Berlin, 12.11.97.

152. HZ, 80 (1898): 156–57.

153. NL Meinecke (Nachtrag 1), Meinecke to Below, Berlin, 30.7.97.
154. "Das Zeitalter der Reizsamkeit," *Gesammelte Schriften*, 7: 512.
155. LW, 364; *cf.* Viikari, *Krise*, 424.
156. *Bericht über die fünfte Versammlung deutscher Historiker zu Nürnberg 12. bis 15. April 1898* (Leipzig, 1898).
157. Schumann, *Historikertage*, 102–19.
158. "Die Entwicklung der deutschen Geschichtswissenschaft vornehmlich seit Herder," Beilage zur *Allgemeinen Zeitung*, Nr. 83 (15.4.98); *cf.* "Die Entwicklungstufen der deutschen Geschichtswissenschaft," ZKg, 5 (1898): 385–438; 6 (1899): 1–45.
159. LW, 379–80.
160. *Bericht über die fünfte Versammlung*, 40–47.
161. NL Harden, Lamprecht to Harden, Leipzig, 21.10.97.
162. NL Lamprecht (Korr. 51), Vogt to Lamprecht, Nuremberg, 5.2.98.
163. NL Lamprecht (Korr. 5), Baldamus to Lamprecht, 25.1.99.
164. NL Lamprecht (Korr. 8), Berger to Lamprecht, Berlin, 25.1.99.
165. Georg Winter, "Karl Lamprecht," *Die Gesellschaft*, 17 (1898): 299.
166. NL Mevissen. Lamprecht to Mevissen, Leipzig, 7.6.98.
167. Schleier, "Der Kulturhistoriker," 21.
168. Althoff was besieged from all sides during the controversy. NL ALthoff (B Nr. 108/1), Lamprecht to Althoff, Leipzig, 4.1.97, 15.9.97; (B Nr. 9/2), Below to Althoff, Münster, 14.3.96; (B Nr. 30/2), Dove to Althoff, Freiburg, 29.7.98; (B Nr. 112/2), Lenz to Althoff, Berlin, 12.10.96.
169. NL Harden, Lamprecht to Harden, Leipzig, 26.4.98.
170. NL Mevissen, Lamprecht to Mevissen, Leipzig, 4.3.98.
171. NL Lamprecht (Korr. 19), Dove to Lamprecht, Freiburg, 25.1.99; NL Dove, Lamprecht to Dove, Leipzig, 23.11.06. Dove had already concluded that Lamprecht's position was untenable. M. Below, *Below*, 74–75.
172. "Geschichtsunterricht und Geschichtswissenschaft," *Pädagogische Zeit- und Streitfragen*, 10 (1899): 1–56, esp. 21–26.
173. NL Bernheim, Lamprecht to Bernheim, Leipzig, 15.11.99. This was the last letter, addressed cooly to "Hochverehrter Herr Kollege." Lamprecht continued, however, to deny his dependence on Comte. MG, 89.
174. NL Meinecke (Nachtrag 1), Meinecke to Below, Berlin, 1.12.97.
175. See Below, "Die städtische Verwaltung des Mittelalters als Vorbild der späteren Territorialverwaltung," HZ, 75 (1895): 404, n. 2.
176. NL Meinecke (Nachtrag 1), Meinecke to Below, Berlin, 1.12.97; Meinecke, *Briefwechsel*, 15–16.
177. "Die neue historische Methode," HZ, 81 (1898): 193–273.
178. See PJb, 92 (1898): 542–51.
179. "Neue historische Methode," 220.
180. Lamprecht, "Herder und Kant als Theoretiker der Geschichtswissenschaft," JbNöSt, 69 (1897): 161–203; *cf.* HZ, 80 (1898): 157.
181. Below, "Neue historische Methode," 244.
182. Ibid., 248, n.
183. Ibid., 247.
184. Ibid., 220.
185. Ibid., 248.
186. Ibid., 242, n.
187. *Cf.* Engelberg, "Methodenstreit," 146.
188. Below, "Neue historiche Methode," 245.
189. NL Liesegang, Lamprecht to Liesegang, Leipzig, 31.7.98.
190. *Die historische Methode des Herrn von Below: Eine Kritik* (Berlin, 1899); *cf.* "Die

Kernpunkte der geschichtswissenschaftlichen Erörterungen der Gegenwart," *Zeitschrift für Socialwissenschaft*, 2 (1899): 11–18.
191. *Historische Methode*, 11.
192. Ibid., 14–15.
193. Ibid., 47.
194. Ibid., 48–49.
195. Ibid., 29.
196. NL Meinecke (Nachtrag 1), Meinecke to Below, Berlin, 22.1.99.
197. NL Meinecke (Nachtrag 1), Meinecke to Below, Berlin, 18.1.99; Meinecke, *Briefwechsel*, 16–17.
198. DLZ, (11.2.99): 247–48; HZ, 82 (1899): 567–68.

8

Banishment

Objektivität und Gerechtigkeit haben nichts miteinander
zu tun.

It is appropriate to return briefly to the theme of tragic heroism, for the dispute
that raged in the German historical profession at the end of the nineteenth
century displayed the classic features of it. The historian's hubris provoked the
wrath of the profession's elders. These men thereupon summoned their young
followers to seek out the hero's flaw and defeat him in battle. The triumphant
contenders were rewarded in the end with distinctions, and the vanquished
apostate was banished.

In no sense does this schema exaggerate the outcome of the *Methodenstreit*.
Without exception, the young scholars who took the field against Lamprecht
were rewarded with professorial chairs—Below in Marburg in 1897, Finke in
Freiburg in 1899, Meinecke at the same institution two years later, Hintze in
Berlin in 1902, Rachfahl in Königsberg in 1903, and Oncken in Giessen in
1906. The banishment of Karl Lamprecht was as complete as could be imposed
within a tradition of *Lehrfreiheit* upon a scholar with lifetime tenure at a German
university. His colleagues shunned him. The professional journals neither published nor reviewed his scholarship. His broad conception of history was declared anathema along with his views on theory and method. His students could
not find positions, for association with him was a stigma that practically ensured
professional failure.

Yet the theme of tragic heroism breaks down once its dénouement requires
that the conquered hero achieve insight into his flaw, resign himself to his fate,
and retire. This role was not for Lamprecht. He never accepted his defeat.
Instead, in the aftermath of the *Methodenstreit* he found personal fulfillment and,
in his own eyes at least, vindication. He brought his vast history of the German
nation to completion. He gained a wider popular readership and more international visibility than any of his colleagues. In Leipzig he constructed an
academic empire dedicated to his own vision of history, and he became a
dominant figure in university politics. And on the eve of war, he reemerged in

the public light as the foreign policy advisor to Germany's leaders. At the end of the drama, this hero was still the most famous historian in Germany.

The German historical profession provided the principal venue and context for Karl Lamprecht's biography during the last two decades of the nineteenth century; and in this period the links between personal history and *Wissenschafts-geschichte* are difficult to separate. The historian's banishment severed these links. The last phase of his biography was set in other arenas, where his activities attracted only occasional notice within the profession. Before following Lamprecht into these other arenas, it is fitting to turn briefly to the efforts of scholars in the historical profession, as well as in several neighboring disciplines, to bury his legacy in the aftermath of the great controversy.

Lamprecht could claim that his opponents had never confronted the issues he had raised, that they had used the flaws in his scholarship as pretexts to evade basic questions of theory and method.[1] He failed, however, to appreciate how these flaws in the end obscured the broader issues and how his own scholarship had defiled his methodological alternatives.[2] The historian's defeat thus rein-forced the profession's commitment to political history and a hermeneutic of sympathetic intuition.

Yet the central issue of *Kulturgeschichte* remained. Although some scholars wished to see the practice of cultural history banned along with Lamprecht, it was impossible to deny that he had enjoyed wide support in the profession, even among academic historians, when he argued that the study of history in Germany had become too riveted on the state, to the neglect of broader social and cultural forces. The problem of cultural history had a practical dimension as well. By virtue of the ministerial directives issued in the early 1890s, social and economic developments figured more prominently in the curricula of the secondary schools than in the course of study offered by historical seminars at the universities. The historical seminars thus failed to provide *Gymnasiallehrer* with either adequate training or appropriate teaching materials in these fields. Lamprecht's appeal in the 1890s was due in large part to the accessibility of his writings for use in the schools; his opponents' alarm reflected the fear that his vision would sow misconceptions in a generation of German secondary students. Pedagogical concerns hence weighed heavily on the profession's leadership as they addressed the problem of cultural history in the wake of the *Methodenstreit*.[3] The challenge, as they saw it, was to domesticate the genre, to remove its noxious features, to disassociate it from Lamprecht, and to bring it more into harmony with the profession's methodological traditions.[4]

Lamprecht himself had made the task easier. His performance had made his own idiosyncratic conception of cultural history the principal casualty of the *Methodenstreit*. The features that he had imposed on the genre—his series of five cultural epochs, his socio-psychic forces, his laws of development, and the principle of immanent causality—were so discredited that a hint of them in a work of historical scholarship was henceforth sufficient to destroy its credibility.

The fate of Kurt Breysig was compelling testimony to this truth.[5] Breysig's early career resembled that of his colleague, Otto Hintze. He trained in Berlin with Treitschke and Schmoller, and like Hintze, he devoted his first major scholarship, under Schmoller's aegis, to the bureaucratic and constitutional development of Brandenburg-Prussia, principally in the era of the Great Elector. In 1896, at the age of thirty, he was granted a tenured extraordinary professorship in Berlin, and he appeared to be on the verge of a brilliant career in the German academy.[6] Then his interests changed. The reversal was not as abrupt as it had impressed his bemused colleagues, for his frustrations with the minutiae of archival scholarship had long been building. Immersion in the writings of Nietzsche in 1895 helped him articulate his discontents and suggested goals more congenial to his expansive and restless intellect. "Higher, ever higher!" read a diary entry in March 1896, in which he first outlined his new plans. "All leads forthwith to the idea of a history of humanity—It cannot be anything less; for religion, art, poetry, science can only be portrayed universally, as a whole."[7]

Breysig's agenda bore a clear resemblance to the one then being worked out in Leipzig. Lamprecht had in fact already come into contact with Breysig, who was close to Liesegang, Hoeniger, and the other economists in Lamprecht's circle of friends in Berlin; and Breysig was one of the finalists for the position in Leipzig that went in 1894 to Marcks (who was himself Breysig's friend).[8] In 1896, as his plans began to take shape, Breysig's relationship with Lamprecht became closer and more complex. He was ten years younger than Lamprecht, but similarities of ambition forged a strong bond, which at times seemed almost filial; it was also marked on both sides by a sense of rivalry and carried the attendant tensions.[9]

Breysig became Lamprecht's loyal ally as the Methodenstreit intensified, for he recognized that his own ambitions were at issue as well. In September 1896 he professed his "solidarity for better or for worse [in Frieden oder Leid]" with his older colleague.[10] Shortly thereafter he began to demonstrate his loyalties. Two articles in the Deutsche Zeitschrift für Geschichtswissenschaft brought the initial statement of his new vision of history.[11] He called for a "developmental history," which was to feature causal analysis, an emphasis on typical behavior and mass phenomena, comparative analysis of long-term developmental sequences, and "the striving for totality." Then he joined Harden's stall of writers, where he commented regularly on historiographical issues, as well as on Burckhardt and Nietzsche (both of whom he worshiped) and on Stefan George, into whose circle of devotees he also wandered for a time.[12]

At the turn of the century Breysig published a vast comparative morphology of the peoples of Europe, which bore the title Cultural History of the Modern Era.[13] He argued that all of these peoples developed, although at different rates and times, through a series of stages that he characterized as ancient, medieval, and modern; this development was, he explained (with a bow to Nietzsche), everywhere governed by the dialectical interplay between the socio-psychic forces of individual self-assertion and devotion to the collective group, in particular to the state.

This survey and the works that he published during the next several years were efforts to bring intellectual unity to the history of the whole world. Breysig displayed a range of vision and imagination (and confusion) that made Lamprecht's look almost confined by comparison. Breysig's scholarship stood out, however, less for its contrasts to Lamprecht's, which seemed minor despite the efforts of both historians to emphasize them, than for its similarities of scope and contour—its emphasis on causality and historical laws, the broad play of socio-psychic forces, developmental stages defined by the growing weight of individualism, and (by no means least) its mystical overtones.[14] Publication of Breysig's *Cultural History of the Modern Era* confirmed in any event, as Goetz recalled, the perception that Lamprecht had won a new disciple.[15]

This perception wrecked Breysig's career. Although he disdained the kind of polemical exchange that had ruined Lamprecht, he was henceforth identified with an approach to history that the profession had proscribed. "Had this project for reform appeared ten or twelve years earlier," Below wrote of the *Cultural History of the Modern Era*, "it probably would have caused a stir." The problem, as Below hardly had to emphasize, was that "the fiasco of another project" had in the meantime "filled most of the public with suspicion against any such enterprise."[16] Professional judgment of Breysig's work ranged from bewilderment to horror; with the exception of Schmoller, his colleagues in Berlin, like Hintze, Meinecke, and Dilthey, found it difficult to defend him.[17] He retained his position in Berlin, but he was isolated in the historical seminar; and his prospects for a chair in history vanished. Like Lamprecht, he became a bogey in the profession, the symbol of history's contamination by what Paul Kehr called in 1913 the "vague principles of philosophy [*vage Philosophemen*]."[18]

Although his pretensions and position within the profession were more modest than Breysig's, Georg Steinhausen was threatened with a similar fate in the aftermath of the *Methodenstreit*. Even before the controversy drew to a close, the liabilities of association with Lamprecht had become apparent to him. He had hoped to set up a "Society for German Cultural History," with the goal of raising money to finance editions of appropriate sources.[19] Recruiting Lamprecht to lead the effort seemed wise when he first became interested in it; by the time a manifesto appeared in 1900, Lamprecht's prominence in the venture ensured its collapse.[20] But Lamprecht's shadow loomed as well over Steinhausen's journal and the broader campaign to provide cultural history with academic respectability.

As the *Methodenstreit* entered its last stages, Steinhausen distanced himself from Lamprecht.[21] It was not a difficult undertaking, for his own conception of cultural history was hardly as broad or systematic as Lamprecht's (nor was it entirely free of the incoherence and antiquarianism that had long characterized the genre). Steinhausen regarded cultural history as a special discipline, defined primarily by the exclusion of politics from its subject matter. In practice, he himself focused on what might today be called *Alltagsgeschichte*, or the history of everyday life—on the social and cultural structures that conditioned the life of the "average person."[22] Although he professed that the goal of cultural history was knowledge of the *Volksseele* or the "internal essence of a people," his vision was less holistic and schematic than Lamprecht's; he was more sensitive to the relationship between class and culture, and he rejected the idea of lawful progression through all-embracing developmental stages.[23]

These points of difference became the theme of a series of critical reviews that Steinhausen addressed to Lamprecht from his journal, which he rechristened in 1903, with a new format and publisher, as the *Archiv für Kulturgeschichte*.[24] Lamprecht accommodated Steinhausen's efforts to back away. In 1905 he greeted Steinhausen's newly published magnum opus, his *History of German Culture*, with a patronizing review that scored Steinhausen's use of "discredited and outmoded concepts," which meant Steinhausen's failure to write cultural history in Lamprecht's fashion.[25] Lamprecht's inclusion of "sociological theory" under the rubric of "discredited and outmoded concepts" was an allusion to Steinhausen's treatment of social class; and it uncovered the scars of the *Methodenstreit*. The skirmish between the two cultural historians failed, in all events, to remove Lamprecht's stigma from Steinhausen's journal; and the absence of academic historians from the ranks of Steinhausen's contributors threatened the future of his whole enterprise.

Attracting these scholars back to the journal required concessions beyond the expulsion of Lamprecht. It was paradoxical that the scholar who arranged the return of academic historians had himself studied with Lamprecht. By the time he joined Steinhausen as editor of the *Archiv für Kulturgeschichte*, however, Walter Goetz had escaped the perils of affiliation with the Leipzig seminar and established himself as the proponent of a more reputable form of cultural history.[26] Although he finished both his doctorate and habilitation in Leipzig, Goetz's real intellectual roots were in Munich, where he worked for several extended periods in the Bavarian Historical Commission and established lasting ties with the country's leading Catholic historians. His experience in Munich recalled Lamprecht's in some respects. Although his early scholarship focused on the political history of Bavaria in the era of the Reformation and the Thirty Years' War, he became fascinated with Burckhardt and turned to the history of art, particularly of the Italian Renaissance.

After completing his habilitation with Marcks and Lamprecht, Goetz taught for six years as *Privatdozent* in Leipzig, where he watched the *Methodenstreit* destroy the collegiality of the historical seminar.[27] In 1901 he fled back to Munich and worked for the next several years in the Historical Commission on an edition of the correspondence of the elector Maximilian I of Bavaria—a project led by Moriz Ritter, whose daughter the young historian married. By the time Goetz received a chair in Tübingen in 1905, however, the Burckhardtian strain in his interests had become paramount, and he had founded his reputation on a series of studies of the Italian Renaissance and Francis of Assisi. On the basis of this work, he had also concluded that *Geistesgeschichte*, the history of great ideas, represented the most viable alternative to Lamprecht's extravagant conception of cultural history. He was thus, beside Lamprecht, the most outspoken academic advocate of *Kulturgeschichte*—and the editor of an important monograph series in this field—when he and Steinhausen entered into negotiations over the future of the *Archiv für Kulturgeschichte*, which had again taken on the look of a *Raritätskasten* and was on the verge of collapse.[28]

In 1909, in the hope of reinvigorating his journal with a new publisher, Steinhausen appealed to the house of B. G. Teubner in Leipzig, whose head was Goetz's close friend, Alfred Giesecke. Giesecke immediately approached Goetz, who in turn persuaded a team of academic historians, including Karl Hampe in Heidelberg, Friedrich von Bezold in Bonn, Carl Neumann in Strassburg, and the Catholic historians Finke and Schulte, to join him on the board of editors of the *Archiv für Kulturgeschichte*.[29] Goetz's elevation in 1911 to the position of coeditor then confirmed the impression that Steinhausen was being eased to the side.[30] Although the intervention of the academics was painful for Steinhausen, it salvaged the journal to which he had devoted his career and lent the undertaking sufficient respectability that talented young historians, such as Karl Alexander von Müller and Willy Andreas, could contribute to it without jeopardizing their professional prospects.[31]

The price that Goetz and his colleagues exacted for placing their imprimatur on *Kulturgeschichte* was a new definition of the field, which clashed not only with Lamprecht's, but also with Steinhausen's.[32] When Goetz announced the terms of the salvage to the journal's readers in 1910, he claimed the field of cultural history.[33] It was essential, he wrote, to clarify the question of cultural history in order to avoid the "degeneration of our discipline." The profession had to recognize the appeal of cultural history to the younger generation, but the field was so broad and amorphous that it offered fertile soil for dilettantes and—as a part of the same species—devotees of Lamprecht's theories. In order to forestall these dangers and provide focus for the future practice of *Kulturgeschichte*, Goetz returned to a familiar theme. He insisted that the "essential center of historical life" resided in the state. "Because the state is the most comprehensive historical force," he explained, "cultural history, in the sense of total history [*Gesamtgeschichte*], will also have to place the state as far as possible in the center of its work, naturally with the reservation that the life of the state, too, is historically conditioned." Cultural history was accordingly to be devoted to "the development of humanity, principally within political groupings." "This conception is not all that far from the view of the political historians," he conceded. Nor was Goetz's conception of method. The great forces that bound together the diverse realms of human experience and related them all to politics, he insisted, were ideas. The challenge facing cultural history was "to work out a methodology for intellectual history [*Geistesgeschichte*]." If any doubts remained about the affinities between Goetz's ideas and Ranke's, they disappeared as Goetz announced that any such methodology had to rest on the foundation of the traditional hermeneutic, or what he called the "historical-critical method."

The purport of Goetz's remarks was to expunge the painful memory of the *Methodenstreit*. His definition of cultural history was fundamentally the same as the one that had emerged out of the exchange between Schäfer and Gothein on the eve of the great controversy. Goetz's principal target was the scholar who had created all the trouble. The matter at hand "for us," he wrote, was "much less to continue Lamprecht's theories than to eliminate them, because most of them stand in the way of developing a fruitful cultural history."[34] But Goetz's definition of "fruitful" cultural history also struck down another troublesome claim, which had surfaced in the pages of Steinhausen's journal during the debate over method. Goetz repudiated the segregation of cultural and political history. Cultural history was instead to be subordinated to political history, at the safe level of subject matter and within the established methodological tradition. The field was to be distinguished principally by its concern for the broad range of affairs, particularly for the intellectual currents, that intersected in the realm of politics.

Goetz's achievement was significant but limited. Although the growing circulation of the journal eased the anxieties of the publisher, Kulturgeschichte, even in this alternative vision, remained a peripheral pursuit in imperial Germany.[35] The journal still did not attract many academic scholars of prominence, nor did the genre shed a reputation for programmatic incoherence that made it a haven for antiquarians and history buffs.

This reputation persisted despite evidence of the great potential in the kind of Kulturgeschichte that Goetz advocated. Ironically, this evidence came from Lamprecht's great enemy (and Goetz's close friend), Friedrich Meinecke. Meinecke never published the extended commentary he planned to write on Lamprecht's work, but Lamprecht nonetheless occupied his thinking after the end of Methodenstreit. Meinecke was convinced, as he wrote in the hundredth volume of the Historische Zeitschrift in 1908, that in spite of its "hybrid combination of historical and philosophical approaches," Lamprecht's challenge had drawn attention to "neglected facts and contexts" and had "in general broadened the field of historical interest."[36] In the belief that comprehending this broadened field demanded a sounder conception of cultural history than Lamprecht's, Meinecke, like Goetz, turned to the history of ideas, particularly to the work of Burckhardt.[37] In 1906, in a short essay on the Swiss scholar's Observations on World History, Meinecke addressed both the strengths and weaknesses of this vision in a way that suggested an agenda.[38] Meinecke admired Burckhardt's originality, the range of his imagination, and his freedom from Kulturschwärmerei—the uncritical faith in progress to which generations of cultural historians like Buckle (and, Meinecke might have added, Lamprecht) had succumbed. Nonetheless, Meinecke concluded, Burckhardt's work suffered from failings common to the genre of cultural history; it was the work of a dilettante—unsystematic, aphoristic, "untroubled" by the demands of "strict scholarship." The problem lay less in Burckhardt's casual research techniques than in his provincialism, a contemplative detachment that smacked of hedonism, and his indifference to the great political events in central Europe that had recently shaped world history. Among these deficiencies, Meinecke found

Burckhardt's antipathy to power the most striking; it limited the relevance of the Swiss historian's view of history for the German profession, whose own advance to "strict scholarship" had passed through the school of the "struggle for state and nation."

Two years later, Meinecke addressed the deficiencies of cultural history again, as he sought to recast this genre in an idiom more appropriate for the German historical profession. The principal theme in his *Cosmopolitanism and the Nation-State* was the political maturation of German national consciousness in the early nineteenth century, the shedding of the cosmopolitan idealism and political quietism that had attached to the idea of the nation, and the coming to terms with the harsh demands of power and the *Staatsnation*, as these were exemplified in the figure of Bismarck.[39] Meinecke's treatise had an important subtext, however, whose theme was linked to the essay on Burckhardt. In Meinecke's eyes, the development of national consciousness corresponded to the maturation of German historiography, as the universalism and cultural emphasis of eighteenth century historical writing gave way to a more sober appreciation of politics and the power of the nation-state. At the culmination of this line of development, as the historiographical analogue to Bismarck, stood Ranke. The book's central chapter bore the title "Ranke and Bismarck."[40] In it Meinecke emphasized the great historian's advance from the "airy" vision of thinkers like Humboldt, Fichte, Schiller, and Novalis, who had "elevated the German nation to a component of universal humanity [*Universal- und Menschheitsnation*]." Ranke's achievement was to "link ideas and realities," to recognize the egotistical motives that drove the actions of states, but also to situate these motives within the universal context that alone gave them historical significance.

Meinecke's book was the German historical profession's great monument to Lamprecht's failure. It represented Meinecke's appropriation of *Kulturgeschichte*, and it marked out the parameters of a genre over which he was soon to preside, in both the *Historische Zeitschrift* and his seminars, until the middle of the twentieth century.[41] He reduced cultural history to the intellectual forces that molded the development of the state; and he insisted that analysis of these forces focus on "the great personalities, the creative thinkers."[42] Meinecke recaptured cultural history within a methodological tradition that featured politics, great ideas, and great historical personalities. Ernst Schulin has aptly described his achievement as the "spiritualization of political history."[43] Ranke, not Lamprecht, was thus the symbol of the "new direction" in German historiography, which in the final analysis comported remarkably well with the old one.

The aftermath of the *Methodenstreit* was rich in irony. While one of Lamprecht's students was teaming with one of Lamprecht's opponents to appropriate what might be called the Burckhardtian strain of his vision of cultural history, another of his opponents was doing the same to its Roscherian component. The dispute over method did nothing to enhance the appeal of economic history within the German historical profession, or to quiet the suspicion that Lamprecht's failings represented merely an extreme case of grave flaws, like material-ism and a penchant for abstraction, which inhered in this genre. No historian gave more vigorous expression to these suspicions than Georg von Below. Shortly after the turn of the century he turned once again on Schmoller, in a venomous attack that suggested a continuing preoccupation with Lamprecht.[44] Below focused on Schmoller's lack of originality, his lax methodology, his advocacy of the Hofrechtstheorie, and his stage-theory of economic growth. However, Schmoller's fundamental failing, in Below's eyes, was also Lam-precht's. Schmoller was a disciple of Comte; he had succumbed to the "delusions of positivism," the attempt to impose the abstract schema of the natural sciences on the past, or, as Below wrote, "the preference for generalizations that stand in no closer relationship to the sources."[45] The tone of this attack was so shrill that it offended even Below's friends in Berlin (who had raised no objection when Lamprecht had been the target of an attack just as shrill).[46] In all events, Below's assault on the country's leading economic historian emphasized the incongruity of a recent reshuffling in the editorial board of another journal.

The Zeitschrift für Sozial- und Wirtschaftsgeschichte bore many resemblances to Steinhausen's journal.[47] It, too, represented part of the effort in the 1890s to extend the practice of history beyond its traditional confines; and it, too, took root on the periphery of the historical profession. It was the creation of a group of young Jewish scholars in Vienna, chief among them Stephan Bauer and Ludo Moritz Hartmann.[48] Their heterodoxy lay (apart from their confessional back-grounds) in their fascination with economic history and patterns of development and in their sympathy for Marxism. Their decision to omit all reference to Kulturgeschichte from the title of the journal suggested a growing attempt already among economic historians to disassociate their scholarship from the wider genre. But the association of the editors with Marxism was nonetheless a grave problem. It fed the worst fears of the academic historians about the ideological consequences of Kulturgeschichte in any form; and it dominated the journal's history in the first years after its establishment in 1893. Like Steinhausen, the editors managed to recruit contributions from several German academics, in-cluding Lamprecht and Breysig; but the venture soon foundered amid academic suspicion and indifference. As a consequence, the journal passed through two publishing houses and ceased appearing in 1900.

Three years later the house of Kohlhammer in Stuttgart took over the journal, reconstituted it as the Vierteljahrschrift für Sozial- und Wirtschaftsgeschichte, and put it under a new team of editors. Bauer and Hartmann remained; their new partner was Below. Below himself later characterized this unlikely development as "a charming joke on world history"; but at the time many observers were confounded.[49] The circumstances surrounding the change remain unclear, but the implications of Below's presence on the editorial board were unmistakable. His role was analogous to Goetz's in the Archiv für Kulturgeschichte; it was to make economic history palatable to the German historical profession, to bring "self-discipline" to a field that, in the words of Below's student, Hermann

Aubin, "desperately needed it."[50] Below's scholarship on medieval municipali-
ties had given him solid credentials in this field, but his concept of economic
history was narrow, governed by his animosities toward materialism and theoretical abstraction, his commitment to the historians' hermeneutic tradition,
and by his belief in the centrality of the state. Unlike the leading younger
historical economists, he had no sympathy for Marx's analysis of economic
development.[51] He regarded economic history as an adjunct to political history.
Economic forces were historically significant to the extent that they bore on the
development of state power; in practice his interests focused on the history of
policies and institutions.[52]

Despite the intellectual and political gulf that separated the journal's editors,
the new arrangement was amicable. But it was an unequal combination. Hartmann and Bauer could not match Below's weight in the profession, for neither
had the remotest prospects of occupying a chair. The two Austrians assembled a
list of contributors that was remarkable for its international breadth; but they
were less successful in winning the cooperation of the economic historians in
Germany whose interests were broader than Below's. For scholars close to
Schmoller (to say nothing of Lamprecht), the prominence of Below in the
journal posed an insuperable obstacle to cooperation, and the reasons were at
least as much personal as intellectual, particularly after Below used the journal as
a forum to renew his attack on the dean of German historical economists.[53] By
the eve of the war, Below had become the driving force in the venture, and in
the name of "protecting genuine historical method" and "preserving the purity
of the discipline," he used the journal to cast his imprint on the practice of
economic history in Germany.[54] Like Goetz and Meinecke, he became the
custodian of one of the principal components of *Kulturgeschichte*.[55]

The *Methodenstreit* did not destroy cultural history in the German historical
profession; it brought instead its final diffusion (and defusion). The historiographical canon was enlarged to allow academic historians to practice what might
be called "mainstream" cultural history, in the form of intellectual and economic history. However, these two subdisciplines were henceforth severed from
one another and became more commonly known by their own names. Both were
also equipped—or as Below preferred to say, "controlled"—with the profession's
traditional methodology and deployed in the service of political history, which
alone was to provide universal categories of analysis.[56] In this form *Kulturgeschichte* was also safe in the secondary schools.[57] As a concession to Steinhausen,
the *Archiv für Kulturgeschichte* continued to provide an outlet for those who
wanted to write about the history of popular culture; but this strain of cultural
history was consigned anew to the profession's periphery, where it languished, as
Gerhard Oestreich has remarked, like a "subterranean current."[58] The fates of
Lamprecht and Breysig warned against the effort to rejoin the fragments of
Kulturgeschichte and to construct a synthesis around a core that was not political.

The German historical profession thus sealed the legacy of Karl Lamprecht. If
their success brought a renewed sense of professional identity, it also emphasized

the isolation of historians from other disciplines whose methods Lamprecht had sought to integrate into the study of the past. Meinecke's intellectual history provided few avenues to philosophy or ethnology; nor did Below's vision of economic history encourage intercourse with scholars who were interested in theories of development or in the formative impact of society and economy on the state. In the aftermath of its own methodological war, the German historical profession thus remained largely aloof from the great issues that occupied scholars in neighboring disciplines at the turn of the century.

The great conflict in the German historical profession, which had already become known as the *Lamprecht-Streit*, was no isolated phenomenon. It represented a phase of a much more comprehensive intellectual debate, which began in Germany at the end of the century. It has commonly been analyzed under the rubric of "the crisis of historicism," which one scholar has recently characterized as "history's loss of its cultural function as the leading discipline in the shaping of opinion."[59] The controversy that marked this crisis was also an exciting spectacle, and it set the parameters of methodological discussions in several academic disciplines for the next decades. In its early stages, Karl Lamprecht was one of the issues, as the conflict in the historical profession converged briefly with the wider debate.

Ernst Troeltsch, who was himself one of the major participants in this wider controversy, once observed that it was basically about the philosophy of history—the "question of the unity, goal, and meaning" of the past.[60] The issue, simply stated, was the objectivity of historical knowledge, the status of the past as the basis for systematic knowledge of the present. The implications were enormous. The critical question was whether the historicity of human action reduced the past to an impenetrable chaos of particulars, which defeated every attempt to generalize, to draw out objective knowledge of historical processes as the foundation for an understanding of contemporary society and culture. The attack on the validity of historical knowledge came in degrees and variations, but an essential similarity linked the growing appeal of formalism in art history, the challenge that Menger issued to the historical economists in the name of neo-classical theory, and the so-called life-of-Jesus problem that plagued Protestant theology.

The problem was already implicit in the work of Ranke. The great historian himself remained untroubled by the implications of his dictum that "every epoch is immediate to God," for it struck him as no anomaly that the ultimate guarantee of history's coherence was theological. This proposition became more unsettling in the age of Nietzsche. During the *Methodenstreit* even Ranke's most devoted followers acknowledged, albeit reluctantly, the metaphysical undertones in the historian's *Ideenlehre*. By the time of the *Methodenstreit*, however, the growing popularity of alternative historical systems based on natural science had exacerbated the problem, insofar as they claimed to discover objective processes in history that German academic scholars found abhorrent. In placing human behavior within the domain of developmental laws, Comte's theory in particular appeared to deny human freedom and to erase the distinction between nature and culture.[61] Marxism, the great problem-child of positivism, featured a vision of historical development that foretold the destruction of culture as German academics knew it.[62] Lamprecht's opponents were able during the *Methodenstreit* to demonstrate the extent to which positivism and Marxism themselves rested on metaphysical premises; but the success of these historians pointed in turn to the problematic foundations of their own beliefs and high-lighted the question of whether any scheme of historical development could dispense with metaphysical postulates.

These uncertainties reverberated far beyond the German historical profession. Most significantly, they fueled methodological discussions within a group of academic disciplines that were becoming known as the social or cultural sciences. These included, among others, economics and the emergent disciplines of sociology, geography, psychology, and anthropology.[63] The challenge was to secure the status of these disciplines as *Wissenschaften* by identifying the objects of inquiry and methodologies that were appropriate to studying the social and cultural contexts of human behavior. This undertaking hinged in turn on establishing the limits beyond which the structures of human action resisted the analytical categories of the natural sciences.

The effort to distinguish these disciplines from the natural sciences began in the 1880s under the banner of Kant. Wilhelm Dilthey attempted to build on the distinctions formulated by the historian Droysen and to define the so-called human sciences (*Geisteswissenschaften*) as the study of meaningful human experience. Dilthey insisted that the object of these sciences was a realm of singularity, contingency, subjectivity, and purposeful action.[64] Objective knowledge of this realm was attainable, but it required, in Dilthey's view, a hermeneutic of sympathetic intuition, or *Verstehen*, which he characterized as the reexperiencing of meaning that had been objectified in cultural products, institutions, and practices—foremost, he believed, in the "workshop of the individual spirit," in the thought of great historical actors, like Schleiermacher, whose early life was the subject of one of Dilthey's own great pieces of scholarship.[65]

In both his historical writings and his theory, Dilthey clung to what might be called a "realist" position, insofar as he believed that the goal of the cultural and social sciences, no less than of the natural sciences, was to represent an objective reality.[66] In his view, the principal distinction between the human sciences and the natural sciences was ontological; it lay in the order of reality that each addressed. In the 1890s, however, Dilthey's views themselves became the object of criticism. Those who pondered the problems of methodology—most prominently Georg Simmel, Wilhelm Windelband, Heinrich Rickert, Emil Lask, and Max Weber—now invoked Kant to distinguish the *Kulturwissenschaften*, as Rickert preferred to call them, not on the basis of the subject matter they addressed, but instead by virtue of the distinct epistemological categories within which they operated.[67] Rickert and other contemporary theorists attempted to work out the principles of concept formation in these disciplines—to define the categories, logic, or grammar of discourse appropriate to what Windelband, in a famous lecture in 1894, labeled the "idiographic" as opposed to the "nomothetic" sciences.[68] However, their insistence on the primacy of epistemology seemed to exclude the possibility of objective knowledge of cultural or social reality (or nature, for that matter), insofar as they insisted that all knowledge was constituted by the mental categories of the observing subject. Although they, like Dilthey, argued that sympathetic intuition was the methodology appropriate to the study of culture and society, they were hard pressed to show how this operation could reflect more than subjective preferences, valuations, and judgments. A lingering belief in universal cultural values shielded Rickert from the relativism implicit in this theory of knowledge. The achievement of Max Weber, who was not so shielded, was to embrace the theory's consequences.[69]

The controversy over method in the social or cultural sciences bore broadly and intensely on the study of history, which in the common use of the term numbered among the Geisteswissenschaften. The neo-Kantian critique undercut the belief that the historian could, if armed with the proper training and methods, produce an objective account of the past. Questioning the reality of cultural values and meanings also cut away the foundations on which traditional concepts of historical development rested; more pertinently, it reduced historical development itself to a concept, an epistemological category, like any other mental structure that provided the past with coherence or purpose.[70]

Given the relevance of this controversy to the academic historians, it is remarkable how little these scholars were interested in or affected by its central issues, even as Lamprecht compelled them to examine the foundations of their own discipline. The "crisis of German historicism" had little directly to do with the German historical profession. Although this crisis provided the context of the Lamprecht-Streit, the broader methodological and philosophical debates intruded little into the profession's own great crisis.

The reasons for the historians' insulation were several. The debate over Lamprecht's theories involved scholars who were as a rule neither broadly trained nor conversant with the debates in other fields. The profession's own history, as well as its parochialism, helped pitch the debate over method at a different, more innocent level than was the case in other disciplines. The question of historical relativism surfaced only briefly, toward the conclusion of the historians' Methodenstreit. The dispute did not challenge the prevalent belief in the reality of historical processes or the objectivity of historical knowledge. In this respect, the Kulturzeitalter fulfilled for Lamprecht the same function as the development of the state did for his enemies. Both represented objective frameworks that endowed the past with meaning and addressed questions of universal value.[71] The outcome of the dispute discredited Lamprecht's schema amid charges that it rested on ideological or metaphysical assumptions; the confident position of his opponents, the proposition that the growth of the state was an objective measure of meaning in history, survived the dispute without examination in light of the same charges.

Thus a significant dialogue between the historians and scholars from other disciplines did not develop, at least prior to the war. Footnotes and casual references in the polemical tracts of historians on both sides of the Methodenstreit showed some familiarity with the arguments of the major theorists of method; but the acquaintance was rarely more than fleeting. Lamprecht's eccentric reading of Kant stood in flat contradiction to the positions of the neo-Kantian philosophers. His approach to the question of historical knowledge was superficially similar to theirs; he, too, spoke of the problematic status of knowledge of the unique and individual in history, but in resolving this problem by means of the lawful progression of collective behavior through cultural epochs, he glided between orders of philosophical argument—and between conflicting philosophical traditions—with a facility that enabled him to appeal to Simmel, Windelband, Schopenhauer, Du Bois-Reymond, John Stuart Mill, and Herbert Spencer in the course of a single article.[72] During the last stage of the Methodenstreit, in his replies to Below in 1899, Lamprecht again demonstrated this facility when he addressed the epistemological issues that Rickert had raised; Lamprecht, however, again attempted to employ Kantian premises to encompass history and natural sciences within a single field of knowledge.[73]

Neo-Kantianism appealed more plausibly to Lamprecht's opponents, who could draw from the arsenal provided by Dilthey and Rickert to parry the attack that Lamprecht was waging in the name of causality on the traditional hermeneutic.[74] Yet, as Georg Iggers has observed, few of these historians appreciated the implications of the methodological issues—the fact that neo-Kantianism posed a graver challenge than Lamprecht to historiographical tradition.[75] Iggers' observation holds even for historians whose interest in questions of methodology was more than casual. Below's reading of Rickert reinforced his confidence that "in the course of time our standards of value are gaining greater objectivity."[76] Meinecke's confidence in the same proposition was tempered but not undermined by his sensitivity to the moral ambiguities of power; and Dilthey's influence underlay his conviction that objective cultural values found embodiment in the thought of great historical figures.[77]

There could be no question about the sympathies of the philosophers themselves.[78] In Lamprecht's historiography they confronted a confused amalgam of the most objectionable doctrines. From the positivists the historian had adopted the principle of lawful development in culture as well as nature; but he had incorporated this principle into a philosophical framework of objective idealism, or what Lask was calling emanationism—a doctrine that conjured up memories of Hegel as it assigned to the concepts of the mind (in the case of Lamprecht's mind, the concepts were called *Kulturzeitalter*) an ontological status higher than the particulars of empirical reality.

Despite the provocations presented by this apparent marriage of Hegel and Comte, the philosophers of method remained on the periphery of the historians' conflict, which pivoted in the end on technical questions of Lamprecht's historical scholarship. More interesting and troubling philosophical questions were at issue elsewhere, especially in psychology, where Windelband and Dilthey were directly involved in the debates over method. The *Methodenstreit* in history was distinguished less for its philosophical sophistication than for its acrimony. This fact reinforced Dilthey's reluctance to become involved in it, despite Meinecke's pleadings and his own acute distaste for Lamprecht.[79] "I must look quietly on," he wrote in 1897 to his friend Paul Yorck von Wartenburg, while scholars are "discussed, praised, upbraided, misunderstood."[80]

Rickert's experience demonstrated the wisdom of Dilthey's reticence. Rickert's epistemological writings undermined the foundations of Lamprecht's historiography, but the philosopher's essays were pitched at such a high level of generalization that Lamprecht himself, doubtless on the strength of a hurried reading, at first reacted positively to one of them.[81] Lamprecht soon recognized, however, that Rickert was no ally, and he turned on the philosopher in a tone with which the historians were by now familiar. Using his own methodological precepts as the standard of comparison, he accused Rickert of "crude logical errors," of standing in "glaring contradiction to genuine scientific thought," and of setting historiography back a century and a half.[82] Rickert concluded that discussion with Lamprecht was "fruitless" and declined to take up the challenge.[83]

Max Weber was more at home in polemics, but he, too, elected to avoid active involvement in the *Methodenstreit*.[84] Still, one shudders to think how Lamprecht might have fared had he, like Rudolf Stammler or Wilhelm Ostwald, been the object of one of Weber's merciless broadsides. Although Lamprecht was spared direct attack, Weber was intensely interested in the debate among the historians. In fact, his great series of methodological essays, which appeared between 1903 and 1907, not only defined a remarkably durable position in the broader methodological debate; they also addressed the principal theoretical issues in the *Lamprecht-Streit* and presented, as Wolfgang Mommsen has pointed out, a penetrating analysis of the failings of both sides.[85] Weber's views on Lamprecht are thus as instructive as they are difficult to sort out from the broader concerns of his methodological writings.[86]

Weber held Lamprecht beneath contempt. In a characteristic outburst in 1905, he dismissed the historian as "a dishonest feuilletonist, who no longer has the slightest right to style himself [*sich geberden*] as a man of scholarship."[87] Weber's favorite epithet for Lamprecht, however, was "dilettante"; and he employed the term so ritually, in his asides and in the rambling footnotes that embellished his essays, that it became almost a code word for the historian and his followers. The venom of reproach was unusual even for Weber, and it suggested the play of several motives. Weber admired Lamprecht's early work in economic history, and he shared the resentments rife among the academic historians over Lamprecht's betrayal of the ethic of scholarship. The bitterness was also a sign of alarm, for Lamprecht's work symptomized a threat to Weber's understanding of sociology. It was not difficult to see the affinities between

Lamprecht's historiography and the progressive evolutionism of scholars like Rudolf Goldscheid, against whom Weber was about to take the field in name of *Wertfreiheit* or value neutrality.[88]

Weber's attack on Lamprecht was oblique. It was launched in the direction of Leipzig, at the historian's *Doktorvater* and the renowned psychologist who was Lamprecht's colleague there. Weber's famous essays on Roscher and Knies were ostensibly a critique of the organic theories of growth that were central in the teachings of these two economists.[89] In fact, the essays demolished the epistemological foundations of every theory of progress and every schema that claimed to reveal objective patterns of historical development. Weber insisted that all such theories imported metaphysics and value judgment in the guise of historical method. In the cases of the two economists, the metaphysics were Hegelian—"borderline emanationism," as Weber characterized Roscher's theories, or "emanationistic logic in a stage of decadence," as he described Knies'.[90] But the methodological confusion was by no means confined to the economists. Weber's essay included an extended criticism of Wundt's theories of lawful psychic development, which, Weber argued, displayed similar failings. In this instance, he remarked, the theories took the "guise of 'objective' psychological observations," but they rested nonetheless on "an a priori philosophical construction about the 'progress' of humanity."[91]

Even as he demolished the foundations of their beliefs, Weber spoke of Roscher and Wundt in a tone of admiration. Wundt he called an "eminent scholar," whose "broad and diverse intellectual work" deserved "extraordinary, grateful respect."[92] Roscher's theories he called the "expression of his mild, discreet, conciliatory personality."[93] But when Weber turned to the epigone of these two scholars, to the historian whose work demonstrated the worst dangers of their confusion, he abandoned all charity. Roscher's work had at least the virtue of originality, impartiality, and a sense of "sober conscientiousness"; once Lamprecht borrowed them, Weber charged, Roscher's ideas were puffed up into "grotesquely dilettantish" constructions and "comical prejudices."[94] Nor, Weber warned, had Wundt fared well in Lamprecht's hands. The psychologist's theories were "nothing short of poison" for the scholarly objectivity of historians who were enticed into concealing their own values, both from themselves and others, in the form of "purportedly psychological categories" and the "false appearance of exactitude." It came then as no surprise when Weber cited Lamprecht's work as a "horrifying example" of this kind of self-deception.[95]

Weber's essays on Roscher and Knies were welcome to the ears of Lamprecht's enemies. Weber placed the indictment of Lamprecht in a broader context and lent it a greater degree of methodological rigor than the historian's opponents had themselves been able to provide. However, in the essays on Roscher and Knies and in several additional pieces on methodology, Weber also subjected the conventional views of the academic historians, whom he persistently (and not without irony) labeled the " 'modern' historians," to an examination that was no less withering for being couched in more temperate terms.[96]

Weber's criticism focused on two vulnerable points. The first was the hermeneutic of *Verstehen*, which, to the extent that it had been examined in the *Methodenstreit*, had taken on the connotations of a spontaneous, quasi-mystical mode of communication between the historian and a realm that was thought to be inaccessible to causal analysis and where cultural meaning resided in individuality and freedom. In his exposition of his own views on historical explanation, or what he called "*deutende Kausalerkenntnis*," Weber stripped the act of *Verstehen* of its mysticism. He analyzed the circumstances that governed it and showed the extent to which no interpretation of cultural meanings, however much it featured singularity and purposeful behavior, could dispense with the logical category of causality insofar as the interpretation related to motivation. "To be sure," he wrote in one of the essays on Roscher and Knies, "there are causal relations without teleology, but there are no teleological concepts without causal rules."[97]

In drawing out similarities of logical structure between the natural and cultural sciences, Weber made a concession to a position that Lamprecht had defended. The second point of his criticism of the "modern" historians also recapitulated an argument that Lamprecht had used, although Weber now directed it at Lamprecht as well. In his famous essay on "Objectivity in the Social Sciences," Weber examined the relationship of history and theory. "Nothing is more dangerous," he wrote, "than the conflation, which has its origins in the prejudices of the naturalists, of theory and history." This proposition looked like the beginning of another swipe at Lamprecht, but Weber continued with the observation that the conflation of theoretical concepts and historical reality took many forms—for example:

> . . . thinking that one has fixed the "real"substance [*Gehalt*], the "essence" of historical reality in those theoretical concepts, or . . . using these concepts as a Procrustian bed into which history is to be constrained, or . . . hypostacizing "ideas" as an "actual [*eigentliche*]" reality that stands behind the flux of appearances, as real "forces" which work themselves out in history.[98]

Weber's criticism left no doubt that he was addressing the confusion that linked Lamprecht and Ranke. His criticism applied alike to the practitioners of the "new" and the "old" history, all of whom subscribed to the fallacy of "realism"— the belief that the concepts with which they organized the past could be free of a priori value judgments and correspond to a historical reality that was objectively given. It had been easy for historians during the *Methodenstreit* to fault Lamprecht for falling victim to this confusion. The sociologist's verdict was that the historians were blind to the same failings in their own work. In his commentary on Eduard Meyer's attempt to articulate a methodological alternative to Lamprecht's, Weber laid bare the ultimate *protestatio fidei* that underlay the writing of history in imperial Germany. "The concept of the 'culture' of a specific people and epoch, the concept of 'Christianity,' of 'Faust,' but also—," and here Weber paused:

. . . something that is easier to overlook—the concept of "Germany" . . . are all, once they are established as objects of historical study, individuals' concepts of value—that is, they are formed with reference to ideas about value.[99]

Weber's observations on the *Methodenstreit* made it clear that he shared Lamprecht's judgment about several other matters. He, too, was struck by the methodological naiveté of the academic historians. "Just how deplorable the state of thinking about the logic of history is," he remarked in one of his essays, was manifest in "the fact that neither historians nor historical methodologists have undertaken the standard studies of this important question."[100] More significantly, Weber thought Lamprecht was right about the parochialism of conventional German historiography and about the need for a comprehensive conception of cultural history.[101] "When one speaks of 'history' alone," Weber wrote in an approving paraphrase of Knies' position, "one must always think in the broadest sense of the word (political, cultural, social history included)."[102]

The famous study that Weber described to Rickert in 1905 as an "essay in cultural history, which you will perhaps find interesting," was thus, as its penultimate footnote confirmed, itself a gloss on the historians' *Methodenstreit*.[103] When Weber alluded at the end of "The Protestant Ethic and the Spirit of Capitalism" to "the type of dilettantes who believe in the 'unity' of the 'social psyche' and its 'reducibility' to a formula," his target was unmistakable.[104] But this essay represented a reckoning not only with Lamprecht, the exemplar of the "type" whose bombastic confusion threatened to discredit the writing of cultural history altogether, but with Schäfer, Goetz, Meinecke, Below, and the other "modern" historians who were attempting to appropriate *Kulturgeschichte* in a way that Weber thought too narrow. Weber's was a remarkable piece of scholarship in a number of respects, not the least as an attempt to employ the ideal type as a means to solve some of the methodological problems that he had identified in the work of the historians. As an exercise in cultural history, however, Weber's work was remarkable not only for establishing a link between material and ideal culture, but for doing so outside the realm of politics.

Like the contemporaneous historical scholarship of his friends Werner Sombart and Ernst Troeltsch, Weber's essay suggested that the broader designs of cultural history might reemerge at the disciplinary juncture where sociology was taking shape.[105] One is tempted to say that their *Kulturgeschichte* was more Lamprechtian in scope than the kind of cultural history then being defined by Meinecke, Goetz, and Below. It was certainly more comprehensive than the historians', and it was more sensitive to the historical interaction among realms of behavior that lay outside the state.

In part for this reason, Weber's scholarship found little sympathy within the historical profession. His methodological essays nonetheless helped seal Lamprecht's ostracism from the academy, where few people any longer took the historian seriously as a scholar. But if Lamprecht ceased to be a force in the German historical profession, he remained a looming presence elsewhere, especially in Leipzig, where his professional banishment had immediate practical ramifications.

As one of the principal nodes in the profession's organizational network, the historical seminar in Leipzig could not have escaped the commotion and acrimony that the *Methodenstreit* visited on relations among professors, *Privatdozenten*, and students in universities throughout the country. But the fact that the main figure in the controversy taught in Leipzig subjected this seminar to a degree of turmoil far beyond what others had to endure.

Lamprecht's performance was of direct concern to his colleagues in Leipzig, especially to Seeliger and Marcks, who not only taught in fields close to his, but sat with him on the editorial board of the *Deutsche Zeitschrift für Geschichtwissenschaft*. Association with Lamprecht was an inescapable result of their proximity, but as the historian's ordeal intensified, both Seeliger and Marcks found this association a source of discomfort, if not a threat to their own reputations.[106] The *Methodenstreit* entered its critical phase not long after the arrival of these two scholars in the seminar; and the good will that both initially bore for their senior colleague soon gave way to hostility, for his position appeared to violate the methodological tenets to which they themselves subscribed. Bonds of loyalty and friendship to Lamprecht's opponents elsewhere in the profession only exacerbated the strain.

Marcks' position was particularly difficult. He was caught between the demands of collegiality with Lamprecht, which included providing advice and comments on manuscripts, and his strong ties to the enemy camp in Berlin, where he had studied.[107] He knew Lenz well and was Meinecke's *Duzfreund*.[108] Maintaining the appearance of impartiality in the dispute required heroic efforts, for both sides were eager to enlist his support.[109] That he maintained cordial relations with Lamprecht as long as he did was a remarkable feat, for sources of friction abounded in even the most routine aspects of life in the seminar.

No group felt the repercussions of the *Methodenstreit* more immediately than did students of history in Leipzig. Completing a doctorate, habilitation, or even the state teaching examinations perforce required these young people to confront faculty committees that included historians on different sides of a paradigmatic dispute.[110] The principal casualties were Lamprecht's students, whose unorthodox topics and casual use of documentation were objectionable to Marcks and Seeliger.[111] Examinations in the seminar thus tended to replicate in microcosm the tensions and misunderstandings that marked the broader methodological controversy.[112] Lamprecht's practice of drawing in readers and examiners from outside the seminar, usually Bücher or August von Miaskowski (the other economist), protected some of his students but further antagonized the colleagues who were circumvented.[113]

Dissension plagued the *Deutsche Zeitschrift für Geschichtswissenschaft* as well.

Personal and intellectual conflicts intruded regularly into editorial decisions, for Seeliger and Marcks were determined to frustrate Lamprecht's hope of turning the journal into a forum for his own variety of cultural history. That the journal even survived its first years was due primarily to Lamprecht's preoccupation with his opponents in Berlin, for he soon lost interest in the routine of editorial work and offered no objections when, in the fall of 1897, Seeliger became sole editor. Seeliger's moves the next year led to the explosion. Determined to rid the journal of all trace of Lamprecht, he removed it to a new publishing house (to Teubner), renamed it the *Historische Vierteljahrschrift*, shifted its emphasis toward political history, and excluded Lamprecht from the editorial board.[114] When in early 1899 Lamprecht accused Seeliger, publicly but without foundation, of deceit in these actions, the two men ceased speaking to one another and henceforth communicated only in writing.[115]

The products of this rupture were a journal without much profile (as even its publisher conceded) and the paralysis of the historical seminar in Leipzig.[116] Tensions had already become acute with the decline of Lamprecht's fortunes in the *Methodenstreit*, the pressures of which registered in the historian's growing impatience, irritability, arrogance, and scarcely disguised longing to abandon the seminar.[117] With the exception of Buchholz, who now taught as extraordinary professor, Lamprecht had lost the affection, as well as the intellectual respect, of most of the seminar by the time the methodological controversy broke off in 1899.[118] Most significantly, in the aftermath of his break with Seeliger, his imperious behavior caused the final erosion of his relations with Marcks.[119]

By the terms of their appointments, Lamprecht and Marcks were to serve in alternate years as directors of the seminar and to oversee the routine matters of allocating space, provisioning the seminar's library, coordinating teaching assignments, and representing the seminar in the wider university. During his first years in Leipzig, Marcks was content to forego his rights and to let Lamprecht serve continuously.[120] The rift between Lamprecht and Seeliger made this arrangement impossible, as Lamprecht attempted to use his powers to expel his colleague from the seminar on the grounds that the auxiliary disciplines, for which Seeliger was responsible, did not need to be organically bound to the seminar.[121] Lamprecht's claim was disinguous, and it raised another issue of growing alarm to Marcks. Seeliger taught most of the courses in medieval history as well, for Lamprecht's teaching interests had pushed with each succeeding volume of his *German History* closer to the modern era, the field in which Marcks' own appointment lay.[122]

In September 1899 Marcks appealed directly to the ministry in order to restore his prerogatives as codirector of the seminar and to block Seeliger's expulsion. But Marcks could not stall Lamprecht's advance into his own area of expertise; nor could he, in the succeeding months, relieve the atmosphere of suspicion and recrimination that permeated the seminar. His escape from Leipzig in the summer of 1901 thus came as no surprise—least of all to Lamprecht, who gave him a final shove. "Can I wish for you to stay in Leipzig now?" read the letter that arrived in Marcks' hands the day before he accepted a call to Heidelberg. "I fear that [our] competition over professional matters, which you for the time being interpret in light of personal antagonisms, is going to become more problematic [schiefer]."[123]

Marcks' departure brought on more problems than it resolved. It removed the only figure who could mediate between Lamprecht and Seeliger—in the literal sense of passing communications from one to the other. In the hopes of maintaining the peace, the ministry agreed in the fall of 1901 to elevate Seeliger to the position of codirector and to dissolve the seminar formally into a section for medieval and constitutional history (for Seeliger) and one for modern and comparative history (for Lamprecht). From offices on opposite ends of the complex of rooms that housed the seminar, the two directors were henceforth to rule independent domains of staff, students, and curriculum, linked only by a common introductory course, a library, and a librarian (whom the ministry was empowered to appoint in the event of disagreement between the two historians).[124]

This bizarre arrangement, which confined contacts between Lamprecht and Seeliger to chance encounters in the common corridor, was too delicate to withstand the addition of a successor to Marcks in the seminar.[125] In fact, it could not even withstand the tensions of finding a successor to Marcks. The dreary negotiations that led in the end to the appointment of Erich Brandenburg demonstrated the extent of Lamprecht's isolation not only in the seminar, but within the wider philosophical faculty. The search committee that the faculty appointed sympathized with Seeliger's desire to hire a modern political historian; but it faced a daunting challenge, for the prospects of finding a scholar whose credentials suited what the ministry of culture described as "the importance of the university of Leipzig" were hardly favorable in view of the disarray in the seminar and the presence in Leipzig of the most notorious figure in the profession.[126] The offer went first in the summer of 1901 to Bezold in Bonn, a historian with impeccable credentials as well as broad interests, who was perhaps the only prominent scholar in the country acceptable to both Lamprecht and Seeliger; but his refusal confirmed the fear that only an inside candidate would accept the position.[127] There were only two of these—Buchholz, who was Lamprecht's candidate, and Brandenburg, then a Privatdozent, who was Seeliger's. Seeliger prevailed. In 1902 Brandenburg was provisionally given the position as an extraordinary professor, and early in 1904, to the accompaniment of Lamprecht's protest and Buchholz's resignation from the seminar, he was named Ordinarius.[128]

Brandenburg's appointment, which gave him the status of deputy director of the seminar, justified Lamprecht's worst fears. Lamprecht's relationship to this student of Max Lenz had been cool from the time of Brandenburg's habilitation in Leipzig, which Marcks had supervised in 1894.[129] Intellectually and temperamentally, Brandenburg stood much closer to Seeliger, and the two combined easily against Lamprecht whenever the affairs of the seminar demanded that the three historians reach a collective decision.[130] Quarrels over space, the library, the division of fees for the introductory course, and—most painfully—the academic performance of Lamprecht's students all attested to the growing turmoil in the seminar.[131]

The problems were too chronic to be confined to the seminar, and they soon entangled the faculty, the ministry of culture, and even the Saxon diet.[132] To the extent that the disputes in the seminar reflected the issues in the *Methoden-streit*, they bore directly on other disciplines represented in the philosophical faculty. For this reason, Lamprecht could count on the sympathy of Wundt and the social scientists, particularly of Bücher and the geographer Ratzel; but his views were anathema to scholars from the more traditional humanistic disciplines, such as the philologists Eduard Sievers and Albert Köster, both of whom sat on the committee that searched for Marcks' successor. August Schmarsow, the art historian, also sat on this committee; and he found Lamprecht's expansive view of history threatening in much the same way as Marcks had. Although Lamprecht had supported Schmarsow's call to Leipzig in 1893, cordiality between the two scholars lasted only a few years, until Schmarsow concluded that Lamprecht's concept of cultural history was in reality, as he later put it, "the general and comparative history of art."[133]

Schmarsow's suspicion of Lamprecht's intentions made him an early observer of developments in the historical seminar, but the chaos in this part of the university soon forced this role onto the entire philosophical faculty.[134] Debates over the seminar's academic appointments, reorganization, administrative policies, and student examinations occupied an inordinate amount of the faculty's time, as this body became a regular court of appeal in the historians' quarrels. The faculty's embroilment reached a scandalizing climax early in 1904, when Lamprecht, who was no longer able to restrain his frustration over the impending appointment of Brandenburg as *Ordinarius*, accused Seeliger of unethical behavior in front of the whole faculty. The faculty, with Schmarsow presiding as dean, voted to censure Lamprecht, who thereupon stormed out of the meeting.[135] A public apology to Seeliger several weeks later ended the incident, but not before the faculty had voted, in Lamprecht's absence, to reject the habilitation of one of his students, Armin Tille.[136]

In the wake of this episode, neither the faculty nor the ministry, which had also grown weary of the war of the historians in Leipzig, was inclined to object to the radical step which alone seemed likely to bring peace. The removal of Lamprecht from the seminar was his own idea. "It has gradually been made completely impossible for me," he wrote in 1904 to the ministry, "to share the same space any longer with a colleague like Seeliger." Lamprecht accordingly called for the "strictest separation of the individual sections" of the seminar in every sense, "scholarly, administrative, and physical [*räumlich*]."[137] After he garnished his demands with threats of resignation, the ministry acceded.[138] In 1905 it divided the seminar anew into autonomous sections, one for Seeliger and Brandenburg and one for Lamprecht, who, over the objections of the other two, was allowed to call his the section for "cultural and universal history," a designation that corresponded to the turn of his interests toward comparative history.[139] A year later the ministry agreed, without even consulting Seeliger or Brandenburg, to move Lamprecht's section into a separate building, despite the manifold difficulties of physically dividing the seminar's infrastructure.[140]

This dénouement was a measure of Lamprecht's tenacity and the extent of his influence in the ministry of culture. It was also a sign of exasperation in Dresden, where officials cared more about tranquillity in the seminar than about the professional feud that had led to the uproar. Their decision meant in practice the creation of a second historical seminar in Leipzig, dedicated to the historiographical agenda of its director. Seeliger and Brandenburg had good reason for alarm, for they knew that this agenda threatened to swallow their own, that Lamprecht's conception of history embraced, as they pleaded in protest to the ministry, "the totality of history."[141] The ministry's decision thus brought yet another paradox to the aftermath of the historians' great controversy over method. Lamprecht's banishment from the profession led to his banishment from the seminar; but if the one signaled an unambiguous defeat, the other represented a great personal victory. Lamprecht's views now acquired a firm organizational footing in Leipzig, where the presence of two competing centers of historical study raised the prospect that the Methodenstreit would henceforth be institutionalized at that university.

During the struggles within the historical seminar, Lamprecht expressed feelings of martyrdom, which, given the ordeals he faced in both the profession and his own faculty, were not altogether unfounded.[142] The early years of the new century were difficult for him. By the end of 1901 the tension in the seminar had so strained his nerves that he had to take medical leave.[143] On more than one occasion he confessed his nostalgia for the Rhineland and his longing to escape from Leipzig, from "our foul little city" and its "envy and narrow-mindedness."[144] However, Lamprecht had no prospect of a professional move at this stage in his career; and his reaction to adversity was in fact entirely in character. He set out on his own. "Then the spirit of father comes over me," he wrote to his brother in January 1904.[145] The invocation of his father at this juncture was significant, not only as evidence of a spirit of defiance, as Herbert Schönebaum has suggested, but also as an indication of associations to which the historian was then alive.[146] "I have endured these attacks," he remarked three weeks later, and "have retired as far as possible into myself alone."[147] Lamprecht's exile from the profession and from the seminar in Leipzig placed him finally in the kind of situation in which he had always felt most comfortable—alone, beyond the confines of authority or convention, be it professional, collegial, or paternal. And here he thrived.

Notes

1. NL Liesegang, Lamprecht to Liesegang, Leipzig, 9.2.98.

2. See Oestreich, "Fachhistorie," 326; H. J. Steinberg, "Lamprecht."

3. See Neubauer, "Die Kulturgeschichte auf höheren Lehranstalten," 257–66; Franz Schnabel, "Inwieweit ist die Kulturgeschichte im Geschichtsunterricht der Oberklassen zu berücksichtigen?" GWU (1987): 733–43. This essay originally appeared, in a slightly different version, in 1914: "Kulturgeschichte im Geschichtsunterricht der Oberklassen," VuG, 4 (1914): 87–97.

4. *Cf.* Rüdiger vom Bruch, "Historiker und Nationalökonomen im Wilhelminischen Deutschland," in Klaus Schwabe, ed., *Deutsche Hochschullehrer als Elite 1815–1945* (Boppard am Rhein, 1988), esp. 127–28.

5. Bernhard vom Brocke, *Kurt Breysig: Geschichtswissenschaft zwischen Historismus und Soziologie* (Lübeck and Hamburg, 1971); vom Brocke, "Kurt Breysig," in Wehler, *Historiker*, 6: 95–116; Gertrud Breysig, *Kurt Breysig: Ein Bild des Menschen* (Heidelberg, 1967); Kurt Breysig, *Aus meinen Tagen und Träumen: Memoiren, Aufzeichnungen, Briefe, Gespräche* (Berlin, 1962); Kurt Breysig, *Gedankenblätter* (Berlin, 1964); vom Bruch, *Wissenschaft*, 370–76.

6. vom Brocke, *Breysig*, 24.

7. Breysig, *Tagen und Träumen*, 92–93.

8. NL Marcks (72), Breysig to Marcks, Berlin, 5.11.95; NL Liesegang, Lamprecht to Liesegang, Leipzig, 16.5.93; vom Brocke, *Breysig*, 25.

9. NL Lamprecht (Korr. 13), Breysig to Lamprecht, Steglitz, 19.2.03; Schmargendorf, 22.11.04; Breysig, *Tagen und Träumen*, 82–87; vom Brocke, *Breysig*, 78–79.

10. NL Lamprecht (Korr. 13), Breysig to Lamprecht, Berlin, 14.9.96. To Marcks he wrote at the same time: "It will not be difficult for me to decide between the banners of Lamprecht and Meinecke." NL Marcks (71), Breysig to Marcks, Berlin, 7.7.96.

11. "Über Entwicklungsgeschichte: Das Objekt," DZfG (Monatsblätter), N. F. 1 (1896/97): 161–74; "Über Entwicklungsgeschichte: Die Methode," ibid., 193–211.

12. NL Harden, Lamprecht to Harden, Leipzig, 16.10.97; vom Brocke, *Breysig*, 69–73.

13. *Kulturgeschichte der Neuzeit: Vergleichende Entwicklungsgeschichte der führenden Völker Europas und ihres sozialen und geistigen Lebens*, 2 vols. (Berlin, 1900–1901).

14. GLA, NL Willy Hellpach (277), Breysig to Hellpach, Wilmersdorf, 20.1.00; Steglitz, 12.6.02; NL Harden, Lamprecht to Harden, Leipzig, 26.1.01; NL Lamprecht (Korr. 13), Breysig to Lamprecht, Wilmersdorf, 18.1.02; Lamprecht, "Entwicklungsstufen," *Zukunft*, 39 (1902): 139–43.

15. Goetz, "Kurt Breysig zum 70. Geburtstag," *Historiker*, 313.

16. Quoted in vom Brocke, *Breysig*, 83.

17. Ibid., 79–101; Breysig, *Tagen und Träumen*, 107.

18. Quoted in Schieder, "Organisation," 276. Despite Bernhard vom Brocke's sympathetic biography, Breysig still suffers from this reputation. See Rüdiger vom Bruch, "Kulturstaat—Sinndeutung von oben?" in Rüdiger vom Bruch et al., eds., *Kultur und Kulturwissenschaft um 1900: Krise der Moderne und Glaube an die Wissenschaft* (Stuttgart, 1989), 63.

19. Steinhausen, "Über den Plan einer zusammenfassenden Quellenpublikation für die deutsche Kulturgeschichte," ZKg, 5 (1898): 439–50.

20. NL Lamprecht (Munich), Aufruf zur Gründung einer "Gesellschaft für Culturgeschichte" für den 1. Januar 1900; NL Lamprecht (Korr. 28), Lamprecht to Heigel, Leipzig, 19.1.99; Schönebaum, "Unausgeführte Vorhaben," 120.

21. ZKg, 6 (1899): 288; ZKg, 8 (1901): 88–93.

22. Steinhausen, "Steinhausen," 243–53; Goetz, *Historiker*, 391–92.

23. NL Lamprecht (Korr. 49), Steinhausen to Lamprecht, Cassel, 9.4.02.

24. AKg, 1 (1903): 361–67; AKg, 3 (1905): 88–91; *cf.* "Zum 50. Band des Archivs für Kulturgeschichte," AKg, 50 (1968): 1–2.

25. Steinhausen, *Geschichte der deutschen Kultur* (Leipzig, 1904); GGA, (1905): 322–34; Steinhausen, "Zur Charakteristik des Historikers Karl Lamprecht," AKg, 3 (1905): 366–71; *cf.* AKg, 2 (1904): 107–11; Steinhausen, "Steinhausen," 265–66.

26. Goetz, "Aus dem Leben eines deutschen Historikers," *Historiker*, 1–87; *cf.* Goetz, "Goetz," in S. Steinberg, 1: 129–68; AKg, 40 (1958): 271–74; HZ, 187 (1959): 731–32; NDB, 6: 582–84; Weber, *Lexikon*, 180–81.

27. NL Lamprecht (Korr. 24), Goetz to Lamprecht, Munich, 27.1.97. Marcks was the principal reader of his *Habilitionsschrift* on Duke Albrecht V of Bavaria. Lamprecht criticized it for—of all things—its biographical failings: "the persons presented are not alive, they appear only in flat relief." UA Leipzig, PA 511, Wülker to Lamprecht et al., Leipzig, 7.5.95. On Goetz in Leipzig, see also Braubach, "Briefe Büchers," 402, n. 49; LW, 445.

28. NL Goetz, Giesecke to Goetz, Leipzig, 12.8.09.

29. "An die Leser des Archivs für Kulturgeschichte," AKg, 8 (1910): 1–3.

30. NL Goetz, Steinhausen to Goetz, Cassel, 9.8.11.

31. Meinecke to Goetz, Freiburg, 31.1.13, in Meinecke, *Briefwechsel*, 38.

32. NL Goetz, Steinhausen to Goetz, Cassel, 7.2.10.

33. "Geschichte und Kulturgeschichte," AKg, 8 (1910): 4–19.

34. Goetz, "Schlusswort," AKg, 8 (1910): 231; *cf.* Lamprecht, "Kulturgeschichte und Geschichte: Erwiderung auf den Aufsatz von W. Goetz," ibid., 225–29.

35. NL Goetz, Giesecke to Goetz, Leipzig, 20.3.11; Steinhausen to Giesecke, 30.5.11 (Abschrift).

36. Meinecke, "Geleitwort zum 100. Bande der Historischen Zeitschrift," HZ, 100 (1908): 6.

37. Schieder, "Historische Zeitschrift," 23.

38. "Jacob Burckhardt, die deutsche Geschichtsschreibung und der nationale Staat," in *Zur Geschichte der Geschichtsschreibung*, ed. Eberhard Kessel (Munich, 1968), 83-87.

39. *Weltbürgertum und Nationalstaat*, ed. Hans Herzfeld (Munich, 1962).

40. Ibid., 244–77.

41. Schulin, "Geistesgeschichte, Intellectual History und Histoire des Mentalités seit der Jahrhundertwende," *Traditionskritik*, 148–49; Schulin, "Meineckes Leben und Werk: Versuch einer Gesamtcharakteristik," ibid., 119; *cf.* Schieder, "Historische Zeitschrift," 33, 50–51.

42. *Weltbürgertum und Nationalstaat*, 24–25.

43. Schulin, "Geistesgeschichte," 148; *cf.* Schulin, "Friedrich Meinecke und seine Stellung in der deutschen Geschichtswissenschaft," in Michael Erbe, ed., *Friedrich Meinecke Heute* (Berlin 1981), esp. 33–37.

44. Georg von Below, "Zur Würdigung der historischen Schule der Nationalökonomie," *Zeitschrift für Sozialwissenschaft*, 7 (1904): 145–85, 221–37, 304–29, 367–91, 451–66, 654–59, 685–86, 710–16, 787–804.

45. Ibid., 327–28, 794.

46. HZ, 93 (1904): 139–40; Otto Hintze, "Gustav v. Schmoller," *Deutsches biographisches Jahrbuch 1917–20* (Berlin and Leipzig, 1928), 133–34; Fritz Hartung, "Gustav von Schmoller und die preussische Geschichtsschreibung," *Schmollers Jahrbuch*, 62 (1938): 295.

47. See Hermann Aubin, "Zum 50. Band der Vierteljahrschrift für Sozial- und Wirtschaftsgeschichte," VSWG, 50 (1963–1964): 1–24.

48. Stephan Bauer, "Ludo M. Hartmann als Mitbegründer der Vierteljahrschrift für

Sozial- und Wirtschaftsgeschichte," VSWG, 18 (1925): 335–39; Günter Fellner, *Ludo Moritz Hartmann und die österreichische Geschichtswissenschaft* (Vienna and Salzburg, 1985), esp. 272–85; Zorn, "'Volkswirtschaft und Kulturgeschichte,'" 469–75; Stieg, 106–7, 110–11. The other two members of the initial editorial board were Emil Szanto and Carl Grünberg. Aubin's attempt to downplay the influence of Marxism on the editors' thinking is not convincing. "Zum 50. Band," 13–15.

49. NL Lamprecht (Korr. 31), Hoeniger to Lamprecht, Berlin, 19.1.03; Below, "Below," 28, 36.
50. Hermann Aubin, "Georg von Below als Sozial- und Wirtschaftshistoriker," VSWG, 21 (1928): 14.
51. Lindenlaub, 281–82.
52. Aubin, "Below," esp. 15–18.
53. NL Lamprecht (Korr. 27), Hartmann to Lamprecht, Vienna, 31.1.03; Below, "Wirtschaftsgeschichte innerhalb der Nationalökonomie," VSWG, 5 (1907): 481–524.
54. Aubin, "Zum 50. Band," 19; Aubin, "Below," 16.
55. Below also became a contributor to the *Archiv für Kulturgeschichte* after Goetz became editor. Below and Marie Schulz, "Briefe von K. W. Nitzsch an W. Maurenbrecher (1861–1880)," AKg, 8 (1910): 305–66, 437–68; "Zur Beurteilung Heinrich Leos," ibid., 9 (1911): 199–209; "Briefe von K. W. Nitzsch an W. Schrader (1868–1880)," ibid., 10 (1912): 25–39.
56. Below, "Wirtschaftsgeschichte innerhalb der Nationalökonomie," 523; *cf.* Below, *Geschichtsschreibung,* 100–101.
57. Schnabel, "Kulturgeschichte," 733–43.
58. Oestreich, "Fachhistorie," 322–23; *cf.* Eulenburg, "*Nachwuchs,*" 48.
59. Hübinger, "Kapitalismus und Kulturgeschichte," 27. See Carlo Antoni, *From History to Sociology: The Transition in German Historical Thinking* (London, 1959); I. S. Kon, *Die Geschichtsphilosophie des 20. Jahrhunderts: Kritischer Abriss,* 2 vols. (Berlin, 1964), esp. 1: 82–157; Ernst Breisach, *Historiography: Ancient, Medieval, and Modern* (Chicago and London, 1983), 326–30; Iggers, *German Conception,* 124–228.
60. Troeltsch, *Historismus,* 12. Troeltsch's volume is also an essential source on the problems of historical method.
61. See Cassirer, 243–55.
62. Frank Fiedler, "Methodologische Auseinandersetzungen in der Zeit des Übergangs zum Imperialismus," in Streisand, *Studien,* 2: 153–78.
63. See Woodruff D. Smith, *Politics and the Sciences of Culture in Germany, 1840–1920* (New York, 1991).
64. Wilhelm Dilthey, *Einleitung in die Geisteswissenschaften: Versuch einer Grundlegung für das Studium der Gesellschaft und der Geschichte. Gesammelte Schriften,* vol. 1 (Stuttgart, 1959). The literature on Dilthey is immense. For an introduction see Michael Ermarth, *Wilhelm Dilthey: The Critique of Historical Reason* (Chicago and London, 1978); H. P. Rickman, *Wilhelm Dilthey: Pioneer of the Human Studies* (Berkeley, 1979). See also Manfred Riedel, *Verstehen oder Erklären? Zur Theorie und Geschichte der hermeneutischen Wissenschaften* (Stuttgart, 1978).
65. Hans-Ulrich Lessing, "Dilthey als Historiker: Das 'Leben Schleiermachers' als Paradigma," in Hammerstein, *Geschichtswissenschaft,* 113–30.
66. See Guy Oakes, "Simmel's Problematic," in Georg Simmel, *The Problems of the Philosophy of History: An Epistemological Essay,* ed. Guy Oakes (New York, 1977), 1–37.
67. Georg Simmel, *Die Probleme der Geschichtsphilosophie* (Leipzig, 1892); Heinrich

Rickert, *Die Grenzen der naturwissenschaftlichen Begriffsbildung: Eine logische Einleitung in die historischen Wissenschaften* (Tübingen and Leipzig, 1902); see also Willey, *Back to Kant*, esp. 131–52.

68. Wilhelm Windelband, "Geschichte und Naturwissenschaft," *Präludien: Aufsätze und Reden zur Philosophie und ihrer Geschichte*, 2 vols. (Tübingen, 1921), 2: 136–60.
69. See Guy Oakes, *Weber and Rickert: Concept Formation in the Cultural Sciences* (Cambridge, MA, and London, 1988); Oakes, "Weber and the Southwest German School: The Genesis of the Concept of the Historical Individual," in Mommsen and Osterhammel, *Weber and His Contemporaries*, 434–46.
70. Eckehard Kühne, "Historisches Bewusstsein in der deutschen Soziologie: Untersuchungen zur Geschichte der Soziologie von der Zeit der Reichsgründung bis zum Ersten Weltkrieg auf wissenssoziologischer Grundlage," Ph.D. dissertation (Marburg, 1971), 328.
71. Lamprecht, "Relativismus," *Zukunft*, 34 (1901): 12–13.
72. Lamprecht, "Was ist Kulturgeschichte?" 80, 89, 90, 93, 103, 136, 144.
73. See Lamprecht, "Kernpunkte," 11–18; cf. *Die kulturhistorische Methode*, 24.
74. PJb, 83 (1896): 91; HZ, 77 (1896): 265; HZ, 78 (1897): 61, 66; JbNöSt, 13 (1897): 667, 687; cf. Metz, *Grundformen*, 475.
75. Iggers, *German Conception*, 197–98.
76. PJb, 92 (1898): 549; DLZ, (11.2.99), 247–48; Below, "Below," 30.
77. See Hajo Holborn, "Wilhelm Dilthey and the Critique of Historical Reason," *Journal of the History of Ideas*, 11 (1950): esp. 116–17; cf. Hughes, *Consciousness and Society*, 200.
78. Below's well-wishers included Paul Laband. M. von Below, *Below*, 75.
79. Breysig, *Tagen und Träumen*, 107.
80. Dilthey to Yorck von Wartenburg, Frühsommer 1897, in *Briefwechsel zwischen Wilhelm Dilthey und dem Grafen Paul Yorck von Wartenburg 1877–1897* (Halle, 1923), 240–41.
81. Rickert, *Kulturwissenschaft und Naturwissenschaft* (Freiburg, 1899); NL Lamprecht (Korr. 35), Lamprecht to Lipps, Leipzig, 22.1.99.
82. Rickert, *Grenzen*, 611–12.
83. Rickert, *Kulturwissenschaft und Naturwissenschaft*, 2d ed. (Tübingen, 1910), 10–11. Erich Rothacker's dissertation could have done little to change Rickert's mind. It attempted to show how Rickert's views comported with a "genetic" approach to history, like Lamprecht's, which featured the entelechial development of cultures. "I believe," Rothacker wrote to Lamprecht with a copy of the dissertation, "that I have written it in the sense you mean, but nowadays one cannot make it clear enough to the philosophers what development really is." NL Lamprecht (Korr. 45), Rothacker to Lamprecht, Munich, 7.5.12; Erich Rothacker, "Über die Möglichkeit und den Ertrag einer genetischen Geschichtsschreibung, im Sinne Karl Lamprechts," Ph.D. dissertation (Tübingen, 1912).
84. See Whimster, 268–83.
85. Wolfgang J. Mommsen, "Max Weber und die historiographische Methode in seiner Zeit," StdSt, 3 (1983): 28–43.
86. The literature on Weber's historical methodology is practically endless. The seminal analyses are Werner Bienfait, *Max Webers Lehre vom geschichtlichen Erkennen: Ein Beitrag zur Frage der Bedeutung des "Idealtypus" für die Geschichtswissenschaft* (Berlin, 1930); Alexander von Schelting, *Max Webers Wissenschaftslehre: Das logische Problem der historischen Kulturerkenntnis. Die Grenzen der Soziologie des Wissens* (Tübingen, 1934), esp. 178–342. Mommsen's article (cf. n. 85) is a good introduction; cf. Guenther Roth, *Politische Herrschaft und persönliche Freiheit* (Frankfurt am Main, 1987), 285–98.

87. GStAM, NL Max Weber (17), Weber to Willy Hellpach, Heidelberg, 5.4.05; *cf.* Hellpach, "Geschichte als Sozialpsychologie," 505.

88. Marianne Weber, *Max Weber: Ein Lebensbild* (Tübingen, 1926), 425–31; Paul Honigsheim, "Die Gründung der deutschen Gesellschaft für Soziologie in ihren geistesgeschichtlichen Zusammenhängen," *Kölner Zeitschrift für Soziologie*, 11 (1959): 3–10. Lamprecht was himself alive to these affinities. He was a member of the German Society for Sociology and an advocate of university chairs in the new discipline. NL Lamprecht (Korr. 24), Lamprecht to Deutsche Gesellschaft für Soziologie, Leipzig, 24.6.12; (Korr. 48), Simmel to Lamprecht, Berlin, 12.7.12; Jerry Z. Muller, *The Other God That Failed: Hans Freyer and the Deradicalization of German Conservatism* (Princeton, 1987), 136.

89. Weber, "Roscher und Knies und die logischen Probleme der historischen National-ökonomie," WL, 1–145.

90. Ibid., 37, 41, 144.

91. Ibid., 56.

92. Ibid.

93. Ibid., 40.

94. Ibid., 24–25, 48.

95. Ibid., 56.

96. "Die 'Objektivität' sozialwissenschaftlicher und sozialpolitischer Erkenntnis," WL, 146–214; "Kritische Studien auf dem Gebiet der kulturwissenschaftlichen Logik," WL, 215–90. In my view, Friedrich Tenbruck underestimates Weber's critical reserve with regard to the "modern" historians. "Max Weber und Eduard Meyer," in Mommsen and Schwentker, 337–79. See also Hans Schleier, "Zu Max Webers Konzeption der historischen Erkenntnis," in Wolfgang Küttler, ed., *Gesellschafts-theorie und geschichtswissenschaftliche Erklärung* (Berlin, 1985), 309–35.

97. WL, 86.

98. Ibid., 195.

99. Ibid., 262.

100. Ibid., 269.

101. Gangolf Hübinger, "Max Weber und die historischen Kulturwissenschaften," in Hammerstein, *Geschichtswissenschaft*, esp. 271–72; Hübinger, "Kapitalismus und Kulturgeschichte," 28, 33–34.

102. WL, 47.

103. Marianne Weber, 357.

104. "Die protestantische Ethik und der Geist des Kapitalismus," in *Gesammelte Aufsätze zur Religionssoziologie*, 4th ed. (Tübingen, 1947), 205–6, n. 3; Hübinger, "Kapitalis-mus und Kulturgeschichte," 34.

105. Ibid., 34–37.

106. StA Dresden, Marcks to KM, Göhren auf Rügen, 19.9.99.

107. NL Marcks (72), Lamprecht to Marcks, Leipzig, 9.3.98; NL Meinecke (25), Marcks to Meinecke, Leipzig, 9.3.96.

108. NL Marcks (72), Lenz to Marcks, Berlin, 12.11.97; NL Meinecke (7), Marcks to Meinecke, Leipzig, 18.8.95.

109. NL Marcks (71), Below to Marcks, Marburg, 1.8.98.

110. LW, 338–39, 370–71.

111. Among the successful dissertations that Lamprecht supervised between 1896 and 1905 were studies of "Das Typische in der Personenschilderung der deutschen Historiker des 10. Jahrhunderts," "Die geschichtliche Weltanschauung W. v. Humboldts im Lichte des klassischen Subjektivismus der Denker und Dichter von Königsberg, Jena und Weimar," and "Die Charakteristik bei Macchiavelli." Schönebaum, "Lamprechtiana," 16–17; Blanke, *Historiographiegeschichte*, 456–66.

112. The most celebrated instance was the clash in 1896 over the habilitation of Ernst Daenell. NL Lamprecht (Korr. 36), Marcks to Lamprecht, Leipzig, 10.10.96.
113. LW, 399–400. One of Lamprecht's doctoral students who survived the ordeal in Leipzig was Otto Hoetzsch.
114. NL Mevissen, Lamprecht to Mevissen, Leipzig, 7.6.98; LW, 371–72.
115. NL Lamprecht (Korr. 47), Seeliger Erklärung, 28.6.99; Seeliger, "Lamprecht," 134; Czok, *Lamprechts Wirken*, 18; LW, 405; HVjs, 1 (1898): 152; HVjs, 2 (1899): 287–88; *cf*. Below, "Neue historische Methode," 194, n. 3.
116. NL Goetz, Giesecke to Goetz, Leipzig, 18.8.09.
117. StA Dresden, VB 10230/11, Lamprecht to Seydewitz, Leipzig, 13.4.99.
118. NL Lamprecht (45), Buchholz to Lamprecht, Paris, 7.1.98.
119. NL Liesegang, Lamprecht to Liesegang, 24.5.98.
120. StA Dresden, VB 10228/1, Seeliger and Marcks to KM, Leipzig, 4.8.99.
121. StA Dresden, VB 10281/203, Waentig to Lamprecht, Dresden, 12.10.99.
122. StA Dresden, VB 10228/1, Marcks to KM, Göhren auf Rügen, 19.9.99; VB 10281/103, Lamprecht, Tableau der historischen Vorlesungen, 1893–1901.
123. UA Leipzig, Phil. Fak., B2/20 (54), Lamprecht to Marcks, Tharandt, 21.5.01 (copy in Marcks' hand); Marcks to Heinze, Leipzig, 22.5.01; NL Lamprecht (Korr. 28), Lamprecht to Heinze, Tharandt, 19.5.01.
124. UA Leipzig, Phil. Fak., B2/20 (54), Lamprecht and Seeliger to Dekan, Leipzig, 11.11.01; ibid., Seminar (Eing. 18.11.01).
125. StA Dresden, VB 10281/103, Lamprecht to Waentig, Leipzig, 2.12.01.
126. *Münchner Allgemeine Zeitung*, Beilage, Nr. 114 (20.5.02).
127. UA Leipzig, Phil. Fak., B2/20 (54), Kommissionssitzung, 10.6.01, 17.6.01; StA Dresden, VB 10281/103, Lamprecht to Hirschfeld, Tharandt, 20.6.01; Hirschfeld to KM, Leipzig, 27.6.01; Schmarsow to KM, Leipzig, 15.2.04. On Bezold, see Srbik, 2: 172–73; NDB, 2: 211; Weber, *Lexikon*, 47–48.
128. UA Leipzig, Phil. Fak., B2/20 (54), PF to KM, Leipzig, 26.1.02; Schmarsow, Beibericht zum Separatvotum Lamprecht betr. Wiederbesetzung des historischen Ordinariats, Leipzig, 22.2.04 (Abschrift); NL Lamprecht (Korr. 15), Buchholz to Lamprecht, Leipzig, 2.1.03.
129. UA Leipzig, PA 124, Urteil über die Habilitationsschrift des Dr. Brandenburg, Leipzig, 11.9.94; Phil. Fak., B2/20 (54), Marcks to Dekan, Leipzig, 25.9.01. On Brandenburg see Srbik, 2: 14; Goetz, *Historiker*, 376–77; NDB, 2: 517; Weber, *Lexikon*, 59–60.
130. StA Dresden, VB 10228/2, Lamprecht to KM, Leipzig, 22.11.06.
131. StA Dresden, VB 10228/2, Lamprecht to KM, Leipzig, 4.4.03; Brandenburg to Lamprecht, Leipzig, 7.7.03; NL Lamprecht (Korr. 33), Köhler to Lamprecht, 25.3.05; (Korr. 50), Tille to Lamprecht, Leipzig, 18.5.04; LW, 516–17.
132. NL Lamprecht (Korr. 50), Tille to Lamprecht, Leipzig, 24.2.06.
133. UA Leipzig, Phil. Fak., PA 555, Kommissionssitzung II, 6.6.15. Wiederbesetzung der Lamprechtschen Professur; NL Lamprecht (Korr. 46), Schmarsow to Lamprecht, 16.8.93; NL Grimm, Lamprecht to Grimm, Leipzig, 15.11.96; BA, Kl. Erw. Nr. 310, Lamprecht to Paul Lindau, Leipzig, 12.6.03. See also A. Schmarsow, "Rückschau beim Eintritt ins siebzigste Lebensjahr," in Johannes Jahn, ed., *Die Kunstgeschichte der Gegenwart in Selbstdarstellungen* (Leipzig, 1924), 135–56; Ernst Ullmann, "August Schmarsow (1853–1936)," in Steinmetz, ed., *Bedeutende Gelehrte in Leipzig*, 1: 109–15. See also Heinrich Dilly, *Kunstgeschichte als Institution: Studien zur Geschichte einer Disziplin* (Frankfurt am Main, 1979), 50. Lamprecht nonetheless drew heavily from Schmarsow's theories of *Raumgestaltung*. E.g., DG, 8: 571–80.
134. UA Leipzig, Phil. Fak., B2/20 (54), Schmarsow to Dekan, Leipzig, 29.11.01; LW, 402–3.

135. UA Leipzig, Phil. Fak., B2/20 (54), Lamprecht to Bücher, Leipzig, 21.1.04; Schmarsow, Beibericht zum Separatvotum Lamprecht betr. Wiederbesetzung des historischen Ordinariats, Leipzig, 22.2.04; NL Bücher, Lamprecht to Bücher, Leipzig, 2.2.04.

136. NL Lamprecht (Korr. 50), Tille to Lamprecht, 26.1.04; LW, 475.

137. StA Dresden, VB 10228/2, Lamprecht to KM, Leipzig, 15.3.04.

138. StA Dresden, VB 10281/203, Lamprecht to Waentig, Leipzig, 3.1.05; Brandenburg to Lamprecht, Leipzig, 5.3.05, 11.3.05; NL Lamprecht (Korr. 15), Buchholz to Lamprecht, Walchensee, 4.4.04; LW, 508.

139. StA Dresden, VB 10228/2, Lamprecht to KM, Leipzig, 17.4.05; Waentig to Direktoren des Historischen Seminars, Dresden, 5.5.05; Seeliger and Brandenburg to KM, Leipzig, 16.11.06. The ancient historian, Curt Wachsmuth, who had remained on the sidelines throughout most of the fight, also received an autonomous section within the seminar.

140. StA Dresden, VB 10228/2, Lamprecht to Seydewitz, Fontainebleau, 16.9.06; Seeliger and Brandenburg to KM, Leipzig, 16.11.06.

141. StA Dresden, VB 10228/2, Seeliger and Brandenburg to KM, Leipzig, 16.11.06.

142. NL Lamprecht (Korr. 28), Lamprecht to Heinze, Tharandt, 19.5.01.

143. StAD, VB 10281/103, Lamprecht to Waentig, Leipzig, 2.12.01.

144. NL Lamprecht (Korr. 59), Lamprecht to Hugo Lamprecht, Leipzig, 11.1.04, 18.3.04; *cf.* MG, foreword.

145. NL Lamprecht (Korr. 59), Lamprecht to Hugo Lamprecht, Leipzig, 11.1.04.

146. LW, 485–86.

147. NL Lamprecht (UL 4), Lamprecht Memorandum [3.2.04].

Part III
The Historian Lives On

9

German History (Reprise)

Glaubt einer Geschichtsschreibung nicht, wenn sie nicht
aus dem Haupte der seltensten Geister herausspringt.

"You know how in Bonn I often lacked the element of repose [*das Verweilende*],"
Lamprecht wrote in 1906 to Alfred Dove. "For my failings I have now
been punished with a general, subjective feeling of mistrust, which is only
slowly disappearing."[1] Lamprecht penned this letter in a moment of critical
introspection that would have been hard to imagine in an earlier period in his
life. He was now fifty and had endured too much in the previous decade to
sustain the exuberance with which he had plunged into the *Methodenstreit*. His
intellectual ambitions had by no means abated; but he had begun to pursue them
with a more serene sense of resolve, which reflected an awareness of his
advancing age and the realization that his views were not going to find acceptance among his professional peers within his lifetime.

To speak of resignation would be to exaggerate, but the historian did look
back with increasing detachment on the controversies that he had unleashed
within the profession. As the conflict receded, so did some of the personal
antagonisms that it had spawned. Lamprecht's resumption of his ties to Dove
was followed by reconciliations in 1906 with Finke and (more remarkably) with
Below, with whom he entered into a cordial correspondence.[2]

Lamprecht's reconciliation with his former enemies indicated anew the absence of malice in his emotional constitution. It also symptomized the dramatic
alteration that the close of the *Methodenstreit* had brought to his status in the
profession. The battle was over. Lamprecht was like the defeated general, who
enjoyed a certain heroic celebrity and respect among some of his former opponents; but he posed no threat to them and exercised no influence. As the
Association of German Historians passed into the control of the academic
scholars who had defeated him, his participation at professional congresses
became more reluctant and infrequent.[3] It also became eccentric; and an air of
pathos attached to his interventions at these meetings.[4]

In these circumstances, the ties of friendship that bound Lamprecht to
individual academic historians, like Dove, Ritter, and Paul Kehr (with whom

his ties extended back to Marburg), survived on the basis of personal affection; professionally, they were as irrelevant as his correspondence with Below.[5] In truth, Lamprecht himself was no longer a relevant factor in the leadership of the German historical profession, nor were the profession's affairs relevant to him. As his interests began to broaden still further beyond the profession's intellectual horizons, he retreated into a local arena.

In the summer of 1898 Lamprecht, his daughters, and Emma Bruch moved back to the middle of Leipzig, into a large apartment that the university owned on the Schillerstrasse. The proximity of his new quarters to the university and the "feeling of comfort" in the place—particularly in the sanctuary of his large new study—were compensation for the return to the ambience of lignite and the pace of city life.[6] The apartment was also closer to the asylum in which his wife resided, so that her weekend visits home became at least more convenient.

Shortly after the move back into town, two events accentuated the bittersweet quality of these visits. In 1900 Lamprecht learned the truth about the circumstances of his marriage—that his wife had already shown symptoms of serious mental disorder before their engagement and that he had been the victim of his mother-in-law's deceit: "*Schöne Sachen das!*"[7] It was of some comfort to him to learn that his wife had herself been innocent to the deception. It was also of some comfort to learn that her father's brother had just died in Strassburg, a rich man. The bulk of the estate, more than a half million marks in securities, passed in 1899 to Mathilde Lamprecht and her husband.[8]

As an *Ordinarius* in a major German university, Karl Lamprecht was financially comfortable to begin with. In addition to his salary, which in 1896 stood at 9,000 marks a year, he could draw on a small capital fund and annuity from his wife's dowry, as well as on fees from his lecture courses, which by 1896 had become very large, and the royalties from his publications, which in the case of the many volumes of his *German History* were also substantial.[9] He had not been altogether free of financial worry, though, for he faced unusual financial burdens in his wife's institutionalization, in supporting a live-in housekeeper, and, during recent years, in dealing with his own health. The inheritance of a "very significant fortune," as he described it, enabled him "to face the future, from a material standpoint, without anxieties."[10] Although it occasioned no major changes in his life style, the money ensured that his wife would never want for care. It also enabled him to guarantee his housekeeper's financial security, to educate his children, and to travel extensively with them. And the money relieved the material, if not the emotional, burdens of providing psychiatric treatment for his daughters, once they, too, began to show signs of emotional illness.[11]

Lamprecht's new wealth solidified his credentials as one of Leipzig's *Honoratioren*, a member of a circle of notables in which the city's leaders of business and government mixed comfortably with scholars from the university. In this milieu, the criteria of status were not measured by the outcomes of scholarly feuds, and Lamprecht's professional notoriety only enhanced his standing. In April 1897, in the heat of the *Methodenstreit*, the king awarded him the Saxon *Ritterkreuz*, first class; seven years later, after he had reaped the scorn of the profession at large and his colleagues in the Leipzig seminar, the Saxon government rewarded him, to his great satisfaction, with the high honorific title of *Geheimer Hofrat*.[12]

The historian was a distinguished figure in Leipzig and a popular personality among the city's elites. He was an extraordinarily interesting man, a gifted conversationalist, the range of whose knowledge was arguably unmatched. As even Seeliger and Marcks could testify, his energy and enthusiasm sowed fascination among those with whom he was not in professional conflict. Another of his colleagues observed that he was gifted "to a remarkable degree" in the art of *Menschenbehandlung*, of exerting influence on others by virtue of his "interests and contacts," which were "many and diverse, if not always deep."[13] "Because he was captivated [*hingenommen*] by the things that occupied him," one civic leader recalled, the historian "awakened excitement about these things and for the way he treated them."[14] His affability and gregariousness among admirers made it easy for Lamprecht to observe the sociable conventions of the city's leading circles. He enjoyed the relaxed company of others, or what he once described as "*Beieinandersein mit Essen und Trinken*."[15]

In Leipzig, as in other localities, the role of *Honoratior* carried both practical and symbolic obligations, whose fulfillment required involvement in a network of local civic and cultural associations. Like many academic scholars, Lamprecht was active in a species of *Verein* that was dedicated to disseminating culture by means of closer contacts between the university and the wider community. He was prominent in a corps of university scholars who presented cycles of lectures to popular audiences.[16] He was a regular speaker at meetings of the local *Lehrerverein*.[17] The frequency and enthusiasm with which he appeared before business groups in Leipzig attested to his admiration for entrepreneurial skills and to the abiding hold on him of Mevissen's vision of a cultured German business elite.[18]

The sudden improvement of his financial position enabled Lamprecht to indulge another of his enthusiasms in a manner that befit a notable. He was one of the city's leading patrons of the arts, a prominent member of groups that supported galleries and museums, theaters and orchestras.[19] His close friends included the two great figures who, as one young contemporary recalled, "permeated the grey city like a magical aura"—the sculptor Max Klinger and Arthur Nikisch, the conductor of the city's renowned Gewandhaus orchestra.[20] Lamprecht's devotion to musical life in Leipzig was particularly intense, and it was more than aesthetic. Like his teaching interests, his musical preferences evolved in step with the progress of his *German History*. By 1904 the regular *Musik-Abende* in the historian's home were featuring the piano music of the late eighteenth century.[21]

Prominence in local cultural and civic life was gratifying. Despite his frequent complaints about the city, strong bonds of loyalty tied the historian to both Leipzig and the kingdom of Saxony, particularly once his prospects for a move elsewhere (which could only mean to Berlin) vanished. Nonetheless, the affairs of the city and state were subordinate to his scholarship, and they occupied him principally on the occasions when they, too, fell into that realm. They often did, for Lamprecht was also a leading patron of Saxon history.

The reputation of the geographer Friedrich Ratzel has fared poorly since his death in 1904. Although he did not himself invent the term, the concept of *Lebensraum* did owe its initial popularity and intellectual respectability to him.[22] Ratzel's defenders have argued persuasively that he cannot be blamed for the abuse of his ideas by a younger generation of geopoliticians and their Nazi disciples.[23] But even his defenders have conceded that Ratzel's work invited misinterpretation. It was riddled with ambiguity, contradiction, and confusion—the failings of a man whose vast range of knowledge corresponded to a penchant for global theory, an impatience with basic levels of analysis, and inattention to questions of detail. Ratzel's inclinations and deficiencies were, in these respects, much like those of his colleague and close friend in Leipzig, Karl Lamprecht.

Like Wilhelm Wundt, another colleague whose grand intellectual design resembled his own, Ratzel came to the study of culture from a background in natural science. Ratzel studied zoology during the 1860s, at a time when the recent publication of Darwin's theories had fired interest in the relationship between natural environment and species variation. Ratzel's road to the academy led, however, through combat in the war of 1870, a stint of journalism, and several years of travel in Europe and America, during which his interests shifted to the impact of the physical environment on the movements of human populations. In Germany, the academic discipline that best matched his interests was geography, and in 1876 he habilitated in this field at the polytechnical university in Munich with a study of Chinese migration into the New World. He thereupon accepted a professorship at the same institution, where he taught for the next ten years.

During Ratzel's tenure in Munich, burgeoning enthusiasm for colonial empire lent popularity and political currency to the study of geography in Germany. At the same time, the discipline itself began to expand into the study of the so-called primitive or natural peoples who inhabited the lands that the colonial enthusiasts coveted.[24] Ratzel was among the early leading figures in the German colonial movement; and he contributed as much as any German scholar to erasing the disciplinary lines between geography and anthropology.[25]

Ratzel laid the foundations of a broader conception of his field in a treatise that he published in 1882 with the suggestive title, *Anthropo-Geographie*.[26] Here he outlined an all-embracing discipline, which, in its claims to construct a bridge between the natural and cultural sciences—between the physical environment and human behavior—recalled the ambitions of some champions of the new field of psychology. Physical surroundings, Ratzel argued, provided the essential context of all human cultures. Like his mentor, Moritz Wagner, he believed that the essential theme of all history was the migration of human groups about the earth. This process was in turn conditioned by the physical location of these groups, the size and quality of space they inhabited, and the natural frontiers they confronted. While Ratzel pleaded that he was no environmental determinist, his language frequently conveyed the impression that natural laws governed the formation, consolidation, and diffusion of the collective traits that defined cultures. He believed, at the very least, that his discipline was nomological, to use Windelband's term. The geographer-anthropologist could chart the regular mechanisms and patterns that characterized both the environmental conditioning of culture and its diffusion through migration.[27]

Publication of this treatise established Ratzel's credentials as the country's leading theoretical geographer. When the chair of Ferdinand von Richthofen fell vacant in Leipzig in 1886, he accepted the call there. Ratzel's scholarship in Leipzig was prodigious, but it was devoted principally to extending and elaborating theories that he had already announced. In his most sensational writings—the ones that later tarnished his reputation—he sought to broaden the scope of his field into "political geography," to establish the relationship between "state and soil," and to argue that political institutions and practices were no less conditioned by physical environment than were other features of human culture.[28] In the last years of his life he turned to natural philosophy.[29] Comte and Spencer retreated before Spinoza and Herder; his vision became more contemplative and aesthetic, not to say mystical. His ruminations turned to the spiritual force that suffused the cosmos and linked the psychic and physical realms, uniting all forms of life with the inorganic world that sustained them.[30]

In Lamprecht, Ratzel recognized a kindred spirit. The tie between the two scholars formed shortly after the historian's arrival in Leipzig in 1891; it was nourished by almost daily conversations and grew into friendship and collaboration. Lamprecht spoke of the geographer as "perhaps my favorite among my Leipzig colleagues."[31] Their similarities of inclination and ambition were already evident before their intellectual bond strengthened during the Methodenstreit and Lamprecht's struggle to escape the accusation that economic determinism lurked in his work. Ratzel's theories about the geographical foundations of culture and politics suggested an alternative position which, in the context of this debate, was more attractive ideologically.[32] Ratzel's influence was evident in Lamprecht's later work, while Lamprecht's influence was evident as the geographer's ideas became more accessible, if not more persuasive, to historians.[33] The deterministic accents in Ratzel's thinking yielded a degree of autonomy to what geographers were calling the "human factor" (Faktor Mensch); his writings dwelt on the reciprocal interaction between the "free human spirit" and the natural environment in shaping the "cultural landscape [Kulturlandschaft]."[34] Like Lamprecht, Ratzel stressed the broad congruities of method and goals between history and the kind of anthropological geography he himself espoused. Both disciplines, he insisted, were interested in questions of historical process;

both used a variety of artefacts, from spears and bows to written records, to study cultural development over time.[35]

These propositions provided the basis for practical collaboration between the two scholars. The concept of "cultural landscape" suggested a division of labor, insofar as one of its elements spoke to the skills of the geographer, the other to those of the cultural historian. The object of this collaboration was implicit in the common interests of the two scholars, too, but it took specific form in response to Lamprecht's frustrations over the problem of regional history in Saxony.

The tensions that had made establishment of the Royal Saxon Commission for History difficult in 1896 continued to trouble the organization's early history. Lamprecht provided most of the energy, but his unorthodox practices found little sympathy among his colleagues on the commission.[36] His solicitation of private funds (from the city fathers of Leipzig, among others) was more successful than his attempt to fix the emphasis of the commission's activities in cultural history, as he understood the term, or to broaden its agenda to include comparative regional history. The commission's meager output during its first five years reflected a series of clashes between Lamprecht and the political historians.[37] The most celebrated was over a project to produce a series of maps—the so-called *Grundkarten*—on which contemporary communal boundaries were to be superimposed onto diagrams of regional river systems. The premise that underlay the project was the perdurability of communal boundaries—the belief that the *Gemeinde* represented a fundamental "spatial unit [*räumliche Einheit*]" and that modern-day boundaries conformed to age-old patterns of settlement, landholding, and administration.[38] The debate in the Saxon historical commission over the value of these maps rehearsed a wider controversy in the press and other local historical societies.[39] Lamprecht was enthusiastic about the project, but he faced the opposition of both the archivist in Dresden and Seeliger in Leipzig, who charged that the whole concept was methodologically unsound.[40]

Seeliger's objections were not unfounded, but the project had acquired special meaning for Lamprecht, who was by now contending with opponents on all fronts. Lamprecht was convinced not only that the *Grundkarten* documented the interdependence of topography and human institutions, but that they symbolized the alliance of history and geography at the most practical level. "Cultural history," he announced in 1898, was so broad in conception, and it "encountered such masses of important materials," that it could hardly achieve its goals "on anything other than a locally restricted, that is, a regional [*landesgeschichtliche*] level."[41] It was perhaps a sign of the historian's preoccupation with the *Grundkarten* that he failed to consider the lethal implications of this proposition for another of his projects, in which he had even more invested.

Early in 1898 Lamprecht persuaded the conference group of local historical societies to endorse the production of *Grundkarten* in principle, as "an indispensable foundation for historical and statistical research."[42] He also approached the geographers at his own university with a proposal for an interdisciplinary institute to promote a comprehensive form of regional history, which they could all endorse and which the Grundkarten seemed to address. Neither Ratzel nor his colleague in the geographical seminar, Wilhelm Sieglin, needed much persuading; and together the three scholars prevailed on the ministry to establish a new institute, whose charge included producing Grundkarten for the kingdom of Saxony and serving as a central clearinghouse of information for similar projects elsewhere.[43]

The historical-geographical seminar in Leipzig, which was officially founded in the fall of 1898, was the first institute for the study of regional history at a German university.[44] It was also one of Lamprecht's most lasting achievements, although much of the credit for its success fell to the young scholar whom the historian recruited to oversee the enterprise. The career of Rudolf Kötzschke demonstrated that even Lamprecht's most able students were unable to escape his shadow.[45] Kötzschke was a product of the university in Leipzig. He studied with Ratzel before completing a doctorate in history in 1889 with Georg Voigt. He seemed fated for a life in secondary teaching before he came under Lamprecht's patronage in 1894. The historian's connections to the Rhineland first brought Kötzschke a commission from the Society for the Study of Rhenish History to edit documents from the abbey of Werden. Then Lamprecht placed him as secretary to the Royal Saxon Commission for History, where he also served as the historian's agent in Dresden.[46] In 1899 he habilitated with Lamprecht on the basis of the work on the Werden abbey, and he was named assistant to the historian, who had just become codirector of the new historical-geographical seminar.

Kötzschke's early career was reminiscent of his patron's. His years of archival work in Dresden and the Ruhr drew his interest to local and regional history, and his work displayed a range of thematic breadth and methodological imagination that recalled Lamprecht's own scholarship in the Rhineland. These parallels were not fortuitous, but the career trajectories of the two scholars then diverged. Kötzschke was too careful and modest to make the grand leap to cultural history on a national scale. Instead, he remained devoted to the regional history of migration, settlement, and cultural dispersion, particularly in Saxony; he thus became one of the leading exponents of a historiographical tradition whose German pioneers were August Meitzen and Wilhelm Arnold, as well as Lamprecht and Ratzel.[47] There is some foundation for calling Kötzschke's scholarship "cultural history in the best sense of the word"; but the boundaries that separated the discipline of history from geography and ethnography virtually disappeared in the work of this historian, who was also an adept in topography, cartography, demography, genealogy, linguistics, architecture, and agronomy.[48] In all events, Kötzschke's work carried the most vital elements of Lamprecht's legacy well into the twentieth century, and it documented the survival, at the level of regional history, of another strain of cultural history.

Lamprecht appreciated the many talents of his student and entrusted most of the affairs of the historical-geographical seminar to him. Kötzschke taught courses in Saxon history, historical geography, and ethnography. He coordinated the preparation of the *Grundkarten* and a series of atlases of Saxon history; in 1902, he became a full member of the Royal Commission for Saxon History, whose secretariat was lodged in the seminar.

Kötzschke also played a role in the achievement of Lamprecht's plan to found a journal of regional history. Conceived as a successor to the journal that had recently fallen into Seeliger's hands, the *Deutsche Geschichtsblätter* began to appear in 1900.[49] The managing editor was Armin Tille, one of Lamprecht's ill-fated advanced students in the historical-geographical seminar, and its editorial board was dominated by Lamprecht's loyalists from the far corners of the profession. The fact that academics like Schulte, Ropp, and Finke were willing at this late date to join this group of archivists, *Gymnasiallehrer* and Austrians attested to an abiding appreciation for Lamprecht's accomplishments as a regional historian. It also suggested the resonance of Lamprecht's and Kötzschke's thinking at the level of local and regional history, for the journal was committed from the start to the broad, interdisciplinary approach that was associated with the Leipzig seminar.[50]

These were nonetheless unhappy times in Leipzig, and Kötzschke experienced first-hand the perils of association with Lamprecht. He could not remain aloof from the turmoil in the historical seminar, particularly after the controversy over the *Grundkarten* brought him into conflict with Seeliger. Twice, in 1899 and 1904, Seeliger blocked Lamprecht's attempts to have Kötzschke promoted to extraordinary professor.[51] Establishment of the historical-geographical seminar afforded him little protection. In fact, the closer Lamprecht sought to integrate this institute into the historical seminar (in the calculation that the geographers would side with him), the more it became itself an object of dispute among the historians.[52] The fact that the two seminars were located in the same complex of offices only confirmed Ratzel's theory that conflicts over space were basic to human culture.[53] Relief for Kötzschke came in the end with the resolution of the crisis in the historical seminar. In 1906, at the urging of Lamprecht and Ratzel's successor, Joseph Partsch—and again over the protests of Seeliger and Brandenburg—the ministry intervened to establish an independent *Seminar für Landesgeschichte und Siedlungskunde* with Kötzschke, whom the ministry now also appointed extraordinary professor, as director.[54]

The arrangement brought peace to one more sector of this troubled university, but it demonstrated anew the extraordinary conditions that prevailed there. Seeliger and Brandenburg, who lost yet another large piece of their seminar's library to an independent institute, eventually exacted a price from Kötzschke for their defeat. Lamprecht's student was forced to wait a quarter-century before he received the *Ordinariat* his scholarship merited. Lamprecht himself stood beyond the reach of his former colleagues, for he controlled his own institute. And as his success in establishing the seminar for regional history suggested, he had important friends elsewhere in the faculty.

Shortly after he joined the faculty in Leipzig in 1891, Lamprecht wrote to Mevissen of the "great advantage" he enjoyed "working here among people in related fields who think much as I do [gesinnungsverwandt]."[55] The presence of a nucleus of eminent scholars who thought much like Lamprecht would have been remarkable at any German university. By the turn of the century, however, the friendship and collaboration among these colleagues in Leipzig had become one of the most extraordinary academic phenomena in imperial Germany.

Leipzig's emergence as a haven for the builders of grand intellectual systems was not altogether accidental. The tradition extended well back into the nineteenth century. Roscher was one of its founders. Another was Gustav Theodor Fechner, the great psychologist and natural philosopher who, on the basis of his famous psychophysical experiments, constructed a Weltbild in which physical and psychic forces were united in parallel operation.[56] The philosophical designs of these two men were basic to the intellectual ambience in Leipzig. During their long careers, they built ties to succeeding generations of scholars whose speculative energy and range of vision matched their own. Fechner's chair passed to Wundt. Roscher recruited Ratzel; he also trained Lamprecht, who in turn recruited Bücher.[57] The congregation of system builders in Leipzig was encouraged in addition by rivalries between the country's two leading universities. Lamprecht's was not the only field in which Leipzig was known as a center of opposition to orthodoxies that were seated in the capital. Ratzel had clashed earlier with Rudolf Virchow and Adolf Bastian over laws of cultural diffusion. Wundt's difficulties with Dilthey likewise invited the conclusion that scholars in Berlin were as dedicated to fortifying the methodological divide between the natural and cultural sciences as scholars in Leipzig were to bridging it.[58]

The similarities in the work of Lamprecht, Bücher, Wundt, and Ratzel ought not be exaggerated. These men worked in separate disciplines; they belonged to what Woodruff Smith has recently characterized as separate communities of discourse, in which different theoretical patterns and methodological issues were central to their scholarship.[59] Nevertheless, they themselves all believed that they were engaged ultimately in a common project. Their goal was to transcend the growing disciplinary fragmentation of the German academy and to fashion at least the rudimentary principles of a single discourse, applicable to every field of knowledge, whether its object be the natural environment, the economy, society, culture, history, ethics, or the human mind. The challenge in each case was to build nomothetic foundations for the human sciences, to establish empirically the regular causal patterns in human behavior that not only bridged the human sciences, but posed analogical equivalents to the laws of natural science.

The project lured these scholars, as it had lured Roscher and Fechner, into an order of speculation that betrayed the limitations of their training in philosophy, which in all cases was largely autodidactic, and made them vulnerable to the charge of dilettantism.[60] They aspired to transcend philosophy, or at least the philosophical antinomies of mind and matter, subject and object, idealism and materialism. The intellectual sources that flowed into their efforts to construct a grand holistic system were familiar; in varying colors and shades, traces surfaced of Darwin, Spencer, and particularly Comte, along with the great German idealists, Herder, Hegel, and Schelling.[61] In the end, most of the Leipzig scholars found refuge in what one might well call an inductive metaphysics or a positivistic idealism; it was ultimately a kind of pan-psychism, which bore the mark of Spinoza and Leibniz.

Because they harbored similar intellectual ambitions and philosophical assumptions, the exchange among these scholars in Leipzig was vigorous. The lines of cross-fertilization in their work were many.[62] Wundt's principles of psychic causality provided the avenue for Lamprecht's flight from materialism. Ratzel's ideas about space and cultural landscapes were fruitful for Bücher, whose theory of growth from stages of domestic to national economy could with little difficulty be cast as a progression through ever larger "economic landscapes."[63]

It was often hard, however, to determine the direction in which the many lines of influence ran, for the exchange among these colleagues did not as a rule take place in writing. They talked. They were close personally and were frequent guests in one another's seminars and homes.[64] And on Friday evenings they met after dinner for coffee in the Cafe Hannes in the Gewandhaus.[65] The regular gatherings of these learned gentlemen led to animated discussions that delighted and fascinated the cafe's other patrons, as the *Kränzchen* became something of an institution in Leipzig. These meetings also provided the scholars with an almost corporate sense of themselves— a fact that lends some basis to calling them the "Leipzig Circle," if not the "Leipzig positivists."[66]

Nevertheless, one should recall Fritz Ringer's observation that interpersonal relations in the German academy were frequently difficult.[67] Despite the similarities of interest among the participants, the emergence of this community of scholars in Leipzig was not spontaneous, nor was it free of friction, even during the circle's period of greatest vitality around the turn of the century. Bücher was the most peripheral and skeptical participant. His ties to Lamprecht had loosened as the historian fell under the sway of Wundt and then began to collaborate with Ratzel. The success of the Leipzig circle was due to a large degree to the force exercised by the boldest, most aggressive, and most eccentric figure of them all.

Little of Wilhelm Ostwald's vast body of work has endured aside from the scholarship in his immediate field of specialization, physical chemistry, for which he earned the Nobel prize in 1909.[68] His principles of "energetics" could not survive the spectacular advances associated with the names of Max Planck and Albert Einstein in theoretical physics.[69] Nor was his attempt to establish these same principles as the foundation for a theory of culture sound enough to weather review by Max Weber.[70]

Ostwald's self-characterization could stand as a fair description of all the Leipzig scholars. In 1923 he wrote of his own "proclivity for regarding every specific problem [*Aufgabe*] straightaway from the perspective of the more general phenomenon under which it could be ordered."[71] The seminal "specific problem" in his own case had to do with the physics and chemistry of catalytic reactions. The results of his experiments led him directly into natural philosophy, to the conclusion that energy, not matter (as most scientists then believed), was the basis of all reality. On the analogy of the laws of thermodynamics, he then deduced the principles of his system of "energetics," whose workings, he insisted, ordered every facet of existence and every field of knowledge according to the intensification and transformation of energy. "The necessary and sufficient precondition of all happenings," he announced, was "differentials in the intensity of available energy"—a general law that applied equally to catalysis and electromagnetism, culture and society, art, genius, and happiness.[72] Finally, Ostwald believed that the principles of energetics implied an ethic, which he formulated in his famous "energetic imperative": "waste not energy—exploit it!" His own multifaceted efforts to reduce the entropy of social, cultural, and political energy extended to pedagogical and penal reform and the promotion of free thought, an international language, and the peace movement.[73]

It was easy to make fun of him. The fallacies in his thinking were transparent. One scientist noted that Ostwald's definition of physical energy alone comprehended seven different meanings of the term.[74] Positing a concept of energy to organize all of reality required an orgy of analogy-building that drained the term of all meaning. "He hangs the word 'energy' around all over the place and thinks he has said something," the physicist Otto Wiener complained.[75] Ostwald's effort also required the dilettante's cheerful ignorance. Weber could not resist a quip about the "imbalance" that seemed to reign in Leipzig, where Lamprecht had "much too much contact with art for purposes of scholarship" and Ostwald had "a little too little." The imbalance persisted, Weber went on, despite the frequent "contact" between the two scholars, which should logically have restored the equilibrium in this particular "intensity differential."[76]

Ostwald was hardly the man to impose intellectual discipline on his friends in Leipzig, but the cohesion and vitality of the *Kränzchen* reflected the deployment of his own enormous energies on behalf of this little community of scholars. The weekly gatherings in the cafe soon encouraged him to establish an additional forum. In 1902 he dedicated his new journal, the *Annalen der Naturphilosophie*, to the pursuit of unified knowledge. The purpose of the journal, as he announced in the first issue, was the "cultivation and development" of the "common ground between philosophy and the individual scholarly disciplines."[77] The result of Ostwald's efforts was one of the most interesting academic journals in imperial Germany—one whose quality and broad interdisciplinary scope enjoyed even Weber's respect, despite the fact that Lamprecht was a contributor (as was Ratzel).[78]

In 1906 Ostwald resigned from the university in Leipzig, retired to his country house (which he called *Haus Energie*), and devoted himself to the causes championed by the Monist League.[79] His withdrawal from Leipzig followed the death of Ratzel in 1904 and the turn of Bücher's interests from economics to journalism as an academic discipline.[80] Much of the spirit drained out of the Leipzig circle thereafter. Lamprecht and Wundt remained as a core, but even their relationship showed the strains of methodological disagreements that developed after the turn of the century.[81] The departure of leading members from the circle was but partially balanced by the occasional presence of younger scholars from the faculty, such as the economist Franz Eulenburg, the philosopher Paul Barth, who had been one of the few from his discipline to defend Lamprecht publicly during the *Methodenstreit*, or the psychologist and philosopher Eduard Spranger, who joined Wundt in Leipzig in 1911.[82]

Although Lamprecht and Ostwald remained in contact after 1906, the chemist's retirement brought an end to the most intensive period of their collaboration.[83] During the *Methodenstreit*, Ostwald helped formulate the terms in which the historian negotiated the transition to idealism. Ostwald's system of energetics was conceived as an alternative to mechanical materialism in the physical sciences, but because his theories featured the play of immaterial forces, Lamprecht found them serviceable to his own needs. Ostwald's influence was most evident in the emphasis that the historian began to place on the intensification of collective psychic energy as the motor of historical change. But the fruits of their many conversations were apparent in Ostwald's work as well, particularly in his studies in the history of science, in which he tried to trace the historical conditions that governed the development and supplantation of reigning scientific theories (in Ostwald's day they were not yet called paradigms).[84] The collaboration between the two men was nurtured by their mutual esteem and broad similarities in interest and temperament. Ostwald himself delivered perhaps the keenest appreciation of their bond when he wrote in 1907 about the "romantic type" of scholar, who possessed a "wealth and diversity of ideas" but preferred to draw "conclusions from conditions insufficiently known," to represent "possibilities as realities," and who was too impatient to allow his ideas "full cultivation and development."[85]

In degrees, Ostwald's description once again fit all of the scholars who made up Lamprecht's circle of friends in Leipzig. These men were instrumental in the evolution of the historian's thinking in the aftermath of the *Methodenstreit*. The "wealth and diversity" of their ideas provided welcome support and stimulation as he refashioned his theories in response to the challenges of the great controversy. However, because they also suffered many of the same deficiencies as he did, these romantics could not help Lamprecht purge his later scholarship of the difficulties that had marred his earlier work.

The *Methodenstreit* prolonged the break that Lamprecht had anticipated in the writing of his *German History*. The contours of the later volumes occupied him nonetheless, even as the controversy compelled him to examine and alter the methodological foundations of his great project. In fact, the preparatory work he did for the succeeding volumes contributed fundamentally to the evolution of his thinking about method, for it complemented the influence of Wundt and his other friends in Leipzig.

The historian planned that the sixth and seventh volumes in the series would cover the seventeenth and eighteenth centuries. He began accordingly in 1895 to immerse himself in the philosophy of this epoch. Here he discovered a great deal that spoke to the methodological issues his opponents had begun to raise. "What riches of intellectual activity during this epoch!" he exclaimed to Mevissen at the end of 1897. "My reverence for the capacity of the human spirit grows from week to week."[86] His encounter with the riches of Spinoza and Leibniz set the stage for his embrace of Wundt's theories in 1896. The evolution of his position over the next several years then registered the progress of his reading into the Goethezeit.[87] "This winter I have been going around with Kant for the first time," he told his brother in March 1897, adding that "I honestly do not know if I have digested him properly."[88] His subsequent methodological arguments persuaded his opponents (if not his friends) that he had digested Kant anything but properly; but his writings at the end of the century did cast a Kantian hue on the theory of immanent historical causality.[89] Lamprecht's fascination with Kant's great contemporary, Herder, also reflected his reading of eighteenth century sources at the end of the 1890s; and such a fascination was more plausible.[90] Once Lamprecht had found a way around Marx through Spinoza and Leibniz, his affinities to Herder became transparent. The concept of the Volksgeist and organic cultural development only required adaptation to a post-Darwinian idiom, in which expressions like biogenesis and "overarching psychic organism" were at home.[91]

Lamprecht's new theory of German history thus emerged out of the several sources to which he turned in confronting his opponents' challenges during the Methodenstreit. To a philosophical framework provided by classical German idealism, the historian fastened a system of psychic mechanics, the principles of which he borrowed from colleagues in Leipzig who were indebted in the end to the same philosophical tradition—from Wundt in the first instance, but also from Ostwald and Ratzel. The emergence of the theory was fitful and riddled with ambiguities and signs of confusion.[92] Despite his many intellectual debts, the historian believed that in the end he had constructed a historical method without theory—or rather, one that had achieved an empirical certainty that transcended all of its own theoretical sources.[93] His psychogenetic method was designed to identify, wholly on the basis of induction, the fundamental collective structures in the nation's past, to demonstrate the psychic character of these structures, and to document their lawful development over time.

The new contours (as well as many of the difficulties) of Lamprecht's methodology were apparent as early as 1896, when his manifesto, "What Is Cultural History?" proclaimed his appropriation of Wundt's theories of psychic causality. Thereafter the historian devoted himself to working out details. During the rest of the Methodenstreit his methodological writings emphasized epistemological questions. With Kant's aid, he had resolved these questions to his own satisfaction by 1902, when he announced that his "period of epistemological molting" was behind him.[94] After 1900 he published less on method and theory, in part because his attentions had returned to writing his *German History*, and in part because he regarded the outstanding theoretical problems as peripheral to an enterprise whose foundations he had already laid. "Doubts about whether I am on the right track have now disappeared for good," he commented in 1901, "and I can now proceed without looking around much to the right or left."[95] His statements on theory now focused on the mechanics of historical development; and they appeared in occasional pieces, prefaces to new editions of his volumes, and in his exchanges with Breysig and Steinhausen.

The problems with which Lamprecht struggled in these writings were neither new nor peripheral. They involved the same polarities that had confounded him during the *Methodenstreit*—the relationship of the material to the spiritual realm, the particular to the general, and the individual to the collectivity. The innovations in his approach to these issues were largely rhetorical. The historian now employed an idiom geared to his belief that the discipline of psychology provided the bridge between history and the universal verities of natural science.[96]

Like Wundt, to whom he owed his fascination with the field, Lamprecht regarded psychology as the "mechanics of the human sciences," the pivotal discipline that had extended the dominion of experiment, induction, causal analysis, and lawful operation into the last spiritual recesses of human behavior, both individual and collective.[97] Lamprecht concluded as well that the great achievements of this discipline had provided historians with both their ultimate challenge and the tools to overcome it. "History is in itself nothing but applied psychology," he wrote.[98] He assumed that studying the operation of these psychological laws over time would demonstrate empirically the laws of history, the developmental patterns that lent coherence to the past.

These assumptions laid heavy claims on psychology—even by the standards of that discipline's practitioners. Lamprecht's claims on the discipline of history were even heavier, as he attempted to work out the specific principles of a "psychic mechanics" that could account for the progression of history through the five cultural epochs, which remained, despite some cosmetic retouching required by his new vocabulary, the cornerstone of his system.[99] The observation that "psychology visibly performs the service of mechanic for history" presupposed that history was tractable to this service—in other words, that history's basic stuff was spiritual, that the *Kulturzeitalter* represented stages in the development of collective mental phenomena.[100] Even though it demanded, as he himself admitted publicly in 1901, an alteration of the views that had informed the first volumes of the *German History*, Lamprecht was comfortable with this premise, for it had provided his first line of defense against the charge of materialism and enabled him to speak of the structures of history in terms that even Dilthey could endorse.[101] "Structures are spiritual in nature," he observed in 1903, "they are the forms of life of socialized human beings which are clothed in certain external, objective forms [*Hüllen*]."[102]

As he examined some of these external, objective forms, however, he encountered an old problem. It was "naturally" necessary, he wrote in 1904, "to make ideal culture and material culture internally comparable, to reduce them, so to speak, to a common denominator," which of course "could only be psychic."[103] The goal, he maintained with an eye to a skeptical Bücher, was accordingly to "spiritualize [psychisiserien]" the stages of economic development, to "emphasize the elements of spiritual development" in economic life, and to reveal how social and economic life was "at the core absolutely [durchaus] socio-psychic and by no means 'material' in nature."[104] The historian's reasoning was that the stages of economic growth corresponded to the development of mental phenomena, and he now isolated the "broadening of the psychic tension between need and satisfaction."[105] His use of the concepts Erweiterung and psychische Spannung was itself broad enough to bring together the ideas of Wundt, Bücher, Ostwald and Ratzel and to erase all distinction between the realms of economy and culture. These terms comprehended, in Lamprecht's parlance, the increase and specialization of production, the geographical expansion and diversification of exchange, the progressive intellectualization of economic drives, and their sublimation into art and scholarship.

Lamprecht was in good company in his fascination with the mental foundations of economic behavior. To speak of interest in this problem as a "need of the times" for a response to Marx is perhaps an exaggeration, but it was a controversial topic among German economists.[106] The controversy had begun decades earlier over the theory of marginal utility. Before it reached a high point several years later in Max Weber's essay on the Protestant ethic, the debate was rekindled at the turn of the century by the publication of Gustav Schmoller's great compendium, the Grundriss der allgemeinen Volkswirtschaftslehre, and by Werner Sombart's massive study of the development of capitalism. Both scholars emphasized the evolution of acquisitive drives in economic development.[107] Lamprecht devoured these volumes, but his most direct debt was to the system of "economic psychology" that the sociologist Gabriel Tarde developed at the same time in France.[108]

Tarde, Schmoller, and Sombart did not, however, furnish Lamprecht's last answer to Marx; and his language betrayed the lingering difficulties of an attempt to treat the material realm as an epiphenomenon of the ideal. At times the historian still wrote as if material circumstances caused spiritual development. He explained that cultural changes "proceeded [hervorgehen] in great part out of economic and social development," that "transitions to new cultural epochs frequently follow transitions to new economic and hence also social forms," and that "great transformations in the area of economy, society, and politics introduced [eingeleitet]" new stages of cultural development.[109]

These observations could be dismissed as residues of Lamprecht's earlier "materialistic" thinking or as signs that he had once again lost track of the train of his own hurried argument, for he appeared to contradict himself repeatedly with assurances that cultural development proceeded according to its own immanent logic. He wrote of the "progression of cultural stages as an inviolable rule of human existence" and of the "internal core" of cultural development, "through which all external events in the final analysis receive character and impetus."[110] As he himself confessed privately, he never fully reconciled these inconsistencies, although as some commentators noted at the time, he appeared to be groping toward a resolution of sorts.[111] At one point he cited "the necessity of absolute coincidence of certain stages of material and spiritual culture."[112] At another, he explained that in any given historical "constellation" "all parts are absolutely determined reciprocally."[113] In the end, Lamprecht seemed headed for a Wundtian (or Fechnerian) resolution; it lay in a kind of psychosocial parallelism, in which each realm of human existence harbored its own "seeds," "potential," or "tendency," which disposed it to develop in harmony with the others, in accordance with the "law of historical relations."[114]

Still, invoking developmental patterns or "inherent developmental tendencies" in this context only compounded the methodological difficulties. The shift from the metaphors of mechanics to those of neo-vitalist biology bespoke the importance of both Darwin and Herder in this stage of Lamprecht's thinking, but it symptomized the move into a different order of inquiry and explanation, which he himself characterized as "social biopsychology."[115] This dreadful term fit the challenge that now awaited the historian whose theory purported not only to describe structural development in biological analogies, but to relate this development to psychological processes conceived in mechanical analogies.

Meeting this challenge required all of Lamprecht's analogical ingenuity. It also overtaxed the repertory of psychological tools with which Wundt had provided him. The historian's differences with his colleague developed over questions of detail, but they grew in importance with the evolution of Lamprecht's ideas about the mechanics of historical change and his increasing interest in accommodating them into a biological explanation of development. Several remarks about the historical variability of laws of psychic mechanics hinted at Lamprecht's discomfort with Wundt's principle that volition was the central psychic process.[116] In Lamprecht's view, volition was the faculty associated with economic activity. His effort to reduce economic development to psychic processes led him to the conclusion that sociopsychic development also affected psychic mechanics, as it brought about the increasing displacement of drives from economic onto artistic and scholarly pursuits. In advanced epochs, volition thus ceded primacy to the more perceptual and intellectual faculties of sensation, imagination, and ideation (or what in German are called *Empfindung* and *Vorstellung*).[117]

Provisioned with this idea, the historian proceeded, as Wundt later put it, "his own way as a psychologist."[118] His way led directly to Theodor Lipps, an important but neglected figure in the history of German psychology—a scholar from whom lines of influence extended to the leading exponents of *Gestalt* psychology and, despite his long polemic with Edmund Husserl, to the strain of philosophy that became known as phenomenology.[119] Lamprecht's first encounter with Lipps was in the 1880s in Bonn, where Lipps was studying philosophy. The two men remained in loose but friendly contact as Lipps moved to chairs in Breslau and Munich and built his reputation as a psychologist with studies of perception, aesthetics, and optical illusion.[120] Lamprecht paid little attention to this scholarship until 1903, when Lipps published a general treatise that suggested a dynamic link between the structures of society and culture and the structures of the mind.[121]

In this book Lipps worked out an elaborate theory of the mind's mechanics, which featured the operation of psychic force (*psychische Kraft*), the appropriation of this force (*Kraftaneignung*) by energy that inhered in all psychic events, and the resultant mental ordering of perceptions and ideas according to a complex set of laws of association and dissociation. Lipps' ideas promised Lamprecht the great link he was seeking.[122] The historian could appropriate fragments of Lipps' system without doing violence to Wundt's basic principles of psychic causality or to Ostwald's ideas about energy. The issue of this marriage, Lamprecht concluded, would be the specific mechanism by which the intensification of psychic energy produced cultural change over time.

Lamprecht published his conclusions in 1905.[123] The focus of his analysis fell on the periods of transition between cultural epochs. Each epoch, he announced, was marked by the prevalence of a "mental order of life [*seelische Lebensordnung*]," "a regulating mental core." In an earlier phase of his thinking, Lamprecht had called this phenomenon a "spiritual diapason," but he now moved to another musical metaphor and spoke of a mental "dominant [*Dominante*]." The debt to Lipps was evident, for this expression referred to mental structure, the complex of psychic associations that lent coherence to the diversity of psychic events in the experience of every individual. Lamprecht then pointed to the difficulties that arose when growing "spiritual excitement, stimulation, occurrences, [and] facts" confronted the mental dominant with a profusion of psychic energy that it was unable to "master." The result, the historian claimed (again with a bow to Lipps), was "dissociations of the mental unity that had until then been prevalent and stronger."

Lamprecht believed that periods of transition between *Kulturzeitalter* were characterized by just this process of psychic dissociation and breakdown of the mental dominant. The symptoms of transition were, he claimed, a general sense of disorientation, passivity, suggestibility, self-deception, and pathologies in the "expression of the personality's energy." These symptoms persisted until the emergence of a new sense of psychic order made possible the adaptation of "mental life" [*Seelenleben*]" to the "intensified [*verstärkte*] world of phenomena, the countless new stimuli." Then, the historian pointed out, "personality, which for a time had been—as it were—taken unaware, repressed, buried" (Lamprecht's terms were "*überrascht, verdrängt, verschüttet*"), "arises again and develops a new dominant." The new cultural epoch was accordingly marked by a "new-won unity of mental functions," which now extended into all areas of cultural expression.

Lamprecht then argued that these psychogenetic transitions were not random, that they conformed to a great overarching pattern of cultural development.[124] In what appeared to be a gloss on Wundt's law of creative synthesis or its variation, the law of historical resultants, he pointed out that because successive mental dominants had to contend with ever more stimulation and energy, the sequence of cultural epochs witnessed a "stronger intensification of mental life, a constantly increasing psychic force, a constantly growing breadth of consciousness." The principal feature of this process was the "lawful self-differentiation of psychic unity," by which the historian meant the progressive differentiation and integration of social groups, the emergence of the individual, and the growth of both the intensity and range of the individual's intellectual activity and control.

In a sympathetic review of these theories, the philosopher Berthold Weiss described in Lamprecht's system a thorough-going symmetry, which was indebted primarily, Weiss thought, to the ideas of Herbert Spencer.[125] The processes of differentiation, integration, and intellectual mastery that marked the grand design of historical development were replicated, Weiss argued, in the course of each of Lamprecht's epochs—and within each realm of cultural activity. A brief but unpursued allusion by Lamprecht to growing intellectual "ossification [Erstarrung]" over the duration of each epoch provided some basis for Weiss' intriguing observation, but the philosopher attributed greater clarity and coherence to the historian's ideas than they could claim. Instead, Lamprecht's attempt to redefine his own discipline as social biopsychology, like his earlier efforts to define a theory of history, had produced an ill-digested compilation of the many ideas from which he had drawn (among them, admittedly, those of Herbert Spencer); but the compilation only confused the methodological issues further.

Two issues stood out. Lamprecht's theory that a profusion of "stimuli [Reize]" occasioned psychic dissociations and the breakdown of an epoch's mental dominant invited once again the charge that spiritual forces were derivative, that material change underlay the mechanics of psychic change. Lamprecht's response was to jump from Lipps' mechanics to biological categories of explanation. The laws of historical development were biological after all. The mental dominant of a Kulturzeitalter was not, Lamprecht insisted, "simply the expression of sociopsychic forces somehow externally stimulated." It was "something in itself: something which carries in itself a certain developmental potential." Therefore, events and outside forces of whatever kind could only accelerate or retard collective psychic development; they could not alter its immanent direction.[126] The mind was, to this extent, an autonomous structure.

Lamprecht's abrupt jump between incommensurable modes of explanation was related to a more basic and familiar problem. Lipps was not a social psychologist. His theories of perception and mental organization were based on the observation of individuals, and he made no claim to explain group mechanics on the basis of these observations. In Lamprecht's eyes, this limitation was irrelevant. The historian had convinced himself that the principles of individual psychology were basic and that they extended, by virtue of the law of historical relations, uniformly to all collective processes. In a breathtaking leap over every intervening level of analysis, he announced that "the elements and laws which the modern psychology of the individual has produced" also governed "the mechanics of the great sociopsychic movements of history."[127]

The flaws in this reasoning converged in Lamprecht's concept of the "mental dominant." The historian applied it interchangeably, with no heed to context, to individual psychic processes, group dynamics of all kinds, and to what would in another vocabulary be called the *Volksseele* and *Zeitgeist*. One passage, in which the historian discussed the consolidation of a new mental dominant, well illustrated the problem:

> And so the whole psyche again becomes free and the master of itself anew, in the appearance of a core of the total personality [*Gesamtpersönlichkeit*]; and it [the psyche] now seeks the highest joy of its existence, in that it progresses to the highest conceivable energetic activation of its functions, under the unified guidance of the dominant. Thereby the newly won unity of its functions remains as the fundamental condition for running free without difficulty [*gradliniges Ausleben*]: and therefore [!] at first a period of idealism approaches.[128]

The principal difficulty in the passage lay in the cloud that hovered over the locus of this psyche and all its powers of agency—whether it was an individual or collective phenomenon (the expression "*Gesamtpersönlichkeit*" was ambiguous), something psychological, cultural, or the free-floating attribute of a historical period.[129] In truth, it was all of these things at once.

Lamprecht's impatient conflation of levels of abstraction was an old habit. Its practical consequence was to erase all methodological distinction between the individual and the aggregate, personal and collective psychology, ontogeny and phylogeny. The formula reduced individuals to generic "developmental examples [*einzelne Entwicklungsexemplare*]," whose existence was governed by the iron laws of Lamprecht's psychologism, this new "natural science of the mind."[130] But Lamprecht's formula also conflated history, psychology, and ideas of organic development to produce, as Eduard Spranger remarked, a "biology of the nation."[131] In this conceptual framework the particular and the general were unified in the nation's "unswerving" morphology through cultural epochs like the stages of an individual life cycle.[132] In theory, as well as in practice, the historian had distilled German history into biography.

Early in 1902, after an interlude of almost seven years, a new volume of Lamprecht's *German History* appeared. It contained a surprise. Instead of resuming in the middle of the seventeenth century, where the fifth volume had stopped, it broke sequence and vaulted over a period of two hundred fifty years to take up in the *Kaiserreich*. The exercise was necessary, Lamprecht explained in the preface, in order to gain a proper comparative perspective on the intervening period, which was to be the theme of subsequent volumes. The next three installments of the *German History*, which appeared between 1902 and 1904, accordingly bore the title of "supplementary volumes" (*Ergänzungsbände*).[133] They offered a vast, sprawling survey of the historian's own era, as well as the first practical illustration of his revised methodology. They also introduced a significant alteration in Lamprecht's schema, in the form of a new epoch of German culture.

That spiritual factors defined this new epoch was immediately clear. The first supplementary volume was devoted to the art, literature, and intellectual currents that characterized a new diapason or dominant, which set in, Lamprecht announced, in the aftermath of the wars of German unification. The survey began with Richard Wagner, whom the historian introduced as both a harbinger and representative figure of the new culture. Wagner's significance lay in his capturing the "most delicate shading of human feelings, particularly of the darker, more unfamiliar, nervous side that is stimulated only by music."[134] This side of human constitution was the central feature of the new cultural period. People became more sensitive, Lamprecht wrote, not only to music, which he called the art form that "works most directly on the nerves," but to aesthetic, emotional, and intellectual stimuli of all kinds. The hallmark of the new epoch was accordingly its "nervousness," the fact that "our nerves have taken on a more conscious life of their own."[135] To characterize this phenomenon and to provide a label for his new cultural period, Lamprecht chose the word *Reizsamkeit*, a neologism (borrowed from Nietzsche) that carried connotations of hypersensitivity to nervous stimulation and which is perhaps best translated as "Excitability."[136]

Wagner was an exemplary figure in another respect, for his synthetic vision of "total art" evoked Wundt's law of psychic relations—another of the era's cultural achievements—which dictated a "close reciprocal connection among all spiritual phenomena" in a given cultural epoch.[137] This law then provided the organizing principle of a long survey, in which the historian drew connections among all phases of ideal culture in the age of Excitability. In graphic art the analogue of the "irritating" new music, with its dissonance and irregular rhythms, was impressionism. Its practitioners, who ranged from Menzel to Böcklin and Liebermann, emphasized the stimulating impact of light and color. In its purest form, the historian explained, "the impression of color is, as it were, directly absorbed at the end of the nerve and coloristically registered."[138] An "intensified sense of reality," a "growing intensity of observation of outward phenomena," and "the penetration of a sense of reality into the soul" marked the onset of a parallel phenomenon in German impressionistic literature, which Lamprecht illustrated in the work of Lilienkron, George, Hofmannsthal, Fontane, Sudermann, and Gerhart Hauptmann.

When the historian turned from the aesthetic forms of culture to the more systematic branches of knowledge, the analogical links weakened and the law of psychic relations began to show signs of strain. The features of the new culture of

Excitability, he argued, were most consonant with the creative arts. The "fragrance [*Duft*], indeed the breath of life of the new spiritual reality [*Dasein*]," first "filled the great realm of *Phantasietätigkeit*." Then, however, the new spiritual life began to "penetrate" and "conquer" the other realms of knowledge.[140] The metaphorical disarray betrayed the danger that the new art posed, in Lamprecht's view, to scholarship. He described how the "foaming over [*Überschäumen*]" of the new aesthetic culture into ethics and religion had produced a new sense of idealism, a fascination with theories of regeneration, aetheticism, mysticism, and heroism.[141] Wagner was again an exemplary figure, as was Nietzsche, whose aphoristic prose read, the historian noted, like modern music.[142] But the prominence of these figures was problematic. Lamprecht's survey of the "half-mystical prophecies," the "exultation and enthusiasm," and the "strong excitement of the feelings and even more the nerves" revealed his discomfort over the currents these thinkers exemplified. The danger, he wrote, was that art in this form might "subjugate" the claims of scholarship to pursue systematic understanding.[143]

The historian's concluding account of the other branches of *Wissenschaft* in the era of Excitability was thus not so much a survey as a call to action. "New times have arrived, a new spiritual life has blossomed," he wrote, "but the systematic investigation of its nature [*Wesen*] has by no means developed far enough."[144] The great challenge faced by the academic disciplines was to extend intellectual control over the broader dimensions of human conduct and to assimilate that side of the human psyche that the era of Excitability had revealed—to understand the "primary processes of stimulation [*Reizvorgänge*] that underly the drives."[145] Lamprecht made no mention of Freud in this connection; in his eyes, the great pioneer in the intellectual mastery of these processes was instead Wundt, whose experimental psychology had laid the foundations for a "decisive, sweeping, convincing" intellectual synthesis of all fields of knowledge under the banner of causality.[146]

In a second supplementary volume, which appeared in 1903, Lamprecht extended the survey to what he had in earlier volumes called material culture, to the economy and society of the German Empire. The volume's principal goal, however, was to erase the distinction between material and ideal culture. Lamprecht here introduced his psychological theory of economic growth. In one of the most remarkable passages in the whole *oeuvre*, he assembled fragments from Sombart, Schmoller, Tarde, Bücher, Haeckel, Ostwald, Ratzel, and Wundt to build a synthesis that was as ingenious as it was porous. Its foundation, he wrote, was a "basic moral drive," the "urge of expediency [*Zweckmässigkeitsbedürfnis*]," which linked the consciousness of human needs with the satisfaction of those needs.[147] Lamprecht declared that the dynamic of economic development was the intensification or the broadening of the "psychological tension between need and satisfaction."[148] The meaning of this proposition remained obscure, but it provided the license for another display of the historian's analogical virtuosity. He insisted that the motif of "growing psychic tension" applied not only to the deferment of personal gratification, but to technological advance, the appearance of trade, the extension of markets (through stages identified by Bücher), the division of labor, and the diversification of production.

Lamprecht had only begun. He now turned the same motif into a conduit to the high culture that he had surveyed in the first supplement. He announced that the basis of the psychic tension that underlay economic development was "nothing other than the drive to preserve and beautify life." "A mere instinct" in the beginning, this drive became "itself intellectualized," as "intellectual elements, mainly conclusions on the basis of moral ideas, intervene between it and its satisfaction."[149] In other words, as he explained in another passage, the "ever more finely conditioned capacity [*Befähigung*]" of the economic drive means ever stronger exertion of the intellect and thus the constantly sharpening acuity of the instruments of knowledge."[150] The key to the historian's feat was the correlation of "tension" and "exertion"—*Spannung* and *Anspannung*. It enabled him to fashion a psychological category amorphous enough to accommodate every aspect of economic growth, along with all the characteristics of intellectual and aesthetic development, which he now defined (still without citing Comte) as the "more reliable replication of the world of phenomena," the broadening of the realm of understanding (*verstandesmässigen Begreifens*), and the development of logical reasoning from a belief in miracles toward its culmination in induction and causality.[151] "Thus in the last analysis," the historian concluded, "the progressive development of the economy and the progressive development of knowledge and technology are only separate aspects [*Sondererscheinungen*] of a single great psychic developmental motif, which can be called essentially the progressive development of the intellect."[152]

After this tour de force had rendered the issue of his materialism meaningless, Lamprecht could speak with impunity about the primacy of economic factors or the "dependence" of intellectual change on economic development. He exercised his impunity in the remainder of his survey of the economy, much of which was keyed to the contemporary debate that the studies of Schmoller, Sombart, and Weber had provoked over the origins and historical significance of modern capitalism.[153] Lamprecht's contribution, which attracted little notice in the academic community, was to declare the whole debate irrelevant. In the formation of the modern economy, he announced, capitalism was "only a secondary factor."[154] The principal vehicle of economic development was instead the institution of "enterprise" (*Unternehmung*), a phenomenon that antedated capitalism. The historian characterized enterprise as a "special form of tension-resolution," which was defined by the synthesis of production and exchange, of manufacture and trade.[155] He traced the modern development of German enterprise from its "wild" beginnings in the late Middle Ages through a "regimented" form in the absolute state of the early modern period, to the "blossoming" of "free enterprise" in the late nineteenth century.[156] At this point, enterprise became everywhere dominant in the economy, and the "intensification" of all phases of entrepreneurial organization and activity justified his speaking, like Ostwald, of an epoch of "energetic enterprise."[157]

Lamprecht turned finally to the social consequences of economic development. He revealed that the "spirit of enterprise" underlay the culture of Excitability. The "extraordinary psychic tensions" called forth by the growth of enterprise had resulted in "psychic intensification," in the "sharpening of economic understanding" and "economic energy."[158] Furthermore, the "spirit of enterprise" left its signature in all other phases of modern life—in the noise and frenetic pace of the city, in materialism, pessimism, and the envy that reigned in the lower classes. This spirit permeated all social strata, from the peasantry and the proletariat to the academic middle class. It operated with special force, however, upon the men whom the historian called the "heroes of free enterprise," the great entrepreneurs who embodied like no other social group the characteristics of the age of Excitability.[159] They were distinguished by their restlessness, their "especially nervous habitus," their "strong sensitivity to stimulation," and by a long list of other traits that suggested the historian's special familiarity with his model. These entrepreneurial heroes possessed the "talent of reforming spirits"; they combined the "richest powers of association with a strong character, and the most delicate sensitivity [leisestes Wittern] for coming things with an energetic will."[160]

The historian's overview of his era's economy, society, and·culture was notable for the absence of politics and the state. Before this feature could be ascribed to a lingering animus against political history, a third and final supplement appeared in 1904, devoted entirely to a survey of contemporary domestic and foreign policy. Lamprecht's opinion of the subject was still admittedly low. "In no sense," he observed, did foreign and domestic policy "constitute the core of 'real' history."[161] Political history had to be traced to its foundations "in the unconscious life-processes of the human condition to which it belongs."[162] "In its whole essence," he continued, now with no fear of the ideological consequences, domestic and foreign policy in the recent past had been "decisively determined by economic and the consequent social developments."[163]

Despite the disclaimer, this volume was (with more than 700 pages) the most massive of the three supplements. It presented a rambling commentary on constitutional, political, and diplomatic developments at the turn of the century, as well as a broad program for reform. An analysis of the programmatic features of the volume will be more pertinent in another context; of greater interest here are several aspects of Lamprecht's effort to link politics to the "unconscious life-processes" that he had described in the preceding supplements.

The yield of this effort was meager. It offered little more than casual pronouncements that the historian failed to develop systematically. His impatience with political history was again evident as he attempted to link domestic politics to the great transformations associated with the development of enterprise in the nineteenth century. The "general political diapason" of the epoch, he wrote, was "democratism."[164] The meaning of this term was unclear. He called it "the

counter-principle to the throne" and used it to suggest growing popular participation in politics. It was evidently related to "socialization," the term that he
invoked to categorize the evolution of the party system. This term was not clear
either, but it appeared to connote the anchoring of traditional ideologies—
which he identified as clericalism, utopianism, legitimism, and legalism—in
specific social groups, or as he himself referred to the process, "the entry of the
parties into the constant and thorough-going confrontation with social problems, from the practical perspectives of a specific group [*Stand*]."[165]

Nor was it immediately clear how the principle of "democratism" comported
with perhaps the most remarkable feature of politics in the era of Excitability.
The historian identified the era's representative political figure as the Kaiser.
William II was, in the historian's view, "without doubt an excitable idealist."
He also resembled the heroic entrepreneurs whom the historian had described
in the previous volume. The Kaiser, too, possessed an "extraordinarily developed power of association;" he was "full of ideas, actively exciting and excitable," impulsive, and yet "devoted with tenacious perseverance to the highest
goals."[166]

Before he could resolve the dialectical tension between the era's political
diapason, the "counter-principle to the throne," and the embodiment of the
same era's *Reizsamkeit*, who sat on the throne, Lamprecht's survey turned to
foreign policy, where the commentary betrayed not a hint of Hegel or, for that
matter, of Marx. The inspiration came instead from Ratzel, as enterprise and
nervousness retreated in the face of geography. Lamprecht emphasized the
"influence of the geographical situation of our homeland" and the "common
spatial destinies of the nation."[167] He argued that "geographical elements"
provided "perhaps the most important conditions for political development" and
cited the impact of these elements on population movements, which he called
"the expansion and contraction of the nation's natural fecundity."[168]

The global catalogue of demands that accompanied this commentary on
foreign policy raised fundamental questions about the historian's understanding
of politics. So did his characterization of the emperor and the basic inconsistencies in his analysis of the historical foundations of his own era. Of Lamprecht's
politics, it suffices here to note that socialist commentators, who had greeted the
early volumes of his *German History*, had reason to conclude, as one of them
wrote of the final supplement, that "the imperialistic ecstasy of the Pan-German
politicians whirls around in the head of the historian Lamprecht."[169]

The supplements to Lamprecht's *German History* raised additional questions
about his understanding of history. The significance of these volumes lay chiefly,
however, in the answers they provided about the historian's assimilation of the
experience of the *Methodenstreit*. Although the research that went into their
preparation was more journalistic than historical, the sheer extent of Lamprecht's scholarship in art, literature, and current affairs was, as Schmoller
commented, astounding.[170] It demonstrated that the historian's energy had not
fallen casualty to the outcome of the dispute.

His penchant for hurried schematization survived, too, as did the attendant difficulties. The problems began with the concept of "*Reizsamkeit*" itself. Its meaning remained ambiguous, not only to hostile reviewers like Mehring, but to the historian himself.[171] Despite the fact that the term described "the era [*Zeit*] of a new culture," which was marked by the appearance of a new diapason, it did not, Lamprecht insisted, represent a new cultural epoch or *Kulturzeitalter*.[172] The era of Excitability referred instead to the "second period of the epoch of Subjectivism," although he never clarified the fine distinction between a "period" and an "epoch." The semantic confusion was the price of his reluctance to redefine the original series of five cultural epochs, which had culminated in Subjectivism and could not have tolerated the addition of a new one. The more ramified periodization thus reflected no "internal displacement" of the original scheme, for "more precise investigations" had, as he assured the reader, confirmed the "periodization which was defined in the 1880s."[173]

Reizsamkeit thus emerged atop an elaborate system of categories, into which the historian could distribute the multitudes of particulars that he had collected from his own era. The schematic profusion was worthy, as one commentator noted, of scholasticism.[174] It reached its height in the volume that attempted to bring order to German high culture. Here the reader wandered through a maze of categories that bore labels like "physiological impressionism," "psychological impressionism," "neuralgic impressionism," "naturalistic impressionism," and "idealistic impressionism." The problem was not so much the routine inconsistency or incompatibility of the historian's categories as it was their eccentricity; and the outcome of the *Methodenstreit* made this problem acute. Lamprecht's historical perspective on the era was, to put it charitably, unique. Analyzing the late poetry of Detlev von Lilienkron as "idealistic impressionism of a physiological character" or the rise of modern capitalism as "the intensification of economic energy" related to no scholarly discourse—other than the one he had himself devised.[175] And in this discourse, the heuristic validity of his categories was not a problem; it was a premise.

Lamprecht was candid about the autodiscursive nature of the *Ergänzungsbände*. He wrote them, as he confessed in the preface to the first one, in the first instance to instruct himself.[176] The principal theme of instruction was the *Methodenstreit*. These volumes represented a belated salvo in the dispute, an attempt to fix its meaning, to situate it in its historical context, and to draw the consequences for his own future.

As its name suggested, *Reizsamkeit* served as the model for a general theory of historical transitions that emphasized the accumulation of psychic stimuli. The transitional character of the era was reflected as well in the organization of the three supplementary volumes. Historical analysis served in each to ground Lamprecht's projections for an impending period of national fulfillment. He foretold the coming of a new political idealism and a sense of solidarity, whose economic foundation would be a new form of "constrained enterprise [*gebundene Unternehmung*]" of cartels and joint-stock companies. Although the proposition did not fit well into the rest of his theories, the leading roles in this transition were to fall to the "*Uebermenschen*," the heroic personalities, like the Kaiser and the great entrepreneurs, who epitomized the age.[177]

An analogous transition was under way in the realm of culture. Fulfillment was to be guided here, too, by "excitable" heroes—by those "exceptional persons of *reizsamer* disposition" who had not been sufficiently appreciated in earlier epochs but who now, in the age of Excitability, "saw before them the most fertile field for personal activity."[178] The role of the culture hero was to fashion the intellectual foundations for renewal, to provide the vision to guide the nation's future in the light of its past. "Our age is unique," Lamprecht wrote, "in that for the first time it fully possesses knowledge of all primitive cultures, as well as a broad overview of the development of the high cultures of humanity." "The insights won from the study of the course of human development," he concluded, "must enable the age to influence the course of the future."[179]

The identity of this hero was transparent.[180] There was but one vision of history equal to the challenges posed by the era of *Reizsamkeit*. Lamprecht's history of this era was thus a final reckoning with his own profession. He portrayed its leaders—his enemies—as the epigones of an earlier generation of historians, whose vision and methods had been shaped by the political imperatives of an epoch now superseded. The *Ergänzungsbände* told of the historian's vindication in the course of German history. They also laid his claim to guide the nation toward its fulfillment in the wake of his own fulfillment, for these volumes signaled the agenda of reform taking shape in Lamprecht's mind even as he completed the final sections of his magnum opus.

In May 1904, when he dispatched a copy of the final *Ergänzungsband* to Althoff, Lamprecht announced that he was "clear about the solution to the problems that await me in the volumes that have yet to appear."[181] The fact that he did not have to confront major new theoretical issues helps account for the subsequent outpouring, which surpassed even the achievement of his great period of productivity in the early 1890s. The last part of the *German History*, which he published between 1904 and 1909, comprised six volumes in nine installments and some 3,700 pages of text. Outlines and drafts of some sections dated from the late 1890s, but most of the effort represented new monuments to the historian's energy and single-mindedness, as well as to his defiance of his professional colleagues.[182] This determination bred its own momentum and sustained him through periods of boredom, which afflicted him increasingly as the project neared its close and his interests turned elsewhere.

The achievement was all the more remarkable for being single-handed. The later volumes rested on no original research, but he wrote them himself and spared his advanced students the exploitation that was already becoming common in the academy.[183] Collaboration was confined, as before, to the distribution of page proofs or portions of manuscripts to his colleagues, friends, and former students; but he could be confident that this practice would produce but minor stylistic suggestions or friendly criticism, which he could incorporate as easily as he could ignore.[184]

The sixth and seventh volumes appeared in three installments between 1904 and 1906. They dealt with the seventeenth and eighteenth centuries, a period that in Lamprecht's scheme marked the later stages of the epoch of Individualism, which had begun in the late fifteenth century. He reminded readers who might have lost track of the argument of the fifth volume that Individualism connoted "the loosening of medievally constrained social forms" and the onset of "a positive, more extensive, greater freedom of the individual founded in the total, real conditions of culture."[185] Now, however, he announced that the term implied a special kind of individual, in whom the ascendancy and autonomy of reason led to spiritual isolation. "Once understanding is viewed as the most essential, if not the only spiritual force, all spiritual experiences are exclusively individual: that is, they are bound to the isolated personality."[186]

The "intellectual isolation of persons," the isolating power of individual reason, defined the diapason of the early-modern era. This motif, which was epitomized in Leibniz's "windowless" monads, linked great systems of rationalist philosophy, like Leibniz's, with the "awakening individualism of the Reformation," as well as with theories of social contract and greater individual expression in art. The era's greatest achievements, Lamprecht noted, came in the realm of *Wissenschaft* or systematic knowledge, in philosophy and the natural sciences, where the triumph of mathematics, mechanics, and deduction broadened human intellectual control over the world and produced the "triumph of spiritual labor over material labor," "the more methodical shaping of the higher forms of human existence."[187]

The attempt to portray the many dimensions of national life as emanations of this diapason produced a number of anomalies. Lamprecht's survey of the triumphant ascent of individual reason accompanied an account of decline in every other phase of the nation's life during the seventeenth and early eighteenth centuries. Towns declined amid war and commercial isolation; so did the urban middle classes, the carriers of the culture of Individualism in the sixteenth century. In the countryside the enserfment of the peasantry presented a spectacle for which the term "Individualism" seemed an improbable description. Against this background, the historian surveyed the general deterioration of cultural expression, or *Phantasietätigkeit*, as the hypertrophy of reason resulted in the "emasculation of poetry and the graphic arts."[188]

Lamprecht's account of general decline seemed to pose another anomaly, for it did not accord with the immanent progressive tendencies postulated in his own laws of development. The resolution of this anomaly required another, mechanical order of explanation.[189] Throughout much of the era of Individualism, the historian explained, Germany was the object of outside influences or, as they were now categorized in his theory, external stimuli or *Reize*. The shift to seaborne commerce fell into this category, as did the material devastation visited by foreign armies. These disasters helped lay the ground for the nation's prolonged submission to cultural intrusions from Italy and France. Germany "displays more the characteristics of a receptive than a creative organism," he wrote of the era, "and its deeper development thus manifests itself in phenomena that deviate often enough from the straight path" of development.[190] The historian's indictment of Italian humanism, which he had issued in the fifth volume, broadened now to other cultural deviations inspired by foreign examples, including all forms of baroque and rococo art, as well as the sterile intellectualism of most of Enlightenment culture. "What we encounter here," he observed of the north German courts of the early eighteenth century, "is empty ceremonial poetry, the twaddle of stale pomp, groveling, cold rhetoric."[191]

Lamprecht's treatment of politics in the age of Individualism recalled the difficulties he had experienced in earlier volumes. As he confessed to Harden, he found the political events of the period to be "rather boring things," and his discussion of them was linked but tangentially to the analysis of social and cultural development.[192] Now his challenge was to accommodate the Borussian gospel, which henceforth supplied the framework for his political narrative. Social and cultural decline thus became the backdrop for political regeneration in the late seventeenth century. Lamprecht's discussion of the rise of absolutism bore the title *Durchbildung*—a word that is difficult to translate but which appeared with increasing frequency in the later volumes to suggest the perfection of developmental potential. His discussion of this phenomenon was nonetheless lucid, thanks largely to Otto Hintze, whose use of ideal types Lamprecht imitated in building a central schematic contrast between the constitutional development of Austria and Brandenburg-Prussia.

Lamprecht argued that the decline of the "national" middle class in the seventeenth century placed the "obligations" of political development on the territorial princes. The Hohenzollerns were the figures of destiny. By the middle of the eighteenth century they had exploited fortune and the advantages of geography to create a state that the historian likened to "a young man, short and sturdily built, in the beginning years of full manhood, well trained in every respect to unfold its power to the utmost."[193] Frederick the Great, whom the historian called the "greatest Hohenzollern," was also the era's exemplary political figure, the "fulfillment of political Individualism."[194] The Frederician state represented in Lamprecht's eyes the last and greatest expression of a theory of state that cast political society as the sum of isolated individuals and imposed the constraints of reason on the absolute ruler.

Lamprecht's survey of German culture in the eighteenth century closed with the harbingers of a new epoch. The revival of commerce in central Europe laid once again the bases of "new life-forms of a purely middle-class society" and hence the social foundations of a vibrant national culture, particularly, he noted, in Hamburg and Leipzig.[195] The hallmark of this new culture was a heightened sensitivity toward the affective dimensions of human behavior, the "unchaining of the imagination" from the shackles of reason.[196] The new motifs were evident in the spread of German pietism, the enthusiasm for Greek (as opposed to Latin) models, in the psychological dramas of Lessing, and above all in the colossal accomplishments of Bach and Händel in a genre that had always best resisted the claims of reason. Frederick the Great's indifference to these new themes was not fortuitous, for they strained the bonds of Individualism. "We stand on a last high cliff," Lamprecht wrote: "the distant view extends already into the realm of the epoch that encloses us today."[197]

In the eighth volume, which appeared late in 1906, Lamprecht introduced his readers into this new "land of Subjectivism." The account suggested, however, that the historian had first to find his own bearings in the new terrain. The difficulty lay in distinguishing the new "Subjectivistic personality" from the old "Individualistic personality." The old one, Lamprecht explained, was "independent in an isolated sense"; there was no thought of its interaction with the rest of the world, in the sense of a "living subject's activation vis-à-vis the objective phenomena of natural and especially of human existence."[198] "In a completely different sense" from that of Individualism, Subjectivism entailed the "freeing of the personality," the liberation of drives, emotions, and creativity.[199] "Fully developed Subjectivistic self-consciousness," the historian observed, led to the realization that one "is not the object, but instead the subject of aesthetic pleasure."[200] Subjectivism meant "knowledge of the world and domination of the world in the broadest" possible sense.[201] It implied moral autonomy and "strengthened spiritual control over oneself and others."[202] Finally, Subjectivism signified the "Durchbildung der Gemeingefühle," the development of "ever stronger feelings of community as against the basic feeling of egotism."[203]

The historian left the impression that he was himself not entirely certain about the distinguishing characteristics of Subjectivism and that he was working out a definition of the new diapason even as he wrote. In the course of an introductory passage and a series of afterthoughts, he pasted together—under the heading of "general intensification of the spiritual diapason"—a list of attributes that were both amorphous and ambiguous enough to accommodate the most diverse phenomena of the new era, whose inception he dated from the middle of the eighteenth century.

Lamprecht's analysis of the transition to Subjectivism was based on the theories that he had formulated earlier with the aid of Theodor Lipps. The transition was provoked, he wrote, by "enormous quantities of new stimuli," which were born of social and economic transformations in the eighteenth century and corresponded to growing psychic "tension between need and need-satisfaction."[204] These stimuli produced the "dissociation of the spiritual condition of Individualism" and triggered an advance to a new, more intensified diapason.[205] The principal locus of this drama was the new national class, the "middle Bürgertum" in the towns of Protestant Germany; it comprised artisans, merchants, and a core of educated officials, Protestant clerics, and scholars who made up the "cultivated public" and sustained the new era's cultural outpouring.

Lamprecht then surveyed the mounuments of early Subjectivism in the work of Kant, Herder, and Goethe. He confirmed the impression, which he had created in the fifth volume, that Kant occupied a seminal position in the new epoch, analogous to Luther's in Individualism. The year 1781, Lamprecht wrote, witnessed the birth of "Subjectivistic metaphysics" in the *Critique of Pure Reason*. Kant's achievement was to turn philosophy away from objects and onto an analysis of "the knowing subject," to identify the constitutive powers of human reason, and announce the "triumphant doctrine of the anthropocentric development of all culture."[206] Herder, whom the historian called the "herald" of the "first great *Weltanschauung* of Subjectivism," descried the developmental foundations of culture.[207] Goethe appeared in Lamprecht's survey as the great writer who traced the progress of Subjectivistic poetry and drama from the excesses of *Sturm und Drang* to their disciplined fulfillment in classicism; he also appeared as the great philosopher of the *Urphänomen*, the "ideas that work behind the objects" of natural science.[208] The historian's enthusiasm for these figures was undisguised, as it was for many of the other pioneers of the new era, like Klopstock, Schiller, and Mozart. The climactic figure in his account, though, was Beethoven, whose creative achievements Lamprecht described as the "highest peaks of development."[209] The role of this genius, he wrote in a long appreciation, was to make music into "what it has to be in an era of Subjectivism, into an art form that expresses innermost life."[210]

The superlatives in the account punctuated Lamprecht's conviction that Subjectivism was a titanic step forward in the nation's development, the unfolding and realization of its immanent potential. The logic of the analysis now required that the historian minimize the impact of foreign influences during the late eighteenth century. This feat became more formidable as the year 1789 approached, but he gave an early indication of his strategy when he, like Voltaire, characterized Rousseau, a Swiss, as "*demi-Allemand.*"[211] Given the standards he set in the next volume, this was but a mild contrivance.

The ninth volume of the *German History* was published early in 1907. It covered the era of the French Revolution and Napoleon, and its principal theme was the politicization of German Subjectivism. The problem, Lamprecht explained, was the retarded realization of the new diapason's political potential. Like the exponents of the new culture, the new national class was politically immature or indifferent, slow to recognize that the "political perfection [*Durchbildung*] of the modern personality" mandated a "democratic" state, which in Lamprecht's definition implied morally free and responsible participants, the "free Subjectivistic perfection of the rule of law," and religious toleration in an "organic" polity suffused and bound by the force of modern patriotism.[212] Absolute monarchy had become an anachronism, the political remnant of Individualism, and a source of decay in the modern era. The historian argued nonetheless that political modernization was well under way in Germany by the end of the eighteenth century. As symptoms of nascent political Subjectivism, he cited the burgeoning of voluntary associations and a political press, efforts to enact pedagogical reform, the incipient emancipation of serfs in Prussia, the early career of Freiherr vom Stein, and the formulation of modern theories of politics by Kant, Schiller, Wilhelm von Humboldt, Fichte, and the Swiss Rousseau.

"Then the French crossed the Rhine."[213] Lamprecht was nearly half-way through the ninth volume before he addressed the impact in Germany of the French upheaval. He portrayed it as a *Reiz*, an outside force whose intrusion—he called it a *Dazwischentreten*—impeded and deflected the Subjectivistic *Durchbildung* of German politics.[214] Like German absolutism, the natural rights theory that animated the revolutionaries in Paris was the "creation of the Individualistic epoch."[215] Its translation into constitutional and administrative reform in occupied Germany was, Lamprecht warned, "at least partially foreign to [German] cultural development and hence always unfruitful in the long run."[216] The enduring reform of German politics took place instead outside the purview of direct French control and in accord with the immanent principles of the nation's own development. At every juncture, whether he was describing municipal reform, the liberalization of enterprise, or the emancipation of the serfs, the historian dismissed the French initiative as superficial or transitory. This effort required evasive maneuvers, the most elaborate of which came in a discussion of agrarian reform. Here the historian depicted the period of French occupation as a fleeting episode by tucking it into a long excursus on the history of the German peasantry, which rambled from the seventh century A.D. to 1848.[217]

The hero of Lamprecht's story was Stein. The Prussian leader represented in the historian's view an "especially German Subjectivistic policy."[218] The October Edict proclaimed the "principal foundations of economic and social Subjectivism."[219] The ensuing reforms brought Prussia to the forefront of political development and established that state's claims to lead the regeneration of the German nation.

Although it was framed in the singular categories of his *Kulturgeschichte*, Lamprecht's description of the reform era in Prussia rehearsed an account that Treitschke and other historians of the Prussian school had rendered familiar. Lamprecht's narrative of the War of Liberation was modeled on the same account. It rivaled Treitschke's in its patriotic pathos, just as it imitated his prose.[220] In passages that were (like Treitschke's) laced with quotes from the war poets, Lamprecht insisted that the war was a *Volkskrieg*, a great popular crusade that mobilized all sectors of the nation in the name of liberation and unification. "What distinguished the beginning battle was the universal participation," he rhapsodized. "The movement which began in Prussia soon expanded by itself, like a contagion, to the west and south."[221] In tracing the betrayal of this great movement, Lamprecht's account followed Treitschke's to Vienna, where Metternich, who had no understanding or sympathy for the principles of Subjectivism, rallied the forces of aristocratic reaction and set the stage for Austria's eventual exclusion from national unification.

"If only I were finished with the *German History*!" wrote Lamprecht to Breysig in May 1907.[222] He had by this time completed the ninth volume and was growing impatient, for he could foresee the end of the entire project. "I am writing day and night on it," he wrote to Ritter earlier the same year.[223] He was also growing tired of it; and he had difficulty concealing either his impatience or his fatigue in the last two volumes, which appeared in three installments between late 1907 and late 1909.

The tenth volume was devoted primarily to the culture of the restoration. The historian charted the parallel development of literature, art, and *Wissenschaft* through stages labeled early romanticism, late romanticism, and realism. Romanticism he characterized as the "first Subjectivistic movement that in the end penetrated all of Germany in equal degrees."[224] It even reached Austria and Bavaria, areas that figured in Lamprecht's account as the nation's most hopeless Catholic backwaters. But this popularity was not an unmixed blessing, for in its early stage romanticism represented a reversion to the mysticism, pathos, and immature enthusiasm of *Sturm und Drang*. The onset of late romanticism after 1830 brought a salutary "cooling-off process," which culminated in the realism of midcentury. Lamprecht's aesthetic judgments were largely those of the minor dramatist and critic Otto Ludwig; his assessment of the era's significance for scholarly thought was his own. "In the realm of *Wissenschaft*," he wrote, the age of Subjectivism was "above all historical."[225] The most enduring achievement of romanticism (and here he echoed Below) was to enshrine historical development as the foundation of scholarship. In sympathetic essays on Ranke, Hegel, Schelling, and several other scholars, Lamprecht traced the general triumph of modern historical consciousness in his own young profession (which he called the "heart of the humanities in the Subjectivistic age"), in philosophy, law, art, and philology, as well as in psychology and the natural sciences, where the formulation of organic theories of development documented the participation of even these disciplines in the epoch's diapason.[226]

The historian then turned with less enthusiasm to the politics of the Restoration. Much of the narrative was listless and only loosely connected to the analytical framework, which again comported with the Borussian account. The challenge, he argued, was to extend the legacy of the War of Liberation and to achieve the national community that Subjectivism prescribed. The principal obstacle was the survival of vestiges of Individualism, not only in the camp of the legitimists but in the "primitive" and "vulgar" doctrines of German liberalism, which rested on "mechanical" theories of natural rights imported from France. The most lucid parts of the volume treated the maturation of the national middle class, the growth of its entrepreneurial component amid the *Durchbildung* of commerce and industry, which Lamprecht analyzed under the rubric of "economic Subjectivism."[227]

The eleventh volume brought the account to a close with some surprises. The first half of this volume, which was published in 1908, began with a discussion of the politics of church-state relations, during which the historian confirmed the suspicion that Subjectivism was a Protestant phenomenon. A conventional political narrative followed to cover the revolution of 1848 and the ensuing reaction. Lamprecht was setting the stage, but not for a conventional dénouement. He first returned to the culture of realism. The progress he documented in the natural sciences, particularly the advances of Darwin and his German disciples, stood in contrast to the signs of general decay that he now identified in the arts. He wrote of the "desiccation of imagination" in prose literature, the "torpidity" of poetry and the drama, of arid historicism and a "realism without ideas" in graphic art, and the erosion of creativity in music which accounted for the popularity of an epigone like Meyerbeer, a Jew.[228] The decline recalled the terminal phases of Individualism a century earlier, and the similarities were not coincidental. The hypertrophy of reason, he noted, "the hegemony of the intellect" over the imagination, again symptomized the breakdown of an old diapason. So did the vogue of pessimism and materialism at midcentury, the breakdown of family bonds and sexual morals, and the increase in the suicide rate. "These are the signs of all declining spiritual periods," he wrote. "The old dominants disappeared; new ones had not yet developed; a condition of moral interregnum began and with it moral anarchy."[229]

This lament rested entirely on the historian's random impressions, and it was a curious way to introduce the political events of the 1860s. These events were the main theme of the eleventh volume's second half, which appeared in 1909 and brought Lamprecht's project to a curious conclusion. His account of the events surrounding the *Reichsgründung* was little more than a hurried schoolbook narrative, much of which was drawn from the standard Borussian surveys. His conclusion, however, marked the break between the Borussians' history of politics and his own. From the perspective of *Kulturgeschichte*, the year 1871 represented an end rather than a beginning; it was situated amid cultural decline and marked the "exiting [*Ausgang*] of the first period of Subjectivism."[230] Bismarck's great achievement failed to still the "nation's drive to unity," which Lamprecht called the "most characteristic and profound political instinct of Subjectivism"; because a significant portion of the German nation remained outside its frontiers, the *Kaiserreich* was not, he announced, the "German state of Subjectivism."[231]

This conclusion forced the historian to extend the narrative beyond 1871. The foundation of the German empire did not alone bring the "first period of Subjectivism" to an end. Lamprecht recounted the diplomatic origins of the Triple Alliance, which he portrayed as a step toward genuine unity among the Germans of central Europe. The *Kulturkampf*, with which the volume then closed, represented the domestic correlate of this alliance. The state's "victory" over what Lamprecht called clericalism, Papalism, and Jesuitism prepared the "consequential Subjectivistic resolution of the relationship between church and state" and represented the "last closure of the history of the first Subjectivistic period of German development."[232]

"So, wherever we look, we can speak of unfulfilled things," he wrote in the end. "The imperfect is really the proper verb tense in which to portray the whole thing."[233] Lamprecht did not need to elaborate, for his *German History* broke off in anticipation of a climax he had already scripted at length. German history awaited its fulfillment in the second period of Subjectivism, the epoch of the Excitable historian.

Lamprecht had had difficulty sustaining his interest in the last volumes, and he was immensely relieved to bring the vast project, which he called his "*oeuvre de longue haleine,*" to an end in the summer of 1909.[234] He spoke of it in the singular, as "my book," and insisted on the unity of its conception and execution. A twelfth volume, which appeared in 1909, documented this claim. Along with a bibliography and index, it contained the original formulation of his life's agenda, the essay on individuality that he had written in Munich in the summer of 1878 but never published.[235]

Lamprecht's claim for the work's unity seemed difficult to reconcile with the many disparities between the volumes published before and after the *Methodenstreit.* The later volumes were riddled with traces of this controversy. The theoretical apparatus was much more elaborate and exposed than in the early volumes, although it conveyed the impression of a greater philosophical migration than had actually taken place. It also corresponded to the much diminished weight of the material realm in the later volumes, where economic development and social stratification were confined to analytical niches titled "Enterprise" and "The Rise of the National Middle Class." The bulk of these volumes was instead given over to political narrative and long discussions of intellectual currents, literature, art, and music; and they often read like program notes for a concert or a museum tour through Lamprecht's favorite works.

The continuities in the work were nonetheless essential. The later volumes can be described in all the same terms as the early ones. They, too, covered a breathtaking range of subjects, from municipal theaters to natural science, from financial administration to pedagogy, and from theology to popular songs. Together with the early volumes, they presented simply the richest history of Germany that had ever been written. It was also the boldest; and the later volumes rivaled their predecessors in employing ingenious analogies to impose a grand interpretive unity on the German past. Lamprecht's *oeuvre* might well have laid claim to greatness had his impatience not subverted its design and execution at every turn. In this respect, too, the later volumes resembled the earlier ones. They were plagued throughout by his haste and carelessness, which resulted in factual errors, heedless (and needless) contradictions, ambiguities, and a chaos of digressions and repetitions. And the flaws in Lamprecht's scholarship, his casual appropriation of other people's work, would have made these volumes rich soil for the successors of Hermann Oncken, except that tilling it no longer offered academic rewards.[236]

To dwell on the historian's failings would serve no purpose. They were part of a personal signature that lent fundamental unity to his work. Another part of that signature is more pertinent. The later volumes of the *German History* continued the story begun in the 1890s. Its main theme was the development of Karl Lamprecht.

The last six volumes of the *German History* traced his intellectual patri-lineage. They contained a gallery of portraits, before which the historian paused to honor the great thinkers who had prepared his way, to acclaim their contribu-tions to his growth and chide them gently for their limitations. The family resemblances were unmistakable. Many of these figures he described as lonely geniuses who had been inadequately appreciated in their own times. There was Spinoza, whose pantheism was predicated on immanent mechanical causality, even though it remained captive to a rationalist metaphysics. The historian's portrait of Leibniz, the other great thinker of the age of Individualism, made note of the same failing but emphasized the centrality of entelechial forces in this philosopher's monadology. Kant, Herder, and Goethe stood out in the section marked "Subjectivism." Herder's accomplishment, although marred in Lamprecht's judgment by a lingering belief in a transcendent God, was to blend the insights of Spinoza and Leibniz with the principle of historical development, which Hegel (whose portrait hung in a later section marked "Romanticism") refined into a dialectical vision that anticipated psychogenesis. Goethe descried the pervasiveness of spirituality and organic development in nature. Kant's intellectual achievement was the most significant of all, for in Lamprecht's view he removed the principle of causality from metaphysics to epistemology. He thus anticipated the dramatic advances in the new science of psychology, which culminated in the triumphs of Wundt.

Most of Lamprecht's forebearers were philosophers, but a small room in the gallery was reserved for historians. Ranke's portrait stood out amid a group of minor scholars, whose limitations were manifest as they groped their way forward from an antiquarian passion for collecting, through a fixation on politics and the deeds of great men, toward a comprehensive view of immanent psychic development.

The grand advance that Lamprecht tracked through the eras of Individualism and Subjectivism was the maturation of German culture. It proceeded on a number of parallel trajectories. Thought progressed from transcendent to im-manent categories of explanation, from recourse to miracles, revelation, and the primitive analogies of myth, through deduction and teleological reasoning in the age of Individualism, to induction and causality under Subjectivism. The corre-late of this advance was the progressive movement from mechanical to genetic and evolutionary modes of thinking. In the creative arts, the process implied broadening fields of perception, the more comprehensive mastery and imagina-tive recreation of the full scope of nature and the human psyche.

These trajectories all converged on Lamprecht. His vision of *Kulturgeschichte* stood as the telos of German cultural development, the synthesis of its every phase. Cultural history offered the nation self-knowledge. It extended the mind's control over the entire panorama of the nation's past. It also identified the nation's immanent potential and, as the supplementary volumes made clear, charted the course of its impending regeneration. In Karl Lamprecht's personal achievement, the German past and future converged.

The historian himself supplied a fitting last word on his *German History*. An afterword to the eleventh volume bade farewell to the reader who had followed him "more or less loyally up to this point." It assured the reader of the "friendy sentiments" of the author, who "in his book has presented, in addition to many other things, a little of himself."[237]

Publishers err. Those who deal in the work of academic scholars are in a special class. While they must attend to the quality of the scholarship they publish, few of them can afford to disregard the market altogether. Because their decisions must reflect two distinct kinds of considerations, they face compounded opportunities for miscalculation.

Alfons Dürr is a case in point. He was the owner of the small publishing house in Leipzig which, at great cost, brought out the four massive volumes of Lamprecht's *Economic Life in the Middle Ages*. While the reviews in the professional journals confirmed Lamprecht's scholarly triumph, the sales figures registered a much more modest commercial achievement. "Relatively speaking, not unfavorable" was Dürr's verdict on the sales, which in 1888, after two years, stood at about 150. He added that "we are still far from covering the production costs."[238] He eventually did cover the costs, but not before he made a colossal mistake. Early in 1890 Lamprecht inquired from Bonn whether Dürr would like to publish a new project, the *German History*, whose first volume was nearing completion. Dürr declined, citing the limited market.[239] The historian thereupon turned to Hermann Heyfelder of the firm of Gaertner in Berlin, who agreed to publish the series.

By 1906, when Heyfelder divested his interest in them, Lamprecht's volumes had sold 70,000 copies.[240] Lamprecht's next publisher, the house of Weidmann in Berlin, had sound instincts for the market, too. By the eve of the war well over 100,000 copies of these volumes were in circulation.[241] Eight of the volumes were in their third edition, five were in their fourth, and one (the first) was in its fifth. Whatever its intellectual flaws, Lamprecht's *German History* was a spectacular commercial success, which gratified its author in the same measure as it baffled and dismayed his opponents.[242]

Lamprecht's success raises the question of his audience. The methodological controversy surely enhanced popular interest in his work. Little can be said with assurance, however, about those whose purchases ran up these sales figures, although fragments of evidence do suggest some tentative conclusions about the kinds of people who made up Lamprecht's reading public.

Academic historians did not. The later volumes of the *German History* not only failed to provoke the renewal that Lamprecht hoped for in the methodological debate; they stimulated no response from his enemies.[243] The leading professional journals—Meinecke's, Delbrück's, and Seeliger's—ignored every installment. Walter Goetz wrote the only significant academic review of Lamprecht's volumes, but he published it in the *Frankfurter Zeitung*.[244] The silence of the historians extended into most other academic fields. Lamprecht's personal ties produced a few scattered notices elsewhere in the scholarly press, but these reviews reflected no serious interest in his work in the academy from which he had been banished. [245]

On the other hand, little evidence supports the view that "workers hungry for education" made up a significant portion of the public which consumed Lamprecht's volumes—even those early volumes that smacked of historical materialism. [246] Lamprecht's retreat into something much different registered quickly in that part of the socialist press that paid attention to cultural stirrings in the bourgeois world. Mehring scored not only Lamprecht's politics, but also his misunderstanding of the driving forces of history and remarked that the supplementary volumes left the reader feeling as if he had subsisted for weeks on a diet of whipped cream and macaroons. [247] To judge from the research of Dieter Langewiesche and Klaus Schönhoven on the holdings in workers' libraries, the interests of workers in historical literature did not extend much beyond popular historical novels. [248] There is, in all events, no indication that Lamprecht's volumes helped fill the shelves of workers' reading rooms. [249]

This absence was not due to the onset of ideological heterodoxy in Lamprecht's work; it suggested instead the social limits of the historian's popular appeal. He admittedly wrote for a broad audience. His volumes were "handy." They were reasonably priced, unburdened with an imposing scholarly apparatus, and written in mannered, sometimes flashy prose, as if they were designed for the same popular press in which Lamprecht sought to promote his own work by planting excerpts and favorable reviews. [250] In the eyes of his opponents, Lamprecht's work pandered to the masses. "The whole thing is so endlessly modern," Oncken complained, "written with superficial dexterity in the most modern *Zeitungsdeutsch* and propped up by means of all the bad arts of cheap showmanship." [251]

Oncken and the others failed to note, however, that Lamprecht's volumes, however skillfully they were packaged and promoted, remained inaccessible to a vast majority of Germans. The *German History* was no introductory survey. It was a vast, rambling compendium addressed at people who were familiar with the basic contours of German history and the monuments of German culture, as well as with foreign languages. The volumes bristled with quotations in Latin, Greek, English, French, and Dutch. Much of the German prose belied Oncken's complaints. Passages confronted the reader with a convoluted style that few newspaper editors would have tolerated. The historian's detailed analyses of the classics of German art, literature, music, and philosophy were written for people who had already encountered these subjects, in the course of an education that extended at least into the upper forms of the secondary schools.

These internal features of the text provided perhaps the most telling clue to the character of the "competent readers" who made up Lamprecht's reading public. His audience was drawn primarily from what one might call the broader reaches of the *Bildungsbürgertum*, those sectors of the German bourgeoisie that were academically educated but not academically employed, the "cultivated" public officials and professionals who subscribed to journals like Harden's, Paul Lindau's *Nord und Süd*, Friedrich Avenarius' *Kunstwart*, or the *Deutsche Rundschau*, which did publish excerpts and reviews of his work.[252] In all likelihood, the core of this social group comprised the historians who worked outside the academy—the archivists, librarians, heads of local and regional historical societies, and the secondary-school teachers who had provided Lamprecht with his most consistent following during the *Methodenstreit*. It is impossible to judge with any certainty the size of the historian's audience—the number of people who actually read at least a portion of the *German History*. A figure of 10,000 to 20,000 is a guess, but it is consistent with this social profile; it also comports with the circulation of journals like Harden's and with the sales figures of Lamprecht's volumes, if one assumes that most of his readers purchased several, if not all, of the nineteen installments that made up the complete work.

This was nonetheless, by contemporary standards, a very large audience. It is tempting to ascribe the historian's popularity to the fact that he spoke to the general concerns and aspirations of this social stratum. Luise Schorn-Schütte has written, for example, that the historian was "extraordinarily sensitive to the socio-political and cultural movement of imperial Germany."[253] Peter Griss has reached a similar conclusion and has argued that Lamprecht's cultural history was "an example of the reaction of the German academic bourgeoisie to the spiritual and social consequences of industrialization, urbanization, and economic expansion."[254] And Karl-Heinz Metz has remarked that Lamprecht's *German History* was an index of the "*Zeitgefühl* of broad sectors" of German society.[255]

These explanations are all plausible but difficult to demonstrate, particularly within the constraints of a biography. Another dimension of the historian's popularity is better documented. He was a symbol and vehicle of discontent within the outer tiers of the German historical profession, where his appeal transcended the flaws in his scholarship. He appealed to those who chafed at the narrowness of the "guild historians"—at what was commonly called *Gelehrtendünkel*—and who believed that the hyperspecialization of academic history neither addressed the social problems that beset the country nor offered a vision that captured the great promise of its future.[256] Lamprecht's history resonated to the mixture of resentment and optimism in these circles, in much the same manner as Oswald Spengler's history later resonated even more broadly to their despair.

Lamprecht's work confronted the big questions of German history. Therein lay one of the principal sources of its appeal. And upon completing his vast survey of the nation's past, the historian turned to even bigger questions.

Notes

1. NL Dove, Lamprecht to Dove, Leipzig, 23.11.06.
2. NL Lamprecht (Korr. 53), Lamprecht to Wenck, Leipzig, 1.5.06; M. von Below, 109–12. The resumption of the tie between Lamprecht and Below was not without a certain pathos, so profound were the misunderstandings between the two scholars. In 1911 Below had a friendly suggestion. "Please don't regard it as presumptuous," he wrote: "think about whether you will not have performed a greater service for our discipline by resuming the kind of monographic work you did in your *Economic Life* than you will by continuing on the path you have followed since then." NL Lamprecht (Korr. 7), Below to Lamprecht, Freiburg, 27.1.11.
3. NL Lamprecht (Korr. 27), Hansen to Lamprecht, Cologne, 21.1.03, 20.3.03; Schumann, 146–47.
4. *Bericht über die siebente Versammlung deutscher Historiker zu Heidelberg, 14. bis 18. April 1903* (Leipzig, 1903), 18–19, 21–23, 35–38; *Bericht über die zehnte Versammlung deutscher Historiker zu Dresden, 3. bis 7. September 1907* (Leipzig, 1908), 18–26; Schumann, 221–24; Metz, *Grundformen*, 468.
5. NL Lamprecht (Korr. 45), Ritter to Lamprecht, Bonn, 5.5.10; (Korr. 33), Kehr to Marianne Lamprecht, Stuttgart, 24.5.15.
6. NL Lamprecht (Korr. 59), Lamprecht to Hugo Lamprecht, Leipzig, July/August 1898.
7. NL Lamprecht (Korr. 59), Lamprecht to Hugo Lamprecht, Leipzig, 31.7.00; LW, 424–25.
8. StA Dresden, VB 10281/203, Kgl. Sächsisches Finanzministerium, Beschluss vom 7. Oktober 1913; NL Lamprecht (R 10), Kgl. Amtsgericht to Else Lamprecht, Leipzig, 29.6.15.
9. NL Lamprecht (Munich), Ehevertrag, Strassburg, 24.5.87 (Abschrift).
10. NL Lamprecht (Munich), Testament, Leipzig, 25.7.10 (Abschrift); NL Lamprecht (R 10), Kgl. Amtsgericht to Else Lamprecht, Leipzig, 29.6.15.
11. NL Goetz (36), Lamprecht to Ritter, Leipzig, 5.1.13; NL Lamprecht (Korr. 58), Emma Bruch to Lamprecht, 21.6.12; (Korr. 10), Lamprecht to Beer, Leipzig, 13.1.14.
12. UA Leipzig, PA 675, Waentig to Lamprecht, Dresden, 15.7.04; StA Dresden, VB 10281/203, Lamprecht to Waentig, New York, 11.10.04.
13. Wilhelm Ostwald, *Lebenslinien: Eine Selbstbiographie*, 3 vols. (Berlin, 1927), 2: 104.
14. NL Lamprecht (M 6), Karl Lamprecht zum Gedächtnis. Trauerfeier in der Universitätskirche zu St. Pauli, 13.5.15, 4.
15. NL Lamprecht (Korr. 59), Lamprecht to Hugo Lamprecht, Leipzig, 17.6.95.
16. NL Lamprecht (Korr. 44), Ratzel to Mitglieder des Ausschusses zur Vorbereitung volksthümlicher Hochschulvorträge in Leipzig, Leipzig, 16.12.96.; cf. vom Bruch, *Wissenschaft*, 262–64; Kittel, *Universität Leipzig*, 38.
17. NL Lamprecht (Korr. 35), Gerner to Lamprecht, 27.8.93; (Korr. 13), Brehn to Lamprecht, Leipzig, 21.1.15.
18. StA Dresden, VB 10230/9, Zweiter Jahresbericht der Handelshochschule zu Leipzig (Leipzig, 1900); NL Mevissen, Lamprecht to Mevissen, Leipzig, 2.12.95; LW, 339–40.
19. NL Liesegang, Lamprecht to Liesegang, Leipzig, 2.12.95; NL Grimm, Lamprecht to Grimm, Leipzig, 6.5.96; NL Lamprecht (Korr. 37), Mayerheim to Lamprecht, Berlin, 25.6.14; (Korr. 47) Schreyer to Lamprecht, Pforta, 14.1.97.
20. NL Lamprecht (Munich), Arthur Nikisch to Else Lamprecht, Leipzig, 2.11.15; NL Lamprecht (Korr. 4), Elsa Asenjeff to Lamprecht, Vorfrühlingsmässe 1908; EB,

2,1: 256; Waldemar Sachs, "Lamprecht und Klinger," *Leipziger Tageblatt*, 5.12.21; Willy Hellpach, *Wirken in Wirren: Lebenserinnerungen*, 2 vols. (Hamburg, 1948–1949), 1: 182.

21. NL Lamprecht (Korr. 55), Wustmann to Lamprecht, Leipzig, 5.12.96; NL Dove, Lamprecht to Dove, Leipzig, 26.2.04.
22. Friedrich Ratzel, "Der Lebensraum: Eine biogeographische Studie," in Karl Bücher et al., eds., *Festgaben für Albert Schäffle zur 70. Wiederkehr seines Geburtstages am 24. Februar 1901* (Tübingen, 1901), 103–89. See Karl-Georg Faber, "Zur Vorgeschichte der Geopolitik: Staat, Nation und Lebensraum im Denken deutscher Geographen vor 1914," in Heinz Dollinger et al., eds., *Weltpolitik, Europagedanke, Regionalismus: Festschrift für Heinz Gollwitzer zum 65. Geburtstag* (Münster, 1982), 389–406; Woodruff D. Smith, "Friedrich Ratzel and the Origins of Lebensraum," *German Studies Review*, 3 (1980): 51–68; Smith, *Sciences of Culture*, 219–33; Michel Korinman, *Quand l'Allemagne pensait le monde: Grandeur et décadence d'une géopolitique* (Paris, 1990), 33–85.
23. Harriet Wanklyn, *Friedrich Ratzel: A Biographical Memoir and Bibliography* (Cambridge, 1961); Gunther Buttman, *Friedrich Ratzel: Leben und Werk eines deutschen Geographen 1844–1904* (Stuttgart, 1977); James M. Hunter, *Perspectives on Ratzel's Political Geography* (Lanham, 1983); Hans-Dietrich Schultz, *Die deutschsprachige Geographie von 1800 bis 1970: Ein Beitrag zur Geschichte ihrer Methodologie* (Berlin, 1980), esp. 182–228.
24. Smith, *Sciences of Culture*, 162–73.
25. Wilhelm E. Mühlmann, *Geschichte der Anthropologie*, 2d ed. (Frankfurt am Main and Bonn, 1968), 124–26; Robert H. Lowie, *The History of Ethnological Theory* (New York, 1937), 119–27.
26. *Anthropo-Geographie oder die Grundzüge der Anwendung der Erdkunde auf die Geschichte* (Stuttgart, 1882); Johannes Steinmetzler, *Die Anthropogeographie Friedrich Ratzels und ihre ideengeschichtlichen Wurzeln* (Bonn, 1956); Hermann Overbeck, "Das politisch-geographische Lehrgebäude von Friedrich Ratzel in der Sicht unserer Zeit (1957)," *Kulturlandschaftsforschung und Landeskunde: Ausgewählte, überwiegend methodische Arbeiten* (Heidelberg, 1965), 60–87; and Overbeck, "Ritter-Riehl-Ratzel: Die grossen Anreger zu einer historischen Landschafts- und Länderkunde Deutschlands im 19. Jahrhundert (1952)," ibid., 88–103.
27. Smith, *Sciences of Culture*, 140–54.
28. *Politische Geographie* (Munich, 1897).
29. Buttmann, 100–109; Schultz, *Deutschsprachige Geographie*, 108–10.
30. *Die Erde und das Leben: Eine vergleichende Erdkunde*, 2 vols. (Leipzig, 1901–1902).
31. BA, Kl. Erw. Nr. 310, Lamprecht to Paul Lindau, Leipzig, 13.12.04; NL Lamprecht (Korr. 44), Ratzel to Lamprecht, Leipzig, 29.1.97; (Korr. 59), Lamprecht to Hugo Lamprecht, Leipzig, 31.3.03; LW, 366, 494; Lamprecht, "Friedrich Ratzel," *Berichte über die Verhandlungen der Königlich Sächsischen Gesellschaft der Wissenschaften zu Leipzig, Philologisch-historische Classe*, 56 (1904): 259–69; Schorn-Schütte, *Lamprecht*, 86–88.
32. See Otto Westphal, *Feinde Bismarcks: Geistige Grundlagen der deutschen Opposition 1848–1918* (Munich and Berlin, 1930), 195–96.
33. Ratzel, "Die Philosophie der Geschichte als Sociologie," *Zeitschrift für Socialwissenschaft*, 1 (1898): 19–25; "Geschichte, Völkerkunde und historische Perspektive," *HZ*, 93 (1904): 1–46. The appearance of this second article caused a stir. "How astonishing that Meinecke accepted it," Breysig wrote to Lamprecht. NL Lamprecht (Korr. 13), Breysig to Lamprecht, Schmargendorf, 22.11.04; Schorn-Schütte, "Territorial-Geschichte," 409–10.
34. Overbeck, "Lehrgebäude," 66–68; Schorn-Schütte, "Territorialgeschichte," 411.

35. Ratzel, "Ethnographie und Geschichtswissenschaft in Amerika, mit einem Zusatz von K. Lamprecht," DZfG, N. F., 2 (1897–1898): 65–74; Ratzel, "Geschichte, Völkerkunde und historische Perspektive," esp. 12–23.

36. NL Mevissen, Lamprecht to Mevissen, Leipzig, 1.4.97; 31.12.98.

37. Lamprecht, "Die Königlich Sächsische Commission für Geschichte," *Berichte über die Verhandlungen der Königlich Sächsischen Gesellschaft der Wissenschaften zu Leipzig, Philologisch-historische Classe*, 52 (1900), 153–67.

38. Ibid., 161.

39. Fritz Curschmann, 'Die Entwicklung der historisch-geographischen Forschung in Deutschland," AKg, 12 (1916): 286–98; *cf.* Schorn-Schütte, "Territorialgeschichte," 406–8.

40. Czok, "Methodenstreit," 20–22.

41. Quoted in Schorn-Schütte, "Territorialgeschichte," 411.

42. NL Lamprecht (UL 12), Ergebnisse der Beratungen der 3. Konferenz von Vertretern landesgeschichtlicher Publicationsinstitute, Nürnberg, 13–15.4.98.

43. StA Dresden, VB 10230/11, Sieglin to KM, 9.7.98; Lamprecht to Waentig, 6.7.98. NL Lamprecht (Korr. 44), Ratzel to Lamprecht, Leipzig, 29.1.97.

44. Czok, "Methodenstreit," 21–22; Herbert Helbig, "Fünfzig Jahre Institut für Deutsche Landes- und Volksgeschichte (Seminar für Landesgeschichte und Siedlungskunde) an der Universität Leipzig," *Berichte zur deutschen Landeskunde*, 19 (1957): 55–77.

45. On Kötzschke see, in addition to Helbig's article, Walter Schlesinger, "Rudolf Kötzschke (1867–1949)," *Zeitschrift für Ostforschung*, 1 (1952): 274–78; Manfred Hellmann, "Zum hundertsten Geburtstag von Rudolf Kötzschke," ibid., 16 (1967): 691–94; Herbert Helbig, "Die Arbeiten Rudolf Kötzschkes," in Werner Emmerich, ed., *Von Land und Kultur: Beiträge zur Geschichte des mitteldeutschen Ostens* (Leipzig, 1937), 9–14; Steinmetz, *Bedeutende Gelehrte in Leipzig*, 251–54; Gerlich, 77–79; Weber, *Lexikon*, 314–15.

46. NL Lamprecht (Korr. 34), Kötzschke to Lamprecht, Dresden, 30.12.96.

47. The tradition was not without its dark side. See Gerhard Heitz, "Rudolf Kötzschke (1867–1949): Ein Beitrag zur Pflege der Siedlungs- und Wirtschaftsgeschichte in Leipzig," in Engelberg, *Karl-Marx Universität*, 2: 262–74; Michael Burleigh, *Germany Turns Eastwards: A Study of Ostforschung in the Third Reich* (Cambridge and New York, 1988).

48. Schlesinger, "Kötzschke," 278.

49. NL Mevissen, Lamprecht to Mevissen, Leipzig, 7.6.98; Tille, "Nachwort," in Kötzschke and Tille, *Karl Lamprecht*, 33–34; Schorn-Schütte, "Territorialgeschichte," 402–5; Gerlich, 73–74.

50. See Kötzschke, "Die Technik der Grundkarteneinzeichnung," *Deutsche Geschichtsblätter*, 1 (1900): 113–31; "Ortsflur, polititscher Gemeindebezirk und Kirchspiel," ibid., 3 (1902): 273–95.

51. Czok, "Lamprecht," 96.

52. StA Dresden, VB 10221/1, Marcks to KM, Göhren auf Rügen, 19.9.99; UA Leipzig, Phil. Fak, B2/20 (54), Seminar (Eing. 18.11.01). The abortive plans of Ratzel and Lamprecht to establish an ethnographic seminar in Leipzig complicated the disputes still further. StA Dresden, VB 10228/2, Ratzel to Lamprecht, Leipzig, 14.7.03; Seeliger to Lamprecht, Leipzig, 14.7.03.

53. StA Dresden, VB 10230/11, Lamprecht to Sieglin to KM, 11.3.99; VB 10228/2, Lamprecht to KM, Leipzig, 28.5.03.

54. StA Dresden, VB 10230/20, Lamprecht to KM, Leipzig, 15.2.06; VB 10228/2, Lamprecht to KM, Leipzig, 6.11.06, Anlage 2, Seeliger and Brandenburg to Lamprecht, Leipzig, 14.11.06; Seeliger and Brandenburg to KM, 16.11.06; Helbig,

"Fünfzig Jahre," 57; Czok, "Methodenstreit," 22–23; Kötzschke, "Das Seminar für Landesgeschichte und Siedlungskunde an der Universtät Leipzig: Ein Rückblick," *Neues Archiv für sächsische Geschichte und Altertumskunde*, 57 (1936): 200–16.
55. NL Mevissen, Lamprecht to Mevissen, Leipzig, 23.12.91.
56. William R. Woodward, "Fechner's Panpsychism: A Scientific Solution to the Mind-Body Problem," *Journal of the History of the Behavioral Sciences*, 8 (1972): 367–86.
57. Buttman, 73.
58. Smith, *Sciences of Culture*, 141–46, 205–8; Ash, 269–72; Lamprecht, "Entwicklungsstufen," 141.
59. Smith, *Sciences of Culture*, 205.
60. Lehmann, "Kant im Spätidealismus," 441.
61. See Simon, *European Positivism*, 244–45, 249–50, 253–54; cf. Schultz, "Moral Force," 77–79.
62. See, for instance, Wundt, *Logik*, 2d ed., 1: 409–10, 424–25, 499–504, 513; 2: 321–28, 451–55, 463, 505.
63. Schorn-Schütte, "Territorialgeschichte," 410.
64. Goetz, "Goetz," 154–55; cf. Ludwig J. Pongratz et al., eds., *Psychologie in Selbstdarstellungen* (Berlin, 1972), 313.
65. Ostwald, *Lebenslinien*, 2: 90, 103; LW, 366.
66. Hunter, *Ratzel*, 41–48; Smith, *Sciences of Culture*, 204–9; Schultz, "Moral Force," 77; Viikari, *Krise*, 215–16.
67. Ringer, *Mandarins*, 55.
68. Jan-Peter Domschke and Peter Lewandrowski, *Wilhelm Ostwald: Chemiker, Wissenschaftstheoretiker, Organisator* (Cologne, 1982); N. I. Rodnyj and J. I. Solowjew, *Wilhelm Ostwald* (Leipzig, 1977); Grete Ostwald, *Wilhelm Ostwald, Mein Vater* (Stuttgart, 1953); Ostwald, "Wilhelm Ostwald," in Raymund Schmidt, ed., *Die Philosophie der Gegenwart in Selbstdarstellungen*, 7 vols. (Leipzig, 1922–1929), 4: 127–61; Herbert Staude, "Wilhelm Ostwald und die physikalische Chemie," in Engelberg, *Karl-Marx-Universität Leipzig*, 1: 481–91; Lothar Striebing, "Wilhelm Ostwald und das Philosophieren der Naturwissenschaftlicher," ibid., 1: 492–504; Günther Lotz et al., eds., *Forschen und Nutzen: Wilhelm Ostwald zur wissenschaftlichen Arbeit* (Berlin, 1982); Ostwald, *Lebenslinien*.
69. Christa Jungnickel and Russell McCormmach, *The Intellectual Mastery of Nature: Theoretical Physics from Ohm to Einstein*, 2 vols. (Chicago and London, 1986), 2: 217–27; Robert John Deltete, "The Energetics Controversy in Late 19th-Century Germany: Helmholtz, Ostwald, and Their Critics," Ph.D. dissertation (Yale University, 1983).
70. Weber, "'Energetische' Kulturtheorien," WL, 376–402.
71. Ostwald, "Ostwald," 130.
72. Ibid., 134; Ostwald, *Energetische Grundlagen der Kulturwissenschaften* (Leipzig, 1909).
73. Ostwald, *Die Forderungen des Tages* (Leipzig, 1910); cf. Chickering, *Imperial Germany*, 124–28.
74. Domschke and Lewandrowski, 47.
75. UB Leipzig, NL Otto Wiener, Wiener to Lamprecht, 20.10.10.
76. WL, 393.
77. "Zur Einführung," *Annalen der Naturphilosophie*, 1 (1902): 1–4.
78. NL Weber (17), Weber to Hellpach, Heidelberg, 27.2.06. This letter appears now in M. Rainer Lepsius et al., eds., *Max Weber: Briefe 1906–1908* (Tübingen, 1990), 40–41.
79. Niles Robert Holt, "The Social and Political Ideas of the German Monist Move-

ment, 1871–1914," Ph.D. dissertation (Yale University, 1967); *cf.* Daniel Gasman, *The Scientific Origins of National Socialism: Social Darwinism in Ernst Haeckel and the German Monist League* (London and New York, 1971).

80. Rüdiger vom Bruch, "Zeitungswissenschaft zwischen Historie und Nationalökonomie: Ein Beitrag zur Vorgeschichte der Publizistik als Wissenschaft im späteren Deutschen Kaiserreich," *Publizistik*, 25 (1980): 579–607; Dietrich Schmidt and Franz Knipping, "Karl Bücher und das erste deutsche Universitätsinstitut für Zeitungskunde," in Engelberg, *Karl-Marx-Universität*, 2: 57–77.

81. See Lamprecht, MG, 19–20; Peter Petersen, *Der Entwicklungsgedanke in der Philosophie Wundts: Zugleich ein Beitrag zur Methode der Kulturgeschichte* (Leipzig, 1908).

82. NL Lamprecht (Korr. 55), Lamprecht to Wundt, Leipzig, 24.6.12; (Korr 5), Barth to Lamprecht, Leipzig, 2.3.05; Barth, "Paul Barth," in Schmidt, *Philosophie der Gegenwart*, 1: 1–20; Barth, "Fragen der Geschichtswissenschaft," *Vierteljahrschrift für wissenschaftliche Philosophie*, 23 (1899): 322–59; Barth, *Die Philosophie der Geschichte als Sociologie* (Leipzig, 1897); NL Lamprecht (Korr. 48), Lamprecht to Spranger, Leipzig, 22.1.12; Spranger to Käthe Hadlich, Leipzig, 16.10.11, in Hans Walter Bähr, ed., *Eduard Spranger: Briefe 1901–1963* (Tübinger, 1978), 54; Schultz, "Moral Force," 79–80.

83. NL Lamprecht (Korr. 40), Ostwald to Lamprecht, Grossbothen, 3.5.10, 5.10.10, 7.12.14; Ostwald, "Meine Freundschaft mit Karl Lamprecht: Geisteswissenschaft und Naturwissenschaft," *Neue Leipziger Zeitung*, 27.6.26; Ostwald, *Lebenslinien*, 2: 103–6; LW, 453–55; *cf.* Lamprecht, MG, 64.

84. NL Lamprecht (Korr. 45), Lamprecht to Ritter, Leipzig, 23.8.07; Ostwald, *Lebenslinien*, 2: 104–5.

85. Ostwald, "Zur Biologie des Forschers," *Forderungen des Tages*, 292–93; Domschke and Lewandrowski, 91–93.

86. NL Mevissen, Lamprecht to Mevissen, Leipzig, 27.12.97.

87. Lamprecht's defense of his techniques of excerpting documents included an unlikely appeal to Goethe's *Farbenlehre*: PJb, 89 (1897): 351.

88. NL Lamprecht, Lamprecht to Hugo Lamprecht, Leipzig, 16.3.97; Schultz, "Moral Force," 9, 20.

89. See K. R. Brotherus, "Sind Kant und Lamprecht unvereinbare Gegensätze?" *Studium Lipsiense: Ehrengabe für Karl Lamprecht* (Berlin, 1909), 1–22.

90. Lamprecht, "Herder und Kant als Theoretiker der Geschichtswissenschaft," JBNöSt, 69 (1897): 161–203.

91. See Jahn, 134.

92. Schleier, "Kulturhistoriker," 23.

93. Czok, "Methodenstreit," 17.

94. "Entwicklungsstufen," 139.

95. NL Althoff (B Nr. 108/1), Lamprecht to Althoff, Leipzig, 20.10.01.

96. See Metz, "'Methodenstreit,'" 12; Cassirer, 281–82.

97. MG, 17.

98. Ibid., 16.

99. Borrowing from Wundt, the historian also added, but then quickly dropped an epoch before symbolism, which he variously called "animism" or "*phantastisch.*" See DG 1 (3): xi, xvi.

100. MG, 18.

101. DG 1 (3): xiv–xv.

102. "Über den Begriff der Geschichte und über historische und psychologische Gesetze," *Annalen der Naturphilosophie*, 2 (1903): 259–60.

103. "Biopsychologische Probleme," *Annalen der Naturphilosophie*, 3 (1904): 445.

104. Ibid., 446; "Über den Begriff der Geschichte," 276–77.

105. "Die Psychisierung der Wirtschaftsstufen," ZKg, 9 (1902): 365–449.
106. Michael Appel, "Der 'Moderne Kapitalismus' im Urteil zeitgenössischer Besprechungen," in Bernhard vom Brocke, ed., Sombarts "Moderner Kapitalismus": Materialien zur Kritik und Rezeption (Munich, 1987), 82.
107. Hübinger, "Kapitalismus und Kulturgeschichte," 34–37; Schorn-Schütte, Lamprecht, 90–93; Lindenlaub, 287.
108. NL Lamprecht (Korr. 59), Lamprecht to Hugo Lamprecht, Wiesbaden, 31.3.02; "Biopsychologische Probleme," 446; Griss, 162. Lamprecht read Tarde's Psychologie économique at the suggestion of Henri Pirenne. Pirenne to Lamprecht, Ghent, 31.12.01, in Bryce Lyon, "The Letters of Henri Pirenne to Karl Lamprecht (1894–1915)," Bulletin de la Commission royale d'histoire, 132 (1966): 212.
109. MG, 52, 105–6.
110. Ibid., 51; "Über den Begriff der Geschichte," 261.
111. NL Lamprecht (Korr. 45), Lamprecht to Ritter, 18.1.08; Franz Eulenburg, "Neuere Geschichtsphilosophie," Archiv für Sozialwissenschaft und Sozialpolitik, 25 (1907): 319–37; Eduard Spranger, Die Grundlagen der Geschichtswissenschaft: Eine Erkenntnistheoretisch-psychologische Untersuchung (Berlin, 1905), 40–48.
112. "Biopsychologische Probleme," 446.
113. "Über den Begriff der Geschichte," 269.
114. MG, 54, 96–97; DG 1 (3): xiv–xv; DG, 8: 590; cf. Spranger, Geschichtswissenschaft, 45; Eulenburg, "Geschichtsphilosophie," 330–31; Spiess, 57–58; cf. Wise, "How Do Sums Count?" 404.
115. "Biopsychologische Probleme," 444; cf. MG, 64.
116. Ibid., 19–20; "Über den Begriff der Geschichte," 270; cf. EB, 1: 452; DG, 6: 163.
117. Lamprecht, "Psychisierung," 421–22; cf. Petersen, Entwicklungsgedanke, 121–22; Spiess, 56–57.
118. Wundt and Klinger, Gedenkblatt, 16–17.
119. See Georg Anschütz, "Theodor Lipps," Archiv für die gesamte Psychologie, 34 (1915): 1–13; Boring, 440–42; C. Müller, "Die Apperzeptionstheorie von W. Wundt und Th. Lipps und ihre Weiterführung in der Gegenwart," Ph.D. dissertation (Münster, 1910).
120. NL Lamprecht (Korr. 35), Lamprecht to Lipps, Leipzig, 22.1.99.
121. Lipps, Leitfaden der Psychologie (Leipzig, 1903).
122. Kötzschke, "Lamprecht," 15; Spiess, 57; Hans Freyer, "Geschichte und Soziologie," Vergangenheit und Gegenwart, 16 (1926): 206; LW, 482–83. Lamprecht's own recollections of his debts to Lipps and Wundt were not entirely accurate. See Guilland, 87, n.1.
123. "Der Übergang zum seelischen Charakter der deutschen Gegenwart: Allgemeine Mechanik seelischer Uebergangszeiten," MG, 51–76.
124. "Zur Psychologie der Kulturzeitalter überhaupt," ibid., 77–102.
125. Berthold Weiss, "Lamprechts Geschichtsphilosophie," Archiv für systematische Philosophie, 12 (1906): 209–24; cf. Spiess, 74–76.
126. MG, 96.
127. Ibid., 15. On the methodological problems see Cassirer's essay "The Theory of Psychological Types in History: Lamprecht," in The Problem of Knowledge, 218–93.
128. MG, 75.
129. Two years later Lamprecht wrote that "gebundene Kulturen" were "Zeiten starker Dissoziation der Gesamtpersönlichkeit." DG, 9: 88.
130. Westphal, Feinde Bismarcks, 190; Cassirer, 289–90; cf. Wise, "How Do Sums Count?" 403.
131. Spranger, Geschichtswissenschaft, 44.
132. MG, 98.

133. *Zur jüngsten deutschen Vergangenheit*, 2 vols. in 3 parts (Berlin, 1902–1904).
134. EB, 1: 8.
135. EB, 1: 59, 65.
136. See Jean Romein, *The Watershed of Two Eras: Europe in 1900*, trans. Arnold J. Pomerans (Middletown, CT, 1978), 447–60. The origins of this concept became the topic of a brief exchange between Lamprecht and Steinhausen, who claimed that he himself was the first to characterize the era in this way, although he used the more conventional word *Reizbarkeit*. AKg, 1 (1903): 362.
137. EB, 1: 70.
138. Ibid., 134.
139. Ibid., 212, 214, 223–4.
140. Ibid., 389.
141. Ibid., 425.
142. Ibid., 408.
143. Ibid., 451.
144. Ibid., 449.
145. Ibid., 428.
146. Ibid., 445.
147. EB, 2, 1: 13, 114.
148. Ibid., 29, 92.
149. Ibid., 66.
150. Ibid., 67.
151. Ibid., 68.
152. Ibid., 112.
153. *Bericht über die siebente Versammlung deutscher Historiker zu Heidelberg*, 18–19; *cf.* Lindenlaub, 291–384.
154. Eb, 2, 1: 49.
155. Ibid., 70.
156. Ibid., 237–238.
157. Ibid., 216.
158. Ibid., 242–43.
159. Ibid., 252.
160. Ibid., 250–52, 263.
161. EB, 2, 2: 44.
162. Ibid., 4.
163. Ibid., 11.
164. Ibid., 18.
165. Ibid., 165, 169, 172.
166. Ibid., 34–35.
167. Ibid., 473, 485.
168. Ibid., 514.
169. Paul Kampffmeyer, *Sozialistische Monatshefte*, 8 (June 1904): 502; *cf.* Kampffmeyer, "Karl Lamprecht und Karl Marx," ibid., 8 (July 1904): 520–26.
170. Schmoller, "Zur Würdigung," 40.
171. Franz Mehring, "Das Zeitalter der Reizsamkeit," *Die Neue Zeit*, 22 (1903–1904): 353–56; also in *Gesammelte Schriften*, 7: 511–15.
172. EB, 1: 3.
173. Ibid., viii.
174. VSWG, 2 (1904): 172; *cf.* Spiess, 20.
175. EB, 1: 222; EB, 2, 1: 58.
176. EB, 1: ix.
177. See MG, 60.

178. EB, 2, 2: 21–2.
179. EB, 1: 414.
180. AKg, 3 (1905): 90; Seeliger, "Lamprecht," 144; Spiess, 18.
181. NL Althoff (Br. Nr. 108/1), Lamprecht to Althoff, Leipzig, 20.5.04.
182. NL Lamprecht (V 1), Disposition für Band 7 der Deutschen Geschichte, 14.6.96; NL Liesegang, Lamprecht to Liesegang, Leipzig, 29.7.97; NL Harden, Lamprecht to Harden, Leipzig, 20.5.04.
183. Most of the minor revisions in subsequent volumes were the work of young scholars whom Lamprecht or his publisher paid. NL Lamprecht (Korr. 19), Lamprecht to Doell, Leipzig, 14.2.10; (Korr. 29), Helmolt to Lamprecht, Munich, 18.11.11; Viikari, *Krise*, 267.
184. NL Lamprecht (Korr. 21), Eulenburg to Lamprecht, Leipzig, 6.3.03; (Korr. 31), Lamprecht to Martin Spahn, Leipzig, 9.9.09; (Korr. 50), Tille to Lamprecht, Leipzig, 12.1.03; NL Harden, Lamprecht to Harden, Bärenburg, 6.7.01.
185. DG, 6: 57.
186. Ibid., 101.
187. Ibid., 67.
188. DG, 7: 391.
189. See Viikari, *Krise*, 320–21.
190. DG, 7: 6.
191. Ibid., 257.
192. NL Harden, Lamprecht to Harden, Leipzig, 21.3.06.
193. DG, 7: 717.
194. Ibid., 776, 801.
195. Ibid., 283.
196. Ibid., 335.
197. Ibid., 383.
198. DG, 8: 4.
199. Ibid., 24.
200. Ibid., 28.
201. Ibid., 33.
202. Ibid., 34.
203. Ibid., 36–37.
204. Ibid., 86, 197.
205. Ibid., 270.
206. Ibid., 46–47.
207. Ibid., 322.
208. Ibid., 382.
209. Ibid., 704.
210. Ibid., 686.
211. Ibid., 251.
212. DG, 9: 40, 75.
213. Ibid., 214.
214. Ibid., 30.
215. Ibid., 308.
216. Ibid., 310.
217. Ibid., 220–35.
218. Ibid., 271.
219. Ibid., 273.
220. Compare, for example, DG, 9: 429 and Heinrich von Treitschke, *Deutsche Geschichte im neunzehnten Jahrhundert*, 5 vols. (Leipzig, 1928), 1: 455; DG, 9: 458 and Treitschke, 1: 523–24; DG, 9: 466 and Treitschke, 1: 560.

221. DG, 9: 414–15.
222. NL Breysig, Lamprecht to Breysig, Leipzig, 13.5.07.
223. NL Lamprecht (Korr. 45), Lamprecht to Ritter, Leipzig, 1.1.07.
224. DG, 10: 20.
225. Ibid., 229.
226. Ibid., 318.
227. Ibid., 433–35.
228. DG, 11: 198, 286, 288, 291.
229. Ibid., 316–17.
230. Ibid., 367.
231. Ibid., 370, 373.
232. Ibid., 628–29.
233. Ibid., 705.
234. NL Lamprecht (UL 6), Denkschrift über die Entwicklung, gegenwärtigen Stand und Zukunft des IKUg (Frühjahr 1914); BA, NL Martin Spahn (31), Lamprecht to Spahn, Leipzig, 30.1.09; NL Dove, Lamprecht to Dove, Leipzig, 18.11.09.
235. NL Lamprecht (H2). The title page of the manuscript carries the notation: "Wiedergefunden c angelesen 2.11.03. Nicht als Ganzes publicierenswert. Wohl aber ev. Einzug in den Registerband."
236. Let a single example suffice:

Heinrich Friedjung, *Der Kampf um die Vorherrschaft in Deutschland 1859 bis 1866*, 2 vols., 2d ed. (Stuttgart, 1898), 1:105–6. "In drei Erlässen vom 12. November, die zur Mitteilung an die preussische Regierung bestimmt waren, wurde ein festes Programm aufgestellt. Es wurde nicht bloss der Augustenburger als künftiger Herzog von Schleswig Holstein namhaft gemacht. . . . Der preussischen Politik wurde der Vorwurf gemacht, sie suche die Angelegenheit der Herzogtümer zu verschleppen."

DG, 11: 444. "In drei Erlässen vom 12. November 1864, die zur Mitteilung an Preussen bestimmt waren . . . wurde der Augustenburger als künftiger Herzog von Schleswig-Holstein namhaft gemacht . . . und Preussen vorgeworfen, es versuche die Angelegenheit der Herzogtümer zu verschleppen."

237. DG, 11: 749.
238. NL Lamprecht (Korr. 20), Dürr to Lamprecht, Leipzig, 29.6.88.
239. NL Lamprecht (Korr, 20), Dürr to Lamprecht, Leipzig, 18.2.90.
240. StA Dresden, VB 10228/2, Lamprecht to Waentig, Fontainebleau, 16.9.06.
241. NL Lamprecht (Korr. 52), Vollert to Lamprecht, Berlin, 7.6.12.
242. NL Dove, Lamprecht to Dove, Leipzig, 14.10.02; NL Lamprecht (Korr. 52), Lamprecht to Vollert, Leipzig, 5.6.12; (Korr. 59), Lamprecht to Hugo Lamprecht, Leipzig, 9.6.02.
243. NL Althoff (B Nr. 108/1), Lamprecht to Althoff, Leipzig, 9.4.03.
244. *Frankfurter Zeitung*, 7.4.01; Goetz, *Historiker*, 296–308; LW, 642–43.
245. Lamprecht's colleague in Leipzig, the librarian Eduard Zarncke commissioned favorable reviews in *Literarisches Zentralblatt*, which he edited. NL Zarncke, Lamprecht to Zarncke, Leipzig, 6.5.04; e.g., LZbl, 52 (1901): 2114–17. Ludo Moritz Hartmann reviewed the first half of the second *Ergänzungsband* in the VSWG, 2 (1904): 166–76; cf. DLZ, 31 (1910): 581–85, where the Austrian archivist, Heinrich Kretzschmayr, published an appreciative review of the whole set. The list of

people to whom Lamprecht himself sent copies of the second supplementary volume included only eight university scholars outside Leipzig, most of whom were still his friends. NL Lamprecht (Korr. 57), Versendungsliste für Deutsche Geschichte Ergänzungsband 2.

246. Engelberg, "Methodenstreit," 151–52.
247. Mehring, "Das Zeitalter der Reizsamkeit," 514.
248. Dieter Langewiesche and Klaus Schönoven, "Arbeiterbibliotheken und Arbeiterlektüre im Wilhelminischen Deutschland," ASg, 16 (1976): 135–204.
249. Walter Hoffmann's survey of the reading regimens of workers between 1906 and 1909 is too selective to be a basis for generalization, but it reveals no trace of Lamprecht, while the name of Ranke appears once. "Die Organisation des Ausleihdienstes in der modernen Bildungsbibliothek," *Volksbildungsarchiv: Beiträge zur wissenschaftlichen Vertiefung der Volksbildungsbestrebungen,* 1 (1910): 308–44.
250. BA, NL Theodor Wolff (14), Lamprecht to Wolff, Leipzig, 11.11.09; NL Lamprecht (Korr. 30), Heyfelder to Lamprecht, Berlin, 7.3.03.
251. "Zur Quellenanalyse," 123.
252. NL Lamprecht (Korr. 4), Avenarius to Lamprecht, Dresden, 7.4.02, 1.4.05; (Korr. 45), Lamprecht to Rodenberg, Leipzig, 3.3.02; NL Harden, Lamprecht to Harden, Bärenburg, 3.7.01.
253. Luise Schorn-Schütte, "Karl Lamprecht und die internationale Geschichtsschreibung," AKg, 67 (1985): 418.
254. Griss, 54.
255. Metz, *Grundformen,* 485.
256. *Zukunft,* 22 (1898): 451.

10

Universal History

Nein, das *Ziel der Menschheit* kann nicht am Ende liegen,
sondern nur *in ihren höchsten Exemplaren*.

For all intents and purposes, the *Methodenstreit* ended in 1899. Occasional attempts to resurrect the methodological issues, at professional meetings or in print, resulted only in echoes. The most noteworthy of these echoes was the lecture that Eduard Meyer, the ancient historian in Berlin, published in 1902, for it produced echoes of its own.[1] Meyer addressed a basic question, which Lamprecht and his opponents had raised in their exchange over the relative status of individual and collective phenomena in history. It was the question of historical significance—the criteria by which the phenomena of the past could be designated historical at all. Meyer argued that the significance of all phenomena was to be judged by the consequences that they produced or by what he called their "effectiveness [*Wirksamkeit*]." "Historical is: what is, or has been effective," he said. "We experience what is effective first of all in the present, when we directly perceive the consequence [*Wirkung*]." The corollary of this principle, he continued, was that the primary object of historical interest was "cultured peoples [*Kulturvölker*]," those who "have been effective in an endlessly higher degree and who still directly affect the present."

Four years later, Meyer's lecture became the foil for one of Max Weber's methodological essays.[2] Weber pointed out that the concept of "effectiveness" depended itself upon the epistemological priorities of the individual historian and that there was, in principle, no reason why a "brawl between two tribes of primitive natives [*Kaffer*] or Indians" might not be as *wirksam* as the battle of Marathon. However, in this essay at least, Weber appeared to endorse as a practical matter the position that Meyer had defended in principle, that the *Kulturvölker* were the most appropriate objects of historical interest and that it would be idle to treat primitive peoples on a par with the Athenians. And to illustrate the futility of such an approach, Weber, like Meyer, pointed with disdain to a series of volumes that had recently begun to appear under the title *Helmolt's History of the World.*[3]

334

Hans Helmolt was a student of Ratzel and Lamprecht. After taking a doctorate in Leipzig in 1891, he worked as an editor for the Society for the Study of Rhenish History. As Lamprecht's professional misfortunes undermined the prospects of his students for academic employment, Helmolt turned to freelance work as an editor and journalist.[4] His most remarkable editorial feat was to assemble a team of thirty-seven collaborators, many of whom were connected with the historical-geographical seminar in Leipzig, in order to write a nine-volume history of the world, which began to appear in 1899.[5] Unorthodox only begins to describe it. It was conceived, as the editor wrote in the preface, "in conscious divergence from all previous works of this kind."[6] It recognized no distinction between history and anthropology. It proceeded on the assumption that all peoples on the planet at all times had histories—a fact concealed in conventional surveys, which portrayed the history of the world as the triumph of modern western culture and power. The basic units in Helmolt's survey were accordingly neither cultural nor political, but geographical; and the inspiration of Ratzel pervaded every volume. "Geography is necessarily the foundation of a comprehensive understanding of world history," Helmolt explained. "The principal goal of such a history is to understand that no single part of humanity develops historically in isolation from its neighbors."[7]

Helmolt's survey remained only a provocation. As late as 1968 a leading German historian described it as "infamous [*berüchtigt*]" and "perverse [*verkehrt*]."[8] Indeed, the project almost seemed calculated to offend conventional thinking, as it traced human history around the globe in a westward parade, which commenced in America and arrived in Germany and western Europe only in the sixth volume. Still, Helmolt's team served early notice that in the writing of world history, no less than in the writing of German history, the standards of historical significance were different in Leipzig than elsewhere.

In Germany at the end of the nineteenth century, "universal history" and "world history" were interchangeable concepts, but the breadth they implied was more philosophical than geographical.[9] The goal was to identify the patterns that ultimately gave meaning to all of human history, but most of the scholars who practiced the genre worked with a restricted definition of both "history" and "human." When Eduard Meyer sought to confine universal history to the cultured peoples, he could appeal to a long and respected historiographical tradition in which he himself was a major figure. Its leading exponent was the country's greatest historian, whose crowning achievement was a major fragment of a *World History*. Here Ranke identified the unifying theme of human history as the swelling movement of culture out of Egypt, via the Middle East, Greece, and Rome into the Germanic Middle Ages—the stage at which the historian's death interrupted this procession before it could reach its destination in the Christian nation-states of modern Europe.[10] When Theodor Lindner carried on the tradition twenty years later, his survey glanced at parts of the globe that Ranke had ignored; but the nonwestern peoples were in the account primarily to highlight the main theme of human history.[11] "West European culture, the crowning of Indo-European culture," Lindner observed in 1901, "strikes us as the most human." And the reason was not, he emphasized, simply "because it is our own."[12]

Even within these confines, however, few German academic historians found the writing or teaching of universal history appealing. The profession's traditions posed formidable impediments. The primacy of the individual and particular in history seemed to exclude cross-cultural comparison, insofar as it dismissed general categories of analysis as questions of philosophy or theology. Problems of historical comparability were especially acute across the broad disparities between what were conventionally known as cultured and noncultured peoples, for this distinction was itself defined, in the manner of Ranke and Meyer, by the exclusion of one of these categories from history.[13] Meyer was hardly alone in believing that primitive peoples were for anthropologists like Ratzel.

The centrality of politics was another part of the historical profession's fortifications against disciplines like Ratzel's, and it accentuated the methodological obstacles to the writing of universal history. Culture implied power. The mark of primitive peoples was their impotence; their want of effective political and military organization signified their cultural destitution and justified their exclusion from history. It also justified their subjugation. Their only escape from anthropology into history lay in their integration into the cultured empires of the west. This reasoning, in which methodological principle blended easily with considerations of high politics, permeated most of the treatments of world history that came out of the German academy.[14] Lindner's survey was merely more subtle than Dietrich Schäfer's apologia, which set the standard in this genre and reduced world history to the diplomatic rivalries among the European colonial powers since the sixteenth century.[15]

Because they drew reigning priorities into question, the debates in Germany over cultural history had important implications for the writing of world history. Schäfer was early alive to the danger. "In truth," he wrote in 1891, during his exchange with Gothein,

one can only speak of coherent historical development in that fraction of humanity that has been located in the so-called oriental-occidental areas during the last four or five thousand years—the fraction that has transplanted its culture to America and Australia in the last centuries and has more or less sporadically extended its influence over the rest of the earth.[16]

This conclusion was a corollary of Schäfer's attack on cultural history, and it rested on the familiar premise that politics provided the only valid criterion and focus of historical scholarship. Insofar as Kulturgeschichte challenged this premise, it encouraged a more comprehensive geographical and chronological conception of world history, as well as greater openness to the methods of anthropologists and geographers. Interest in cultural history did not, however, lead straight to universal history on these terms. Burckhardt's Observations on World History made clear—as did the contents of Steinhausen's journal—that even among those who opposed Schäfer, the standards of culture, and hence of cultural history, were western if not specifically German.[17] Nonetheless, the advocates of a broader view of world history in Germany were to be found alongside the cultural historians on the peripheries of the historical profession, where they encountered the same kinds of prejudices. Most of the efforts to include nonwestern peoples in world history were from the pens of marginal scholars, who produced vast surveys for popular audiences and contributed to collaborative projects like Helmolt's, which were dismissed in academic circles as *Buchbindersynthesen*.[18]

Kurt Breysig's experience was once again instructive. He did draw the connection between *Kulturgeschichte* and a variety of *Universalgeschichte* that deserved the name. In the first years of the new century, he published a series of articles in Harden's journal in which he argued that the developmental phases that he had identified in the history of the European peoples were valid everywhere on earth. These phases accordingly offered a framework for the comparative study of all the world's peoples.[19] In 1905 he attacked Ranke's "geographically so ill [*übel*] constrained idea" of a world history, and he elaborated on his own schema. It rested upon a much-expanded concept of politics, which Breysig attempted to deprive of evaluative connotations. The histories of all peoples, he argued, proceeded in parallel, although at different times and rates, through a series of stages, each characterized by successively broader and more integrated forms of "quasi-political [*staatsähnlichen*]" or political organization, from the family to the modern state.[20] Two years later, he published the first volume of what was to be the exposition of these stages in a massive history of humanity.[21]

Breysig had already gone too far for his colleagues. His attempt in 1909 to establish an interdisciplinary institute for comparative historical research in Berlin collapsed in the face of the concerted resistance of that university's historians. Eduard Meyer led the opposition and mobilized all of the profession's prejudices. Breysig's plan, he reported, was a "disastrous mistake [*verhängnisvoller Irrweg*]." Introducing students of history to the problems of ethnology would only sow "confusion and wild dilettantism in their heads." Besides, Meyer concluded, the kinds of peoples whom Breysig proposed to study, "North American and Australian tribes," "simply have no history."[22]

The word "dilettantism" was the flag, for Meyer was by now practiced in the vocabulary of Max Weber. The plan for an institute of comparative history in Berlin touched on other issues and personalities. Breysig was a pioneer in trying to frame the terms on which a comparative history of all the world's peoples might be written, but he was not alone in this effort. Indeed, his plan for the institute might well have fared better if there had not been a precedent.

In 1899 the *Frankfurter Zeitung* invited Lamprecht to review the first volume of Helmolt's survey of world history. The result was a curious essay.[23] It addressed the volume only long enough to praise it, although without much conviction, as a "partial payment." Lamprecht found the cosmopolitan scope and innovative organization congenial, but not the narrative format to which the authors remained wedded. The bulk of the historian's review consisted of his own ruminations about a payment-in-full, a "comparative cultural history of the world." He explained that the basis of such a history would have to be those "moments which are replicated in the fate of every people and are common to the development of all human communities." Once these moments had been identified, historians could isolate the elements in each people's history that were of significance for the "character of universal historical development." The great challenge for a comparative cultural history of the world thus lay, he concluded, "in the development of a theory [Lehre] of typical cultural stages and the application of this theory to the fate of every individual nation."

As this essay made clear, Lamprecht had himself been thinking about world history for some time.[24] His interest in the subject was another product of the Methodenstreit. It first surfaced in 1896, when his article "What Is Cultural History?" injected still another provocation into the controversy.[25] Here Lamprecht pointed out that his opponents' fixation on politics and the singularity of historical processes made a comparative history of humanity inconceivable. His own alternative view suffered no such deficiency. Cultural history, he wrote, featured a theory of "typical national development" and "regularly recurring developmental moments"; the genre accordingly offered the comparative criteria necessary for writing the history of the nations of the world.[26] By the end of this manifesto, little doubt remained about the contours of Lamprecht's "typical national development." "The historical periods which I have inferred empirically from the course of German history," he announced, "can be found empirically as well, mutatis mutandis, at least in the history of the nations of the European west and the peoples of classical antiquity."[27]

This proposition then became a secondary theme in the Methodenstreit. Lamprecht's opponents all rejected it in favor of the view that world history was itself a singular process, that the "individual nations," as Hintze put it, "represent distinct developmental stations in a larger whole."[28] And it needed no emphasis that this "larger whole" was the culture that the modern west embodied. The unity of world history complemented the uniqueness of each nation's history, so that it was idle to speak of "typical" or "normal" patterns of development. "What, after all, is a 'normally developed people'?" Below asked, confident that there was no answer to his question.[29] Lamprecht's view thus clashed with the reigning principle because it was both too singular and not singular enough. It appeared to isolate the history of every nation but at the same time to lock them all into parallel patterns of development.

Lamprecht's defeat in the Methodenstreit resulted in the profession's rejection of his ideas about world history, too; but he himself was no more prepared to abandon these ideas than he was the rest of his methodology. In fact, as his German History progressed to its conclusion and the challenge presented by this project receded, the methodological problems of a world history moved into the center of his interest.[30] It is tempting to portray this transition as a logical, if not a necessary, stage in Lamprecht's own development. The historian himself regarded it in these terms.[31] In 1904 he wrote to his brother of the "broader problems" that he was beginning to confront. "After I have risen from regional to national history," he went on, these problems could "naturally only be of a world-historical character."[32] The progressive broadening of the historian's field of focus was thus to culminate in what he described in 1906 as his "real task," the preparation of a comparative history on a universal scale.[33]

The task represented a culmination in more than one sense. It signaled the onset of the ultimate stage in a process of personal development, which, as the historian's portrayal of the nation's history had made clear, was measured in the broadening of the human intellect. "One always does best when one sticks to one's own development [*Selbsterziehung*]. And in this respect I am only in the beginning," he confessed to Dove in 1906. "Only now are the real problems coming—those that pertain to world history."[34] The historian turned his gaze beyond the confines of national history, out onto a field that knew practically no bounds. The significance of this motif was not lost on his closest friends, who followed this, his final venturing out. The purview of the historian now underwent, Wundt remarked, "an expansion almost into the unlimited."[35] *Ungemessen* was the suggestive term that Bücher used to describe the "uncharted areas" into which Lamprecht's interests were broadening.[36]

The turn to world history was of enormous significance for the historian in one other respect. It promised his vindication. In a revealing letter to Ritter in 1907, he admitted that "*at first* the whole disposition of the *German History* is or was nothing but an enormous hypothesis." Certainty, he explained, lay only in the realization that "my hypothesis applies to cultures that are altogether divergent from the German," so that he began to look into the history of other cultures, "simply in order to dispell my doubts."[37] Lamprecht's admission was not altogether candid. He was convinced of the validity of his theories long before his interests turned to world history, and the doubts he intended to dispel were not his own, but those of his opponents. The letter to Ritter nonetheless pointed to one of the great attractions of world history for Lamprecht, as well as to the agenda that he attached to it from the beginning. The expansion into world history represented the historian's final rejoinder to his opponents in the *Methodenstreit*, for in his own eyes at least, an account of all the world's cultures would confirm his views about German history.

Lamprecht's heavy but indiscriminate reliance on ethnological research in the first volume of the *German History* implied from the start—indeed it presupposed—that his developmental schema was valid in more than the German case.[38] He did not pursue this reasoning until provoked by the methodological controversy, but even then he was too preoccupied with other issues to work out more than the outlines of a methodology of universal history. His ideas on the subject emerged in more detail only after the conclusion of the controversy; and they reflected the evolution of his methodological views in the direction of "social biopsychology" during the early years of the new century. They also reflected his ongoing intellectual exchange with two figures in his orbit. Ratzel's influence on his views was direct, particularly on his thinking about primitive stages of cultural development.[39] Breysig's significance lay more in identifying problems than in offering solutions, for his definition of developmental phases employed criteria that were too political for Lamprecht's taste.[40]

Lamprecht removed all doubt about his intentions in 1901, when the first volume of the German History appeared in a third edition. "The author's studies in universal history," read the preface, "have reached a point where the assertion is justified" that

> the psychic developmental stages, which were initially discovered in the development of the German nation [Volksgemeinschaft] through epochs of Symbolic, Typical, Conventional, Individual, and Subjective mental life, are valid absolutely [schlechthin] everywhere and replicate themselves in the development of every people on earth, without exception.[41]

This breathtaking proposition formed the foundation of Lamprecht's vision of universal history. The claim that he had undertaken the studies necessary to sustain it empirically was pure fantasy; and it could hardly disguise the historian's resort to a familiar practice, which had invited the quip that he was trying, like Baron von Münchhausen, to pull himself out of the swamp by his own pigtail.[42] Universal history—the history of every phase of human life at every moment in time and in every corner of the planet—confirmed Lamprecht's series of Kulturzeitalter; but this self-same series alone made universal history intelligible. On the most extravagant scale, Lamprecht arrived where he had begun; his conclusion was his premise.

The historian's transition to universal history was smooth. It basically extended his method to a broader purview. The cultural epochs with which he had brought schematic order to the German past were to be imposed on the histories of all national groups. German history was paradigmatic.[43] In its broad contours, the cultural morphology of every nation passed lawfully, as he wrote in 1904 with respect to Japan, through "the same series of developmental stages of mental and material culture."[44] Variations in the timing and pace of this process, as well as in the idiosyncratic features of each example of national development—its "special tone" or "characteristic coloration"—could be traced to the effects of collective temperament (Beanlagung) and to a range of environmental determinants, in which geographical factors, or what Lamprecht, like Ratzel, called the Raumfrage, stood out.[45]

However, because the new project entailed a vast broadening of both the temporal and spatial dimensions of analysis, it made acute a number of problems that the historian had not confronted as long as his interests were confined to national history. Explaining full cycles of cultural development required greater attention to the phases at the temporal extremes—an extension of the range of historical analysis both backward, into the origins of culture, and forward into the phases of its decline. This undertaking posed problems of sources that were formidable enough to daunt most historians, who were less imaginative than

Lamprecht. Collaboration with Ratzel had confirmed his confidence that the fruits of ethnological research into the "primitive peoples" of Africa and Oceania offered valid bases for conclusions about the historical beginnings of every human culture, whether German, ancient Greek, or Japanese.[46]

This proposition was bold, but it was less daring than another avenue by which the historian proposed to approach the early development of culture. The theory that ontogeny recapitulates phylogeny—that the individual life cycle corresponds to group development—already had a long history when Lamprecht first encountered it in Roscher's hands in the 1870s.[47] Lamprecht's claim to a small place in this history rests on his effort to exploit the theory's practical implications. On the premise that primitive culture corresponded to childhood, he became interested in child psychology.[48] He also assembled a large collection of children's drawings in the library of his seminar, where he set his students to work on them, expecting that these documents of early visual perception would offer keys to the first stages of all cultural development.[49] The availability of these artefacts in turn encouraged his conviction that art, or what he called the visual products of *Phantasietätigkeit*, offered the most reliable indices of cultural development.

The historian found cultural decline a less interesting facet of universal history. Lamprecht was no Spengler. Decline cast a shadow over the telos he had identified in his own nation's history. The *German History* moved on an upward trajectory, charting fulfillment, both political and personal. "Creative forward movement alone is the soul of human development," he wrote in the ninth volume.[50] He never worked out a schema for "typical" cultural development beyond the Subjective epoch. His occasional remarks about "the most mature and hypermature" cultures rested on phylogenetic parallels with old age and his readings into the history of late imperial China.[51]

The emphasis on normal cycles of development in Lamprecht's thinking nonetheless invited the charge that he lacked a real concept of a world history, that his schema encompassed instead a plurality of hermetically sealed national histories, each of which unfolded in parallel. There was some truth to the charge, but it was easy to exaggerate.[52] Patterns of cross-cultural influence occupied a prominent place in his theory, where, like everything else, they were classified, endowed with exotic labels, and assembled into an imposing compendium of laws.[53] The historian distinguished, for example, between "renaissances," which aligned cultural transmissions along a temporal axis (as younger cultures assimilated features of older ones), and "receptions," which referred to the spatial axis (to transmissions between contemporary cultures). He described these transmissions as "osmotic phenomenona" and drew distinctions among "endosmoses," "exosmoses," and "diosmoses." He announced the rule that the most durable transmissions—those of the greatest universal significance— occurred in a "mental medium" and involved the products of ideal culture, which were more easily conveyed than their social or economic "vessels [*Hüllen*]."[54]

Yet methodological considerations limited the analytical weight that the historian could assign to these transmissions, whatever he chose to call them. In his conceptual vocabulary, particularly after its modification to accommodate Lipps' theories, cross-cultural influences operated—regardless of their source, character, or duration—as external "stimuli [Reize]" on the culture that received them. Their reception was accordingly regulated by the laws of psychic mechanics.[55] At this point, however, Lamprecht again encountered difficulties inherent in the incommensurability of the categories of explanation that he sought to employ. The laws of cultural interaction were mechanical, in his view, but the higher laws of every nation's cultural development were biological: the basic patterns remained immanent in the succession of Kulturzeitalter. Once again, Lamprecht's escape was to argue that cultural transmissions could accelerate, retard, or affect secondary characteristics of national development but not alter its basic contours.[56]

Lamprecht had laid out most of the methodological foundations for a universal history by 1905 in a series of articles and lectures, as well as in passages of his German History.[57] Like the other facets of his theory, it was imposing in its range and imaginative audacity. And it raised profound problems. The historian himself characterized his schema as the "national course of human history and the normal course of national developments."[58] It differed fundamentally from the conventional view, which emphasized the singular, cumulative progress of human culture through a succession of select historical civilizations, each of which had a characteristic attribute to add (the usual way stations included the monotheistic Jews, the rational Greeks, the political Romans, and the free Germans). Lamprecht's vision was more open and less invidious. It accorded to every people on earth the dignity of participation in a common human process, and it defined cultural disparity more as a question of timing than inherent inferiority.[59]

Still, the question persists whether the centrality of the "normal nation" in Lamprecht's schema did not in the end defy an attempt to articulate a unified vision of world history. His own efforts to confront this problem were unconvincing. He spoke of a "general law of fruitful universal-historical coherence [Zusammenhang]" without specifying the nature of this coherence.[60] He likewise observed that "above the development of the nations, there stands the universal unfolding of a great, singular development of humanity," to which he added only that this singular process "provides an absolute standard for every national development."[61] Lamprecht's agenda compelled him to emphasize the autonomous replication of his own Kulturzeitalter. These epochs seemed to provide the only common theme in human history, for the historian also had to deemphasize the significance of cross-national bonds, such as religion, that might have constituted other, less schematic sources of unity in world history.

In the last analysis, however, the difficulty lay deeper. Lamprecht's vision of universal history did not lack unity; but its unity was not historical. The move into world history accentuated a problem that lurked just under the surface in his

German History. It had to do with the ontological status of the subjects that populated Lamprecht's history of the world, the nations whose collective psychic development constituted the universal theme in his panorama. He failed to recognize it as a problem. "Whether one seeks a substratum for psychic events and phenomena in a hypothetical *Volkseele,*" he wrote in 1907, "is a secondary question, in fact, from a scholarly standpoint, almost a trivial [*gleichgültig*] question."[62] Trivial it was not. In Lamprecht's eyes, though, it was not a historical question—the *Volk* was not a historical phenomenon.

Because of the heterogeneity of the sources that fed into it, Lamprecht's grand scheme of universal history is difficult to characterize. The label "naturalism" is only partially just. "Natural philosophy" is at least as accurate. The collective subjects of Lamprecht's history were natural phenomena. Nations transcended history, as did the laws that governed their cultural growth. The historian drove historical contingency, the central premise of his opponents' position, to the margins of analysis, where it was subordinated to the laws of psychic mechanics, which were in turn subsumed under the sway of the higher principles of cultural biology. The energy that drew people together into national communities and then molded their collective development was primordial. "How it arose, where it came from, he did not ask." Seeliger isolated the problem when he spoke of this "creative *Urkraft,*" which in Lamprecht's thinking was a "permanently given factor [*Grösse*]," the "power that constituted and gave form to history."[63] Its operation thus exempted both the fact of nationality and the immanent contours of cultural development from the play of historical circumstance.

Because this power was ideal, Lamprecht was less tempted than some of his colleagues to wander in one direction to which his preference for biological metaphors pointed. His remarks on the subject of race were never entirely consistent.[64] In the logic of his theories, however, biological factors were secondary or contingent, like geography and climate; they could affect the circumstances but not the fundamental direction of cultural development through the *Kulturzeitalter.* A physiological explanation of cultural development was unacceptable, not only because it rested on materialistic assumptions, but also because the idea of permanent cultural difference undercut the schematic unity of his own view.[65] "Racial differences," he insisted, were subordinate to the "fundamental common elements of our human nature."[66]

There was a Herderian grandeur to Lamprecht's vision. The voice of each people accented the great common chorus of national development.[67] But the common elements were fundamental, and they represented the ultimate unity in this vision, which in the end owed more to Leibniz than to Herder. The unity was entelechial. The immanent teleology in the historian's system lay in the progressive unfolding, broadening, and self-realization of the intellect in a national context. This process united every individual, at every time and every place, along a single continuum of development. Lamprecht's *Kulturzeitalter,* the great product of one individual's intellect, defined the principle that embraced everyone who ever lived within a single shared experience—his own.

Lamprecht made it clear that this principle was ahistorical in a celebrated lecture he delivered in October 1904. Here he told of the common developmental phases that every nation underwent. He also explained how he knew of them. "By eliminating the singular and individual elements!" "With complete methodological certainty," the historian declared, he could compare the individual cultural epochs of various nations "without, given the nature of this comparison, paying any attention to chronology or locality [terrestrische Lokalisierung]."[68] Ernst Cassirer was not the only commentator to rub his eyes at this assertion. In order to identify the underlying principle in history, Lamprecht had suspended history. The result, as Cassirer pointed out, was not a theory of history at all, but a "scientific 'nowhere' (utopia) and 'nowhen' (uchronia)."[69]

"Abstraction from time and space, gentlemen!" It was a remarkable conclusion in a lecture on historical method. That the lecture occasioned little consternation among the audience was due to another of its remarkable features. Lamprecht delivered it in New York City.

Karl Lamprecht's international fame at the turn of the century was second only to Ranke's and perhaps Theodor Mommsen's. The historical profession in Germany was but one site of methodological conflict at the turn of the century. As controversies flared in other lands over similar historiographical issues, Lamprecht became, like Ranke, an international symbol of professional conflict.

The history of these controversies elsewhere touches Lamprecht's biography only tangentially.[70] As in Germany, Ranke was the symbol of history's professionalization in France, Britain, and the United States. In these countries, too, the process featured the enshrinement of what Georg Iggers has called a "factological" approach, the conviction that the retrieval of the particulars of the past, if undertaken with the proper training and spirit of objectivity, would produce a scientifically valid picture of "how it really happened."[71] And as in Germany, professional historians invoked Ranke's sanction for a hermeneutic of Verstehen and for a view that emphasized free moral action in history and the centrality of the state as an object of inquiry.

The attack on these principles developed elsewhere at roughly the same time as in Germany. It grew out of similar frustrations, particularly among younger scholars, over the parochialism of the methodology associated with Ranke's name—its inability to address social and economic problems in an age of industrial conflict or to accommodate the explanatory models of the natural sciences. Lamprecht did not directly inspire this attack anywhere outside Germany, but his onslaught on Ranke's views in his own country was highly publicized elsewhere; and it made him a symbol and source of encouragement to historians, like the advocates of the "New History" in the United States or the scholars around Henri Berr's journal Révue de synthèse historique in France, who were engaged in campaigns of their own to broaden the discipline. In these countries, the campaigns played out in an intellectual climate less hostile than that in Germany to the idea of a social science, and in less beleaguered conditions in the historical profession.[72] As a consequence, the reception of Lamprecht's work, although by no means uncritical, became broader and more enthusiastic among academic historians abroad than at home.

Lamprecht was alive to the paradox. Even before his defeat at home and the turn of his interests to world history, he had established foreign contacts to an extent unusual among German academic historians, some of whom, like Below, regarded his international prominence with alarm.[73] Lamprecht was a fixture at international congresses, a champion of international cooperation in causes that he advocated at home, such as publishing historical documents and the *Grundkarten*.[74] In 1901 he broadened the scope of the monograph series that he edited for Perthes to encompass the history of the world; and he attempted to turn the series into a showcase of international scholarship. The volumes of Henri Pirenne's *History of Belgium* became his greatest triumph, as well as the foundation of a long friendship between the two historians.[75] Another distinguished friend was the Dutch historian P. J. Blok, whose *History of the Netherlands* also appeared in translation in Lamprecht's series. Ties of friendship and intellectual affinity bound Lamprecht as well to Berr, Georges Blondel, and Gabriel Monod in France; to Paul Fredericq and Guilliaume Des Marez in Belgium; and to the American historian William E. Dodd, who had taken a doctorate in Leipzig in 1898.[76] Lamprecht's seminar in Leipzig was a mecca for foreign students, over whom the historian exercised particular care. A number of them came from parts of Europe, such as Norway, Finland, and Poland, where national sentiment was perforce cultural rather than political, so that the *Kulturgeschichte* associated with Leipzig was more congenial to them than the variety of history taught at other German universities.[77]

Lamprecht cultivated these contacts in the course of extensive travels abroad, which he undertook for purposes of both research and recreation. He regularly vacationed with his daughters in France, Italy, and Greece. He believed in familiarizing himself with the places he wrote about, and some of the most vivid passages in the early volumes of his *German History* were the fruits of trips to Scandinavia and the Baltic, the Low Countries, Austria, and east-central Europe. These excursions remained confined to the European continent until 1904, when the historian embarked on the research trip that became the travel adventure of his life.

In a sense, the idea of convening an international scholarly congress to examine the unity of all knowledge originated in Leipzig, even though the venue of this gathering was to be St. Louis, Missouri. Hugo Münsterberg, the man who was most responsible for the idea, studied with Wundt in Leipzig in the early 1880s.[78] His career subsequently led to a lectureship in psychology in Freiburg and finally, in 1897, to Harvard, where William James recruited him to direct that university's laboratory of experimental psychology. The professional migrations of this talented young scholar brought a series of ruptures, which started with his abandonment of Judaism and led to a lingering sense of emotional and intellectual uneasiness. The effort to soften the impact of these breaks occupied him for the rest of his life. He continued to revere Wundt after rejecting his teacher's psychophysical parallelism for a theory of autonomous motor processes. His rejection of Wundt's metaphysics culminated in a conversion to neo-Kantianism, which took place in Freiburg under Rickert's influence; yet he could not abandon his belief in the final unity of knowledge, and he used a logic more taxionomic than deductive to link the categories of knowledge in a schematic metaphysics.[79] Lingering ties to his homeland remained problematic, too; and in the United States he devoted himself less to scholarship than to promoting German-American friendship.

His political and philosophical interests converged in his plan for a scholarly congress to meet in conjunction with the Universal Exposition that was to commemorate the centenary of the Louisiana Purchase in St. Louis in 1904.[80] Münsterberg was well connected to the organizers of the event. He persuaded them to issue expense-paid invitations to the world's "leaders of thought" to come to St. Louis for a week in September 1904. The assembled scholars were to consider the correlations among all their fields, as he put it, to "fill the sciences of our time with the growing consciousness of belonging together, with the longing for fundamental principles."[81] In Münsterberg's eyes, the conference was also to be a baptism for American scholarship, and he had no doubt about who should preside. Armed with invitations, he arrived in central Europe in the summer of 1903, where, with Althoff's blessing, he recruited a spectacular assemblage of German and Austrian talent, which included Max Weber, Ferdinand Tönnies, Ernst Troeltsch, Werner Sombart, Adolf Harnack, Max Dessoir, Ludwig Boltzmann, Karl Budde, Albert Penck, and Wilhelm Waldeyer.[82] Münsterberg failed to persuade Wundt to attend, so the delegation from Leipzig comprised the minerologist Ferdinand Zirkel, the philologist Sievers, Ostwald (as a philosopher), and—as the lone historian in the German group—Karl Lamprecht.[83]

Lamprecht accepted this invitation with mixed feelings. He had no affection for most of the scholars in the German contingent, who in turn could imagine no figure less appropriate than Lamprecht to represent the German historical profession abroad. But the New World offered its own attractions, and Lamprecht planned to spend little time in the midst of his German colleagues. An invitation to deliver a series of lectures after the congress at Columbia University, the bastion of the New History, portended a sympathetic reception in America.[84] He anticipated, though, that the period before the congress would be the most significant part of the journey. "It won't be a so-called pleasure trip, but probably a hard one, full of strains," he told his brother on the eve of his departure. "Nonetheless," he added, "I go gladly, for I see that the business is professional."[85] He was referring to his new interests. He intended, as he explained in justifying a leave of absence to the ministry, to "get to know the country to the extent necessary for purposes of world history."[86] To prepare himself for the adventure, he consulted with Ratzel, who had not only traveled extensively in the United States as a young man, but was adept in the ethnography of colonial cultures.

The historian arrived in New York City aboard the *Kaiser Wilhelm II* on 3 August 1904. Equipped with his Baedeker and a camera, he plunged immediately into the hinterland on a far-flung expedition, which taxed his physical stamina and yielded more impressions than even he could easily assimilate. His itinerary led by boat up the Hudson, into Canada, then by train into Michigan, Illinois, Wisconsin, across the northern Great Plains, and over the Rocky Mountains to the very ends of the earth, to Victoria and Vancouver, Seattle and Portland, thence to San Francisco and Los Angeles, back north to Sacramento, and eastward to St. Louis.

Like the many other German academics who made the pilgrimage to the New World in these years, Lamprecht carried a lot of cultural baggage, which was ill suited to the "raw stimuli [*rohe Reize*]" that assaulted his sensitivities throughout his American experience.[87] Whether the subject was architecture, food, women, the train system, or a language he found difficult to understand, comparisons with home could only be invidious. America was a crude place— massive, noisy, monotonous, materialistic, tasteless, superficial, and naive. German settlements in Wisconsin, "*deutsches Farmerland*," could provide but small oases of order and cultivation in a landscape whose very topography symbolized the problem. "Americans," he noted from the train that carried him southward through the Cascade mountains, "will require ages to bestow on the natural face of their country [*"Natur ihres Landes"*], whose primal magic they have removed in the basest way, the tender charms [*Reize*] of a cultured land."[88]

In such a mood Lamprecht arrived in late September in St. Louis to participate in what was becoming known to skeptics as the "Münsterbergian circus."[89] Here another travel adventure of sorts awaited him. Before he could take the seat assigned him on the podium next to Charles Baxter Adams, he had to wander through the labyrinth of compartments into which Münsterberg had ordered human knowledge. Woodrow Wilson presided over his "division" (B, Historical Science), William M. Sloane and James Harvey Robinson over his "department" (3, Political and Economic History), Charles Homer Haskins over his "section" (C, Medieval).[90] On 21 September Lamprecht addressed a small audience in English on "Historical Development and the Present Character of the Science of History."[91]

Then he left St. Louis without participating in the other festivities of the congress.[92] He headed east and spent most of the rest of his American sojourn in New York City, Washington, D.C., Boston, and central Pennsylvania. The highlight of the journey came late in October, at the jubilee at Columbia University to celebrate the 150th anniversary of the founding of King's College. Here Lamprecht presented his theories of social biopsychology and universal history in a cycle of lectures (in German) before a largely sympathetic audience that included James Harvey Robinson, Charles A. Beard, and Carl Becker.[93] The university then removed any doubts about Lamprecht's triumph, when, to his immense pride, it awarded him an honorary doctorate of law.

By the time the historian set sail for Europe in November, his impressions of

America had changed. The easy condescension that had guided him on his westward journey yielded to more balanced but disquieting thoughts, for he had concluded that the cultural deficiencies he had witnessed were joined with enormous power and vitality in a people "destined for greatness."[94] This realization affected his thinking in several ways. The impact of the American experience on his political views is best postponed. Two other aspects of his experience are of more immediate interest.

Lamprecht went to America with the agenda of an ethnographer. Extending his theories into universal history mandated study of cultural development in a country that had originally been colonized by more advanced cultures. The journey was thus devoted in the first instance to the quest for an American culture, which he pursued in museums, theaters, and bookstores and in institutions of higher learning wherever he traveled. The quest was confined. Excepting a brief excursion into Virginia and the District of Columbia, his travels brought no contact with non-white Americans. The results were nonetheless troubling, for they were not easily reconciled with his theory of culture and the epochs of its development.

Lamprecht found no American culture. Despite their strong sense of national consciousness, he concluded that Americans displayed "no real culture of their own."[95] This judgment rested on his impressions of the products of their "*Phantasietätigkeit*," the indices provided in American art, drama, literature, and music. The historian could find little to distinguish any of it. If original, it was trivial, like popular music; at its best it was derivative. American painters trained in Europe. Edward MacDowell "tried to compose in an American fashion," but he, like other American composers, remained "almost completely under the spell of European imitation."[96] Washington Irving displayed a "genuinely American sense of grotesque humor," but because of his debt to English culture of the eighteenth century, he was "not yet American."[97] Walt Whitman's thought was "fundamentally un-American."[98] Poe had a similar problem. The historian praised him as the "first great lyricist of the New World" but posed the rhetorical question: "Is the mystical pathos of his sensitivity, the romanticism which lightens the day, the melodrama of his diction characteristically [*gemeinhin*] American?"[99]

The difficulty, Lamprecht believed, inhered in the colonial experience of this vast land, its ethnic and regional diversity, and the westward movement of its population. All these circumstances had overwhelmed the higher cultures of the colonizers, as well as the brief flowering of a coherent "Yankee culture" in colonial New England. But a solution lay at hand, he thought, in the tremendous expansion of American enterprise, which was already giving out the "intensive economic stimuli" that were the "essential foundation for the development of modern psychic life."[100] Thus, in spite of the meager yield of his investigations in American theaters, museums, and music halls, the historian descried in the artistic output of the previous quarter-century "the traces of a new, now genuinely American culture."[101]

The materialistic accents in Lamprecht's projection for America's cultural arrival were less troublesome than some other features of this analysis. It remained obscure what characteristics of a work of art, literature, or music would justify its description as "culture" or, for that matter, as "American." The suspicion is difficult to suppress, though, that these labels rehearsed the historian's own aesthetic preferences. His encounter with American culture raised additional problems. The consolidation of an American culture was to be the defining prerequisite for the emergence of an American nation. "The new nation will not exist without culture," he announced.[102] The voice was Baron von Münchhausen's, for Lamprecht's theory stipulated that the development of culture took place only within a national framework. However, the observation about the American nation was, in a literal sense, only the beginning of the methodological conundrum. The logic of Lamprecht's theory of the *Kulturzeitalter* also required that only upon its consolidation could American culture commence its lawful morphology. "We are just now on the eve of an autonomous [*eigene*] cultural development," he noted.[103] But he failed then to specify where this development was to begin, if not where his theory demanded—in the same Symbolic epoch where the Germanic tribes had started some 2,000 years earlier. A hint that cultures of different epochs could perhaps coexist simultaneously within the same society, like geological strata, suggested that the historian had briefly taken note of the problem, but this suggestion threatened to raise still graver difficulties for a theory of periodization.[104]

Lamprecht did not dwell on the American recalcitrance to his theories. These theories were, in all events, too hard set and basic to his intellectual and emotional constitution to admit the modification that the American experience would have required. Besides, his interest was more excited by another chapter of his American odyssey.

He visited colleges and universities. In addition to Columbia, his destinations included Yale, Harvard, Vassar, West Point, Johns Hopkins, Pennsylvania, Chicago, Stanford, and the public universities of Wisconsin and California. Much of what he encountered at these institutions added to his bemusement over American culture. At Columbia his hosts took him to a football game. "I have had enough of these things to last a lifetime," he wrote. "The dumb, ox-like collisions of the two teams" were perhaps less objectionable to this German scholar than the "disciplined, frenetic howling of the thousands of on-lookers." A student rally at the Greek theater in Berkeley likewise left him wondering whether the way German students anesthetized themselves with alcohol was any worse than the anesthesia that American students administered on themselves by screaming.[105]

Other aspects of American academic life he found more attractive. He was struck by the intensity of instruction in small classes, in which students were encouraged to think independently. He was struck even more by the corporate spirit that seemed to reign on American campuses, the ties of loyalty that bound students to their institution not only throughout their studies, but afterward, when they supported it financially. The fact that "lots of money is donated" left a deep impression.[106] The corporate spirit extended, Lamprecht believed, to the faculty, where the ambience was less intolerant and cliquish than in Germany and where scholars were united in an ethic of scholarship that demanded that "the truth must conquer, and it will as long as research and publication take place without prejudice."[107]

Lamprecht returned to Europe with enduring impressions, as well as a host of new friends and contacts.[108] Although his methodological views underwent no significant change in response to his encounter with American culture, his experiences in the New World affected his agenda in other important ways. Of most immediate consequence were lessons he drew from higher education in the United States. Aspects of American academic life, he concluded, were worth emulating.

The historical seminar to which Lamprecht returned in Leipzig displayed nothing of the corporate solidarity that had impressed him in American universities. It was already on the verge of terminal crisis when he left in the summer of 1904 for America. His return to it early in 1905 precipitated the negotiations that eventuated, eighteen months later, in the ministry's decision to remove Lamprecht to quarters in a separate building.

The formal dissolution of the seminar followed in 1907. Convinced, as it told the feuding directors, that only their "complete separation" would resolve the problem, the ministry agreed to turn Lamprecht's section into a separate "seminar for cultural and universal history." Beginning in 1908, it was to be autonomous, bound only nominally to the rest of what was henceforth called the historical institute—the seminars of Seeliger, Brandenburg, and a new ancient historian, Ulrich Wilcken.[109]

The arrangement resembled the dissolution of a marriage, and so did the disputes that followed among the historians over the disposition of the community property. They fought over the *Privatdozenten*. They fought over Kötzschke's seminar and its library. Before they could agree on an equitable division of the libraries, they were reduced to quarreling on a book-by-book basis.[110] The students, the children of this divorce, suffered as well. Not only were they compelled to pay additional fees for multiple memberships in the seminars, but they discovered that taking introductory course work in one seminar could lead to their exclusion from advanced courses in the other.[111]

Throughout the disputes over the future of the seminars, Lamprecht's behavior was by no means blameless. But he emerged in the end with a victory that astounded his colleagues in Leipzig and suggested the extent of the German historical profession's isolation, both in its own country and the rest of the world. Lamprecht had several advantages. He was a tenacious advocate of his own cause. He was well practiced in the skills of lobbying in Dresden, and he was not above resorting to dissimulation or misrepresentation.[112] He also had from the start a clear concept of what he wanted, as well as a practical agenda.

His experience in the United States had suggested both a new model for his seminar and novel ways to find financial support for it.

Lamprecht had begun to plan his course of action as soon as it became evident, shortly after his return from the United States, that he would be given his own seminar. Several months after the ministry's final decision, he presented his plans in an unlikely forum, in his last address before the Association of German Historians, which met in Dresden in September 1907.[113] Here he announced that the "historical-political direction" of scholarship was in decline, and he drew the pedagogical consequences. The curriculum in history seminars would in the future have to emphasize cultural and universal history. Instruction must "naturally" begin with German cultural history. Then, he explained, the perspective of students was to be broadened to comprehend "everything that falls into the realm of the human potential." Courses on the cultural history of China, Japan, and the United States were to follow. To support these offerings and a variety of others, seminar libraries were to include sections on German, Germanic, Scandinavian, English, and Slavic history, the history of the Latin peoples, Indian and pre-Columbian American cultures, the history of the world's religions, and a (small) section for ethnology. The auxiliary disciplines were to include a section for instruction in source criticism, geography, economics, sociology, the philosophy of law, ethics, and religion, and another section for "genetic psychology," by which Lamprecht meant social psychology, child psychology, and the "psychology of human developmental periods—youth, maturity, old age."

Lamprecht's presentation astonished an audience that was dominated by representatives of the "historical-political direction," whose decline he foretold. Rachfahl heckled him from the floor during the address.[114] Many others in the audience were offended when Lamprecht recommended photographs of his own trip to America as source material for lectures on American cultural history. Georg Kaufmann gave voice to the skepticism of these historians when he observed that "Lamprecht's path is too broad; the power of humans is not great enough to proceed along it without straying."[115] In the eyes of Kaufmann and his friends, Lamprecht had already strayed hopelessly; but these scholars all underestimated their colleague's power to proceed alone down the broad path he had charted.

Lamprecht was a pioneer. The seminar he described in Dresden was to be the first institute devoted to world history at a German university. Bringing it to life required a pioneering feat of another kind, an achievement that was the envy of Lamprecht's peers and a model for academic entrepreneurs ever since. The campaign began in January 1906, when the historian exploited his long-standing ties to the Rhenish business community to raise 6,000 marks for library purchases in Leipzig.[116] As the ministry in Dresden pondered the future of his seminar, Lamprecht behaved, as one East German commentator noted, "like a genuine flexible bourgeois" and plied the skills of persuasion he had learned from Mevissen and the academic fund-raisers in the United States.[117] His principal targets were civic notables and business leaders in Leipzig.[118] By early 1907, he had raised close to 40,000 marks, a figure that included the value of his large personal library, which he proposed to donate to his seminar.[119]

The success of the private fund-raising raised the historian's stock in Dresden, as did his ties to the royal house.[120] The ministry responded by providing the seminar with two stories of a magnificent old building in the middle of town, the so-called Golden Bear, which had once been the residence of the eighteenth-century literary theorist, Johann Christof Gottsched, as well as headquarters of the music publisher Breitkopf und Haertel. It was also next door to Wundt's institute. Officials in Dresden agreed in addition to move Kötzschke's seminar into rooms in the building (a decision that scored another defeat for Seeliger) and to provide an additional 18,000 marks for the library.[121] Late in 1907, in response to "many a letter, many an inquiry" (and many an appearance), Lamprecht's campaign acquired a momentum of its own.[122] "The cause is attracting far more attention than I thought," he confessed to Harden.[123] Donations of money, books, and other artefacts flowed in from far and near. Former students responded, as did friends from France and Belgium. The Carnegie Foundation provided a subsidy for the library.[124] A local publisher underwrote the purchase of oriental books.[125] The emperor of China donated a collection of 5,000 volumes to the library, while the American government sent busts of George Bancroft and William H. Prescott.[126] The most gratifying news came from Berlin, where Althoff, in an old man's gesture of affection for an errant protégé, intervened from retirement, only weeks before his death late in 1908, to help persuade the chancellor, Bernhard von Bülow, to provide a grant of 10,000 marks to Lamprecht's new seminar in the name of the Kaiser.[127]

By the time Lamprecht moved into his new quarters at the end of 1908, he had amassed a small fortune in donations and subscriptions. The ministry was still inclined to be generous. In addition to the seminar's ample annual budget, it authorized 80,000 marks toward establishing the library and remodeling the Golden Bear into "an artistic creation" according to the historian's specifications, which included a separate telephone hook-up, special lighting in the courtyard, and double doors on all the work rooms for insulation against noise.[128] The ministry's most dramatic gesture came in January 1909 as a response to the news from Berlin of the imperial subsidy. To Lamprecht's enormous satisfaction and the consternation of his colleagues, the ministry granted the new seminar an extraordinary degree of administrative autonomy from the university's philosophical faculty, as well as a special link to Dresden. Lamprecht's seminar became the Royal Saxon Institute for Cultural and Universal History at the University of Leipzig.[129]

These were the most gratifying moments in the historian's life. "I have spent the entire holiday in my new seminar, arranging books!—even while the construction workers hammered away here and there," Lamprecht wrote to Ritter in January 1909. "And in this mechanical activity, days, hours, almost weeks have flown by so fast that I have become more indifferent to the special features of the regular holidays than I have ever been before or will hopefully ever be again."[130] Instruction began in the new institute early in 1909, but construction work delayed its formal opening until May, when several hundred students, benefactors, friends, and colleagues gathered in the Golden Bear to help the historian celebrate his own triumph.[131] In his address at the dedication, Lamprecht emphasized the significance of the occasion for the history of his discipline. He portrayed his new institute as the successor to the instructional models developed by Ranke in Berlin and Noorden in Leipzig; its mission, he said, was to transcend the specialization that had distinguished these seminars in an earlier era, to develop the "scholarly motifs that are suited to establishing the connections among the separate disciplines."[132] That the occasion was also of enormous significance for the historian's own history was well known to most of those in his audience, who were nonetheless ill prepared for the way he alluded to it:

> When I now look back on my life from the high-point I have reached, onto all the many struggles and storms, I feel the need to say one thing to my dear young friends at just this hour. That which has carried me through all the severity of my life and struggle is the Word: Not that I believe, but that I know that my redeemer liveth.

Lamprecht was not known to be a religious man. The festive mood at the dedication dampened, Schönebaum reports, amid confusion over the identity of the historian's redeemer.[133]

The frequency with which religious metaphors were subsequently employed to describe Lamprecht's new institute suggested that this confusion was needless. Alfred Dove called the historian "the founder of a scholarly sect."[134] Another observer pointed with less irony to a "new gospel" and the "apostle of a new history."[135] Even deprived of its religious overtones, though, the founding of the Institute for Cultural and Universal History was a moment of personal vindication and fulfillment. After 1908 it became incongruous to speak of the pathos of Karl Lamprecht. He now ruled an academic empire in Leipzig, where his theories inspired both devotion and a far-flung program of research and instruction.

Lamprecht had anticipated that completion of the *German History* would enable him to proceed immediately to an ambitious plan of research in world history. Three areas were of special interest. Fascinated, like many others, by Japan's defeat of Russia in the Far East and by the analogies that this event suggested to the recent German past, the historian planned to trace more fully the rise of what he regarded as a young oriental culture through the developmental stages that his theory prescribed.[136] The history of China, a culture that Lamprecht (again like many others) thought to be in decline, was to provide a basis for extending his theory beyond the developmental as well as the geographical limits of the German case.[137] Finally, his interest in the United States grew out of both his personal experiences in that land and his belief in its paradigmatic significance for the formation of colonial cultures.[138]

None of these projects came to fruition. Beyond an account of his trip to America, which included a brief, impressionistic overview of American cultural history, his published work comprised only derivative surveys and a few cursory efforts, based largely on the research of his students, to show that the early development of Chinese and Japanese art progressed as it was supposed to.[139] A plan to write a survey of world history never progressed beyond outlines.[140] The final volume of the *German History* was thus Lamprecht's last major piece of published scholarship. But its appearance also coincided with the establishment of his institute, which marked a change in the way he operated. "The problems of universal history are pushing me ever further onward," he wrote shortly after the opening of the institute. He also confessed that these problems were too great for someone his age to confront alone: "Here there is nothing else to do but to organize research."[141]

That the research he organized would bear his personal stamp was self-evident—his own indignant protests to the contrary notwithstanding.[142] The Institute for Cultural and Universal History was conceived, constructed, and guided by its director's vision of history. As he told an international congress of historians in Berlin in 1908, the "comprehensive structure of hypotheses" within which his institute would operate featured the periodization of "history as psychic development." The function of his institute, he continued, was to "assemble completely independent material as conclusive evidence [*zu einem stärksten Beweis*] for the validity of periodization."[143]

Lamprecht's hypotheses, or what he insisted on calling his "principles," were never in question.[144] Validating them was an exercise in celebration. However hermetic or idiosyncratic (or wrong), these principles inspired imperial Germany's most open, practical, and fruitful agenda for the study of world history. In their grandest tautology, Lamprecht's theories offered the analytical categories for the cross-cultural comparisons whose purpose was to confirm his theories. But these theories also provided a rationale for the comparative historical study of every people on earth.

In the summer semester of 1909, Lamprecht's institute opened its insulated doors to more than 100 students. Within a year its membership stood at 320—more than the combined enrollments of the other historical seminars in Leipzig.[145] As they might have in the United States, these students passed under the guidance of instructors and advisors through a structured curriculum, which was modeled on principles similar to those Lamprecht had introduced into the historical seminar in the 1890s.[146] At the beginning of each semester, all students were invited to consult personally with the director, who assured them of his wish "to be useful to them in the planning of their studies."[147] In addition, a special office advised the students about their course work and informed the director about concerns of the students.[148]

Lamprecht himself taught the basic lecture course, which was required of all beginning students. It introduced them to the methodological principles that were to guide their subsequent work in the institute. The course also molded a significant segment of the historian's reading public. Required materials included volumes of the *German History*, made available to students at a discount, and other standard Lamprechtian texts.[149] The rest of the first tier of the curriculum comprised smaller introductory courses (*Uebungen*) designed to orient students for advanced study and to fulfill the needs of students who anticipated careers in secondary teaching. These courses covered various topics in *Kulturgeschichte*, such as socioeconomic history, legal history, and the cultural history of the eighteenth and nineteenth centuries.[150]

Students then passed to a second level of instruction, where they took courses devoted primarily to national histories, or to what Lamprecht called the "singular method." Offerings included (in 1909) topics in French and Chinese cultural history and the history of social movements in the nineteenth century. In 1913 students could choose among topics in English and Italian cultural history, heresy and millennarianism in the late Middle Ages, and Marx and historical materialism. The third and most advanced tier of instruction emphasized the "comparative method"—the comparative history of individual branches of culture, as well as aggregate strains of cultural development.[151] Here, for example, students encountered courses on the comparative ethical and expressive development of children in selected west European cultures, the ethnology of the Middle Ages, the development of the epic, and, at the knee of the director, the comparative history of German and Japanese art.

The instructors in the Institute for Cultural and Universal History were a corps of disciples, young scholars whose sympathy for the director's theories invited the charge that they were his *Handlanger*, or pliant creatures.[152] Lamprecht's denials rang hollow. Many of the instructors were his former students, who could have found academic employment nowhere else. The autonomy of the institute afforded Lamprecht absolute powers of appointment, which allowed him to flaunt the faculty's traditions. Most of his instructors had not habilitated; one taught in a local *Gymnasium*, another had no doctorate. Perhaps because they constituted such a singular body within the university, the bond that linked them seemed almost familial.[153] The bond was in fact familial in the case of one of them, Johannes Goldfriedrich, who was married to Lamprecht's niece. All of the instructors were devoted to the director, who modeled their responsibilities along the lines of an American academic department.[154] They participated in planning the curriculum and, within this framework, were free to choose their own offerings. Consensus reigned nonetheless on the fundamental principles that were to guide instruction in the institute. As one of the instructors confessed to Lamprecht in 1911, the purpose of his course was to direct "work which can promote your ideas."[155]

The same principles guided activity at the ultimate tier of Lamprecht's institute, which was devoted to research. The advanced students who came to Lamprecht's institute (many of them from abroad) were set to work on a range of subjects limited only by the director's imagination. "Lamprecht gave me an enormous program of work," one of these students recalled of his regimen, which required reading in the full range of German history in order to draw out the contrasts among the cultural epochs.[156] Students mined the past for traces of these epochs. A majority of them did so within German history, but of the sixty doctoral students whom Lamprecht supervised after his emancipation from the historical seminar, nearly a quarter wrote on topics that corresponded to the historian's broadening interests in the Orient, the United States, and the history of primitive peoples.[157]

Even within his own realm, however, Lamprecht's freedom to promote his vision of history was limited. His institute shielded him and his disciples only partially from the claims of the university's philosophical faculty and the historical profession at large. In Leipzig, both of these institutions were embodied in Lamprecht's former colleagues in the historical seminar, who had accepted their defeat at his hands almost with a sense of relief but had hardly changed their opinion of his scholarship. Lamprecht was not able to evade them, for his institute could not challenge the faculty's prerogative to award degrees in history and to appoint the committees that examined his students. The themes of some of these students' dissertations justified the inclusion of Bücher, the geographer Partsch, or some other sympathetic colleague as the second reader; but in many cases the appointment of Seeliger or Brandenburg to this role guaranteed the continuation of the paradigmatic conflicts that had destroyed the historical seminar.[158]

A new series of contested doctoral promotions and habilitations thus occupied the faculty from the moment Lamprecht's institute opened. The case of Adolf Rein, the first in the series, displayed the typical features of the problem. His dissertation on the origins of autobiography in the German Middle Ages purported to trace the evolution of this genre through Lamprecht's epochs. Lamprecht was pleased with the result and recommended acceptance; Seeliger and Brandenburg thought otherwise.[159] Neither of them could understand how an autobiographical fragment by Ludwig the Bavarian was "Typical," while another by Rudolf of Habsburg was "Individualistic." The methodological premises of the dissertation were all Lamprechtian, Brandenburg reported: "[T]he interpretations and commentaries are for the most part statements of the author's taste and they prove nothing." With the committee split, the question went before the philosophical faculty, where Lamprecht lost badly despite his plea that he was the only scholar in the faculty qualified to judge a work of cultural history.

Rein, who later recalled that he had fallen "into the cross fire between the historiographical fronts," survived by switching to a safe topic in political history.[160] Others among Lamprecht's students were less fortunate. Most vulnerable were those who were not habilitated at the time of their appointment as instructors in the institute and who then sought to repair the deficiency in their credentials by habilitating with the director. These cases stirred faculty resentments, so the cross fire was intense; and several young scholars, including Goldfriedrich, fell victim to it.[161]

Well might Lamprecht argue that his colleagues did not understand the methods or standards of scholarship that prevailed in his institute.[162] But the argument carried little force. He attempted in vain to find relief in the appointment of another scholar of reliable sympathies, who could join him on the committees that supervised his students.[163] Seeliger and Brandenburg blocked his effort to install Kötzschke in this role.[164] The two historians also won an important victory in Dresden late in 1913, when they deprived Lamprecht of a new extraordinary professorship which the ministry had just created in west European history.[165] The ministry's decision was a painful blow to a scholar whose influence in Dresden had been an advantage. It further shifted the political balance among the Leipzig historians against Lamprecht, and it came at a bad time, for the Institute for Cultural and Universal History was attracting unfavorable attention elsewhere.

The establishment of an institute for Lamprecht was difficult for the rest of the German historical profession to ignore. It was also difficult to comprehend. Reactions were everywhere envious, and they ran from grudging admiration (from scholars like Finke) to revulsion.[166] The preponderance of the latter sentiment was evident in the failure of attempts to establish similar institutes elsewhere, first by Breysig in Berlin and then by Bernheim in Greifswald.[167] Some of the animus was directed at Lamprecht's sovereign control of his institute, but most of it concerned issues of scholarly integrity, such as the instructors' lack of qualifications, the insufficiency of language training, and the centrality of children's drawings in the institute's library—to say nothing of the director's methodological views.[168] Academic historians were reluctant, however, to vent their feelings in public about the spectacle in Leipzig. The terms on which the *Methodenstreit* broke off seemed to demand their silence lest public criticism encourage Lamprecht to revive the polemic. Nor was this an imaginary danger, as Ernst Troeltsch learned in 1909 when he broke the ban in the *Historische Zeitschrift* with a review of the dissertation of Felix Günther, one of Lamprecht's students.[169] Although Troeltsch recognized the virtues of this work, which dealt with the emergence of anthropology in eighteenth century Germany, he concluded, much as Seeliger or Brandenburg might have, that the "ravages" of Lamprecht's categories had sapped the work of most of its value. Günther's fate was thus a useful example of the "running amok [*Verwilderung*]" that Lamprecht's "new method" was encouraging and how this method threatened "to turn learned and talented works into babble [*verworrenes Gerede*]." Amid protestations of his distaste for polemics, Lamprecht thereupon published a rejoinder in two different journals and encouraged his student to respond to Troeltsch's charges in an angry pamphlet.[170] Troeltsch chose not to reply.

The episode confirmed the wisdom of the profession's silence. The obverse of the same strategy was the quiet ostracism of virtually every young scholar who was identified with the institute or its director. Other than Goetz, Ernst Daenell was the only student who habilitated with Lamprecht and then found a chair at a German university before the war; and he left Leipzig in 1897, early enough to avoid association with the institute.[171] Lamprecht was tireless in promoting the careers of his advanced students, both within his institute and outside, but the situation was hopeless. Even if they survived the cross fire in Leipzig, these young scholars could aspire at best to employment in journalism, archives, or in local historical societies, like those to which Lamprecht had ties in Cologne and Dresden.

The profession's leadership broke the ban of silence on only one other occasion, early in 1914, when compromising testimony about affairs in Leipzig arrived from an unexpected quarter. In November 1912 Arley Barthlow Show, who taught history at Stanford, delivered the presidential address to the Pacific Coast Branch of the American Historical Association in Berkeley. The address was about Lamprecht. Show had studied in Leipzig at the turn of the century and had returned for several visits, so he held the credentials to offer a penetrating judgment. He portrayed Lamprecht as a would-be messiah, an apostle who had an unwavering "faith in his own creed" and "proclaimed his new evangel to scholars of his native land." Show characterized the Institute for Cultural and Universal History as the domain of the apostle's disciples, "men of his own choosing, men thoroughly filled with his own ideas and methods," a "new school" dedicated to "a highly organized propaganda for the new culture history." Show also analyzed the conception that underlay this history and concluded that it was "little short of absurd": "speculative, metaphysical, intuitional, poetical, what you will; but not inductive, therefore not scientific, and not historical."[172]

Show's strictures, which were published in the United States in October 1913, were aimed not only at Lamprecht but at Lamprecht's friends in the United States. To Lamprecht's enemies in Germany, who cared little about the American context of the address, Show looked like the ideal witness to reveal long-known but unspoken truths about Lamprecht's institute—the outsider with the inside knowledge. As soon as he learned of the speech, Seeliger arranged for its translation and publication in a journal edited by one of his former students.[173] Convinced that the article portended a definitive end to the *Methodenstreit*—even (or particularly) in Leipzig—Seeliger then urged Delbrück to reopen the *Preussische Jahrbücher* to the methodological debate. With the lesson of Troeltsch before him, Delbrück declined. He advised Seeliger, as Meinecke had once counseled Below, that "scholarship always fights in vain against charlatans and must allow them to die on their own barrenness."[174] Delbrück did allow Seeliger to reprint a brief notice from his own journal, the *Historische Vierteljahrschrift*, which announced the publication of Show's article in German and recommended "very special attention" to "this voice from abroad and from the New World, where the 'new direction' seemed to have won full success."[175]

Lamprecht was shocked. His emotional armor was much too thick to permit the thought that Show had delivered a telling indictment of his life's work. Nor did his anger over Seeliger's role in the affair matter much, for the relationship of these two men could not grow any worse.[176] He was shocked mainly by the provenance of the attack, for Seeliger had gauged correctly the importance that Lamprecht attached to the American reception of his theories. In the light of strong public support from the students and instructors in his institute, however, the historian contented himself with a brief public statement in the hope that the impact of the attack would be limited in Dresden.[177]

Lamprecht had become accustomed to both the studied indifference of the profession's leaders and the machinations of his local colleagues. He allowed neither to affect his plans for the expansion of historical studies in his institute. The continuing effort to build the institute's endowment—a resource beyond the reach of his enemies—brought him in contact with businessmen, philanthropists, embassies, heiresses, and even the Nobel committee after some of his friends nominated his institute (at his request, although in vain) for the peace prize.[178] He used much of the money he raised to recruit foreign scholars to teach the history of their own lands in tandem with German instructors. The reluctance of the ministry to fund positions for foreigners initially limited the program to team-taught courses with young scholars from England, France, and the United States.[179]

Recruiting foreign scholars represented one of Lamprecht's responses to the charge that his institute offered insufficient language training. He also placed renewed emphasis on the history of visual perception, a facet of the institute's work that seemed to minimize the significance of language. Lamprecht was convinced that the development of visual perception was "the most accessible part of human history."[180] The "universal clarity [*Anschaulichkeit*]" of visual art, as he wrote in 1913, was "disturbed by no medium like language."[181] This principle had guided his own research as early as the 1880s, when he wrote on the evolution of medieval ornamentation. Now it highlighted the importance of the children's drawings in the institute's library. By 1914 Lamprecht had built the collection to more than 200,000, and he began to encourage his advanced students to work in it.[182]

Although many questions remained about the mission of his institute and many battles remained to be fought over its staffing and competence, Lamprecht had by the eve of the war built one of imperial Germany's most impressive academic empires—certainly its most unusual one. His institute had spilled out from the confines of the Golden Bear into the next building; it now housed not only the Institute for Cultural and Universal History, but also Kötzschke's seminar for *Landesgeschichte und Siedlungskunde*, a new seminar for east Asian studies, and still another—this time from the theological faculty—for the comparative history of religions.[183] The library of Lamprecht's institute alone comprised (in addition to the children's drawings) over 30,000 volumes, the bulk of which were on modern cultural and intellectual themes.[184] The resources of this empire were marshaled to offer a coherent program of research and instruction, which guided students down the path first trod by the director himself, from regional and national history to ever more comprehensive intellectual vistas.[185]

Lamprecht incorporated other disciplines into his empire with an ease that bespoke the capaciousness of his vision and his ambition to create the methodology for a unified field of knowledge. While his enemies in Leipzig sounded the alarm over the academic imperialism of this "putative universal genius," even more sympathetic observers were struck by the resemblance of his institute to a small university.[186] In truth, no field of study was irrelevant to Lamprecht's grand schema of history, which all other academic disciplines were to serve, as Josef Engel has remarked, as "applied sciences."[187] Lamprecht's vision implied the reform not only of his own discipline, but of the whole academy.

Notes

1. Eduard Meyer, "Zur Theorie und Methodik der Geschichte," in Meyer, *Kleine Schriften*, 2d ed., 2 vols. (Halle, 1924), 1: 1–67.
2. Weber, "Kritische Studien auf dem Gebiet der kulturwissenschaftlichen Logik," WL, 215–90.
3. WL, 274; Meyer, 37.
4. NL Lamprecht (Korr. 29), Helmolt to Lamprecht, Leipzig, 14.2.05.
5. Hans F. Helmolt, ed., *Weltgeschichte*, 9 vols. (Leipzig and Vienna, 1899–1907).
6. Ibid., 1: v.
7. Helmolt, "Die Anordnung des Stoffes," ibid., 1: 19.
8. Alfred Heuss, *Zur Theorie der Weltgeschichte* (Berlin, 1968), 31.
9. See Ernst Schulin, "Einleitung," in Schulin, ed., *Universalgeschichte* (Cologne, 1974), esp. 28–32; Schulin, *Traditionskritik*, 183–88; Joseph Vogt, *Wege zum historischen Universum: Von Ranke bis Toynbee* (Stuttgart, 1961), 11–22.
10. Krieger, 320–43; *cf.* Eberhard Kessel, "Rankes Idee der Universalhistorie," HZ, 178 (1954): 269–308.
11. Theodor Lindner, *Weltgeschichte seit der Völkerwanderung*, 9 vols. (Stuttgart, 1906–1916).
12. Lindner, *Geschichtsphilosophie: Einleitung zu einer Weltgeschichte seit der Völkerwanderung* (Stuttgart, 1901), 107.
13. See Hans Schleier, "Zu den Theorien über die Entwicklung der Gesellschaft im spätbürgerlichen deutschen Geschichtsdenken," in Ernst Engelberg and Wolfgang Küttler, eds., *Formationstheorie und Geschichte: Studien zur historischen Untersuchung von Gesellschaftsformationen im Werk von Marx, Engels und Lenin* (Vaduz, 1978), 612–18.
14. See McClellan, *German Historians and England*; Willy Schenk, *Die deutsch-englische Rivalität vor dem ersten Weltkrieg in der Sicht deutscher Historiker: Missverstehen oder Machtstreben?* (Aarau, 1967).
15. Dietrich Schäfer, *Weltgeschichte der Neuzeit*, 2 vols. (Berlin, 1907); *cf.* Graf Yorck von Wartenburg, *Weltgeschichte in Umrissen*, 4th ed. (Berlin, 1901).
16. Schäfer, "Geschichte und Kulturgeschichte," 339.
17. Vogt, 19–21.
18. For instance, Otto Kaemmel, ed., *Spamers Illustrierte Weltgeschichte, mit besonderer Berücksichtigung der Kulturgeschichte*, 4th ed., 10 vols. (Leipzig, 1902).
19. vom Brocke, *Breysig*, 53–61.

20. *Der Stufenbau und die Gesetze der Welt-Geschichte* (Berlin, 1905).
21. *Die Geschichte der Menschheit: Die Völker ewiger Urzeit. Die Amerikaner des Nordwestens und des Nordens* (Berlin, 1907).
22. vom Brocke, *Breysig*, 76–101, quotations from 95.
23. "Eine Weltgeschichte nach neuen Grundsätzen," *Frankfurter Zeitung*, 24.9.99. The review appears also in *Die kulturhistorische Methode*, 39–46.
24. I have dealt with aspects of this problem in "Karl Lamprechts Konzeption einer Weltgeschichte," *Archiv für Kulturgeschichte*, 73 (1991): 437–52. See also Spiess, 176–86.
25. The first hint of Lamprecht's interest in world history came in an allusion to cross-cultural influences in the pamphlet, "Alte und neue Richtungen," 79. A statement of long-term goals from late in 1893 contained no mention of world history. NL Liesegang, Lamprecht to Liesegang, Leipzig, 30.11.93.
26. "Was ist Kulturgeschichte?" 97–100.
27. Ibid., 130.
28. Hintze, "Ueber individualistische und kollektivistische Geschichtsauffassung," 66; *cf.* Rachfahl, "'Kollektivistische' Geschichtswissenschaft," 675.
29. Below, "Neue historische Methode," 255.
30. BA, Kl. Erw. Nr. 310, Lamprecht to Lindau, Leipzig, 7.12.03; Staatsbibliothek Preussischer Kulturbesitz, Berlin, NL Breysig, Lamprecht to Breysig, Leipzig, 15.7.05.
31. NL Lamprecht (Korr. 48), Lamprecht, Meine Tätigkeit nach Vollendung der Deutschen Geschichte und die Absichten meines Alters, August 1914.
32. NL Lamprecht (Korr. 59), Lamprecht to Hugo Lamprecht, Leipzig, 7.6.04; *cf.* Griss, 31, 165.
33. NL Lamprecht (Korr. 53), Lamprecht to Wenck, Leipzig, 1.5.06.
34. NL Dove, Lamprecht to Dove, Leipzig, 23.11.06.
35. Wundt and Klinger, *Gedenkblatt*, 10.
36. Bücher, *Worte zum Gedächtnis*, 10.
37. NL Lamprecht (Korr. 45), Lamprecht to Ritter, Leipzig, 23.8.07.
38. E.g., DG, 1: 188.
39. Ratzel, "Geschichte, Völkerkunde und historische Perspektive," esp. 7–9, 12–16, 18–23.
40. NL Breysig, Lamprecht to Breysig, Leipzig, 15.7.05, April 1906; Lamprecht, "Entwicklungsstufen," 141.
41. DG, 1 (3): x–xi.
42. Rachfahl, "'Kollektivistische' Geschichtswissenschaft," 674; *cf.* EB, 1: 450.
43. MG, 103.
44. "Biopsychologische Probleme," 447.
45. "Begriff der Geschichte," 264; MG, 113.
46. "Begriff der Geschichte," 581; MG, 122.
47. Lamprecht, *Beiträge*, 58; Schultz, "Moral Force," 19.
48. NL Hellpach (72), Lamprecht to Hellpach, 14.12.01.
49. StA Dresden, VB 10281/203, Lamprecht to Waentig, Leipzig, 10.1.05; Lamprecht, Aufforderung zum Sammeln von Kinderzeichnungen, Elberfeld, 12.3.05; NL Lamprecht (Korr. 45), Lamprecht to Ritter, Leipzig, 24.11.07.
50. DG, 9: 148.
51. NL Lamprecht (Korr. 41), Lamprecht to Philippi, Leipzig, 30.4.13; MG, 120–21; Kötzschke, "Karl Lamprecht," 21; LW, 468, 542.
52. Below, "Neue historische Methode," 256, n. 1.; Seeliger, "Lamprecht," 136.
53. MG, 111–13.
54. "Über den Begriff der Geschichte," 275–76; *cf. Americana*, 98.

55. MG, 114.
56. Ibid., 115. Lamprecht disguised the problem by simply calling biological analogies mechanical.
57. "Universalgeschichtliche Probleme vom sozialpsychologischen Standpunkte," MG, 103–30; cf. "Zur universalgeschichtlichen Methodenbildung," Abhandlungen der philologisch-historischen Classe der Königlich-Sächsischen Gesellschaft der Wissenschaften, 27 (1909): 33–63. The latter essay is in Schleier, Alternative, 374–404.
58. MG, 126.
59. See Karl H. Metz, "Historisches 'Verstehen' und Sozialpsychologie: Karl Lamprecht und seine 'Wissenschaft der Geschichte,'" Saeculum: Jahrbuch für Universalgeschichte, 33 (1982): esp. 103–4.
60. MG, 115.
61. "Über den Begriff der Geschichte," 262.
62. "Universalgeschichtliche Methodenbildung," 638.
63. Seeliger, "Lamprecht," 141.
64. See EB, 2,2: 463; cf. "Nationalismus und Universalismus in Deutschland," Dokumente des Fortschritts, 1 (1907–1908): 5–10; "Über auswärtige Kulturpolitik," Mitteilungen des Verbandes für internationale Verständigung, 8 (1913): 6–7.
65. MG, 86.
66. NL Lamprecht (Korr. 45), Lamprecht to Rothacker, Leipzig, 1.2.12.
67. Jahn, "Lamprecht," 135–38; Doren, 365; Arens, 307.
68. MG, 91–93.
69. Cassier, 288.
70. For surveys see Luise Schorn-Schütte, "Karl Lamprecht und die internationale Geschichtsschreibung," AKg, 67 (1985): 417–64; Schorn-Schütte, Lamprecht, 287–337; Hans Schleier, "Zur internationalen Stellung Karl Lamprechts," Wissenschaftliche Beiträge der Ernst-Moritz-Arndt-Universität Greifswald zur Nordeuropa Forschung: 7. Gesellschaftswissenschaftliches Seminar DDR-Finnland (Greifswald, 1982), 4–13; Georg Iggers, "The 'Methodenstreit' in International Perspective: The Reorientation of Historical Studies at the Turn from the Nineteenth to the Twentieth Century," StdSt, 6 (1984): 21–32.
71. Iggers, "International Perspective," 22; cf. Iggers, "Image of Ranke," 17–40.
72. On France see the persuasive analysis of Lutz Raphael, "Historikerkontroversen im Spannungsfeld zwischen Berufshabitus, Fächerkonkurrenz und sozialen Deutungsmustern: Lamprecht-Streit und französischer Methodenstreit der Jahrhundertwende in vergleichender Perspektive," HZ, 251 (1990): 325–63. See also Christian Simon's extended analysis, which emphasizes the similarities in the historiography on both sides of the Rhine: Staat und Geschichtswissenschaft.
73. NL Marcks (71), Below to Marcks, Marburg, 5.4.98.
74. NL Mevissen, Lamprecht to Mevissen, Leipzig, 2.1.98; Pirenne to Lamprecht, Ghent, 12.2.97, in Lyon, "Letters," 207; Luise Schorn-Schütte, "Karl Lamprecht: Wegbereiter einer historischen Sozialwissenschaft?" in Hammerstein, Geschichtswissenschaft, 176.
75. See Bryce Lyon, Henri Pirenne: A Biographical and Intellectual Study (Ghent, 1974), 128–34; Schorn-Schütte, Lamprecht, 320–28.
76. NL Lamprecht (Munich), Lamprecht to Else Lamprecht, Leipzig, 23.12.06; NL Lamprecht (Korr. 19), Dodd to Lamprecht, Ashland, Virginia, 8.2.02; (Korr. 38), Lamprecht to Monod, Bonn, n.d; Robert Dallek, Democrat and Diplomat: The Life of William E. Dodd (New York, 1968), 17–23.
77. Lamprecht's students included Halvdan Koht, Waslaw Sobieski, and Gunnar Palander. See Koht, "Aus den Lehrjahren eines Historikers," WaG, 13 (1965): 149–65; Matti Viikari, "Die Tradition der finnischen Geschichtsschreibung

und Karl Lamprecht," StdSt, 6 (1984): 33–43; Schorn-Schütte, *Lamprecht*, 328–36.

78. See Phyllis Keller, *States of Belonging: German-American Intellectuals and the First World War* (Cambridge, MA, 1979), 7–118; Margaret Münsterberg, *Hugo Münsterberg: His Life and Work* (New York and London, 1922).

79. Bruce Kuklick, *The Rise of American Philosophy: Cambridge, Massachusetts, 1860–1930* (New Haven and London, 1977), 203–8.

80. See George Haines, IV and Frederick H. Jackson, "A Neglected Landmark in the History of Ideas," *Mississippi Valley Historical Review*, 34 (1947–1948): 201–20; Jurgen Herbst, *The German Historical School in American Scholarship: A Study in the Transfer of Culture* (Ithaca, 1965), 207–15; Guenther Roth, "Americana: Bildungsbürgerliche Ansichten und auswärtige Kulturpolitik im Wilhelminischen Deutschland," in Roth, *Politische Herrschaft und Persönliche Freiheit* (Frankfurt am Main, 1987), esp. 181–82.

81. Münsterberg, "The Scientific Plan of the Congress," Howard J. Rogers. ed., *Congress of Arts and Sciences: Universal Exposition, St. Louis, 1904*, 6 vols. (Boston and New York, 1905–1906), 1: 93.

82. See Ostwald, *Lebenslinien*, 2: 411–12.

83. The decision to invite Lamprecht was due probably to the suggestion of James Harvey Robinson: Schorn-Schütte, *Lamprecht*, 295, n. 37.

84. LW, 480. Robinson was probably responsible for this invitation, too.

85. NL Lamprecht (Korr. 59), Lamprecht to Hugo Lamprecht, Leipzig, 24.7.04.

86. StA Dresden, VB 10281/203, Lamprecht to KM, Leipzig, 17.12.03.

87. Lamprecht, *Americana: Reiseeindrücke, Betrachtungen, Geschichtliche Gesamtansicht* (Freiburg, 1906).

88. Ibid., 38.

89. Keller, 38.

90. Rogers, *Congress*, 1: 54–76.

91. Ibid., 2: 111–24.

92. LW, 493. Neither Lamprecht's published account of his American journey nor the notes in his papers make mention of his participation in the congress. NL Lamprecht (L 29), Amerikareise, Tagebuchblätter 1904); cf. *Americana*, 48.

93. Columbia University, Nicholas Murray Butler Collection, Lamprecht to Butler, Manhattan, 16.10.04; NL Lamprecht (Korr. 29), Columbia University in the City of New York. The lectures were published simultaneously in German, as *Moderne Geschichtwissenschaft*, and in English as *What Is History? Five Lectures in the Modern Science of History* (New York, 1905).

94. *Americana*, 64.

95. Ibid., 71, 103.

96. Ibid., 132.

97. Ibid., 120.

98. Ibid., 134.

99. Ibid., 121.

100. Ibid., 131.

101. Ibid., 124.

102. Ibid., 147.

103. Ibid., 142–3.

104. Ibid., 102.

105. Ibid., 88.

106. Ibid., 90.

107. Ibid., 91.

108. NL Lamprecht (Korr. 2), George B. Adams to Lamprecht, New Haven, 19.11.06;

(Korr. 13, 2), James Bryce to Lamprecht, London, 21.2.05; (Korr. 44), Lamprecht to Präsident of Rice Institut, Houston, Leipzig, 4.7.12; Butler Papers, Butler to Lamprecht, 11.1.11.

109. StA Dresden, VB 10228/2, KM to Lamprecht and Seeliger, Dresden, 11.1.07; Lamprecht and Seeliger, Protocol, Leipzig, 25.7.07.

110. StA Dresden, VB 10228/2, Lamprecht to KM, Leipzig, 5.8.07.

111. StA Dresden, VB 10228/3, Lamprecht to KM, Leipzig, 18.7.08; Seeliger, Brandenburg, and Wilcken to KM, Leipzig, 18.12.08.

112. In the summer of 1906 Lamprecht lied when he assured the ministry that he had been negotiating with Seeliger and Brandenburg over the physical separation of his section from theirs. StA Dresden, VB 10228/2, Lamprecht and Seeliger, Protocol, Leipzig, 25.7.07.

113. "Zur Ausgestaltung der universalgeschichtlichen Studien im Hochschulunterricht," Bericht über die zehnte Versammlung deutscher Historiker zu Dresden, 3. bis 7. September 1907 (Leipzig, 1908), 18–23; cf.Lamprecht, "Universalgeschichte auf der Hochschule," Zukunft, 60 (1907): 432–39.

114. LW, 539.

115. Bericht über die zehnte Versammlung, 24. See also Schumann, Historikertage, 224–27.

116. NL Lamprecht (UL 10), An die Gönner eines künftigen Seminars für Kultur- und Universalgeschichte, Leipzig, 26.10.07.

117. Heinz Weissbach, "Die Entwicklung des Instituts für Kultur-und Universalgeschichte bzw. der Abteilung Allgemeine Geschichte der Neuzeit des Instituts für Allgemeine Geschichte von 1909 bis 1969: Ein Beitrag zu einer Institutschronik," 2 vols. (Diplomarbeit, Karl-Marx-Universität Leipzig, 1979), 1: 13; cf. Metz, Grundformen, 469.

118. NL Lamprecht (M4a) contains of list of Gönner, which comprises twenty-one entries from Leipzig, none from Cologne, and eight from Frankfurt am Main. It is not clear, however, when this list was assembled.

119. NL Lamprecht (Korr. 45), Lamprecht to Ritter, Leipzig, 1.1.07; StA Dresden, 10228/2, Lamprecht to KM, Leipzig, 11.6.07.

120. NL Lamprecht (Munich), Johann Georg to Lamprecht, Dresden, 24.4.07, 11.1.09; Weissbach, 13, 15.

121. NL Lamprecht (UL 10), An die Gönner.

122. Lamprecht, "Ein neues Historisches Institut," Zukunft, 68 (1909): 348.

123. NL Harden, Lamprecht to Harden, Leipzig, 12.9.07.

124. Schorn-Schütte, Lamprecht, 306.

125. StA Dresden, VB 10230/21, Lamprecht to KM, Leipzig, 27.5.14.

126. Lamprecht, "Ein neues Historisches Institut," 349.

127. NL Althoff (B Nr. 108/1), Lamprecht to Althoff, Schierke, 29.8.08; Lamprecht to Bülow (Entwurf, October 1908); Weissbach, 1: 13.

128. UA Leipzig, RA 900 (II), Lamprecht to Rentenamt, Leipzig, 15.1.09; 2.2.09, 22.2.09; NL Lamprecht (M6), Karl Lamprecht zum Gedächtnis, 27; NL Lamprecht (UL 10), An die Gönner.

129. UA Leipzig, Phil. Fak., B/14.19, Bd. 1, KM to PF, Dresden, 19.1.09.

130. NL Lamprecht (Korr. 45), Lamprecht to Ritter, Leipzig, 4.1.09.

131. Rudolf Kötzschke et al., Studium Lipsiense: Ehrengabe Karl Lamprecht, dargebracht aus Anlass der Eröffnung des Königlichen Sächsischen Instituts für Kultur- und Universalgeschichte bei der Universität Leipzig (Berlin, 1909).

132. Lamprecht, "Ein neues Historisches Institut," 341–50. The speech is also in Zwei Reden zur Hochschulreform (Berlin, 1910).

133. LW, 571–72.

134. Dove, "Lamprecht," 313.

135. Arley Barthlow Show, "Die Kulturgeschichtsschreibung Karl Lamprechts," VuG, 4 (1914): 67.

136. NL Lamprecht (Korr. 59), Lamprecht to Hugo Lamprecht, Leipzig, 23.10.05; (Korr. 4), Asakawa to Lamprecht, Hanover, N.H., 5.1.05; NL Goetz (174), Lamprecht to Ritter, Leipzig, 27.12.09; EB, 2,2: 695; Kötzschke, "Lamprecht," 21.

137. NL Harden, Lamprecht to Harden, Fontainebleau, 19.9.06; NL Lamprecht (Korr. 45), Lamprecht to Ritter, Paris, 26.9.06.

138. Lamprecht, *Americana*, 125, n. 1.

139. "Europäische Expansion," *Zukunft*, 65 (1908): 141–53; "Zur universalgeschichtlichen Methodenbildung," 55–58; "Rede des antretenden Rektors Dr. Karl Lamprecht," *Rektorenwechsel an der Universität Leipzig am 31. Oktober 1910* (Leipzig, n.d.), 15–36.

140. NL Lamprecht (Pl 10), Entwürfe zur Weltgeschichte; LW, 468, 542.

141. NL Lamprecht (Korr. 45), Lamprecht to Ritter, Leipzig, 6.7.09.

142. StA Dresden, KM 10228/2, Lamprecht to KM, Leipzig, 22.11.06.

143. "Die kultur- und universalgeschichtlichen Bestrebungen an der Universität Leipzig," IWWKT, 2 (1908): 1141–50. This lecture is reprinted in Schleier, *Alternative*, 365–73, where the quotations are on 367–68. See also Karl Dietrich Erdmann, *Die Oekumene der Historiker: Geschichte der Internationalen Historikerkongresse und des Comité International des Sciences Historiques* (Göttingen, 1987), 72–79.

144. NL Lamprecht (Korr. 67a), Lamprecht, "Erklärung," VuG, No. 9 (1. Beilage) 1914.

145. StA Dresden, VB 10228/3, Seeliger to Brandenburg to KM, Leipzig, 17.1.13; NL Lamprecht (Munich), Lamprecht to Else Lamprecht, Leipzig 6.5.10; *cf.* Czok, "Lamprecht," 97.

146. Herbert Schönebaum, "Karl Lamprechts hochschulpädagogische Bestrebungen," *Zeitschrift für Pädagogik*, 2 (1956): 11.

147. NL Lamprecht (UL 6), Geschichte bei der Universität Leipzig: Lehrplan für das Winter-Semester 1909 auf 1910.

148. StA Dresden, VB 10281/203, Ordnung des Verwaltungspersonals im IKUg: Vorlage für den künftigen Bericht ans Ministerium [1915]; Weissbach, 27.

149. NL Lamprecht (L 1), Übungen, WS 1908/9, Vorkurs; (Korr. 30), Heyfelder to Lamprecht, Freiburg, 23.10.05; Lamprecht, *Einführung in das historische Denken* (Leipzig, 1912).

150. NL Lamprecht (UL 6), Kgl. Sächsisches Institut für Kultur- und Universalgeschichte, Lehr- und Arbeitsplan für das Wintersemester 1913/14.

151. Jahn, "Lamprecht," 139–40.

152. NL Dove, Lamprecht to Dove, Leipzig, 13.12.07; Weissbach, 1: 137–46.

153. NL Lamprecht (M6), Karl Lamprecht zum Gedächtnis, 28.

154. NL Lamprecht (Korr. 67a), Erklärung der Dozenten.

155. NL Lamprecht (Korr. 34), Kretzschmar to Lamprecht, Leipzig, 19.11.11.

156. Rein, Politik und Universität, 11.

157. Schönebaum, "Lamprechtiana," 17–19. The subjects included ancient Chinese and Japanese art, the American Constitutional Convention, and the mental development of black children.

158. LW, 626–27.

159. NL Lamprecht (UL 4), Doubletten zum Fall Rein (1909).

160. Rein, Politik und Universität, 20–22.

161. NL Lamprecht (Korr. 24), Brandenburg to Lamprecht. Leipzig, 23.10.11; (Korr. 32), Lamprecht to PF, Leipzig, 27.11; (UL 4), Lamprecht to Köster, Leipzig, 4.6.12. See Blanke, *Historiographiegeschichte*, 466–74.

162. UA Leipzig, Rep. I/1, Nr. 104, Bd. 1., Lamprecht to Heinrici, Leipzig, 10.11.11.

163. StA Dresden, VB 10230/21, Lamprecht to KM, Bad Kösen, 3.1.13.

164. NL Lamprecht (UL 4), Beilage (Kötzschkes Teilnahme an den Promotionen 1914).

165. NL Lamprecht (UL 4), Beck to Lamprecht, Dresden, 11.12.13; LW, 659.

166. Finke, "Finke," 108.

167. StA Dresden, VB 10281/203, Helmolt to Waentig, Dresden, 18.12.09.
168. Georg von Below, "Kulturgeschichte und kulturgeschichtlicher Unterricht," HZ, 106 (1911): 96–105; AKg, 8 (1910): 231–32; vom Brocke, Breysig, 93, 95.
169. HZ, 103 (1909): 122–27.
170. Lamprecht, "Herr Professor Troeltsch," DLZ, 30 (1909): 3071–72; LZbl, 60 (1909): 1479–80; Felix Günther, Troeltsch-Heidelberg und die Lamprechtsche Richtung: Eine Entgegnung (Leipzig, 1909). See Friedrich Wilhelm Graf, "Ernst Troeltsch: Kulturgeschichte des Christentums," in Hammerstein, Geschichtswissenschaft, esp. 136–37.
171. NL Lamprecht (Korr. 18), Daenell to Lamprecht, Münster, 19.6.14; Weber, Lexikon, 98.
172. Arley Barthlow Show, "The New Culture-History in Germany," The History Teacher's Magazine, 4 (1913): 215–21.
173. Arley Barthlow Show, "Die Kulturgeschichtsschreibung Karl Lamprechts," VuG, 4 (1914): 65–87. Fritz Friederich, the editor, did a dissertation with Seeliger in 1898 (Lamprecht was the second reader).
174. NL Delbrück, Delbrück to Seeliger, Berlin, 13.5.14 (Briefkonzeptbuch 31).
175. Seeliger, "Über die Kulturgeschichtsschreibung Karl Lamprechts," PJb, 156 (1914): 539–42; "Zusatz des Herausgebers," ibid., 542–44.
176. NL Lamprecht (Korr. 10), Lamprecht to Berr, Leipzig, 30.4.14; LW, 683–88.
177. NL Lamprecht (Korr. 67a), Erklärung der Dozenten; Erklärung der Studenten; Lamprecht, "Erklärung," VuG, no. 9 (1. Beilage) 1914; LW, 686–88.
178. NL Lamprecht (Korr. 34), Lamprecht to Koht, 19.1.12; (Korr. 35, 2), Lamprecht to Lewald, Leipzig, 23.7.12; (Korr. 38), Lamprecht to Gabriel Monod, Leipzig, 1.2.12; (Korr. 27, 2), Lamprecht to Baronin Schroeder, 6.8.13.
179. NL Lamprecht (Korr. 52), Lamprecht to Ward, Leipzig, 20.1.12; (UL 6), Lamprecht to Salinger, Leipzig, 4.8.13; Schmaltz to Lamprecht, Dresden, 2.8.13.
180. NL Lamprecht (Korr. 44), Lamprecht to Riemann, 12.11.14.
181. NL Lamprecht (Korr. 39), Lamprecht to Nadler, 26.9.13.
182. NL Lamprecht (UL 6), Lamprecht to KM, Leipzig, 16.11.14; cf. Erich Franke, Die geistige Entwicklung der Negerkinder: Ein Beitrag zur Frage nach den Hemmungen der Kulturentwicklung (Leipzig, 1915).
183. NL Lamprecht (UL 6), IKUg, Lehr- und Arbeitsplan für das Winter-Semester 1913/14; LW, 680.
184. UA Leipzig, Phil. Fak., PA 511, Kommissionssitzung II, 6.6.15, Wiederbesetzung der Lamprechtschen Professur.
185. NL Lamprecht (UL 6), Lamprecht to Schmaltz, Leipzig, 1913 ("nicht vollendet").
186. LW, 551; Goetz, "Goetz," 164–65; cf. Show, "Culture-History," 221.
187. Engel, "Universitäten," 368.

11

Academic Reform

[I]ch weiss keinen besseren Lebenszweck, als am Grossen und Unmöglichen, *animae magnae prodigus*, zugrunde zu gehen.

He was heavy-set and of medium height. He had brown eyes and wore glasses. His beard was dark brown when he grew it in the 1880s, but by the end of the century the strains of the *Methodenstreit* had whitened both beard and hair to give him an avuncular appearance.[1]

Although his physical stature was unimposing, Karl Lamprecht radiated a sense of energy and power so compelling that the word "charisma" does not seem out of place. His friends and colleagues attested to it; so did his extraordinary success in raising money among civic and business leaders. The most dramatic tributes to it came, though, from his most captive and captivated audience, his students. "He is the best teacher among all the German professors I know," wrote Halvdan Koht, the Norwegian historian who studied in Leipzig in the late 1890s. "One will not easily find another example of his practical knack, his characteristic ability to make everything so clear and plausible that it is indelibly imprinted in the memory."[2] Adolf Rein praised Lamprecht's "unusual gift of making dead things come alive."[3] Kötzschke recalled a "teacher of quite uncommon effectiveness," whose lectures were delivered in "an exuberant style" and presented a "rich diversity of intellectual content which easily burst the bounds of conventional forms."[4] Another student spoke of the "magic" that the teacher "exercised on the young students of history."[5] The American student, William E. Dodd, wrote of the "immense influence" that Lamprecht exerted over students in Leipzig.[6]

These testimonies also made it clear that the sources of Lamprecht's fascination for students were the same traits that earned him the opprobrium of his professional peers. Students who had been weaned on political history delighted in the extraordinary range of Lamprecht's coverage and his ability to impose coherence on the most diverse features of the past. Hendrik de Man, who took a doctorate in Leipzig with Bücher early in the new century, was struck by Lamprecht's penchant for "grand, bold syntheses" and his ability to "awaken excitement and enthusiasm" among his students.[7] Kötzschke, who on many occasions observed the awakening of this excitement amid cascades of daring analogies, described the sense of wonderment that fell upon students when their professor, in the course of presenting some "grand overview or comparing phenomena that seemed remote," "revealed astonishing relationships, unanticipated connections."[8]

The strength of Lamprecht's rapport with students had already been evident in Bonn. In Leipzig he became a celebrity, and his lectures became spectacles that bore comparison (not the least in his own mind) with Treitschke's in Berlin.[9] Even before the *Methodenstreit* brought him national notoriety, Lamprecht's lectures attracted hundreds of people.[10] After the turn of the century it became difficult to find auditoriums large enough to contain the throngs of students, as well as the auditors from town (male and female) who wanted to experience Lamprecht.[11] They were treated to scenes like the one Koht described of the historian pacing the stage, gesticulating with his whole body, shoving the lectern aside to make more room, illustrating a point on the blackboard or by means of some "telling anecdote in a drastic figure of speech." "One did not forget what he said," Koht added, for it was "simply unmatched" "how he could, with but few words, paint a landscape or, so to speak, embody an intellectual climate [*Zustand*] or even throw a shimmer of understanding onto the secrets of higher mathematics."[12]

The fact that Lamprecht became a national celebrity during the late 1890s only enhanced the excitement in the auditorium. His lectures were another arena in the methodological controversy. He conveyed to his students the sense that history was being made in his classroom, that the "new direction," whose prophet stood before them, was emerging before their eyes. "We young ones read each of his passionate polemics as soon as it appeared," Gustav Radbruch recalled, "and took his side, quickly convinced."[13] The proselytizing admittedly did not convince all of his students. Dodd, a less impressionable outside observer than Koht, concluded that Lamprecht was "a man of prodigious vanity," although this judgment perhaps reflected a student's frustration at being turned away from one of Lamprecht's oversubscribed seminars.[14]

The students who did manage to enroll in these advanced courses discovered an additional range of pedagogical qualities that set Lamprecht apart from most of his colleagues. His rapport with his advanced students was like that of an older friend, who was wise yet young enough to enjoy the company of students and to understand their problems, both academic and personal.[15] His periodic consultations with students in the Institute for Cultural and Universal History extended a long-standing practice. As he had in Bonn, he frequently accompanied his students to the tavern after the institute closed. His excursions with advanced students to places like Wittenberg and Schulpforta, which had figured in his own intellectual maturation, was another sign of his affection for his disciples. Hendrik de Man was one of the more skeptical participants in these outings, but he confessed that he never again looked with the same eye at the interior of a church after Lamprecht took him through the cathedral in Naumburg.[16]

Lamprecht was a devoted teacher, whose inventiveness scorned the bounds of convention. The use of travel photographs as visual aids failed to impress his professional colleagues in Dresden in 1907, but it was a staple feature of instruction in Leipzig.[17] Lamprecht's institute acquired the most modern machinery then available for the reproduction and slide projection of photographs.[18] The historian consulted with his friends on the faculty about teaching techniques; and his appearances as an auditor in the lectures of his colleagues served pedagogical as well as research interests, before these visitations became such a spectacle that some of the faculty asked him to stay away.[19]

The distinction between scholarship and pedagogy was never sharp in Lamprecht's thinking. His course offerings corresponded to the progress of his *German History* toward his own day. Offerings in the history of the United States and the Orient likewise marked the outward turn of his research interests. He often lectured directly from his own manuscripts, some of which in fact gestated on the podium.[20] He lectured in much the same way as he wrote, so that new insights found their way as quickly, and as little assimilated, into his lecture notes as they did into his book manuscripts.[21]

Lamprecht's students were more willing than his professional peers to forgive the confusion and inconsistencies that resulted from this practice. Students made up his most loyal and appreciative audience. They constituted a forum in which his claim to be winning the *Methodenstreit* was compelling, and their significance to him grew as his professional misfortunes accumulated. He took pride and encouragement in his pedagogical success, which was advertised in his spectacular enrollments; and he found the company of admiring students a growing source of pleasure and rejuvenation.[22] In these circumstances, the historian's attention turned to the institution that provided their education.

Lamprecht's tenure at the university of Leipzig coincided with a difficult period of growth, in which the institution endured all the strains and dislocations that marked the transformation of German higher education in this era generally.[23] The roots of the transformation, in Leipzig as elsewhere, were demographic and economic.[24] More students enrolled in the university than ever before. Their backgrounds were more diverse, and their professional aspirations were geared to the demands and opportunities of a burgeoning industrial economy. Accommodating these pressures required more money and space, a larger corps of instructors, and major adjustments in the curriculum and governance.

When Lamprecht was appointed to the faculty in Leipzig in the summer semester of 1891, some 3,200 students were matriculated in the university. On the eve of the opening of the Institute for Cultural and Universal History in 1909, the figure had risen to more than 4,400, forty-four of whom were women.[25] The increase in enrollments in Leipzig lagged somewhat behind the national average, for the university's most dramatic growth had come earlier, as had the shift in the composition of the student population toward the sons of the commercial and industrial middle classes.[26] The wealthier, better connected, and more "illiberal" students continued to congregate in student corporations of several descriptions, of which there were some sixty in Leipzig; but in 1896 independent students, whose social backgrounds tended to be more modest, began to organize in the so-called free student association (*Freie Studentenschaft*) or *Finkenschaft*—the first such organization in the country.[27]

Changes in the distribution of students among the faculties also corresponded to national trends, although they were more pronounced in Leipzig. The number of students enrolled in the medical, legal, and theological faculties declined absolutely between 1891 and 1908—most significantly (over 40 percent) in the theological faculty, which in 1908 enrolled but 300 students.[28] The expansion of the student body was concentrated in the philosophical faculty, where enrollments grew by over 200 percent during the same period. The growth was heavy in the natural and social sciences—in the institutes for physics, applied chemistry, and the so-called *Staatswissenschaften*, as well as in geography and economics. The most spectacular growth reflected the dramatic impact that the universities' own expansion had on secondary education. The largest increases in enrollments came in the humanistic disciplines, in which secondary teachers traditionally trained—in German and the Romance languages, classical philology, philosophy, and in history, where Lamprecht (who was admittedly no traditional humanist) was alone responsible for much of the increase.[29]

The expansion of the faculty failed to keep pace with the increase in enrollments in Leipzig, where the ratio of students to teachers was significantly higher than the national average.[30] In 1893 the instructional staff comprised 193 scholars; by 1908 the teaching corps had grown only to 223.[31] These figures concealed significant imbalances within the faculty. Only two of the thirty new instructors were *Ordinarien*; the rest were extraordinary professors and *Privatdozenten*. In 1908 the *Nichtordinarien* thus constituted close to three-quarters of the teaching staff. In this respect, too, conditions in Leipzig conformed to a national trend—particularly among the larger urban universities—toward entrusting instruction to this auxiliary staff of underpaid and insecure scholars, many of whom were unhappy over their prospects for long-term apprenticeship in positions that excluded them from the rights and benefits of full faculty status.[32]

Because it offered an avenue to new professorial chairs, these apprentice scholars greeted the university's growing specialization, which was as much a part of academic life in Leipzig as it was elsewhere. The professional homes of the instructors, chair holders, and *Nichtordinarien* alike were in laboratories, clinics, seminars, and institutes that were devoted in the first instance to research, much of it collective. These were the basic units in what Adolf Harnack characterized in 1905 as the *Grossbetrieb der Wissenschaft*.[33] Twenty-two of them were established in Leipzig between 1891 and 1908, in disciplines from English and musicology to Old Testament theology and theoretical physics—and cultural and universal history.[34] The proliferation and dispersion of these institutes in buildings throughout the old town and beyond encouraged the compartmentalization of the university; it also raised difficult questions about the coherence of the curriculum and the proper relationship between basic research and the instruction of the majority of students, who were oriented to the more practical demands posed by state examinations.

Finally, the growing weight of institutes of specialized research also affected the governance of the university in Leipzig in much the same manner as it did in other universities.[35] The loss of a sense of intellectual and corporate community among the faculty symptomized another problem, which the establishment of Lamprecht's institute laid bare. The new seminars and institutes were the creations not of the faculty but of the ministry of culture, which provided their funding, prescribed their missions and staffing, and, in theory at least, supervised their operations. This practice benefited individual scholars who were adept in negotiating with the ministry. However, it also deprived the faculty of corporate power over its own affairs and brought the university under bureaucratic control from the capital, where the university's budget contended not only with the Saxon diet, but with competing demands for research funds from the state's technical university in Dresden, the mining academy in Freiberg, and several other public agencies, like the Royal Saxon Academy of Sciences and the Royal Commission for Saxon History.[36] Extensive corporate assets—in property, forests, and other endowments—had ensured the university a measure of fiscal autonomy until the late nineteenth century, when the transformation of the institution began in earnest; but by 1906 the university depended on the Saxon government for 80 percent of its funding.[37]

Lamprecht witnessed the transformation of the university first-hand. He encountered a significant portion of the increased student body in his own lectures and seminars. He observed the pressures that heavy enrollments visited on *Nichtordinarien*, and he was well acquainted with the inequities these scholars faced; his attempts to secure the promotions of three extraordinary professors who taught in the historical seminar—Arndt, Buchholz, and Kötzschke—brought reminders of his own earlier frustrations in Bonn. He was also more sensitive than most of his colleagues to the efforts of the unincorporated students to organize; perhaps the memory of his unhappy encounter with the *Burschenschaften* in Göttingen persuaded him to become faculty "protector" of the free student association.[38] Finally, Lamprecht experienced the compartmentalization and bureaucratization of the university; in fact, his Institute for Cultural and Universal History was a classic illustration of the opportunities that this aspect of the university's transformation offered.

Although he was a major beneficiary of the university's compartmentalization, Lamprecht's life work represented a rebellion against the intellectual parochialism that this trend both symptomized and promoted. His every instinct resisted the fragmentation of knowledge. His historical vision featured the synchronized progress of every field of inquiry—from botany to theology—

through the *Kulturzeitalter* toward the goal of a common methodology, which, he was confident, would be founded in the era of *Reizsamkeit* on the principles of psychogenetic development. Collaboration with Wundt, Ratzel, Bücher, and Ostwald encouraged the historian's confidence and constituted an informal front against the university's intellectual fragmentation; collaboration also suggested the general terms on which remote disciplines, such as chemistry and economics, could be accommodated in a unified methodology.

During the first years of the new century, however, Lamprecht was preoccupied with demolishing the residual bonds that had unified the historians in Leipzig. He had little occasion to consider the broader implications of his vision for the organization of the university until his journey to the United States excited his interest. The sense of corporate unity that seemed to pervade American colleges and universities, the bonds of institutional loyalty among students and alumni, the collegiality and selfless devotion of the faculty to the unprejudiced "investigation of truth"—to the "genuine mission of the university"—all suggested a formula for the reform of the academy at home.[39] And he found the formula the more compelling because he was convinced that his own theory of history represented the truth whose unprejudiced investigation would unify the German university. Those observers who spoke of the Institute for Cultural and Universal History as a "mini-university" were closer to the truth than they realized. Lamprecht regarded his own empire as a microcosm of the reformed German university, the harbinger of the new basic unit in German academic education, which would bring students and faculty together in a coordinated program of instruction and research founded on a comprehensive new intellectual paradigm.

Buoyed by the founding of his institute, the historian began late in 1909, both publicly and in representations to the ministry, to address the broad failings of the German academy and to offer a program for its reform.[40] It was essential, he announced, to bring higher education into step with principles of the "new times" (by which he meant the era of Excitability), which demanded an increase in the "intensity of instruction [*Intensität des Lehrbetriebes*]."[41] The central problem, he argued, lay in the humanistic disciplines, which "essentially determined the signature of the whole university."[42] Here the resources were the most inadequate, the pressure of enrollments the most severe, and, as comparisons with institutions of higher learning in the United States revealed, the organization of research and practical instruction was the most outmoded. But the root of the problem, he charged, lay deeper, in the reluctance of the German humanities to embrace the "powerful transformation of our scholarly thinking," which had set in at the end of the previous century and had already revolutionized the natural sciences.[43] In the humanistic disciplines the counterpart of this transformation had to be the historicization of every field of inquiry. "Historicization is complete in the language fields and in the political and social sciences," he wrote in a circular to his faculty colleagues at the end of the year. The same process was "now seizing hold of [*ergreift*] the philological disciplines" and had in fact already transformed the "oldest and most developed" of these disciplines, classical philology.[44]

It was already clear from these observations where Lamprecht's campaign was heading. The transformation in the humanities was to bring them all together as subfields of a common historical discipline, whose final principles were the historian's own. "The historicization of the humanities will culminate [*abschliessen*] in the perfection [*Durchbildung*] of the general comparative disciplines," he continued in the same circular, "like cultural history and general social psychology." The individual humanistic disciplines were henceforth to supply the "substructure" for the comprehensive intellectual framework that Lamprecht had defined. This role mandated the "growing intensity of investigation" into the distinctive subject matter of each discipline, as well as honing in the arts of historical interpretation.

The organizational changes that Lamprecht proposed were designed to enhance the intensity of research and instruction so defined.[45] Each discipline was to be organized in a reformed seminar, which offered, in place of large lectures, an expanded number of small classes (*Uebungen*), planned and taught by a collegial staff of instructors, most of them *Privatdozenten*, among whom the director was but *primus inter pares*. The courses were to be organized in tiers, in order to balance the demands of instruction and research and to lead the students through the discipline systematically and under close supervision. The elementary courses, which were devoted to an introduction to the subject matter and principles of interpretation, were designed for students who were preparing for midlevel teaching examinations or the equivalent. Advanced courses were to cover more specialized themes and prepare students for higher-level teaching examinations. The most advanced tier of the institute's activity, which was devoted to pure research, was the preserve of the apprentice scholars. To finance these reforms, particularly the expanded instructional staff, Lamprecht called for raising student fees; but in return he also proposed to extend the principles of collegiality to the students, to give them a voice in the seminars' governance, and to encourage the emergence of a "genuine productive cooperative."[46]

The practical details of Lamprecht's plans to reform the humanities left no doubt about his ultimate design, at least to anyone who had visited the Golden Bear. The Institute for Cultural and Universal History was, as the historian later confessed, to be the "mother institute."[47] Its children were to be similar units in the other humanistic disciplines, where curricula, instruction, and governance were to be reorganized in the light of Lamprechtian precepts. Moreover, these disciplines, no less than his own, were to be enlisted in the service of a familiar intellectual agenda; the destiny of all the children was to generate—each in its own way—raw material in order to provide additional substance to the grand psychogenetic synthesis over which the scholars in Lamprecht's own institute presided. To use Karl-Heinz Metz's metaphors, Lamprecht's project cast the university's other disciplines in the role of subcontractors, providers of semifinished products for the grand edifice that the historian was constructing.[48]

When he first announced them, these ideas represented only the unconventional preferences of a lone member of the faculty. The practical chances of action on them appeared negligible. The historian's plans required far more financial support than increased student fees were going to provide; and the ministry had already indulged Lamprecht's imagination to a lavish degree. In addition, the historian's proposals for the reform of curriculum and governance invaded the prerogatives of the faculty, particularly the philosophical faculty, both individually and as a body. Predictably, his initial inquiries among the scholars whom his plans most affected generated little enthusiasm. [49]

Lamprecht's advocacy of these plans in fact only intensified the suspicion and antagonism that his earlier conduct had earned him in the philosophical faculty. He had little patience for this body's traditions and conventions. Some of his colleagues had long found his drive and self-assurance offensive; and the ranks of his opponents had already begun to grow before the turmoil of the *Methodenstreit*. [50] The methodological position that the historian defended during this controversy was anathema to most of the humanists in the philosophical faculty, as well as to some members of other faculties who had trained in similar traditions of interpretation. The most significant of these scholars was the church historian in the theological faculty, Theodor Brieger, who was close both intellectually and personally to Max Lenz. [51] The extent of Lamprecht's isolation in his own faculty registered in the votes that went against him whenever his conflicts with Marcks, Seeliger, and Brandenburg spilled over into this broader forum. Most of the philosophical faculty held Lamprecht responsible for the chaos in the historical seminar; and many of them resented the extraordinary benefits he reaped in the aftermath.

The historian did have friends. His closest ties were to his colleagues in the *Kränzchen*, particularly to Wundt, Ratzel, and Ostwald. This group was too small, however, to form the nucleus of a power bloc, even before the death of Ratzel in 1904 and the resignation the next year of Ostwald, who had also made a practice of offending the faculty's corporate sensitivities. [52] Admiration for Lamprecht's efforts to promote cooperation among the dispersed units of the university tended to grow in proportion to the distance from the core of humanists whom these efforts seemed to threaten most directly. He found support among natural scientists in the philosophical faculty, such as the physicists Theodor Des Courdes and Otto Wiener, as well as among scholars in other faculties, such as the theologian Rudolf Kittel and the director of the university's obstetrics clinic, Paul Zweifel. [53] His ties to several of these scholars were strengthened by membership in a small faculty club called the "Peonie." [54]

Lamprecht's weakness within his own faculty appeared nonetheless to confine his influence within his own institute and to frustrate his wider hopes for the reform of the humanities. The surprise that the historian professed over the political spectacle that now unfolded in Leipzig was thus doubtless genuine. [55] So was the dismay within the philosophical faculty, over whose angry opposition Lamprecht took over leadership of the university in 1910.

In Leipzig, as in most other German universities, the office of rector, the highest elective position in the faculty, had become largely ceremonial. In an era when a small permanent staff of bureaucrats oversaw the day-to-day business of the institution, and when the most important administrative channels linked individual faculty members directly to the ministry, the office was a symbolic relic of the university's earlier autonomy.[56] The rector was elected by all the *Ordinarien* in the four subfaculties for a term of but one year.[57] He represented the university on public occasions; within the university his responsibilities comprised a number of areas that affected the faculty as a whole, such as student affairs and the regulation of relations among the subfaculties. Most of these responsibilities he fulfilled in his role as president of the academic senate, which comprised the university's sixty-seven chair holders.

The office rotated each year among the subfaculties—by tradition, among former deans of these bodies. This tradition alone seemed to exclude Lamprecht, who had held no faculty office higher than *Prokanzler*, a minor position that required his overseeing, like a "dry bureaucrat," the paperwork of doctoral promotions in 1899–1900.[58] The historian had no prospects for being elected dean of his own subfaculty, where his enemies outnumbered his champions. In his case, however, tradition never carried much weight. By 1910, when the rotation returned to the philosophical faculty, his feats of fund-raising and lobbying in Dresden on behalf of his own institute had made him the most visible member of the university community. Over the opposition of most of his own subfaculty, his friends elsewhere, primarily in the legal and medical faculties, launched a campaign that led in July to his election as rector for the academic year 1910–1911.[59]

Lamprecht's term promised to be no ordinary tenure in that office, for he did not intend to rest content with its ceremonial functions. "One must remember that the word 'rector' comes from '*regere*'," he pointed out, "and that means 'to rule.'"[60] In his inaugural address in October 1910, at the commencement of the winter semester, he made it clear that he regarded his election as a mandate to put into practice the reforms that he had earlier advocated. He lectured his assembled colleagues about the "most universal connections which recur within human spiritual life throughout history." To keep abreast of the changes in contemporary spiritual life, he continued, the humanistic disciplines would have to undergo "a transformation of their methods and the means and organization of their instruction" as a prelude to the general reorganization of the university.[61] To this end, Lamprecht called for the restructuring of the seminars, increased participation of the *Nichtordinarien* in their governance, and the establishment of institutes modeled after his own.[62] The new rector saw no need to remain coy or to spare the feelings of Seeliger and Brandenburg, who now sat at his feet. The reform of the university was to occur under the banner of cultural history. It was, he said, the "mission of scholarship to illuminate the gaze into the future," but history itself had revealed that "*Kulturgeschichte* is far more qualified for this mission than political history or any other branch of historical studies."

Academic life now became exciting in Leipzig. Lamprecht's onslaught on the university's traditions was in many respects reminiscent of his challenge to the methods, organization, and parochial traditions of the German historical profession. The university's "intellectual horizon" had, he concluded, "become downright narrow."[63] Innovation, the institution's route "to a higher horizon," again implied opening, broadening, and inclusion; traditional disciplines were to be integrated within a universal paradigm; established institutional structures and pedagogical methods were to be redesigned; and marginal groups were to be drawn into the life of the institution. It was another far-reaching and imaginative call for reform—in order, in the end, to serve a personal agenda. The parallels extended farther. In the university, too, tradition had powerful defenders; and they mobilized, virtually on the morrow of Lamprecht's inauguration, in order to frustrate his plans, although they proved to be less successful than the leaders of the historical profession had been.

The turmoil began almost immediately within one of the marginal realms of the university. The rector bore no responsibility for the incident that occasioned it, although he was linked to one of the parties to the dispute. The free student association had become a force in student politics in Leipzig, a champion of student grievances, and an aggressive rival of the corporations.[64] The association set up a casino and work-referral service for its members, as well as a lending library and a cooperative bookstore in which students could purchase texts (such as Lamprecht's *German History*) at a discount.[65] It also claimed to represent all unincorporated students, whether they were members of the association or not, in the university's formal celebrations and in agencies of student government. This claim was controversial. So was the cycle of lectures by leaders of several German political parties, which the association sponsored in the fall of 1910. Addresses by a Free Conservative and a Progressive proceeded without incident; when the social democrat Eduard Bernstein spoke in November, it produced an uproar, as local patriots sent petitions to Dresden and Berlin to denounce not only the students who held the meeting but the rector who defended their action.[66]

In the wake of the Saxon government's decision henceforth to prohibit socialist speakers at the university, and amid a flurry of petitions from students and instructors, the future of the free student association became an urgent item on the agenda of the university senate. These students had made themselves vulnerable. The association's claim to represent all unincorporated students had produced protests from students who did not wish to belong; but this issue screened deeper suspicions. "The motto of the free student association is the politicization of the student," warned Seeliger, who, like many of his fellow senators, looked upon Bernstein as a much graver symptom of this problem than the Free Conservative.[67] When, in May 1911, negotiations between the senate and the students reached an impasse over the question of representation, the senate voted to dissolve the association.

The vote was a minor defeat for Lamprecht, who was still the protector of this organization—a fact that no doubt figured in the minds of some of the senators. In the aftermath, however, the rector engineered one of his enduring achievements, a solution to the free students' principal grievance. There was no student constitution or formal organization of student government in Leipzig. A student council, which had been established in 1904 on the initiative of the free students, had collapsed in 1909 in an atmosphere of suspicion among students and faculty, and among incorporated and unincorporated students. These suspicions were still alive in the summer of 1911 when Lamprecht negotiated an elaborate settlement among all the parties. It established a general student council (*Allgemeiner Studentenausschuss*, or AStA) as the representative body of the entire student body and empowered it to administer special fees, which the university collected from all students; the council in turn was to comprise two committees, which were elected separately by the incorporated and unincorporated students and which governed the affairs specific to these two constituencies.[68]

Although the agreement embodied principles that free student associations had advocated around the country for years, the settlement in Leipzig set a precedent; other universities quickly imitated the "Leipzig movement."[69] Lamprecht was proud of the achievement, for he sympathized with the aims of the free students, and the agreement represented a significant part of a wider plan to make students a more active component of the university community. Several other projects served the same design. A program of matinee concerts performed for the university by students of the choral society and the *collegium musicum* would, Lamprecht anticipated, encourage students to take on burdens "for the great academic community to which they belong."[70] The university's office of academic advising, another institution that he founded on their behalf, extended a precedent established by Althoff in Berlin and emulated in the Institute for Cultural and Universal History.[71]

Lamprecht's attempt to address the grievances of another marginal sector of the university community encountered more entrenched resistance. References in his inaugural address to the plight of the *Nichtordinarien* had encouraged a public debate; they also encouraged the local branch of the Association of Honorary Professors, Extraordinary Professors, and *Privatdozenten* to renew demands for a fixed schedule of salaries, representation in organs of faculty governance, participation in the planning of the curriculum, and for the formal right to supervise doctoral work.[72] These demands now enjoyed the sympathy of the rector, who was close to some of the leaders of this association and regarded the disadvantaged status of these people as a *kleine soziale Frage*; Lamprecht could also expect tangible benefits from the presence of Kötzschke on the doctoral committees of his own students.[73] His goal was "organically to integrate" junior faculty into the university's "professional code of obligations," in the calculation that "broader and more explicitly defined obligations" would "in and of themselves entail corresponding rights."[74] The rector could do little more for these scholars, however, than call for reports on conditions in the four subfaculties. The deans, who spoke for the chair holders, were happy with the

status quo and resisted all concessions on the grounds that the demands of the
junior faculty were, as the dean of the theological faculty reported, "impermissi-
ble and impractical."[75]

Lamprecht's engagement on behalf of students and junior faculty reflected a
vision of the "small academic state" that he proposed to construct in Leipzig.[76]
This vision had prominent American features. Lamprecht's admiration for
American higher education was well known; and during his tenure as rector he
attempted to foster an American presence in Leipzig. He encouraged the
International Student Association, in which Americans were the principal
contingent.[77] He also attempted to exploit his connections to Columbia University in order to establish a regular exchange of scholars between the two
institutions.[78] He could not, however, break Berlin's monopoly on the American exchange programs with both Columbia and Harvard; and his efforts
yielded but one American visitor, a Germanist from Wisconsin, for a single
semester in 1912.[79]

Shortly after his inauguration, the rector staged an exhibit of pictures in the
great aula of the university on the "progress of American universities."[80] Those
who visited the exhibit were well prepared for his next project. Late in 1910 he
persuaded the univesity's business office to purchase a large plot of land to the
south of the city, in the outlying district of Probstheida. Here, far removed from
"the commotion of big-city life," he proposed to construct a "grand academic
settlement" on the model of an American campus, like the one that had
impressed him in Palo Alto.[81] The rector took this idea more seriously than most
of his faculty, who reacted, he noted, with a "special kind of smile" whenever he
raised the subject.[82] In consultation with American colleagues, however, he
began to plan the removal of the university to the new park, where the
instructional facilities, like the layout of faculty and student housing, would be
designed to promote a community of learning.[83] The costs of constructing this
community promised to be prohibitive, though; and no one took seriously the
rector's suggestion that selling the university's property in the middle of town
would finance the campus without the "slightest difficulty."[84] The idea proceeded no further.

Lamprecht was meanwhile occupied with a more significant project. The
cornerstone of his tenure in office would, he hoped, be the reorganization of the
university's seminars, again on the model of American academic departments
(and his own institute). These units were to be consolidated into institutes along
broader disciplinary boundaries. Their curricula were to be restructured in tiers,
so that chair holders presided over research at the highest levels, while more
basic levels of instruction were entrusted to junior faculty, whose compensation
was to come not only in participation in faculty governance but in positions that
carried regular salaries.[85]

The rector was already in negotiations with the ministry over funding this
plan when, on the eve of his inauguration, news from Berlin put the project in a
different light.[86] In October 1910, the Kaiser announced a campaign to mobilize

public and private resources in order to endow a group of research institutes, to be called the Kaiser Wilhelm Society for the Advancement of Science.[87] These institutes signaled the most ambitious effort yet to marry basic scientific research to the needs of an advancing industrial society.[88] Lamprecht could legitimately claim to be a pioneer in bringing together public and private monies in support of academic scholarship, but he judged the marriage in the capital from a different perspective than the organizers. "Naturally," he wrote to Berlin two days after the Kaiser's announcement, the new institutes should include, "at the top of the list," one for universal history; he also volunteered his own services as an advisor to the project, noting that he was "perhaps the only person in Germany who has practical and organizational experience" in the area of research institutes.[89] His offer went unheeded. However, as it became clear that the Berlin institutes would serve the natural sciences, Lamprecht recognized another opportunity.

To the ministry, his colleagues, and the public, Lamprecht now spoke of the "grave danger" that developments in the capital posed to the prestige of both Leipzig and its university.[90] It was imperative, he argued, to establish an analogous complex of research institutes in Leipzig—devoted not to the natural sciences, where the costs were immense and the Prussians' advantage was already established. The opportunity lay instead in the humanities, where a "clear advantage over Berlin seems attainable," particularly in view of the presence in Leipzig of two institutes, one for experimental psychology and another for cultural and universal history, which "anticipated the ideal of the research institute" that the Kaiser had proclaimed.[91]

The ministry was receptive to his arguments and promised in principle to support the plan. Lamprecht then began to mobilize private money. Once again he approached the city's civic and business leaders in the hope of capitalizing an endowment. To potential donors, who, he was confident, "would not let themselves be shamed by Prussia," he emphasized the economic advantages that his project offered the city.[92] He enticed some of the donors with the prospect of the honorific title *Kommerzienrat*, before university officials protested that the whole campaign was taking on the "character of a business deal."[93] Within four months, Lamprecht had nonetheless secured commitments for almost half a million marks.[94]

He attempted meanwhile to generate support among his faculty colleagues for a complex of research institutes whose core would be Wundt's and his own.[95] A key additional component was to be an institute for ethnology, attached to the city's anthropological museum; its role was to provide a bridge over the "whole field of human psychogenesis"—from its most primitive expressions (which were to fall to Wundt), through the ethnologists' preserves in the lower or "natural" cultures, to the higher cultural levels, where Lamprecht's own team of scholars was to concentrate.[96] In addition, an institute for comparative linguistics would focus on the "individual paths of human development from the most general and highest perspective."[97] An institute for comparative religious history would do the same; it would also secure the support of the theological faculty for the project. A psychogenetic museum, attached to Lamprecht's own institute, would then crown the whole edifice.

These negotiations proceeded informally among scholars from whom Lamprecht could expect sympathy. But when, in May 1911, he first laid his ideas before the senate formally in his role as rector, the response could hardly have surprised him.[98] The resistance came from the philosophical faculty. Lamprecht's concession of superiority in the natural sciences to Berlin antagonized some of his own allies. One senator, a zoologist, remarked that the condition of some of the humanities seminars in Leipzig was "wretched" and that Berlin had "a decidedly higher standing in the humanities than in the natural sciences." Seeliger, a hardened observer of Lamprecht's tactics—a man who also could have been excused a sense of déja vu—raised the issue of Lamprecht's scholarship and warned against granting him the power, single-handedly and for his own eccentric designs, to select and lavish funds on other units of the university. Seeliger, though, faced the same disadvantage that he had during earlier negotiations over the future of the historical seminar. Lamprecht had raised the money. Not only had the rector laid the basis of a large private endowment, but he had elicited promises of an annual sum of 75,000 marks from Dresden and an additional 20,000 from the city government to support the ethnological institute. Although the senators expressed concern lest "foreign elements invade the university"—in other words, lest the private donors demand a voice in the affairs of the institutes—few of them were prepared to turn down the money.[99]

Lamprecht emerged with a victory from his first confrontation with the faculty, but the lines of fracture had been defined. Although the senate authorized his continuing negotiations with the ministry on behalf of the five institutes that he himself had identified, opposition to his plans broadened and became more bitter within the philosophical faculty.[100] At the end of May, sixteen members of this faculty protested formally to the ministry. The realization of the rector's plans, they warned, would bring grave harm to the university; it would cast on the whole institution the stamp of a "distinct scholarly tendency," which (and here they did not exaggerate) "is not shared by many members of the faculty and has encountered broad opposition in the world of learning."[101] The money could be much better employed, they argued, to support the existing seminars.

Lamprecht's opponents once again betrayed their want of a compelling alternative vision, but they made up 40 percent of the philosophical faculty, and they included not only the historian's usual enemies, like Seeliger, Brandenburg, and Schmarsow, but most of the university's leading humanists. The ministry, which was itself becoming nervous about the prominence of psychogenesis in Lamprecht's plans, could not disregard the protest of these scholars and in June directed the philosophical faculty to devise a solution acceptable to all parties.[102] This directive undermined Lamprecht's position and compelled him to negotiate with his opponents, who now had the votes to set up a special committee to reconsider the whole plan.[103]

In retreat, Lamprecht thereupon persuaded his leading benefactors to reassign their donations to his personal control.[104] This ploy was a measure of the untenability of his position within his own faculty. His colleagues first learned of the maneuver in November 1911, when the special committee recommended replacing his whole concept with a single loose umbrella organization, made up of existing seminars and charged with "promoting scholarly research in the whole area of the humanities, without preference to any particular areas or methods."[105] At this point Lamprecht revealed that the private donations had been restricted to supporting "comparative cultural studies" and that he himself was empowered to define this concept.[106] He now stood alone amid the storm that accompanied the faculty's discovery that, as one member protested, they "could say absolutely nothing about the whole project." Lest the whole plan collapse, Lamprecht backed down in the face of what he himself described as the "sheer fury" of his colleagues.[107] He agreed to join a delegation to ask the donors to reassign their gifts once again—now to underwrite research institutes devoted to disciplines that the faculty itself had designated as "cultural studies."

Lamprecht was no longer rector of the university when this stormy scene took place. The expiration of his term at the end of October 1911 reduced the momentum behind the campaign for the research institutes.[108] It also limited his influence in the ensuing struggle, which finally led, in June 1914, to the establishment of a pale Saxon counterpart to the Kaiser Wilhelm Society. The bitter negotiations pitted Lamprecht against most of the faculty in competition for the favor of the donors and the ministry. Both sides lost. The faculty robbed the project of the idiosyncratic intellectual focus that Lamprecht had proposed, but the price was to dissipate the financial rewards he had promised.

The product of these negotiations, the King Friedrich August Foundation for Scientific Research in Leipzig, was a hybrid creation.[109] Its administrative structure rewarded Lamprecht's disdain for his colleagues. The foundation was not directly connected to the university, and the board that administered the endowment included but two members of the faculty amid representatives of the donors, the city, and the Saxon Academy of Sciences. The foundation's charge reflected a victory of sorts for the faculty, which had liberated most of the private donations from Lamprecht's control. In place of Lamprecht's five linked institutes, the foundation established twenty-two autonomous research centers, which were attached to existing units of the university and committed to humanistic research more conventionally defined.[110] Among all these centers, the foundation was to distribute about 100,000 marks annually from the private endowment and the public subsidies.[111]

Lamprecht objected to both the financial and intellectual fragmentation that accompanied the proliferation of research institutes in Leipzig. "Little is recognizable any longer of the original happy idea," he complained in 1912, as he regarded the "monstrous creation" that his colleagues were putting together.[112] Yet the historian salvaged a little. He retained enough influence in the ministry to help a few of his friends receive institutes of their own.[113] He also kept control of the single most generous private donation, and he earmarked its proceeds for the institutes in universal history, ethnology, and psychology, which had constituted the core of his original design.[114]

Despite the success of the faculty in diluting Lamprecht's concept, the King Friedrich August Foundation was known justly as the historian's creation.[115] It was another monument to his energy, imagination, and unconventionality; and the meager outcome of his labors demonstrated anew the institutional controls that discouraged heterodoxy and innovation in the German academy. The history of the Kaiser Wilhelm Society in Berlin suggests that these controls frustrated research in the natural sciences as well, although on a scale that the humanists could only envy. Three months before the establishment of the Saxon foundation, the annual budget of a single component of the Kaiser Wilhelm Society, the Institute for Chemistry, was set at more than all the Saxon institutes' combined.[116] A month after the establishment of the Saxon foundation, moreover, the outbreak of the war further restricted the support for humanistic research in Leipzig. In another sign of the faculty's distaste for the whole project, the academic senate voted in August 1914 to divert all the funds from the institutes to meet the "pressing obligations" of war.[117] The institutes formally opened nonetheless in November, but the circumstances of war limited their operations until inflation wiped out the endowment.[118]

In one of his last official acts as rector, Lamprecht journeyed north with his younger daughter in the summer of 1911 to represent his university at jubilees of the universities of Christiana in Norway and St. Andrew's in Scotland, where he also received two additional honorary doctorates. As they had during his American trip, the official celebrations provided the occasion for an extended travel adventure, which led the historian this time through Norwegian fjords, the Scottish highlands (where he found caber-tossing more to his taste than American football), and the Inner Hebrides.[119]

Although a bitter conflict with his faculty awaited him, Lamprecht returned home in October in a serene mood to render account of his term as rector.[120] "On the whole I look back with satisfaction on the year," he wrote early in 1912, "for I have fully accomplished the great bulk of my ideals."[121] To Pirenne he reported that he had been able to "introduce my principal ideals for university reform, so that they will now without exception be put into practice."[122] Although he exaggerated his success, he had achieved more in his year in office than any rector in memory.[123] And if his program was, as Wundt remarked, like a "kaleidoscopic picture," much of which anticipated the future, some of his accomplishments, such as the student constitution, had an immediate and lasting impact.[124]

Lamprecht paid a heavy price for his efforts. Most of his plans were unorthodox, and the centerpiece of his administration, the campaign on behalf of the research institutes, antagonized the faculty and left many of them, like Seeliger, grateful that a rector's term of office was too short "to cause further havoc."[125] But the conflict over the institutes persisted beyond Lamprecht's rectorate; and within a year Seeliger, who had lost all sense of gratitude, was formally protesting "in the name of the university and in the name of all of the colleagues affected that the Institute for Cultural and Universal History is being paraded before us as a model."[126] Seeliger remained an extreme case, but enmity for the former rector was rife in Leipzig. In his later years, Bücher recalled, Lamprecht "had the effect of a red flag on a majority" of the faculty.[127]

Perhaps because he recognized the futility of his position or had become preoccupied with other things, Lamprecht fought out the campaign over the research institutes with less energy and conviction than he had displayed in his earlier battles. "I stand isolated," he wrote in 1914: "here and there I still have a remnant of friendship, if not support, and I look down upon this world like an Arab on the tracks of a camel in the desert."[128] Detachment was not due to fatigue alone, however. Repeated clashes with his colleagues had convinced him that the university was as resistant to his ideas as was the historical profession. So he sought a wider forum.

Many of his ideas about academic reform bore on a category of problems that some experts had by the turn of the century begun to address as a distinct field of inquiry. They called it *Hochschulpädagogik* or the pedagogy of higher education. The field was oriented to the systematic study—at the universities—of instructional methods appropriate for the universities, where the assumption had traditionally reigned that research bred its own proper techniques of communication and where questions of pedagogy had occupied no place in the curriculum.[129]

Lamprecht's interest in questions of pedagogy was deep and long-standing. It took shape during his apprenticeship as a *Gymnasiallehrer* under the tutelage of Oskar Jaeger in Cologne. Pedagogical issues, in the secondary schools as well as the universities, lurked in the background of the controversies among the academic historians in the 1890s; and Lamprecht's great popularity among secondary teachers was reward for his sensitivity to their concerns about modernizing the curriculum and instruction in history, as well as for his attempt to integrate these teachers into the profession by means of the Association of German Historians. In Leipzig his efforts to link the academy to the teaching community extended—via his activity in the *Lehrerverein* and *Volkshochschule*—to elementary teachers, a large number of whom also enrolled in his courses as participants in a special program that the university made available to qualified graduates of the local *Lehrerseminare*.[130] Lamprecht was, as a consequence, not only open to innovation in his own teaching; he was conversant with the major issues and theories of pedagogical reform. The curricular changes that he instituted at every opportunity at the university, the introduction of systematic steps toward more advanced levels of instruction, had Herbartian underpinnings.[131]

The appreciation that the historian enjoyed among teachers contrasted with the disdain of his academic colleagues, and it led him during his rectorate to ponder the reform of the secondary schools. Here opposition promised to be less entrenched to recasting the humanities on foundations which alone, he believed, could provide pedagogical coherence. He thus called for "a more psycho-logically mediated approach" in secondary education, which he again under-stood to mean cultural history.[132] Aside from courses in geography, ethnology, and religious history (which would supplant traditional instruction in religion), the central feature of his reformed curriculum was to be integrated instruction in languages and cultural history—an idea that found no support at the university, where one philologist, a self-described opponent of "all blurring of disciplinary boundaries," once characterized it as serving "herring with whipped cream."[133]

Despite the currency of such views among his academic colleagues, Lam-precht was too much a product of German academic culture to believe that reform of the secondary schools could dispense with the initiative of the universities. As pedagogical questions moved to the center of his agenda in the aftermath of his rectorate, his attention thus turned to new strategies for the reform of higher education. He first became interested in a new national organization that offered the prospect of translating to other German universities the reforms that he had initiated in Leipzig.

The transformation of German higher education at the end of the nineteenth century made institutional coordination both more urgent and complicated. New problems—from the admission of women and the rights of Nichtordinarien to degree requirements and the competing demands of the technical universities—were national (if not international) in scope; and they strained the competence of the ministries of culture, which governed higher education in each federal state, no less than they challenged the residual autonomy of individual institutions of higher learning. However, because greater coordina-tion of academic policy threatened established prerogatives and jurisdictions, opposition was entrenched in the more traditional university faculties, which resisted further control from the ministry, and in ministries in the smaller states, which resisted further control from Berlin.

These problems made consultations among leaders of German higher educa-tion difficult. It was symptomatic of the difficulties that the first such consulta-tions were among officials from the ministries, which Althoff dominated as long as he ruled in Prussia. Regular "unofficial" conferences among rectors at Prussian universities began in 1903, but only in 1913 did national meetings take place; and rectors from the technical universities continued to meet separately until 1916.[134] In these circumstances, attempts to organize new forms of consultation among German educators had an unconventional, if not oppositional, flavor. The most significant of these attempts were the congresses of university faculty members, the Hochschullehrertage, which began to meet in 1907 and tended to attract scholars from nontraditional disciplines and non-Prussian universities; out of their ranks the Association of German University Teachers (Verein

Deutscher Hochschullehrer) emerged as an umbrella organization.[135] Pedagogical issues provided another, even more unconventional avenue toward interfaculty consultation. In 1910, the Society for the Pedagogy of Higher Education (*Gesellschaft für Hochschulpädagogik*) was founded in order to bring scholars from universities, technical universities, and business schools together with students and laypeople who were interested in problems of curriculum and instruction.[136]

Despite the prominence of Bücher and several of his other Leipzig friends in these efforts, Lamprecht paid them only passing attention until his interests turned toward reforming the university.[137] The immediate stimulus for his involvement was unexpected and happy. Ernst Bernheim's interest in pedagogical questions was long-standing; in fact, it was one of the impediments to his advancement in a profession where textbooks in historical methodology, however effective and successful, did not carry the weight of more traditional scholarship. Bernheim served as rector of the university of Greifswald and was a leading figure in the efforts to establish a national organization of university faculty members. In 1910, he responded to one of Lamprecht's manifestos on academic reform by breaking the silence that had reigned between the two scholars for more than a decade.[138]

Thus by the end of his rectorate, Lamprecht was well aware of the various projects to build links among academic reformers. In his final month in office, he presented his ideas about humanistic research institutes to the *Hochschullehrertag*, which met in Dresden to consider the ramifications of the founding of the Kaiser Wilhelm Society.[139] But given the unconventionality of his views, his preferences for another forum were not difficult to anticipate. In the fall of 1911 he became, at Bernheim's suggestion, the national chairman of the new *Gesellschaft für Hochschulpädagogik*, in which he saw a more promising vehicle for the broader realization of the very designs that the faculty was mobilizing to block in Leipzig.

In November 1911, in the midst of his confrontation with his colleagues in Leipzig over the research institutes, Lamprecht outlined his ideas about the society of which he had just become chairman. To Bernheim he announced, in an allusion to his own institute, that the precondition for improving instructional methods at the universities was the "development of university institutes and seminars to higher forms of education." In order to achieve this end, he called for a new fund-raising campaign among rich benefactors (he was now thinking of Andrew Carnegie, whom he had met in Scotland, and Friedrich Krupp); he also proposed merging the society with the rectoral conferences and the other interfaculty organizations and expanding the undertaking to include all of German-speaking Europe. The object, he explained, was to turn the Society for the Pedagogy of Higher Education into an "authority of such imposing weight" that state agencies would accede to its demands.[140]

Bernheim's skeptical reaction to these proposals foretold another round of frustration for Lamprecht.[141] The other major faculty organization, the Association of University Teachers, resisted the historian's call for a merger.[142] Problems also developed within the Society for the Pedagogy of Higher Education itself. The reputation of this organization was shaky from the start. It was known, in the words of an official in the Saxon ministry of culture, "as a thoroughly unnecessary creation," "founded by younger instructors who are dissatisfied and vain" and supported by "elements who want to play a role."[143] Nonetheless, the organization had attracted a number of prominent scholars who were known for their progressive views in politics as well as pedagogy, including Wilhelm Foerster and Franz von Liszt from Berlin, Fritz Stier-Somlo from Bonn, Rudolf Eucken from Jena, and Paul Natorp and Martin Rade from Marburg. These scholars, however, resisted Lamprecht's designs for the organization. The agent of their resistance was another in a long succession of sticklers for convention, protocol, and detail whom the historian seemed to encounter at every station of his life. Hans Schmidkunz, who held a doctorate in philosophy, was the driving force in the organization—its founder, theoretician, executive secretary (*Geschäftsführer*) in Berlin, and the editor of its journal, the *Zeitschrift für Hochschulpädagogik*.[144] Lamprecht's broad plans for academic reform challenged Schmidkunz's power in the organization as well as his sense of its mission, which was confined to promoting the establishment of pedagogical seminars at the universities. Schmidkunz regarded the board of directors, over which Lamprecht presided, as a decorative body; and he conveyed his views to the historian in a tone that made cooperation between the two men impossible.[145]

In other respects, too, Lamprecht's involvement with this organization was reminiscent of earlier episodes in his life. His interest in the society proved ephemeral once he discovered that opposition to his plans was again seated in the university of Berlin, where, as he complained to Harden, a nimbus of *beati possidens* bred resistance to all manner of reform.[146] When he learned that Schmidkunz enjoyed the support of Liszt and the other academics in Berlin (as well as Bernheim), Lamprecht's enthusiasm for the cause evaporated.[147] The only event of significance that occurred during his term of office was a national congress of the organization, which he hosted in October 1912 in Leipzig, in spite of the antipathy of both the ministry and most of his own faculty. The meeting was notable for the absence of all the academics from Berlin and the absence of research institutes from the agenda, which focused instead on new instructional materials and techniques in physics, mathematics, minerology, and philology.[148] When the congress also ratified Schmidkunz's definition of the organization's goals, Lamprecht resigned from the chairmanship. From the historian's perspective, the highlight of the meeting was a personal reunion with Bernheim, with whom his relationship remained cordial thereafter, despite Bernheim's support for Schmidkunz.[149]

Lamprecht remained on the society's board of directors, but this organization ceased to figure much in his calculations. His restless campaign for academic reform turned elsewhere instead.[150] Because allies in the academy were difficult to find, he again became an independent advocate and plunged into several well-publicized academic controversies.[151] He spoke out in favor of creating university chairs in sociology.[152] But he also took Wundt's side in a brief polemical exchange with the sociologist Georg Simmel, whose proposal to bar experimental psychologists from chairs in philosophy represented a fundamental challenge to his own views about the reform of the humanities curriculum.[153] Public debates surrounding the establishment of municipal universities in Hamburg and Frankfurt afforded additional opportunities to promote his ideas.[154] So did the intriguing discussions about converting the *Technische Hochschule* in Dresden into a university to rival the one in Leipzig.[155] On these occasions, however, the historian spoke for no organization or constituency, least of all his own university or profession. It might thus have been possible to dismiss Karl Lamprecht as a lonely and eccentric voice, had not his advocacy of academic reform become part of a much broader campaign, which by the outbreak of the war had vaulted him into a prominent place in German politics.

Notes

1. NL Lamprecht (L 35), Polizeilicher Ausweis, Leipzig, 12.3.15; Ostwald, *Lebenslinien*, 1: 103.
2. Koht, 152–53.
3. Rein, Politik und Universität, 13.
4. Kötzschke, "Lamprecht," 27.
5. Tille, "Nachwort," 29.
6. Dallek, 18.
7. Hendrik de Man, *Gegen den Strom: Memoiren eines europäischen Sozialisten* (Stuttgart, 1953), 78.
8. Kötzschke, "Lamprecht," 27.
9. NL Treitschke, Lamprecht to Treitschke, Leipzig, 9.12.94; Schönebaum, "Hochschulpädagogische Bestrebungen," 6.
10. NL Lamprecht (Korr. 59), Lamprecht to Hugo Lamprecht, Leipzig, 1.5.96, 1.11.05; NL Mevissen, Lamprecht to Mevissen, Leipzig, 27.11.06.
11. UA Leipzig, Rep. I/XVI/IIA, Nr. 19, Sitzung des akademischen Senats, 11.12.07 (Punkt V: Dr. Lamprechts Antrag auf Beschaffung eines grösseren Hörsaales); StA Dresden, VB 10228/2, Lamprecht to KM, Leipzig, 22.11.06; NL Lamprecht (Korr. 35), Levinstein to Lamprecht, Leipzig, 3.3.05; Czok, "Lamprechts Wirken," 19. *Cf.* Elsa Asenijeff, *Tagebuchblätter einer Emancipierten* (Leipzig, 1902).
12. Koht, 154–55.
13. Gustav Radbruch, *Der innere Weg: Aufriss meines Lebens* (Stuttgart, 1951), 47.
14. Dallek, 18.
15. Tille, "Nachwort," 30–31.
16. Man, *Gegen den Strom*, 78.
17. NL Lamprecht (Munich), Demonstrationsmaterial zum Vortrag von Professor Lamprecht über Ausgestaltung der universalgeschichtlichen Studien im Hochschulunterricht (1907).
18. LW, 566–67.
19. UB Leipzig, NL Otto Wiener, Lamprecht to Wiener, Leipzig, 6.1.03; NL Lamprecht (Korr. 49), Studniczka to Lamprecht, Leipzig, 4.5.08.

20. NL Lamprecht (Korr. 30), Pierer'sche Hofbuchdruckerei to Lamprecht, Altenburg, 31.1.03; LW, 515–16.
21. NL Hellpach (72), Lamprecht to Hellpach, Schierke, 29.12.11.
22. NL Lamprecht (M6), Karl Lamprecht zum Gedächtnis. Trauer-Salamander, 20.5.15; LW, 475–76.
23. See W. Stieda, "Die Königlich Sächsische Universität Leipzig," in W. Lexis, ed., *Die Universitäten im Deutschen Reich* (Berlin, 1904), 503–34; McClelland, *State, Society, and University*, 233–321; Konrad H. Jarausch, ed., *The Transformation of Higher Learning, 1860–1930: Expansion, Diversification, Social Opening, and Professionalization in England, Germany, Russia, and the United States* (Chicago, 1983).
24. For a comprehensive case study of this transformation in institutions of higher learning in Baden, see Reinhard Riese, *Die Hochshule auf dem Wege zum wissenschaftlichen Grossbetrieb: Die Universität Heidelberg und das badische Hochschulwesen 1860–1914* (Stuttgart, 1977); *cf.* Karl-Heinz Manegold, *Universität, Technische Hochschule und Industrie: Ein Beitrag zur Emanzipation der Technik im 19. Jahrhundert unter besonderer Berücksichtigung der Bestrebungen Felix Kleins* (Berlin, 1970).
25. Franz Eulenburg, *Die Entwicklung der Universität Leipzig in den letzten hundert Jahren: Statistische Untersuchungen* (Leipzig, 1909), 194.
26. Ibid., 204–5.
27. Czok, "Höhepunkt," 223; Konrad H. Jarausch, *Students, Society, and Politics in Imperial Germany: The Rise of Academic Illiberalism* (Princeton, 1982), 278–80.
28. Eulenburg, *Entwicklung*, 194.
29. Ibid., 112–13.
30. Lothar Burchardt, "Deutsche Wissenschaftspolitik an der Jahrhundertwende: Versuch einer Zwischenbilanz," GWU, 26 (1975): 273.
31. Czok, "Höhepunkt," 224.
32. Eulenburg, *Nachwuchs*, 34–35; Paulsen, *Universitäten*, 127–37; *cf.* Rüdiger vom Bruch, "Universitätsreform als soziale Bewegung: Zur Nicht-Ordinarienfrage im späten deutschen Kaiserreich," GG, 10 (1984): esp. 74–77; vom Bruch, *Wissenschaft, Politik und öffentliche Meinung: Gelehrtenpolitik im Wilhelminischen Deutschland (1890–1914)* (Husum, 1980), 122–28.
33. Adolf Harnack, "Vom Grossbetrieb der Wissenschaft," in Harnack, *Aus Wissenschaft und Leben*, 2 vols. (Giessen, 1911), 1: 10–20.
34. Eulenburg, *Entwicklung*, 112–13.
35. Alexander Kluge, *Die Universitäts-Selbstverwaltung* (Frankfurt am Main, 1958), 93–96.
36. Frank R. Pfetsch, *Zur Entwicklung der Wissenschaftspolitik in Deutschland 1750–1914* (Berlin, 1974), 57–58.
37. Eulenburg, *Entwicklung*, 187, 213–16.
38. NL Wolff (14), Lamprecht to Wolff, Leipzig, 15.2.02; LW, 302–3.
39. Lamprecht, *Americana*, 91.
40. StA Dresden, VB 10281/203, Lamprecht to KM, Leipzig, 6.12.09; Lamprecht, "Zur Fortbildung unserer Universitäten," IWWKT, 3 (1909): 1539–54; LW, 576–77, 580–83; *cf.* Ludwig Langerbeck, "Die Universitätsreformpläne Karl Lamprechts," in Engelberg, *Karl-Marx-Universität*, 2: 39–48.
41. Lamprecht, "Zur Fortbildung," 1540–42.
42. Lamprecht, *Rektoratserinnerungen*, 11.
43. "Rede des antretenden Rektors Dr. Karl Lamprecht," *Rektorenwechsel an der Universität Leipzig am 31. Oktober 1910* (Leipzig, n.d.), 16–17.
44. NL Lamprecht (UL 6), Lamprecht, Leitmotive für eine Diskussion über die Weiterbildung der geisteswissenschaftlichen Forschungsinstitute, wie sie sich aus collegialen Gesprächen ergeben haben (Weihnachten, 1909).

45. Ibid.; LW, 582; Langerbeck, 46.
46. Lamprecht, "Zur Fortbildung," 1552–54.
47. Lamprecht, *Rektoratserinnerungen*, 68.
48. Metz, *Grundformen*, 470.
49. LW, 583.
50. NL Lamprecht (Korr. 15), Buchholz to Lamprecht, Walchensee, 4.4.04; Breysig, *Tagen und Träumen*, 84; LW, 233–34.
51. NL Lamprecht (Korr. 59), Lamprecht to Hugo Lamprecht, Leipzig, 27.7.97; NL Harden, Lamprecht to Harden, Leipzig, 5.1.98.
52. LW, 500.
53. NL Wiener, Lamprecht to Wiener, Leipzig, 11.3.05; NL Lamprecht (Munich), Schoenebaum to Rose-Schütz, Leipzig, 29.1.1962; Smith, *Sciences of Culture*, 275.
54. NL Lamprecht (Korr. 54), Windisch to Lamprecht, Leipzig, 18.10.14.
55. Lamprecht, *Rektoratserinnerungen*, 5; Schönebaum, "Unausgeführte Vorhaben," 120.
56. Paulsen, *Universitäten*, 94–95; Kluge, *Selbstverwaltung*, 149–68.
57. Rudolf Kötzschke, "Universität Leipzig," in Michael Doeberl, et al., eds., *Das akademische Deutschland*, 5 vols. (Berlin, 1930–1931), 1: 298–99.
58. NL Grimm, Lamprecht to Grimm, Leipzig, 25.7.99.
59. LW, 599–600.
60. Lamprecht, *Rektoratserinnerungen*, 10.
61. "Rede des antretenden Rektors Dr. Karl Lamprecht," *Rektorenewechsel an der Universität Leipzig am 31. Oktober 1910* (Leipzig, n.d.), 31. The speech is also in Lamprecht, *Zwei Reden zur Hochschulreform* (Berlin, 1910).
62. Lamprecht, "Rede des antretenden Rektors," 32.
63. Lamprecht, *Rektoratserinnerungen*, 11.
64. UA Leipzig, Rep. II/XVI/III F Nr. 1, Präsidium der Leipziger Finkenschaft to Rektorat, Leipzig, 31.10.96; *cf.* Werner Mahrholz, "Geschichtliche Stellung der Freistudententschaft," in Doeberl, *Das akademische Deutschland*, 2: 593–99; Paul Ssymank, "Geschichtlicher Verlauf der freistudentischen Bewegung," ibid., 599–600.
65. Lamprecht, *Rektoratserinnerungen*, 40.
66. Ibid., 41–42; LW, 607–8; Langerbeck, 42–43.
67. UA Leipzig, Rep. I/XVI/IIA Nr. 19, Sitzung des akademischen Senats, 15.2.11.
68. UA Leipzig, Rep. I/XVI/IIA Nr. 19, Sitzung des akademischen Senats, 25.10.11; Lamprecht, *Rektoratserinnerungen*, 42–46; Langerbeck, 43–44.
69. NL Lamprecht (Korr. 52), Lamprecht to F. Weber, Leipzig, 4.3.12; (Korr. 55), Kurt Wulff to Lamprecht, Berlin, 25.7.14; Lamprecht, *Rektoratserinnerungen*, 47, n. 1; *cf.* Jarausch, *Students*, 380–81.
70. NL Lamprecht (Korr. 46), Lamprecht to Schering, Leipzig, 9.2.12.
71. NL Lamprecht (Korr. 41), Pazkowski to IKUg, Berlin, 3.5.12; Weissbach, 1: 31; *cf.* vom Brocke, "System Althoff," 68.
72. StA Dresden, VB 10281/25, Vereinigung der Honorarprofessoren, aussordentlichen Professoren und Privatdozenten an der Universität Leipzig to KM, Leipzig, 23.1.08; NL Lamprecht (Korr. 62), Hofmann, DS über die Rechte der ausserordentlichen Professoren und über die nächsten Ziele und Aufgaben der medizinischen Fakultät, Leipzig, 1.11.11; *cf.* vom Bruch, "Universitätsreform als soziale Bewegung," 83–84.
73. Lamprecht, *Rektoratserinnerungen*, 70–71.
74. NL Lamprecht (Korr. 62), Lamprecht, Zur Fortbildung des mittleren und höheren Schulwesens [n.d.].
75. NL Lamprecht (Korr. 62), Hauck to Akademischer Senat, Leipzig, 21.6.11;

Strohal to Lamprecht, Leipzig, 23.6.11; Kittel to Akademischer Senat, Leipzig, 12.12.11.
76. Lamprecht, *Rektoratserinnerungen*, 7.
77. NL Lamprecht (Korr. 33), Lamprecht to Keppl, Leipzig, 9.1.12; UA Leipzig, Rep. II/XVI/III F Nr. 1, Bergmann, "Der Internationale Studenten-Verein an der Universität Leipzig"; Anje Fellenberg, "Zur Stellung ausländischer Studenten an der Universität Leipzig in den Jahren 1900 bis 1914" (Diplomarbeit, Karl-Marx-Universität Leipzig, 1979), 13–14.
78. NL Lamprecht (Munich), Nicholas Murray Butler to Lamprecht, Dresden, 20.9.10; Butler Papers, Lamprecht to Butler, 16.2.11.
79. Butler Papers, Butler to Lamprecht, 11.1.11; LW, 604; *cf.* Harnack, "Vom Grossbetrieb," 10–20. On the exchanges see Bernhard vom Brocke, "Der deutsch-amerikanische Professorenaustausch: Preussische Wissenschaftspolitik, internationale Wissenschaftsbeziehungen und die Anfänge einer deutschen auswärtigen Kulturpolitik vor dem Ersten Weltkrieg," *Zeitschrift für Kulturaustausch*, 31 (1981): 128–82.
80. NL Lamprecht (Korr. 52), Lamprecht to Waentig, n.p., n.d. (fall 1910); (Korr. 50), Tombo to Lamprecht, New York, 24.11.11; Lamprecht, *Rektoratserinnerungen*, 13–14.
81. UA Leipzig, RA Nr. 1582/I, Ankauf weiterer Areals in Leipzig-Probstheida und Zuckelhausen für Zwecke der Universität. Lamprecht first devised the plan as a student in Leipzig, when his professors asked how he would solve problems of overcrowding, which the university was then beginning to experience. His idea thus antedated Althoff's proposal to remove the university in Berlin to Dahlem. Lamprecht, *Rektoratserinnerungen*, 47–55; Schönebaum, "Hochschulpädagogische Bestrebungen," 10; Langerbeck, 44; *cf.* vom Brocke, "System Althoff," 58.
82. Lamprecht, *Rektoratserinnerungen*, 55.
83. NL Lamprecht (B), Vorentwurf zu dem Bebauungsplan für die Verlegung der Leipziger Universität nach Probstheida; (Korr. 50), Tombo to Lamprecht, New York, 6.4.11; (UL 2), Lamprecht to Matheusius, Leipzig, 23.4.13.
84. Lamprecht, *Rektoratserinnerungen*, 54.
85. Butler Papers, Lamprecht to Butler, Leipzig, 7.6.12; NL Lamprecht (Korr. 52), Lamprecht to Ward, Leipzig, 14.6.12; Kötzschke, "Lamprecht," 23.
86. StA Dresden, VB 10281/203, Lamprecht to KM, Leipzig, 15.10.10.
87. See Bernhard vom Brocke, "Die Kaiser-Wilhelm Gesellschaft im Kaiserreich: Vorgeschichte, Gründung und Entwicklung bis zum Ausbruch des Ersten Weltkrieges," in Rudolf Vierhaus and Bernhard vom Brocke, eds., *Forschung im Spannungsfeld von Politik und Gesellschaft: Geschichte und Struktur der Kaiser-Wilhelm-/Max-Planck-Gesellschaft* (Stuttgart, 1990), 17–162; Lothar Burchardt, *Wissenschaftspolitik im Wihleminischen Deutschland: Vorgeschichte, Gründung und Aufbau der Kaiser-Wilhelm-Gesellschaft zur Förderung der Wissenschaften* (Göttingen, 1975); Günter Wendel, *Die Kaiser-Wilhelm-Gesellschaft 1911–1914: Zur Anatomie einer imperialistischen Forschungsgesellschaft* (Berlin, 1975).
88. See Lothar Burchardt, "Halbstaatliche Wissenschaftsförderung im Kaiserreich und in der frühen Weimarer Republik," in Gunter Mann and Rolf Winau, eds., *Medizin, Naturwissenschaft, Technik und das Zweite Kaiserreich* (Göttingen, 1977), 35–51; Frank Pfetsch, "Scientific Organisation and Science Policy in Imperial Germany, 1871–1914: The Foundation of the Imperial Institute of Physics and Technology," *Minerva*, 8 (1970): 557–80; Jeffrey Allan Johnson, *The Kaiser's Chemists: Science and Modernization in Imperial Germany* (Chapel Hill and London, 1990).
89. NL Lamprecht (Korr. 10), Lamprecht to Bethmann Hollweg, Leipzig, 13.10.10.

90. "Eine Versicherungsprämie," *Leipziger Neueste Nachrichten*, 30.10.10.
91. UA Leipzig, Rep. I/I Nr. 104, Bd. 1, Lamprecht Notiz, Leipzig, 15.11.10; Lamprecht RS, Leipzig, 10.1.11.
92. Ibid.
93. NL Lamprecht (UL 10), Riemar to Lamprecht, Leipzig, 8.3.11; Burgdorff to Lamprecht, Leipzig, 19.3.11.
94. UA Leipzig, Rep. I/I Nr. 104, Bd. 1, Zusammenstellung der bei der Universitäts-Rentenamts-Kasse zur Begründung von Forschungs-Instituten eingelieferten Spenden nach dem Stande am 11.10.11.
95. NL Lamprecht (UL 10), Lamprecht to Beck, Leipzig, 18.11.10; (UL 2), Protokoll über die am 7.12.10 erfolgte Sitzung der akademischen Verwaltungsdeputation.
96. NL Lamprecht (UL 2), Weule to Rat der Stadt Leipzig, Leipzig, 8.12.10.
97. Ibid.
98. UA Leipzig, Rep. I/XVI/IIA Nr. 19, Sitzung des akademischen Senats, 3.5.11.
99. NL Lamprecht (UL 10), Lipsius et al. to KM, Leipzig, 5.5.11, Abschrift.
100. NL Lamprecht (UL 10), DS betreffend die Entwicklung von Forschungsinstituten an der Universität Leipzig (May 1911).
101. NL Lamprecht (UL 10), Lipsius et al. to KM, Leipzig [29.5.11], Abschrift.
102. NL Lamprecht (UL 10), Beck to Akademischer Senat, Dresden, 29.6.11; Wundt to Lamprecht, Leipzig, 1.7.11.
103. UA Leipzig, Rep. I/I Nr. 104, Bd. 1, Sitzung von Sr. Magnifizens dem derzeitigen Rektor eingeladenen Ordinarien und Professoren zur Besprechung über Forschungsinstitute und Hebung der Lehrgänge und Lehrmittel der geisteswissenschaftlichen Institute, 12.7.11.
104. NL Lamprecht (UL 10), Scholle DS, Leipzig, 10.7.11.
105. UA Leipzig, Rep. I/I Nr. 104, Bd. 1, Leskien et al. to Akademischer Senat, Leipzig, 6.11.11.
106. UA Leipzig, Rep. I/I Nr. 104, Bd. 1, Sitzung der Senatskommission in Sachen der Förderung wissenschaftlicher Forschungen und Unterhaltung von Forschungsinstituten, 25.11.11.
107. NL Lamprecht (Korr. 9), Lamprecht to Bernheim, Leipzig, 14.11.11.
108. LW, 630–31, 657–58.
109. UA Leipzig, Rep. I/I Nr. 104, Bd. 2, Urkunde über die König-Friedrich-August-Stiftung für wissenschaftliche Forschung zu Leipzig, Leipzig, 31.1.14; Hans Haas, "König-Friedrich-August Stiftung für wissenschaftliche Forschung zu Leipzig (Sächsische Staatliche Forschungsinstitute)," in Ludolf Brauer et al., eds., *Forschungsinstitute: Ihre Geschichte, Organisation und Ziele*, 2 vols. (Hamburg, 1930), 1: 374–86.
110. NL Lamprecht (UL 10), Forschungsinstitute 1914; Haas, 376.
111. Ibid., 379.
112. NL Lamprecht (Korr. 46), Lamprecht to Schmaltz, Leipzig, 7.12.12; (Korr. 6), Lamprecht to Beck, Leipzig, 5.5.14.
113. NL Lamprecht (Korr. 44), Lamprecht to Hinrichsen, Leipzig, 14.5.14; (Korr. 46), Lamprecht to Schering, Leipzig, 17.3.14.
114. NL Lamprecht (Korr. 10), Lamprecht to Hans Meyer, Leipzig, 28.7.13; UA Leipzig, Rep. I/I Nr. 104, Bd. 2, Zusammenstellung der zur Errichtung von Forschungsinstituten bei der Universität Leipzig eingegangenen Spenden, Leipzig, 29.6.14; Verzeichnis der zur Verfügung stehenden Gelder.
115. Haas, 376.
116. Johnson, *Kaiser's Chemists*, 159–74.
117. UA Leipzig, Rep. I/I Nr. 104, Bd. 2, Otto Meyer to Direktoren der Forschungsinstitute, Leipzig, 2.9.14.

118. UA Leipzig, Rep. I/I Nr. 104, Bd. 2, KM to Akademischer Senat, Dresden, 21.10.14; Haas, 384; vom Brocke, "Kaiser-Wilhelms Gesellschaft," 58–59.
119. NL Lamprecht (Korr. 45), Lamprecht to Ritter, Schottland, 24.9.11; Lamprecht, Rektoratserinnerungen, 16–34; LW, 623–24.
120. "Rede des abtretenden Rektors Dr. Karl Lamprecht: Bericht über das Studienjahr 1910/11," Rektorenwechsel an der Universität Leipzig am 31. Oktober 1911 (Leipzig, n.d.), 1–22.
121. NL Lamprecht (Korr. 22), Lamprecht to Franck, Leipzig, 3.2.12.
122. NL Lamprecht (Korr. 42), Lamprecht to Pirenne, Leipzig, 14.1.12.
123. NL Lamprecht (Korr. 48), Lamprecht, Meine Tätigkeit nach Vollendung der Deutschen Geschichte und die Absichten meines Alters, August 1914.
124. Wundt, Gedenkblatt, 7.
125. Seeliger, "Lamprecht," 135.
126. NL Lamprecht (UL 4), Lamprecht to Dekan der PF, Leipzig, 17.12.12.
127. Braubach, "Aus Briefen Karl Büchers," 401–2; UA Leipzig, Rep. I/I Nr. 104, Bd. 1, Lamprecht to Heinrici, Leipzig, 10.11.11.
128. NL Lamprecht (Korr. 13), Lamprecht to Brüggemann, Leipzig, [1914].
129. Paulsen, Universitäten, 279–86.
130. Lamprecht, Rektoratserinnerungen, 37; Johannes Kretzschmar, "Zum Gedächtnis Karl Lamprechts," Leipziger Lehrerzeitung, 22 (1915): 354–57; "Volksthümliche Hochschulkurse," Zukunft, 20 (1897): 13–15.
131. Kretzschmar, 357; cf. EB, 2,2: 419.
132. NL Lamprecht (Korr. 62), Lamprecht, Vorschläge für eine erweiterte Fortbildung der Mittelschulen [1910–1911?]; Zur Fortbildung des mittleren und höheren Schulwesens [1910–1911?].
133. NL Lamprecht (Korr. 34), Köster to Lamprecht, Leipzig, 12.2.12.
134. Wilhelm Schlink, "Rektorenkonferenz und Verband der Deutschen Hochschulen," in Doeberl et al., Das akademische Deutschland, 3: 589–90.
135. Hans Gerber, Das Recht der wissenschaftlichen Hochschulen in der jüngsten Rechtsentwicklung, 2 vols. (Tübingen, 1965), 1: 12–3; 2: 9–10; Riese, Hochschule, 328–34; vom Bruch, Wissenschaft, 114–21.
136. See Erich Leitner, "Die hochschulpädagogische Bewegung in ihrem Verhältnis zur Hochschulreform," in Erich Leitner et al., eds., Die pädagogische Herausforderung der Universität 1898–1934: Studien zur Gesellschaft für Hochschulpädagogik (Weinheim, 1990), 31–45; Dietrich von Queis, "36 Jahre Hochschuldidaktik: Die erste hochschulpädagogische Bewegung 1898–1934," ibid., 47–75; Friedemann Schmithals, "Die Gesellschaft für Hochschulpädagogik als Modellfall für die Institutionalisierungsprobleme der Hochschul-Pädagogik," ibid., 78–96.
137. EB, 2,2: 456.
138. NL Lamprecht (Korr. 9), Bernheim to Lamprecht, Greifswald, 31.3.10. See Gerhard Roger, "Ernst Bernheims organisatorische und theoretische Leistung in der Hochschulpädagogischen Bewegung," Karlheinz Jackstel, ed., Studien zur Geschichte der Hochschulpädagogik (II) (Halle, 1989), 5–15. Bernheim's review of Lamprecht's Moderne Geschichtswissenschaft insisted again on the author's debt to Comte, but praised the work as a "service in the broadening and deepening of our historiography." Kritische Blätter für die gesamte Sozialwissenschaften, 2 (1905): 113–15. Lamprecht was not appeased. He described Bernheim's as a "standpoint fundamentally opposed to mine." StA Dresden, VB 10281/203, Lamprecht to Waentig, Leipzig, 17.4.05.
139. Rüdiger vom Bruch, "Wissenschaftspolitik, Kulturpolitik, Weltpolitik: Hochschule und Forschungsinstitute auf dem Deutschen Hochschullehrertag in Dresden 1911," Horst-Walter Blanke and Jörn Rüsen, eds., Vom historischen Seminar zum histori-

schen Forschungsinstitut: Zur Transformation des Historismus (Paderborn, 1992), esp. 10–19.

140. NL Lamprecht (Korr. 9), Lamprecht to Bernheim, Leipzig, 14.11.11; (Korr. 62), Wiegandt to Lamprecht, Leipzig, 24.10.11; Lamprecht to Ladewig, Leipzig, 21.3.12.
141. NL Lamprecht (Korr. 9), Bernheim to Lamprecht, Greifswald, 25.11.11.
142. NL Lamprecht (Korr. 62), Lamprecht to Klein, Leipzig, 30.1.12; (Korr. 55), Lamprecht to Wundt, Leipzig, 24.6.12.
143. StA Dresden, VB 10273/11, Burgsdorff to Beck, Leipzig, 30.6.12.
144. Gerhard Hahn and Karlheinz Jackstel, "Hochschulpädagogische Theorieentwicklung und Innovation—Zum Wirken von Hans Schmidkunz," Karlheinz Jackstel and Erich Leitner, eds., *Studienreform und Hochschuldidaktik 1890–1933: Konzepte, Kontroversen, Kompromisse* (Zeitschrift für Hochschuldidaktik, Sonderheft 13) (Vienna, 1990), 99–109.
145. NL Bernheim, Lamprecht to Bernheim, Leipzig, 24.4.12; NL Lamprecht (Korr. 62), Lamprecht to Sternberg, Leipzig, 14.5.12.
146. NL Harden, Lamprecht to Harden, Leipzig, 2.7.12; NL Lamprecht (Korr. 37), Lamprecht to Meyer [1914].
147. NL Bernheim, Lamprecht to Bernheim, Leipzig, 26.3.12; Lamprecht to Bernheim, Berlin, 9.4.13.
148. StA Dresden, VB 10273/11, Lamprecht to KM, Leipzig, 24.6.12; 3. Tagung der "Gesellschaft für Hochschulpädagogik": Liste der Teilnehmer; *Leipziger Tageblatt*, 19.10.12; NL Lamprecht (Korr. 62), Einladung zur dritten Tagung der "Gesellschaft für Hochschulpädagogik" in Leipzig.
149. LW, 654.
150. NL Bernheim, Lamprecht to Bernheim, Leipzig, 23.12.13.
151. NL Lamprecht (UL 10), Lamprecht, Forschungsinstitute nach Leipziger System; (Korr. 49), Lamprecht to Stange, Leipzig, 2.12.14; Lamprecht, "Gärung und Klärung im Hochschulgebiet," *Frankfurter Zeitung*, 6.5.14.
152. NL Lamprecht (Korr. 24), Lamprecht to Deutsche Gesellschaft für Soziologie, Leipzig, 24.6.14; Muller, 136.
153. NL Lamprecht (Korr. 36), Heinrich Meier to Lamprecht, Göttingen, 17.10.13; Lamprecht, "Eine Gefahr für die Geisteswissenschaften," *Zukunft*, 83 (1913): 16–24, 421–29; Simmel, "An Herrn Professor Karl Lamprecht," ibid., 230–34.
154. NL Lamprecht (Korr. 62), Lamprecht to Neumann, Leipzig, 9.12.13; StA Dresden, VB 10281/203, *Dresdner Anzeiger*, 11.6.13; cf. Friedrich Wilhelm Graf, "Rettung der Persönlichkeit: Protestantische Theologie als Kulturwissenschaft des Christentums," in vom Bruch, *Kultur und Kulturwissenschaften um 1900*, 108.
155. NL Lamprecht (Korr. 21), Lamprecht to Elster, Leipzig, 21.1.13; (Korr. 50), Lamprecht to Tille, Leipzig, 14.7.12; LW, 666–69.

12

Culture and Policy

[D]as Unhistorische und das Historische ist gleichermassen
für die Gesundheit eines einzelnen, eines Volkes und einer
Kultur nötig.

"Historians had a special influence in a historically minded time," Thomas
Nipperdey has recently observed of the German empire. They were "bestowers
of identity, explicators, interpreters, fashioners of the future."[1] In the culture of
the German educated middle class at least, this proposition was so well rooted
that it survived even the turmoil that the historians inflicted upon themselves in
the 1890s. In truth, none of the parties to the *Methodenstreit* questioned the
principle that the past sanctioned the present, that history offered the most valid
font of orientation for the affairs of state, and that professional historians were
uniquely qualified, as the custodians of the past, to offer political guidance.

This conviction made historians the most politically active group of academic
scholars in imperial Germany. Yet they, like other academic scholars, were
loath to call their activity political. "Scholars can and shall not make politics,"
wrote one of the academy's foremost spokesmen, Friedrich Paulsen, who cited
the academic scholar's "habitus of theoretical indifference" to the give-and-take
of politics. The theoretical activity central to scholarship, he declared, "easily
creates a certain indecisiveness, a kind of abulia, an inclination to doubt."[2]
Paulsen was also one of the more sensitive and open-minded of the academy's
spokesmen, so his views offer powerful testimony to the success of German
scholars in a hegemonic enterprise, which was to exclude an order of political
belief—about which they were anything but indifferent—from the very rubric
of politics.

Nipperdey offers additional testimony of the same kind when he writes of the
"metapolitical" dimension of these beliefs—the fact that they addressed a
self-evident, implicit set of values and norms thought to reside in a realm of
"culture," which transcended partisan dispute and imposed obligations on the
entire community.[3] The prominence of historians in the interpretation of
culture documented the historical sanction to which these values and norms laid
claim. In practice, however, *Kultur*, so defined, symbolized the aspirations and

394

anxieties of the Protestant *Bildungsbürgertum*, from which most academic scholars were recruited; and the practical, political implications of the concept registered in the empassioned intervention of these scholars into debates over issues of confession, the constitution, social and educational reform, foreign policy, and national security.[4]

An animus against partisan politics nonetheless inhered in this construction of culture. It was especially marked among the academic historians once the activism of the Prussian school yielded to neo-Rankeanism and the more aloof modes of engagement it implied. Yet this posture, too, entailed practical commitments, just as it recommended special avenues of political intervention to the historians who claimed to interpret and defend German culture. Most scholars eschewed association with the political parties. Their activism tended instead to find vent in journalism and in causes that were styled as "national" and hence nonpartisan. This category included a carefully orchestrated propaganda campaign on behalf of the battle fleet at the turn of the century, as well as activity in patriotic societies, such as the German School Association, the German Colonial Society, and the Eastern Marches Society.[5] Scholars in the capital were a special case. Proximity to the corridors of power encouraged more direct forms of political intervention—at court, in the ministries, and in central bureaucratic offices.

The historical profession's great renegade was another special case. While he shared most of the "metapolitical" assumptions of his colleagues and observed most of the conventional forms of political action, Lamprecht's views on politics were too intimately linked to his historiography to remain orthodox. Professional isolation nurtured his political eccentricity, until it found expression in a personal crusade, which was remarkable for its style and agenda and for the brief notoriety it attracted.

Karl Lamprecht's political education was in most respects unexceptional. The rectory where he grew up breathed a moderate strain of conservatism not uncommon among the lower Lutheran clergy in Prussia. His father read the *Kreuzzeitung* but greeted happily the national settlement that sealed the dramatic events of midcentury.[6] The boy's seminal impressions of politics were born of these same events. His earliest recollections were of the celebration in Jessen, when he was five, of the coronation of William I as king of Prussia. The wars of unification intruded into his experience at the age of nine, when his father took him to watch Danish prisoners of war at work on the fortifications at Wittenberg. The boy witnessed the campaign of 1866 more immediately, for Jessen was a minor way station in the movement of Prussian troops into and out of Saxony; and a general briefly took up quarters in the rectory.[7] When Lamprecht experienced the campaign of 1870 at boarding school, the patriotic excitement and frustration of a boy too young to participate were tempered by the news that a teacher and a former classmate had lost their lives in the field.[8]

Lamprecht spent the early years of the new *Kaiserreich* at Schulpforta, where the curriculum and life-style were calculated to reinforce the basic conceptions of patriotism and civic virtue that he had imbibed at home. At the same time, his monarchism and Protestantism, which were central to these conceptions, became more militant in the atmosphere of conflict that accompanied the *Kulturkampf* and the repression of the budding socialist movement. His mentor at boarding school, the rector Friedrich Wilhelm Herbst, encouraged this direction in his thinking, for the older man was convinced that socialism and Catholicism threatened the achievement of 1871.[9]

Lamprecht's university studies affected his political beliefs more indirectly. Failure to join a *Burschenschaft* in Göttingen spared him exposure to the xenophobia and ferocious political intolerance that student corporations were breeding in their members. Experience in the army cured him of any temptation to romanticize military life.[10] In the political ambience that prevailed at the universities in both Göttingen and Leipzig, however, his basic convictions remained intact even as his intellectual and emotional maturation brought him into conflict with authority on several fronts. His challenge to the statolatry of the historical profession did not extend to the symbols of authority or the configuration of power in the Bismarckian state. Nor did his conflict with paternal authority, which became manifest in his growing distance from Christianity, cause him to question either his confessional preferences or his commitment to the civic virtues implied by German Protestantism. When Noorden recommended Lamprecht to Sybel in 1880 as an "entirely Protestant Prussian," who was filled with "serious moral" and "upright monarchical convictions [*Gesinnung*]," his words echoed a formula that described successful socialization into the political culture of the new *Reich*.[11]

The most distinctive phase of Lamprecht's political education occurred in the Rhineland. Gustav von Mevissen was in this respect, too, his mentor. The goals and energy of Mevissen's politics were alike congenial to the young historian. The older man's activism was directed toward shaping a new civic elite in the marriage of enterprise and culture—a union that required the vision of the scholar to mobilize the energy of the businessman in the service of the nation's collective destiny. Mevissen seemed himself to embody this union, and his influence on Lamprecht was indelible. It made the historian a lifelong admirer of Germany's enterpreneurial class, with which he later entertained closer and more extensive contacts than perhaps any other academic in the country.[12] Mevissen's vision also underlay the historian's belief in the active civic obligations of academic scholarship, as well as Lamprecht's abiding admiration for an earlier generation of activist historians who had honored these obligations— foremost among them Mevissen's friend Treitschke.

The demands of scholarly apprenticeship in the Rhineland nonetheless left the historian little time for political activism, save for his work in the Society for the Study of Rhenish History, which both he and Mevissen regarded as a civic undertaking. Lamprecht's involvement in electoral politics in 1887, as a speaker on behalf of local candidates of the national *Kartell*, remained but an episode.[13]

He affiliated with none of the established parties, although the views of National Liberals most approximated his own.

At the time of his departure from the Rhineland at the end of the decade, Lamprecht's political views were more orthodox than the views on historical method that were then gestating. His monarchism and his reverence for Bismarck were unqualified, but these convictions had become virtual badges of honor among young academic scholars, as had the anticlericalism and genteel antisemitism that accented his devotion to the symbols of authority in the new state.[14] However, the seeds of unconventionality had been planted. Friendship with Mevissen had established in Lamprecht's mind the vital moral bond between politics and historical scholarship. In the controversies that occupied him in the next decade this bond was intensified and transformed, as politics became subsumed in historiography.

The *Methodenstreit* was about politics. The avidity with which Lamprecht's opponents tore into the early volumes of his *German History* was due in good part to the perception that these volumes were subversive. In this respect, Mehring's acclaim was the most devastating comment on Lamprecht's scholarship, for it was singularly stationed to nourish this perception. The historian's transgression was to write as if material forces were fundamental to German history and thus to connive, even if unconsciously, in the onslaught then being waged in the name of Marxism against the political foundations of the new German empire.

This charge of subversiveness was based on a profound and willful misreading of Lamprecht's early volumes, which the historian admittedly encouraged with his own eclecticism and confusion. He was no materialist. In ways he himself probably failed to realize, both the historical subject and the processes that he described in these volumes were ideal, moral phenomena. The narrative structure of his history was fully congruent with the secular theology that the Prussian school of historians had formulated to legitimize Bismarck's achievement, as well as with the structures of power and authority that had emerged out of it.[15] Lamprecht's, no less than Droysen's or Sybel's, was a story of decline from medieval splendor, halting regeneration under the banner of Luther and the Hohenzollerns, and redemption by force of arms.

Yet in ways that remained unnoticed, or at least unmentioned in the *Methodenstreit*, Lamprecht's vision of history generated a more ambivalent kind of tension with the structure of authority in the new empire. Although the ontology of the German nation remained confused in the historian's mind, the premises of his *Kulturgeschichte* excluded a political definition and made the settlement of 1871 problematic as the telos of German history. Whether it was defined as a cultural, moral, or natural entity, the nation transcended the frontiers of the new German state. This incongruity was the avenue through which Lamprecht's activism first emerged, for in a manner that recalled the critical energy of Treitschke's generation of historians, it identified the unfulfilled obligations of the German past. The same incongruity also cast the question of subversiveness in a different light, for in Lamprecht's view, the laws of the nation's own history disclosed the transience and insufficiency of the political structure created in 1871.

The problematic implications of this position emerged only slowly amid the political conflicts of the early twentieth century. Because it did not contest the national symbols, the view was far easier for a young historian to embrace in the early 1890s than was historical materialism. The embrace became increasingly evident in those early volumes of the German History that Lamprecht wrote in Leipzig, where he had made some new political friends.

The city of Leipzig played host to the militant forces that gathered at both extremes of German politics during the early Wilhelmine epoch. At one pole was the most radical socialist newspaper in the country, Bruno Schönlank's Leipziger Volkszeitung. At the other was Paul Liman's Leipziger Neueste Nachrichten, the voice of the city's right-wing forces and an advocate, as one young witness recalled, of "the most hot-headed nationalism."[16] The university gravitated toward the latter pole. While a few young intellectuals from the editorial staff of the Volkszeitung (like Hendrik de Man) studied at the university, Liman's was by a wide margin the journal of choice among students and faculty. The university was also the center of one of the largest and most active local networks of patriotic societies in the country. With the enthusiastic support of Liman's paper, these groups, which together comprised several thousand of the city's wealthier and better educated inhabitants, forged a coalition among the parties of the right, principally the National Liberals and the anti-Semites, in an effort to exclude socialists from the municipal government. University scholars were prominent fixtures on local executive boards of the patriotic societies, while student corporations furnished large contingents to the membership of these organizations.[17]

Leipzig was also the hub of the Pan-German League. Founded in Berlin in 1891, this organization was the most aggressive exponent of the new nationalism that had emerged in Germany in the 1880s out of popular agitation to promote the idea of overseas empire and to support German communities outside the Reich, which were embroiled in ethnic conflict in the Habsburg monarchy and elsewhere in eastern Europe.[18] The basis of the League's program was an ethnic or völkisch rather than a political definition of the German nation; and this proposition underlay the organization's demands for a more "dynamic" German foreign policy and for the "consolidation of all Germans around the world."

After an initial period of instability, the League reconsolidated in 1893 when the leadership devolved to Leipzig. The new national chairman was Liman's friend, Ernst Hasse, the director of the Saxon Statistical Bureau in Leipzig. Hasse also held an extraordinary professorship at the university. His deputy was one of his former students, Adolf Lehr. Together these two men oversaw the expansion of the national organization in the second half of the decade; in Leipzig they also built one of the largest local chapters in the country, which included several of Hasse's colleagues from the university, among them Ratzel and the chemist Johannes Wislicenus, who had been one of the League's original founders.[19]

The chapter also included Lamprecht. The skepticism that the historian professed in 1892 to Pirenne about this organization evidently faded, for he soon found the League to be a cordial political outlet for his energy.[20] Treitschke's legacy of patriotic activism weighed heavily on him during his early years in Leipzig, when he concluded that his *German History* offered a vehicle for allowing scholarship, as he wrote to Althoff, "to speak to broad segments of the nation."[21] The Pan-German League exuded a sense of vitality, which appealed to Lamprecht's sense of his own mission; and the League's program corresponded to the imperatives that inhered in his conception of German history. It is not clear when or under whose influence he joined, but signs of his interest in the organization began to surface in 1893, after which he quickly became one of the League's prized resources from the ranks of the academic historians—a distinction he shared with another of Treitschke's disciples, Dietrich Schäfer.[22]

Lamprecht's principal service to the organization was his scholarship. In the third and fourth volumes of his *German History*, which he published in 1893 and 1894 (at a time when his opponents were accusing him of abetting the socialists), passages read like glosses on the program of the Pan-German League. The historian announced that Flanders and Holland represented "a special formation of the German being [*Wesen*]" and warned of the *deutschfeindlich* character of Czech and Polish nationalist ambitions (this in the fourteenth century).[23] In the section of the fifth volume that appeared in 1894, he wrote of the dissemination of Luther's writings throughout "Pan-Germany [*Alldeutschland*]".[24] The language of these passages featured the same rhetoric and imagery that pervaded the Pan-Germans' propaganda, although Lamprecht's partiality for foreign words put the League's goal of linguistic purity beyond his reach. His "pioneers of German culture," in this case the settlers who conquered the Hungarian plains in the twelfth century, were not the correct *Vorkämpfer* of Pan-German parlance, but *Pioniere*.[25]

The most intense period of Lamprecht's engagement was in the mid-1890s, when the aura of the League's politics hovered over much of his work, including the early polemics of the *Methodenstreit*.[26] Political considerations figured large in his initiatives during the early *Historikertage* which preceded the establishment of the Association of German Historians.[27] The presence of Swiss, Austrian, Flemish, and Dutch historians at these meetings was calculated, as he explained in the spring of 1894, to promote "the common spiritual interests among Germans [*deutsch-geistige Interessen*], which transcend the Reich's boundary posts," for "a spiritual Pan-Germanism can only be of value to our future."[28] The historian's network of contacts in Austria grew during the course of these meetings; and it was based upon political as well as methodological sympathies.[29] The support he enjoyed among Austrian historians during the *Methodenstreit* emphasized the affinities between *Kulturgeschichte* and *völkisch* nationalism, as did the politics of some of his students and allies in Germany, such as Liesegang, Buchholz, Ernst Daenell, Otto Hoetzsch, Benno Hilliger, and Armin Tille.[30]

Even at its height, however, Lamprecht's engagement on behalf of the Pan-German League was restricted. He was a leading figure in Leipzig's patriotic milieu, and his obligations placed heavy burdens on his time. He was in great demand to write for the popular press and to address student audiences on patriotic occasions.[31] Like other academics who joined patriotic societies, he was an enormous asset, a *Dekorationsperson*, whose status alone made him a popular speaker at meetings. Other organizations sought to exploit this principle. He was active in a local veteran's association and Leipzig's chapter of the Eastern Marches Society, as well as in a group that called itself the *Patriotenbund* and raised money to build monuments around the city.[32] When the naval agitation began in earnest at the end of the decade, Lamprecht was a leading member of the "Free Association for Naval Lectures," which coordinated the participation of German academics in this campaign.[33]

The commitments of the *Honoratior* limited the time and energy that Lamprecht could expend on the Pan-German League. His affiliation loosened gradually over the next several years for other reasons as well. He was not a pliant follower. He clashed with the League's leadership over the so-called *Umsturzvorlage*, the package of laws against subversion that the government put before the Reichstag in 1895.[34] Of greater significance were his reservations over the evolution of the League's posture at the end of the decade and the growing stridency of its criticism of government policy. The League's position smacked of partisanship, and it threatened to compromise Lamprecht's understanding of his own political role, which was to address political questions on the authority of his scholarship.[35] The League's drift into "national opposition" raised additional issues of authority, for it brought the organization into conflict with the government to a degree uncomfortable to Lamprecht, whose public deference to the symbols of political authority was so great that it occasionally embarrassed and annoyed his colleagues.[36]

The historian's growing distance from the Pan-German League in the late 1890s was due as well to his preoccupation with defending his theories of history during the last stages of the *Methodenstreit*. When his attention returned to broad questions of politics in the aftermath of this controversy, his vision betrayed the impact of the great personal crisis he had just endured. The bond between politics and historical scholarship acquired a new emphasis and urgency. The proposition that politics represented the fulfillment of history's obligations implied now the vindication of his own vision of historical development. The historian's politics were henceforth geared to a personal agenda that was too eccentric for the programmatic constraints of the Pan-German League or, for that matter, any other political organization in imperial Germany.

The supplementary volumes to his *German History*, which Lamprecht published shortly after the turn of the century, revealed that he had not abandoned his ambitions to succeed Treitschke as the tribune of the nation.[37] These volumes represented his political manifesto. They contained his most comprehensive commentary on politics to date, an extended analysis of the historical background of the political struggles in his own era of Excitability, and a set of prescriptions for their resolution. The volumes also revealed the dependence of the historian's politics on his historiography. The resemblances were methodological as well as conceptual. Eclecticism, inconsistency, and a set of idiosyncratic premises made his view of politics as unconventional as his theory of history.

The passages on foreign policy were the most conventional, at least in the sense that they seemed to attach the imprimatur of history to the program of the Pan-German League. The laws of history required that Germany become an "expansive state [*Expansionsstaat*]," he wrote.[38] His description of the imperatives that inhered in this stage of historical development rehearsed a familiar catalogue of demands. The list included the consolidation of Germans on the continent (preferably by means of a central-European customs union), German settlement in southeast Europe, Asia, and South America, kindling cultural solidarity among Germans abroad, African colonies, commercial expansion, and a battle fleet. But Lamprecht lacked the ruthless consistency of the Pan-Germans' ideologues; and in many of these passages he vacillated between extravagance and caution. He appeared to abjure future German territorial acquisitions in Europe, but only until his attention turned to the "Germanic states" in the west and to "some kind of *Anschluss*" of Holland "to Germany."[39] He spoke of the "unchained *Unkultur*" of the Slavs in the Habsburg monarchy and the threat that the "Slavic storm [*Ansturm*]" posed there to the ethnic integrity of German communities.[40] Several pages later he observed, in tones less cordial to the Pan-Germans, that "geographical conditions seem to point to close cultural cooperation between Slavs and Germans."[41]

Lamprecht's vacillations were due, as usual, to his carelessness—to his hasty failure to perceive the repeated contradictions into which he had stumbled. This time, however, the inconsistencies also reflected a significant transformation that had taken place in his thinking about politics. His commentary on foreign policy had by now taken root in a much broader vision of politics, which might be described, like his historiography, as a new discourse, in which a special logic displaced more conventional language and categories of analysis (and rules of consistency).

Lamprecht's survey of politics in the era of Excitability was a rhapsody on the theme of regeneration. The hallmark of the transition to the "expansionist state" was, in his view, the development of a "new idealism," which would also suffuse domestic politics, transcend traditional sectorial divisions, and produce a renewed sense of national solidarity. Everywhere he looked, the historian descried trends that marked—in their analogous operation—the singularity, power, and pervasiveness of this regenerative process. He found indices in the centralization of government, in the development of the "constrained" enterprise of joint stock companies and cartels, in the corporate organization of society into trade unions, cooperatives, and voluntary associations, in the moderation of social conflict with the advance of social reform, and in the attenuation of confessional antagonisms in the emergence of what he called a "new piety," a "higher and freer form of religious life."[42]

Lamprecht's description of this process clearly implied a program of domestic reform to encourage political centralization, industrial enterprise, and moderate social reform.[43] Some features of his vision resembled ideas that were being vetted in the Pan-German League about the renewal of national solidarity at home. Most notably, he spoke like the Pan-Germans of the "more far-sighted and educated" sectors of the nation and hinted that the claims of the Gebildeten to national leadership justified reform of the Reichstag suffrage.[44] Yet Lamprecht wrote in an almost Saint-Simonian spirit of optimism and generosity that was foreign to the League's discussion of domestic affairs, where the language of national regeneration cloaked conspiratorial anxieties and threats of repression aimed at socialists, Catholics, and national minorities of all descriptions.[45] Lamprecht, by contrast, accepted the salience of "democratism" in contemporary politics (even though he failed to define the concept clearly). He embraced the kind of state-driven social reform promoted by his colleagues in the Verein für Sozialpolitik; and he offered a prescient analysis of the forces that were fostering the national integration of both social democracy and Catholicism.

Susan Schultz has recently emphasized just these themes in situating Lamprecht's ideology of national solidarity and reform within a broader intellectual critique of liberalism, in which Wundt, Schmoller, and Otto von Gierke also participated. Like them, she writes, Lamprecht was convinced that

> egoism and arbitrary freedom ("negative" liberalism, in Schmoller's terminology) could and would tear asunder the German Reich. Freedom must be endowed with a collectivistic, ethical limitation: arbitrary freedom could only be circumvented by an awareness of past and present collectivistic, ethical forces.[46]

The argument is compelling, insofar as it identifies the intellectual sources of a central theme in Lamprecht's writings, particularly in the supplements and the later volumes of the German History. The argument is also misleading. To the extent that it implies the primacy of political concerns in Lamprecht's theories of history, it inverts his own priorities.[47] The central theme of Lamprecht's history was not his politics; the central theme of Lamprecht's politics was his history.

"Both domestic and foreign policy," he wrote, "are in the first instance derivative phenomena [Folgeerscheinungen]."[48] Lamprecht's words must be taken seriously, for in practice this principle guided his thinking about politics as well as his writing of political history. The political changes he described represented but one facet of a more fundamental cultural and moral transformation that beckoned as the fulfillment of German history in the era of Excitability. The "new idealism" that animated politics in this era was the derivative of the new spiritual diapason. It corresponded to the era's nervous energy, vitality, and the self-awareness it had achieved in the intellectual mastery of nature and human affairs—in the formulation of a triumphant historical synthesis called *Kulturge-schichte*, which embraced and integrated every branch of human knowledge. From this perspective, politics was at once (only) the expression and the instrument of imperatives that inhered in this singular vision of the nation's history. Lamprecht's history alone lent intelligibility to politics; politics in turn validated Lamprecht's history.

Prescribing a program for reform on the basis of this understanding of politics posed the same kinds of methodological difficulties that the historian had encountered earlier in debates with Rachfahl and Hintze over the collective constraints on human agency. Portraying regeneration as the outcome of pro-found "socio-psychic" forces implied the futility of intervention or prescriptions of any kind. The historian's renewed attempt to resolve these difficulties sug-gested that the earlier debates had made an impression on him.[49] Now he called out the heroes. "The leadership of a hero and master [*Helden und Herrn*]" was required, he announced at the conclusion of his survey, to meet the "next challenges of the *Expansionsstaat*."[50] Likewise, he wrote, domestic politics de-manded *ein Individuum*, a "statesman of great scale," "great political persons."[51] Lamprecht's description made it clear, however, that the greatness of these men lay precisely in their sensitivity to the historical forces that molded them—in their "instinct for coming things," their "intuition for the future," and their "unconscious comprehension" of the "great developmental motifs and laws that govern human communities."[52]

Lamprecht's survey of his own era read like an extended essay on heroism. The giants of politics, of whom the Kaiser was the exemplary figure, joined the Mevissen-like heroes of enterprise and the great artists and scholars (whom he called the "entrepreneurs of scholarship") to form a new elite.[53] These men embodied the spirit, vitality, and energy of the era of *Reizsamkeit*, but their challenge was at the same time their constraint: they were to provide commit-ment and discipline for this spirit and to impel their epoch along the course prescribed by the "great developmental laws" of its own history. And it was self-evident that this role implied a special kind of heroism for the custodian of that history in Leipzig.

It is uncertain when Lamprecht left the Pan-German League, for the break was not abrupt. The last notice of his presence on the executive board of the Leipzig chapter appeared in 1902, shortly after the end of the League's agitation on behalf of the Boers, in which he had participated.[54] His relations with Hasse and other leaders of the organization remained friendly; in fact, traces of Lamprecht's thinking surfaced in Hasse's own manifesto on politics, his *Deutsche Politik*, fragments of which appeared between 1905 and 1908 as a semi-official statement of the League's position.[55] By this time, however, Hasse had already come under the influence of the man whose growing prominence in the League exacerbated the very tendencies that the historian had found objectionable. Heinrich Class, the young lawyer from Mainz who succeeded Lehr at Hasse's side in 1901, embodied the traits of a new generation of nationalists who were turning the Pan-German League into a symbol of pugnacity, racist antisemitism, and loud contempt for the men who ruled the country.[56]

Lamprecht's gradual withdrawal from the Pan-German League brought him briefly into the vicinity of another organization whose program was more cordial to his thinking about both the monarch and social policy. Friedrich Naumann's political beliefs gestated in a setting different from those of Lamprecht, and they reflected a more complex and troubled retreat from Protestant Christianity; but by the turn of the century the two men had reached significant points of convergence. The brief career of Naumann's National-Social Association was devoted to revitalizing the monarchy as a symbol of national integration under the banner of imperial expansion, democratic suffrage, and social reform—a program that Naumann and his followers called, in a more innocent age, "national socialism."[57]

The historian's link to Naumann's circle was Max Maurenbrecher, the son of Lamprecht's colleague in Bonn and Leipzig, Wilhelm Maurenbrecher. The two first met in Bonn in the home of the elder Maurenbrecher, when the son was a boy. Max Maurenbrecher subsequently took a doctorate in theology and a second degree in history in Leipzig, where he studied with Wundt, Bücher, and Lamprecht.[58] He then embarked on a political career. Like many young German Protestant liberals in the 1890s, he found Naumann to be the most exciting figure in German politics, and in 1901 he became the salaried executive secretary to the National-Social Association.

Maurenbrecher had tried in vain for several years to interest Lamprecht in Naumann's efforts. The near-simultaneous publication of the historian's first supplement to the German History and Naumann's manifesto, Demokratie und Kaisertum, encouraged another attempt. Early in 1902, Maurenbrecher invited the historian's attention to the parallels in these two documents. The inescapable consequence of Lamprecht's conclusions, he argued, was that a "strong commitment to social and national ideals" was "the only way to overcome the subjectivistic degeneration of our present-day culture."[59] Naumann himself then issued a shrewd appeal to the historian's sense of his own mission. "The application of your method to the present times must encourage, in a most effective way, the course implied by our national-social ideas," he wrote. "History in your sense implies political activity in ours."[60] After hearing this music, Lamprecht agreed to lecture to the next annual congress of Naumann's group. Then, after Maurenbrecher attempted to prescribe the theme of his talk, the historian became annoyed and changed his mind.[61] The decision was due in part to lingering reservations about the open partisanship of Naumann's organization; but it also reflected the more fundamental difficulty of bridling Lamprecht's strong but eccentric political impulses in any way.

The issue of Lamprecht's more active cooperation with the Naumann circle became moot the next year, when the National-Social Association dissolved into the left-liberal Freisinnige Vereinigung and Maurenbrecher migrated to the

Social Democratic party.[62] Lamprecht nonetheless portrayed Naumann's efforts as a symptom of the era's idealism, the "perfection [*Durchbildung*] of a selfless social instinct"; and passages in the later supplements on the Kaiser and social policy registered the historian's continuing enthusiasm for some of Naumann's ideas.[63]

The encounter with Naumann hardly subdued Lamprecht's enthusiasm for *Weltpolitik* and other foreign policy extravagances, for at the time there was little to distinguish Naumann in this respect from the Pan-German League.[64] The historian's retreat from arrogant nationalism marked the completion of his withdrawal from the Pan-German League and a major transition in his political thinking. Harbingers of the transition were to be found in the supplementary volumes, where admonishments against presumption, narrow-mindedness, and dogmatism in foreign policy were directed at Hasse and his friends.[65] The decisive event, however, took place several months after the publication of the last supplement in 1904, when Lamprecht went to America.

The sojourn in the United States shook the historian's assumptions about politics more than it did his views on historical method. His critical remarks about the undermining of German ethnic identity, the disappearance of German culture, and the diminishing political role of German-Americans in the New World were part of a standard Pan-German lament; but the conclusions he drew were not.[66] The experience dissolved Lamprecht's confidence in the correlation of culture and power—the comfortable belief, which he shared with the Pan-Germans, that German cultural superiority legitimized the nation's claims to world power. In the United States he could discover only the primitive beginnings of a national culture; but he found signs everywhere of the immense power that was awakening in the New World and awaited only the development of an indigenous culture before it overwhelmed the limited political and military resources of the Old World.[67]

"Well may Germany seem small in comparison," he wrote.[68] This observation captured the central lesson that Lamprecht drew from his experience in the New World. The remark betrayed his apprehension over the growing anomaly of culture and power. Events outside Europe implied the political decline of the world's most historically advanced cultures, and—of more immediate import—it foretold practical constraints on German power. Resolving this anomaly now became the historian's central political occupation. The effort immediately required adjustments in his political commentary, which he undertook despite the difficulty of accommodating them to his theory of historical development.

Allusions to "Teutonic culture" signaled an initial adjustment, which he formulated even as he traversed the North American continent. He first sounded the theme in Oregon. He expressed relief to observe that the "Germanic or Teutonic type predominates" amid the ethnic mixture he encountered in Portland.[69] Variations echoed in subsequent references to a "general Teutonic type," to the "deep religiosity of the Teutons" in the United States, and to "Teutonic-American public morality."[70] By the end of the account, the historian left the impression that the emerging American culture was going to be Teutonic.

The meaning of this proposition was not clear, for it made little sense in the framework of his own theories. Because he rejected the categories in which some Pan-Germans had begun to speak of a Germanic or Teutonic racial community, the attributes he cited, like religiosity, public morality, or "general Teutonic" characteristics, could refer only to a Teutonic nation, a cultural "substratum" or formation, which had never existed and had not yet emerged in America. Efforts to define such a formation only added to the confusion. When he described the Germans and the Dutch as historic Teutons, the adjustment to his theory could be read as merely semantic, for he could appeal to the Pan-German dimension of his own scholarship; he could do so with less plausibility, however, when he sought to include "the Scandinavians" in the same category.[71] When he enlarged the family of "Teutonic daughter-nations" to include the English, he exceeded in one blow the claims of his own scholarship, the wildest pretensions of the Pan-German League, and the logic of his own argument, announced in an earlier passage, that a "strictly Germanic, Teutonic impression" implied "everything but English."[72]

These contortions once again suggested how resistant America was to his historical theories. But he passed immediately on to the political implications of his encounters with the Teutons. The practical bond among Lamprecht's "Teutonic nations" was the colonization of North America. Common participation in the settlement of the continent had linked the colonizers in a community with the emergent nation, whose culture they had together spawned. The American nation "will be a Teutonic one; and this fact affords the English, Scandinavians, and Germans [and presumably the Dutch] a decisive lead over the rest of the population in contributing to this new formation."[73] This fact also implied the vehicle to tame the challenge of the New World and to arrest the decline of German power. "The Teutons are born for one another," he proclaimed, "together they will dominate [beherrschen] the world." "Teutons" had metamorphosed once again, however, into a political category; it referred now expressly to a constellation of power among Germany, England, and the United States, which the historian characterized as the "three great Teutonic nations."[74]

Lamprecht returned from America sobered yet exhilarated. "I have learned a lot, but perhaps more important, unlearned a lot."[75] His discovery of a Teutonic community marked the first stage in an advance beyond the arrogance, parochialism, and Pan-German fixations of his earlier commentaries. With these constraints now shed, his perspective on politics expanded in step with the broadening of his methodological interests into universal history, a process that his American adventure had also encouraged.

The new accents in his politics were almost immediately apparent. "It behooves an old, cultured nation like ours not to confine itself to affairs at home," he wrote in the preface to the account of his American journey, which he published in 1906. "The earthly cosmos, the human world, has shifted. And a good part of our national future depends on whether we quickly understand the changes involved and draw the necessary consequences."[76] A series of articles and speeches over the next several years read like addenda to the *Ergänzungs-bände*, as did passages in the later volumes of his *German History*.[77] He examined the development of a "human community based on the division of labor," the internationalization of trade, communications, and culture, and the emergence of new powers in Asia and North America.[78] The necessary consequence of these developments was what he variously called a "new cosmopolitanism" or a "practical cosmopolitanism," a sense of national pride paired with awareness, cooperation, and respect for other cultures. "Our cosmopolitan feelings are balanced against our national feelings," he observed in 1906, "and we do not find that the one could exist without the other."[79]

Lamprecht wrote as if these conclusions were natural corollaries to the theory of universal history that he had already worked out; but he never examined systematically their theoretical ramifications. He implied that the new cosmopolitanism represented a phenomenon specific to the age of Excitability—a higher stage in the development of national consciousness. This consciousness, whose object was a "new humanity filled with international elements," had logically to reflect the common human experience of national development through five historical epochs.[80] In truth, all of these propositions were problematic. It was not clear from his commentary whether Germany occupied this stage of development alone, or how consciousness of the "new humanity" could emerge simultaneously among nations at disparate stages of cultural development, or how an international culture could form at all, given the basic national autonomy of cultural development.

Lamprecht ignored these problems, too. He was more interested in the practical challenges and opportunities with which the "upsurging [*emporflam-mende*] unity of human relations" confronted the "paradigmatic nation."[81] Germany represented, in the historian's view, the most unalloyed and farthest advanced case of "normal national development."[82] But historical distinction carried privilege and responsibility; the pioneer's was a preceptive role. Germany, he wrote, had a "special" role in the world, "national and universal at the same time," which corresponded to the nation's achievement and "special endowments [*Veranlagung*]."[83] The "purified" national pride of the "new cosmopolitanism" was the consciousness of the "special value of the nation and of special national gifts," whose "development, maintenance, and propagation in the world" defined the nation's great obligation.[84] "The world is too poor in originality," he declared, "to dispense with the special German genius."[85] "The German spirit alone is universal, directed toward binding," he wrote in 1906 in the *German History*; it was "a spirit of lawfulness and conciliating compromise, and therefore destined to create a culture that is to unify everything that was, is, and will be great on earth."[86]

The historian did not need to explore the character of the "German genius" in much detail. That it was cultural was obvious. Nor did it require a great leap for him to conclude that Germany's obligation lay in a cultural crusade, a mission to disseminate the nation's great achievements to the rest of the world, to preside over an impending transition prescribed by the laws of history, and to lead the advance toward the "highest moral human community."[87] The rewards would be great. The mission promised both security and national self-awareness, the "tasty fruit" that he described as the "clear, secure, honorable conscious-ness" of the nation's "own power and its rightful place in the circle of its sister-nations."[88] But the final significance of Germany's mission was, as this formulation revealed, to restore the correlation of culture and power, albeit in a new equation. In an era of growing international solidarity, the historian reasoned, German culture was a more effective guarantor of German power, security, and "well-conceived national interests" than were the German armed forces.[89]

This reasoning drew out the political dimension of the far-flung agenda that had taken shape in the historian's mind around plans for historiographical and academic reform. The object now was to guide policy in directions charted by the imperatives of historical development. As Lamprecht conceived it, this was itself a pedagogical undertaking. Its goal was to promote a "new national ethic," a "higher idealism," by educating the thinking of those who most mattered in the formulation of policy—the nation's cultured elite, "die Gebildete der Nation," who, as he explained to Bücher, were to be "properly enlightened about the so decisive present phase of development."[90] Bücher was skeptical, for he well recognized that words like "proper enlightenment" and "phase of development" masked the real core of Lamprecht's agenda. Political reform, like academic reform, was ultimately the instrument of another crusade, whose object was to promulgate and ratify a vision of history.

Early in 1907, in a letter to Althoff, Lamprecht reflected about his own political commitments. "I am not a politician and never will be one," he wrote, "but I am occasionally roused to show that a more solidly based and—I think—more passionate political position is possible on the basis of my historical point of view."[91] This conviction had underlain the historian's political activism from the beginning of his career, and it did not change upon his departure from the Pan-German League; nor did the belief, which he had shared with the Pan-Germans, that the country's educated elites had a special obligation in the shaping of policy. By 1907, however, the specifics of his "political position" had changed, as had his interpretation of the imperatives that inhered in his own "historical point of view." He gave a clear signal of the change when he disavowed the League's Anglophobia and prescribed closer German ties to England and the United States, declaring that the Teutons collectively repre-sented the "cement that holds the contemporary human world together."[92]

The most dramatic sign of the new direction in Lamprecht's political thinking came in an address that he delivered in June 1909.[93] Here he called for a basic reorientation of German policy. "We, more than any other nation on earth, have become too used to reckoning only with antiquated, military methods." Effective policy, he said, required other, more subtle means, directed toward the protection of cultural superiority, the recognition of the legitimate claims of others, and—"shining in the background"—"a general cultural ideal" that encompassed at least European civilization. "Today," he concluded, "we are talking about things that we can group together under the name of cultural policy."

One of the remarkable features of this address was that the historian presented it to the annual meeting of the Association for Germandom Abroad (*Verein für das Deutschtum im Ausland*). This organization was the successor of the German School Association, and it was, next to the Pan-German League, perhaps the most significant advocate of *völkisch* nationalism in Germany. Lamprecht appealed to the sentiments of this organization when he recommended a "cultural policy" as the most effective way to solidify ties among Germans throughout the world. But he offended the sentiments of many in his audience when he commented favorably about the efforts of some of his own new-found political friends, who were pursuing "the new ideal of a cultural policy" at peace congresses.

The new tones in Lamprecht's commentary on world politics had quickly drawn the attention of the leaders of the German peace movement, who had for years been advocating international cooperation, organization, and the peaceful arbitration of international conflict. Because their cause implied the limitation of national sovereignty, their campaign was marked by more fervor than success; and its leaders had constantly to contend with attacks that the Pan-Germans and other patriots directed at their patriotism, realism, and even their sanity.[94]

The convocation of the two Hague conferences, in 1899 and 1907, lent a degree of credibility to the peace movement's campaign. So did Alfred Hermann Fried's attempt to purge the campaign of the moralism that had originally animated it and to portray pacifism as a *Wissenschaft*, a systematic analysis of recent history in which the peace movement's goals represented the logical, if not inevitable, outcome of the internationalization of trade, communications, and cultural contacts, as well as the only reasonable response to the growing destructiveness of military technology. Prior to the Hague conferences, the peace movement had enjoyed virtually no sympathy within the German academy. Fried's achievement was to provide the movement with a more plausible program, which appealed to a small group of jurists and other academic scholars whose interest in international law and arbitration had been kindled at the Hague.

The similarity between Fried's theories and the new accents in Lamprecht's views was coincidental, but it encouraged the evolution of the historian's thinking toward the kind of political internationalism that the peace movement advocated. Fried's vision was at once Herderian and utilitarian. When he wrote of an international community, or what he called the "organization of the world," he implied the elimination of neither national units nor competitive relations among them; he envisaged instead an international organization that was empowered to adjudicate disputes among its members, so that international rivalries could be diverted from the waste of war and the arms race into more constructive modes. Lamprecht was less inclined than Fried to speculate about institutional particulars, but he concluded that Fried's theories addressed in a different idiom the historical trends he had himself identified. The "new cosmopolitanism," he announced in 1910, was "the apostle and intimate friend [Vertrauter] of every peace movement."[95]

Lamprecht first drifted into the vicinity of the peace movement in 1906. He joined the Anglo-German Conciliation Committee (Deutsch-englisches Verständigungskomitee), an organization founded by English and German pacifists in 1905, but which expanded beyond these circles in the aftermath of the first Moroccan crisis, when it coordinated a series of celebrated exchange visits among leaders from politics, business, journalism, and the academy.[96] Lamprecht's contacts within this milieu then grew, and he became, along with Wilhelm Ostwald, the German peace movement's foremost academic supporter. He joined other internationalist organizations and wrote for journals close to the peace movement.[97] He began to correspond regularly with the movement's leaders and to offer advice on strategy. In Fried's journal he characterized the peace movement as the "most sublime blossom of European political culture."[98] To Bertha von Suttner, the grande dame of the peace movement, he explained that Kulturgeschichte had made the history of warfare obsolete and that his institute in Leipzig was "designed to contribute to peace and progress among nations."[99]

The pacifists were not accustomed to kind words from German scholars or to their movement's modest advance into the German academy, which followed. The inspiration for the founding of the German Association for International Conciliation, the Verband für internationale Verständigung, in 1911 came from Fried, but the main figures in the organization were a group of academic jurists, among them Emmanuel von Ullmann, Ludwig von Bar, Georg Jellinek, Franz von Liszt, and Walther Schücking.[100] These scholars, most of whom were known as political progressives, had a professional interest in arbitration and international law, but they also believed that a campaign to foster "an understanding of questions of international law" in the German public at large would help counterbalance the Pan-German League and ease tensions born of naval competition and the renewed crisis in North Africa. Their program was broad and innocuous enough to attract some 300 academics and politicians, most of whom were less interested in international law than in encouraging stability in German policy. In this group were some of the most famous scholars in the country, including Max and Alfred Weber, Ernst Troeltsch, Georg Simmel, Adolf Harnack, Paul Natorp, Hermann Cohen, and Alfred Vierkandt.

Lamprecht was a prominent figure in this organization, but his hopes for turning it into an instrument of his own agenda were short-lived.[101] At the behest of Schücking, whom he knew personally, he signed the initial public appeal and then joined the executive committee.[102] His participation was complicated, however, by the difficulty of his relations with some of the other academics. Aside from Max Lehmann (whose politics were more progressive than his historiography), he was the lone historian among the academics. But few of the other scholars had much sympathy for him, and fewer still regarded the *Verband für internationale Verständigung* in the same light as he did, as an expression of the "new cosmopolitanism."[103]

Lamprecht's participation in this organization soon disclosed his isolation, but it was notable nonetheless. His address to the *Verband*'s first national congress in October 1912 was an occasion to restate his position on German policy and to give it a label that became a *topos* of public discussion in the last years of peace. He called for promoting international understanding by means of a "cultural foreign policy [*auswärtige Kulturpolitik*]."[104] He spoke now of the systematic dissemination of culture as the indispensable foundation for economic expansion and the peaceful penetration of political influence abroad: "If any principles of practical politics today can long claim validity, they are that a cultural foreign policy, which is destined to unite and bring peace to the nations, can only rest on competition for the highest moral and intellectual treasures of humanity." The danger was that other countries, particularly the French, British, and Americans, had awakened earlier than Germany to the importance of cultural policy. "We Germans may not remain behind," he said, for "our nation, the nation of philosophers and pedagogues, is called to take over an especially important role."

Lamprecht's address was unobjectionable to this point, but the bulk of it had to do with prerequisites of a cultural foreign policy. And here the historian staked familiar claims. A "cultural foreign policy," he explained, implied "forthwith universal cultural history," for "only a clear understanding of the one allows hope for the fully successful perfection [*Durchbildung*] of the other." He pointed out that cultural foreign policy was inherently a question of cultural exchange, in other words, of "receptions," "renaissances," and "osmoses" among different cultural communities. The politician who aspired to pursue such a policy consequently required the assistance of scholars who could provide "universal knowledge of human cultural development" and of the mechanics that had historically governed cultural exchanges. German historical scholarship, he concluded, had performed great things during national unification in the nineteenth century: "May it intercede no less gloriously and decisively in the movement toward the unity of humanity in the twentieth century!"

Lamprecht delivered this address in Heidelberg, where many in the audience found it an embarrassment. The scholars there who had dealt with him before, like Troeltsch and Max Weber, recognized all the code words and were pained to be associated in any way with Lamprecht's theories of history—whatever the merits of his ideas about foreign policy.[105] The organizers were embarrassed, too, although less by the body of the historian's speech than by an aside that threatened to wreck the whole meeting. In a preface to his remarks on cultural foreign policy, Lamprecht made it clear, in an ill-tempered rebuff to a visiting French ambassador of good will, that returning Alsace-Lorraine to France was nowhere on the agenda of any German foreign policy.[106]

Six months later, Lamprecht repeated the performance when he threw an international congress of historians in London into consternation with menacing talk of war.[107] The incidents in London and Heidelberg suggested the limits of the "new cosmopolitanism." They also suggested the paradox—not to say contradiction—in what George Hallgarten has called Lamprecht's "antinomian universalism," a credo in which internationalism appeared in an intriguing blend with the aggressive pursuit of national interest.[108]

The paradox was deceptive, for it marked deep continuities in the historian's thinking. The evolution of Lamprecht's political position, from the Pan-Germans to the peace movement, had been less dramatic than it seemed. The political assumptions that had attracted him to the Pan-German League twenty years earlier were rooted in his historiography; and they did not change. He continued to believe in the ethnic foundations of history and politics, in the eventual political consolidation of the German nation in Europe, and in the validity of German claims to cultural hegemony and colonial empire. His advocacy of the peace movement, international organization, and the "new cosmopolitanism" was designed to promote these claims peacefully and hence, given the limits of German military power, more effectively than the Pan-Germans' policies of provocation.

These continuities were now reformulated in Lamprecht's concept of a "cultural foreign policy." It called for the employment of what he had called as early as 1904 "the instruments of national spiritual and scholarly power."[109] He reasoned that the triumphant advance of German culture would breed admiration and sympathy in foreign countries for the nation's achievements, at the same time that it nourished pride and self-consciousness among Germans around the globe. Conversely, he believed that such a policy would erode resistance to the peaceful realization of the nation's legitimate political claims, at the same time that it laid the foundations for an international community in which Germany would enjoy preeminence. It was a singular amalgam, which was at least as much to the taste of the patriots in the *Verein für das Deutschtum im Ausland* as it was to the members of the *Verband für internationale Verständigung*.[110]

Lamprecht accommodated arguments and expectations from the full spectrum of imperial German politics with a facility that raises another problem. It is tempting to portray him as the *Realpolitiker*, the cynical imperialist who pursued expansionist policies, as one commentator has written, with "simply a refinement of the methods."[111] To do so, however, is to misrepresent him. As he himself often confessed, he was no politician. His politics were naive and visionary, and he was often blind to the practical implications of the positions he took. His historical vision supplied both his political agenda and the idiosyncratic set of categories in which he understood political processes; concepts like regeneration, fulfillment, community, and idealism guided his political thinking; and the relationship of power to culture was never disingenuous in his mind. The historian thus struck more seasoned politicians as a curious figure, even as they tried to exploit his ideas about a cultural foreign policy.

Talk of cultural regeneration abounded in Germany during the early years of the new century. The topic had become, as Rüdiger vom Bruch has noted, "a modish trend," in which a colorful variety of middle-class reformers indulged with almost religious fervor.[112] The so-called culture movement comprised vegetarians and teetotalers, racists and theosophists, devotees of "ethical culture," and academic proponents of the new *Kulturwissenschaften*. The variations on the theme were legion, but in an era of social and political malaise, most of these reformers understood *Kultur* to mean values connoted by the term *Bildung*; and their concept of "regeneration" implied a program of civic education, a campaign to revitalize these values as the moral foundation of the nation and import them into sectors of German society that had hitherto proved resistant.[113]

Lamprecht was one of the first to study the historical significance of this movement, which he portrayed as a manifestation of the new idealism of *Reizsamkeit*. He was also a loud voice in the same chorus. The capaciousness of his interests—and the leniency with which his vision accommodated incongruous ideas—appealed to reformers of diverse persuasions, who hoped to recruit him to causes like monism, the Wickersdorf movement, the new science of "political anthropology," and—on the urging of Elisabeth Foerster-Nietzsche— to the "Foundation for the Promotion of Atheism."[114] But Lamprecht was not a reliable ally. As his experience with the Pan-Germans, Naumann's group, and the peace movement revealed, his own ideas about cultural regeneration were too geared to his own theories of history to allow more than cursory or casual association with other reformist causes. His significance in the history of the campaign for cultural reform in imperial Germany lay rather in his efforts to direct this campaign toward questions of foreign policy and to bring it to the notice of the country's rulers.

Lamprecht preferred the route of the political independent to the seats of power. Like many academics, he was convinced that his counsel enjoyed the special authority of his scholarship and hence a privileged claim to the attention of the men who ruled. Sending copies of the *Ergänzungsbände* to the Kaiser and chancellor was more than a ritual, for much of the political manifesto that these volumes contained was addressed to these men. The supplements were the first in a stream of political documents, speeches, and articles that the historian dispatched to Bernhard von Bülow, of whom he had a high, if credulous regard.[115] These documents, as he explained in early 1906, were to demonstrate what "a historian of my views can infer from the current situation about the on-going political education of the nation."[116]

Bülow's encouragement was confined to bland praise for the historian's ability to instill "a more profound understanding of our situation."[117] Lamprecht was nonetheless heartened enough to place himself in the service of the short-lived parliamentary coalition that bore the chancellor's name. The result was a series of speeches and articles in which Bülow could, he admitted, "find many of my own thoughts in a new light."[118] Closer observers than Bülow could also detect traces of the broader concerns that the historian shared with other cultural reformers, as well as signs of where his German History then stood. The issue at hand, Lamprecht now argued, was the "politicization of society."[119] This was not the most fortunate term he could have chosen, for he had to insist that it did not mean the submission of the government to parliamentary control. "Politicization" implied instead the "organization of society," specifically the modernization of the forces opposed to clericalism and socialism. The challenge, Lamprecht explained, was to reconcile the "fundamental conditions of political life," which had emerged with Subjectivism at the end of the eighteenth century and were embodied in the reforms of Stein. "Freedom of the individual personality" was one of these "fundamental conditions"; the "organization of the masses" was the other. The historian's leap to the twentieth century was swift, but it required only identifying the liberals in Bülow's bloc with the one principle and the Conservatives with the other.

Lamprecht was gratified by the brief notoriety that his commentary brought him, but he had reason to question the wisdom of such direct engagement in partisan issues. He had no real platform or allies, nor was he well situated, in Leipzig, to proffer counsel in Berlin. His efforts on behalf of Bülow's financial reform in 1908 proved futile, and shortly afterward the parliamentary coalition that he had characterized in such extravagant terms collapsed.[120] In the meantime, however, he had begun to explore another political avenue that lay closer to his professional concerns and promised more tangible rewards. He discovered that access to power led through culture.

The mediator was his former patron. Friedrich Althoff's career was dedicated to the political utility of culture; and no official was more alive to the potential assets offered to German foreign policy by the towering prestige of German scholarship. Between 1903 and 1906, on the eve of his retirement, he introduced a number of international exchange programs—for scholars, teachers, and students—that were calculated to exploit this potential.[121] Althoff's ideas were well known to Lamprecht, and they accorded with the historian's own thinking about the civic mission of German scholarship. Lamprecht had himself played a role in the most spectacular triumph of Althoff's strategy, at the St. Louis Exposition in 1904. Two years later, he approached Althoff with a plan that would "without fail be of benefit to modern German policy." A condensation of his German History, he wrote, translated into English and French for distribution abroad, would provide "our policy" with the "strong literary support abroad" that it required.[122]

Although nothing came of this project, it helped lay a basis for a proposition that Lamprecht put to Althoff in a long interview in the summer of 1908. The historian reported on the success of the campaign to found the Institute for Cultural and Universal History in Leipzig. He also emphasized the political significance of this undertaking. The new institute that he envisaged would, he claimed, result in "a significant strengthening of German intellectual influence" by introducing foreign scholars to forms of instruction that reflected "specific German intellectual development."[123] Althoff was by now retired, but he was still a pivotal figure in the bureaucratic network in the capital, so his endorsement of Lamprecht's request for federal financial support opened doors. In November Lamprecht lectured in Berlin in support of Bülow's financial reform. There he met with the chancellor, who rewarded all his efforts with the subsidy for the Institute of Cultural and Universal History.

The historian's tour of the capital in November 1908 included another important stop, at the office of the federal state secretary of the interior. He and its occupant had not been in contact for more than thirty years, since they had left Schulpforta and then studied briefly at the same time in Leipzig.[124] The immediate topic of Lamprecht's interview with Theobald von Bethmann Hollweg was the subsidy for the Leipzig institute. The discussion soon turned to broader questions of history, culture, and policy; and it continued in the course of an extended correspondence over the next six and a half years.[125] The bond between the two men was based on more than shared personal experience and the perception of each that the other might be of practical use. The affection, although not free of mutual flattery, was genuine on both sides.[126] Lamprecht's vision, confidence, and sense of dynamism complemented Bethmann's remarkable blend of calculation and melancholy, caution and fantasy. In the historian's company, the minister appeared to let down his reserve. "It was astounding," Lamprecht wrote of one of their subsequent interviews, how "he approached me with trust and opened up to me inwardly."[127]

Bethmann's elevation to the chancellorship in July 1909 changed the stakes, if not the dynamics, of the relationship. In the conviction that Bethmann was, as the historian later put it, Germany's "first chancellor of intellect" and a representative of the new idealism, Lamprecht undertook a campaign to instruct the new chancellor in the arts of political heroism and to instruct the public in its virtues.[128] Six months after Bethmann took office, the historian descried "an undoubtedly strongly historically [*sic*] developed intelligence" in Bethmann's "striving constantly to comprehend things in the broadest context, in the strong current of their accumulation [*Auflauf*]" and "in their own inherent principles."[129] Observers like Franz Mehring, who scoffed at Lamprecht's "genuflection" before the chancellor, were uninitiated into the language that the two men shared.[130] "What you say about the modern role of history is certainly very apt," came the response from Berlin. And "what you said about me," Bethmann continued, "accurately describes my conception of the ideal mission of a statesman, if not what I am now."[131]

These words were well chosen to encourage Lamprecht's belief that a kindred soul now ruled in Berlin and that he himself was linked in a special relationship to the highest councils of state. The thought that he had become the confidante and intellectual advisor to the chancellor complimented his sense of his own importance and lent an air of pathos to the awkward discretion with which he drew attention to his "fairly intimate connections."[132] He was thus flattered to be an instrument of Bethmann's domestic agenda during the debates over the reform of the Prussian suffrage in 1910.[133]

Lamprecht was not entirely innocent, for he expected in return that Beth-mann Hollweg would be an instrument of another agenda. In the first years of Bethmann's tenure in office, this agenda featured matters of academic reform, primarily the effort to promote Lamprecht's own institute as a model for restruc-turing research and instruction in the humanities at German universities. So, for Bethmann's instruction, the historian emphasized the political ramifications of this undertaking. Late in 1910 he drew the chancellor's attention to the "experiments in Saxony" and explained that modern civic education demanded the "transformation [Umbildung] of humanistic instruction" on a "historical-psychological" basis.[134]

A year later the historian prepared a long memorandum in which he addressed this theme again, now with accents that reflected the evolution of his interests during his tenure as rector in Leipzig.[135] He portrayed academic reform as a matter of national urgency. The conclusion had found acceptance everywhere, he reported, that a general reform of scholarship, the creation of "new forms and institutions," was indispensable. The expectation was rife in other countries "that secure and successful progress in new scholarly directions"—and here he emphasized "both methods and scholarly institutions"—"must proceed from Germany"; the nation would otherwise renounce "an essential and effective and specially legitimate means of participating in the development of humanity." The most urgent needs were to reform seminars and institutes according to the Leipzig model and to coordinate the administration of higher education—specifically to enlarge existing faculty organizations and consultative bodies to include universities throughout German-speaking Europe.

This memorandum was the basis of a long interview between Bethmann and Lamprecht in Berlin in January 1912.[136] The chancellor was in a lugubrious mood, for dramatic socialist gains in federal elections were at that time com-pounding the depression brought on by attacks from Conservatives and Pan-Germans against his diplomacy in the Moroccan crisis. In these circumstances, Bethmann could generate but mild interest in the reorganization of the German academy, and he suggested passing the historian's proposals on to the Prussian ministry of culture (where they could expect little sympathy).[137] The chancellor preferred to ruminate on general questions of domestic and foreign policy, and he was interested in Lamprecht's impressions of the peace movement, as well as his thoughts about "a more powerful cultural policy for Germany externally."[138]

It would be an exaggeration to say that Lamprecht emerged from this inter-view with a mandate from Bethmann Hollweg, just as it was an exaggeration for the historian to describe the chancellor shortly later, to Fried, as a "Bundesgenos-se of the peace movement."[139] The interview nonetheless marked the beginning of a new political role for Lamprecht, as well as greater official interest in the kinds of internationalist causes in which he had become active. Although his influence was much more limited than he himself believed, there was henceforth less pathos in the historian's claims to speak with the chancellor's authority about the importance of culture as an instrument of foreign policy. He became a

"*Vertrauensmann*" of sorts, who furnished information and advice to the chancellery about the organizations with which he had become associated. He also cleared at least some of his activities in Berlin and withdrew from membership in one international organization, the *Office central des Nationalités*, when the foreign office concluded that a "certain mistrust" was "appropriate."[140]

Lamprecht now became a minor participant in the fierce debates that raged over foreign and military policy in Germany during the last years of peace.[141] The controversy accompanied the passage through the Reichstag of two enormous arms bills, and it featured a nationalist fronde that the Pan-Germans spearheaded against Bethmann Hollweg's government.[142] Stripped of its connections to his historiography, Lamprecht's concept of a "cultural foreign policy" corresponded to the position that the beleaguered chancellor staked out in defense of his own cautious diplomacy and his efforts at conciliation with Britain.

The historian's activities coalesced with other facets of a campaign to deflect the attacks of the patriots on the chancellor's integrity and political competence. Lamprecht's views were consistent with those of a number of publicists close to the chancellor—including Paul Rohrbach, Hans Plehn, and Bethmann's advisor Kurt Riezler—who were attempting to lay the intellectual foundations for a "liberal" or "ethical" imperialism, whose object was to be, as Plehn formulated it, a "German world-policy without war."[143] Like Lamprecht's, their strategy recommended "moral conquests," the peaceful German penetration of foreign lands by means of schools, scholarly exchanges, and cultural contacts abroad.[144] The strategy also put a premium on the so-called *Auslandsvereine* or private friendship societies, like the German-Chinese Association and the German Committee for the Near East, which emerged in droves on the eve of the war with the quiet encouragement of the German foreign office.[145]

While Lamprecht joined several of these societies, his interests and energy were principally engaged in providing Bethmann's position, as he understood it, with the most compelling justification he could conceive, the imprimatur of cultural history.[146] He renewed his call for a "new idealism" and republished most of the second and third *Ergänzungsbände* with but minor modifications, evidently in the belief that the chancellor's idealism comported with the Pan-German coloration of the original volumes.[147] The cloying portrait that Lamprecht published in 1913 of the "modern idealist" who sat on the imperial throne was less to the taste of the Pan-Germans, who had drawn the Kaiser's "personal rule" into the scope of their attack; but the book was part of the same campaign, and passages in it rested on "intimate information" that the chancellor had fed to the author.[148] Of greater significance in this context was Lamprecht's address in Heidelberg to the *Verband für internationale Verständigung* in October 1912, for it injected the term "cultural foreign policy" into the debate. The frequency with which the address was reprinted in the press—in the semi-official *Deutsche Revue*, among other places—suggested that both the term and the concept had the chancellor's endorsement.[149]

The historian was dissatisfied, however, with the role of semi-official propagandist for the regime and with the regime's indifferent pursuit of the policies he had prescribed. He believed that his organizational talents could be put to better use. For all the consternation it had caused in Heidelberg, the connection between cultural foreign policy and universal history remained axiomatic in his mind. He was convinced that he himself had laid the academic foundations for such a policy in his own institute in Leipzig, where young scholars from abroad trained in the appropriate methodologies alongside historians from Germany and returned home "filled with good will, frequently with great enthusiasm for Germany."[150]

Lamprecht's discontents surfaced in a memorandum that he submitted to "the first chancellor of the new idealism" in May 1913.[151] Its theme was the deficiency of German policy. The historian pointed out that west European nations had already turned a "positive, creative cultural foreign policy" into "one of the most important instruments of their whole foreign policy," while the process was only in its incipient stages in Germany. To close the gap, it was essential to define "a really complete program" on the basis of scholarly study of "systems of cultural foreign policy." The forces to undertake this study, he noted, were "available in rich quantity" from the ranks of the "middle generation of scholars"; and he appended a list of ten such scholars from the ranks of his own students and friends—a group whose expertise stretched from the Orient to the Balkans and who needed, as he assured Bethmann, "only to be harnessed."

Bethmann's response came in late June, as the Reichstag entered the final stages of deliberation over his government's second *Wehrvorlage* in as many years.[152] The response was cautious, but it was couched in terms that he knew would appeal to Lamprecht, who was unlikely in any event to be discouraged by the incongruity between its contents and its timing. "I am, like you, convinced of the importance, indeed the necessity of a cultural foreign policy," declared the German chancellor. He lamented that Germans underestimated the "finer means" of diplomacy—what the French were calling the "imperialism of the idea." To repair the problem and to conduct a "cultural policy in the grand style" required, he wrote, that the "spiritual leaders of modern Germany" generate the "support and cooperation of the educated sectors" of society. "The world-political future of our nation will thank you"—and here he meant Lamprecht personally—"for everything that you do to excite and encourage" this support.

Receipt of this *wunderschönen* letter encouraged Lamprecht now to venture into Berlin's bureaucratic politics in an effort to build organizational support for his own concept of a cultural foreign policy.[153] The effort was handicapped from the start, however, for it demanded political skills beyond those he had practiced in Dresden. The fact that his principal allies in this venture were a group of engineers itself indicated the nature of the problem.

Lamprecht had known Conrad Matschoss for several years. Matschoss was best known as the author of popular and scholarly studies on the history of the steam engine. He taught the history of technology at the technical university in

Berlin, where he was also deputy director of the Association of German Engineers, that profession's major interest group.[154] In June 1913, at the same time that Bethmann's letter arrived, this organization convened in Leipzig for its annual congress; and at Matschoss' invitation, Lamprecht delivered an address. After the historian had lectured the assembled engineers about the coming "idealism of economic life and technology," he asked Matschoss, a widely traveled man who had developed a worldwide network of contacts, to help him found an organization whose goal would be to promote "German economic exports by cultivating esteem for [German] culture" abroad.[155]

Emphasizing the "practical" economic motif in the venture was not to Lamprecht's own taste, but it was a price worth paying for the support of Matschoss and the other directors of the Association of German Engineers. The headquarters of this organization in Berlin became the center of a campaign in the fall of 1913 to interest other groups in Lamprecht's plan. The difficulty was that the historian's conception of a cultural foreign policy comprehended a vast catalogue of undertakings, which threatened to collide with the interests and activities of dozens of other organizations, both public and private. Under the rubric of promoting "the spiritual export of knowledge," he hoped to coordinate the operations of German business and cultural organizations in foreign lands, to support German schools abroad, to attract foreigners to institutions of higher learning in Germany, to arrange exchange programs for scholars and tours for German artists abroad, to oversee the scholarly study of German communities abroad, and—certainly not least—to foster pedagogical reform at home and abroad.[156] The initial signs were nonetheless hopeful. The economist Robert Hoeniger, Lamprecht's old comrade-in-arms in the war with Below, joined the campaign as a representative of the organization with the most reason for concern, the Association for Germandom Abroad, whose principal occupation was raising money for German schools in foreign countries. More heartening, however, was the interest shown in the project by the German government.

Bethmann Hollweg had been more reticent than Lamprecht about their ties. Aside from a few officials in the chancellery, such as Kurt Riezler and Arnold Wahnschaffe, few people in the federal government were privy to the contents of the interviews or correspondence between the two.[157] In August 1913, the chancellor introduced Lamprecht, albeit indirectly, to a broader circle of his colleagues.[158] In a circular to the federal secretaries of the interior, the treasury, and foreign affairs, Bethmann made it clear that his remarks to Lamprecht about the need for a cultural foreign policy were more than cosmetic. "Projects and organizations whose goal is to make foreign culture accessible to Germans, or conversely to promote German cultural life abroad," he told his colleagues, "are not, in my estimation, everywhere experiencing the appreciation and support they deserve." The moral and economic rewards of a cultural foreign policy (and he used Lamprecht's term) were nowhere more apparent than in China, where, he noted, many cultural organizations were already at work. The chancellor called for the "consolidation and common development" of all these forces, and he instructed his colleagues to consult with one another and with the "agencies, societies, scholars, and businessmen concerned."

Although the antecedents of this circular reached far beyond Lamprecht, Bethmann clearly regarded the historian as someone to be consulted. In the other bureaucratic offices, however, the circular encountered little but skepticism and—particularly in the foreign office—anxiety over jurisdictional incursions from rival agencies; so when a new memorandum arrived from Leipzig in December with a plan for a "Society to Promote a German Cultural Foreign Policy," the chancellor himself broke the bureaucratic inertia.[159] His office first authorized Lamprecht to publish in the *Vossische Zeitung*, the so-called June letter, in which Bethmann had written of the "importance, indeed the necessity of a cultural foreign policy."[160] Then Wahnschaffe, the undersecretary in the chancellery, coaxed reluctant officials in the foreign office to talk to the historian.[161]

The interview, which took place on 23 December, laid bare the practical difficulties of Lamprecht's plan.[162] He proposed that his new society encompass three different sorts of activities: it was to serve as a clearinghouse among existing cultural organizations, promote German language courses abroad, and sponsor the study of the history of Germandom abroad. His interlocutors were not impressed. They pronounced the whole project impractical and ill conceived, although they objected particularly to those aspects of it that intruded into their office's jurisdiction over German elementary and secondary schools abroad.

Lamprecht left the interview cheered nonetheless; he had heard only what he wanted to hear. The foreign office's position on the foreign schools allowed him to unveil the plan's vital core to Bethmann (if not to Matschoss). "The spiritual expansion of our nation around the world," he wrote in late December to the chancellor, was an "educational question of the highest rank."[163] It had to do with the German academy. "If German influence is to have an impact on the mentality of the spiritual leaders of other countries, it is necessary to develop this influence above all in the realm of the nation's most advanced instruction in history, and that means at the universities." The goal was a "new *Weltbild*," a "universal conception," which could be achieved in the "humanistic institutes of our universities"—if, he added, these institutes were "improved [*fortgebildet*] or founded for this purpose." Least any doubts linger, the historian suggested the expenditure of 180,000 marks annually to establish a Kaiser-Wilhelm Institute for Cultural and Universal History in Berlin.[164] He did not have to nominate a director.

The historian was in euphoria when he submitted this remarkable proposal. As he had anticipated, publication of his letter from the chancellor had created a sensation in the press; and his public association with Bethmann lent credibility to his pretensions to exert influence in the highest councils of state. In these circumstances it was easy for him to conclude, as he wrote to Dove at New Year's in 1914, that "my divergent conception of history is beginning to dominate [*beherrschen*] part of our politics."[165] The completion of his life's agenda, the dominion of the new history in the citadel of the old, beckoned in the Kaiser's name.

The reverie quickly dissolved. Like many others before him, Bethmann Hollweg learned of the hazards of association with Lamprecht. He had authorized publication of the "June letter" but not the historian's gloss, which claimed that the letter (which Riezler had drafted) presented a "personal portrait" of the chancellor, as well as evidence of his "acute thinking" and "moderation honed by experience." The ensuing controversy in the press predictably resurrected the Pan-Germans' charge that Bethmann was too weak and muddle-headed to hold office. The term "culture-babble [*Kulturgeschwätz*]" typified the tone of editorial commentary in the right-wing press.[166] Lamprecht's "*Renommage mit Kanzlerbriefen*" (as he himself described it) and his relentless importunities, of which the proposal for the institute was merely the most extravagant, cost him the respect and good will of Wahnschaffe and Riezler in the chancellery, who joined the foreign office in counseling Bethmann against further encouragement (to say nothing of financial support) for the historian.[167]

The final blow to Lamprecht's standing in official circles came from his colleagues in the profession. The publication of the "June letter" came as an unhappy surprise to a group of historians who had tried for years to forget about Lamprecht. "Long live tragic irony!" wrote Marcks to Meinecke when he learned of the link between Lamprecht and the chancellor.[168] In January Max Lenz published a backhanded slap, in which he endorsed the idea of a cultural foreign policy but, in a clear allusion to Lamprecht's prominence in the venture, warned historians to be mindful of a "sense of their mission" and not to become "dumb."[169] When Bethmann consulted the Berlin Academy of Sciences about Lamprecht's request for support, Dietrich Schäfer drafted a report that declared Lamprecht's influence on students to be "confusing and misleading."[170] Several weeks later another professional indictment arrived in the chancellery, when Hans Delbrück sent over a copy of Arley Show's withering assessment of Lamprecht's institute in Leipzig.[171]

Bethmann's response to Lamprecht now turned "dilatory," and the other agencies followed his lead.[172] The historian's call for an institute of universal history was scattered for burial, along with a proposal for stipends for the Leipzig institute, in the files of several agencies.[173] The foreign office became "very reserved" and ignored Lamprecht's efforts in favor of the *Auslandsvereine*, like the new German-Turkish Association, whose leaders were better known and whose goals were better defined.[174]

The government's decision to back away condemned Lamprecht's efforts to futility. In early February 1914, when he and Matschoss convened a meeting of businessmen and politicians in Berlin to discuss the plans for their new organization, no officials attended and an institute for universal history was nowhere on the agenda.[175] In addition to the representatives of several friendship societies, the meeting included Hermann Paasche and Richard Eickhoff from the Reichstag, Otto Hoetzsch, Ernst Jäckh, and Otto von Hentig, the chairman of the

Association for Germandom Abroad. These men were seasoned enough to recognize the snub from the government. They were also interested in practical, business-oriented results and found much to criticize in Lamprecht's amorphous, unfunded project, which now comprised a clearinghouse to coordinate and distribute information to cultural organizations already working abroad, a proposal to promote German language instruction and traveling lectures, and a society to study the history of Germandom abroad. After protracted discussion it was, as one delegate commented, difficult to "get a clear picture of how the project will have an impact."

Lamprecht was beginning to share the doubts himself. He had not been open with all his colleagues about his own ultimate designs, and as the prospects for an institute for universal history receded before the more practical challenges of putting the organization together, he began to lose interest in the project. He was, as he wrote to one of his colleagues, a representative of a "specially spiritual standpoint in cultural foreign policy."[176] Close readers of his manifesto on behalf of the new organization, which appeared in April in the *Frankfurter Zeitung*, could recognize the signs.[177] Here he deprecated the role of economic calculation in cultural foreign policy. It was understandable, he wrote, that the "economic element" would initially preponderate during the "transition from a purely economic foreign policy to a cultural foreign policy." Now, however, in the "decisive moment," when a "true cultural policy" was emerging, he insisted that the "spiritual movement" "must receive its due."

Lamprecht withdrew to Leipzig as a secretariat in Berlin, funded in part by a gift from Mevissen's daughter, oversaw the tedious effort to constitute the several components of the Society to Promote a Cultural Foreign Policy.[178] Incoherence continued to plague the campaign, and the historian's involvement at a distance only exacerbated the problem. At his urging, but against the advice of his collaborators in Berlin, one component, a Society for the Study of Germandom Abroad, was hurriedly called to life in April in order to indicate progress.[179] This society was the only tangible product of Lamprecht's efforts on behalf of a cultural foreign policy. Questions about its mission, funding, and its relationship to the broader organization (and to the Association for Germandom Abroad) remained unclarified when, four months later, it dissolved in the circumstances of war.

Karl Lamprecht's immersion into high politics was little more than a curiosity in the history of the origins of the First World War. Although his campaign has earned him a prominent place in the annals of German cultural foreign policy in the twentieth century, he had no discernible impact on German policy or on the forces that were building for war in Germany and elsewhere. He owed his brief prominence to the fortunes of his acquaintance with the chancellor, whose sympathy for his ideas on policy was probably genuine but limited by powerful political constraints. Lamprecht's ideas on politics were guileless and eccentric. They brought elements of conflicting traditions into an uneasy marriage; and they were anchored in his historiography, which prescribed an agenda that made political action difficult on any but his own terms and antagonized those whose political views were more conventional. The historian's sojourn in politics thus foundered in circumstances that recalled the defeat of his campaigns to revolutionize the profession and to restructure the academy. Before he could ponder the lessons of his repeated failures, however, regeneration beckoned a last time.

Notes

1. Nipperdey, *Deutsche Geschichte 1866–1918*, 592.
2. Paulsen, *Universitäten*, 325.
3. Nipperdey, *Deutsche Geschichte 1866–1918*, 591; see also Ringer, *Mandarins*, esp. 113–27; vom Bruch, "Kulturstaat," 63–102.
4. The Bible on this theme is Rüdiger vom Bruch's, *Wissenschaft, Politik und öffentliche Meinung*. See also his "Historiker und Nationalökonomen im Wilhelminischen Deutschland," 105–50; McClelland, *German Historians and England*; Schenk, *Die deutsch-englische Rivalität*.
5. For the literature on the patriotic societies see Roger Chickering, *We Men Who Feel Most German: A Cultural Study of the Pan-German League, 1886–1914* (London, 1984). The statistics I compiled in this study are too fragmentary to support more than tentative generalizations about the preferences of German *Ordinarien* in the patriotic societies. Of the twenty-five localities I used for comparison, only four— Berlin, Breslau, Leipzig, and Munich—were university towns. Cf. vom Bruch, "Historiker und Nationalökonomen," 143–45; vom Bruch, *Wissenschaft*, 428–32.
6. KE, 67; DG, 11: 362.
7. KE, 26, 60, 68; DG, 11: 361.
8. NL Lamprecht (Korr. 59), Lamprecht to Hugo Lamprecht, Pforta, 1.9.70; Schönebaum, "Verbundenheit," 36; KE, 15.
9. Weymar, *Selbstverständnis*, 204.
10. NL Lamprecht (Korr. 59), Lamprecht to Hugo Lamprecht, Bonn, 10.7.80; LW, 27–28.
11. Noorden to Sybel, 5.1.80, in Noorden, 610–11.
12. Engelberg, "Methodenstreit," 140–42.
13. NL Lamprecht (Korr. 25), Franz Grouven to Lamprecht, Euskirchen, 12.2.87; (Korr. 47), Lamprecht to Sering, Bonn, 13.2.87.
14. NL Lamprecht (Korr. 59), Lamprecht to Hugo Lamprecht, Bonn, 14.11.80; NL Bernheim, Lamprecht to Bernheim, n.p., 23.6.92; NL Liesegang, Lamprecht to Liesegang, Leipzig, 8.7.96; LW, 148.
15. See Hoffmeister, 15.
16. Hellpach, *Wirken*, 201–3.
17. Ratzel was active in the Colonial Society, Seeliger in the School Association, and Marcks in the Eastern Marches Society. Buttmann, 81; Kötzschke, "Seeliger," 495; cf. Chickering, *We Men*, 144.
18. Ibid., esp. 44–73.
19. Smith, *Sciences of Culture*, 203.
20. Schorn-Schütte, "Lamprecht und die internationale Geschichtsschreibung," 439, n. 70.
21. NL Althoff (B Nr. 108/1), Lamprecht to Althoff, Leipzig, 24.1.94; NL Treitschke, Lamprecht to Treitschke, Leipzig, 9.12.94; cf. DG, 1 (2): v, vii.
22. NL Lamprecht (Korr. 25), Wislicenus to Lamprecht, Leipzig, 27.6.93, 9.7.93;

(Korr. 31), Howard to Lamprecht, Leipzig, 10.1.93; (Korr. 37), Meyer to Lamprecht, Leipzig, 28.11.93; (Kr. 10), Liesegang to Lamprecht, Berlin, 18.1.94. See also Otto Bonhard, *Geschichte des Alldeutschen Verbandes* (Leipzig and Berlin, 1920), 180–81; Hans Krause, "Die alldeutsche Geschichtsschreibung vor dem ersten Weltkrieg," in Streisand, *Studien*, 2: 202–3; Chickering, "Weber and Schäfer"; Hoffmeister, 21, 96; Schultz, "Moral Force," 80.

23. DG, 3: 297; DG, 4: 413. Other instances abounded. See DG, 3: 366, 384; DG, 4: 75, 137, 141, 418–19, 474.

24. DG, 5: 258; *cf.* Hoffmeister, 52.

25. DG, 3: 227. Not that he ignored the problem. In one passage he deplored the "Einströmen französischer Wörter" into the Flemish language in the fifteenth century. DG, 4: 137; *cf.* EB, 1: 266. See also Bonhard, 136. On the language of radical nationalism, see Chickering, *We Men*, 74–101.

26. E.g., *Alte und neue Richtungen*, 2–3.

27. NL Treitschke (7), Lamprecht to Treitschke, Leipzig, 17.10.93; Lamprecht, "Historikertag und Umsturzvorlage," *Zukunft*, 11 (1895): 203–4; *cf.* Griss, 35.

28. NL Althoff (B Nr. 108/1), Lamprecht to Althoff, Leipzig, 3.4.94.

29. NL Lamprecht (L 25), Tagebuchnotizen, Reise nach Oesterreich, October-November 1894; *cf.* Rupert Hobiger, "Oesterreich bei Karl Lamprecht," Ph.D. dissertation (Vienna, 1939).

30. NL Lamprecht (Korr. 15), Buchholz to Lamprecht, Walchensee, 5.9.06; (Korr. 18), Daenell to Lamprecht, Berlin, 29.11.12; (Korr. 56), Zwiedineck-Südenhorst to Lamprecht, Graz, 24.7.95; NL Liesegang, Lamprecht to Liesegang, Leipzig, 24.5.98; *Bericht über die vierte Versammlung deutscher Historiker zu Innsbruck*, 5–8; Lyon, *Pirenne*, 110–11; LW, 332, 423.

31. NL Lamprecht (V 1), Verein deutscher Studenten to Lamprecht, Leipzig, 31.12.92; Lamprecht, "Zum Gedächtnis Heinrichs von Treitschke," *Zukunft*, 16 (1896): 108–12; "Eine Festrede," *Zukunft*, 26 (1899): 137–43; Schönebaum, "Unausgeführte Vorhaben," 119; LW, 235, 436, 518.

32. NL Lamprecht (Korr. 58), Lamprecht to Hugo Lamprecht, Leipzig, 5.4.95; (Korr. 67a), Deutscher Ostmarkenverein to Lamprecht, Berlin, n.d. [early 1895]; NL Grimm, Lamprecht to Grimm, Leipzig, 28.4.96. The historian evidently saw no conflict between membership in the Ostmarkenverein and the Jablinowski Society.

33. NL Harden, Lamprecht to Harden, 16.2.00; LW, 422; Lamprecht, "Die Entwicklung des wirtschaftlichen und geistigen Horizonts unserer Nation," in Gustav Schmoller et al., eds., *Handels- und Machtpolitik: Reden und Aufsätze im Auftrage der Freien Vereinigung für Flottenvorträge* (Stuttgart, 1990), 1: 39–62; *cf.* Wolfgang Marienfeld, *Wissenschaft und Schlachtflottenbau in Deutschland 1897–1906* (Frankfurt, 1957).

34. NL Lamprecht (Korr. 33), Lehr to Lamprecht, Berlin, 6.3.95.

35. See Lamprecht, "Die Gesellschaft Jesu," *Zukunft*, 10 (1895): 449; vom Bruch, *Wissenschaft*, 79.

36. Schmoller, "Zur Würdigung," 29–30; Schumann, 52; Dallek, 21; *cf.* Chickering, *We Men*, 62–69. Unlike the Pan-Germans, Lamprecht never regarded Bismarck as a symbol of opposition. His reverence for the chancellor survived a brief but strained visit to Friedrichsruh in 1895, when Bismarck objected to his ideas about alternatives to the settlement of 1866. NL Lamprecht (Munich), Walter Goetz to Marianne Lamprecht, Tübingen, 20.4.18.

37. LW, 520.

38. DB, 2,2: 737.

39. EB, 2,2: 469, 484, 509.

40. Ibid., 490–92.

41. Ibid., 539–40.
42. Ibid., 202.
43. Viikari, *Krise*, 263; Hoffmeister, 74, 111.
44. EB, 2,2: 705; *cf.* EB, 1: 471.
45. Hoffmeister, 120.
46. Schultz, "Moral Force," 169.
47. Schultz is not the only one to do so. See Hoffmeister, 49, 80, 112; *cf.* Viikari, *Krise*, 412.
48. EB, 2,2: 44.
49. Viikari, *Krise*, 260; Hoffmeister, 77.
50. EB, 2,2: 737.
51. Ibid., 166.
52. Ibid., 166–67.
53. Ibid., 15; DG, 11: 352; *cf.* Viikari, *Krise*, 403; Hoffmeister, 22.
54. LW, 422–23.
55. NL Lamprecht (Korr. 28), Hasse to Lamprecht, Leipzig, 2.1.97; (Korr.35), Langhans to Lamprecht, Gotha, 16.1.02; (Korr. 24), Julius Goebel to Lamprecht, Cambridge, Mass., 24.7.07; *cf.* Chickering, *We Men*, 74–101.
56. Ibid., esp. 214–18; Bonhard, 181; *cf.* EB, 1: 147.
57. See Peter Theiner, *Sozialer Liberalismus und deutsche Weltpolitik: Friedrich Naumann im Wilhelminischen Deutschland (1860–1919)* (Baden-Baden, 1983); Dieter Düding, *Der Nationalsoziale Verein 1896–1903: Der gescheiterte Versuch einer parteipolitischen Synthese von Nationalismus, Sozialismus und Liberalismus* (Munich and Vienna, 1972); Richard Nürnberger, "Imperialismus, Sozialismus und Christentum bei Friedrich Naumann," HZ, 152 (1950): 525–48.
58. NDB, 16: 434–35.
59. NL Lamprecht (Korr. 36), Max Maurenbrecher to Lamprecht, Schöneberg, 9.1.02, 19.3.02; LW, 466.
60. NL Lamprecht (Korr. 39), Naumann to Lamprecht, Schöneberg, 21.3.02.
61. LW, 467; Theiner, 95.
62. The story had an interesting sequel. Maurenbrecher's job disappeared in 1903. Lamprecht thereupon made him a generous loan and became one of the first in a series of scholars to support Maurenbrecher financially. NL Lamprecht (Korr. 36), Max Maurenbrecher to Lamprecht, Schöneberg, 23.7.03; NL Harden, Lamprecht to Harden, Leipzig, 24.7.03; *cf.* Dieter Fricke, "Nationalsoziale Versuche zur Förderung der Krise der Sozialdemokratie: Zum Briefwechsel zwischen Max Maurenbrecher und Friedrich Naumann 1910–1913," *Beiträge zur Geschichte der Arbeiterbewegung*, 25 (1983): 538–39.
63. *Cf.* EB, 2,2: 399.
64. Düding, 73; *cf.* Chickering, *Imperial Germany*, 248–52.
65. EB, 2,2: 588, 626–27, 693.
66. NL Lamprecht (L 29), Amerikareise, Tagebuchblätter 1904, e.g., 5.9.04, where the remarks are more belligerent than in the published version; *cf. Americana*, 44–45; Chickering, *We Men*, 88–89.
67. *New York Times*, 9 October 1904.
68. *Americana*, 84; *cf.* DG, 11: 703.
69. *Americana*, 37.
70. Ibid., 64, 105, 128.
71. Ibid., 99.
72. Ibid., 38, 85.
73. Ibid., 146.
74. Ibid., 83.

75. Ibid., 92.
76. Ibid., 5–6.
77. Lamprecht, *Freiheit und Volkstum: Worte zur heutigen politischen Lage* (Cologne, 1906); Lamprecht, "Nationalismus und Universalismus in Deutschland," *Dokumente des Fortschritts*, 1 (1907–1908): 5–10; Lamprecht, "Europäische Expansion in Vergangenheit und Gegenwart," *Geschichte der Neuzeit, Ullsteins Weltgeschichte*, vol. 6 (Berlin, 1910), 599–625; DG, 8: 60–61; *Americana*, 131.
78. StA Dresden, VB 10281/103, Aus einer Rede von Professor Dr. LL.D. Lamprecht vor der Leipziger Studentschaft, December 1907.
79. *Freiheit und Volkstum*, 11.
80. NL Lamprecht (Korr. 6), Lamprecht to Beck, Leipzig, 23.4.14.
81. StA Dresden, VB 10281/103, Aus einer Rede von Professor Dr. LL.D. Lamprecht vor der Leipziger Studentschaft, December 1907.
82. See MG, 103; *cf.* Griss, 119.
83. "Nationalismus und Universalismus," 10.
84. DG, 8: 60–61.
85. *Americana*, 8.
86. DG, 8: 501.
87. StA Dresden, VB 10281/103, Aus einer Rede von Professor Dr. LL.D. Lamprecht vor der Leipziger Studentschaft, December 1907.
88. "Nationalismus und Universalismus," 10.
89. "Europäische Expansion," 621.
90. NL Bücher, Lamprecht to Bücher, 4.8.10 (copy in NL Lamprecht (Korr. 14); NL Lamprecht (Korr. 21), Lamprecht to Egger, Leipzig, 23.5.14; Lamprecht, "Rede des antretenden Rektors," 36.
91. NL Althoff (B Nr. 108/1), Lamprecht to Althoff, 8.2.07.
92. StA Dresden, VB 10281/103, Aus einer Rede von Professor Dr. LL.D. Lamprecht vor der Leipziger Studentschaft, December 1907. Lamprecht's advocacy of this diplomatic alignment probably owed something to the cordial relationship he established in the United States with the historian, James Bryce, who in 1906 was appointed British ambassador to Washington. NL Lamprecht (Korr. 31). Bryce to Lamprecht, London, 21.2.05; *cf. Americana*, 83.
93. Herbert Schönebaum, "Karl Lamprechts Mühen um innere und äussere Kulturpolitik," WaG, 15 (1955): 143–44; LW, 572–74.
94. Roger Chickering, "War, Peace, and Social Mobilization in Imperial Germany: Patriotic Societies, the Peace Movement, and Socialist Labor," in Charles Chatfield and Peter van den Dungen, eds., *Peace Movements and Political Cultures* (Knoxville, 1988), 3–22. On the history of the peace movement see, in addition to my *Imperial Germany and a World Without War*, Karl Holl, *Pazifismus in Deutschland* (Frankfurt am Main, 1988); Dieter Riesenberger, *Geschichte der Friedensbewegung in Deutschland: Von den Anfängen bis 1933* (Göttingen, 1985).
95. "Europäische Expansion," 621; *cf.* Lamprecht, *Die Nation und die Friedensbewegung* (Berlin, 1914).
96. NL Lamprecht (Korr. 35), Lamprecht to Lübke, Leipzig, 11.7.12; LW, 549; Hoffmeister, 99; Chickering, *Imperial Germany*, 312–15; *cf.* Gerald Deckart, "Deutsch-englische Verständigung: Eine Darstellung der nichtoffiziellen Bemühungen um eine Wiederannäherung der beiden Länder zwischen 1905 und 1914," Ph.D. dissertation (Munich, 1967).
97. NL Lamprecht (Korr. 35), Lamprecht to Lindau, Leipzig, 22.4.13; (Korr, 37), Meyer to Lamprecht, Berlin, 20.3.08; Lamprecht, "Nationalismus und Universalismus."
98. "Die Nation und die Friedensbewegung," *Die Friedenswarte*, 12 (1910): 41–44; *cf.*

Lamprecht, *Die Nation und die Friedensbewegung* (Berlin, 1914); Chickering, *Imperial Germany*, 138.

99. Ibid.; NL Lamprecht (Munich), Bertha von Suttner to Lamprecht, Vienna, 6.10.09.

100. Roger Chickering, "A Voice of Moderation in Imperial Germany: The 'Verband für internationale Verständigung,' 1911–1914," *Journal of Contemporary History*, 8 (January 1973): 147–64; Chickering, *Imperial Germany*, 148–62.

101. See Otfried Nippold, *Meine Erlebnisse in Deutschland vor dem Weltkriege (1909–1914)* (Berne, 1918), 19.

102. BA, NL Schücking (58), Lamprecht to Schücking, 9.12.08; Entwurf der Statuten des Verbandes für internationale Verständigung.

103. Chickering, *Imperial Germany*, 136, 154. The historian and pacifist Ludwig Quidde was initially among the officers, but he was not an academic scholar.

104. "Über auswärtige Kulturpolitik," *Mitteilungen des Verbandes für internationale Verständigung*, 8 (1913): 3–14. The text is also in Kurt Düwell, *Deutschlands auswärtige Kulturpolitik 1918–1932: Grundlinien und Dokumente* (Cologne and Vienna, 1976), 255–67; *cf.* ibid., 14–19.

105. Lamprecht's speech did nothing to assuage the skepticism which Weber expressed during this meeting about the whole organization. See Paul Honigsheim, *On Max Weber* (New York and East Lansing, 1968), 13.

106. Lamprecht, "Auswärtige Kulturpolitik und Geschichtswissenschaft," *Mitteilungen des Verbandes für internationale Verständigung*, 1 (1913): 8; NL Lamprecht (Korr. 61), Lamprecht to D'Estournelles de Constant, n.p., n.d. [October 1912]; Adolf Wild, *Baron d'Estournelles de Constant (1852–1924): Das Wirken eines Friedensnobelpreisträgers für die deutsch-französische Verständigung und europäische Einigung* (Hamburg, 1973), 392–93.

107. Erdmann, *Oekumene*, 87.

108. George W. F. Hallgarten, *Imperialismus vor 1914*, 2 vols. (Munich, 1951), 2: 314.

109. EB, 2,2: 553.

110. See E. Mencke-Glückert, "Zur Vollendung von Karl Lamprechts deutscher Geschichte," *Das Deutschtum im Ausland*, (March 1910): 122–30.

111. Hoffmeister, 95; *cf.* Engelberg, "Methodenstreit," 145; Guilland, 22–23.

112. Rüdiger vom Bruch, *Weltpolitik als Kulturmission: Auswärtige Kulturpolitik und Bildungsbürgertum in Deutschland am Vorabend des Ersten Weltkrieges* (Paderborn, 1982), 40. See also Nipperdey, *Deutsche Geschichte 1866–1918*, 507–30; Chickering, *Imperial Germany*, 122–31.

113. vom Bruch, "Kulturstaat," 63–101.

114. NL Lamprecht (Korr. 5), Lamprecht to Barthels, Leipzig, 8.7.14; (Korr. 22), E. Foerster-Nietzsche to Lamprecht, Weimar, 12.3.12; (Korr. 40), Lamprecht to Ostwald, Leipzig, 7.12.14; (Korr. 55), L. Woltmann to Lamprecht, Eisenach, 4.3.03. And in the same category: NL Lamprecht (Munich), Karl May to Lamprecht, Radebeul, 12.9.06.

115. "The phlegmatic one who complements the Kaiser well." NL Lamprecht (Korr. 59), Lamprecht to Hugo Lamprecht, 19.11.02.

116. PAAA, Deutschland 122, Bd. 6, Lamprecht to Bülow, Leipzig, 9.1.06.

117. Ibid., Bülow to Lamprecht, Berlin, 18.12.05.

118. PAAA, Deutschland 125, Bd. 4, Bülow to Lamprecht, Berlin, 2.0.07.

119. Ibid., Lamprecht to Bülow, Leipzig, 5.2.07; Lamprecht, "Die künftige Politisierung der Gesellschaft," *Berliner Tageblatt*, 15.1.07; *cf. Freiheit und Volkstum*, 10.

120. NL Lamprecht (Munich), Bülow to Lamprecht, Berlin, 25.4.09; Lamprecht, "Finanz und Finanznot des alten Deutschen Reiches," *Die Reichsfinanzreform: Ein Führer* (Berlin, 1908), 1–10.

121. vom Brocke, "Professorenaustausch," 128–46; vom Brocke, "System Althoff," 46.
122. NL Althoff (B Nr. 108/1), Lamprecht to Althoff, Fontainebleau, 19.9.06.
123. NL Althoff (B Nr. 108/1), Lamprecht to Althoff, Schierke, 29.8.08; Lamprecht to Bülow (October 1908], Entwurf.
124. The claim that Bethmann Hollweg and Lamprecht were close at Pforta and remained so thereafter is wrong. It first appeared in Hermann Kötschke, *Unser Reichskanzler: Sein Leben und Wirken*, 5th ed. (Berlin, 1916), 19; *cf.* Klaus Hildebrand, *Bethmann Hollweg: Der Kanzler ohne Eigenschaften?* (Düsseldorf, 1970), 27–28. On the eve of his death, the historian wrote to the chancellor: "You know very well that our relationship in Schulpforta was by no means secure and well grounded; what separated us was probably more in the nature of social prejudice [*Vorurteile verschiedenartiger Standesanschauungen*] than personal aversion." NL Lamprecht (Korr. 11), Lamprecht to Bethmann Hollweg, Leipzig, 29.4.15.
125. NL Lamprecht (Korr. 59), Lamprecht to Hugo Lamprecht, Leipzig, 18.11.08; NL Lamprecht (Munich), Bethmann Hollweg to Lamprecht, Berlin, 23.12.08; StA Dresden, VB 10230/21, Bethmann Hollweg to Lamprecht, Berlin, 5.5.09.
126. NL Lamprecht (Munich), Bethmann Hollweg to Marianne and Else Lamprecht, Berlin, 19.7.17. Here Bethmann spoke of Lamprecht as "*mein verstorbener Freund.*"
127. NL Lamprecht (Korr. 29), Lamprecht to Helmolt, Leipzig, 9.2.12.
128. NL Lamprecht (Korr. 11), Lamprecht to Bethmann Hollweg, Leipzig, 29.4.15.
129. "Historia vitae magistra," *Berliner Tageblatt*, 7.1.10; LW, 583.
130. Mehring, "Paranoia professoris magistra," *Die Neue Zeit*, 28 (1909–1910): 545–48 (*Gesammelte Schriften*, 7: 516–19).
131. NL Lamprecht (Korr. 11), Bethmann Hollweg to Lamprecht, 8.1.10 (Kopie).
132. NL Lamprecht (Korr. 29), Lamprecht to Helmolt, Leipzig, 2.2.12; NL Harden, Lamprecht to Harden, Leipzig, 23.2.10.
133. Lamprecht, "Deutsche Ideale," *Zukunft*, 71 (1910): 114–19.
134. NL Lamprecht (Korr. 11), Lamprecht to Bethmann Hollweg, Leipzig, 13.10.10.
135. StA Dresden, VB 10281/203, Lamprecht to Bethmann Hollweg, Leipzig, January 1912. Abschrift.
136. NL Lamprecht (Korr. 29), Lamprecht to Helmolt, Leipzig, 9.2.12; (Korr. 22), Lamprecht to Fried, Leipzig, 16.2.12.
137. NL Lamprecht (Korr. 46), Lamprecht to Schmalz, Leipzig, 10.1.12; (Korr. 37), Lamprecht to Mayer, Leipzig, 29.1.12.
138. Butler Papers, Lamprecht to Butler, Leipzig, 12.1.12.
139. NL Lamprecht (Korr. 22), Lamprecht to Fried, Leipzig, 13.1.12.
140. NL Lamprecht (Korr. 22), Lamprecht to van der Frier, Leipzig, 8.3.12; PAAA, Eur. gen. Nr. 37, Bd. 14, Schoen to Bethmann Hollweg, Paris, 28.3.12; Bethmann Hollweg to Lamprecht, Berlin, 3.4.12.
141. See Rüdiger vom Bruch, "Krieg und Frieden: Zur Frage der Militarsierung deutscher Hochschullehrer und Universitäten im späten Kaiserreich," in Jost Dülffer and Karl Holl, eds., *Bereit zum Krieg: Kriegsmentalität im wilhelminischen Deutschland 1890–1914* (Göttingen, 1986), 74–98; vom Bruch, "'Militarismus,' 'Realpolitik' und 'Pazifismus.' Aussenpolitik und Aufrüstung in der Sicht deutscher Hochschullehrer (Historiker) im späten Kaiserreich," MGM, no. 1 (1986): 37–58; Klaus Wernecke, *Der Wille zur Weltgeltung: Aussenpolitik und Öffentlichkeit im Kaiserreich am Vorabend des Ersten Weltkrieges* (Düsseldorf, 1970).
142. Chickering, *We Men*, 253–98.
143. NL Lamprecht (Korr. 45), Lamprecht to Rohrbach, Leipzig, 2.12.14; LW, 660–61; *cf.* J. J. Ruedorffer [Kurt Riezler], *Grundzüge der Weltpolitik in der Gegenwart* (Stuttgart and Berlin, 1914), 251–52. See vom Bruch, *Weltpolitik*, 69–89; Düwell,

22–25; Walter Mogk, *Paul Rohrbach und das 'Grössere Deutschland': Ethischer Imperialismus im Wilhelminischen Zeitalter* (Munich, 1972), esp. 159–83; Hoffmeister, 159.

144. Gerhard A. Ritter, "Motive und Organisationsformen der internationalen Wissenschaftsbeziehungen und die Anfänge einer auswärtigen Kulturpolitik im deutschen Kaiserreich vor dem Ersten Weltkrieg," in Lothar Kettenacker et al., eds., *Studien zur Geschichte Englands und der deutsch-britischen Beziehungen: Festschrift für Paul Kluke* (Munich, 1981), 153–200.

145. PAAA, Deutschland 126b, Bd. 1, Lilienthal to Waldthausen, Berlin, 6.6.12; Bethmann Hollweg to Schinekel, Berlin, 22.7.12; Jürgen Kloosterhuis, "Deutsche auswärtige Kulturpolitik und ihre Trägergruppen vor dem Ersten Weltkrieg," in Kurt Düwell and Werner Link, eds., *Deutsche auswärtige Kulturpolitik seit 1871* (Cologne and Vienna, 1981), 7–35.

146. NL Lamprecht (Korr. 36), Marc to Lamprecht, Munich, 15.5.14; *cf.* A. Ritter (Winterstetten), *Berlin-Baghdad: Neue Ziele mitteleuropäischer Politik* (Munich, 1916), 63.

147. *Deutsche Geschichte der jüngsten Vergangenheit und Gegenwart*, 2 vols. (Berlin, 1912–1913).

148. NL Lamprecht (Korr. 47), Lamprecht to Schücking, Leipzig, 22.10.13; LW, 662–63; Lamprecht, *Der Kaiser: Versuch einer Charakteristik* (Berlin, 1913); *cf.* Lamprecht, "Staatsform und Politik im Lichte der Geschichte," *Handbuch der Politik*, 1 (5) (Berlin, 1912): 759–60.

149. vom Bruch, *Weltpolitik*, 97.

150. NL Lamprecht (UL 6), Lamprecht to Salinger, Leipzig, 4.8.13.

151. BA, R43F, RK Nr. 4, Bd. 5, Lamprecht to Bethmann Hollweg, Leipzig, 19.5.13. A copy is in PAAA, Deutschtum im Ausland Nr. 5, Bd. 1. The letter is reprinted along with Bethmann's response in vom Bruch, *Weltpolitik*, 147–51.

152. BA, R43F, RK Nr. 4, Bd. 5, Bethmann Hollweg to Lamprecht, Berlin, 21.6.13. A copy is in PAAA, Deutschtum im Ausland Nr. 5, Bd. 1.

153. BA, R43F, RK Nr. 4, Bd. 5, Lamprecht to Wahnschaffe, Leipzig, 11.12.13. Rüdiger vom Bruch has analyzed this episode and reprinted many of the relevant documents in *Weltpolitik als Kulturmission*, 90–122, 147–209.

154. NL Lamprecht (Korr. 36), Matschoss to Lamprecht, Berlin, 28.9.10; NDB, 16: 385–87; *cf.* Wolfgang König, "Die Ingenieure und der VDI als Grossverein in der wilhelminischen Gesellschaft 1900 bis 1918," in Karl-Heinz Ludwig and Wolfgang König, eds., *Technik, Ingenieure und Gesellschaft: Geschichte des Vereins deutscher Ingenieure 1856–1981* (Düsseldorf, 1981), 275–76, 287; Kees Gispen, *New Profession, Old Order: Engineers and German Society, 1815–1914* (Cambridge, 1989).

155. NL Lamprecht (Korr. 36), Lamprecht to Matschoss, Leipzig, 14.10.13; BA, R43F, RK Nr. 4, Bd. 5, Lamprecht, Darlegung der bisher in kleinem Kreise erörterten An- und Absichten (Leipzig, December 1913); PAAA, Deutschtum im Ausland Nr. 5, Bd. 1; vom Bruch, *Weltpolitik*, 155–59; Lamprecht, "Die Technik und die Kultur der Gegenwart," *Zeitschrift des Vereins deutscher Ingenieure*, 57 (1913): 1523–26.

156. BA, R43F, RK Nr. 4, Bd. 5, Lamprecht, Darlegung der bisher in kleinem Kreise erörterten An- und Absichten.

157. Karl Dietrich Erdmann, ed., *Kurt Riezler: Tagebücher, Aufsätze, Dokumente* (Göttingen, 1972), 48; Wernecke, 306; *cf.* Bernd F. Schulte, *Die Verfälschung der Riezler Tagebücher* (Frankfurt am Main, 1985), 174.

158. BA, R43F, RK Nr. 4, Bd. 5, Bethmann Hollweg RS, Hohenfinow, 5.8.13. Also in PAAA, Deutschtum im Ausland Nr. 5, Bd. 1; vom Bruch, *Weltpolitik*, 152–53.

159. BA, R43F, RK Nr. 4, Bd. 5, Lamprecht to Bethmann Hollweg, Leipzig, 8.12.13;

Lamprecht, Darlegung der bisher in kleinem Kreise erörterten An- und Absichten; PAAA, Deutschtum im Ausland, Nr. 5, Bd. 1, AA to Bethmann Hollweg, Berlin, 30.10.13; vom Bruch, Weltpolitik, 100.

160. BA, R43F, RK Nr. 4, Bd. 5, Lamprecht to Wahnschaffe, Leipzig, 11.12.13.

161. BA, R43F, RK Nr. 4, Bd. 5, Wahnschaffe to Lamprecht, Berlin, 18.12.13.

162. PAAA, Deutschtum im Ausland, Nr. 5, Bd. 1, Lamprecht, "Zweite DS," Leipzig, 30 December 1913.

163. Ibid.

164. BA, R43F, RK Nr. 4, Bd. 5, Lamprecht to Bethmann Hollweg, Leipzig, 31.12.13; vom Bruch, Weltpolitik, 174–75.

165. NL Dove, Lamprecht to Dove, Leipzig, 3.1.13 [sic].

166. PAAA, Deutschland 122 Nr. 16, Bd. 5, Eisendecher to Bethmann Hollweg, Karlsruhe, 12.12.13; "Der Reichskanzler über 'äussere Kulturpolitik,'" Kreuzzeitung, Nr. 582 (12.12.13); Wernecke, 306–7; vom Bruch, Weltpolitik, 100–101, 109; cf. Eberhard von Vietsch, Bethmann Hollweg: Staatsmann zwischen Macht und Ethos (Boppard, 1969), 292.

167. BA, R43F, RK Nr. 4, Bd. 5, Lamprecht to Bethmann Hollweg, Leipzig, 4.1.14; Wahnschaffe to Bethmann Hollweg, Berlin, 6.1.14; NL Lamprecht (Korr. 43), Lamprecht to Planitz, Leipzig, 7.7.13. Riezler's pseudonymous Grundzüge der Weltpolitik appeared in a series that Lamprecht and Helmolt edited, but the identity of the author remained the playfully guarded secret of the chancellery. Lamprecht sent a review of the book to Riezler, who thanked the historian for the "critique of the book, which is well known to me." NL Lamprecht (Korr. 32), Riezler to Lamprecht, Grosses Hauptquartier, 26.10.14.

168. vom Bruch, Weltpolitik, 91.

169. Max Lenz, "Rückblick und Ausblick," Der Tag, 4.1.14. A copy is in the chancellery files.

170. Leo Stern et al., eds., Die Berliner Akademie der Wissenschaften in der Zeit des Imperialismus, 3 vols. (Berlin, 1975–1979), 1: 98. The account does not make clear the date or context of Schäfer's report, but it was likely drafted in connection with requests that Lamprecht made in January 1914.

171. BA, R43F, RK Nr. 4, Bd. 6 (7–9); vom Bruch, Weltpolitik, 91.

172. BA, R43F, RK Nr. 4, Bd. 5, Bethmann Hollweg to Lamprecht, Berlin, 21.1.14.

173. BA, R43F, RK Nr. 4, Bd. 5, Wahnschaffe to Bethmann Hollweg, Berlin, 31.1.14.

174. NL Lamprecht (Korr. 61), Lamprecht to Matschoss, n.p., n.d. [February 1914]; Lamprecht to Nippold, Leipzig, 27.2.14.

175. NL Lamprecht (Korr. 61), Besprechung über Massnahmen zur Förderung deutscher auswärtiger Kulturpolitik am 6.2.14. The protocol is reprinted in vom Bruch, Weltpolitik, 176–95.

176. NL Lamprecht (Korr. 48), Lamprecht to Siegismund, Leipzig, 24.2.14.

177. "Zur auswärtigen Kulturpolitik," Frankfurter Zeitung, 12.4.14; also in vom Bruch, Weltpolitik, 196–201.

178. NL Lamprecht (Korr. 37), Lamprecht to Mathilde Mevissen, Leipzig, 1.5.14; (Korr. 61), Lamprecht to Sevin, Leipzig, 18.3.14; Matschoss to Lamprecht, 7.4.14.

179. NL Lamprecht (Korr. 61), Sevin to Lamprecht, 17.4.14; (Korr. 67a), Gesellschaft für Erforschung des Deutschtums im Ausland, Aufruf, Berlin and Leipzig, April 1914; (Korr. 61), Lamprecht et al., RS, Berlin, June 1914.

13

Interruptions

Dächtet ihr gross vom Volke, so wäret ihr auch barmherzig
gegen dasselbe und hütet euch wohl, euer historisches
Scheidewasser ihm als Lebens- und Labetrank anzubieten.

The World Exhibition of the Book Trade and Graphics, or BUGRA, opened in
Leipzig in May 1914. Even by the standards of this city, where large-scale fairs
and exhibitions were staple occurrences, it was an impressive spectacle. Eighty-
four pavilions housed exhibits from all over the world on the technologies of
printing, book production, graphic design, photography, and the manufacture of
paper products. A building called the House of Culture contained the most
intriguing part of the exhibition. Its theme was the cultural history of the world.
By means of graphic sources of every description—primitive oriental woodcuts,
Buddhist scriptures, Turkish incunabula, and children's drawings from around
the world—a main exhibit and eight subsidiary presentations documented the
parallel development of all the world's cultures through a common series of
historical epochs, which corresponded to stages in the economic development
of each.[1]

It was only fitting that the House of Culture became known as the Lamprech-
tianum. The exhibits were a tribute to the historian's vision, as well as to his
organizational talent. The effort occupied him and the staff of his institute for
more than a year and required lengthy negotiations with hundreds of scholars
around the world, as well as with several levels of officialdom and Eugen
Diederichs, one of BUGRA's other participants, who agreed to publish a series
of guidebooks that members of Lamprecht's team had prepared for the exhibits.[2]

BUGRA was a local triumph, but it was one of the historian's few sources of
gratification in a trying period of his life. The cooling of his relationship to the
chancellor, which fatally undercut his campaign for a cultural foreign policy,
was the first in a string of setbacks that befell him in the early months of 1914.
The translation of Show's article was particularly distressing, for it made clear to
observers outside the historical profession the extent of his isolation within it.
The article not only confirmed the skepticism of Riezler and others in the
chancellery about Lamprecht; it compromised the historian's standing in

431

Dresden.[3] Officials in the ministry of culture declined to support him during a series of bitter disputes with his colleagues in Leipzig in the spring of 1914, as the faculty blocked his attempt to create an extraordinary professorship for his institute, excluded him from the planning of a new colonial institute, and rejected the dissertations of two more of his doctoral students.[4]

Walter Goetz's essay was the last blow. Of all the academic historians in Germany, Goetz was the most sympathetic to Lamprecht's goals (if not his methods), but in the early summer of 1914 he aimed an attack at Leipzig. Goetz's essay, which was titled "Historical Instruction and Historical Research Institutes," appeared in the same journal that had carried Show's indictment several months earlier.[5] Goetz joined a chorus of historians who were calling for a national historical research institute on the model of the Kaiser Wilhelm Society. Here he endorsed most of Lamprecht's ideas about the need to broaden and coordinate teaching and advanced research in history. He did so, however, without once mentioning Lamprecht's name or the Institute for Cultural and Universal History. "Much of what you are talking about has already been realized in my institute," Lamprecht pointed out to the author.[6] But the article was not calculated to flatter. Goetz concluded with a warning to his colleagues, lest good ideas, "which are in the air," fall into the wrong hands and the "eccentricity of a single individual" (and here he did not have to mention names) result in a research institute "which would not have the character of an organization common to German historical scholarship."

Lamprecht was used to this kind of treatment, but he was becoming discouraged amid the mounting reminders of his isolation. In these circumstances, the possibility of an escape from Leipzig became more attractive. His name surfaced in the press in connection with a chair in Hamburg; and although he had no chance of appointment there (the chair went to Max Lenz), he was more interested in it than his public denials suggested.[7] An invitation to spend a semester at the University of Wisconsin, as Carl Schurz Professor, offered a respite that he was tempted to accept but for the requirement that he lecture in English.[8] He soon regretted his decision not to accept, and as his difficulties with his colleagues increased during the spring of 1914, he began to contemplate a more drastic form of escape through resignation from the faculty.[9]

The historian was tired. He turned fifty-eight in February 1914. As his sixtieth birthday approached, a growing consciousness of age exacerbated his feelings of frustration and isolation. "Present times demand much of a person," he reflected to a friend in March 1914, "conflict is exhausting and the so-called *Zeitgeist* is cruel especially to those who are growing old."[10] Fatigue affected central facets of his activity. He could no longer work long hours in the evening; and in his institute he complained of being overworked and out of touch with his students.[11]

Nor was his private life exempt from distress. In the fall of 1913 he had a serious disagreement with the tax officials over the liabilities accruing from his wife's inheritance.[12] His wife's condition was stable, but it brought him little consolation.[13] His daughters, who were now in their mid-twenties, remained at home in the care of Emma Bruch. The historian wrote of his pleasure as he watched them grow up to be a "pair of gallant human beings," but his professions masked lingering anxieties that his "children," as he persisted in calling these women, were going to suffer their mother's fate.[14]

Early in May 1914 Lamprecht found an escape of sorts. The pressures on him made the noise and pace of life in the city center difficult to bear, so he rented a small summer house on the outskirts of the city, in Stötteritz near the new monument to the Battle of Nations. Although the move required him and his family to make frequent commutes into town by tram, the house afforded fresh air and sunshine in a semirural setting; and it was near his wife's asylum.[15] The summer of 1914 promised to be restful.

"We here have lived through the most wonderful days," wrote Lamprecht of the experiences of that summer: "a single great feeling of moral elevation, a soaring of religious sentiments, in short, the ascent of a whole people to the heights."[16] The outbreak of war in early August took him by surprise, but it quickly transported him into the euphoria in which men of education and property in Leipzig, and elsewhere, followed the conflict in its first weeks. These were "holy days," he declared, "days of endless uplift," which he experienced like "a rapture of tremendous happiness."[17]

The historian plunged into the war effort. Although he still held a commission in the *Landwehr*, he was too old for active service in uniform. Like other academics of his generation, he devoted his energies instead to the mobilization of morale on the home front and to the defense of the German cause among his colleagues abroad. He thus joined forces with many of the most renowned figures in the German intellectual world, as well as with some of his former enemies.[18] However, despite his prominence in this effort and his gestures to solidarity with his new allies, his own exertions were still geared to a unique vision of history and to a no less unique reform agenda. Consequently, even amid the general enthusiasm over the war, he remained an eccentric participant.

Lamprecht's commentary on the war reflected the volatility of his impressions during the early months of the conflict, as the censors established their claims to an interpretive monopoly. Much of his commentary rehearsed themes that other writers were injecting into public discussion, albeit in different categories. However, Lamprecht's commentary also betrayed the strains that the war and the censors' interpretations of it placed on his historical categories.

In a heroic gesture to the *Burgfrieden*, the historian purged his commentary of most of the foreign words; he also refashioned his *Kulturzeitalter* in the more conventional labels that he had introduced and then neglected in the third volume of his *German History*. He now wrote of "ancient times," "middle ages," "modern times," and "contemporary times."[19] The subdivisions he employed in this periodization revealed, however, that the sacrifice was merely cosmetic, for as he insisted in his most extended statement, the war required "a new awareness [*einer anderen Kenntnis*] of our history," which was geared to the conceptual vocabulary of a "cultural-political standpoint."[20] From this standpoint, the war broke out at a climactic moment in the nation's cultural development, as the great tendencies of the period "since about 1750" had just culminated in the fusion of *Volk und Staat* in an "ever stronger, inseparable unity," a community permeated by the spirit of the new idealism and a consciousness of the nation's universal mission to provide cultural leadership in the world.[21] The war was hence opportune. "Should it be a question of a leading place for our nation in the world politically and culturally," he concluded, "then it would be hard to achieve otherwise than by means of war at just this time and under just these circumstances."[22]

The historian found it easier to graft the war onto his categories of German cultural history than to explain some of the broader historical implications of the conflict. The difficulty reflected the limitations of his scheme of universal history, for the parallel development of national cultures failed to provide a compelling explanation for the constellation of forces in 1914—the alliance of the advanced west European cultures with Russia or the loyalty of the western Slavs and the Turks to the German-Austrian alliance. Lamprecht attempted early in the war to use racial categories to resolve the problem. He wrote of the struggle of "Germandom," "Romandom," and "Slavdom," and of a "Mongolian-Tatar-infected Russia," which he, like many others, believed had initiated the struggle; but he quickly retreated from these categories once he realized that they raised even more intractible anomalies—on the order of a Germanic blood community in which "only England stands aside."[23]

The historian then appropiated another theme from the public discourse on the origins and significance of the war. He argued that the basic conflict was between two *Kulturkreise* or cultural groups, the Anglo-French and the German, and he suggested that the former had entered its historical decline. The key was an element of calculation and cunning (*List*), which had (since Shakespeare's time, he explained) taken over Anglo-French morality to a much greater degree than it had the more rigorous and innocent German ethical constitution. The Anglo-French experience suggested that at a higher stage of historical development a "certain cultural hypertrophy [*Verbildung*]" or "decadence [*zersetzende Entwicklung*]" set in.[24] This argument resonated with the dichotomies that other German writers were drawing between "civilization" and "culture" and between "traders" and "heroes"; it also anticipated motifs that Spengler developed at the end of the war. Lamprecht himself clouded the historical issues, though, when he suggested in the same breath that a "freedom from moral scruples" had been a feature of the "Celtic character" since the days of Caesar.

Whatever difficulties it posed for his conception of universal history, the war required but minor adjustments in Lamprecht's political thinking. The evolution of his position before the war, his drift from the Pan-German League toward the peace movement, was based principally on considerations of means, the calculation that German claims could be more effectively pursued by policies of conciliation and cultural penetration than by force of arms. The outbreak of armed conflict nullified this calculation, at least temporarily; and it drew him back into the proximity of the Pan-Germans in championing a war to achieve these claims.

The rhetoric in which the historian referred to German claims ceded nothing to the Pan-Germans in extravagance. He wrote of *Weltansprüche*, "a position of world domination [*Weltherrschaft*]," and the "beginning of Germanic hegemony in Europe."[25] That these claims carried far-reaching territorial implications seemed clear, if only on the strength of passages about central Europe and Flemish Belgium in the supplements to his *German History*, which he had republished unaltered on the eve of the war. After the outbreak of the war, however, he was reluctant to address specific questions of territorial expansion. His public reserve was due to the censors and to pressure from the chancellery and the foreign office, which he continued to consult despite the disappointments of the spring.[26] But his reticence also reflected a basic feature of his thinking about the war. He paid little attention to the divisive issues that were already animating the war-aims debate in Germany; questions of territory, resources, reparations, and domestic political reform did not much interest him.

Lamprecht understood the war on his own terms. The conflict did not shake the convictions that underlay his historiography. Even in war, he believed, politics was a derivative sphere of human history, and the ultimate issues at stake in the conflict were cultural. "National power will in the last analysis be won only by spiritual means, as all of history attests."[27] So read his impatient gloss on a draft program of war aims, which a proponent of annexations sent him in September 1914. Lamprecht reasoned that the expansion of German rule was bound to remain ephemeral if it lacked the requisite cultural foundations—if it were not based on the self-conscious promotion of the superior national ideals that sanctioned German expansion.

Familiar themes surfaced in this proposition. In Lamprecht's eyes, the war demonstrated the urgency of a cultural foreign policy, as he himself had defined the term, and it validated the reforms that he had long advocated as the indispensable basis of such a policy. "For efforts to reform the pedagogy of the universities," he wrote to Bernheim in October, "it is now, in my view, an extraordinarily favorable time, and one should exploit it in every respect."[28] As this remarkable assertion revealed, the primary significance of the conflict lay for him in the opportunities it provided for the continuation of a personal crusade that had appeared frustrated on the war's eve. Allusions to "elevating the spiritual position of our nation to the heights of its mission" or to "the most necessary practical prerequisites of a comprehensive world policy" were ritual preludes to calls for university reform, research institutes in the humanities, and more cultural and universal history at all levels of instruction.[29] In the historian's view, these imperatives transcended even the outcome of the conflict. "In the event that the fate of the war is decided in our favor," he wrote early in the conflict, "a situation will be created in which the nation will most urgently require a broadening of historical studies into universal history."[30]

Lamprecht's appreciation of the war comported to a degree with the more conventional categories in which other writers were framing a range of agendas; but his thinking was too idiosyncratic to sustain durable alliances with any of them. In this respect, too, the war represented no hiatus in his experience. Along with Wundt, Ostwald, Max Klinger, Eduard Meyer, Heinrich Finke, and Max Lenz, he affixed his signature to the infamous "Declaration of the Ninety-Three," the defiant proclamation "To the World of Culture" in which the leaders of German art and scholarship defended German militarism and German actions in Belgium, including the shelling of Louvain, in the name of German culture.[31] Lamprecht also participated briefly in the Cultural Association of German Scholars and Artists (*Kulturbund deutscher Gelehrter und Künstler*), which the anatomist Wilhelm Waldeyer (whom he had met in St. Louis) recruited among the signatories of this declaration in hopes of exploiting their contacts abroad to promote sympathy for the German cause.[32]

Lamprecht's prominence in this venture had uncomfortable repercussions. It earned him the censure of Waldeyer, who objected for tactical reasons to even the most abstract allusions in public to German leadership in postwar central Europe.[33] These strictures came too late to save the historian from the consequences of his intemperate defense of the actions of the German army. His international fame now proved a liability and made him a natural symbol abroad of the militarization of the German professoriate.[34]

Lamprecht's notoriety created burdens at home, too. He paid a price for the ambiguity and extravagance of some of his pronouncements, as well as for his reputation as a man who "can write articles better and faster than anyone else."[35] Solicitations for his support arrived from organizations that represented a broad variety of opinion in the emerging debate over war aims and political reform, from Nordic regenerationists on the right to the *Bund neues Vaterland* on the left.[36] Most of these overtures the historian ignored. His principal vehicle was instead a cycle of lectures designed to satisfy what he called a "genuine mania for learning [*Lernwut*]" in the public at large.[37] Under the auspices of the university in Leipzig and the Saxon government, he toured the kingdom with an inventory of lectures on behalf of his reform projects. Proposals to expand instruction in cultural history at all levels accompanied calls for creating a special section for cultural foreign policy in the German foreign office, and—until Waldeyer cautioned him—for establishing a central European confederation under German leadership after the war.[38] Teachers' organizations provided the most responsive forum, as the historian attempted to broaden his campaign to the capital and the national press.[39]

"Evidently the war has stirred you to the depths and raised you to an activity keener even than your wont," wrote Benjamin Ide Wheeler, one of the scholars whom the historian was cultivating in the neutral lands.[40] The war did invigorate Lamprecht, and his frenetic activity in its support signaled the rekindling of his crusade. "I am genuinely a happy man in these difficult times," he wrote to

Ritter at the end of 1914, "for I see much that is important, much for which I have fought for so long, growing and thriving."[41] His fervor sustained him through mounting evidence of the war's cost. Aside from his niece's husband, no members of his immediate family were under arms; but close friends on both sides of the front were not spared. The war gutted his institute of instructors and students alike; and by the end of the year some twenty of them had fallen in combat, many at Langemarck.[42] Plans for a new journal of universal history fell casualty to the war, as did his institute's monograph series, his royalties from the *German History*, and BUGRA.[43] So, for all intents and purposes, did the new humanistic research institutes at the university, which were founded formally in November.

Developments abroad brought additional grounds for concern. Lamprecht's efforts to defend Germany among his American friends appeared to have little effect; and he learned that one of his former students, who was living in the United States, had taken his own life in despair over the German cause.[44] The news from Belgium at the end of 1914 was even more disquieting. In Ghent, his friends Pirenne and Fredericq led the faculty boycott that closed down the university in protest against the German occupation. The German authorities thereupon seized the two scholars as hostages, nominally to secure a tribute to cover the costs of occupation.[45] Lamprecht, who had in all innocence expected that his friendship with these two men could survive the German invasion of their country, besieged the chancellor and helped secure their release in early January 1915.[46] Whether or not they knew of Lamprecht's good offices, Pirenne and Fredericq could not forgive him his signature on the "Declaration of the Ninety-Three" or his collaboration in German efforts to reopen the university in Ghent with a Flemish faculty.[47]

Lamprecht's intervention on behalf of his Belgian colleagues was nonetheless one of the few occasions when he experienced success in the central agencies of the German government. The quiet demise in August of his project to establish a Society to Promote a Cultural Foreign Policy went unlamented in official circles. Establishment of a Central Division for Service Abroad (*Zentralstelle für Auslandsdienst*) within the foreign office preempted all his efforts to revive the project in the new circumstances of war. In hopes of expanding his base of operations beyond Leipzig, he proposed in October to create an official agency, to be called a *Nachrichtendienst*, in order to coordinate countrywide lecture cycles by a team of scholars of his choosing.[48] This project collapsed on the opposition of the chancellery, the foreign office, and the Prussian ministry of culture.[49] So did the next proposal from Leipzig, which envisaged commissioning German scholars to edit the historical documents of foreign countries. The purpose of the project, the historian explained to the foreign office, was to promote the German cause abroad by introducing the "German spirit and a German sense of scholarship into the historical writing" of other countries.[50] After he had reviewed this proposal at the chancellor's request (and Lamprecht's), Riezler pronounced the historian the "*comble* of the impractical."[51]

This view was shared everywhere in the top levels of the German government.

Still, these officials could not ignore him. He was tenacious. From their previous experience, they knew that he would, as he told Waldeyer, "go ahead by myself."[52] Officials could also judge the size of Lamprecht's popular following, for a tract that he wrote in October, on the historical significance of the war, had gone through seventeen editions by early 1915.[53] As the historian's disappointments accumulated in the fall of 1914, he became more outspoken in his criticism of German diplomacy. "How many difficulties might we have been spared in the last months if my requests and suggestions of the last years had really found a sympathetic hearing in the foreign office."[54] His remarks in public were less pointed than this complaint to the chancellery in December. But the cautious notes in his commentary at the end of the year did suggest the onset of doubts about the wisdom of German policy, while his repeated calls for a section for cultural foreign policy were without question a critical barb at the foreign office.[55]

In a gesture of mollification, as well as to secure his support for Flemish separatism, the government organized a grand tour of the western front for him in March 1915. The ostensible purpose of the visit was to lecture to the support troops in the rear of the second German army, to which his former pupil, Carl Theodor Deichmann, was attached. The list of his appointments with the commanding general of that army, the governor-general of occupied Belgium, the German foreign minister, the chancellor, and the Kaiser suggested another reason for the tour. This treatment was designed to flatter the historian and dispel his doubts about German policy. It succeeded. On 19 March he arrived with what he admitted was a "rather vague" program in St. Quentin, where the second army was headquartered.[56] There he spent two exhilarating weeks in the daily company of flyers and other junior officers, who responded to him like admiring students, and among the army's highest-ranking soldiers in the evenings. On the 19th he dined with the commanding general, Karl von Bülow; the next day he spent twenty minutes discussing the history and politics of the Flemish problem with the Kaiser.[57]

The sojourn brought Lamprecht back to a part of Europe that had been the theme of his doctoral dissertation thirty-five years earlier; and the cultural historian succumbed to the temptation to study the land anew with a more practiced eye. But this eye was captive to his exhilaration and to his beliefs about the nature of the cultural forces that were locked in conflict. The fleeting impressions that he collected in northern France validated the German presence there and trivialized the burdens of occupation. On the basis of "intimate information," he concluded that the local population, though given to abstract complaints about the war, was "by and large happy" and had "nothing to criticize," for the German administration was vorzüglich—friendly, honest, and productive, if a little pedantic.[58]

In this frame of mind, the historian journeyed north on 30 March to Brussels, where he found corroboration for his impressions. "They are happy with us," he noted of that city's residents, "even if they don't admit it; and they would, if they could express themselves freely, concede the superiority of the German administration over the French."[59] He persisted in this conviction despite some painful evidence to the contrary. In Brussels he met with his friend, the historian Guilliaume Des Marez, who like Pirenne and Fredericq was embittered over Lamprecht's public defense of the invasion of his country. When Lamprecht cheerfully observed that the Belgians seemed happy with the German regime, Des Marez replied that but for the German troops, Lamprecht would not be safe in the city.[60] Then Lamprecht traveled to Ghent, to console Pirenne who, in the wake of his captivity, had lost a son in battle. Here Lamprecht learned that a friendship of a quarter-century had fallen casualty; the Belgian historian turned him away at the door.[61]

Lamprecht returned saddened but unchastened to Brussels in order to present his views about another problem to high German officials. His impressions in occupied Belgium confirmed (as the German government had reason to expect) a long-standing conviction that he had been unable to embrace in public during the war. The concept of a Belgian nationality he pronounced a "very empty and vague thought, beyond all political feasibility."[62] He was convinced that the conflict between Walloons and Flemings had deep roots in the historical antagonism between French and German culture; and it was so fundamental that its containment demanded some form of permanent German protectorate over Belgium after the war. On 4 April he reported these conclusions to the German governor-general in Brussels, Moritz von Bissing. This interview went well, for the two men agreed "entirely" on the Belgian question. Bissing, Lamprecht reported, "knew how to mobilize my knowledge of Belgium for his purposes."[63]

Buoyed by the experience, the historian prepared for an interview the next day in Brussels with the German foreign minister, Gottlieb von Jagow. He expected to reveal a comprehensive political design.[64] Its foundation was to be a German *Reich* "which accords with European requirements"; its precondition was the "definitive conquest [*Besiegung*]" of England, "so that there can be no doubt of its inferiority." The position of Germany was to be anchored in an autarchic confederation among the Germanic states of Europe, along with Turkey, Italy, Egypt, Central Africa, and China. The links among these states were to be solidified "above all" by "ample, brilliant cultural exchange of the highest order." The Chinese alliance was pivotal, he believed, for it would ensure German "military superiority [*Uebergewalt*] over the world."

This design represented Lamprecht's most extravagant, extended, and concrete (not to say practical) statement of war aims. It made the Pan-Germans' programs look modest by comparison. It was also a significant departure from both the substance and accents of his earlier pronouncements, in private as well as public. It betrayed signs of his experience at the front, the impact of all its excitement, disappointments, and strain on a man whose political views were volatile in any case. However, before he could lay out his views to Jagow, the historian collapsed.

Lamprecht's health intrudes little into his biography until the end. On few occasions in his life did he suffer from physical ailments serious enough to require more than routine professional attention. Finally, though, he fell victim to an affliction so sudden and virulent that questions persist to this day about its nature.

Unlike his brother Georg, Lamprecht escaped the diseases that were still the scourge of childhood in mid-nineteenth century Germany. Although his father was diabetic, the boy inherited no significant physical disorders from his parents, save his weak eyesight, which compelled him to wear glasses at the age of fifteen.[65] His two most significant episodes of ill health accompanied periods of intense emotional strain. In the early 1880s, he endured chronic gastritis, which the doctors diagnosed variously as a stomach or intestinal disorder, although it might well have been an ulcer.[66] His condition correlated in all events with the furious pace of his life in the Rhineland, as he labored to establish a foot in the historical profession. Physical afflictions also complicated the professional crisis of the late 1890s. The gastrointestinal disorder returned in the wake of a bronchial infection serious enough to require surgery.

Once these crises abated, Lamprecht's health improved, and it remained sound for the next decade and a half. Although completing his *German History* required another extended period of furious exertion, he survived it with but minor bouts of illness. He was fortunate, as he himself recognized.[67] Despite the solicitude of Ostwald, who warned him against the imprudent expenditure of his energy, the historian took few precautions in the interest of his health.[68] He lived well. He indulged regularly in the pleasures of good food, drink, and cigars—marks and privileges of the German academic bourgeoisie. A friend once noted that his idea of a concession to chronic indigestion was to warm his beer before drinking it.[69] His growing corpulence testified to his life-style, as well as to his lack of a regimen of physical exercise after 1896, when he retired from the active army reserves and ceased participating in annual maneuvers.[70] As his frequent travels attested, he nonetheless had enormous physical energy, most of which he expended in his study, where he labored late into the night. He seldom rested, but when he did, he slept well.[71] He was, he boasted, one of the few passengers to sleep through an Atlantic storm on his way back to Europe from America in November 1904.[72]

Symptoms of advancing age became more noticeable after 1909 and the completion of his magnum opus. He suffered from mild arthritis and became easily fatigued. His eyes weakened and required rest.[73] Thoughts of his own death occupied him more frequently, although he had pondered this subject intermittently since early in the century, when he revised his will to accommodate his wife's inheritance and purchased grave sites for himself and her on the grounds of Schulpforta.[74] However, the ailments of which he was now complaining were neither serious nor uncommon in a man in his late fifties; and on the eve of the war the historian could report that his health was basically sound.[75]

Despite the concerns of his doctor over his renewed exertions during the war, the claim that Lamprecht worked himself to death is more picturesque than plausible.[76] The reality was more prosaic. Upon his arrival in northern France in March 1915 he fell victim to severe indigestion.[77] The condition persisted, and two weeks later, on 5 April, he collapsed in Brussels. He rallied his strength that evening for his interview with Jagow but left for Germany the next day, canceling the interview which had been scheduled for him with Bethmann Hollweg in Charleroi.[78] After a brief stop in Cologne, where his lifeless appearance shocked the friends who met him, he returned to Leipzig.[79]

The reports of the symptoms are too fragmentary to permit more than a guess about the nature of the historian's malady. The perplexity of the physicians in Leipzig matched the confusion of his friends, who diagnosed the problem variously as acute leukemia, anemia, or a disorder of the liver and kidneys, if not sheer exhaustion.[80] The affliction was certainly abdominal; and there were signs of internal bleeding.[81] The symptoms are consistent with the perforation and temporary sealing off of an ulcer on 5 April, followed by abscess, leakage, and progressive anemia, which killed him.

Lamprecht himself recognized the extremity of his condition, which left him too weak to work. "I sit here in my small coffin," he wrote to his daughter, "and have nothing to do with the world."[82] On 17 April he contacted Schulpforta about his grave. At the end of the month the doctors moved him to the hospital, where his condition deteriorated. He died on 10 May 1915.

He scripted his own exit.[83] At the memorial service at the university chapel on 13 May, members of the Gewandhaus orchestra, with Nikisch conducting, played the funeral march from the *Eroica*. Lamprecht had earlier characterized Beethoven's symphony as a musical portrait of "the passage of genius through this world of imperfection—its heroic struggle to realize and exert its innermost essence, the moment of its apparent defeat, but then its joyful recovery and final victory in an ideal world."[84] The symphony was a tribute from the hero of one era to the hero of another. At the casket the next day, in Schulpforta, the chaplain read texts that Lamprecht had himself selected for the occasion. The passage from 1 Corinthians 13 contained the historian's final reading of his own life:

> For we know in part, and we prophesy in part.
>
> But when that which is perfect is come, then that which is in part shall be done away.
>
> When I was a child, I spake as a child, I thought as a child; but when I became a man, I put away childish things.
>
> For now we see through a glass, darkly; but then face to face: now I know in part; but then shall I know even as also I am known.

Notes

1. "Die 'Bugra 1914,'" *Die Post*, 6.5.14; Karl Soll, "Lamprechts Grundausstellung," *Vossische Zeitung*, 10.7.14; LW, 689–92.
2. NL Lamprecht (Munich), Internationale Ausstellung für Buchgewerbe und Graphik, Leipzig 1914, Kulturgeschichtliche Abteilung: Organisation, Arbeitsplan und Mitgliederliste bearbeitet nach dem Stand vom 1. Juli 1913; NL Lamprecht (Korr. 60), Lamprecht to Schramm, Leipzig, 10.1.14; Diederichs to Lamprecht, Jena, 11.7.14.
3. StA Dresden, VB 10281/203, Marianne Lamprecht, Mein Vaters wissenschaftliche Entwicklung . . . [1915]. The glosses on this document revealed the doubts of officials in the ministry about Lamprecht's whole concept.
4. StA Dresden, VB 10281/203, Lamprecht to Beck, Leipzig, 24.4.14; NL Lamprecht (Korr. 6), Lamprecht to Beck, Leipzig, 21.3.14; (Korr. 52), Lamprecht to Beck, Leipzig, 5.5.14; LW, 693–95.
5. "Historischer Unterricht und historische Forschungsinstitute," VuG, 4 (1914): 205–11; StA Dresden, VB 10281/203, Lamprecht to KM, Leipzig, 15.8.14.
6. NL Lamprecht (Korr. 24), Lamprecht to Goetz, Leipzig, 20.8.14.
7. NL Lamprecht (Korr. 27), Lamprecht to *Leipziger Neueste Nachrichten*, Leipzig, 3.10.13; (Korr. 47), Lamprecht to Baronin Schroeder, 6.8.13; (Korr. 62), Lamprecht to Neumann, Leipzig, 9.12.13.
8. NL Lamprecht (Korr. 21), Lamprecht to Eucken, Leipzig, 23.2.14; (Korr. 51), Vantirre to Lamprecht, Madison, 31.3.14.
9. NL Lamprecht (Korr. 67a), Lamprecht to KM, Leipzig, 22.4.14; LW, 697.
10. NL Lamprecht (Korr. 53), Lamprecht to Wenck, Leipzig, 19.3.14.
11. BA, NL Goetz (36), Lamprecht to Ritter, Leipzig, 5.1.13; StA Dresden, VB 10230/21, Lamprecht to KM, Leipzig, 3.5.13.
12. StA Dresden, VB, 10281/203, Finanzministerium Beschluss vom 7.10.13.
13. Franz Arens has hinted at the possibility of a romantic involvement at this time in the historian's life: Arens, "Lamprecht," 318. The suggestion rests on a dubious reading of Eduard Spranger's obituary: *cf.* Spranger, "Lamprechts Geschichtsauffassung," 174.
14. NL Lamprecht (Korr. 45), Lamprecht to Ritter, Leipzig, 14.6.12.
15. NL Lamprecht (Korr. 45), Lamprecht to Ritter, Leipzig, 20.5.14; (Korr. 49), Lamprecht to Springmann, Leipzig-Stötteritz, 6.5.14.
16. NL Lamprecht (Korr. 26), Lamprecht to Guthe, Leipzig, 14.10.14.
17. NL Lamprecht (Korr. 46), Lamprecht to Schmaltz, Leipzig, 21.8.14; (Korr. 12), Lamprecht to Blok, Leipzig, 5.9.14.
18. Klaus Schwabe, *Wissenschaft und Kriegsmoral: Die deutschen Hochschullehrer und die politischen Grundfragen des Ersten Weltkrieges* (Göttingen, 1969); Fritz Klein, "Die deutschen Historiker im ersten Weltkrieg," in Streisand, *Studien*, 2: 227–47; John A. Moses, "Pan-Germanism and the German Professors, 1914–1918," *Australian Journal of Politics and History*, 15 (December 1969): 45–60.
19. Lamprecht, *Deutscher Aufstieg 1750–1914: Einführung in das geschichtliche Verständnis der Gegenwart* (Gotha, 1914), 7, 13, 17–18.
20. Ibid., iii.
21. Ibid., 41–43.
22. Ibid., 43.
23. Lamprecht, *Zur neuen Lage* (Leipzig, 1914), 10–11; *cf. Deutscher Aufstieg*, 5–6.
24. Lamprecht, "Rückblick und Ausblick," *Die Woche*, 17 (2.1.15): 1–4.
25. NL Lamprecht (Korr. 13), Lamprecht to Breysig, Leipzig, 27.8.14; "Zur neuen

Lage," 15; "Geistige Mobilmachung," *Akademische Rundschau*, 2 (1914): 564, cited in vom Bruch, *Kulturmission*, 93.

26. NL Lamprecht (Korr. 46), Lamprecht to Salvadori, Leipzig, 10.11.14; (Korr. 61), Lamprecht to Waldeyer, Leipzig, 11.12.14; *cf.* Lamprecht, "Belgien und wir," *Berliner Tageblatt*, Nr. 665, 25.12.14.

27. NL Lamprecht (Korr. 63), Hermann Schumacher, Entwurf einer Denkschrift, Bonn, 5.9.14, Abschrift; *cf.* Lamprecht, "Krieg und Kultur," *Illustrierte Zeitung*, 1.10.1914.

28. NL Lamprecht (Korr. 9), Lamprecht to Bernheim, Leipzig, 15.10.14.

29. StA Dresden, VB 10281/203, Lamprecht to KM, Leipzig, 15.8.14; NL Lamprecht (Korr. 54), Lamprecht to Witting, 5.10.14; (Korr. 35), Lamprecht "Erziehungsfragen und Hochschulprobleme" (16.1.15).

30. NL Lamprecht (Korr. 5), Lamprecht to Baum, Leipzig, 14.8.14.

31. Bernhard vom Brocke, "'Wissenschaft und Militarismus': Der Aufruf der 93 'An die Kulturwelt!' und der Zusammenbruch der internationalen Gelehrtenrepublik im Ersten Weltkrieg," in W. M. Calder, III, et al., eds., *Wilamowitz nach 50 Jahren* (Darmstadt, 1985), 649–719; LW, 724–5.

32. NL Lamprecht (Korr. 61), Waldeyer to Lamprecht, Berlin, 30.12.14; *cf.* vom Brocke, "'Wissenschaft und Militarismus,'" 664.

33. NL Lamprecht (Korr. 61), Waldeyer to Lamprecht, Berlin, 9.12.14.

34. vom Brocke, "'Wissenschaft und Militarismus,'" 685–7; Schwabe, *Wissenschaft und Kriegsmoral*, 200, n. 103.

35. NL Lamprecht (Korr. 21), Stein to Eulenburg, Frankfurt am Main, 5.10.14.

36. NL Lamprecht (Korr. 12), Walter van der Bleek to Lamprecht, Wilmersdorf, 12.10.14; (Korr. 39), Naumann to Lamprecht, Berlin, 27.1.15; Lamprecht to Leonard Nelson, Leipzig, 20.10.14; (Korr. 61), Tepper-Laski to Lamprecht, Berlin, 26.1.15.

37. StA Dresden, VB 10281/203, Lamprecht to Schmaltz, 5.10.14.

38. StA Dresden, VB 10281/203, Lamprecht, Wünsche und Vorschläge für die nächste deutsche Zukunft in kurzer Formulierung; NL Lamprecht (Korr. 61), Lamprecht to Waldeyer, Leipzig, 11.12.14; Lamprecht, "Die Vorträge im kommenden Winter," *Akademische Rundschau*, 3 (1914): 1–3.

39. NL Lamprecht (Korr. 31), Hirzel to Lamprecht, Leipzig, 4.12.14; (Korr. 35), Lamprecht to Leipziger Lehrerverein, Leipzig, 22.2.15; (Korr. 39), Lamprecht to Nostiz, Leipzig, 19.11.14; (Korr. 51), Gesellschaft Urania to Lamprecht, Berlin, 19.11.14.

40. NL Lamprecht (Korr. 53), Wheeler to Lamprecht, Berkeley, 11.1.15.

41. NL Lamprecht (Korr. 45), Lamprecht to Ritter, Leipzig, 2.12.14.

42. NL Lamprecht (Korr. 45), Lamprecht to Ritter, Leipzig, 25.12.14; LW, 711.

43. NL Lamprecht (Korr. 51), Voigtländer to Lamprecht, Berlin, 10.9.14; (Korr 52), Vollert to Lamprecht, Berlin, 3.9.14; (Korr. 60), Diederichs to Lamprecht, Jena, 11.8.14; Schönebaum, "Unausgeführte Vorhaben," 120.

44. NL Lamprecht (Korr. 4), Amort to Lamprecht, Brooklyn, 23.10.14; (Korr. 16), Lamprecht to Burgess, Leipzig, 8.2.15; (Korr. 21), Lamprecht to Eliott and Butler, Leipzig, n.d.

45. NL Lamprecht (Korr. 27), Hansen to Lamprecht, Cologne, 29.1.15; LW, 716; Lyon, *Pirenne*, 209–10.

46. NL Lamprecht (Korr. 42), Lamprecht to Pirenne, Leipzig, 31.8.14; (Korr. 11), Bethmann Hollweg to Lamprecht, Grosses Hauptquartier, 4.1.15.

47. NL Lamprecht (Korr. 31), Hoeniger to Lamprecht, Brandenburg, 17.1.15; (Korr. 42), Lamprecht to Wirth, Leipzig, 13.1.14; Lyon, *Pirenne*, 216–17.

48. BA, R43F, RK Nr. 4, Bd. 6, Lamprecht to Bethmann Hollweg, Leipzig, 22.9.14; NL Lamprecht (Korr. 18), Daenell to Lamprecht, Münster, 9.10.14.

49. BA, R43F, RK Nr. 4, Bd. 6, Wahnschaffe to Lamprecht, Berlin, 10.14; Kornika (?) to Wahnschaffe, 17.10.14.
50. PAAA, Deutschland 163, Lamprecht to Mumm, Leipzig, 28.12.14.
51. Ibid., Riezler to AA, Grosses Hauptquartier, 14.1.15.
52. NL Lamprecht (Korr. 61), Lamprecht to Waldeyer, Leipzig, 12.11.14.
53. *Deutscher Aufstieg*, 17th ed. (Gotha, 1915).
54. NL Lamprecht (Korr. 61), Lamprecht to Wahnschaffe, Leipzig, 2.12.14.
55. vom Brocke, "'Wissenschaft und Militarismus,'" 685–7; *cf.* Lamprecht, "Deutschland und der Orient," in Hugo Grothe, ed., *Deutsche Kultur in der Welt* (Leipzig, 1914), 1–2.
56. NL Lamprecht (L 35), Reisenotizen, March/April 1915. Kriegsschauplatz; (H 60), Lamprecht, Reise nach dem Kriegsschauplatz (Kriegserinnerungen), 11. The historian planned to publish this memoir of his tour when he returned. Galley proofs were ready when the army blocked publication, primarily on account of his intemperate remarks about Belgium. NL Lamprecht (H 60), Dirr to Marianne Lamprecht, Brussels, 16.9.15. Efforts of the historian's daughters to publish the account after the war were also fruitless, because, as one sympathetic editor explained, it pertained to "a time when most of us thought quite differently about the course of things than we do today." (H 60), Soll to Else Lamprecht, Berlin, 29.3.19.
57. NL Lamprecht (L 35), Gespräch mit K., 20.3.15; (H 60), Reise nach dem Kriegsschauplatz, 46–60.
58. Ibid., 10, 23 ii–6, 44–45.
59. Ibid., 61.
60. Lyon, *Pirenne*, 218.
61. LW, 720. Lyon's account makes no mention of this visit, although it does recount Pirenne's turning Hoeniger, another former German friend, away at the door in January 1915. Schönebaum's account is based on more intimate knowledge and is consistent with a passage in Lamprecht's own memoir: "The experiences that I had in these days belong to the most difficult that I have ever had to overcome one after another in a short time." Reise nach dem Kriegsschauplatz, 63. See also Bryce and Mary Lyon, eds., *The Journal de guerre of Henri Pirenne* (Amsterdam, 1976), 9–10.
62. Ibid., 64–66.
63. Ibid., 66–67.
64. Ibid., 69–71.
65. LW, 20–21.
66. NL Lamprecht (Korr. 59), Lamprecht to Hugo Lamprecht, Bonn, 28.7.86.
67. DG, 11: 748.
68. Ostwald, "Freundschaft"; LW, 453.
69. NL Lamprecht (L 3a), Zimmer to Marianne Lamprecht, Zehlendorf, 6.8.15.
70. LW, 302.
71. NL Goetz (36), Lamprecht to Ritter, Leipzig, 5.1.13.
72. *Americana*, 93.
73. NL Goetz (174), Lamprecht to Ritter, Leipzig, 22.10.09; NL Lamprecht (Korr. 45), Lamprecht to Ritter, Schloss Labers, 20.9.10; (Korr. 59), Lamprecht to Else Lamprecht, Leipzig, 13.5.12.
74. LW, 476, 681.
75. NL Lamprecht (Korr. 24), Lamprecht to Gneisse, Leipzig, 3.7.14.
76. UA Leipzig, Phil. Fak., PA 675, Lamprecht to KM, Leipzig, 23.2.15, Abschrift; Kötzschke, "Lamprecht," 1; Bücher, *Worte zum Gedächtnis*, 12; LW, 736; Engelberg, "Methodenstreit," 151.
77. NL Lamprecht (Munich), Lamprecht to Else and Marianne Lamprecht, St. Quentin, 19.3.15.

78. NL Lamprecht (H 60), Dirr to Marianne Lamprecht, Brussels, 11.9.15; LW, 720.
79. NL Lamprecht (Korr. 18), Deichmann to Marianne Lamprecht, Mehlen, 28.5.15.
80. Breysig, *Tagen und Träumen*, 84; LW, 722; *cf.* Metz, *Grundformen*, 473; Schleier, "Der Kulturhistoriker," 30.
81. Schönebaum, who saw him upon his return, reports that "every drop of blood had disappeared from his face" as his strength ebbed. LW, 721.
82. NL Lamprecht (Munich), Lamprecht to Else Lamprecht, Leipzig, 28.4.15.
83. NL Lamprecht (M6), Karl Lamprecht zum Gedächtnis. Begräbnis in Schulpforta bei Naumburg, 14.5.14.
84. DG, 8: 695.

Bibliography

ARCHIVAL SOURCES

Badisches Generallandesarchiv, Karlsruhe
  Nachlass Willy Hellpach
  Nachlass Erich Marcks
Bayerische Staatsbibliothek, Munich
  Autographensammlung
  Heyse-Archiv
  Krumbacheriana
Bundesarchiv, Koblenz
  Akten der (Alten) Reichskanzlei
  Nachlass Walter Goetz (Nachlass Moriz Ritter)
  Nachlass Maximilian Harden
  Nachlass Paul Lindau
  Nachlass Walther Schücking
  Nachlass Martin Spahn
  Nachlass Gottfried Traub
  Nachlass Theodor Wolff
Columbia University, New York
  Nicholas Murray Butler Papers
Deutsche Staatsbibliothek, Berlin
  Nachlass Hans Delbrück
  Nachlass Heinrich von Treitschke
Geheimes Staatsarchiv Preussischer Kulturbesitz, Berlin-Dahlem
  Nachlass Friedrich Meinecke
Geheimes Staatsarchiv Preussischer Kulturbesitz, Merseburg (formerly Zentrales Staatsarchiv, Merseburg)
  Nachlass Friedrich Althoff
  Nachlass Gustav Schmoller
  Nachlass Heinrich von Sybel
  Nachlass Max Weber
Hessische Landesbibliothek, Wiesbaden
  Nachlass Erich Liesegang
Hessisches Staatsarchiv, Marburg
  Nachlass Hermann Grimm
Historisches Archiv der Stadt Köln
  Akten der Gesellschaft für Rheinische Geschichtskunde
  Nachlass Gustav von Mevissen
Karl Lamprecht, Private Papers, Munich
Politisches Archiv des Auswärtigen Amtes, Bonn
  Deutschland 122 No. 6, 125, 126b, 163
  IV A. Deutschtum im Ausland No. 5

Eur. Gen. No. 37
Vereinigte Staaten von Amerika No. 16
Staatsarchiv Dresden
  Ministerium für Volksbildung: Kultusministerium—Universität Leipzig
  Historisches Seminar
  Institut für Kultur- und Universalgeschichte
  Personalakten Lamprecht, Erich Brandenburg
  Professoren- und Dozentenvereinigungen
Staatsarchiv Oldenburg
  Nachlass Hermann Oncken
Staatsbibliothek Preussischer Kulturbesitz, Berlin
  Nachlass Kurt Breysig
Universitätsarchiv Bonn
  Akten des königlichen Curatoriums der Rheinischen Friedrich-Wilhelms-Universität
  Personalakt Lamprecht
  Akten der philosophischen Fakultät
Universitätsarchiv Leipzig
  Akademischer Senat
  Institut für Kultur- und Universalgeschichte
  Ordentliche Professur für neuere Geschichte
  Personalakten Karl Lamprecht, Max Lehmann, Erich Marcks, Walter Goetz
  Philosophische Fakultät
  Rentamt
Universitätsbibliothek, Bonn
  Autographen-Sammlung: Karl Lamprecht-Richard Pick
  Nachlass Carl Justi
  Nachlass Karl Lamprecht
  Nachlass Aloys Schulte
Universitätsbibliothek, Freiburg i. Br.
  Nachlass Alfred Dove
Universitätsbibliothek, Leipzig
  Akten der Jablonowski Gesellschaft
  Nachlass Karl Bücher
  Nachlass Rudolf Hildebrand
  Nachlass Otto Mayer
  Nachlass Friedrich Ratzel
  Nachlass Herbert Schönebaum
  Nachlass Wilhelm Stieda
  Nachlass Otto Wiener
  Nachlass Eduard Zarncke

PUBLISHED SOURCES

Bähr, Hans Walter, ed. *Eduard Spranger: Briefe 1901–1963*. Tübingen, 1978.
Bericht über die dritte Versammlung deutscher Historiker in Frankfurt am Main. Stuttgart, 1895.
Bericht über die fünfte Versammlung deutscher Historiker zu Nürnberg, 12. bis 15. April 1898. Leipzig, 1898.
Bericht über die siebente Versammlung deutscher Historiker zu Heidelberg, 14. bis April 1903. Leipzig, 1903.

Bericht über die vierte Versammlung deutscher Historiker zu Innsbruck, 11. bis 14. September 1896. Leipzig, 1897.

Bericht über die zehnte Versammlung deutscher Historiker zu Dresden, 3. bis 7. September 1907. Leipzig, 1908.

Bericht über die zweite Versammlung deutscher Historiker in Leipzig. Stuttgart, 1894.

Braubach, Max. "Aus Briefen Karl Büchers an Aloys Schulte: Ein Beitrag zur deutschen Wissenschaftsgeschichte zwischen 1890 und 1925." Brunner, Otto et al., eds. *Festschrift Hermann Aubin zum 80. Geburtstag*. 2 vols. Wiesbaden, 1965. 1: 375–402.

———. "Zwei deutsche Historiker aus Westfalen: Briefe Heinrich Finkes an Aloys Schulte." *Westfälische Zeitschrift* 118 (1968): 9–114.

Briefwechsel zwischen Wilhelm Dilthey und dem Grafen Paul Yorck von Wartenburg 1877–1897. Halle, 1923.

Dove, Alfred. *Ausgewählte Aufsätze und Briefe*. Ed. Friedrich Meinecke. 2 vols. Munich, 1925.

Erdmann, Karl-Dietrich. "Geschichte, Politik und Pädagogik—aus den Akten des deutschen Historikerverbandes." *Geschichte in Wissenschaft und Unterricht* 19 (1968): 2–21.

Erdmann, Karl Dietrich, ed., *Kurt Riezler: Tagebücher, Aufsätze, Dokumente*. Göttingen, 1972.

Hirsch, Paul, ed. "Briefe namhafter Historiker an Harry Bresslau." *Die Welt als Geschichte* 14 (1954): 223–41.

Lepsius, M. Rainer et al., eds. *Max Weber: Briefe 1906–1908*. Tübingen, 1990.

Meinecke, Friedrich. *Ausgewählter Briefwechsel*. Ed. Ludwig Dehio and Peter Classen. Stuttgart, 1962.

AUTOBIOGRAPHY

Asenijeff, Elsa. *Tagebuchblätter einer Emancipierten*. Leipzig, 1902.

Barth, Paul. "Paul Barth." Ed. Schmidt. *Philosophie der Gegenwart* 1: 1–20.

Below, Georg von. "Georg von Below." Ed. S. Steinberg. 1: 1–49.

Brentano, Lujo. *Mein Leben im Kampf um die soziale Entwicklung Deutschlands*. Jena, 1931.

Breysig, Kurt. *Aus meinen Tagen und Träumen: Memoiren, Aufzeichnungen, Briefe, Gespräche*. Berlin, 1962.

———. *Gedankenblätter*. Berlin, 1964.

Bücher, Karl. *Lebenserinnerungen: 1847–1890*. Tübingen, 1919.

Finke, Heinrich. "Heinrich Finke." Ed. S. Steinberg. 1: 91–128.

Goetz, Walter. "Walter Goetz." Ed. S. Steinberg. 1: 129–70.

Hellpach, Willy. *Wirken in Wirren: Lebenserinnerungen*. 2 vols. Hamburg, 1948–49.

Koht, Halvdan. "Aus den Lehrjahren eines Historikers." *Die Welt als Geschichte* 13 (1953): 149–65.

Lamprecht, Karl. *Kindheitserinnerungen*. Gotha, 1918.

———. *Rektoratserinnerungen*. Ed. Arthur Köhler. Gotha, 1917.

Lehmann, Max. "Max Lehmann." Ed. S. Steinberg. 1: 207–32.

Man, Hendrik de. *Gegen den Strom: Memoiren eines europäischen Sozialisten*. Stuttgart, 1953.

Meinecke, Friedrich. *Autobiographische Schriften*. Ed. Eberhard Kessel. Stuttgart, 1969. 3–134.

Nippold, Otfried. *Meine Erlebnisse in Deutschland vor dem Weltkriege (1909–1914)*. Berne, 1918.

Ostwald, Wilhelm. "Meine Freundschaft mit Karl Lamprecht: Geisteswissenschaft und Naturwissenschaft." *Neue Leipziger Zeitung*. 27.6.26.

———. "Wilhelm Ostwald." Ed. Schmidt. *Die Philosophie der Gegenwart*. 4: 127–61.

————. *Lebenslinien: Eine Selbstbiographie.* 3 vols. Berlin, 1927.
Rachfahl, Felix. "Felix Rachfahl." Ed. S. Steinberg. 2: 199–222.
Radbruch, Gustav. *Der innere Weg: Aufriss meines Lebens.* Stuttgart, 1951.
Rein, G. A. *Politik und Universität,* diktiert 1975–76.
Schmarzow, A. "Rückschau beim Eintritt ins siebzigste Lebensjahr." Jahn, Johannes, ed. *Die Kunstgeschichte der Gegenwart in Selbstdarstellungen.* Leipzig, 1924. 135–56.
Schmidt, Raymund, ed. *Die Philosophie der Gegenwart in Selbstdarstellungen.* 7 vols. Leipzig, 1922–29.
Steinberg, Sigfrid, ed. *Die Geschichtswissenschaft der Gegenwart in Selbstdarstellungen.* 2 vols. Leipzig, 1925.
Steinhausen, Georg. "Georg Steinhausen." Ed. S. Steinberg. 1: 233–74.
Wilhelm II. *Aus meinem Leben.* Berlin and Leipzig, 1927.
Wundt, Wilhelm. *Erlebtes und Erkanntes.* 2d ed. Stuttgart, 1921.

LAMPRECHTIANA

"Die ältesten Nachrichten über das Hof- und Dorfsystem, speziell am Niederrhein," *Zeitschrift des Bergischen Geschichtsvereins* 16 (1880): 191–99.
Alte und neue Richtungen in der Geschichtswissenschaft. Berlin, 1896.
Americana: Reiseeindrücke, Betrachtungen, Geschichtliche Gesamtansicht. Freiburg, 1906.
"Das Arbeitgebiet [sic] geschichtlicher Forschung." *Die Zukunft* 15 (1896): 25–28.
"Der Ausgang des geschichtswissenschaftlichen Kampfes." *Die Zukunft* 20 (1897): 195–208.
Ausgewählte Schrifen zur Wirtschafts- und Kulturgeschichte und zur Theorie der Geschichtswissenschaft. Ed. Herbert Schönebaum. Aalen, 1974.
"Über auswärtige Kulturpolitik." *Mitteilungen des Verbandes für internationale Verständigung* 8 (1913): 3–14.
"Zur auswärtigen Kulturpolitik." *Frankfurter Zeitung* 12.4.14.
"Über den Begriff der Geschichte und über historische und psychologische Gesetze." *Annalen der Naturphilosophie* 2 (1903): 255–78.
Beiträge zur Geschichte des französischen Wirthschaftslebens im elften Jahrhundert. Leipzig, 1878.
"Belgien und wir." *Berliner Tageblatt* No. 665, 25.12.14.
"Der Bilderschmuck des Codex Egberti zu Trier und des Codex Epternacensis in Gotha." *Jahrbücher des Vereins von Alterthumsfreunden im Rheinland* 70 (1881): 56–112.
"Bilderzyklen und Illustrationstechnik im späteren Mittelalter." *Repertorium für Kunstwissenschaft* 7 (1883): 405–15.
"Biopsychologische Probleme." *Annalen der Naturphilosophie* 3 (1904): 442–48.
Deutsche Geschichte. 12 vols. Berlin and Freiburg, 1891–1909.
Deutsche Geschichte der jüngsten Vergangenheit und Gegenwart. 2 vols. Berlin, 1912–13.
"Deutsche Ideale." *Die Zukunft* 71 (1910): 114–19.
Deutscher Aufstieg 1750–1914: Einführung in das geschichtliche Verständnis der Gegenwart. Gotha, 1914.
Deutsches Wirtschaftsleben im Mittelalter: Untersuchungen über die Entwicklung der materiellen Kultur des platten Landes auf Grund der Quellen. Zunächst des Mosellandes. 3 vols. Leipzig, 1885–86.
"Deutschland und der Orient." Ed. Hugo Grothe. *Deutsche Kultur in der Welt.* Leipzig, 1914. 1–2.
Einführung in das historische Denken. Leipzig, 1912.
"Die Entstehung der Willebriefe und die Revindication des Reichsgutes unter Rudolf von Habsburg," *Forschungen zur deutschen Geschichte* 21 (1881): 1–19.
"Die Entwickelung des wirtschaftlichen und geistigen Horizonts unserer Nation." Ed.

Gustav Schmoller et al. *Handels- und Machtpolitik: Reden und Aufsätze im Auftrage der Freien Vereinigung für Flottenvorträge.* Stuttgart, 1900. 1: 39–62.

"Die Entwicklung der deutschen Geschichtswissenschaft vornehmlich seit Herder." *Beilage zur Allgemeinen Zeitung* No. 83, 15.4.98.

"Die Entwicklungsstufen der deutschen Geschichtswissenschaft." *Zeitschrift für Kulturgeschichte* 5 (1898): 385–438; 6 (1899): 1–45.

"Entwicklungsstufen." *Die Zukunft* 39 (1902): 139–43.

"Europäische Expansion in Vergangenheit und Gegenwart." *Geschichte der Neuzeit. Ullsteins Weltgeschichte*, vol. 6. Berlin, 1910. 599–625.

"Europäische Expansion." *Die Zukunft* 65 (1908): 141–53.

"Eine Festrede." *Die Zukunft* 26 (1899): 137–43.

"Finanz und Finanznot des alten Deutschen Reiches." *Die Reichsfinanzreform: Ein Führer.* Berlin, 1908. 1–10.

"Zur Fortbildung unserer Universitäten." *Internationale Wochenschrift für Wissenschaft, Kunst und Technik* 3 (1909): 1539–54.

"Fränkische Ansiedelungen und Wanderungen im Rheinland." *Westdeutsche Zeitschrift für Geschichte und Kunst* I (1882): 123ff.

"Fränkische Wanderungen und Ansiedlungen im Rheinland." *Zeitschrift des Aachener Geschichtsvereins* 4 (1882): 189–250.

Freiheit und Volkstum: Worte zur heutigen politischen Lage. Cologne, 1906.

"Friedrich Ratzel." *Berichte über die Verhandlungen der Königlich Sächsischen Gesellschaft der Wissenschaften zu Leipzig, Philosogisch-historische Classe* 56 (1904): 259–69.

"Gärung und Klärung im Hochschulgebiet." *Frankfurter Zeitung* 6.5.14.

"Zum Gedächtnis Heinrichs von Treitschke." *Die Zukunft* 16 (1896): 108–12.

"Eine Gefahr für die Geisteswissenschaften." *Die Zukunft* 83 (1913): 16–24, 421–9.

"Die gegenwärtige Lage der Geschichtswissenschaft." *Die Zukunft* 14 (1896): 247–55.

"Geistige Mobilmachung." *Akademische Rundschau* 2 (1914): 563–5.

"Die geschichtswissenschaftlichen Probleme der Gegenwart." *Die Zukunft* 17 (1896): 247–55; 300–11.

"Die Gesellschaft Jesu." *Die Zukunft* 10 (1895): 499–55.

"Gustav von Mevissen als Förderer der Geschichtswissenschaft," *Nationalzeitung* No. 551, 1899.

"Herder und Kant als Theoretiker der Geschichtswissenschaft." *Jahrbücher für Nationalökonomie und Statistik* 69 (1897): 161–203.

"Herr Professor Troeltsch." *Deutsche Literaturzeitung* 30 (1909): 3071–72; *Literarisches Zentralblatt* 60 (1909): 1479–80.

"Die Herrlichkeit Erpel: Ein wirtschafts-, sozial- und verfassungsgeschichtliches Paradigma." *Beiträge zur Geschichte vornehmlich Kölns und der Rheinlande. Zum 80. Geburtstage Gustav v. Mevissens.* Cologne, 1895. 1–26.

Die historische Methode des Herrn von Below: Eine Kritik. Berlin, 1899.

"Historia vitae magistra." *Berliner Tageblatt* 7.1.10.

"Historikertag und Umsturzvorlage." *Die Zukunft* 11 (1895): 203–4.

"Individualität, Idee und sozialpsychische Kraft in der Geschichte." *Jahrbücher für Nationalökonomie und Statistik* 68 (1897): 880–900.

Initial-Ornamentik des VIII. bis XIII. Jahrhunderts. Leipzig, 1882.

"Die Kernpunkte der geschichtswissenschaftlichen Erörterungen der Gegenwart." *Zeitschrift für Socialwissenschaft* 2 (1899): 11–18.

"Die Königlich Sächsische Commission für Geschichte." *Berichte über die Verhandlungen der Königlich Sächsischen Gesellschaft der Wissenschaften zu Leipzig, Philologisch-historische Classe* 52 (1900): 153–67.

"Krieg und Kultur." *Illustrierte Zeitung* 1.10.1914.

"Die kultur- und universalgeschichtlichen Bestrebungen an der Universität Leipzig."

Internationale Wochenschrift für Wissenschaft, Kunst und Technik 2 (1908): 1141–50.
Die kulturhistorische Methode. Berlin, 1900.
"Die künftige Politisierung der Gesellschaft." *Berliner Tageblatt* 15.1.07.
"Meine Gegner." *Die Zukunft* 21 (1897): 109–21, 199–208, 240–52.
Menzel, Karl, et al., eds. *Die Trierer Adahandschrift.* Leipzig, 1889.
Moderne Geschichtswissenschaft: Fünf Vorträge. Freiburg im Breisgau, 1905.
Die Nation und die Friedensbewegung. Berlin, 1914.
"Die Nation und die Friedensbewegung." *Die Friedenswarte* 12 (1910): 41–44.
"Nationalismus und Universalismus in Deutschland," *Dokumente des Fortschritts* 1 (1907–8): 5–10.
Zur neuen Lage. Leipzig, 1914.
"Neuere Litteratur zu den historisch-methodologischen Erörterungen," *Deutsche Zeitschrift für Geschichtswissenschaft* n.F. 2 (1897–98): 121–25.
"Ein neues Historisches Institut." *Die Zukunft* 68 (1909): 341–50.
"Die Psychisierung der Wirtschaftsstufen." *Zeitschrift für Kulturgeschichte* 9 (1902): 365–449.
"Recht und Wirtschaft zur Frankenzeit." *Historisches Taschenbuch* 2 (1882): 43–67, 76–89.
"Rede des abtretenden Rektors Dr. Karl Lamprecht: Bericht über das Studienjahr 1910/11." *Rektorenwechsel an der Universität Leipzig am 31. Oktober 1911.* Leipzig, n.d., 1–22.
"Rede des antretenden Rektors Dr. Karl Lamprecht." *Rektorenwechsel an der Universität Leipzig am 31. Oktober 1910.* Leipzig, n.d., 15–36.
"Review of Inama-Sternegg, *Deutsche Wirtschaftsgeschichte des 10. bis 12. Jahrhunderts.*" *Jahrbücher für Nationalökonomie und Statistik* 64 (1895): 294–98.
"Rückblick und Ausblick." *Die Woche* 17 (2.1.15): 1–4.
Schleier, Hans, ed. *Karl Lamprecht: Alternative zu Ranke. Schriften zur Geschichtstheorie.* Leipzig, 1988.
Skizzen zur rheinischen Geschichte. Leipzig, 1887.
"Staatsform und Politik im Lichte der Geschichte." *Handbuch der Politik* 1 (5) (Berlin, 1912): 747–60.
"Die Technik und die Kultur der Gegenwart." *Zeitschrift des Vereins deutscher Ingenieure* 57 (1913): 1523–26.
"Universalgeschichte auf der Hochschule." *Die Zukunft* 60 (1907): 432–39.
"Zur universalgeschichtlichen Methodenbildung." *Abhandlungen der philologisch-historischen Classe der Königlich-Sächsischen Gesellschaft der Wissenschaften* 27 (1909): 33–63.
"Zum Unterschiede der älteren und jüngeren Richtungen der Geschichtswissenschaft." *Historische Zeitschrift* 77 (1896): 257–61.
"Der Ursprung des Bürgertums und des städtischen Lebens in Deutschland," *Historische Zeitschrift* 67 (1891): 385–424.
"Verse und Miniaturen aus einer Evangelienhandschrift der Kölner Dombibliothek." *Neues Archiv der Gesellschaft für ältere deutsche Geschichtskunde* 9 (1884): 620–23.
"Volksthümliche Hochschulkurse." *Die Zukunft* 20 (1897): 13–15.
"Zur Vorgeschichte des Consensrechtes der Kurfürsten." *Forschungen zur deutschen Geschichte* 23 (1883): 63–116.
"Die Vorträge im kommenden Winter." *Akademische Rundschau* 3 (1914): 1–3.
"Was ist Kulturgeschichte? Beitrag zu einer empirischen Historik." *Deutsche Zeitschrift für Geschichtswissenschaft* N.F. 1 (1896–97): 75–150.
"Eine Weltgeschichte nach neuen Grundsätzen," *Frankfurter Zeitung* 24.9.99.
"Eine Wendung im geschichtswissenschaftlichen Streit." *Die Zukunft* 18 (1897): 23–33.
What Is History? Five Lectures in the Modern Science of History. New York, 1905.

"Zwei Notizen zur ältesten deutschen Geschichte." *Zeitschrift des Bergischen Geschichts-vereins* 16 (1880): 173–90.
Zwei Reden zur Hochschulreform. Berlin, 1910.
Zwei Streitschriften, den Herren H. Oncken, H. Delbrück, M. Lenz zugeeignet. Berlin, 1897.

JOURNALS

Annalen der Naturphilosophie
Archiv für Kulturgeschichte
Deutsche Geschichtsblätter
Deutsche Literaturzeitung
Deutsche Zeitschrift für Geschichtswissenschaft, Neue Folge, 1–2 (1896–98)
Die Zukunft
Göttinger Gelehrte-Anzeigen
Historische Vierteljahrschrift
Historische Zeitschrift
Jahrbücher für Nationalökonomie und Statistik
Jahresberichte für Geschichtswissenschaft
Literarisches Zentralblatt
Preussische Jahrbücher
Vierteljahrschrift für Sozial- und Wirtschaftsgeschichte
Westdeutsche Zeitschrift für Geschichte und Kunst
Zeitschrift für Kulturgeschichte

CONTEMPORARY LITERATURE (UP TO 1916)

Allgemeine Deutsche Biographie
Aly, Friedrich. "Der Einbruch des Materialismus in die historischen Wissenschaften." *Preussische Jahrbücher* 81 (1895): 199–214.
Anschütz, Georg. "Theodor Lipps." *Archiv für die gesamte Psychologie* 34 (1915): 1–13.
Arnold, Wilhelm. "Zur Geschichte des Rheinlands." *Westdeutsche Zeitschrift für Geschichte und Kunst* 1 (1882): 1–35.
Barth, Paul. "Fragen der Geschichtswissenschaft." *Vierteljahrschrift für wissenschaftliche Philosophie* 23 (1899): 322–59.
———. *Die Philosophie der Geschichte als Sociologie.* Leipzig, 1897.
Baur, Wilhelm. *Das deutsche evangelische Pfarrhaus: Seine Gründung und sein Bestand.* Bremen, 1878.
Below, Georg von. "Zur Beurteilung Heinrich Leos." *Archiv für Kulturgeschichte* 9 (1911): 199–209.
———. "Briefe von K. W. Nitzsch an W. Schrader (1868–1880)." *Archiv für Kulturgeschichte* 10 (1912): 25–39.
———. "Zur Entstehung der deutschen Stadtverfassung." *Historische Zeitschrift* 58 (1887): 193–244; 59 (1888): 193–247.
———. *Der Höniger-Jastrow'sche Freundeskreis.* Düsseldorf, 1892.
———. "Kulturgeschichte und kulturgeschichtlicher Unterricht." *Historische Zeitschrift* 106 (1911): 96–105.
———. "Die neue historische Methode." *Historische Zeitschrift* 81 (1898): 193–273.
———. "Über Theorien der wirtschaftlichen Entwicklung der Völker, mit besonderer Rücksicht auf die Stadtwirtschaft des deutschen Mittelalters." *Historische Zeitschrift* 86 (1901): 1–77.
———. "Wirtschaftsgeschichte innerhalb der Nationalökonomie." *Vierteljahrschrift für Sozial- und Wirtschaftsgeschichte* 5 (1907): 481–524.

————. "Zur Würdigung der historischen Schule der Nationalökonomie." *Zeitschrift für Sozialwissenschaft* 7 (1904): 145–85, 221–37, 304–29, 367–91, 451–66, 654–59, 685–86, 710–16, 787–804.

Below, Georg von, and Schulz, Marie. "Briefe von K. W. Nitzsch an W. Maurenbrecher (1861–1880)." *Archiv für Kulturgeschichte* 8 (1910): 305–66, 437–68.

Bernheim, Ernst. *Geschichtsforschung und Geschichtsphilosophie.* Göttingen, 1880.

————. "Geschichtsunterricht und Geschichtswissenschaft." *Pädagogische Zeit- und Streitfragen* 10 (1899): 1–56.

————. *Lehrbuch der historischen Methode.* Leipzig, 1889.

————. *Lehrbuch der historischen Methode.* 2d ed. Leipzig, 1894.

————. *Lehrbuch der historischen Methode und der Geschichtsphilosophie.* 3d ed. 2 vols. Leipzig, 1908.

Bezold, Friedrich von. *Geschichte der deutschen Reformation.* Berlin, 1890.

Bleuler, Josef. *Dementia Praecox oder die Gruppe der Schizophrenien.* Leipzig, 1911.

Breysig, Kurt. "Über Entwicklungsgeschichte: Das Objekt." *Deutsche Zeitschrift für Geschichtswissenschaft* N.F. 1 (1896/97) (Monatsblätter): 161–74.

————. "Über Entwicklungsgeschichte: Die Methode." *Deutsche Zeitschrift für Geschichtswissenschaft* N.F. 1 (1896/97) (Monatsblätter): 193–211.

————. *Die Geschichte der Menschheit: Die Völker ewiger Urzeit. Die Amerikaner des Nordwestens und des Nordens.* Berlin, 1907.

————. *Kulturgeschichte der Neuzeit: Vergleichende Entwicklungsgeschichte der führenden Völker Europas und ihres sozialen und geistigen Lebens.* 2 vols. Berlin, 1900–1901.

————. *Der Stufenbau und die Gesetze der Welt-Geschichte.* Berlin, 1905.

Brotherus, K. R. "Sind Kant und Lamprecht unvereinbare Gegensätze?" Koetzschke, ed. *Studium Lipsiense: Ehrengabe für Karl Lamprecht.* Berlin, 1909.

Bücher, Karl. *Die Entstehung der Volkswirtschaft: Vorträge und Versuche.* Tübingen, 1893.

————. *Worte zum Gedächtnis an Karl Lamprecht.* Leipzig, 1916.

Burckhardt, Jacob. *The Civilization of the Renaissance in Italy: An Essay.* New York, 1954.

Caro, J. "Die europäische Staatengeschichte von Heeren, Ukert und Giesebrecht." Ed. Karl Lamprecht. *Allgemeine Staatengeschichte.* Gotha, 1907. 3–12.

Curschmann, Fritz. "Die Entwicklung der historisch-geographischen Forschung in Deutschland." *Archiv für Kulturgeschichte* 12 (1916): 129–63, 285–325.

Dilthey, Wilhelm. *Einleitung in die Geisteswissenschaften: Versuch einer Grundlegung für das Studium der Gesellschaft und der Geschichte. Gesammelte Schriften.* vol. 1. Stuttgart, 1959.

————. *Gesammelte Schriften.* 14 vols. Berlin and Stuttgart, 1921–66.

————. "Ideen über eine beschreibende und zergliedernde Psychologie." *Sitzungsberichte der Akademie der Wissenschaften zu Berlin 1894.* Berlin, 1894. 1309–1407.

Dopsch, Alfons. "Stand der Forschung auf dem Gebiete der älteren deutschen Verfassungs- und Sozialgeschichte." *Die Geisteswissenschaften* 12 (1913–1914): 323–27.

Doren, Alfred. "Karl Lamprechts Geschichtstheorie und die Kunstgeschichte." *Zeitschrift für Aesthetik und allgemeine Kunstwissenschaft* 11 (1916): 353–89.

Droysen, Johann Gustav. "Die Erhebung der Geschichte zum Rang einer Wissenschaft." *Historische Zeitschrift* 9 (1863): 1–22.

————. *Historik: Rekonstruktion der ersten vollständigen Fassung der Vorlesungen (1857) Grundriss der Historik in der ersten handschriftlichen (1857/58) und in der letzten gedruckten Fassung (1882).* Ed. Peter Leyh. Stuttgart-Bad Cannstatt, 1977.

Ebbinghaus, Hermann. "Über erklärende und beschreibende Psychologie." *Zeitschrift für Psychologie* 6 (1896): 161–205.

Erben, Wilhelm. "Die Entstehung der Universitäts-Seminare." *Internationale Wochenschrift für Wissenschaft, Kunst und Technik* 7 (1913): 1247–64, 1335–47.

Eulenburg, Franz. *Der "akademische Nachwuchs": Eine Untersuchung über die Lage und die*

Aufgaben der Extraordinarien und Privatdozenten. Leipzig and Berlin, 1908.

————. *Die Entwicklung der Universität Leipzig in den letzten hundert Jahren: Statistische Untersuchungen.* Leipzig, 1909.

————. *Die Frequenz der deutschen Universitäten: Von ihrer Gründung bis zur Gegenwart.* Leipzig, 1904.

————. "Neuere Geschichtsphilosophie." *Archiv für Sozialwissenschaft und Sozialpolitik* 25 (1907): 283–337.

Finke, Heinrich. *Genetische und klerikale Geschichtsauffassung: Eine Antwort an Professor Dr. Karl Lamprecht.* Münster, 1897.

————. *Die kirchenpolitischen und kirchlichen Verhältnisse zu Ende des Mittelalters nach der Darstellung K. Lamprechts: Eine Kritik seiner "Deutschen Geschichte."* Rome, 1896.

Franke, Erich. *Die geistige Entwicklung der Negerkinder: Ein Beitrag zur Frage nach den Hemmungen der Kulturentwicklung.* Leipzig, 1915.

Friedjung, Heinrich. *Der Kampf um die Vorherrschaft in Deutschland 1859 bis 1866.* 2 vols. 2d ed. Stuttgart, 1898.

Gabert, Erich. "Karl Lamprechts Theorie der Geschichtswissenschaft: Darstellung und Versuch einer psychologischen Analyse." Ph.D. dissertation, Leipzig, n.d.

Goetz, Walter. "Historischer Unterricht und historische Forschungsinstitute." *Vergangenheit und Gegenwart* 4 (1914): 205–11.

Gothein, Eberhard. *Die Aufgaben der Kulturgeschichte.* Leipzig, 1889.

————. *Wirtschaftsgeschichte des Schwarzwaldes und der angrenzenden Landschaften.* Strassburg, 1892.

Guilland, Antoine. "Karl Lamprecht." *Revue historique* 121 (1916): 83–108.

Günther, Felix. *Troeltsch-Heidelberg und die Lamprechtsche Richtung: Eine Entgegnung.* Leipzig, 1909.

Hannak, E. "Lamprechts Deutsche Geschichte und die neue Richtung in der Geschichtswissenschaft." *Zeitschrift für das österreichische Gymnasium* (1897): 293–308.

Hansen, Joseph. *Gustav von Mevissen.* 2 vols. Berlin, 1906.

Harnack, Adolf. "Vom Grossbetrieb der Wissenschaft." *Aus Wissenschaft und Leben.* 2 vols. Giessen, 1911. 1: 10–20.

Hartmann, Eduard von. *Die Selbstzersetzung des Christentums und die Religion der Zukunft.* Berlin, 1874.

Hashagen, Justus. "Gustav von Mevissen," *Allgemeine deutsche Biographie.* Leipzig, 1907. 53: 772–88.

Helmolt, Hans F., ed. *Weltgeschichte.* 9 vols. Leipzig and Vienna, 1899–1907.

Hinneberg, Paul. "Die philosophischen Grundlagen der Geschichtswissenschaft." *Historische Zeitschrift* 60 (1889): 18–55.

Hintze, Otto. "Über individualistische und kollektivistische Geschichtsauffassung." *Historische Zeitschrift* 78 (1897): 60–67.

Hoeniger, Robert. *Professor Georg von Belows "Detailpolemik": Ein Nachwort zu dessen Arbeiten über städtische Verfassungsgeschichte.* Berlin, 1892.

Höhlbaum, Konstantin. "Gustav von Mevissen." *Historische Zeitschrift* 94 (1899): 72–79.

Jastrow, Ignaz. "Erwiderung betreffend die 'Jahresberichte der Geschichtswissenschaft.'" *Mitteilungen aus der historischen Litteratur* 17 (1889): 92–116.

————. "Karl Wilhelm Nitzsch und die deutsche Wirtschaftsgeschichte." *Schmollers Jahrbuch* 8 (1884): 148–71.

Jodl, Friedrich. *Die Culturgeschichtsschreibung: Ihre Entwickelung und ihr Problem.* Halle, 1878.

Kaemmel, Otto, ed. *Spamers Illustrierte Weltgeschichte, mit besonderer Berücksichtigung der Kulturgeschichte.* 4th ed. 10 vols. Leipzig, 1902.

Kampffmeyer, Paul. "Karl Lamprecht und Karl Marx." *Sozialistische Monatshefte* 8 (July 1904): 520–26.

Kappstein, Theodor. "Karl Lamprecht." *Reclams universum* 33 (1915): 218–22.

Koehne, Carl. *Der Ursprung der Stadtverfassung in Worms, Speier und Mainz.* Breslau, 1890.

König, Edmund. W. *Wundt als Psycholog und als Philosoph.* Stuttgart, 1902.

Kötschke, Hermann. *Unser Reichskanzler: Sein Leben und Wirken.* 5th ed. Berlin, 1916.

Kötzschke, Rudolf. "Gerhard Seeliger." *Historische Vierteljahrschrift* 20 (1922): 482–96.

———. "Karl Lamprecht." Ed. Kötzschke and Tille. *Karl Lamprecht.* 1–28.

———. "Ortsflur, polititscher Gemeindebezirk und Kirchspiel." *Deutsche Geschichtsblätter* 3 (1902): 273–95.

———. "Die Technik der Grundkarteneinzeichnung." *Deutsche Geschichtsblätter* 1 (1900): 113–31.

———. "Verzeichnis der Schriften Karl Lamprechts." Ed. Karl Bücher. *Worte zum Gedächtnis an Karl Lamprecht.* Leipzig, 1916. 13–27.

Kötzschke, Rudolf, et al. *Studium Lipsiense: Ehrengabe Karl Lamprecht, dargebracht aus Anlass der Eröffnung des Königlichen Sächsischen Instituts für Kultur- und Universalgeschichte bei der Universität Leipzig.* Berlin, 1909.

Kötzschke, Rudolf, and Tille, Armin. *Karl Lamprecht: Eine Erinnerungsschrift der deutschen Geschichtsblätter.* Gotha, n.d.

Kretzschmar, Johannes. "Zum Gedächtnis Karl Lamprechts." *Leipziger Lehrerzeitung* 22 (1915): 354–57.

Kuhnert, Adolf. *Der Streit um die geschichtswissenschaftlichen Theorien Karl Lamprechts.* Gütersloh, 1906.

Lenz, Max. *Geschichte der Königlichen Friedrich-Wilhelms-Universität zu Berlin.* 4 vols. Halle, 1910–1918.

Lexis, W., ed. *Die Universitäten im Deutschen Reich.* Berlin, 1904.

Lindner, Theodor. *Geschichtsphilosophie: Einleitung zu einer Weltgeschichte seit der Völkerwanderung.* Stuttgart, 1901.

———. *Weltgeschichte seit der Völkerwanderung.* 9 vols. Stuttgart, 1906–1916.

Lipps, Theodor. *Leitfaden der Psychologie.* Leipzig, 1903.

Lorenz, Ottokar. "Die 'bürgerliche' und die naturwissenschaftliche Geschichte," *Historische Zeitschrift* 39 (1878): 458–85.

———. *Die Geschichtswissenschaft in Hauptrichtungen und Aufgaben kritisch erörtert.* Berlin, 1886.

Lotze, Hermann. *Mikrokosmus: Ideen zur Naturgeschichte und Geschichte der Menschheit.* 4th ed. 3 vols. Leipzig, 1884–1888.

Mehring, Franz. "Deutsche Geschichte." *Die Neue Zeit* 12 (1893–1894): 443–48, 475–80.

———. *Gesammelte Schriften.* 15 vols. Berlin, 1980.

———. "Paranoia professoris magistra." *Die Neue Zeit* 28 (1909–1910): 545–48.

———. "Das Zeitalter der Reizsamkeit." *Gesammelte Schriften,* 7: 511–15.

Meinecke, Friedrich. "Geleitwort zum 100. Bande der Historischen Zeitschrift." *Historische Zeitschrift* 100 (1908): 1–10.

———. "Jacob Burckhardt, die deutsche Geschichtsschreibung und der nationale Staat." Ed. Eberhard Kessel. *Zur Geschichte der Geschichtsschreibung.* Munich, 1968. 83–87.

———. *Weltbürgertum und Nationalstaat.* Ed. Hans Herzfeld. Munich, 1962.

Mencke-Glückert, E. "Zur Vollendung von Karl Lamprechts deutscher Geschichte." *Das Deutschtum im Ausland* (March 1910): 122–30.

Meyer, Eduard. "Zur Theorie und Methodik der Geschichte." *Kleine Schriften.* 2d ed. 2 vols. Halle, 1924. 1: 1–67.

Müller, C. "Die Apperzeptionstheorie von W. Wundt und Th. Lipps und ihre Weiterführung in der Gegenwart." Ph.D. dissertation. Münster, 1910.

Müller, Johannes. *Die wissenschaftlichen Vereine und Gesellschaften Deutschlands im neunzehnten Jahrhundert: Bibliographie ihrer Veröffentlichungen.* 2 vols. Berlin, 1883–1917.

Neubauer, F. "Die Kulturgeschichte auf den höheren Lehranstalten." *Zeitschrift für das Gymnasialwesen* 41 (1896–1897): 257–66.

Nietzsche, Friedrich. "Vom Nutzen und Nachteil der Historie für das Leben." Ed. Karl Schlechta. *Werke.* 6 vols. Munich and Vienna, 1980. 1: 209–85.

Nitzsch, Karl Wilhelm. *Geschichte des deutschen Volkes bis zum Augsburger Religionsfrieden.* 2d ed. Stuttgart, 1959.

Oncken, Hermann. *Lamprechts Verteidigung: Eine Antwort auf Zwei Streitschriften.* Berlin, 1898.

———. "Zur Quellenanalyse modernster deutscher Geschichtsschreibung." *Preussische Jahrbücher* 89 (1897): 83–125.

Ostwald, Wilhelm. *Energetische Grundlagen der Kulturwissenschaften.* Leipzig, 1909.

———. *Die Forderungen des Tages.* Leipzig, 1910.

Paulsen, Friedrich. *Die deutschen Universitäten und das Universitätsstudium.* Berlin, 1902.

———. *Geschichte des gelehrten Unterrichts auf den deutschen Schulen und Universitäten vom Ausgang des Mittelalters bis zur Gegenwart.* 2d ed. 2 vols. Berlin and Leipzig, 1896–1897.

Petersen, Peter. *Der Entwicklungsgedanke in der Philosophie Wundts: Zugleich ein Beitrag zur Methode der Kulturgeschichte.* Leipzig, 1908.

Pirenne, Henri. "Une polémique historique en Allemagne." *Revue historique* 62 (1897): 50–57.

Rachfahl, Felix. "Deutsche Geschichte vom wirthschaftlichen Standpunkt." *Preussische Jahrbücher* 83 (1896): 48–96.

———. "Max Lenz und die deutsche Geschichtswissenschaft." *Historische Zeitschrift* 123 (1921): 189–220.

———. "Review of Karl Lamprecht, *Deutsche Geschichte.* 5. Bande, 2. Hälfte." *Mitteilungen des Instituts für oesterreichische Geschichtsforschung* 17 (1896): 468–78.

———. "Über die Theorie einer 'kollektivistischen' Geschichtswissenschaft." *Jahrbücher für Nationalökonomie und Statistik* 68 (1897): 659–89.

Ranke, Leopold von. *Weltgeschichte, IX,* 2. Ed. Alfred Dove. Leipzig, 1888.

Ratzel, Friedrich. *Anthropo-Geographie oder die Grundzüge der Anwendung der Erdkunde auf die Geschichte.* Stuttgart, 1882.

———. *Die Erde und das Leben: Eine vergleichende Erdkunde.* 2 vols. Leipzig, 1901–1902.

———. "Ethnographie und Geschichtswissenschaft in Amerika, mit einem Zusatz von K. Lamprecht." *Deutsche Zeitschrift für Geschichtswissenschaft* N.F., 2 (1897–1898): 65–74.

———. "Geschichte, Völkerkunde und historische Perspektive." *Historische Zeitschrift* 93 (1904): 1–46.

———. "Der Lebensraum: Eine biogeographische Studie." Bücher, Karl, et al., eds. *Festgaben für Albert Schäffle zur 70. Wiederkehr seines Geburtages am 24. Februar 1901.* Tübingen, 1901. 103–89.

———. "Die Philosophie der Geschichte als Sociologie." *Zeitschrift für Socialwissenschaft.* 1 (1898): 19–25.

———. *Politische Geographie.* Munich, 1897.

Rickert, Heinrich. *Die Grenzen der naturwissenschaftlichen Begriffsbildung: Eine logische Einleitung in die historischen Wissenschaften.* Tübingen and Leipzig, 1902.

Riehl, Wilhem Heinrich. *Die bürgerliche Gesellschaft.* Ed. Peter Steinbach. Frankfurt am Main, 1976.

Riezler, Kurt [pseud. J. J. Ruedorffer]. *Grundzüge der Weltpolitik in der Gegenwart.* Stuttgart and Berlin, 1914.

Ritter, Moriz. *Deutsche Geschichte im Zeitalter der Gegenreformation und des Dreissigjährigen Krieges (1555–1648)*. Stuttgart, 1889.

———. "Der Streit zwischen politischer und Kulturgeschichte." *Beilage zur Münchner Allgemeinen Zeitung*. No. 262 (1893).

Rogers, Howard J., ed. *Congress of Arts and Sciences: Universal Exposition, St. Louis, 1904*. 6 vols. Boston and New York, 1905–1906.

Roscher, Wilhelm. *System der Volkswirtschaft: Die Grundlagen der Nationalökonomie*. 13th ed. Stuttgart, 1875.

Rothacker, Erich. *Über die Möglichkeit und den Ertrag einer genetischen Geschichtsschreibung im Sinne Karl Lamprechts*. Leipzig, 1912.

Schäfer, Dietrich. *Aufsätze, Vorträge und Reden*. 2 vols. Jena, 1913.

———. *Das eigentliche Arbeitsgebiet der Geschichte*. Jena, 1888.

———. *Geschichte und Kulturgeschichte: Eine Erwiderung*. Jena, 1891.

———. *Weltgeschichte der Neuzeit*. 2 vols. Berlin, 1907.

Schaumkell, Ernst. *Geschichte der deutschen Kulturgeschichtsschreibung*. Leipzig, 1905.

Schmoller, Gustav. "Die Beurteilung Rankes durch K. Lamprecht." *Sitzungsberichte der Historischen Gesellschaft zu Berlin*. 258. Sitzung, 8.6.96.

———. *Grundriss der allgemeinen Volkswirtschaftslehre*. 2 vols. Leipzig, 1900–1904.

———. "Die soziale Entwickelung Deutschlands und Englands hauptsächlich auf dem platten Lande des Mittelalters." *Schmollers Jahrbuch* 12 (1888): 203–18.

———. "Zur Würdigung von Karl Lamprecht." *Schmollers Jahrbuch* 39 (1916): 27–54.

Schnürer, Gustav. "Lamprechts Deutsche Geschichte." *Historisches Jahrbuch* 18 (1897): 88–116.

———. "Zum Streite über Lamprechts deutsche Geschichte." *Historisches Jahrbuch* 21 (1900): 776–85.

Schwann, Mathieu. "Lamprechts Deutsche Geschichte." *Die Zukunft* 15 (1896): 120–25.

Seeliger, Gerhard. "Karl Lamprecht." *Historische Vierteljahrschrift* 19 (1919–1920): 133–44.

———. "Über die Kulturgeschichtsschreibung Karl Lamprechts." *Preussische Jahrbücher* 156 (1914): 539–42.

Show, Arley Barthlow. "Die Kulturgeschichtsschreibung Karl Lamprechts." *Vergangenheit und Gegenwart* 4 (1914): 65–87.

———. "The New Culture-History in Germany." *The History Teacher's Magazine* 4 (1913): 215–21.

Simmel, Georg. "An Herrn Professor Karl Lamprecht." *Die Zukunft* 83 (1913): 230–34.

———. *Die Probleme der Geschichtsphilosophie*. Leipzig, 1892.

———. *The Problems of the Philosophy of History: An Epistemological Essay*. Ed. Guy Oakes. New York, 1977.

Spiess, Emil Jakob. *Die Geschichtsphilosophie von Karl Lamprecht*. Erlangen, 1912.

Spranger, Eduard. *Die Grundlagen der Geschichtswissenschaft: Eine Erkenntnistheoretisch-psychologische Untersuchung*. Berlin, 1905.

———. "Karl Lamprechts Geschichtsauffassung." *Sonntagsbeilage zur Vossischen Zeitung* No. 23 (6 June 1915): 173–76.

Steinhausen, Georg. "Der Streit um die Kulturgeschichte." *Die Nation* No. 51 (19.9.96): 763–66.

———. *Geschichte der deutschen Kultur*. Leipzig, 1904.

———. *Geschichte des deutschen Briefes: Zur Kulturgeschichte des deutschen Volkes*. 2 vols. Berlin, 1889–1891.

Stieda, W. "Die Königlich Sächsische Universität Leipzig." Ed. Lexis. *Die Universitäten im Deutschen Reich*. 503–34.

Sybel, Heinrich von. "Georg Waitz." *Vorträge und Abhandlungen*, 309–13.
———. *Vorträge und Abhandlungen*. Ed. Konrad Varrentrapp. Munich and Leipzig, 1897.
———. "Worte der Erinnerung an Julius Weizsäcker." *Vorträge und Abhandlungen*, 315–20.
Tille, Armin. "Nachwort." Ed. Kötzschke and Tille. *Karl Lamprecht*. 29–35.
Treitschke, Heinrich von. *Deutsche Geschichte im neunzehnten Jahrhundert*. 5 vols. Leipzig, 1928.
Weber, Max. "'Energetische' Kulturtheorien." *Wissenschaftslehre*. 376–402.
———. *Gesammelte Aufsätze zur Wissenschaftslehre*. Ed. Johannes Winckelmann. Tübingen, 1982.
———. "Kritische Studien auf dem Gebiet der kulturwissenschaftlichen Logik." *Wissenschaftslehre*. 215–90.
———. "Die 'Objektivität' sozialwissenschaftlicher und sozialpolitischer Erkenntnis." *Wissenschaftslehre*. 146–214.
———. "Die protestantische Ethik und der Geist des Kapitalismus." *Gesammelte Aufsätze zur Religionssoziologie*. 4th ed. Tübingen, 1947. 17–206.
———. "Roscher und Knies und die logischen Probleme der historischen Nationalökonomie." *Wissenschaftslehre*. 1–145.
Weiss, Berthold. "Lamprechts Geschichtsphilosophie." *Archiv für systematische Philosophie* 12 (1906): 209–24.
Wenzelburger, K. Theodor. *Geschichte der Niederlande*. 2 vols. Gotha, 1879–1886.
Windelband, Wilhelm. "Geschichte und Naturwissenschaft." *Präludien: Aufsätze und Reden zur Philosophie und ihrer Geschichte*. 2 vols. Tübingen, 1921. 2: 36–60.
Wines, Roger, ed. *Leopold von Ranke, The Secret of World History: Selected Writings on the Art and Science of History*. New York, 1981.
Winter, Georg. "Die Begründung einer sozialstatistischen Methode in der deutschen Geschichtsschreibung durch Karl Lamprecht." *Zeitschrift für Kulturgeschichte*. 1 (1893–1894): 196–219.
———. *Geschichte des dreissigjährigen Krieges*. Berlin, 1893.
———. "Karl Lamprecht." *Die Gesellschaft* 17 (1898): 296–314.
Wundt, Wilhelm. "Über die Definition der Psychologie." *Philosophische Studien* 12 (1896): 1–66.
———. *Ethik: Eine Untersuchung der Tatsachen und Gesetze des sittlichen Lebens*. Stuttgart, 1886.
———. *Logik: Eine Untersuchung der Prinzipien der Erkenntnis und der Methoden wissenschaftlicher Forschung*. 2 vols. Stuttgart, 1880–1883; 2d ed. 2 vols. Stuttgart, 1894–1895.
———. *System der Philosophie*. Leipzig, 1889.
———. *Völkerpsychologie: Eine Untersuchung der Entwicklungsgesetze von Sprache, Mythus und Sitte*. 10 vols. Leipzig, 1900–1920.
Wundt, Wilhelm, and Klinger, Max. *Karl Lamprecht: Ein Gedenkblatt*. Leipzig, 1915.
Yorck von Wartenburg [Paul Graf]. *Weltgeschichte in Umrissen*. 4th ed. Berlin, 1901.

SECONDARY LITERATURE (SINCE 1916)

Albisetti, James C. *Secondary School Reform in Imperial Germany*. Princeton, 1983.
Alter, Peter. "Eberhard Gothein." Ed. Wehler. *Historiker*. 8: 40–55.
Anderson, Paula Relyea. "Gustav von Schmoller (1838–1917)." Ed. Halperin. *Essays*. 289–317.
Antoni, Carlo. *From History to Sociology: The Transition in German Historical Thinking*. London, 1959.

Appel, Michael. "Der 'Moderne Kapitalismus' im Urteil zeitgenössischer Besprechungen." Ed. Bernhard vom Brocke. *Sombarts "Moderner Kapitalismus": Materialien zur Kritik und Rezeption*. Munich, 1987. 67–85.

Arens, Franz. "Karl Lamprecht." *Preussische Jahrbücher* 203 (1926): 191–213, 306–28.

Arieti, Sylvano, and Brody, Eugene B., eds. *American Handbook of Psychiatry*. 2d ed. 7 vols. New York, 1974–1981.

Arnold, Alfred. *Wilhelm Wundt: Sein philosophisches System*. Berlin, 1980.

Ash, Mitchell G. "Academic Politics in the History of Science: Experimental Psychology in Germany, 1879–1914." *Central European History* 13 (1980): 255–86.

Aubin, Hermann. "Aufgaben und Wege der geschichtlichen Landeskunde." Ed. Fried. *Landesgeschichte*. 38–52.

———. "Georg von Below als Sozial- und Wirtschaftshistoriker." *Vierteljahrschrift für Sozial- und Wirtschaftsgeschichte* 21 (1928): 1–31.

———. "Zum 50. Band der Vierteljahrschrift für Sozial- und Wirtschaftsgeschichte." *Vierteljahrschrift für Sozial- und Wirtschaftsgeschichte* 50 (1963–1964): 1–24.

Baron, Samuel H. "Psychological Dimensions of the Biographical Process." Ed. Samuel H. Baron and Carl Pletsch. *Introspection in Biography: The Biographer's Quest for Self-Awareness*. Hillsdale, NJ, 1985. 1–31.

Barthel, Heinz, et al. "Karl Bücher: Seine politische und wissenschaftliche Stellung." Ed. Engelberg. *Karl-Marx-Universität*. 2: 78–91.

Bauer, Stephan. "Ludo M. Hartmann als Mitbegründer der Vierteljahrshrift für Sozial- und Wirtschaftsgeschichte." *Vierteljahrschrift für Sozial- und Wirtschaftsgeschichte* 18 (1925): 335–39.

Bayertz, Kurt. *Wissenschaftstheorie und Paradigmabegriff*. Stuttgart, 1981.

Below, Georg von. *Die deutsche Geschichtsschreibung von den Befreiungskriegen bis zu unseren Tagen: Geschichtsschreibung und Geschichtsauffassung*. Munich and Berlin, 1924.

Below, Minnie von. *Georg von Below: Ein Lebensbild für seine Freunde*. Stuttgart, 1930.

Bemporad, Jules R., and Pinsker, Henry. "Schizophrenia: The Manifest Symptomology." Ed. Arieti. *Handbook*. 3: 524–39.

Benjamin, Walter. "Unpacking My Library: A Talk about Book Collecting." Ed. Hannah Arendt. *Illuminations*. New York, 1969.

Berglar, Peter. "Harden und Rathenau: Zur Problematik ihrer Freundschaft." *Historische Zeitschrift* 210 (1969): 75–94.

Beuchelt, Eno. *Ideengeschichte der Völkerpsychologie*. Meisenheim am Glan, 1974.

Beuys, Barbara. "Die Pfarrfrau: Kopie oder Original?" Ed. Greiffenhagen. *Pfarrhaus*. 47–61.

Bezold, Friedrich von. *Geschichte der Rheinischen Friedrich-Wilhelms-Universität von der Gründung bis zum Jahre 1870*. Bonn, 1920.

Bienfait, Werner. *Max Webers Lehre vom geschichtlichen Erkennen: Ein Beitrag zur Frage der Bedeutung des "Idealtypus" für die Geschichtswissenschaft*. Berlin, 1930.

Bigler, Robert M. *The Politics of German Protestantism: The Rise of the Protestant Church Elite in Prussia, 1815–1848*. Berkeley and Los Angeles, 1972.

Blanke, Horst Walter. *Historiographiegeschichte als Historik*. Stuttgart-Bad Cannstatt, 1991.

———. "Die Wiederentdeckung der deutschen Aufklärungshistorie und die Begründung der Historischen Sozialwissenschaft." Ed. Wolfgang Prinz and Peter Weingart. *Die sog. Geisteswissenschaften: Innenansichten*. Frankfurt am Main, 1990. 105–33.

Blanke, Horst Walter, Fleischer, Dirk, and Rüsen, Jorn. "Theory of History in Historical Lectures: The German Tradition of *Historik*, 1750–1900." *History and Theory* 23 (1984): 331–56.

Blättner, Fritz. *Das Gymnasium: Aufgaben der höheren Schule in Geschichte und Gegenwart*. Heidelberg, 1960.

Bock, Klaus Dieter. *Strukturgeschichte der Assistentur: Personalgefüge, Wert- und Zielvorstellungen in der deutschen Universität des 19. und 20. Jahrhunderts.* Düsseldorf, 1972.

Böckenförde, E. W. *Die deutsche verfassungsgeschichtliche Forschung im 19. Jahrhundert: Zeitgebundene Fragestellungen und Leitbilder.* Berlin, 1961.

Boehm, Laetitia, and Müller, Rainer A., eds. *Universitäten und Hochschulen in Deutschland, Österreich und der Schweiz: Eine Universitätsgeschichte in Einzeldarstellungen.* Düsseldorf, 1983.

Bonhard, Otto. *Geschichte des Alldeutschen Verbandes.* Leipzig and Berlin, 1920.

Bonner Gelehrte: Beiträge zur Geschichte der Wissenschaften in Bonn. Geschichtswissenschaften (150 Jahre Rheinische Friedrich-Wilhelms-Universität zu Bonn 1818–1968). Bonn, 1968.

Boockmann, Hartmut, et al. *Geschichtswissenschaft und Vereinswesen im 19. Jahrhundert: Beiträge zur Geschichte historischer Forschung in Deutschland.* Göttingen, 1972.

Boring, Edwin G. *A History of Experimental Psychology.* New York, 1950.

Bormann-Heischkeil, Sigrid. "Die soziale Herkunft der Pfarrer und ihrer Ehefrauen." Ed. Greiffenhagen. *Pfarrhaus.* 149–74.

Braubach, Max. "Carl von Noorden 1833–1883." *Bonner Gelehrte.* 162–69.

———. *Kleine Geschichte der Universität Bonn 1818–1968.* Bonn, 1968.

———. *Landesgeschichtliche Bestrebungen und historische Vereine im Rheinland.* Cologne and Opladen, 1955.

Breisach, Ernst. *Historiography: Ancient, Medieval, and Modern.* Chicago and London, 1983.

Breysig, Gertrud. *Kurt Breysig: Ein Bild des Menschen.* Heidelberg, 1967.

Brinckmann, Carl. *Gustav Schmoller und die Volkswirtschaftslehre.* Stuttgart, 1937.

Bringmann, Wolfgang G., et al. "Wilhelm Wundt 1832–1920: A Brief Biographical Sketch." *Journal of the History of the Behavioral Sciences* 11 (1975): 287–97.

Bringmann, Wolfgang G., et al., eds. *Wundt Studies: A Centennial Collection.* Toronto, 1980.

Bruford, Walter Horace. *The German Tradition of Self-Cultivation: "Bildung" from Humboldt to Thomas Mann.* Cambridge, 1975.

Brunner, Otto. *Land und Herrschaft: Grundfragen der territorialen Verfassungsgeschichte Oesterreichs im Mittelalter.* Darmstadt, 1970.

Bucholz, Arden. *Hans Delbrück and the German Military Establishment: War Images in Conflict.* Iowa City, 1985.

Burchardt, Lothar. "Deutsche Wissenschaftspolitik an der Jahrhundertwende: Versuch einer Zwischenbilanz." *Geschichte in Wissenschaft und Unterreicht* 26 (1975): 271–89.

———. "Halbstaatliche Wissenschaftsförderung im Kaiserreich und in der frühen Weimarer Republik." Ed. Gunter Mann and Rolf Winau. *Medizin, Naturwissenschaft, Technik und das Zweite Kaiserreich.* Göttingen, 1977. 35–51.

———. *Wissenschaftspolitik im Wiheleminischen Deutschland: Vorgeschichte, Gründung und Aufbau der Kaiser-Wilhelm-Gesellschaft zur Förderung der Wissenschaften.* Göttingen, 1975.

Burleigh, Michael. *Germany Turns Eastwards: A Study of Ostforschung in the Third Reich.* Cambridge and New York, 1988.

Busch, Alexander. *Die Geschichte des Privatdozenten: Eine soziologische Studie zur grossbetrieblichen Entwicklung der deutschen Universitäten.* Stuttgart, 1959.

Büsch, Otto, and Erbe, Michael, eds. *Otto Hintze und die moderne Geschichtswissenschaft.* Berlin, 1983.

Bussmann, Walter. "Heinrich von Sybel (1817–1895)." *Bonner Gelehrte.* 93–103.

Buttmann, Gunther. *Friedrich Ratzel: Leben und Werk eines deutschen Geographen 1844–1904.* Stuttgart, 1977.

Cassirer, Ernst. *The Problem of Knowledge.* New Haven, 1969.

Chickering, Roger. *Imperial Germany and a World Without War: The Peace Movement and German Society, 1892–1914.* Princeton, 1975.

———. "Karl Lamprechts Konzeption einer Weltgeschichte." *Archiv für Kulturgeschichte* 73 (1991): 437–52.

———. "Max Weber und Dietrich Schäfer." Ed. Mommsen und Schwentker. *Max Weber und seine Zeitgenossen.* 462–75.

———. "An Uninvited Guest." Ed. James van Horne Melton and Hartmut Lehmann. *Paths of Continuity: Central European Historiography from the 1930s through the 1950s.* Cambridge, 1993.

———. "A Voice of Moderation in Imperial Germany: The 'Verband für internationale Verständigung,' 1911–1914." *Journal of Contemporary History* 8 (January 1973): 147–64.

———. "War, Peace, and Social Mobilization in Imperial Germany: Patriotic Societies, the Peace Movement, and Socialist Labor." Ed. Charles Chatfield and Peter van den Dungen. *Peace Movements and Political Cultures.* Knoxville, 1988. 3–22.

———. *We Men Who Feel Most German: A Cultural Study of the Pan-German League, 1886–1914.* London, 1984.

———. "Young Lamprecht: An Essay in Biography and Historiography." *History and Theory* 28 (1989): 198–214.

Cooper, Arnold M. "Narcissism." Ed. Arieti. *Handbook.* 7: 297–316.

Craig, Gordon. "Delbrück: The Military Historian." Ed. Peter Paret. *Makers of Modern Strategy: From Machiavelli to the Nuclear Age.* Princeton, 1986. 326–53.

Czok, Karl. "Der Höhepunkt der bürgerlichen Wissenschaftsentwicklung, 1871 bis 1917." Ed. Lothar Rathmann. *Alma mater lipsiensis: Geschichte der Karl-Marx-Universität Leipzig.* Leipzig, 1984. 191–228.

———. "Karl Lamprecht (1856–1915)." Ed. Steinmetz. *Bedeutende Gelehrte.* 1: 91–99.

———. *Karl Lamprechts Wirken an der Universität Leipzig.* Berlin, 1984.

———. "Der Methodenstreit und die Gründung des Seminars für Landesgeschichte und Siedlungskunde 1906 an der Universität Leipzig." *Jahrbuch für Regionalgeschichte* 2 (1967): 11–26.

Dallek, Robert. *Democrat and Diplomat: The Life of William E. Dodd.* New York, 1968.

Danziger, Kurt. "The Positivist Repudiation of Wundt." *Journal of the History of the Behavioral Sciences* 15 (1979): 205–30.

———. "Wundt and the Two Traditions in Psychology." Ed. Rieber. *Wundt.* 73–87.

———. "Wundt's Psychological Experiment in the Light of His Philosophy of Science." *Psychological Research* 42 (1980): 109–22.

Deckart, Gerald. "Deutsch-englische Verständigung: Eine Darstellung der nichtoffiziellen Bemühungen um eine Wiederannäherung der beiden Länder zwischen 1905 und 1914." Ph.D. dissertation. Munich, 1967.

Dehio, Ludwig. "Ranke and German Imperialism." *Germany and World Politics in the Twentieth Century.* London, 1965. 38–71.

Deist, Wilhelm, ed. *Militär und Innenpolitik im Weltkrieg 1914–1918.* 2 vols. Düsseldorf, 1970.

Deltete, Robert John. "The Energetics Controversy in Late 19th-Century Germany: Helmholtz, Ostwald, and Their Critics." Ph.D. dissertation. Yale University, 1983.

Demandt, Alexander. "Natur- und Geschichtswissenschaft im 19. Jahrhundert." *Historische Zeitschrift* 237 (1983): 37–66.

Deutsch, Robert, and Weber, Wolfgang. "Marginalisierungsprozesse in der deutschen Geschichtswissenschaft im Zeitalter des Historismus." *Schweizerische Zeitschrift für Geschichte* 35 (1985): 174–97.

Diamond, Solomon. "Buckle, Wundt, and Psychology's Use of History." *Isis* 75 (1984): 143–52.

———. "Selected Texts from Writings of Wilhelm Wundt." Ed. Rieber. *Wundt.* 155–77.

Dilly, Heinrich. "Entstehung und Geschichte des Begriffs Historismus—Funktion und Struktur einer Begriffsgeschichte." *Geschichte allein ist zeitgemäss.* Giessen, 1978.

———. *Kunstgeschichte als Institution: Studien zur Geschichte einer Disziplin.* Frankfurt am Main, 1979.

Doeberl, Michael, et al., eds. *Das akademische Deutschland.* 5 vols. Berlin, 1930–1931.

Domschke, Jan-Peter, and Lewandrowski, Peter. *Wilhelm Ostwald: Chemiker, Wissenschaftstheoretiker, Organisator.* Cologne, 1982.

Dopsch, Alfons. "Zur Methodologie der Wirtschaftsgeschichte." *Kultur- und Universalgeschichte: Walter Goetz zu seinem 60. Geburtstag.* Leipzig and Berlin, 1927. 518–38.

Dotterweich, Volker. *Heinrich von Sybel: Geschichtswissenschaft in politischer Absicht (1817–1861).* Göttingen, 1978.

Düding, Dieter. *Der Nationalsoziale Verein 1896–1903: Der gescheiterte Versuch einer parteipolitischen Synthese von Nationalismus, Sozialismus und Liberalismus.* Munich and Vienna, 1972.

Düwell, Kurt. *Deutschlands auswärtige Kulturpolitik 1918–1932: Grundlinien und Dokumente.* Cologne and Vienna, 1976.

Eagleton, Terry. *Marxism and Literary Criticism.* Berkeley and Los Angeles, 1976.

Eisermann, Gottfried. *Die Grundlagen des Historismus in der deutschen Nationalökonomie.* Stuttgart, 1956.

Engel, Eduard. *Deutsche Stilkunst.* Vienna and Leipzig, 1922.

Engel, Josef. "Die deutschen Universitäten und die Geschichtswissenschaft." *Historische Zeitschrift* 189 (1959): 223–378.

Engelberg, Ernst. "Zum Methodenstreit um Karl Lamprecht." Ed. Streisand. *Studien.* 2: 136–52.

Engelberg, Ernst, et al., eds. *Karl-Marx-Universität Leipzig 1409–1959: Beiträge zur Universitätsgeschichte.* 2 vols. Leipzig, 1959.

Erbe, Michael, ed. *Friedrich Meinecke Heute.* Berlin, 1981.

Erdmann, Karl-Dietrich. *Geschichte, Politik und Pädagogik: Aufsätze und Reden.* Stuttgart, 1970. 384–407.

———. *Die Oekumene der Historiker: Geschichte der Internationalen Historikerkongresse und des Comité International des Sciences Historiques.* Göttingen, 1987.

Erikson, Erik H. *Childhood and Society.* 2d ed. New York, 1963.

———. *Identity: Youth and Crisis.* New York, 1968.

Ermarth, Michael. *Wilhelm Dilthey: The Critique of Historical Reason.* Chicago, 1978.

Eschler, Erhard. "Wilhelm Wundt (1832–1920)." Ed. Steinmetz. *Bedeutende Gelehrte.* 1: 79–84.

Faber, Karl-Georg. "Ausprägungen des Historismus." *Historische Zeitschrift* 228 (1979): 1–22.

———. "Zur Vorgeschichte der Geopolitik: Staat, Nation und Lebensraum im Denken deutscher Geographen vor 1914." Ed. Heinz Dollinger et al. *Weltpolitik, Europagedanke, Regionalismus: Festschrift für Heinz Gollwitzer zum 65. Geburtstag.* Münster, 1982. 389–406.

Faulenbach, Bernd, ed. *Geschichtswissenschaft in Deutschland: Traditionelle Positionen und gegenwärtige Aufgaben.* Munich, 1974.

Fellenberg, Anje. "Zur Stellung ausländischer Studenten an der Universität Leipzig in den Jahren 1900 bis 1914." Diplomarbeit, Karl-Marx-Universität Leipzig, 1979.

Fellner, Günter. *Ludo Moritz Hartmann und die österreichische Geschichtswissenschaft: Grundzüge eines paradigmatischen Konfliktes.* Vienna and Salzburg, 1984.

Ferber, Christian von. *Die Entwicklung des Lehrkörpers der deutschen Universitäten und Hochschulen 1864–1954.* Göttingen, 1956.

Fiedler, Frank. "Methodologische Auseinandersetzungen in der Zeit des Übergangs zum Imperialismus." Ed. Streisand. *Studien.* 2: 153–78.

Fiedler, Ralph. *Die klassische deutsche Bildungsidee: Ihre soziologischen Wurzeln und pädagogischen Folgen.* Weinheim, 1972.

Fischel, W. J. "Der Historismus in der Wirtschaftswissenschaft dargestellt an der Entwicklung von Adam Müller bis Bruno Hildebrand." *Vierteljahrschrift für Sozial- und Wirtschaftsgeschichte* 47 (1960): 1–31.

Fischer, Dietrich. "Die deutsche Geschichtswissenschaft von Droysen bis Hintze in ihrem Verhältnis zu Soziologie." Ph.D. dissertation. Cologne, 1966.

Frank, Walter. "Apostata: Maximilian Harden und das wihleminische Deutschland." *"Höre Israel!": Studien zur modernen Judenfrage.* Hamburg, 1941. 15–108.

Frevert, Ute. *Ehrenmänner: Das Duell in der bürgerlichen Gesellschaft.* Munich, 1991.

Freyer, Hans. "Geschichte und Soziologie." *Vergangenheit und Gegenwart.* 16 (1926): 201–11.

Fricke, Dieter. "Nationalsoziale Versuche zur Förderung der Krise der Sozialdemokratie: Zum Briefwechsel zwischen Max Maurenbrecher und Friedrich Naumann 1910–1913." *Beiträge zur Geschichte der Arbeiterbewegung.* 25 (1983): 537–48.

Fried, Pankraz, ed. *Probleme und Methoden der Landesgeschichte.* Darmstadt, 1978.

Fröchling, Jürgen. "Georg von Below—Stadtgeschichte zwischen Wissenschaft und Ideologie." *Die alte Stadt* 6 (1979): 54–85.

Frye, Northrop. "Historical Criticism: Theory of Modes." *Anatomy of Criticism: Four Essays.* Princeton, 1971.

Gadamer, Hans-Georg. *Truth and Method.* New York, 1975.

Gasman, Daniel. *The Scientific Origins of National Socialism: Social Darwinism in Ernst Haeckel and the German Monist League.* London and New York, 1971

Geramb, Viktor von. *Wilhelm Heinrich Riehl: Leben und Wirken (1823–1897).* Salzburg, 1954.

Gerber, Hans. *Das Recht der wissenschaftlichen Hochschulen in der jüngsten Rechtsentwicklung.* 2 vols. Tübingen, 1965.

Gerlich, Alois. *Geschichtliche Landeskunde: Genese und Probleme.* Darmstadt, 1986.

Gestrich, Andreas. "Erziehung im Pfarrhaus." Ed. Greiffenhagen. *Pfarrhaus.* 63–82.

Gilbert, Felix. *History: Politics or Culture: Reflections on Ranke and Burckhardt.* Princeton, 1990.

Gilbert, Felix, ed. *The Historical Essays of Otto Hintze.* New York, 1975.

Gispen, Kees. *New Profession, Old Order: Engineers and German Society, 1815–1914.* Cambridge, 1989.

Goebel, Klaus. "Des Kaisers neuer Geschichtsunterricht: Änderungen des preussischen Lehrplans 1915 und ihre Vorgeschichte." *Geschichte in Wissenschaft und Unterricht* 25 (1974): 709–17.

Goetz, Walter. *Historiker in meiner Zeit: Gesammelte Aufsätze.* Graz, 1957.

———. "Moriz Ritter (1923–1940)." *Historische Zeitschrift* 131 (1925): 472–95.

Götz, Wolfgang. "Historismus. Ein Versuch zur Definition des Begriffs." *Zeitschrift des Deutschen Vereins für Kunstwissenschaft* 24 (1970): 196–212.

Gooch, G. P. *History and Historians in the Nineteenth Century.* Boston, 1959.

Gothein, Marie Luise. *Eberhard Gothein: Ein Lebensbild.* Stuttgart, 1931.

Graefe, Friedrich, ed. *Max Lenz zum Gedächtnis: Lebenslauf und Gedenkaufsätze.* Berlin, 1935.

Graf, Friedrich Wilhelm. "Ernst Troeltsch: Kulturgeschichte des Christentums." Ed. Hammerstein. *Geschichtswissenschaft.* 131–52.

———. "Rettung der Persönlichkeit: Protestantische Theologie als Kulturwissenschaft des Christentums." Ed. vom Bruch. *Kulturwissenschaften.* 103–31.

Greiffenhagen, Martin, ed. *Das evangelische Pfarrhaus: Eine Kultur- und Sozialgeschichte.* Stuttgart, 1984.

Griss, Peter. *Das Gedankenbild Karl Lamprechts: Historisches Verhalten im Modernisierungsprozess der "Belle Epoque."* Bern, 1987.

Haas, Hans. "König-Friedrich-August-Stiftung für wissenschaftliche Forschung zu Leipzig (Sächsische Staatliche Forschungsinstitute)." Brauer, Ludolf, et al., eds. *Forschungsinstitute: Ihre Geschichte, Organisation und Ziele.* 2 vols. Hamburg, 1930. 1: 374–86.

Habermas, Jürgen. *Strukturwandel der Öffentlichkeit: Untersuchungen zu einer Kategorie der bürgerlichen Gesellschaft.* Neuwied and Berlin, 1962.

Hahn, Gerhard, and Jackstel, Karlheinz. "Hochschulpädagogische Theorieentwicklung und Innovation—Zum Wirken von Hans Schmidkunz." Ed. Karlheinz Jackstel and Erich Leitner. *Studienreform und Hochschuldidaktik 1890–1933: Konzepte, Kontroversen, Kompromisse. Zeitschrift für Hochschuldidaktik,* Sonderheft 13. Vienna, 1990. 99–109.

Haines, George, IV, and Jackson, Frederick H. "A Neglected Landmark in the History of Ideas." *Mississippi Valley Historical Review* 34 (1947–1948): 201–20.

Hallgarten, George W. F. *Imperialismus vor 1914.* 2 vols. Munich, 1951.

Halperin, S. William, ed. *Essays in Modern European Historiography.* Chicago and London, 1970.

Hammerstein, Notker, ed. *Deutsche Geschichtswissenschaft um 1900.* Stuttgart, 1988.

Hardtwig, Wolfgang. "Geschichtsinteresse, Geschichtsbilder und politische Symbole in der Reichsgründungsära und im Kaiserreich." Ed. Ekkehard Mai and Stephan Waetzoldt. *Kunstverwaltung, Bau- und Denkmal-Politik im Kaiserreich.* Berlin, 1981. 47–74.

———. "Geschichtsreligion—Wissenschaft als Arbeit—Objektivität: Der Historismus in neuer Sicht." *Historische Zeitschrift* 252 (1991): 1–32.

———. *Geschichtsschreibung zwischen Alteuropa und moderner Welt: Jacob Burckhardt in seiner Zeit.* Göttingen, 1974.

———. "Von Preussens Aufgabe in Deutschland zu Deutschlands Aufgabe in der Welt: Liberalismus und borussianisches Geschichtsbild zwischen Revolution und Imperialismus." *Historische Zeitschrift* 231 (1980): 265–324.

———. "Die Verwissenschaftlichung der Geschichtsschreibung und die Aesthetisierung der Darstellung." Ed. Reinhart Koselleck et al. *Formen der Geschichtsschreibung.* Munich, 1982. 147–91.

Hartmann, Volker. *Die deutsche Kulturgeschichtsschreibung von ihren Anfängen bis W. H. Riehl.* Marburg, 1971.

Hartung, Fritz. "Gustav von Schmoller und die preussische Geschichtsschreibung." *Schmollers Jahrbuch* 62 (1938): 277–302.

Heimpel, Hermann. "Über Organisationsformen historischer Forschung in Deutschland." *Historische Zeitschrift* 189 (1959): 139–222.

Heitz, Gerhard. "Rudolf Kötzschke (1867–1949): Ein Beitrag zur Pflege der Siedlungs- und Wirtschaftsgeschichte in Leipzig." Ed. Engelberg. *Karl-Marx Universität.* 2: 262–74.

Helbig, Herbert. "Die Arbeiten Rudolf Kötzschkes." Ed. Werner Emmerich. *Von Land und Kultur: Beiträge zur Geschichte des mitteldeutschen Ostens.* Leipzig, 1937. 9–14.

———. "Fünfzig Jahre Institut für Deutsche Landes- und Volksgeschichte (Seminar für Landesgeschichte und Siedlungskunde) an der Universität Leipzig." *Berichte zur deutschen Landeskunde* 19 (1957): 55–77.

———. *Universität Leipzig.* Frankfurt am Main, 1961.

Hellmann, Manfred. "Zum hundertsten Geburtstag von Rudolf Kötzschke." *Zeitschrift für Ostforschung* 16 (1967): 691–94.

Hellpach, Willy. "Geschichte als Sozialpsychologie, zugleich eine Epikrise über Karl Lamprecht." *Kultur- und Universalgeschichte: Walter Goetz zu seinem 60. Geburtstage.* Leipzig and Berlin, 1927. 501–17.

Herbst, Jurgen. *The German Historical School in American Scholarship: A Study in the Transfer of Culture.* Ithaca, 1965.

Herkless, John L. "Meinecke and the Ranke-Burckhardt Problem." *History and Theory* 9 (1970): 290–321.

———. "Ein unerklärtes Element in der Historiographie von Max Lenz." *Historische Zeitschrift* 222 (1976): 81–104.

Hildebrand, Klaus. *Bethmann Hollweg: Der Kanzler ohne Eigenschaften?* Düsseldorf, 1970.

Hinrichs, Carl. *Ranke und die Geschichtstheologie der Goethezeit.* Göttingen, 1954.

Hintze, Otto. "Gustav von Schmoller." *Deutsches Biographisches Jahrbuch* (1917–1920): 124–34.

Hirsch, Emanuel. *Geschichte der neueren evangelischen Theologie in Zusammenhang mit den allgemeinen Bewegungen des europäischen Denkens.* 5 vols. Gütersloh, 1964.

Hirsch, Felix. "Hermann Oncken and the End of an Era." *Journal of Modern History* 18 (1946): 148–58.

Hobiger, Rupert. "Oesterreich bei Karl Lamprecht." Ph.D. dissertation. Vienna, 1939.

Hoffmann, Walter. "Die Organisation des Ausleihdienstes in der modernen Bildungsbibliothek." *Volksbildungsarchiv: Beiträge zur wissenschaftlichen Vertiefung der Volksbildungsbestrebungen,* 1 (1910): 55–72, 227–344; 2 (1911): 29–132, 389–424; 3 (1913): 319–74.

Hoffmeister, Kay. "Karl Lamprecht: Seine Geschichtstheorie als Ideologie und seine Stellung zum Imperialismus." Ph.D. dissertation. Göttingen, 1956.

Hohendahl, Peter Uwe. *Literarische Kultur im Zeitalter des Liberalismus 1830–1870.* Munich, 1985.

Holborn, Hajo. "Der deutsche Idealismus in sozialgeschichtlicher Beleuchtung." *Historische Zeitschrift* 174 (1952), 359–84.

———. "Wilhelm Dilthey and the Critique of Historical Reason." *Journal of the History of Ideas* 11 (1950): 93–118.

Holl, Karl. *Pazifismus in Deutschland.* Frankfurt am Main, 1988.

Hollinger, David. "T. S. Kuhn's Theory of Science and Its Implications for History." *American Historical Review* 78 (1973): 370–93.

Holt, Niles Robert. "The Social and Political Ideas of the German Monist Movement, 1871–1914." Ph.D. dissertation. Yale University, 1967.

Honigsheim, Paul. "Die Gründung der deutschen Gesellschaft für Soziologie in ihren geistesgeschichtlichen Zusammenhängen." *Kölner Zeitschrift für Soziologie* 11 (1959): 3–10.

———. *On Max Weber.* New York and East Lansing, 1968.

Hubatsch, Walther. "Wilhelm Maurenbrecher 1838–1893." *Bonner Gelehrte.* 155–61.

Hübinger, Gangolf. "Kapitalismus und Kulturgeschichte." Ed. vom Bruch. *Kulturwissenschaften.* 25–43.

———. "Max Weber und die historischen Kulturwissenschaften." Ed. Hammerstein. *Geschichtswissenschaft.* 269–81.

Hübinger, Paul Egon. *Das Historische Seminar der Rheinischen Friedrich-Wilhelms-Universität zu Bonn: Vorläufer, Gründung, Entwicklung. Ein Wegstück deutscher Universitätsgeschichte.* Bonn, 1963.

Hübschmann, Siegfried. "Karl Lamprecht." *Mitteldeutsche Lebensbilder.* Magdeburg, 1929. 4: 405–15.

Hughes, H. Stuart. *Consciousness and Society: The Reorientation of European Social Thought, 1890–1930.* New York, 1958.

Hunter, James M. *Perspectives on Ratzel's Political Geography.* Lanham, 1983.

Iggers, Georg G. *The German Conception of History: The National Tradition of Historical Thought from Herder to the Present.* 2d ed. Middletown, CT, 1983.

———. "Heinrich von Treitschke." Ed. Wehler. *Historiker.* 2: 66–80.

———. "Historicism." *Dictionary of the History of Ideas.* 2 (1973): 456–64.

———. "The Image of Ranke in American and German Historical Thought." *History and Theory* 2 (1962): 17–40.

————. "The 'Methodenstreit' in International Perspective: The Reorientation of Historical Studies at the Turn from the Nineteenth to the Twentieth Century." *Storia della Storiographia* 6 (1984): 21–32.

Iggers, Georg G., and Powell, James M., eds. *Leopold von Ranke and the Shaping of the Historical Discipline.* Syracuse, NY, 1990.

Jagow, Kurt, ed. *Dietrich Schäfer und sein Werk.* Berlin, 1925.

Jahn, Georg. "Die historische Schule der Nationalökonomie und ihr Ausklang—Von der Wirtschaftsgeschichte zur geschichtlichen Theorie." Ed Antonio Montaner. *Geschichte der Volkswirtschaftslehre.* Cologne and Berlin, 1967, 41–50.

————. "Karl Lamprecht als Wirtschafts- und Kulturhistoriker: Zur 100. Wiederkehr seines Geburtstages." *Schmollers Jahrbuch* 76 (1956): 129–42.

Jameson, Frederic. *The Political Unconscious: Narrative as a Socially Symbolic Act.* Ithaca, 1981.

Jarausch, Konrad H. "The Institutionalization of History in 18th-Century Germany." Ed. Hans Erich Bödeker et al. *Aufklärung und Geschichte: Studien zur deutschen Geschichtsschreibung im 18. Jahrhundert.* Göttingen, 1986. 25–48.

————. *Students, Society, and Politics in Imperial Germany: The Rise of Academic Illiberalism.* Princeton, 1982.

Jarausch, Konrad H., ed. *The Transformation of Higher Learning, 1860–1930: Expansion, Diversification, Social Opening, and Professionalization in England, Germany, Russia, and the United States.* Chicago, 1983.

Jeismann, Karl-Ernst. *Das preussische Gymnasium in Staat und Gesellschaft: Die Entstehung des Gymnasiums als Schule des Staates und der Gebildeten 1787–1817.* Stuttgart, 1974.

Johnson, Jeffrey Allan. *The Kaiser's Chemists: Science and Modernization in Imperial Germany.* Chapel Hill and London, 1990.

Jungnickel, Christa, and McCormmach, Russell. *The Intellectual Mastery of Nature: Theoretical Physics from Ohm to Einstein.* 2 vols. Chicago and London, 1986.

Kaufhold, Karl Heinrich. "Gustav von Schmoller (1838–1917) als Historiker, Wirtschafts- und Sozialpolitiker und Nationalökonom." *Vierteljahrschrift für Sozial- und Wirtschaftsgeschichte.* 75 (1988): 217–52.

Kehr, Ekart. "Moderne deutsche Geschichtsschreibung." Ed. Hans-Ulrich Wehler. *Der Primat der Innenpolitik: Gesammelte Aufsätze zur preussisch-deutschen Sozialgeschichte im 19. und 20. Jahrhundert.* Berlin, 1976, 254–67.

Keller, Phyllis. *States of Belonging: German-American Intellectuals and the First World War.* Cambridge, MA, 1979.

Kernberg, Otto. "Pathological Narcissism in Middle Age." *Internal World and External Reality: Object Relations Theory Applied.* New York and London, 1980. 135–54.

————. *Borderline Conditions and Pathological Narcissism.* New York, 1975.

Kessel, Eberhard. "Rankes Idee der Universalhistorie." *Historische Zeitschrift* 178 (1954): 269–308.

Kittel, Rudolf. *Die Universität Leipzig und ihre Stellung im Kulturleben.* Dresden, 1924.

Klaiber, Ludwig. "Verzeichnis der Schriften Georg von Belows." *Aus Sozial- und Wirtschaftsgeschichte: Gedächtnisschrift für Georg von Below.* Stuttgart, 1928. 343–55.

Klein, D. B. *A History of Scientific Psychology: Its Origins and Philosophical Backgrounds.* New York and London, 1970.

Klein, Fritz. "Die deutschen Historiker im ersten Weltkrieg." Ed. Streisand. *Studien.* 2: 227–47.

Kleinertz, Everhard. "Joseph Hansen (1862–1943)." Hansen, Joseph. *Preussen und Rheinland von 1815 bis 1915: Hundert Jahre politischen Lebens am Rhein.* Cologne, 1990. 273–325.

Kloosterhuis, Jürgen. "Deutsche auswärtige Kulturpolitik und ihre Trägergruppen vor dem Ersten Weltkrieg." Ed. Kurt Düwell and Werner Link. *Deutsche auswärtige Kulturpolitik seit 1871.* Cologne and Vienna, 1981. 7–35.

Kluge, Alexander. *Die Universitäts-Selbstverwaltung*. Frankfurt am Main, 1958.

Knapp, T. "Zur Geschichte der Landeshoheit." *Württembergische Vierteljahrshefte für Landesgeschichte* 38 (1932): 9–112.

Kocka, Jürgen. "Otto Hintze." Ed. Wehler. *Historiker*. 3: 41–64.

König, Wolfgang. "Die Ingenieure und der VDI als Grossverein in der wilhelminischen Gesellschaft 1900 bis 1918." Ed. Karl-Heinz Ludwig and Wolfgang König. *Technik, Ingenieure und Gesellschaft: Geschichte des Vereins deutscher Ingenieure 1856–1981*. Düsseldorf, 1981.

Kötzschke, Rudolf. "Nationalgeschichte und Landesgeschichte." Ed. Fried. *Landesgeschichte*. 13–37.

——. "Das Seminar für Landesgeschichte und Siedlungskunde an der Universität Leipzig." *Neues Archiv für sächsische Geschichte und Altertumskunde* 57 (1936): 200–16.

——. "Universität Leipzig." Ed. Doeberl. *Das akademische Deutschland* 1: 289–308.

Kohut, Heinz. *The Analysis of the Self: A Systematic Approach to the Psychoanalytic Treatment of Narcissistic Personality Disorders*. New York, 1971.

——. *Self Psychology and the Humanities: Reflections on a New Psychoanalytic Approach*. New York and London, 1985.

Kohut, Thomas. *William II and the Germans: A Study in Leadership*. New York, 1991.

Kon, I. S. *Die Geschichtsphilosophie des 20. Jahrhunderts: Kritischer Abriss*. 2 vols. Berlin, 1964.

Korinman, Michel. *Quand l'Allemagne pensait le monde: Grandeur et décadence d'une géopolitique*. Paris, 1990.

Kraul, Margret. *Das deutsche Gymnasium 1780–1980*. Frankfurt am Main, 1974.

Krause, Hans-Thomas. "Die alldeutsche Geschichtsschreibung vor dem ersten Weltkrieg." Ed. Streisand. *Studien*. 2: 190–226.

——. "Dietrich Schäfer: Vom Schüler Treitschkes zum ideologischen Wegbereiter des ersten Weltkrieges." Ph.D. dissertation. Halle/Wittenberg. 1968.

Krieger, Leonard. *Ranke: The Meaning of History*. Chicago, 1977.

Krill, Hans-Heinz. *Die Ranke Renaissance: Max Lenz und Erich Marcks*. Berlin, 1962.

Kuczynski, Jürgen. *Studien zu einer Geschichte der Gesellschaftswissenschaften*. 10 vols. Berlin, 1975–1978.

Kuhn, Thomas S. *The Essential Tension: Selected Studies in Scientific Tradition and Change*. Chicago and London, 1977.

Kühne, Eckehard. "Historisches Bewusstsein in der deutschen Soziologie: Untersuchungen zur Geschichte der Soziologie von der Zeit der Reichsgründung bis zum Ersten Weltkrieg auf wissenssoziologischer Grundlage." Ph.D. diss. Marburg. 1971.

Kuklick, Bruce. *The Rise of American Philosophy: Cambridge, Massachusetts, 1860–1930*. New Haven and London, 1977.

Kultermann, Udo. *Geschichte der Kunstgeschichte: Der Weg einer Wissenschaft*. Frankfurt am Main, 1981.

Kupisch, Karl. *Die Hieroglyphe Gottes: Grosse Historiker der bürgerlichen Epoche von Ranke bis Meinecke*. Munich, 1967.

La Vopa, Anthony J. "Vocations, Careers, and Talent: Lutheran Pietism and Sponsored Mobility in Eighteenth-Century Germany." *Comparative Studies in Society and History* 28 (1986): 255–86.

Langerbeck, Ludwig. "Die Universitätsreformpläne Karl Lamprechts." Ed. Engelberg. *Karl-Marx-Universität*. 2: 39–48.

Langewiesche, Dieter, and Schönoven, Klaus. "Arbeiterbibliotheken und Arbeiterlektüre im Wilhelminischen Deutschland." *Archiv für Sozialgeschichte* 16 (1976): 135–204.

Leary, David E. "German Idealism and the Development of Psychology in the Nineteenth Century." *Journal of the History of Philosophy* 18 (1980): 309–10.

Lee, Dwight E., and Beck, Robert N. "The Meaning of Historicism." *American Historical Review* 59 (1954): 568–77.

Lehmann, Gerhard. *Geschichte der Philosophie, VIII: Die Philosophie des neunzehnten Jahrhunderts.* 2 vols. Berlin, 1953.

———. "Kant im Spätidealismus und die Anfänge der neukantischen Bewegung." *Zeitschrift für philosophische Forschung* 10 (1963), 438–56.

Lehmann, Hartmut. "'Das ewige Haus': Das lutherische Pfarrhaus im Wandel der Zeiten." Ed. H. Look. *"Gott kumm mir zu hilf": Martin Luther in der Zeitenwende.* Berlin, 1985. 177–200.

Leitner, Erich. "Die hochschulpädagogische Bewegung in ihrem Verhältnis zur Hochschulreform." Ed. Leitner. *Herausforderung.* 31–45.

Leitner, Erich, et al., eds. *Die pädagogische Herausforderung der Universität 1898–1934: Studien zur Gesellschaft für Hochschulpädagogik.* Weinheim, 1990.

Lepenies, Wolf. *Die Drei Kulturen: Soziologie zwischen Literatur und Wissenschaft.* Munich and Vienna, 1985.

Lessing, Hans-Ulrich. "Dilthey als Historiker: Das 'Leben Schleiermachers' als Paradigma." Ed. Hammerstein. *Geschichtswissenschaft.* 113–30.

Lewald, Ursula. "Karl Lamprecht 1856–1915." *Bonner Gelehrte.* 231–53.

———. "Karl Lamprecht und die Rheinische Geschichtsforschung." *Rheinische Vierteljahrsblätter* 21 (1956): 279–304.

Lindenfeld, David F. *The Transformation of Positivism: Alexius Meinong and European Thought, 1880–1920.* Berkeley and Los Angeles, 1980.

Lindenlaub, Dieter. *Richtungskämpfe im Verein für Sozialpolitik: Wissenschaft und Sozialpolitik im Kaiserreich vornehmlich vom Beginn des "neuen Kurses" bis zum Ausbruch des ersten Weltkrieges (1890–1914).* Wiesbaden, 1967.

List, Günther. "Historische Theorie und nationale Geschichte zwischen Frühliberalismus und Reichsgründung." Ed. Faulenbach. *Geschichtswissenschaft.* 35–53.

Lukács, Georg. *Theorie des Romans.* Berlin, 1963.

Lyon, Bryce. *Henri Pirenne: A Biographical and Intellectual Study.* Ghent, 1974.

———. "The Letters of Henri Pirenne to Karl Lamprecht (1894–1915)." *Bulletin de la Commission royale d'histoire* 132 (1966): 161–231.

Lyon, Bryce, and Lyon, Mary, eds. *The Journal de guerre of Henri Pirenne.* Amsterdam, 1976.

Maclean, Michael J. "Johann Gustav Droysen and the Development of Historical Hermeneutics." *History and Theory* 21 (1982): 347–66.

Mahrholz, Werner. "Geschichtliche Stellung der Freistudententschaft." Ed. Doeberl. *Das akademische Deutschland.* 2: 593–99.

Manegold, Karl-Heinz. "Das 'Ministerium des Geistes': Zur Organisation des ehemaligen preussischen Kultusministeriums." *Die deutsche Berufs- und Fachschule* 63 (1967): 512–24.

———. *Universität, Technische Hochschule und Industrie: Ein Beitrag zur Emanzipation der Technik im 19. Jahrhundert unter besonderer Berücksichtigung der Bestrebungen Felix Kleins.* Berlin, 1970.

Mann, Günter. "Geschichte als Wissenschaft und Wissenschaftsgeschichte bei Du Bois-Reymond." *Historische Zeitschrift* 213 (1980): 75–100.

Marcks, Friedrich. *Oskar Jäger.* Berlin and Leipzig, 1930.

Marhold, Wolfgang. "Die soziale Stellung des Pfarrers." Ed. Greiffenhagen. *Pfarrhaus.* 175–94.

Marienfeld, Wolfgang. *Wissenschaft und Schlachtflottenbau in Deutschland 1897–1906.* Frankfurt, 1957.

McClelland, Charles E. *The German Historians and England: A Study in Nineteenth-Century Views.* Cambridge, 1971.

————. "Zur Professionaliserung der akademischen Berufe in Deutschland." Ed. Werner Conze and Jürgen Kocka. *Bildungsbürgertum im 19. Jahrhundert: Bildungssystem und Professionalisierung in internationalen Vergleichen.* Stuttgart, 1985. 233–47.

————. *State, Society and University in Germany 1700–1914.* Cambridge, 1980.

Meinecke, Friedrich. *Die Entstehung des Historismus.* Munich, 1959.

Meinhardt, Günther. *Die Universität Göttingen: Ihre Entwicklung und Geschichte von 1734–1974.* Göttingen, 1977.

Meischner, Wolfram, and Eschler, Erhard. *Wilhelm Wundt.* Cologne, 1979.

Meisner, Heinrich Otto. "Otto Hintzes Lebenswerk." *Historische Zeitschrift* 164 (1941): 66–90.

Mertens, Lothar. "Das Privileg des Einjährig-Freiwilligen Militärdienstes." *Militärgeschichtliche Mitteilungen* No. 1 (1986): 59–67.

Metz, Karl-Heinz. *Grundformen historiographischen Denkens: Wissenschaftsgeschichte als Methodologie. Dargestellt an Ranke, Treitschke und Lamprecht.* Munich, 1979.

————. "Historisches 'Verstehen' und Sozialpsychologie: Karl Lamprecht und seine 'Wissenschaft der Geschichte.'" *Saeculum: Jahrbuch für Universalgeschichte* 33 (1982): 95–104.

————. "Der 'Methodenstreit in der deutschen Geschichtswissenschaft (1891–99)': Bemerkungen zum sozialen Kontext wissenschaftlicher Auseinandersetzungen." *Storia della Storiografia* 6 (1984): 3–20.

Miller, Alice. *Das Drama des begabten Kindes und die Suche nach dem wahren Selbst.* Frankfurt am Main, 1983.

Mischel, Theodore. "Wundt and the Conceptual Foundations of Psychology." *Philosophy and Phenomenological Research* 31 (1970–1971): 1–26.

Mogk, Walter. *Paul Rohrbach und das 'Grössere Deutschland': Ethischer Imperialismus im Wilhelminischen Zeitalter.* Munich, 1972.

Mommsen, Wolfgang J. "Max Weber und die historiographische Methode in seiner Zeit." *Storia della Storiografia* 3 (1983): 28–43.

————. "Ranke and the Neo-Rankean School in Imperial Germany: State-Oriented Historiography as a Stabilizing Force." Ed. Iggers and Powell. *Ranke.* 124–40.

Mommsen, Wolfgang J., and Osterhammel, Jürgen, eds. *Max Weber and His Contemporaries.* London, 1987.

Mommsen, Wolfgang J., and Schwentker, Wolfgang, eds. *Max Weber und seine Zeitgenossen.* Göttingen, 1988.

Moses, John. "Pan-Germanism and the German Professors, 1914–1918." *Australian Journal of Politics and History* 15 (December 1969): 45–60.

Mühlmann, Wilhelm E. *Geschichte der Anthropologie.* 2d ed. Frankfurt am Main and Bonn, 1968.

Müller, Detlef K. *Sozialstruktur und Schulsystem: Aspekte zum Strukturwandel des Schulwesens im 19. Jahrhundert.* Göttingen, 1977.

Muller, Jerry Z. *The Other God That Failed: Hans Freyer and the Deradicalization of German Conservatism.* Princeton, 1987.

Münsterberg, Margaret. *Hugo Münsterberg: His Life and Work.* New York and London, 1922.

Murphy, Gardner, and Kovach, Joseph K. *Historical Introduction to Modern Psychology.* New York, 1972.

Mütter, Bernd. "Die Geschichtswissenschaft in der alten Universität und Akademie Münster von der Aufklärung bis zum Historismus (1773 bis 1902)." *Westfälische Zeitschrift* 126/27 (1978): 158–61.

————. *Die Geschichtswissenschaft in Münster zwischen Aufklärung und Historismus.* Münster, 1980.

Nipperdey, Thomas. "Die anthropologische Dimension der Geschichtswissenschaft."

Gesellschaft, Kultur, Theorie: Gesammelte Aufsätze zur neueren Geschichte. Göttingen, 1976. 33–58.

―――. *Deutsche Geschichte 1800–1866: Bürgerwelt und starker Staat.* Munich, 1984.

―――. *Deutsche Geschichte 1866–1918: Arbeitswelt und Bürgergeist.* München, 1990.

―――. "Historismus und Historismuskritik heute." Ed. Eberhard Jäckel and Ernst Weymar. *Die Funktion der Geschichte in unserer Zeit.* Stuttgart, 1975. 82–95.

Noble, Thomas F. X. *The Republic of St. Peter: The Birth of the Papal State, 680–825.* Philadelphia, 1984.

Noorden, Werner von. "Carl von Noorden, ein akademisches Leben." 2nd version, 1944. Ms. in NL Schönebaum.

Novick, Peter. *That Noble Dream: The Objectivity Question in the American Historical Profession.* Cambridge and New York, 1988.

Nürnberger, Richard. "Imperialismus, Sozialismus und Christentum bei Friedrich Naumann." *Historische Zeitschrift* 152 (1950): 525–48.

O'Boyle, Leonore. "Klassische Bildung und soziale Struktur in Deutschland zwischen 1800 und 1848." *Historische Zeitschrift* 207 (1968): 584–608.

Oakes, Guy. *Weber and Rickert: Concept Formation in the Cultural Sciences.* Cambridge, MA, and London, 1988.

―――. "Weber and the Southwest German School: The Genesis of the Concept of the Historical Individual." Ed. Mommsen and Osterhammel. *Weber and His Contemporaries.* 434–46.

Oesterreich, Helga. "Die Geschichtswissenschaft an der Universität Münster." Ed. Heinz Dollinger. *Die Universität Münster 1789–1980.* Münster, 1980. 347–74.

Oestreich, Gerhard. "Die Fachhistorie und die Anfänge der sozialgeschichtlichen Forschung in Deutschland." *Historische Zeitschrift* 208 (1969): 320–63.

Oexle, Otto Gerhard. "Ein politischer Historiker: Georg von Below." Ed. Hammerstein. *Geschichtswissenschaft.* 283–312.

Ostwald, Grete. *Wilhelm Ostwald: Mein Vater.* Stuttgart, 1953.

Overbeck, Hermann. "Das politisch-geographische Lehrgebäude von Friedrich Ratzel in der Sicht unserer Zeit (1957)." *Kulturlandschaftsforschung und Landeskunde: Ausgewählte, überwiegend methodische Arbeiten.* Heidelberg, 1965. 60–87.

―――. "Ritter-Riehl-Ratzel: Die grossen Anreger zu einer historischen Landschafts- und Länderkunde Deutschlands im 19. Jahrhundert (1952)." *Kulturlandschaftsforschung und Landeskunde: Ausgewählte, überwiegend methodische Arbeiten.* Heidelberg, 1965. 88–103.

Pabst, Klaus. "Historische Vereine und Kommissionen in Deutschland bis 1914." *Vereinswesen und Geschichtspflege in den böhmischen Ländern.* Munich, 1986. 13–38.

Petersen, Peter. *Wilhelm Wundt und seine Zeit.* Stuttgart, 1925.

Pfetsch, Frank R. *Zur Entwicklung der Wissenschaftspolitik in Deutschland 1750–1914.* Berlin, 1974.

―――. "Scientific Organisation and Science Policy in Imperial Germany, 1871–1914: The Foundation of the Imperial Institute of Physics and Technology." *Minerva* 8 (1970): 557–80.

Philippsborn, Leo. "Carl von Noorden, ein deutscher Historiker des 19. Jahrhunderts." Ph.D. dissertation. Göttingen, 1963.

Plessner, Hellmut. "Zur Soziologie der modernen Forschung und ihrer Organisation in der deutschen Universität." *Diesseits der Utopie.* Frankfurt, 1974. 121–42.

Pongratz, Ludwig J. *Problemgeschichte der Psychologie.* Munich, 1984.

Pongratz, Ludwig, J.; et al., eds. *Psychologie in Selbstdarstellungen.* Berlin, 1972.

Popper, Annie M. "Karl Gotthard Lamprecht (1856–1815)." Ed. Halperin. *Essays.* 119–42.

Porter, Theodore M. "Lawless Society: Social Science and the Reinterpretation of

Statistics in Germany, 1850–1880." Ed. Lorenz Krüger et al. *The Probabilistic Revolution*. 2 vols. Cambridge, MA, 1987. 1: 351–76.

———. *The Rise of Statistical Thinking, 1820–1900*. Princeton, 1986.

Poulantzas, Nicos. *Fascism and Dictatorship: The Third International and the Problem of Fascism*. London, 1974.

Premerstein, A. von, et al. "Zur Geschichte des Historischen Seminars." Ed. H. Hermelink and S. A. Kaehler. *Die Philipps-Universität zu Marburg 1527–1927: Fünf Kapitel aus ihrer Geschichte. Die Universität Marburg seit 1866 in Einzeldarstellungen*. Marburg, 1927. 735–41.

Pusch, Oskar. *Von Below: Ein deutsches Geschlecht aus dem Ostseeraum*. Dortmund, 1974.

Queis, Dietrich von. "36 Jahre Hochschuldidaktik: Die erste hochschulpädagogische Bewegung 1898–1934." Ed. Leitner. *Herausforderung*. 47–75.

Rado, Sandor. "Obsessive Behavior: So-Called Obsessive-Compulsive Neurosis." Ed. Arieti. *Handbook*. 3: 195–208.

Raphael, Lutz. "Historikerkontroversen im Spannungsfeld zwischen Berufshabitus, Fächerkonkurrenz und sozialen Deutungsmustern: Lamprecht-Streit und französischer Methodenstreit der Jahrhundertwende in vergleichender Perspektive." *Historische Zeitschrift* 251 (1990): 325–63.

Rappard, H. V. "A Monistic Interpretation of Wundt's Psychology." *Psychological Research* 42 (1980): 123–34.

Redlich, Fritz. "Academic Education for Business: Its Development and the Contribution of Ignaz Jastrow." *Steeped in Two Cultures: A Selection of Essays*. New York and Evanston, 1971. 199–257.

Reichel, Waltraut. *Studien zum Wandel von Max Lehmanns preussisch-deutschen Geschichtsbild*. Göttingen, 1963.

Reill, Hans Peter. *The German Enlightenment and the Rise of Historicism*. Berkeley and Los Angeles, 1975.

Richter, Wilhelm. *Der Wandel des Bildungsgedankens: Die Brüder von Humboldt, das Zeitalter der Bildung und die Gegenwart*. Berlin, 1971.

Rickman, H. P. *Wilhelm Dilthey: Pioneer of the Human Studies*. Berkeley, 1979.

Rieber, R. W., et al., eds. *Wilhelm Wundt and the Making of a Scientific Psychology*. New York and London, 1980.

Riedel, Manfred. *Verstehen oder Erklären? Zur Theorie und Geschichte der hermeneutischen Wissenschaften*. Stuttgart, 1978.

Riese, Reinhard. *Die Hochschule auf dem Wege zum wissenschaftlichen Grossbetrieb: Die Universität Heidelberg und das badische Hochschulwesen 1860–1914*. Stuttgart, 1977.

Riesenberger, Dieter. *Geschichte der Friedensbewegung in Deutschland: Von den Anfängen bis 1933*. Göttingen, 1985.

Ringer, Fritz K. *The Decline of the German Mandarins: The German Academic Community 1890–1933*. Cambridge, MA, 1969.

Ritter, Gerhard. "Zum Begriff der 'Kulturgeschichte.'" *Historische Zeitschrift* 171 (1951): 293–302.

———. "Die deutschen Historikertage." *Geschichte in Wissenschaft und Unterricht* 4 (1953): 513–21.

———. "Motive und Organisationsformen der internationalen Wissenschaftsbeziehungen und die Anfänge einer auswärtigen Kulturpolitik im deutschen Kaiserreich vor dem Ersten Weltkrieg." Ed. Lothar Kettenacker et al. *Studien zur Geschichte Englands und der deutsch-britischen Beziehungen: Festschrift für Paul Kluke*. Munich, 1981. 153–200.

Ritter, Moriz. *Die Entwicklung der Geschichtswissenschaft an den führenden Werken betrachtet*. Berlin and Munich, 1919.

Ritzel, Gerhard. "Schmoller versus Menger: Eine Analyse des Methodenstreits im Hinblick auf den Historismus in der Nationalökonomie." Ph.D. dissertation. Basel, 1950.

Robinson, David. "Wilhelm Wundt and the Establishment of Experimental Psychology, 1875–1914: The Context of a New Field of Scientific Research." Ph.D. dissertation. University of California, Berkeley, 1987.

Rodnyj, N. I., and Solowjew, J. I. *Wilhelm Ostwald.* Leipzig, 1977.

Roger, Gerhard. "Ernst Bernheims organisatorische und theoretische Leistung in der Hochschulpädagogischen Bewegung." Ed. Karlheinz Jackstel. *Studien zur Geschichte der Hochschulpädagogik (II).* Halle, 1989. 5–15.

Romein, Jean. *The Watershed of Two Eras: Europe in 1900.* Middletown, CT, 1978.

Rorty, Richard. *Philosophy and the Mirror of Nature.* Princeton, 1979.

Roth, Guenther. "Americana: Bildungsbürgerliche Ansichten und auswärtige Kulturpolitik im Wilhelminischen Deutschland." *Politische Herrschaft und Persönliche Freiheit.* Frankfurt am Main, 1987. 175–201.

———. *Max Weber's Vision of History.* Berkeley and Los Angeles, 1979.

Rürup, Reinhard. "Ludwig Quidde." Ed. Wehler. *Historiker.* 3: 124–47.

Rüsen, Jörn. *Begriffene Geschichte: Genesis und Begründung der Geschichtstheorie J. G. Droysens.* Paderborn, 1969.

———. *Historische Vernunft: Grundzüge einer Historik I. Die Grundlagen der Geschichtswissenschaft.* Göttingen, 1983.

Sachs, Waldemar. "Lamprecht und Klinger." *Leipziger Tageblatt* 5.12.21.

Sachse, Arnold. *Friedrich Althoff und sein Werk.* Berlin, 1928.

Schäfer, Ulla G. *Historische Nationalökonomie und Sozialstatistik als Gesellschaftswissenschaften.* Cologne and Vienna, 1971.

Schefold, Bertram. "Karl Bücher und der Historismus in der deutschen Nationalökonomie." Ed. Hammerstein. *Geschichtswissenschaft.* 239–67.

Scheibler, Hans Carl, and Wülfrath, Karl, eds. *Westdeutsche Ahnentafeln.* Vol. 1. Weimar, 1939.

Schelting, Alexander von. *Max Webers Wissenschaftslehre: Das logische Problem der historischen Kulturerkenntnis. Die Grenzen der Soziologie des Wissens.* Tübingen, 1934.

Schenk, Willy. *Die deutsch-englische Rivalität vor dem ersten Weltkrieg in der Sicht deutscher Historiker: Missverstehen oder Machtstreben?* Aarau, 1967.

Schieder, Theodor. "Die deutsche Geschichtswissenschaft im Spiegel der Historischen Zeitschrift." *Historische Zeitschrift* 189 (1959): 1–73.

———. "Organisation und Organisationen der Geschichtswissenschaft." *Historische Zeitschrift* 237 (1983): 265–87.

Schleier, Hans. "Die Auseinandersetzung mit der Rankeschen Tradition Ende des 19. Jh. in Deutschland: Die deutschen Historiker und die Herausforderungen an die Geschichtswissenschaft." *Jahrbuch für Geschichte* 32 (1985): 271–87.

———. "Zur internationalen Stellung Karl Lamprechts." *Wissenschaftliche Beiträge der Ernst-Moritz-Arndt-Universität Greifswald zur Nordeuropa-Forschung: 7. Gesellschaftswissenschaftliches Seminar DDR-Finnland.* Greifswald, 1982. 4–13.

———. "Der Kulturhistoriker Karl Lamprecht, der 'Methodenstreit' und die Folgen." Ed. Schleier. *Lamprecht.* 7–45.

———. "Zu Max Webers Konzeption der historischen Erkenntnis." Ed. Wolfgang Küttler. *Gesellschaftstheorie und geschichtswissenschaftliche Erklärung.* Berlin, 1985. 309–35.

———. "Die Ranke-Renaissance." Ed. Streisand. *Studien.* 2: 99–135.

———. *Sybel und Treitschke: Antidemokratismus und Militarismus im historisch-politischen Denken grossbourgeoiser Geschichtsideologen.* Berlin, 1965.

———. "Zu den Theorien über die Entwicklung der Gesellschaft im spätbürgerlichen deutschen Geschichtsdenken." Ed. Ernst Engelberg and Wolfgang Küttler. *Formations-theorie und Geschichte: Studien zur historischen Untersuchung von Gesellschaftsformationen im Werk von Marx, Engels und Lenin.* Vaduz, 1978.

Schleier, Hans, ed. *Karl Lamprecht: Alternative zu Ranke. Schriften zur Geschichtstheorie.* Leipzig, 1988.

Schlesinger, Walter. "Rudolf Kötzschke (1867–1949)." *Zeitschrift für Ostforschung* 1 (1952): 274–78.

Schlink, Wilhelm. "Rektorenkonferenz und Verband der Deutschen Hochschulen." Ed. Doeberl. *Das akademische Deutschland.* 3: 589–96.

Schmidt, Dietrich, and Knipping, Franz. "Karl Bücher und das erste deutsche Universitätsinstitut für Zeitungskunde." Ed. Engelberg. *Karl-Marx-Universität.* 2: 57–77.

Schmidt, Roderich. "Arnold Schaefer 1819–1883." *Bonner Gelehrten,* 170–89.

Schmithals, Friedemann. "Die Gesellschaft für Hochschulpädagogik als Modellfall für die Institutionalisierungsprobleme der Hochschul-Pädagogik." Ed. Leitner. *Herausforderung.* 78–96.

Schnabel, Franz. *Deutsche Geschichte im neunzehnten Jahrhundert: Die Erfahrungswissenschaften.* Freiburg i Br., 1965.

————. *Deutsche Geschichte im neuzehnten Jahrhundert: Die protestantischen Kirchen in Deutschland.* Freiburg i. Br., 1965.

————. "Inwieweit ist die Kulturgeschichte im Geschichtsunterricht der Oberklassen zu berücksichtigen?" *Geschichte in Wissenschaft und Unterricht* (1987): 733–43.

————. "Kulturgeschichte im Geschichtsunterricht der Oberklassen." *Vergangenheit und Gegenwart* 4 (1914): 87–97.

Schnädelbach, Herbert. *Geschichtsphilosophie nach Hegel: Die Probleme des Historismus.* Munich, 1974.

————. *Philosophy in Germany, 1831–1933.* Cambridge, 1984.

Scholz, Johannes. *Geschichte der Burschenschaft Germania in Göttingen während der Jahre 1871–1893.* Neustrelitz, 1931.

Schönebaum, Herbert. "Carl von Noorden und Wilhelm Maurenbrecher im Austausch über die geistige Entwicklung des jungen Karl Lamprecht." *Archiv für Kulturgeschichte* 44 (1962): 379–87.

————. "Gustav Mevissen und Karl Lamprecht: Zur rheinischen Kulturpolitik von 1880–1890." *Rheinische Vierteljahrsblätter* 17 (1952): 180–96.

————. Heinrich von Treitschke und Karl Lamprecht: Dr. Erich Madsack gewidmet zu seinem 70. Geburtstag am 25. September 1959 (Privatdruck). In NL Lamprecht (Munich).

————. "Karl Lamprecht: Leben und Werk eines Kämpfers um die Geschichtswissenschaft 1856–1915." Unpublished ms. 1956. Copies in UB Bonn and Leipzig.

————. "Karl Lamprecht und Ernst Bernheim." *Archiv für Kulturgeschichte* 43 (1963): 217–39.

————. "Karl Lamprechts hochschulpädagogische Bestrebungen." *Zeitschrift für Pädagogik* 2 (1956): 1–16.

————. "Karl Lamprechts Mühen um innere und äussere Kulturpolitik." *Welt als Geschichte* 15 (1955): 137–52.

————. "Karl Lamprechts Verbundenheit mit seiner Heimat jenseits der 'Kindheitserinnerungen.'" *Heimatkalender für den Kreis Jessen 1956.* Jessen, 1956.

————. "Karl Lamprechts wissenschaftlicher Anruf an Rheinland und Sachsen und an die gesamte deutsche Nation." *Hamburger Mittel- und Ostdeutsche Forschungen.* Hamburg, 1957. 139–65.

————. "Lamprechtiana: Verzeichnis der Schriften Karl Lamprechts und der von ihm in Referat und Korreferat betreuten Dissertationen." *Wissenschaftliche Zeitschrift der Karl-Marx-Universität Leipzig* 5 (1955–1956): 7–21.

————. "Unausgeführte Vorhaben wissenschaftlicher und kulturpolitischer Art und die Forschungsinstitute Karl Lamprechts." *Forschungen und Fortschritte* 33 (1959): 117–23.

————. "Vom Werden der Deutschen Geschichte Karl Lamprechts." *Deutsche Vierteljahrschrift für Literaturwissenschaft und Geistesgeschichte* 25 (1951): 94–111.

Schorn-Schütte, Luise. *Karl Lamprecht: Kulturgeschichtsschreibung zwischen Wissenschaft und Politik.* Göttingen, 1984.

————. "Karl Lamprecht und die internationale Geschichtsschreibung." *Archiv für Kulturgeschichte* 67 (1985): 417–64.

————. "Karl Lamprecht: Wegbereiter einer historischen Sozialwissenschaft?" Ed. Hammerstein. *Geschichtswissenschaft.* 153–91.

————. "Stadt und Staat. Zum Zusammenhang von Gegenwartsverständnis und historischer Erkenntnis in der Stadtgeschichtsschreibung der Jahrhundertwende." *Die alte Stadt* 10 (1983): 228–66.

————. "Territorialgeschichte—Provinzialgeschichte—Landesgeschichte: Ein Beitrag zur Wissenschaftsgeschichte der Landesgeschichtsschreibung." Ed. Helmut Jäger et al. *Civitatum communitas: Studien zum europäischen Städtewesen.* Cologne and Vienna, 1984. 390–416.

Schulin, Ernst. "Friedrich Meinecke und seine Stellung in der deutschen Geschichtswissenschaft." Ed. Erbe. *Meinecke.* 25–49.

————. "Geistesgeschichte, Intellectual History und Histoire des Mentalités seit der Jahrhundertwende." *Traditionskritik,* 144–62.

————. "Meineckes Leben und Werk: Versuch einer Gesamtcharakteristik." *Traditionskritik,* 117–32.

————. *Traditionskritik und Rekonstruktionsversuch.* Göttingen, 1979.

Schulin, Ernst, ed. *Universalgeschichte.* Cologne, 1974.

Schulte, Bernd F. *Die Verfälschung der Riezler Tagebücher.* Frankfurt am Main, 1985.

Schultz, Dietrich. *Die deutschsprachige Geographie von 1800 bis 1970: Ein Beitrag zur Geschichte ihrer Methodologie.* Berlin, 1980.

Schultz, Susan D. "History as a Moral Force against Individualism: Karl Lamprecht and the Methodological Controversies in the German Human Sciences, 1880–1914." Ph.D. dissertation. University of Chicago, 1985.

Schulze, Winfried. *Deutsche Geschichtswissenschaft nach 1945.* Munich, 1989.

————. "Friedrich Meinecke und Otto Hintze." Ed. Erbe. *Meinecke.* 122–36.

————. "Otto Hintze und die deutsche Geschichtswissenschaft um 1900." Ed. Hammerstein. *Geschichtswissenschaft.* 323–39.

————. *Soziologie und Geschichtswissenschaft: Einführung in die Probleme der Kooperation beider Wissenschaften.* Munich, 1974.

Schumann, Peter. *Die deutschen Historikertage von 1893 bis 1937: Die Geschichte einer fachhistorischen Institution im Spiegel der Presse.* Göttingen, 1975.

Schwabe, Klaus. "Hermann Oncken." Ed. Wehler. *Historiker.* 2: 81–97.

————. *Wissenschaft und Kriegsmoral: Die deutschen Hochschullehrer und die politischen Grundfragen des Ersten Weltkrieges.* Göttingen, 1969.

Seeliger, Gerhard. "Karl Lamprecht." *Historische Vierteljahrschrift* 19 (1919–1920): 133–44.

Seifert, Friedrich. *Der Streit um Karl Lamprechts Geschichtsphilosophie: Eine historisch-kritische Studie.* Augsburg, 1925.

Selle, Götz von. *Die Georg-August-Universität zu Göttingen 1737–1937.* Göttingen, 1937.

Sellnow, Werner. *Gesellschaft-Staat-Recht: Zur Kritik der bürgerlichen Ideologien über die Entstehung von Gesellschaft, Staat und Recht.* Berlin, 1963.

Shapiro, David. *Neurotic Styles.* New York and London, 1965.

Simon, Christian. *Staat und Geschichtswissenschaft in Deutschland und Frankreich 1871–1914.* Bern, 1988.

Simon, Ernst. *Ranke und Hegel*. Munich, 1926.

Simon, W. M. *European Positivism in the Nineteenth Century: An Essay in Intellectual History*. Ithaca, 1963.

Skalweit, Stephan. "Moriz Ritter 1840–1923." *Bonner Gelehrte*. 209–24.

Smith, Woodruff D. "Friedrich Ratzel and the Origins of Lebensraum." *German Studies Review* 3 (1980): 51–68.

————. *Politics and the Sciences of Culture in Germany, 1840–1920*. New York, 1991.

Spieler, Karl-Heinz. *Untersuchungen zu Johann Gustav Droysens "Historik."* Berlin, 1970.

Srbik, Heinrich Ritter von. *Geist und Geschichte vom deutschen Humanismus bis zur Gegenwart*. 2 vols. Munich and Salzburg, 1951.

Ssymank, Paul. "Geschichtlicher Verlauf der freistudentischen Bewegung." Ed. Doeberl. *Das akademische Deutschland*. 2: 599–600.

Stählin, Karl. "Erich Marcks zum Gedächtnis." *Historische Zeitschrift* 160 (1930): 496–533.

Staude, Herbert. "Wilhelm Ostwald und die physikalische Chemie." Ed. Engelberg. *Karl-Marx-Universität*. 1: 481–91.

Steinberg, Hans-Josef. "Karl Lamprecht." Ed. Wehler. *Historiker*. 1: 58–68.

Steinmetz, Max, ed. *Bedeutende Gelehrte in Leipzig*. 2 vols. Leipzig, 1965.

Steinmetzler, Johannes. *Die Anthropogeographie Friedrich Ratzels und ihre ideengeschichtlichen Wurzeln*. Bonn, 1956.

Stern, Leo, et al., eds. *Die Berliner Akademie der Wissenschaften in der Zeit des Imperialismus*. 3 vols. Berlin, 1975–1979.

Stieg, Margaret F. *The Origin and Development of Scholarly Historical Periodicals*. University, Alabama, 1986.

Streisand, Joachim, ed. *Studien über die deutsche Geschichtswissenschaft*. 2 vols. Berlin, 1965.

Striebing, Lothar. "Wilhelm Ostwald und das Philosophieren der Naturwissenschaftlicher." Ed. Engelberg. *Karl-Marx-Universität*. 1: 492–504.

Tenbruck, Friedrich H. "Max Weber und Eduard Meyer." Ed. Mommsen and Schwentker. *Weber und seine Zeitgenossen*. 337–79.

Terdiman, Richard. *Discourse/Counter-Discourse: The Theory and Practice of Symbolic Resistance in Nineteenth-Century France*. Ithaca, 1985.

Theiner, Peter. *Sozialer Liberalismus und deutsche Weltpolitik: Friedrich Naumann im Wilhelminischen Deutschland (1860–1919)*. Baden-Baden, 1983.

Thimme, Annelise. *Hans Delbrück als Kritiker der Wilhelminischen Epoche*. Düsseldorf, 1955.

Titze, Hartmut. "Die zyklische Überproduktion von Akademikern im 19. und 20. Jahrhundert." *Geschichte und Gesellschaft* 10 (1984): 92–121.

Troeltsch, Ernst. *Der Historismus und seine Probleme: Das logische Problem der Geschichtsphilosophie*. Tübingen, 1922.

Turner, R. Steven. "The Growth of Professorial Research in Prussia, 1818 to 1848—Causes and Context." Ed. Russell McCormmach. *Historical Studies in the Physical Sciences*. Philadelphia, 1971. 3: 137–82.

————. "Historicism, *Kritik*, and the Prussian Professoriate, 1790 to 1840." Ed. Mayotte Bollack et al. *Philologie und Hermeneutik im 19. Jahrhundert*. 2 vols. Göttingen, 1983. 2: 450–77.

————. "The Prussian Universities and the Concept of Research." *Internationales Archiv für Sozialgeschichte der deutschen Literatur* 5 (1980): 68–93.

Ullmann, Ernst. "August Schmarzow (1853–1936)." Ed. Steinmetz. *Bedeutende Gelehrte*. 1: 109–15.

van Hoorn, Willem, and Verhave, Thom. "Wundt's Changing Conceptions of a General and Theoretical Psychology." Ed. Bringmann. *Wundt Studies.* 71–113.

Vierhaus, Rudolf. "Bildung." Ed. Otto Brunner et al. *Geschichtliche Grundbegriffe: Historisches Lexikon zur politisch-sozialen Sprache in Deutschland.* 6 vols. Stuttgart, 1972–1990. 1: 508–551.

———. "Kulturgeschichte." Ed. Klaus Bergmann et al. *Handbuch der Geschichtsdidaktik.* 3d ed. Düsseldorf, 1985. 187–90.

———. "Ranke und die Anfänge der deutschen Geschichtswissenschaft." Ed. Faulenbach. *Geschichtswissenschaft.* 17–34.

———. *Ranke und die soziale Welt.* Münster, 1957.

Vietsch, Eberhard von. *Bethmann Hollweg: Staatsmann zwischen Macht und Ethos.* Boppard, 1969.

Viikari, Matti. *Die Krise der "historistischen" Geschichtsschreibung und die Geschichtsmethodologie Karl Lamprechts.* Helsinki, 1977.

———. "Die Tradition der finnischen Geschichtsschreibung und Karl Lamprecht." *Storia della Storiographia* 6 (1984): 33–43.

Vogler, Günter. "Max Lehmann." Ed. Streisand. *Studien.* 2: 57–95.

Vogt, Joseph. *Wege zum historischen Universum: Von Ranke bis Toynbee.* Stuttgart, 1961.

vom Brocke, Bernhard. "Der deutsch-amerikanische Professorenaustausch: Preussische Wissenschaftspolitik, internationale Wissenschaftsbeziehungen und die Anfänge einer deutschen auswärtigen Kulturpolitik vor dem Ersten Weltkrieg." *Zeitschrift für Kulturaustausch* 31 (1981): 128–82.

———. "Hochschul- und Wissenschaftspolitik in Preussen und im Deutschen Kaiserreich 1882–1907: Das 'System Althoff.'" Ed. Peter Baumgart. *Bildungspolitik in Preussen zur Zeit des Kaiserreichs.* Stuttgart, 1980. 9–118.

———. "Die Kaiser-Wilhelm Gesellschaft im Kaiserreich: Vorgeschichte, Gründung und Entwicklung bis zum Ausbruch des Ersten Weltkrieges." Ed. Rudolf Vierhaus and Bernhard vom Brocke. *Forschung im Spannungsfeld von Politik und Gesellschaft: Geschichte und Struktur der Kaiser-Wilhelm-/Max-Planck-Gesellschaft.* Stuttgart, 1990. 17–162.

———. "Kurt Breysig." Ed. Wehler. *Historiker.* 6: 95–116.

———. *Kurt Breysig: Geschichtswissenschaft zwischen Historismus und Soziologie.* Lübeck and Hamburg, 1971.

———. "'Wissenschaft und Militarismus': Der Aufruf der 93 'An die Kulturwelt!' und der Zusammenbruch der internationalen Gelehrtenrepublik im Ersten Weltkrieg." Ed. W. M. Calder, III, et al. *Wilamowitz nach 50 Jahren.* Darmstadt, 1985. 649–719.

vom Bruch, Rüdiger. "Die deutsche Hochschule in der historischen Forschung." Ed. Dietrich Goldschmidt et al. *Forschungsgegenstand Hochschule: Überblick und Trendbericht.* Frankfurt and New York, 1984. 1–27.

———. "Gustav Schmoller." Ed. Hammerstein. *Geschichtswissenschaft.* 219–38.

———. "Gustav Schmoller." Ed. Wolfgang Treue and Karlfried Gründer. *Berlinische Lebensbilder: Wissenschaftspolitik in Berlin. Minister, Beamte, Ratgeber.* Berlin, 1987. 175–93.

———. "Historiker und Nationalökonomen im Wilhelminischen Deutschland." Ed. Klaus Schwabe. *Deutsche Hochschullehrer als Elite 1815–1945.* Boppard am Rhein, 1988.

———. "Krieg und Frieden: Zur Frage der Militarsierung deutscher Hochschullehrer und Universitäten im späten Kaiserreich." Ed. Jost Dülffer and Karl Holl. *Bereit zum Krieg: Kriegsmentalität im wilhelminischen Deutschland 1890–1914.* Göttingen, 1986. 74–98.

———. "Kulturstaat—Sinndeutung von oben?" Ed. vom Bruch. *Kulturwissenschaft.* 63–101.

———. "'Militarismus,' 'Realpolitik' und 'Pazifismus.' Aussenpolitik und Aufrüstung in der Sicht deutscher Hochschullehrer (Historiker) im späten Kaiserreich." *Militärge-*

schichtliche Mitteilungen No. 1 (1986): 37–58.

———. "Universitätsreform als soziale Bewegung: Zur Nicht-Ordinarienfrage im späten deutschen Kaiserreich." *Geschichte und Gesellschaft* 10 (1984): 72–91.

———. *Weltpolitik als Kulturmission: Auswärtige Kulturpolitik und Bildungsbürgertum in Deutschland am Vorabend des Ersten Weltkrieges.* Paderborn, 1982.

———. *Wissenschaft, Politik und öffentliche Meinung: Gelehrtenpolitik im Wilhelminischen Deutschland (1890–1914).* Husum, 1980.

———. "Wissenschaftspolitik, Kulturpolitik, Weltpolitik: Hochschule und Forschungs- institute auf dem Deutschen Hochschullehrertag in Dresden 1911." Ed. Horst-Walter Blanke and Jörn Rüsen. *Vom historischen Seminar zum historischen Forschungsinstitut: Zur Transformation des Historismus.* Paderborn, 1992. 1–28.

———. "Zeitungswissenschaft zwischen Historie und Nationalökonomie: Ein Beitrag zur Vorgeschichte der Publizistik als Wissenschaft im späteren Deutschen Kaiserreich. *Publizistik* 25 (1980): 579–607.

vom Bruch, Rüdiger, Graf, Friedrich Wilhelm, and Hübinger, Gangolf, eds. *Kultur und Kulturwissenschaft um 1900: Krise der Moderne und Glaube an die Wissenschaft.* Stutt- gart, 1989.

Walsh, W. W. *Philosophy of History: An Introduction.* New York, 1960.

Wanklyn, Harriet. *Friedrich Ratzel: A Biographical Memoir and Bibliography.* Cambridge, 1961.

Weber, Christof. "Heinrich Finke zwischen akademischer Imparität und kirchlichem Antiliberalismus." *Annalen des Historischen Vereins für den Niederrhein* 186 (1983): 139–65.

Weber, Marianne. *Max Weber: Ein Lebensbild.* Tübingen, 1926.

Weber, Wolfgang. *Biographisches Lexikon zur Geschichtswissenschaft in Deutschland, Oester- reich und der Schweiz: Die Lehrstuhlinhaber für Geschichte von den Anfängen des Faches bis 1970.* Frankfurt am Main, 1984.

———. *Priester der Klio: Historisch-sozialwissenschaftliche Studien zur Herkunft und Karriere deutscher Historiker und zur Geschichte der Geschichtswissenschaft 1800–1970.* Frankfurt am Main, Bern, New York, 1984.

Wehler, Hans-Ulrich. *Deutsche Gesellschaftsgeschichte: Von der Reformära bis zur industriel- len und politischen "Deutschen Doppelrevolution" 1815–1845/49.* Munich, 1987.

———. "Professionalisierung in historischer Perspektive." *Geschichte und Gesellschaft* 6 (1980): 311–25.

Wehler, Hans-Ulrich, ed. *Deutsche Historiker.* 9 vols. Göttingen, 1972–81.

———. *Ludwig Quidde, Caligula: Schriften über Militarismus und Pazifismus.* Frankfurt am Main, 1977.

Weissbach, Heinz. "Die Entwicklung des Instituts für Kultur-und Universalgeschichte bzw. der Abteilung Allgemeine Geschichte der Neuzeit des Instituts für Allgemeine Geschichte von 1909 bis 1969: Ein Beitrag zu einer Institutschronik." 2 vols. Diplo- marbeit, Karl-Marx-Universität Leipzig, 1979.

Weller, B. Uwe. *Maximilian Harden und die "Zukunft."* Bremen, 1970.

Wendel, Günter. *Die Kaiser-Wilhelm-Gesellschaft 1911–1914: Zur Anatomie einer im- perialistischen Forschungsgesellschaft.* Berlin, 1975.

Wenger, Pierre. *Grundzüge der Geschichtsschreibung von Erich Marcks.* Zürich, 1950.

Werdermann, Hermann. *Die deutsche evangelische Pfarrfrau: Ihre Geschichte in vier Jahrhun- derten.* 3d ed. Witten, 1935.

Wernecke, Klaus. *Der Wille zur Weltgeltung: Aussenpolitik und Öffentlichkeit im Kaiserreich am Vorabend des Ersten Weltkrieges.* Düsseldorf, 1970.

Westphal, Otto. *Feinde Bismarcks: Geistige Grundlagen der deutschen Opposition 1848– 1918.* Munich and Berlin, 1930.

———. "Max Lenz (1850–1932)." *Hansische Geschichtsblätter* 57 (1932): 29–37.

Weymar, Ernst. *Das Selbstverständnis der Deutschen: Ein Bericht über den Geist des Geschichtsunterrichts der höheren Schulen im 19. Jahrhundert.* Stuttgart, 1961.

Whimster, Sam. "Karl Lamprecht and Max Weber: Historical Sociology within the Confines of a Historians' Controversy." Ed. Mommsen and Osterhammel. *Weber and His Contemporaries.* 268–83.

White, Hayden. *Metahistory: The Historical Imagination in Nineteenth-Century Europe.* Baltimore and London, 1973.

———. *The Content of the Form: Narrative Discourse and Historical Representation.* Baltimore and London, 1987.

Wild, Adolf. *Baron d'Estournelles de Constant (1852–1924): Das Wirken eines Friedensnobelpreisträgers für die deutsch-französische Verständigung und europäische Einigung.* Hamburg, 1973.

Willemsen, Carl Arnold. "Alfred Dove 1844–1916." *Bonner Gelehrte,* 254–59.

Willey, Thomas E. *Back to Kant: The Revival of Kantianism in German Social and Historical Thought, 1860–1914.* Detroit, 1978.

Winkel, Harald. *Die deutsche Nationalökonomie im 19. Jahrhundert.* Darmstadt, 1977.

Winnicott, D. W. "Playing: Creative Activity and the Search for the Self." *Playing and Reality.* London and New York, 1971. 53–64.

Wise, M. Norton. "How Do Sums Count? On the Cultural Origins of Statistical Causality." Ed. Lorenz Krüger et al. *The Probabilistic Revolution.* 2 vols. Cambridge, MA, 1987. 1: 395–425.

Woodward, William R. "Fechner's Panpsychism: A Scientific Solution to the Mind-Body Problem." *Journal of the History of the Behavioral Sciences* 8 (1972): 367–86.

Young, Harry F. *Maximilian Harden, Censor Germaniae: The Critic in Opposition from Bismarck to the Rise of Nazism.* The Hague, 1959.

Zorn, Wolfgang. "Eberhard Gothein 1853–1923." *Bonner Gelehrte.* 260–71.

———. "'Volkswirtschaft und Kulturgeschichte' und 'Sozial- und Wirtschaftsgeschichte': Zwei Zeitschriften in der Vorgeschichte der VSWG 1863–1900." *Vierteljahrschrift für Sozial- und Wirtschaftsgeschichte* 72 (1985): 457–75.

Index

Academy of Sciences (Bavarian), 71, 86;
  Historical Commission, 35, 258
Academy of Sciences (Prussian), 91, 421
Academy of Sciences (Saxon), 115, 371,
  381
Acta Borussica, 230, 250n. 105
Adaldag (archbishop of
  Hamburg-Bremen), 133
Adams, Charles Baxter, 347
Albrecht V (duke of Bavaria), 278n. 27
Alldeutscher Verband. See Pan-German
  League
Allgemeiner Deutscher Schulverein. See
  German School Association
Allgemeiner Studentenausschuss, 377
Alte Pinakothek, 53
Althoff, Friedrich, 63n. 102, 99nn. 40,
  41, 102nn. 116, 117, 118, 122,
  104n. 164, 112, 116, 172n. 94,
  173n. 112, 226, 252n. 168, 311, 346,
  377, 384, 390n. 81, 399, 408; and
  Lamprecht, 85–87, 93, 96, 114, 150,
  158, 181, 241, 352, 414–15
American Historical Association (Pacific
  Coast Branch), 358
Andreas, Willy, 259
Anglo-German Conciliation Committee,
  410
Annalen der Naturphilosophie, 296
Archiv für Kulturgeschichte, 258–60,
  262–63, 279n. 55, 336
Aristotle, 54, 198
Arndt, Wilhelm, 115, 161–62, 165,
  194, 371
Arnold, Wilhelm, 78, 80, 83, 149, 292
Association for Germandom Abroad,
  409, 412, 419, 422
Association of German Engineers, 419
Association of German Historians, 167,
  178, 216, 240, 286, 351, 383, 399
Association of German University
  Teachers, 384–85
Association of Honorary Professors,
  Extraordinary Professors, and
  Privatdozenten (Leipzig), 377

Aubin, Hermann, 263, 278–79n. 48
Aufklärung, 25
Augsburg, Religious Peace of, 71
Auslandsvereine, 417, 421
Auswärtige Kulturpolitik. See Cultural
  foreign policy
Avenarius, Friedrich, 198, 323

Bach, J. S., 314
Bancroft, George, 352
Bar, Ludwig von, 410
Barth, Paul, 297
Bastian, Adolf, 294
Battle of Nations, 433
Bauer, Stephan, 262–63
Baumann, J. J., 40
Baumgarten, Hermann, 113, 162, 235
Beard, Charles A., 347
Bebel, August, 40
Becker, Carl, 347
Becker, Wilhelm, 76
Beethoven, Ludwig van, 441
Below, Georg von, 74, 109, 140–41n. 34,
  153–55, 163, 166–67, 168n. 4,
  168–69n. 17, 171nn. 85, 87,
  172nn. 90, 98, 175–76, 181–83, 187,
  192, 194, 206n. 18, 216–17, 220–21,
  229–30, 237, 247n. 48, 254, 257,
  267, 271, 279n. 55, 280n. 78, 286–87,
  317, 324n. 2, 338, 345, 358, 419;
  contra Lamprecht, 146–51, 159–61,
  178, 242–45, 262–64
Benjamin, Walter, 7, 57
Berlin Historical Society, 228
Berlin, technical university, 419
Berlin, university, 31, 35, 75, 88, 90,
  113, 147, 157–58, 172n. 94, 187,
  219, 227, 230, 235, 254, 256–57,
  289, 337, 353, 357, 368, 377–78;
  Institute for Comparative Historical
  Research, 337; Lamprecht and,
  160–62, 165, 167, 178–82, 294,
  379–80, 386
Bernheim, Ernst, 39–41, 44, 50,
  63nn. 101, 105, 79, 99n. 40, 120,

122–23, 126, 156, 163, 166, 193, 222, 228–30, 241–42, 247n. 41, 249nn. 99, 100, 252n. 173, 357, 385–86, 392n. 138, 435
Bernstein, Eduard, 376
Berr, Henri, 344
Bethmann Hollweg, Theobald von, 16, 415–22, 428n. 124, 431, 437–38, 441
Bezold, Friedrich von, 154, 235–37, 259, 274
Bismarck, Otto von, 69, 157, 162–63, 219, 261, 318, 396–97, 424n. 36
Bismarck-Jahrbuch, 163
Bissing, Moritz von, 439
Blâtand, Harald (king of Denmark), 133
Bleuler, Eugen, 95
Blok, P. J., 78, 345; *History of the Netherlands*, 345
Blondel, Georges, 345
Böckh, August, 29
Böcklin, Arnold, 305
Boer War, 403
Boltzmann, Ludwig, 346
Bonn, university, 38, 45, 69–72, 113, 195, 219, 259, 274, 302, 386; Lamprecht and, 72–74, 76–77, 83–87, 94, 96–97, 115, 122, 162, 368, 371
Brandenburg, Erich, 164, 274–75, 293, 350, 356–57, 364n. 112, 374–75, 380
Bredow, Gabriel Gottfried, 26
Breitkopf und Haertel, 352
Brentano, Lujo, 114, 140n. 32
Breslau, university, 87, 96, 113, 140–41n. 34, 182, 219–20, 302
Bresslau, Harry, 163
Breysig, Kurt, 166, 170n. 57, 256–57, 262–63, 277nn. 10, 18, 316, 325n. 33, 337, 340, 357; *Cultural History of the Modern Era*, 256–57
Brieger, Theodor, 374
Bruch, Emma, 117, 141n. 53, 223, 287, 433
Brunner, Heinrich, 149
Brunner, Otto, xiii, 168n. 13
Bryce, James, 426n. 92
Bücher, Karl, 91, 93, 157, 208–9n. 99, 300, 306–7, 339, 356, 367, 372, 383, 385, 404, 408; and Lamprecht, 114, 161, 194–95, 227, 272, 275, 294–95, 297

Buchholz, Gustav, 164, 194, 273–74, 371, 400
Buckle, T. H., 32, 40, 90, 198, 229, 260
Budde, Karl, 346
BUGRA, 431, 437
Bülow, Bernhard von, 352, 413–15, 427n. 115
Bülow, Karl von, 438
Bund neues Vaterland, 436
Burckhardt, Jacob, 43, 89, 153, 155, 220, 256, 258, 260–61, 336; *Civilization of the Renaissance in Italy*, 53; Lamprecht and, 52–54, 79, 93, 120, 127–28; *Observations on World History*, 260, 336
Burschenschaften, 24, 371, 396
Busch, Wilhelm, 74, 115

Caesar, Julius, 434
California, University of, 349
Caligula, 165
Carnegie, Andrew, 385
Carnegie Foundation, 352
Carolingians, 54, 80, 82, 124, 148, 163, 184
Cassirer, Ernst, 88, 344
Central Division for Service Abroad, 437
Charlemagne, 137
Charles V (emperor), 235
Chicago, University of, 349
Christiana, university, 382
Christoph of Oldenburg (count), 235
Class, Heinrich, 403
Clausewitz, Carl von, 147, 182
Cohen, Hermann, 410
Coligny, Gaspard de, 162
Columbia University, 346–47, 349, 378
Comte, Auguste, 40, 49, 90, 120, 198, 205, 229, 241–42, 249n. 100, 252n. 173, 262, 265, 267, 290, 295, 307, 392n. 138
Conrad II (emperor), 133
Conze, Werner, xiii
Cornelius, Carl Adolf, 52, 71
Council of Constance, 216
Counter-Reformation, 70–71, 235
Cultural Association of German Scholars and Artists, 436
Cultural foreign policy, 411–12, 417–22, 431, 435, 438
Cultural history, xii, 104n. 164, 115,

117–19, 133, 138, 149, 151–54, 159,
165–66, 177, 180, 185–87, 199–205,
214, 218, 220, 222, 238, 245, 273,
275, 291–92, 316, 318, 320, 373,
375, 384, 397, 399, 403, 410, 417,
431, 435–36; in aftermath of
Methodenstreit, 255–64, 271; early
history of, 87–93; support for,
154–57, 227–33, 345; and universal
history, 336–38, 351, 355
Cuny, Ludwig von, 85
Curtius, Ernst, 181

Daenell, Ernst, 282n. 112, 357, 400
Dahlmann, Friedrich Christoph, 70, 166
Dargun, Ralph, 142n. 83
Darmstädter Bank for Commerce and
Industry, 69
Darwin, Charles, 90, 198, 205, 289,
295, 298, 301; *The Origin of
Species*, 32·
"Declaration of the Ninety-Three,"
436–37
Deichmann, Carl Theodor, 68, 74, 438
Deichmann, Theodor, 68–69, 94, 117
Deichmann, Wilhelm Ludwig, 67–68
Delbrück, Hans, 161–62, 181, 183, 222,
235, 237–40, 250nn. 116, 122,
251n. 147, 321, 358, 421
Des Courdes, Theodor, 374
Des Marez, Guilliaume, 345, 439
Dessoir, Max, 346
Deutsch-englisches Verständigungskomitee.
See Anglo-German Conciliation
Committee
Deutsche Geschichtsblätter, 293
Deutsche Kolonialgesellschaft. See German
Colonial Society
Deutsche Literaturzeitung, 172n. 90, 183
Deutsche Revue, 417
Deutsche Rundschau, 323
*Deutsche Zeitschrift für
Geschichtswissenschaft*, 159, 165, 167,
179, 192, 256, 272
Deutscher Ostmarkenverein. See Eastern
Marches Society
Deutsches Theater, 192
Deutsches Wirtschaftsleben im Mittelalter.
See German Economic Life in the Middle
Ages
Diederichs, Eugen, 431
Dilthey, Wilhelm, 153, 155, 199, 232,

242–43, 250n. 116, 257, 265–68,
294, 299
Dodd, William E., 345, 367–68
Döllinger, Ignaz, 71
Dorpat, university, 71
Dove, Alfred, 87, 96, 99n. 47, 111, 113,
140n. 32, 149, 167, 241, 252n. 171,
286, 339, 353, 420
Dresden, technical university, 371, 387
Droysen, Johann Gustav, 31–33, 35–37,
40–41, 75, 87, 112, 152–53, 155,
157, 166, 230, 265, 397
Drumann, Wilhelm, 88
Du Bois-Reymond, Emil, 40, 90, 198, 267
Dürer, Albrecht, 124, 128, 203
Dürr, Alfons, 321
Düsseldorf, Academy of Art, 86

Eagleton, Terry, 24
Eastern Marches Society, 395, 400,
423n. 17, 424n. 32
Ebbinghaus, Hermann, 199
Eichhorn, Karl Friedrich, 149
Eickhoff, Richard, 421
Einstein, Albert, 295
Elizabeth I (queen of England), 162
Elster, Ludwig, 91
Engel, Eduard, 144n. 132
Engel, Josef, 34, 360
Engelhus, Dietrich, 72, 98n. 35
Engels, Friedrich, 123, 127, 175
Erasmus, Desiderius, 128
Erdmannsdörffer, Bernhard, 90, 152,
219–20
Erich (king of Sweden), 133
Erikson, Erik, 6
Erler, Georg, 115
Eucken, Rudolf, 386
Eulenburg, Franz, 297
Europäische Staatengeschichte, 166
Excitability, era of, 305–6, 308–10,
330n. 136, 401–3, 407, 413

Faber, Karl-Georg, xii
Faust, 56, 139, 270
Fechner, Gustav Theodor, 45, 196, 294,
301
Feuerbach, Ludwig, 198
Fichte, J. G., 3, 15, 26, 189, 261, 316
Finke, Heinrich, 216–17, 221, 223,
246n. 17, 247nn. 30, 32, 254, 259,
286, 293, 357, 436

Finkenschaft. See Free student association
Fischer, Fritz, xii
Foerster, Wilhelm, 386
Foerster-Nietzsche, Elisabeth, 413
Fontane, Theodor, 305
Foundation for the Promotion of
  Atheism, 413
Francis of Assisi, 258
Franco-Prussian War, 23, 219, 289
Frankfurt, university, 387
Frankfurter Zeitung, 321, 337, 422
Frederick II (Prussian king), 157, 230,
  313–14
Frederick III (German king), 131
Frederick Barbarossa, 124
Frederick William, Great Elector, 256
Fredericq, Paul, 345, 437, 439
Free Association for Naval Lectures, 400
Free student association, 370, 371,
  376–77
Freiberg i. S., mining academy, 371
Freiburg i. Br., university, 162, 241,
  254, 345
Freie Studentenschaft. See Free student
  association
Freie Vereinigung für Flottenvorträge. See
  Free Association for Naval Lectures
Freisinnige Vereinigung, 404
French Revolution, 25–26, 315
Frensdorff, Ferdinand, 39
Freud, Sigmund, 306
Freyer, Hans, xiii
Freytag, Gustav, 71, 87–88, 180,
  227; *Bilder aus der deutschen
  Vergangenheit*, 88
Fried, Alfred Hermann, 409–10, 416
Friederich, Fritz, 366n. 173
Friedrich August III (king of Saxony),
  381–82
Friedrich-Wilhelms *Gymnasium*,
  Cologne, 68
Frye, Northrop, 136

Gadamer, Hans-Georg, 29
Gaertner Verlag, 321
George, Stefan, 256, 305
German Association for International
  Conciliation, 410–12, 417
German Colonial Society, 395, 423n. 17
German Committee for the Near East,
  417
German Economic Life in the Middle Ages,

81–83, 85–87, 93–94, 96, 109, 117,
  124, 127, 142n. 83, 146, 149–50,
  159, 247n. 43, 321, 324n. 2
German *History*, 122, 138, 140n. 13,
  150–51, 158–61, 175–78, 183–84,
  187, 192–94, 224, 229–30, 241,
  251n. 127, 273, 287–88, 309,
  332n. 236, 338–43, 345, 353–55,
  369, 376, 397–400, 402, 404, 407,
  414, 433, 435, 437, 440; audience,
  321–23; preparation of volumes 1–5,
  117–22; preparation of volumes 6–11,
  297–304; volume 1, 122–24, 238–39,
  321, 339–40; volume 2, 124–25;
  volume 3, 125–26, 399; volume 4,
  126–27, 183–85, 199–200, 217, 399;
  volume 5, 127–29, 192, 217, 220–22,
  235–36, 399; volumes 6 and 7, 200,
  312–14; volume 8, 314–15; volume 9,
  315–16; volume 10, 317; volume 11,
  317–19; volume 12, 319, 354;
  supplements, 304–11, 320, 322,
  400–405, 407, 413, 417, 435
German School Association, 395, 409,
  423n. 17. *See also* Association for
  Germandom Abroad
German Society for Sociology, 281n. 88
German-Chinese Association, 417
German-Turkish Association, 421
Gesellschaft für Hochschulpädagogik. See
  Society for the Pedagogy of Higher
  Education
Gesellschaft für Rheinische Geschichtskunde.
  See Society for the Study of Rhenish
  History
Gess, Felician, 115
Gestalt psychology, 301
Gewandhaus orchestra (Leipzig), 288,
  441
Ghent, university, 437
Gierke, Otto von, 83, 149, 159,
  251n. 147, 402
Giesebrecht, Wilhelm, 52, 93, 166
Giesecke, Alfred, 259
Giessen, university, 113, 254
Goethe, Johann Wolfgang, 13, 25, 138,
  162, 298, 314, 320, 328n. 87
Goetz, Walter, 71, 115, 164, 257–60,
  262–63, 271, 278n. 27, 279n. 55, 321,
  357, 432
Goldfriedrich, Johannes, 355–56, 437
Goldscheid, Rudolf, 269

Görres-Gesellschaft, 216, 218
Gothein, Eberhard, 78, 83, 91, 93, 113, 140n. 32, 152–55, 185, 214, 229, 232, 260, 336. See also Schäfer, Dietrich
Göttingen, university, 149, 158, 195, 216, 222, 249n. 100; Lamprecht and, 22–24, 37–45, 50–51, 55, 115, 229, 371, 396
Gottsched, Johann Christof, 352
Grauert, Hermann, 163
Greifswald, university, 45, 99n. 40, 122, 193, 216, 219, 357, 385
Grenzboten, 71
Grimm, Hermann, 46, 181, 186, 225, 232
Griss, Peter, 323
Grünberg, Carl, 278–79n. 48
Grundkarten, 291–93, 345
Günther, Felix, 357
Gustav Adolf, 219

Haeckel, Ernst, 198, 306
Hague peace conferences, 409
Halle (-Wittenberg), university, 44, 88, 90, 96, 183
Hallgarten, George, 412
Hamburg, university, 387, 432
Hampe, Karl, 259
Händel, Georg Friedrich, 314
Handelshochschule (Cologne), 69
Hansen, Joseph, 246n. 17
Hanssen, Georg, 39, 50, 83
Harden, Maximilian, 192–94, 205, 226, 232, 237–40, 256, 313, 323, 337, 352, 386
Hardtwig, Wolfgang, 26
Harless, Woldemar, 76
Harnack, Adolf, 217–18, 346, 370, 410; History of Dogma, 217
Hartmann, Eduard von, 42, 56
Hartmann, Ludo Moritz, 166, 262–63, 332n. 245
Harvard University, 345, 349, 378
Haskins, Charles Homer, 347
Hasse, Ernst, 398, 403, 405; Deutsche Politik, 403
Hassel, Paul, 164, 291
Hauptmann, Gerhart, 305
Heeren, August Ludwig, 166
Hegel, G. W. F., 3, 28, 31, 33, 41, 46–49, 52, 69, 92, 119, 135, 197–98, 205, 267, 269, 295, 309, 317, 320

Hegel, Karl, 93
Heidelberg, university, 259, 274
Heigel, Karl Theodor von, 216
Heimpel, Hermann, 75, 98n. 35
Heller von Hellwald, Friedrich, 90
Hellpach, Willy, 225–26
Helmholtz, Heinrich von, 196, 198
Helmolt, Hans, 335, 337, 430n. 167
Helmolt's History of the World, 334–35, 337
Helmstedt, university, 26
Henne am Rhyn, 88
Hentig, Otto von, 421
Heraclitus, 198
Herbart, Johann Friedrich, 41, 197, 383
Herbst, Friedrich Wilhelm, 17, 67–68, 396
Herder, J. G., 41, 48, 88, 90, 119, 153, 205, 240, 242–43, 290, 295, 298, 301, 314, 320, 343, 409
Hettner, Felix, 77
Heyfelder, Hermann, 321
Hildebrand, Bruno, 46, 48, 90–91, 121, 194
Hilliger, Benno, 400
Hinneberg, Paul, 93, 156, 172n. 90, 220
Hintze, Otto, 151, 167, 170n. 57, 230–34, 243, 250n. 105, 254, 256–57, 313, 338, 403
Historical Society for the Lower Rhine, 77
Historikertage, 167, 399; Munich (1893), 166; Leipzig (1894), 167; Frankfurt a.M. (1895), 167; Innsbruck (1896), 216, 228; Nuremberg (1898), 240; Dresden (1907), 351, 369
Historische Vierteljahrschrift, 273, 293, 321, 358
Historische Zeitschrift, 35, 45, 148–49, 156–57, 165, 171n. 85, 172n. 98, 206n. 22, 260–61; contra Lamprecht, 112, 149, 159–60, 178–80, 182, 191–92, 220, 230, 239, 242, 244–45, 321, 357
Historischer Verein für den Niederrhein. See Historical Society for the Lower Rhine
Hochschullehrertage, 384–85
Hochschulpädagogik, 383–86
Hoeniger, Robert, 93, 150, 161, 172n. 90, 181, 247n. 41, 251n. 127, 256, 419, 444n. 61
Hoetzsch, Otto, 282n. 113, 400, 421
Hofmannsthal, Hugo von, 305

Hofrechtstheorie, 148–49, 160, 262
Hohenstaufen dynasty, 125
Hohenzollern dynasty, 313, 397
Höhlbaum, Konstantin, 76, 140n. 30
Humboldt, Wilhelm von, 26, 29, 235, 261, 316
Hume, David, 234
Husserl, Edmund, 41, 301
Hutten, Ulrich von, 133

Iggers, Georg G., 31, 267, 344
Ihering, Rudolf von, 23
Inama-Sternegg, Karl Theodor, 82, 91, 93, 149
Institut für Kultur- und Universalgeschichte. See Institute for Cultural and Universal History
Institut für österreichische Geschichte, 163
Institute for Cultural and Universal History, xiv, 352–59, 368–75, 377–79, 383, 385, 410, 414–16, 421, 431–32, 437
International Student Association, 378
Irving, Washington, 348
Ivo, Bishop of Chartres, 44, 46, 50

Jablonowski Society of Sciences (Royal), 115, 424n. 32
Jäckh, Ernst, 421
Jaeger, Oskar, 68, 383
Jaffé, Philip, 87, 112
Jagow, Gottlieb von, 439, 441
Jahrbücher für Nationalökonomie und Statistik, 92–93
James, William, 198, 345
Jameson, Frederic, 135
Janssen, Johannes, 89, 182, 216, 218–20; *Geschichte des deutschen Volkes*, 89
Jastrow, Ignaz, 91, 93, 150, 247n. 41
Jeismann, Karl-Ernst, 14
Jellinek, Georg, 410
Jena, university, 17n. 2, 154, 386
Joachimsthal *Gymnasium* (Berlin), 22
Johann Georg (king of Saxony), 115, 164, 288
Johns Hopkins University, 349

Kaiser Wilhelm Society for the Advancement of Science, 379, 381–82, 385, 432
Kaiser-Wilhelm Gesellschaft zur Förderung der Wissenschaften. See Kaiser Wilhelm

Society for the Advancement of Science
Kant, Immanuel, 41, 56, 137–39, 197–98, 228, 265–67, 314–16, 320, 346; *Critique of Pure Reason*, 189, 315; Lamprecht and, 189, 205, 244–45, 267, 298
Karlsruhe, technical university, 152, 194
Kaufmann, Georg, 140–41n. 34, 351
Kaufmann, Richard, 91
Kautsky, Karl, 175
Kehr, Ekart, 176
Kehr, Paul, 257, 286
Kernberg, Otto, 63–64n. 119, 105n. 179
Kiel, university, 182
King Friedrich August Foundation for Scientific Research, 381–82
King's College (Columbia University), 347
Kittel, Rudolf, 374
Klinger, Max, 288, 436
Klopstock, Friedrich Gottlieb, 15, 315
Knies, Karl, 46, 48, 90–91, 153, 269–71
Kohl, Horst, 163
Kohlhammer Verlag, 262
Köhne, Carl, 166
Koht, Halvdan, 367–68
Kohut, Heinz, 19n. 45
Kolb, Georg Friedrich, 88
König-Friedrich-August Stiftung für wissenschaftliche Forschung. See King Friedrich August Foundation for Scientific Research
Königsberg, university, 71, 140–41n. 34, 147, 183, 254
Koser, Reinhold, 113, 157, 162, 167
Köster, Albert, 275
Köstlin, Julius, 238
Kötzschke, Rudolf, 292–93, 350, 352, 357, 359, 367–68, 371, 377
Kraepelin, Ernst, 95
Kretzschmayr, Heinrich, 332n. 245
Kreuzzeitung (Neue Preussische), 395
Krieger, Leonard, 213
Krupp, Friedrich, 385
Kuczynski, Jürgen, xiii
Kugler, Bernhard, 216
Kuhn, Thomas, 245
Külpe, Oswald, 198–99
Kulturbund deutscher Gelehrter und Künstler. See Cultural Association of German Scholars and Artists

Kulturgeschichte. See Cultural history
Kulturkampf, 23, 89, 216, 318, 396
Kulturprotestantismus, 219, 396
Kunstwart, 323

Laband, Paul, 280n. 78
Lamprecht, Emilie (née Limburg), 3–4,
    18n. 11, 19n. 45, 74, 94, 97n. 6
Lamprecht, Karl Georg, 2, 4, 5–6, 9,
    11, 17, 18–19n. 22, 20n. 50, 440
Lamprecht, Karl Hugo, 4–5, 9–10, 43,
    50, 63n. 117, 68, 74, 86, 94–95, 112,
    116, 141n. 53, 193, 237, 276, 298,
    346
Lamprecht, Karl Nathaniel, 2–17,
    17n. 2, 18n. 22, 19n. 45, 20n. 50,
    22–23, 43–44, 52, 56, 68, 97n. 6,
    111, 122, 138, 276, 395, 440
Lamprecht, Mathilde (née Mühl),
    95–96, 111–12, 116, 140n. 14, 187,
    223, 287, 432, 440
Landwehr, 58n. 12, 433
Lange, F. A., 198
Langemarck, 437
Langewiesche, Dieter, 322
Lask, Emil, 265, 267
Lebensraum, 289
Lehmann, Max, 99n. 40, 102n. 118,
    112–13, 116, 149, 157–62, 171n. 80,
    178, 182, 195, 205nn. 4, 7, 222, 228,
    410
Lehr, Adolf, 398, 403
Lehrerseminare (Leipzig), 383
Lehrerverein (Leipzig), 288, 383
Leibniz, Gottfried Wilhelm, 41, 119,
    197–98, 200, 205, 295, 298, 312,
    320, 343
Leipzig, university, xiv, 87, 113–15,
    157–59, 195, 220, 225, 228, 239–40,
    254, 269, 290, 292–96, 326n. 52,
    335, 345, 353–54, 360, 367–72,
    374–85, 387, 390n. 81, 396, 398,
    404, 415, 432, 436; historical seminar,
    115–16, 158, 161–65, 194, 258,
    272–76, 350–51, 353, 357–58;
    historical-geographical seminar,
    292–93, 335; *Historische Abende*, 164;
    Lamprecht as student, 44–46, 50–52,
    55; Lamprecht and faculty politics,
    372–83; seminar for cultural and
    universal history, 350; *Seminar für
    Landesgeschichte und Siedlungskunde*,

293, 350, 352, 359. *See also* Institute
    for Cultural and Universal History
Leipzig, *Volkshochschule*, 383
"Leipzig Circle," 295–97, 374
"Leipzig movement," 377
Leipziger Neueste Nachrichten, 398
Leipziger Volkszeitung, 398
Lenz, Max, 113, 147, 224, 229, 234–35,
    247nn. 36, 41, 43, 250–51n. 122, 272,
    274, 374, 432, 436; contra Lamprecht,
    161–62, 181–82, 218–23, 235,
    237–39, 421
Leo, Heinrich, 88, 92, 166
Leopold (prince of Prussia), 86
Lessing, Gotthold Ephraim, 314
Liebermann, Max, 305
Liebknecht, Wilhelm, 40
Liesegang, Erich, 93, 161, 172n. 90,
    176, 181, 187, 194, 200, 206n. 29,
    226–27, 233, 256, 400
Lilienkron, Detlev von, 305, 310
Liman, Paul, 398
Lindau, Paul, 323
Lindner, Theodor, 37–38, 335–36
Lipps, Theodor, 301–3, 314, 329n. 122,
    342
Liszt, Franz von, 386, 410
Literarisches Zentralblatt, 332n. 245
Loersch, Hugo, 76
Lorenz, Ottokar, 89
Lotze, Rudolf Hermann, 41–42, 45, 48,
    50, 119, 225
Louis XIV (king of France), 162
Ludwig the Bavarian, 356
Ludwig, Otto, 317
Lukács, Georg, xi, xiv
Luther, Martin, 8, 11, 43, 57, 89,
    128–29, 137, 139, 157, 182, 219–21,
    315, 397, 399

MacDowell, Edward, 348
Mach, Ernst, 198
Man, Hendrik de, 367–68, 398
Marathon, battle of, 334
Marburg, university, 45, 97, 99n. 40,
    102n. 118, 111–13, 115–16, 122,
    140–41n. 34, 147, 150, 157, 163,
    219, 254, 386
Marcks, Erich, 162–64, 192, 194–95,
    206n. 22, 208n. 87, 219, 256, 258,
    272–75, 277n. 10, 278n. 27, 288, 374,
    421, 423n. 17

Marx, Karl, 40, 54, 120–22, 135, 175, 229, 262–63, 298, 300, 309, 355, 397
Matschoss, Conrad, 418–21
Maurenbrecher, Max, 404, 425n. 62
Maurenbrecher, Wilhelm, 70–74, 83, 86, 98n. 30, 113, 115–16, 147, 404
Maurer, Georg von, 83, 149
Maximilian I (Bavarian elector), 258
Maximilian I (emperor), 127
Maximilian II (king of Bavaria), 28
Mehring, Franz, xiii, 175–76, 181, 187, 240, 310, 322, 397, 415
Meinecke, Friedrich, 35, 38, 74, 112, 151, 171n. 85, 178, 186–87, 193, 206nn. 18, 22, 216, 233, 247n. 48, 250n. 116, 254, 257, 263–64, 272, 277n. 10, 325n. 33, 421; contra Lamprecht, 179–80, 182, 191, 220, 230–31, 241–42, 244–45, 268, 321, 358; *Cosmopolitanism and the Nation-State*, 261; and cultural history, 260–61, 267, 271
Meitzen, August, 83–85, 91, 104n. 164, 159, 181, 292
Melanchthon, Philipp, 15
Menger, Karl, 91, 264
Menzel, Adolf, 203, 305
Menzel, Karl, 72–73, 83, 86–87
Messmer, J. A., 53
Methodenstreit, xii, xiv, 18–19n. 22, 286, 288, 290, 297–99, 309–10, 319, 321, 323, 334, 338–39, 357–58, 367–69, 374, 394, 397, 399, 400; course of, 175–253; aftermath, 254–83; preliminaries, 146–74
Metternich, Clemens von, 316
Mettlach (abbey), 80
Metz, Karl-Heinz, 9, 323, 373
Mevissen, Gustav von, 68–69, 72–79, 84, 94, 96, 98n. 29, 100n. 59, 102n. 122, 111, 114, 116, 126, 129, 135, 158–59, 161, 165, 167, 288, 294, 298, 351, 396–97, 403
Mevissen, Mathilde, 65n. 163, 422
Meyer, Eduard, 270, 334–37, 436
Meyerbeer, Giacomo, 318
Miaskowski, August von, 91, 272
Mill, John Stuart, 267
Ministry of culture (Prussian), 36, 85, 87, 384, 416, 437. See also Althoff, Friedrich

Ministry of culture (Saxon), 44, 162–64, 274–76, 292–93, 346, 350–52, 357, 359, 371–72, 374–75, 378–82, 386, 432, 442n. 3
Mommsen, Theodor, 35, 75, 181, 187, 344
Mommsen, Wolfgang, xiii, 268
Monist League, 296, 413
Monod, Gabriel, 345
Monumenta Historica Germaniae, 35, 37
Morgan, Lewis Henry, 123, 142n. 83
Moritz (duke of Saxony), 15
Moroccan crisis (1905–6), 410
Moroccan crisis (1911), 410, 416
Möser, Justus, 89
Mozart, Wolfgang Amadeus, 315
Mühl, Gustav, 95
Müller, Karl Alexander von, 259
Münchner Allgemeine Zeitung, 113
Munich, polytechnical university, 289
Munich, university, 22, 35, 52, 71, 93, 163, 216, 302
Münster, academy, 96, 140–41n. 34, 150, 216, 217
Münsterberg, Hugo, 199, 345, 346, 347
Münzer, Thomas, 129

Napoleon, 75, 198, 219, 315
Nasse, Erwin, 86
National Assembly (Frankfurt, 1848–49), 69
National Liberals, 397–98
National-Social Association, 404
Nationalsozialer Verein. See National-Social Association
Natorp, Paul, 386, 410
Naudé, Albert, 157, 162, 167
Naumann, Friedrich, 404, 413; *Demokratie und Kaisertum*, 404
Nazis, 289
Neo-Kantianism, 266–67, 346
Neo-Rankeanism, 189–90, 213, 220, 241, 395
Neue Zeit, 175
Neumann, Carl, 259
"New History," 344, 346
Niehbuhr, Barthold Georg, 29, 70
Niese, Benedictus, 112
Nietzsche, Friedrich, xi, 15, 256, 264, 305–6
Nikisch, Arthur, 288, 441
Nipperdey, Thomas, 12, 26, 294

Nitzsch, Karl Wilhelm, 35, 82–83, 88, 92, 149, 168–69n. 17
Nobel prize: chemistry, 295; peace, 359
Noorden, Carl von, 45–46, 51–52, 64n. 127, 67, 70, 72, 83–84, 87, 98n. 30, 115, 353, 396
Nord und Süd, 323
Novalis, 261

October Edict, 316
Oestreich, Gerhard, xii, 154, 263
Office central des Nationalités, 417
Olaf (king of Norway), 133
"Old Catholics," 71
Oldenbourg, Rudolf, 179
Oncken, Hermann, 235–37, 239, 241–42, 250–51n. 122, 251n. 127, 254, 319, 322
Oncken, Wilhelm, 113
Oregon, 347, 405
Ostwald, Wilhelm, 114, 268, 295–98, 300, 302, 306, 308, 346, 372, 374, 410, 436, 440
Otto I (emperor), 70
Ottonian dynasty, 124–25, 184

Paasche, Hermann, 421
Pan-German League, 309, 398–406, 408–10, 412–13, 416–17, 421, 424n. 36, 434, 439
Partsch, Joseph, 293, 356
Parzifal, 139
Patriotenbund (Leipzig), 400
Pauli, Reinhold, 39
Paulsen, Friedrich, 181, 394
Peace movement, xi, 296, 409–10, 412–13, 416, 434
Peasants' War, 129, 165, 221
Penck, Albert, 346
Pennsylvania, University of, 349
"Peonie," 374
Pericles, 17
Perthes, Friedrich, 166–67, 250n. 105, 345
Pertz, Georg Heinrich, 37
Pfister, Johann Karl, 166
Pflugk-Harttung, Julius von, 102n. 118
Philip II (king of Spain), 162
Pirenne, Henri, 78, 166, 227, 329n. 108, 345, 382, 399, 437, 439, 444n. 61; *History of Belgium*, 166, 345
Planck, Max, 295

Plehn, Hans, 417
Poe, Edgar Allan, 348
Prescott, William H., 352
Preussische Jahrbücher, 181–83, 192, 235, 239, 321, 358
Prometheus, 56, 226
Prüm (abbey), 80
Prussian historical school, 33, 48, 136, 157, 195, 219, 241, 313, 316–18, 395, 396–97
Prussian state archive, 35, 112, 178

Quetelet, L. A. J., 207n. 60
Quidde, Ludwig, 159, 165, 427n. 103

Rachfahl, Felix, 182–87, 189, 191, 193, 200, 207nn. 39, 56, 216, 220–22, 233–34, 237, 243, 250n. 116, 254, 351, 403
Radbruch, Gustav, 368
Rade, Martin, 386
Ranke, Heinrich, 30
Ranke, Leopold von, xiii, 15, 23, 45–49, 52, 61n. 59, 66n. 169, 88, 90, 92, 112, 138, 151, 153, 157, 162, 166, 180, 182, 184–85, 219–20, 228, 236, 241–42, 244, 259, 261, 264, 317, 320, 333n. 249, 335, 337, 344; *German History in the Era of the Reformation*, 236; *Ideenlehre*, 29, 30, 43, 184, 190, 201, 233, 235, 242, 264; Lamprecht and, 43, 58, 67, 87, 93, 118, 127–28, 159, 176–77, 189–91, 201, 214, 233–35, 270; *World History*, 335; and the professionalization of history, 27–39, 75, 135, 213, 353
"Ranke Renaissance," 34, 219
Ratzel, Friedrich, 114, 157, 179, 275, 289–90, 292–96, 298, 306, 309, 326n. 52, 335–36, 339–41, 346, 372, 374, 399, 423n. 17; *Anthropo-Geographie*, 289
Reformation, 54, 56, 81, 126, 128, 137, 139, 217, 220–22, 235, 238, 258, 312
Reichstag, 216, 400, 402, 417–18
Reichstagsakten, 38
Rein, Adolf, 356, 367
Reinhardt, Max, 192
Reizsamkeit. See Excitability, era of
Révue de synthèse historique, 344
Rheinische Eisenbahn, 69, 70, 76, 79

Ricardo, David, 47
Richthofen, Ferdinand von, 290
Rickert, Heinrich, 243–44, 265,
   267–68, 271, 280n. 83, 346
Riehl, Wilhelm Heinrich, 22, 39, 52,
   88, 93
Riezler, Kurt, 417, 419, 421, 430n. 167,
   431, 437; *Grundzüge der Weltpolitik*,
   430n. 167
Ringer, Fritz, 295
Ritschl, Albrecht, 23
Ritter, Moriz, 63n. 102, 71, 73–74, 84,
   87, 94, 96, 103n. 128, 108, 111, 147,
   160, 224, 229–30, 235–37, 241, 258,
   286, 317, 339, 352, 437
Robinson, James Harvey, 347,
   363nn. 83, 84
Rohrbach, Paul, 417
Romanticism, 119, 242–43
Ropp, Goswin Freiherr von der, 113,
   140n. 30, 140–41n. 34, 293
Roscher, Wilhelm, 45–46, 48–55, 77,
   79, 85, 90–91, 110, 113–14, 118–21,
   140n. 32, 157, 194, 203, 225, 261,
   269–70, 294, 341
Rothacker, Erich, 280n. 83
Rousseau, Jean-Jacques, 315–16
Rudolf of Habsburg (emperor), 73, 80,
   126, 133, 356

St. Andrew's University, 382
St. Maximin (abbey), 80
Saint-Simon, Claude Henri de, 402
Salian dynasty, 124
Savigny, Friedrich Karl von, 46
Saxon Commission for History (Royal),
   164, 167, 291–93, 358, 371
Saxon Statistical Bureau, 398
Scala, Rudolf von, 216, 228
Schaafhausen Bank, 69
Schaefer, Arnold, 72, 77, 83, 195
Schäfer, Dietrich, 180, 271, 336, 399,
   421, 430n. 170; contra Gothein,
   151–55, 185, 214, 229, 232, 260
Scharnhorst, Gerhard von, 112
Scheffer-Boichorst, Paul, 172n. 94, 181
Schelling, Friedrich Wilhelm Joseph, 3,
   41, 295, 317
Scherr, Johannes, 88, 96
Schiller, Friedrich von, 261, 315–16
Schleiermacher, Friedrich, 3, 8, 29, 42,
   46, 241, 265

Schmarsow, August, 275, 282n. 133, 380
Schmidkunz, Hans, 386
Schmoller, Gustav, 90–93, 118,
   142n. 83, 149–51, 156, 158, 161,
   230, 249n. 92, 250n. 116, 256–57,
   262–63, 300, 306–7, 309, 402;
   *Grundriss der allgemeinen
   Volkswirtschaftslehre*, 300; Lamprecht
   and, 51, 76–77, 82–85, 159, 166–67,
   181, 227–28, 241
Schmollers Jahrbuch, 91–92
Schnürer, Gustav, 218
Schönberg, Gustav, 91
Schönebaum, Herbert, xiv, 17n. 2, 39,
   64n. 127, 65n. 142, 240, 276
Schönhoven, Klaus, 322
Schönlank, Bruno, 398
Schopenhauer, Arthur, 56, 267
Schorn-Schütte, Luise, 323
Schücking, Walther, 410
Schulin, Ernst, 261
Schulpforta, 2, 15–17, 22–23, 66n. 169,
   67, 74, 94, 368, 395, 415, 428n. 124,
   440–41
Schulte, Aloys, 168n. 17, 195, 227, 259,
   293
Schultz, Susan, 402
Schulze, Johannes, 36
Schulze, Winfried, 231
Schybergson, M. G., 166
Seeliger, Gerhard, 163, 165, 173n. 112,
   192, 194, 225, 272–75, 288, 291,
   293, 321, 350, 352, 356–58,
   364n. 112, 366n. 173, 374–76, 380,
   383, 423n. 17
Seven Years' War, 157
Seydewitz, Paul von, 164
Shakespeare, William, 434
Show, Arley Barthlow, 358, 421,
   431–32
Sickel, Theodor, 163
Siebeck, Paul, 165
Sieglin, Wilhelm, 292
Sievers, Eduard, 275, 346
Simmel, Georg, 265, 267, 387, 410
Sloane, William M., 347
Smith, Adam, 47
Smith, Woodruff, 294
Socialism, 34, 167, 175, 376, 398–99,
   402, 405, 416
Society for German Cultural History,
   257

Society for the History of the Mark Brandenburg, 75
Society for the Pedagogy of Higher Education, 385–86
Society for the Study of Germandom Abroad, 422
Society for the Study of Rhenish History, 76–78, 83, 86, 100n. 59, 111–12, 147–48, 164, 292, 335, 358, 396
Society to Promote a Cultural Foreign Policy, 420, 422, 437
Sohm, Rudolf, 149
Solomon, Felix, 164
Sombart, Werner, 271, 300, 306–7, 346
Spencer, Herbert, 40, 198, 267, 290, 295, 303
Spengler, Oswald, 323, 341, 434
Spinoza, Baruch, 41, 119, 197–98, 200, 290, 295, 298, 320
Spranger, Eduard, 31, 297, 304, 442n. 13
Springer, Anton, 52, 53, 78, 114
Stammler, Rudolf, 268
Stanford University, 349, 358, 378
Stein, Karl Freiherr vom, 157, 315–16, 414
Steinhausen, Georg, 154–56, 192, 227, 257–60, 262–63, 330n. 136, 336; History of German Culture, 258
Stenzel, Gustav, 166
Stieda, Wilhelm, 91
Stier-Somlo, Fritz, 386
Stieve, Felix, 216
Stintzing, Zitta von, 94
Strassburg, university, 51, 90, 97, 113, 259
Sturm und Drang, 315, 317
Sudermann, Hermann, 305
Suttner, Bertha von, 410
Sven (king of Denmark), 133
Sybel, Heinrich von, 33, 35, 37, 45–46, 69–72, 75, 90, 93, 98n. 29, 99n. 40, 112, 157, 162, 164, 171n. 82, 172n. 98, 173n. 112, 178–79, 181, 187, 206n. 18, 219; and Lamprecht, 72, 84, 149, 159, 179, 396–97
Szanto, Emil, 278–79n. 48

Tacitus, 123
Taine, Hippolyte, 40, 90
Tarde, Gabriel, 300, 306, 329n. 108
Tenbruck, Friedrich 281n. 96
Teubner, B. G. (Verlag), 259, 273

Thirty Years' War, 71, 236, 258
Tille, Armin, 275, 293, 400
Tirpitz, Alfred von, 219
Tönnies, Ferdinand, 346
Treitschke, Heinrich von, 33, 35, 69, 71, 136, 152, 157, 179, 185–87, 192, 200, 206n. 29, 220, 230, 239, 256, 316, 368; Lamprecht and, 84–85, 161–62, 180–81, 396–97, 399, 401; German History in the Nineteenth Century, 136, 316
Triple Alliance, 318
Troeltsch, Ernst, 25–26, 46, 264, 271, 346, 357–58, 410–11
Tübingen, university, 38, 45, 96, 152, 216, 258

Ukert, Friedrich August, 166
Ullmann, Emmanuel von, 410
Ullmann, Heinrich, 216
Umsturzvorlage, 400
United States Military Academy (West Point), 349
Universal Exposition (St. Louis, 1904), 346, 413, 436

Varrentrapp, Conrad, 97, 113, 147, 219
Vassar College, 349
Vatican archives, 216
Verband deutscher Historiker. See Association of German Historians
Verband für internationale Verständigung. See German Association for International Conciliation
Verein Deutscher Hochschullehrer. See Association of German University Teachers
Verein für das Deutschtum im Ausland. See Association for Germandom Abroad
Verein für Sozialpolitik, 90, 154, 402
Vienna, Peace of, 27, 75
Vierhaus, Rudolf, 12
Vierkandt, Alfred, 410
Vierteljahrschrift für Sozial- und Wirtschaftsgeschichte, 262–63, 279n. 48
Vierteljahrschrift für Volkswirtschaft und Kulturgeschichte, 89
Virchow, Rudolf, 294
Voigt, Georg, 52–53, 113, 292
Voltaire, 88, 315
Vom Brocke, Bernhard, xii
Vom Bruch, Rüdiger, 413

Vormärz, 31
Vossische Zeitung, 420

Wachsmuth, Curt, 23, 39, 115, 283n.139
Wachsmuth, Wilhelm, 88
Wagner, Adolf, 181
Wagner, Moritz, 289
Wagner, Richard, 305–6
Wahl, Adalbert, 170n.57
Wahnschaffe, Arnold, 419–21
Waitz, Georg, 23, 35, 37–38, 40, 42, 69, 75, 77, 82, 93, 152, 195, 230
Waldeyer, Wilhelm, 346, 436, 438
Walsh, W. W., 25
War of Liberation, 316, 317
Warnkönig, Theodor, 39
"*Was ist Kulturgeschichte?*" See "What Is Cultural History?"
Wattenbach, Wilhelm, 35, 93, 163
Weber, Alfred, 410
Weber, Ernst Heinrich, 196
Weber, Max, xii, xiii, 47, 49, 233, 265, 295–96, 300, 307, 334, 337, 346, 410–11, 427n.105; and Lamprecht, 268–71, 411; "Objectivity in the Social Sciences," 270; "The Protestant Ethic and the Spirit of Capitalism," 271, 300; "Roscher and Knies and the Logical Problems of Historical National Economy," 269–71
Weidmann Verlag, 321
Weiland, Ludwig, 149
Weiss, Berthold, 303
Weiszäcker, Julius, 37–38, 42, 44–45, 65n.142, 83–85, 113, 163, 216, 230
Wenzelburger, K. Theodor, 236–37
Werden (abbey), 292
Westdeutsche Zeitschrift für Geschichte und Kunst, 77–78, 111–12, 159, 165
Westphalia, Peace of, 71, 122, 136
"What Is Cultural History?" 200, 204–5, 215, 224, 230, 233, 298, 338
Wheeler, Benjamin Ide, 436
Whimster, Sam, 129
White, Hayden, 136, 226
Whitman, Walt, 348
Wickersdorf movement, 413
Wiener, Otto, 296, 374
Wilcken, Ulrich, 350

William I (king of Prussia, German emperor), 162, 395
William II (king of Prussia, German emperor), 71, 87, 165, 309, 311, 352, 378–79, 403, 405, 413, 417, 421, 427n.115, 438
William of Orange, 230
Wilson, Thomas Woodrow, 347
Windelband, Wilhelm, 41, 243, 265, 267–68, 290
Winter, Georg, 159, 236–37, 239, 241
Wisconsin, 378, 432
Wisconsin, University of, 349, 378, 432
Wislicenus, Johannes, 399
Wolf, Adam, 89
Wolf, Friedrich August, 26, 29
World Exhibition of the Book Trade and Graphics. See BUGRA
World War I, 382, 422
Wundt, Wilhelm, 41, 45, 51, 114, 195–205, 209n.115, 210nn.119, 130, 215, 222, 224–25, 227, 230, 233, 269, 275, 289, 294–95, 297–303, 305–6, 320, 328n.99, 329n.122, 339, 345–46, 352, 372, 374, 379, 382, 387, 402, 404, 436; *Völkerpsychologie*, 198

Yale University, 349
Yorck von Wartenburg, Paul, 268

Zarncke, Eduard, 332n.245
Zeitschrift für deutsche Kulturgeschichte. See *Zeitschrift für Kulturgeschichte*
Zeitschrift für Hochschulpädagogik, 386
Zeitschrift für Kulturgeschichte, 89, 154–55, 192, 262. See also *Archiv für Kulturgeschichte*
Zeitschrift für Sozial- und Wirtschaftsgeschichte, 262. See also *Vierteljahrschrift für Sozial- und Wirtschaftsgeschichte*
Zentralstelle für Auslandsdienst. See Central Division for Service Abroad
Zimmer, Friedrich, 68, 74
Zimmermann, Wilhelm, 127
Zirkel, Ferdinand, 346
Zukunft, Die, 192–93, 208n.92, 232, 237, 239, 323, 337
Zurich, polytechnical university, 96
Zweifel, Paul, 374